AF876384

ESSENTIALS OF BUSINESS LAW

2024 Release

Anthony L. Liuzzo, J.D., MBA, Ph.D.
Professor Emeritus, Wilkes University

Ruth C. Hughes, J.D.
Wilkes University Wilkes-Barre, Pennsylvania

Mc Graw Hill

ESSENTIALS OF BUSINESS LAW

Published by McGraw Hill LLC, 1325 Avenue of the Americas, New York, NY 10019.

This book is printed on acid-free paper.

2 3 4 5 6 7 8 9 CPI 29 28 27 26 25

ISBN 978-1-266-91482-9
MHID 1-266-91482-X

Cover Image: *Shutterstock/MarinaGrigorivna*

mheducation.com/highered

Dedication

To the many students who have enriched our profession and our lives.
May this book give relevant knowledge for the upcoming
generation of students so that they can change
the world for the better.

"Education is the most powerful weapon you can use to
change the world."

Nelson Mandela,
social activist, statesman, and former president of South Africa

ABOUT OUR AUTHORS

Courtesy of Ruth Hughes

Ruth Calhoun Hughes, J.D. Ruth Hughes serves as Associate Professor of Business Law at Wilkes University in Wilkes-Barre, Pennsylvania.

Hughes is a licensed attorney and received her JD from Washington and Lee University in Lexington, Virginia, and her BA in economics from Tulane University in New Orleans, Louisiana.

She began her career as an attorney specializing in corporate transactions in New York City and Wilkes-Barre, Pennsylvania. She was director of the Small Business Development Center in Wilkes-Barre for many years before joining the faculty of the Sidhu School of Business and Leadership at Wilkes University in 2013.

Her research interests, publications, and presentations include the areas of environmental sustainability in business, equity crowdfunding, and emerging trends in securities laws. She serves as a reviewer for several academic publications.

Hughes is an active member of many university, professional, and community organizations. She is married to Richard Hughes and the proud mother of three children, Callie, Ellen, and Richard.

Courtesy of Anthony L. Liuzzo

Anthony L. Liuzzo, J.D., MBA, Ph.D. Dr. Anthony L. Liuzzo is Professor Emeritus at Wilkes University where, until his retirement in 2017, he served as Professor of Business and Economics and Chairperson of the Business Programs of Arizona.

Dr. Liuzzo is an attorney and economist. He earned his Ph.D. in business administration, Master of Philosophy in economics, and MBA in management and organizational behavior from New York University; his Juris Doctor in law from St. John's University; and his Bachelor of Science in marketing from Fordham University in New York City.

During his career, Dr. Liuzzo specialized in public policy issues, employment law, and holiday retail sales forecasting. He has been cited on numerous occasions in hundreds of publications–including CNN, Fox News, *Forbes,* the *New York Times, USA Today,* the *Arizona Republic,* the *New York Daily News,* the *Philadelphia Daily News,* the *Chicago Tribune,* the *Washington Times,* the *Cincinnati Enquirer,* the *Pittsburgh Post-Gazette,* the *Detroit News,* the *Christian Science Monitor,* and the *San Francisco Examiner*–for his views on legal and business issues.

Prior to his retirement, Dr. Liuzzo was the author of several editions of the popular textbook, *Essentials of Business Law,* and its accompanying assessment materials, mobile applications, and instructor's manual, published by McGraw Hill.

David B. Moore Photography

Dr. Liuzzo was also the author of several books and numerous articles that have appeared in scholarly and professional journals. He has served as editor of a scholarly journal and has been instrumental in creating several successful small businesses.

Dr. Liuzzo has testified as an expert witness in numerous civil and criminal trials and has appeared before state legislatures for his insights into pending regulations. He served as a member of many professional and community organizations, and as a member and officer of several boards of directors.

Brief CONTENTS

Contents

Evlakhov Valeriy/Shutterstock

Hisham Ibrahim/Photodisc/Getty Images

Chip Somodevilla/Getty Images

Ryan McVay/Getty Images

Jim Arbogast/Getty Images

Design Pics

Brian A Jackson/Shutterstock

Radius Images/Getty Images

Photodisc/Getty Images

ColorBlind Images/Blend Images LLC

Digital Vision/Getty Images

M Stock/Alamy Images

sirtravelalot/Shutterstock

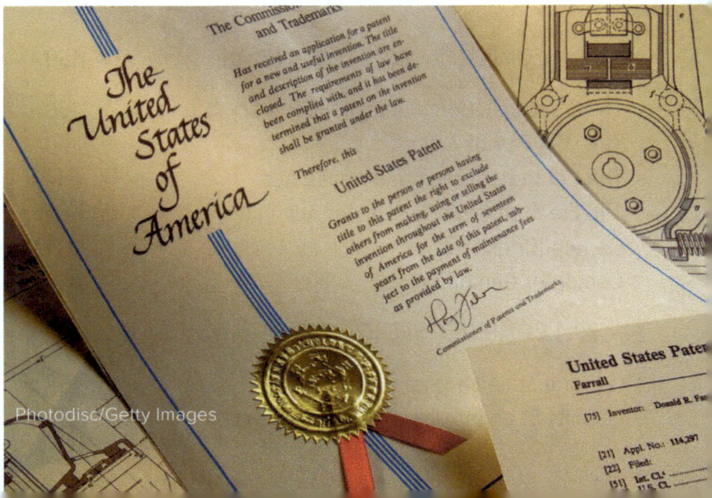

Photodisc/Getty Images

Mark Dierker/
McGraw Hill

DW labs Incorporated/ Shutterstock

Kim Steele/Photodisc/Getty Images

BananaStock/ Getty Images

Preface

ACKNOWLEDGEMENT AND THANK YOU TO TONY LIUZZO

After great service to the Business Law community, our colleague Tony Liuzzo has announced that he is retiring from authorship of future editions of *Essentials of Business Law*. For me, Tony has always been "the author" of this text and I was honored when he asked me to co-author the text with him. I gratefully joined this effort and learned so much from Tony as we worked together. Tony, thank you for your mentorship to me. Perhaps even more important, though, has been your vision for this textbook which has introduced so many students to business law. Enjoy your retirement and thank you!

Ruth Calhoun Hughes

WELCOME TO *ESSENTIALS OF BUSINESS LAW*

The new, 2024 release edition of the *Essentials of Business Law* program continues to be a practical, concise, and broad-based introduction to the vibrant field of business law. While continuing to offer all of the features that have made the 11 prior editions successful, this new edition includes a chapter on the areas of law affected by social media, updated content, and enhanced support materials. Both the traditional areas of law, such as contracts and property, and the emerging areas of law, such as e-commerce and environmental, are covered in short, informative chapters written to capture the essence of each topic. The objective of the text throughout its coverage is ease–ease of use, ease of teaching, ease of assessment, and ease of understanding. It has been developed for those seeking a more fundamental overview of the concepts and principles that are vital to the understanding of business law.

NOTE TO STUDENTS

The 2024 release of *Essentials of Business Law* covers the latest developments in the legal field. This text will help you discover a wealth of information and learning opportunities that will give you a clear understanding of business law topics. The text will also help you identify, explain, and apply the principles of business law in your daily life and in the larger world in which you live. The world of business is continually changing, especially with the advent and evolution of the global marketplace. The concepts and principles presented in the text will assist you in understanding those changes as they relate to business law.

The chapters in *Essentials of Business Law* are organized in a concise and easy-to-read way. Numerous examples applying the law to real-world situations will assist you in understanding important concepts, whereas key term definitions are provided throughout the text for your reference. The end-of-chapter assessments will help you apply your knowledge and gauge your understanding of the material as you progress, and the extra resources accompanying the text will provide useful and easy-to-use tools to supplement your appreciation of the material.

NOTE TO INSTRUCTORS

What sets *Essentials of Business Law* apart from other programs available is its concise organizational nature and supplementary materials. Chapters are succinct, making it simple for you to plan presentations and teach the course. Each chapter offers an abundance of assessment tools that will help you evaluate your students' progress. The new edition offers expanded coverage of current or emerging areas in the business law field, including legal ethics and laws applying to social media, e-commerce, and health care law. In addition, the number of key terms has been increased to include both legal and nonlegal definitions. As a result, *Essentials of Business Law* offers you and your students the coverage of essential topics that many larger, more expensive book programs miss entirely. The 2024 release edition has been expanded and updated to include a variety of teaching tools that make it simple for you to organize your classroom discussions, effectively communicate the important business law concepts in each chapter, and assess your students' grasp of the material. The book is accompanied by an Instructor Resource Center, complete with an Instructor's Manual, a Test Bank, and PowerPoint slides for each chapter. Each tool makes planning and teaching the course easier than ever.

CHANGES TO THIS EDITION

CHAPTER 1

Our System of Law has been revised as follows:

- Updated the state adoptions of the Uniform Commercial Code.
- Included multiple-choice questions designed to reinforce learning objectives.

CHAPTER 2

Ethics and the Law has been revised as follows:

- Updated Section 2.3 to clarify that ethical issues are not enforceable in court.
- Included multiple-choice questions designed to reinforce learning objectives.

CHAPTER 3

Criminal Law has been revised as follows:

- Clarified the definition of a crime to highlight the goal of public protection.
- Updated the terminology in 3.1 regarding reproductive rights and LGBTQ rights to ensure inclusivity of the categories that accurately reflect current law.
- Included multiple-choice questions designed to reinforce learning objectives.

CHAPTER 4

Tort Law has been revised as follows:

- Clarified language in 4.1 distinguishing between a tort and a crime.
- Changed Example 4.1 to a more inclusive example of libel.
- Changed Example 4.10 to a clearer example of conversion.
- Clarified the definition of negligence in the text of 4.7.
- Removed sentence in 4.7 referring to general numbers of lawsuits involving automobiles.
- Included multiple-choice questions designed to reinforce learning objectives.

CHAPTER 5

Constitutional Law has been revised as follows:

- Changed the opening quote.
- Changed Example 5.1 to an updated example of preemption.
- Included multiple-choice questions designed to reinforce learning objectives.

CHAPTER 6

Administrative Law has been revised as follows:

- Included multiple-choice questions designed to reinforce learning objectives.

CHAPTER 7

Introduction to Contracts has been revised as follows:

- Updated the title in the quote at the beginning of the chapter.
- Updated Section 7.8 to reflect current status of smart contracts and their use.
- Included multiple-choice questions designed to reinforce learning objectives.
- Changed Legal Research Using Technology question 51 to focus on creation of smart contracts on a blockchain platform.

CHAPTER 8

Offer and Acceptance has been revised as follows:

- Clarified how offer and acceptance occurs with smart contracts.
- Included multiple-choice questions designed to reinforce learning objectives.

CHAPTER 9

Mutual Agreement has been revised as follows:

- Included multiple-choice questions designed to reinforce learning objectives.

CHAPTER 10

Consideration has been revised as follows:

- Example 10.9 has been updated with a change of gender.
- Included multiple-choice questions designed to reinforce learning objectives.
- Changed Case question 44 to be a specific example of gratuitous consideration, *Alden v. Presley.*

CHAPTER 11

Competent Parties has been revised as follows:

- Updated the quote at beginning of the chapter.
- Changed terminology related to mental capacity to reflect current language.
- Included multiple-choice questions designed to reinforce learning objectives.

CHAPTER 12

Legal Purpose of Contracts has been revised as follows:

- Updated the general status of state gambling regulation to reflect expansion of legal gambling under state laws.
- Updated the section on usurious agreements to reflect that fewer states are regulating maximum interest rates.
- Clarified definition of monopoly power.
- Included multiple-choice questions designed to reinforce learning objectives.

CHAPTERS 13, 14, AND 15

All of these chapters now include multiple-choice questions designed to reinforce learning objectives.

CHAPTER 16

Transfer of Title has been revised as follows:

- Clarified 16.4 to include role of risk of loss in title transfers.
- Included multiple-choice questions designed to reinforce learning objectives.

CHAPTERS 17, 18, 19, AND 20

These chapters now include multiple-choice questions designed to reinforce learning objectives.

CHAPTER 21

Creditors Rights and Bankruptcy has been revised as follows:

- Included a new quote at the beginning of the chapter.
- Included multiple-choice questions designed to reinforce learning objectives.

CHAPTER 22

Introduction to Commercial Paper has been revised as follows:

- Updated learning outcome 22.7 to include digital applications.
- Added explanation of role of peer-to-peer digital applications in Section 22.7 with an updated list of example applications.
- Added new Thinking Critically about the Law question 40 focused on whether peer-to-peer digital applications should be regulated by the EFTA.
- Included multiple-choice questions designed to reinforce learning objectives.

CHAPTERS 23, 24, AND 25

These chapters now include multiple-choice questions designed to reinforce learning objectives. Chapter 24 also includes more inclusive language with regard to married couples, replacing "husband and wife" with "spouses."

CHAPTER 26

Landlord–Tenant Relations has been revised as follows:

- Section 26.3 was revised to explain the ban on evictions during COVID-19 due to public health considerations.
- Added Thinking Critically about the Law question 40 to address whether the government should be allowed to restrict evictions due to public health considerations.
- Included multiple-choice questions designed to reinforce learning objectives.

CHAPTER 27

Wills, Intestacy, and Trusts has been revised as follows:

- Added a new quote at the beginning of the chapter.
- Included multiple-choice questions designed to reinforce learning objectives.

CHAPTER 28

Intellectual Property has been revised as follows:

- Updated information in Section 28.2 Patents regarding the ability to patent DNA strains.
- Included multiple-choice questions designed to reinforce learning objectives.

CHAPTER 29

Computer Privacy and Speech has been revised as follows:

- Clarified the standard for constitutional right to privacy in Section 29.1.
- Updated the status of state laws regulating use and access to data.
- Updated the laws regulating online gambling.
- Included multiple-choice questions designed to reinforce learning objectives.

CHAPTER 30

Social Media and the Law has been revised as follows:

- Updated the opening quote.
- Added subsection to 30.5 Removal of Accounts.
- Included multiple-choice questions designed to reinforce learning objectives.

CHAPTER 31

Conducting Business in Cyberspace has been revised as follows:

- Added a new quote at beginning of the chapter to focus on blockchain.
- Renamed 31.1 Business, the Internet, and Blockchain to explain the emerging role of blockchain technology in the business landscape.
- Revised Thinking Critically about the Law question 33 to reflect the increase in the offering limits for equity crowdfunding.
- Included multiple-choice questions designed to reinforce learning objectives.

CHAPTER 32

The Employer–Employee Relationship has been revised as follows:

- Added a new quote at the beginning of the chapter.
- Clarified the need for documentation in 32.6 Employee References.
- Clarified that states and local municipalities have enacted minimum wage higher than the federal minimum wage.
- Included multiple-choice questions designed to reinforce learning objectives.

CHAPTER 33

Employment Law has been revised as follows:

- Updated Section 33.2 to reflect the U.S. Supreme Court ruling applying the protection against gender discrimination in employment to discrimination based on sexual orientation and gender identity.
- Included multiple-choice questions designed to reinforce learning objectives.

CHAPTERS 34 AND 35

These chapters now include multiple-choice questions designed to reinforce learning objectives. Chapter 35 also has a new opening quote.

CHAPTER 36

International Business Law has been revised as follows:

- Updated the status of the USMCA.
- Updated the list of European Union members.
- Included multiple-choice questions designed to reinforce learning objectives.

CHAPTER 37

Business and the Environment has been revised as follows:

- Added a new opening quote.
- Revised Section 37.5 to clarify the standard for negligence.
- Included multiple-choice questions designed to reinforce learning objectives.

CHAPTER 38

Health Care Law has been revised as follows:

- Added a new opening quote.
- Included multiple-choice questions designed to reinforce learning objectives.

SUPPLEMENTARY MATERIALS

The Constitution of the United States can be found in the Appendix.

Acknowledgments

We would like to extend our sincere appreciation to the following individuals:

- To the reviewers who have contributed their time and ideas to the development of the 2024 release:

Bonnie Bolinger
Ivy Tech Community College

Joyce Brooks
King's College

Jeff Bruns
Bacone College

Murray Brunton
Central Ohio Technical College

Barbara Desautels
Hesser College

Konstantinos Diamantis
Tunxis Community College

Donna Donathan
Huntington Junior College

Richard Gendler
Florida Atlantic University

John Gray
Faulkner University

Denise Greaves
Herzing College

Diane Hagan
Ohio Business College

Christie Highlander
Southwestern Illinois College

Thomas Hughes
University of South Carolina

Jill Jasperson
Utah Valley University

Steven Kaber
Baldwin-Wallace College

Jill Kingsbury
Metropolitan Community Colleges–Maple Woods

Gilbert Logan
Bryant & Stratton College

Kirsten Mast
The College of Idaho

Debra McCarthy
Central Lakes College

James McCord
Huntington Junior College

Donna McCurley
Gadsden State Community College

Victoria Miller
Piedmont Technical College

Kristin Mueller
Ivy Tech Community College

William Padley
Madison Area Technical College

Elisabeth Sperow
California Polytechnic State University

Cathy Steiner
DuBois Business College

Fran Tannenbaum
NVCC Woodbridge Campus

Matthew Thisse
Dorsey Business Schools

Lori Whisenant
C.T. Bauer College of Business University of Houston

Robert Wible
Bradford School

Finally, this content was but a raw, unsold manuscript until the skilled publishing team refined it. Our manuscript benefited immeasurably from the guidance of the multiple levels of skill provided to us by McGraw Hill. We respect and honor our Managing Director, Rebecca Olson; Executive Portfolio Manager, Kathleen Klehr; Product Developer, Eva Lopez of Agate Publishing; Marketing Manager, Nate Anderson; and Content Project Managers, Sherry Kane and George Theofanopoulos.

A GUIDED TOUR

The 2024 release of *Essentials of Business Law* is designed to ensure that students will not only learn fundamental applications of business law, but also will be able to put those basics into practice after reading a multitude of real-world examples and performing several skill assessment activities.

"A concise, well written, introduction into Business Law that focuses on essential knowledge regarding the various topics. An excellent textbook for college students embarking into the subject of Business Law."

–Fran Tannenbaum, Northern Virginia Community College: Woodbridge Campus

CHAPTER OPENING QUOTE

Each chapter opens with a lighthearted but thoughtful quote. The quotes come from a variety of sources, including famous judges, lawyers, entertainers, and businesspeople.

OUR SYSTEM OF LAW

"As long as I have any choice, I will stay only in a country where political liberty, toleration, and equality of all citizens before the law are the rule."

Albert Einstein,
noted scientist

Rubberball/Getty Images

LEARNING OUTCOMES

After studying this chapter and completing the assessment, you will be able to

1.1 Discuss the application of law in today's world.

1.2 Provide examples of how this application of law affects (a) one's personal or social operations, and (c) governments.

1.3 Identify the principal sources of law in the United States.

1.4 Explain the reasons for the preparation of the Uniform Commercial Code.

1.5 Cite and describe the major classifications of law.

1.6 Distinguish moral law from legal obligations.

1.7 Describe the structure of our federal and state court systems.

LEARNING OUTCOMES

Learning Outcomes outline the focus of the chapter and provide a roadmap for the material ahead. Each is tied directly to a main heading in the chapter, as well as a corresponding Chapter Summary point, to help reiterate important topics throughout.

LEGAL TERMS

Legal Terms are identified at the beginning of each chapter, as well as in the margins where they first appear in the text. They offer expanded coverage to ensure students are comfortable with the language after completing the course.

LEGAL terms

- plaintiff
- defendant
- *stare decisis*
- common law
- precedent
- case law
- statutory law
- ordinance
- administrative law
- Uniform Commercial Code (UCC)
- moral law
- jurisdiction

EXAMPLE 2.1

▸ BP Oil operated a drilling facility in the Gulf of Mexico that exploded, killing 11 workers and creating a devastating oil spill that had an enormous negative impact on the ecosystem of the Gulf. BP Oil was accused of using shortcuts in its well capping system and also appears to have had an inadequate response system in place for the spill.

EXAMPLES

Examples throughout the chapter help students understand concepts in a real-world context. Each creates a scenario that ties directly to a key topic, ensuring students will be able to recognize and apply what they have learned in their careers.

"I particularly like these examples because they are real-life cases that explain the material that the student just read. My students have said the examples help them to understand the Principles of Law."

–Kristin Mueller, Ivy Tech Community College

CHAPTER SUMMARY

2.1 Examples of how ethics in our world have negatively affected business practices include investors acting on insider information, accounting scandals, investment fraud, businesses polluting our natural habitat, and individuals acting unethically in the development of medical and electronic technology. The expansion of global markets also raises some ethical predicaments for business professionals.

2.2 Morals are concerned with an individual person's beliefs as to right and wrong. Ethics is about the standards and principles for the behavior of individuals within a society. Values are beliefs or standards considered worthwhile.

2.3 Legal mandates are imposed on individuals or groups by authorities or governments. In contrast, ethical considerations generally spring from within individuals or organizations. However, ethical beliefs are the foundation of many of our laws.

2.4 Business firms respond to ethical concerns by acts of corporate responsibility and the formulation of codes of ethics, or credos. Educational institutions offer courses and workshops and expand their existing programs. Governments enact legislation and create programs to protect consumers and the environment and to ensure ethical behavior of business firms and the government itself. Trade and professional associations develop guidelines for business and professional members.

2.5 Some ways business can ensure ethical practices include integrating corporate codes of ethics and relying on whistleblowers. Corporate codes of ethics vary from one firm or industry to another. Whistleblowing is the exposing of an unethical situation to an authority or the media.

CHAPTER SUMMARIES

Chapter Summaries correspond to particular performance objectives and chapter headings, making quick reference and retention of key concepts easy.

CHAPTER ONE
ASSESSMENT

MATCHING LEGAL TERMS

Match each of the numbered definitions with the correct term in the following list.

a. administrative law	g. executive order	m. *stare decisis*
b. appellate court	h. moral law	n. trial court
c. civil law	i. original jurisdiction	o. Uniform Commercial Code
d. common law	j. plaintiffs	
e. criminal law	k. precedents	
f. defendants	l. statutory law	

1. A legally binding directive issued by the president. 1. _____
2. The portion of the law based on the decisions of the old English courts. 2. _____
3. A judicial body that has original jurisdiction in cases involving state law. 3. _____
4. Court decisions that later courts tend to follow. 4. _____
5. Those who bring suit against others. 5. _____
6. A judicial body empowered by law to review the findings of a lower judicial body. 6. _____
7. The practice of a court to follow previous decisions. 7. _____

CHAPTER ASSESSMENTS

Chapter Assessments sharpen students' critical thinking, decision making, teamwork, technology, and communication skills and aid in student retention. Assessments include:

- Matching Key Terms
- True/False Quiz
- Multiple Choice Quiz
- Discussion Questions
- Thinking Critically about the Law
- Case Questions
- Case Analysis
- Legal Research

ADDITIONAL MCGRAW HILL CONNECT

EVERGREEN

Content and technology are ever-changing, and it is important that you can keep your course up to date with the latest information and assessments. That's why we want to deliver the most current and relevant content for your course, hassle-free.

Essentials of Business Law is moving to an Evergreen delivery model, which means it has content, tools, and technology that is updated and relevant, with updates delivered directly to your existing McGraw Hill Connect® course. Engage students and freshen up assignments with up-to-date coverage of select topics and assessments, all without having to switch editions or build a new course.

POLLING

Every learner has unique needs. Uncover where and when you're needed with the new Polling tool in McGraw Hill Connect®! Polling allows you to discover where students are in real time. Engage students and help them create connections with your course content while gaining valuable insight during lectures. Leverage polling data to deliver personalized instruction when and where it is needed most.

APPLICATION-BASED ACTIVITIES

The 2024 release contains Application-Based Activities for Business Law. This digital feature provides students valuable practice using problem-solving skills to apply their knowledge

to realistic scenarios. Students progress from understanding basic concepts to using their knowledge to analyze complex scenarios and solve problems. Application-Based Activities have been developed for the most often taught topics (as ranked by instructors) in the business law course. These unique activities are assignable and auto-gradable in Connect.

UWORLD CPA REVIEW

UWorld
YOUR WORLD OF LEARNING

McGraw Hill has partnered with UWorld CPA Review, a global leader in CPA Exam preparation, to provide students a smooth transition from the accounting classroom to successful completion of the CPA Exam. While many aspiring accountants wait until they have completed their academic studies to begin preparing for the CPA Exam, research shows that those who become familiar with exam content earlier in the process have a stronger chance of successfully passing the CPA Exam. Accordingly, students using these McGraw Hill materials will have access to sample CPA Exam multiple-choice questions from UWorld CPA Review, with expert-written explanations and solutions. All questions are either directly from the AICPA or are modeled on AICPA questions that appear in the exam. Instructors may assign the auto-gradable UWorld CPA Review multiple-choice questions in Connect. McGraw Hill and UWorld CPA Review are dedicated to supporting every accounting student along their journey, ultimately helping them achieve career success in the accounting profession. For more information about the full UWorld CPA Review program, exam requirements, and exam content, visit https://accounting.uworld.com/cpa-review/

MCGRAW HILL'S SMARTBOOK® 2.0

Available within Connect, SmartBook 2.0 is an adaptive learning solution that provides personalized learning to individual student needs, continually adapting to pinpoint knowledge gaps and focus learning on concepts requiring additional study. SmartBook 2.0 fosters more productive learning, taking the guesswork out of what to study, and helps students better prepare for class. With the ReadAnywhere mobile app, students can now read and complete SmartBook 2.0 assignments both online and offline. For instructors, SmartBook 2.0 provides more granular control over assignments with content selection now available at the concept level. SmartBook 2.0 also includes advanced reporting features that enable instructors to track student progress with actionable insights that guide teaching strategies and advanced instruction, for a more dynamic class experience.

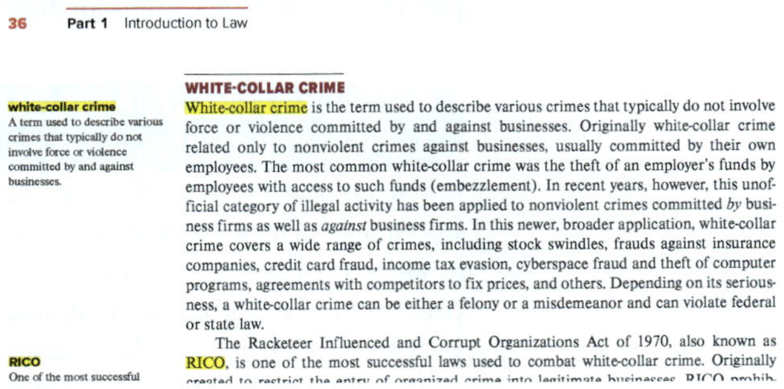
36 **Part 1** Introduction to Law

white-collar crime
A term used to describe various crimes that typically do not involve force or violence committed by and against businesses.

RICO
One of the most successful

WHITE-COLLAR CRIME

White-collar crime is the term used to describe various crimes that typically do not involve force or violence committed by and against businesses. Originally white-collar crime related only to nonviolent crimes against businesses, usually committed by their own employees. The most common white-collar crime was the theft of an employer's funds by employees with access to such funds (embezzlement). In recent years, however, this unofficial category of illegal activity has been applied to nonviolent crimes committed *by* business firms as well as *against* business firms. In this newer, broader application, white-collar crime covers a wide range of crimes, including stock swindles, frauds against insurance companies, credit card fraud, income tax evasion, cyberspace fraud and theft of computer programs, agreements with competitors to fix prices, and others. Depending on its seriousness, a white-collar crime can be either a felony or a misdemeanor and can violate federal or state law.

The Racketeer Influenced and Corrupt Organizations Act of 1970, also known as RICO, is one of the most successful laws used to combat white-collar crime. Originally

PROCTORIO REMOTE PROCTORING & BROWSER-LOCKING CAPABILITIES

Remote proctoring and browser-locking capabilities, hosted by Proctorio within Connect, provide control of the assessment environment by enabling security options and verifying the identity of the student.

Seamlessly integrated within Connect, these services allow instructors to control the assessment experience by verifying identification, restricting browser activity, and monitoring student actions.

Instant and detailed reporting gives instructors an at-a-glance view of potential academic integrity concerns, thereby avoiding personal bias and supporting evidence-based claims.

READANYWHERE® APP

Read or study when it's convenient with McGraw Hill's free ReadAnywhere® app. Available for iOS and Android smartphones or tablets, give users access to McGraw Hill tools including the eBook and SmartBook® or Adaptive Learning Assignments in McGraw Hill Connect®. Students can take notes, highlight, and complete assignments offline–all their work will sync when connected to Wi-Fi. Students log in with their Connect username and password to start learning–anytime, anywhere!

OLC-ALIGNED COURSES: IMPLEMENTING HIGH-QUALITY INSTRUCTION AND ASSESSMENT THROUGH PRECONFIGURED COURSEWARE

In consultation with the Online Learning Consortium (OLC) and our certified Faculty Consultants, McGraw Hill has created preconfigured courseware using OLC's quality scorecard to align with best practices in online course delivery. This turnkey courseware contains a combination of formative assessments, summative assessments, homework, and application activities, and can easily be customized to meet an individual instructor's needs and desired course outcomes. For more information, visit https://www.mheducation.com/highered/olc.

TEST BUILDER IN CONNECT

Available within McGraw Hill Connect®, Test Builder is a cloud-based tool that enables instructors to format tests that can be printed, administered within a Learning Management System, or exported as a Word document. Test Builder offers a modern, streamlined interface for easy content configuration that matches course needs, without requiring a download.

Test Builder allows you to:

- access all test bank content from a particular title.
- easily pinpoint the most relevant content through robust filtering options.
- manipulate the order of questions or scramble questions and/or answers.
- pin questions to a specific location within a test.
- determine your preferred treatment of algorithmic questions.
- choose the layout and spacing.
- add instructions and configure default settings.

Test Builder provides a secure interface for better protection of content and allows for just-in-time updates to flow directly into assessments.

WRITING ASSIGNMENT

Available within McGraw Hill Connect®, the Writing Assignment tool delivers a learning experience to help students improve written communication skills and conceptual understanding. Assign, monitor, grade, and provide feedback on writing more efficiently and effectively.

CREATE YOUR BOOK, YOUR WAY

McGraw Hill's Content Collections Powered by Create® is a self-service website that enables instructors to create custom course materials–print and eBooks–by drawing upon McGraw Hill's comprehensive, cross-disciplinary content. Choose what you want from our high-quality textbooks, digital products, articles, cases, and more. Combine it with your own content quickly and easily, and tap into other rights-secured, third-party content such as cases, articles, readings, cartoons, and labs. Content can be arranged in a way that makes the most sense for your course, and you can select your own cover and include the course name and school information as well. Choose the best format for your course: color print, black-and-white print, or eBook. The eBook can be included in your Connect course and is available on the free ReadAnywhere® app for smartphone or tablet access as well. When you are finished customizing, you will receive a free digital copy to review in just minutes! Visit McGraw Hill Create®–www.mcgrawhillcreate.com–today and begin building!

McGraw Hill connect®

A complete course platform

Connect enables you to build deeper connections with your students through cohesive digital content and tools, creating engaging learning experiences. We are committed to providing you with the right resources and tools to support all your students along their personal learning journeys.

65%
Less Time Grading

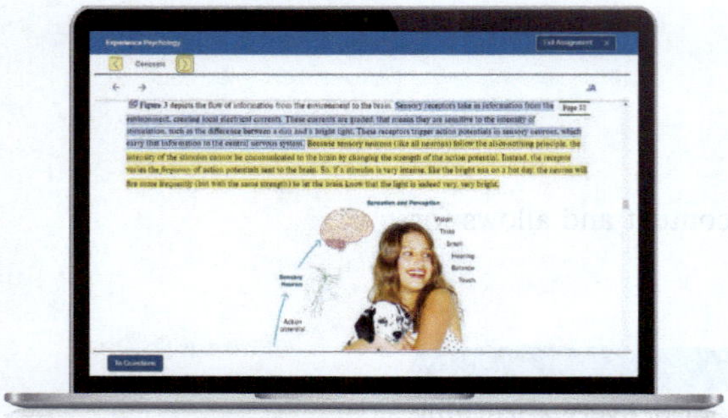

Laptop: Getty Images; Woman/dog: George Doyle/Getty Images

Every learner is unique

In Connect, instructors can assign an adaptive reading experience with SmartBook® 2.0. Rooted in advanced learning science principles, SmartBook 2.0 delivers each student a personalized experience, focusing students on their learning gaps, ensuring that the time they spend studying is time well spent.
mheducation.com/highered/connect/smartbook

Study anytime, anywhere

Encourage your students to download the free ReadAnywhere® app so they can access their online eBook, SmartBook® 2.0, or Adaptive Learning Assignments when it's convenient, even when they're offline. And since the app automatically syncs with their Connect account, all of their work is available every time they open it. Find out more at **mheducation.com/readanywhere**

> ***"I really liked this app—it made it easy to study when you don't have your textbook in front of you."***
> Jordan Cunningham, a student at *Eastern Washington University*

Effective tools for efficient studying

Connect is designed to help students be more productive with simple, flexible, intuitive tools that maximize study time and meet students' individual learning needs. Get learning that works for everyone with Connect.

SUPPORT AT every step

Education for all

McGraw Hill works directly with Accessibility Services departments and faculty to meet the learning needs of all students. Please contact your Accessibility Services Office, and ask them to email **accessibility@mheducation.com**, or visit **mheducation.com/about/accessibility** for more information.

Affordable solutions, added value

Make technology work for you with LMS integration for single sign-on access, mobile access to the digital textbook, and reports to quickly show you how each of your students is doing. And with our Inclusive Access program, you can provide all these tools at the lowest available market price to your students. Ask your McGraw Hill representative for more information.

Solutions for your challenges

A product isn't a solution. Real solutions are affordable, reliable, and come with training and ongoing support when you need it and how you want it. Visit **supportateverystep.com** for videos and resources both you and your students can use throughout the term.

Updated and relevant content

Our new Evergreen delivery model provides the most current and relevant content for your course, hassle-free. Content, tools, and technology updates are delivered directly to your existing McGraw Hill Connect® course. Engage students and freshen up assignments with up-to-date coverage of select topics and assessments, all without having to switch editions or build a new course.

ESSENTIALS OF
BUSINESS LAW

PART 1

Introduction to Law

Hisham F. Ibrahim/Getty Images

chapter 1
Our System of Law

LEARNING OUTCOMES

After studying this chapter and completing the assessment, you will be able to

1.1 Discuss the application of law in today's world.

1.2 Provide examples of how this application of law affects (a) one's personal or social life, (b) business or business operations, and (c) governments.

1.3 Identify the principal sources of law in the United States.

1.4 Explain the reasons for the preparation of the Uniform Commercial Code.

1.5 Cite and describe the major classifications of law.

1.6 Distinguish moral law from legal obligations.

1.7 Describe the structure of our federal and state court systems.

LEGAL terms

- plaintiff
- defendant
- *stare decisis*
- common law
- precedent
- case law
- statutory law
- ordinance
- administrative law
- Uniform Commercial Code (UCC)
- moral law
- jurisdiction

OUR SYSTEM OF LAW

"As long as I have any choice, I will stay only in a country where political liberty, toleration, and equality of all citizens before the law are the rule."

Albert Einstein,
noted scientist

Rubberball/Getty Images

1.1 THE LAW IN OUR WORLD

The U.S. Supreme Court Building.
Pixtal/AGE Fotostock

When students in their 20s were asked to say the first thing that came to mind when they heard the word *law,* responses included "cops and robbers," "courtroom," "narcs," "drug raid," "legislators," "speed limit," and "traffic violation." Without doubt, the impressions that most people have of the law are influenced not so much by actual experience, but by the way the law is portrayed on television and in movies. Sometimes the picture is distorted. Justice always seems to triumph, the "good guys" usually win, and the "bad guys" ultimately are caught and punished–a view that society wishes were true.

Unfortunately, movies and television shows provide the only picture many people get of the law. What people do not see are the many day-in, day-out applications of the law that deal with such ordinary matters as an automobile driver charged with having caused injury to another driver or one corporation suing another corporation over responsibility for defective merchandise. In real life, the administration of justice can be much less exciting than is often portrayed. There are areas of the law that do not hinge on clear-cut "right" or "wrong" but on an ill-defined middle ground. Still, justice and law are hallmarks of a free society in today's world.

The fact of the matter is that our system of law functions largely outside the spotlight of public attention. Every business day, in every city, town, and village in this country, courts are in session, juries are being selected, and attorneys are busy seeking favorable decisions for their clients, who might be either a plaintiff, the person who brings a lawsuit against another, or a defendant, the person against whom a lawsuit is brought or who is charged with a violation of the law.

plaintiff
The party who begins a lawsuit by filing a complaint in the appropriate court.

defendant
The party against whom a lawsuit is brought and from whom recovery is sought.

Although the ordinary applications of law are not quite as exciting as a television drama, it is important to understand certain essential legal principles because they affect both one's business and one's personal life. Accountants, for example, need to know that if they do their work carelessly and cause someone to sustain a loss, they could be sued. Just as important, a person who is planning to rent an apartment or buy a home needs to know their legal rights as they relate to property.

No one person can possibly know the entire body of law. Even learned judges and lawyers tend to specialize in certain fields of law. The average person should, however, strive to understand some of the general principles of law, how to avoid common problems and pitfalls, and when to seek professional help.

The law presented in this text deals primarily with the general principles of law and their applications to business. Some chapters focus on personal applications of the law, however, and others treat ethical aspects of personal and business behavior.

1.2 APPLICATIONS OF LAW

The effects of law are felt throughout society. Indeed, some aspects of the law apply to all persons, institutions, and organizations.

PERSONAL APPLICATIONS OF LAW

Imagine, for a moment, how the law affects just one day in people's lives. The alarm clock that awakens them in the morning is set to a time that is regulated by a law establishing standard time zones. Various federal and state laws regulate the purity and wholesomeness of their breakfast foods. The clothing they wear is labeled in compliance with governmental regulations. Their right to drive a car is regulated by state laws, and speed limits and other traffic laws are often the responsibility of state or local officials. People are assured that no one else may occupy their homes while they are away at school or work because the law protects their property rights. The safety and freedom they enjoy are possible because they live in a nation of order–and that order is a result of laws passed for the benefit of the people and the protection of their rights.

BUSINESS APPLICATIONS OF LAW

If people's personal lives are influenced by law, think of how much more businesses, and those who work for businesses, are affected by law. Every business must comply with many federal, state, and local laws that are primarily aimed at regulating business activity. A firm that wishes to set up business in a particular community may find that there are laws that prohibit such activities. For example, local zoning ordinances might prohibit the operation of a noisy factory in a residential area. State and federal laws prohibit or regulate the operation of certain businesses that might pollute the environment. Still other laws require that businesses provide safe working conditions for employees or demand that only qualified persons perform certain jobs. State laws, for instance, require that barbers and pharmacists pass examinations to be licensed.

GOVERNMENT APPLICATIONS OF LAW

Legislatures at all levels of government pass many laws that apply only to businesses and individuals, but some laws apply specifically to governments. For example, the federal government may pass a law that provides funding for building highways or for low-income housing. The same law may require that states, counties, or municipalities maintain them.

1.3 SOURCES OF LAW

The ever-changing body of law that affects everyone in our country has arisen from a number of sources. As a result, laws sometimes conflict with one another. The way these conflicts are resolved will be discussed in this chapter.

CONSTITUTIONAL LAW

In our country, the principles and ideals that protect individual liberty and freedom are incorporated in the Constitution of the United States (the federal Constitution). This historic document gives the federal government certain reasonable powers and, at the same time, clearly limits the use of those powers. In addition, each state has a constitution of its own that gives certain powers to the various levels of government within that state. Like the federal Constitution, state constitutions provide safeguards for the rights of individuals within that particular state. You will learn more about the Constitution of the United States and the important foundation it provides to our legal system in Chapter 5 (see Appendix).

The Constitution of the United States.
Comstock/Getty Images

EXECUTIVE ORDERS

An executive order is a legally binding directive issued by the president with the intent to change the manner in which federal agencies and officials operate so as to improve the practices of the federal government. Perhaps the most historically significant example of an executive order was President Lincoln's *Emancipation Proclamation,* an order issued on January 1, 1863, proclaiming all people enslaved to be forever free, and ordering all segments of the executive branch to treat these persons as free. Other more recent executive orders include those issued in response to the COVID-19 pandemic in 2020.

TREATIES

A treaty is a written agreement between two or more countries that serves to establish terms of an international relationship. Treaties become legally binding when they are approved by two-thirds of the Senate (see Chapter 36).

COMMON LAW

After the Revolutionary War, one of the most difficult tasks faced by our newly independent nation was to establish a system of law. Because the original states were formerly English colonies, it is not surprising that the new states adopted the system of laws that had been used in England for hundreds of years–that is, relying on previous legal decisions when similar disputes arose. This practice of relying on previous decisions is known as *stare decisis*, which means "to stand on decided cases." The English system is known as the common law and still influences legal decisions in the United States today.

stare decisis
The practice of relying on previous decisions in which similar disputes arose.

common law
The body of recorded decisions that courts refer to and rely upon when making later legal decisions.

PRECEDENT

A precedent is a court decision on which later courts rely in similar cases. In some instances, a court may be influenced by precedent; in other cases it may not. Whether a court follows a precedent, or decides to overrule it, depends on the court that has ruled on the case and whether the previous case was decided by the highest court in the same state. Decisions made by the U.S. Supreme Court, for example, must be followed by other courts.

precedent
A model case that a court can follow when facing a similar situation.

Court decisions are recorded in writing so that lawyers and judges can refer to them in preparing or hearing a case. These decisions are published in books called reporters, and many of these decisions are available online. Each case decision is identified by a citation, which includes the names of the parties involved followed by the volume number, the name of the reporter, and the beginning page number of the case. For example, the case of *Milkovich v. News-Herald,* 473 N.E.2d 1191, is reported in volume 473 of the *Northeastern Reporter, Second Series,* beginning on page 1191.

Court decisions are published in books called reporters.
Jim Sugar/Corbis Documentary/Getty Images

CASE LAW

Sometimes a statute or a common law precedent may be difficult to apply to certain cases or, with the passing of time, may take on a different meaning. An existing statute or an accepted precedent may be based on outmoded standards of justice. In such cases, a court may disregard earlier interpretations of a statute or a principle of common law, or it may interpret them differently. The court's decisions in these cases influence later cases because they too become precedents that may be followed in similar cases. The effects of these decisions have been called case law.

case law
The effects of court decisions that involve the same or similar facts.

STATUTORY LAW

Both federal and state constitutions are general statements of the powers of governments and the rights of individuals. The specific applications of powers and rights are provided for in laws enacted by federal, state, and local governments. Each state constitution provides for a legislature that represents the people. These legislatures have the power to enact laws so long as they do not conflict with either the federal or the state constitution. The laws passed by Congress and by state legislatures are called statutes, and the field of law that deals with these statutes is known as statutory law. A law that is passed by a local government, such as a city council, is often called an ordinance.

Not only do statutes provide the specific applications of the powers and rights in the constitutions, they also allow governments to respond to particular circumstances. For example, when the federal and state constitutions were written, cellular telephones and automobiles were not even imagined, much less matters to be regulated. Yet after these were developed, various legislatures passed statutes that restricted the use of cellular telephones while driving.

statutory law
The field of law involving statutes, which are laws passed by Congress or by state legislatures.

ordinance
A law that is passed by a local government, such as a city council.

ADMINISTRATIVE LAW

Protection of the rights and freedom of individuals and organizations is well established by the federal and state constitutions, by statutory law, and by common law. Still, today's complex society and system of justice present special needs that require certain laws that include their own administrative machinery. Sometimes when a federal, state, or local legislative body enacts a law, it also sets up an organization to establish rules and enforce them. Administrative law is the body of rules, regulations, and decisions created by administrative agencies.

administrative law
The body of rules, regulations, and decisions created by administrative agencies.

The practice of establishing specialized administrative agencies has several advantages. For example, it relieves the police and the courts from having to establish and enforce regulations that are often highly technical. Administrative agencies include federal agencies such as the National Labor Relations Board, state agencies such as public service commissions, and local agencies such as boards of health. These agencies have in common the authority to establish rules that have the force of law, to maintain "courts" that are often called appeal boards, and to conduct "trials" that are often called hearings. Because administrative law has become such an important part of our legal system, an entire chapter will be devoted to it (see Chapter 6).

1.4 UNIFORM COMMERCIAL CODE

When the United States was primarily a farming nation and there was relatively little commerce among states, it did not matter that the state constitutions and statutes differed from state to state. As trade among the states increased, however, so did the problems caused by the conflict in business laws among the different states. For example, businesspeople knowing the laws of their state had little difficulty so long as customers were all from the same state. But when business was conducted with customers in many states, they had to know the law in all of them.

To help solve this problem, the Uniform Commercial Code (UCC) was prepared in 1952 by the National Conference of Commissioners on Uniform State Laws. The UCC is a set of laws that govern various commercial transactions and are designed to bring uniformity to the laws of the states. Since then, all 50 states have adopted the UCC as part of their state law. Not every state has adopted the entire UCC, and often state courts have differing interpretations of their UCC sections. This book will refer to the most widely used version of UCC sections.

Uniform Commercial Code (UCC)
A set of laws that govern various commercial transactions and that is designed to bring uniformity to the laws of the states.

1.5 CLASSIFICATION OF LAWS

The various laws, regardless of origin, can be grouped into several broad classifications, each of which represents a legal specialty. Frequently, a lawyer will specialize in one of these areas.

- *Constitutional law* is the study of the federal Constitution, its interpretation by the federal courts, and its relationship to existing laws.
- *Civil law* is the study of the rights and obligations of individuals and includes the law of property, the law of contracts, and the law of torts.
- *Criminal law* is concerned with acts against society (criminal acts) and the regulation of criminal activity.
- *Administrative law* is concerned with the conduct of governmental administrative agencies and their regulations. Examples are tax laws and laws dealing with transportation and trade.
- *International law* is concerned with the conduct of nations in their relations with other nations.

1.6 MORAL LAW

moral law
The "law" concerned with the unenforceable obligations that people have to one another.

Since earliest times, people have recognized that they are to a certain extent responsible for one another and have obligations to one another beyond those required by the law. For example, a person who sees someone drowning has a moral obligation to try to save them, and a person who hears someone screaming for help in the night has a moral duty to at least call the police. Such obligations are based on moral law—that is, the "law" concerned with the unenforceable obligations that people have to one another. Many legal obligations are based on moral obligations, but not all moral obligations are legally enforceable; a person's conscience is often the only means of enforcement.

Moral law refers to the unenforceable obligations that people have to one another.
MC3 Dylan McCord/US Navy

1.7 A SYSTEM OF COURTS

Some of our laws came from sources that were not originally concerned with human freedom. However, most legal scholars agree that today's laws provide adequate protection of the rights of the individual. But the mere existence of laws is not enough.

There must be a means of administering the law to protect the rights of individuals and businesses and to curtail the activities of wrongdoers. In this country, courts and governmental agencies have been established to administer the law. The federal and state constitutions and the entire body of written law would be of little value to individuals and businesses if there were no provision for enforcing the law. Police alone cannot fulfill this function. The federal and state constitutions provide for the establishment of a system of courts that ensure citizens' rights and enforce federal and state statutes.

COURT JURISDICTION

The authority or power of a court to hear cases, as granted by a constitution or legislative act, is known as the court's jurisdiction. A court may be limited in its powers to certain kinds of cases or to certain geographical areas. A court has original jurisdiction if it is authorized to hear and decide a case when it is first presented. If a court has the power to review the decisions of another court, it has appellate jurisdiction (the authority to hear appeals).

jurisdiction
The authority of a court, as granted by a constitution or legislative act, to hear and decide cases.

Courts that are given the power to hear only certain kinds of cases have special jurisdiction. Examples are family courts, traffic courts, and tax courts.

FEDERAL COURTS

The U.S. Constitution provides for a federal court system: "The judicial power of the United States, shall be vested in one Supreme Court, and in such inferior courts as the Congress may from time to time ordain and establish."

The court system that has developed has various levels. The Supreme Court of the United States is the highest court in the federal system. It serves as the court of original jurisdiction for certain kinds of cases, such as those in which a state is one of the parties. The Supreme Court rules on the constitutionality of laws by hearing selected cases that test those laws. The Supreme Court also hears appeals from the highest state courts. However, the Court actually hears only a small percentage of appeals because it has no legal obligation to review decisions of lower courts, except in very limited cases.

The federal district courts have original jurisdiction in cases involving federal statutes and in cases when the parties are citizens of different states and the amount involved is greater than $75,000. There are a total of 94 federal district courts–each state having at least one.

Most appeals from the district courts go to one of the 13 circuit courts of appeals. The decisions of the circuit courts are usually final, although further appeal to the U.S. Supreme Court is possible. Appeals of the decisions of federal administrative agencies, such as the Federal Trade Commission (FTC), are also made to the U.S. Circuit Courts of Appeals.

The federal court system also includes specialized courts that hear only certain kinds of cases. Three of these specialized courts are the U.S. Tax Court, the U.S. Bankruptcy Court, and the U.S. Claims Court. Figure 1.1 gives an overview of the federal court system. For a complete listing, maps, and information regarding the court system, visit: http://www.uscourts.gov/court_locator.aspx.

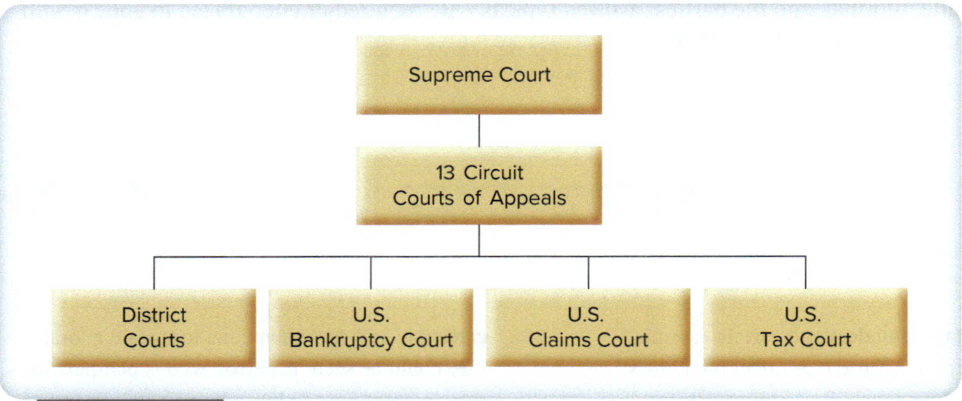

FIGURE 1.1 The Federal Court System

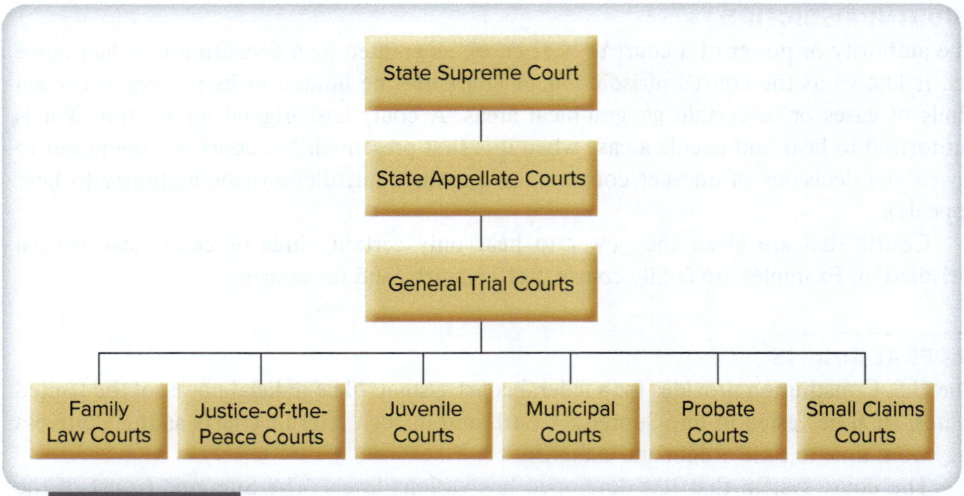

FIGURE 1.2 The State Court System

STATE COURTS

State court systems vary, but there are certain basic similarities in all state court systems. All states have general trial courts, which are courts of original jurisdiction, authorized to hear cases not otherwise restricted to specialized courts. General trial courts handle nearly all important disputes involving contracts, criminal law, and corporations. Trial courts in a state may be large municipal courts, with such specialized areas of jurisdiction as traffic violations, juvenile conduct, and domestic relations, or they may be small justice-of-the-peace courts called magistrate courts, established to hear certain minor violations of law.

If one of the parties in a case feels that they did not have a fair trial in the court of original jurisdiction, they can, with the aid of an attorney, seek an appeal in a state appellate court, which hears appeals from the trial courts. The names of appellate courts vary in different states. Beyond the courts of appeals are higher-level courts, often called supreme courts, which make final determinations on matters of law. In some less populous states that have no intermediate court of appeals, the state supreme court also serves as a court of appeals. Figure 1.2 gives an overview of the state court system.

Many communities have special courts to handle cases involving small amounts of money. Where these courts exist, there is usually a limit, ranging from $2,500 to $25,000, on the amount of the claim. Because there is a limit on the amount of money that can be involved, these courts are often called small claims courts. The proceedings usually are quite informal, and the parties involved typically are required or encouraged to appear without lawyers to represent them.

CHAPTER SUMMARY

1.1 It is important to understand certain essential legal principles because they affect both one's business and personal life. Accountants, for example, need to know that if they do their work carelessly and cause someone to sustain a loss, they could be sued. A person who is planning to rent an apartment or buy a home needs to know their legal rights as they relate to property.

1.2 Examples of how the application of law affects a person's personal and social life can be seen everywhere from the foods eaten, the medicines used, the goods purchased, to the clothing worn. Examples of how the law affects business can be seen in zoning ordinances, regulation of environmental pollution, and licensing laws. Examples of how the law affects the federal government include laws providing for funding for building highways or for low-income housing, or requiring that states, counties, or municipalities maintain them.

1.3 The sources of law in the United States are the Constitution, executive orders, treaties, common law, precedent, case law, statutory law, and administrative law.

1.4 To address conflicts in business law among states, the UCC was prepared in 1952. The UCC is a set of laws that govern various commercial transactions and are designed to bring uniformity to the laws of the states.

1.5 Law in the United States is typically classified as constitutional law, civil law, criminal law, administrative law, and international law.

1.6 Moral law is concerned with the unenforceable obligations that people have to one another; legal obligations are those required by enacted statutes and other laws.

1.7 The structure of the federal and state court systems includes courts of original jurisdiction (federal district courts and state courts) and appeals courts (federal circuit courts of appeals, the U.S. Supreme Court, and state appellate courts).

CHAPTER ONE ASSESSMENT

MATCHING LEGAL TERMS

Match each of the numbered definitions with the correct term in the following list.

a. administrative law
b. appellate court
c. civil law
d. common law
e. criminal law
f. defendants
g. executive order
h. moral law
i. original jurisdiction
j. plaintiffs
k. precedents
l. statutory law
m. *stare decisis*
n. trial court
o. Uniform Commercial Code

1. A legally binding directive issued by the president. **1.** _____

2. The portion of the law based on the decisions of the old English courts. **2.** _____

3. A judicial body that has original jurisdiction in cases involving state law. **3.** _____

4. Court decisions that later courts tend to follow. **4.** _____

5. Those who bring suit against others. **5.** _____

6. A judicial body empowered by law to review the findings of a lower judicial body. **6.** _____

7. The practice of a court to follow previous decisions. **7.** _____

8. The category of law concerned with acts against society. 8. _____

9. The authorization of a judicial body to hear certain types of cases when they are first brought to court. 9. _____

10. The legal specialty concerned with the rights and obligations of individuals. 10. _____

11. A group of laws dealing with business transactions in a consistent manner that have been adopted by most of the states. 11. _____

12. The legal specialty concerned with the relationship between businesses or individuals and government agencies. 12. _____

13. The branch of the law concerned with the laws passed by Congress and by state legislatures. 13. _____

14. The law concerned with the unenforceable obligations that people have to one another. 14. _____

15. Those against whom a suit is brought or who are charged with a violation of the law. 15. _____

TRUE/FALSE QUIZ

Indicate whether each of the following statements is true or false:

16. In our country, the principles and ideals guarding our individual liberty are presented in the common law. 16. _____

17. Statutes are laws passed by state and federal legislatures. 17. _____

18. The kind of law that results when a court disregards an existing statute, an accepted precedent, or a principle of common law, or interprets them differently, with the result that a new precedent is established, is known as precedent law. 18. _____

19. The purpose of the Uniform Commercial Code is to provide uniform laws for all states to regulate business transactions in the states. 19. _____

20. Unenforceable obligations that people have to one another are considered to be an aspect of moral law. 20. _____

21. The authority of a court, as granted by a constitution or legislative act, is known as the court's jurisdiction. 21. _____

22. If a court has the power to review the decisions of another court, it has original jurisdiction. 22. _____

MULTIPLE CHOICE QUIZ

Choose the correct answer from the choices given after each question.

23. Common law is defined as (a) the body of law common to all 50 states (b) the body of law common to the majority of the 50 states (c) the body of law recorded from previous court decisions (d) the body of law enacted by the legislature. **23.** _____

24. Which of the following is not a source of law that is enforced by state or federal governments in the United States? (a) Moral law (b) Case law (c) Statutory law (d) Administrative law. **24.** _____

25. What recommended body of laws has been enacted to regulate business law by all 50 states? (a) The Uniform Business Code (b) The Uniform Commercial Code (c) The Uniform Regulatory Code (d) The Uniform Legal Code. **25.** _____

26. Moral law is defined as (a) law defined by moral obligations not enforceable by law (b) law defined by moral obligations enforceable by law (c) law defined by religious authority only (d) law defined by legislatures as moral law. **26.** _____

27. Federal district court opinions are appealed to (a) state supreme courts (b) federal circuit courts (c) federal specialized courts (d) state circuit courts. **27.** _____

28. The power of a court to hear a case is known as (a) jurisdiction (b) *stare decisis* (c) precedent (d) advocacy **28.** _____

29. Federal Courts hear cases that involve (a) any state or federal claim (b) only federal claims (c) federal claims and claims by citizens of different states (d) only state claims. **29.** _____

30. The highest level court in the federal system is (a) the D.C. Circuit Court (b) any state supreme court (c) the U.S. Senate (d) the U.S. Supreme Court. **30.** _____

31. Laws passed by legislatures are known as (a) statutory law (b) case law (c) administrative law (d) moral law. **31.** _____

32. Laws passed by local governments, such as city councils, are usually known as (a) statutes (b) ordinances (c) administrative regulations (d) case decisions. **32.** _____

DISCUSSION QUESTIONS

Answer the following questions and discuss them in class.

33. Describe what contemporary society would be like without the system of laws that currently exists.

34. Explain how law affects (a) people's personal or social lives and (b) business or business operations.

35. Identify the principal origins of law in the United States.

36. Cite and describe the major classifications of law.

37. Distinguish moral law from legal obligations.

38. Can common law and statutory law operate side by side? What are the advantages of each?

THINKING CRITICALLY ABOUT THE LAW

Answer the following questions, which require you to think critically about the legal principles that you learned in this chapter.

39. Personal Applications of Law Many applications of law primarily affect individuals, such as buying or selling personal property. Critique the amount and kinds of protection provided to individuals and whether you think that the law provides too much protection, limiting individual freedom, or too little protection against harm. What are some examples?

40. Business Applications of Law Consider the numerous laws that affect businesses and evaluate the regulatory climate in which they operate. Does it seem that there are too many regulations or too few? Explain your answer.

____

____

41. Government Regulation of Governments Various levels of government enact laws that affect other levels of government. Explain the reason for such seemingly inefficient interrelationships and offer an opinion of whether there might be other ways to achieve the same objectives.

____

____

42. *Stare Decisis* The legal concept of *stare decisis,* which means "to stand on decided cases," is an important factor in our system of law. Is it possible that previous cases, or precedents, do not always embody the exact same issues, concepts, and present-day circumstances as the current case to which the earlier one is applied and by which the current one is judged? What would you suggest as an alternative to the use of precedents?

____

____

43. A Question of Ethics Normally there are no prosecutions for "padding" an expense account, yet it is considered unethical. Should such activity be prosecuted more forcefully?

____

____

CASE QUESTIONS

Study each of the following cases. Answer the questions that follow with Yes or No.

44. Precedent Ferguson was arrested for possession of a small quantity of marijuana in a state where it was illegal. He argued at his trial that the highest court in a neighboring state had ruled a similar law invalid, which would be a binding precedent.

a. Is Ferguson correct in his belief? **a.** _____

b. Can a state's highest court rule that the law of another state is not binding in its own state? **b.** _____

c. Does a precedent in one state affect the law in another? **c.** _____

45. Jurisdiction A television station aired a broadcast containing insulting remarks about a local official. The official had the broadcaster charged under a state statute that prohibited making defamatory remarks on public airwaves. The broadcaster argued that the statute was in conflict with the U.S. Constitution's guaranty of free speech. The public official countered that the statute was legal and enforceable.

a. Can states enact laws that limit free speech? **a.** _____

b. Can defamatory remarks be made illegal? **b.** _____

c. Can a state statute be in conflict with the U.S. Constitution? **c.** _____

46. Civil Law Phipps became involved in a case of mistaken identity. A local merchant falsely accused her, in front of people who knew her, of shoplifting. Phipps was charged but not convicted. Angry and embarrassed, yet not wanting to spend money for an attorney, she acted as her own attorney and sued the merchant for false arrest in small claims court.

a. Can Phipps act as her own attorney? **a.** _____

b. Does small claims court have jurisdiction in this case? What other facts do you need to know? **b.** _____

c. Is there a dollar limit on the kind of case that can be brought to small claims court? **c.** _____

CASE ANALYSIS

Study each of the following cases carefully. Briefly state the principle of law and your decision.

47. Interpretation of Statute Muscarello illegally sold marijuana, which he transported in a small truck. Police discovered a handgun in the locked glove compartment of the truck. A provision in the firearms chapter of the federal law demands a five-year required prison term for persons who use or carry a firearm during or related to trafficking in drugs. Muscarello claimed that because the gun was in the locked glove compartment of the truck, it did not fall within the description of the word *carry* as used in the statute and that he was not subject to the required five-year prison term. *Did Muscarello violate the firearms chapter of the criminal code?* [*Muscarello v. United States,* 118 S. Ct. 1911 (1998)]

Principle of Law:

____

____

Decision:

____

____

48. Contract Essentials Without first obtaining the required marriage license, Evelyn and Joseph Carabetta were married in a religious ceremony. Thereafter, they lived together as husband and wife. They raised four children, all of whose birth certificates listed Joseph Carabetta as their father. At no time did either party ever deny that they were married. In an action to dissolve the marriage, Evelyn Carabetta claimed that the lack of a marriage license made the marriage void. *Does the lack of a marriage license make the marriage void?* [*Carabetta v. Carabetta,* 438 A.2d 109 (Connecticut)]

Principle of Law:

____

____

Decision:

____

____

LEGAL RESEARCH

Complete the following activities. Share your findings with the class.

49. Working in Teams In teams of three or four, interview the owners or managers of small businesses to determine the levels of laws—federal, state, or local—to which the firm is subject. Further, ask the interviewee to provide examples.

____

____

50. Using Technology Using the Internet and search engines, investigate the operation of small claims courts in your community or one nearby. Determine the kinds of cases typically heard and the limit in dollars involved in cases that these courts are authorized to hear.

____

____

chapter 2 Ethics and the Law

LEARNING OUTCOMES

After studying this chapter and completing the assessment, you will be able to

2.1 Cite some examples of how unethical behavior in our world has negatively affected business practices.

2.2 Distinguish among ethics, morals, and values. Cite influences on group and individual values.

2.3 Discuss the relationship between law and ethics.

2.4 Discuss the different types of ethical reasoning and provide examples of responses to ethical issues by business firms, educational institutions, governments, and trade and professional associations.

2.5 Discuss some ways businesses can ensure ethical practices.

LEGAL terms

- morals
- ethics
- values
- Sarbanes–Oxley Act
- code of ethics
- stakeholders
- whistleblower
- duty-based reasoning
- outcome-based reasoning

ETHICS AND THE LAW

"There may be times when we are powerless to prevent injustice, but there must never be a time when we fail to protest."

Elie Wiesel, writer, Nobel laureate, and Holocaust survivor

Evlakhov Valeriy/Shutterstock

2.1 UNETHICAL BEHAVIOR IN OUR WORLD

The news abounds with examples of unethical behavior in business, including poor treatment of employees, using insider information for personal gain, violation of consumer interests, and environmental damage from operations.

EXAMPLE 2.1

▶ BP Oil operated a drilling facility in the Gulf of Mexico that exploded, killing 11 workers and creating a devastating oil spill that had an enormous negative impact on the ecosystem of the Gulf. BP Oil was accused of using shortcuts in its well capping system and also appears to have had an inadequate response system in place for the spill.

Examples of unethical behavior in professions or government may also affect business. Technology and expansion of global markets have presented businesses with a new array of ethical questions and corresponding unethical behavior. For example, advances in genetics, cloning technology, and the use of stem cells in medical science have all raised ethical issues that were unknown even a decade earlier. Internet, computer technology, and social media have all prompted discussions of ethical issues surrounding privacy and free speech (see Chapters 29 and 30). The expansion of global markets has created new ethical issues as well. Is it ethical for an American company to do business with a company in an undemocratic country or one that engages in systemic racial segregation?

EXAMPLE 2.2

▶ The Rev. Leon Sullivan was a director of the General Motors Corporation who proposed that American companies should ensure that equal employment would be available regardless of race in its South African operations, even though South Africa had laws in place at that time requiring racial segregation. These principles were eventually adopted by several hundred other companies doing business in South Africa.

2.2 MORALS, ETHICS, AND VALUES

While morals, ethics, and values may seem synonymous, the three terms have different meanings.

Morals are individual and societal beliefs as to what is right and wrong. Ethics consist of the standards and principles that govern the behavior of individuals within a society. Both ethics and morals derive from values—that is, the beliefs or standards that underlie an individual and society's beliefs.

Individual and group values are influenced by religion, traditions, and customs. Values may be influenced by a variety of factors from one's culture—those of a nation or an ethnic group. The American culture, for example, holds that such characteristics as freedom, individualism, family life, fair play, hard work, and honesty are important. On the other hand, the values held by a subculture—for example, employees of a corporation or a department within a company—may differ from those of the larger culture.

morals
Beliefs about behavior as judged by society.

ethics
The philosophical study of what is right and wrong, good and bad.

values
Beliefs or standards considered worthwhile, and from which a society derives its moral rules.

Ethical principles have been the foundation of many of our laws.
Stockbyte/Getty Images

2.3 THE RELATIONSHIP BETWEEN LAW AND ETHICS

Legal mandates are imposed on individuals or groups by authorities or governments. Ethical considerations, on the other hand, generally spring from within individuals or organizations. However, ethical ideas have been the foundation of much of the legislation enacted by federal, state, and local governments.

EXAMPLE 2.3

Senior executives at Enron, a multimillion-dollar energy company, and its accounting firm, Arthur Anderson LLP, employed a variety of questionable accounting practices, deception, and attempts to influence politicians and the media to boost their stock price and resulting executive benefits. Executives who knew the company was headed for bankruptcy quietly sold their shares in the company while encouraging employees to retain and even buy additional shares. After Enron's eventual collapse, some senior executives, including the CEO, tried to argue that they were unaware of any illegal activity.

Sarbanes–Oxley Act
A federal statute that placed an onus on upper management to monitor closely the financial dealings and disclosures of their firms and that established a board to oversee accounting practices in the United States.

As a result of cases like Enron, Congress passed the Sarbanes-Oxley Act in 2002, which placed a greater responsibility on upper management to closely monitor the financial dealings and disclosures of their firms. The law also established a board to oversee accounting practices in the United States. The board reports to the Securities and Exchange Commission, a federal agency.

Consider the role of ethics in the laws that protect consumers against misleading advertising, deceptive labeling, and price-fixing, as well as laws enacted to protect investors from misleading financial information and fraud. These laws are clearly based on ethical considerations. Court decisions, too, are frequently influenced by ethics as judges and juries examine the facts of a case and form beliefs about the parties and issues involved.

A distinction between law and ethics is that legal mandates are usually more precise. The law requires individuals and organizations to behave in specified ways, requiring or prohibiting certain acts and are enforceable by courts. Ethical issues may be multifaceted, and violations are not enforceable by courts or the government.

EXAMPLE 2.4

The YumBurger chain was faced with the legal requirement of paying its employees a specified minimum wage. It could have simply fulfilled that requirement. However, the management decided, based on ethical considerations, to increase the pay of their workers beyond the mandated wage, feeling the required minimum was inadequate. While this decision might be commendable from an ethical standpoint, it could involve several other ethical issues as well: The cost of the extra pay might result in higher prices for consumers or reduced earnings for shareholders.

2.4 ETHICAL REASONING AND RESPONSES

APPROACHES TO ETHICAL REASONING

Approaches to ethical reasoning can be broadly grouped into two categories: duty-based reasoning and outcome-based reasoning. Duty-based reasoning requires that ethical decisions should be based on the consequences of actions and has a corresponding implication that an unethical decision is one that violates the rights of others. For example, an owner of a company may feel that they have a duty to provide fair pricing for a product to the consumer because the consumer has a right to a fair price. Outcome-based reasoning, in contrast, requires analysis of decisions based on creating the greatest good for the most number of people. For example, a company agrees to subsidize the price of milk at a relatively low rate by increasing the price of a more expensive cheese product that the company also sells. The market for milk is much larger, with a diverse income range of purchasers, while the market for the cheese product is smaller and wealthier.

duty-based reasoning Ethical reasoning that is based on consequences of actions.

outcome-based reasoning Ethical reasoning based on creating the greatest good for the most people.

The growing awareness of the importance of ethics is evident in the responses of businesses, educational institutions, governments, and trade and professional associations.

RESPONSES OF BUSINESS FIRMS

There is increasing concern about ethics in the business world. Some of this concern is undoubtedly the result of enlightened self-interest, as when corporate executives say that ethical practices are simply good business practices. For example, in voluntarily paying its workers more than the legally required minimum wage, YumBurger may attract scarce workers in a tight labor market; if it packages its products in an environmentally friendly container, it may attract more purchasers who are environmentally conscious. Other executives may be interested in ethical practices because of the favorable publicity it gives their firms. Corporations may now be more concerned about the possible legal consequences of unethical behavior because of new legislation and more severe penalties for violations.

EXAMPLE 2.5

- Johnson & Johnson was confronted with a crisis when people in the Chicago area began dying of cyanide poison after taking the firm's Tylenol capsules. Although no connection between the poison and Tylenol was established, Johnson & Johnson recalled the product at great cost. James Burke, chairman and CEO at the time of the crisis, said that the established ethics credo was invaluable during this crisis because everyone in the firm knew the standard of ethics required of them, and personnel at various levels were able to make the necessary decisions quickly.

RESPONSES OF EDUCATIONAL INSTITUTIONS

Educational institutions have responded to the increased need to examine ethics by adding courses, workshops, and programs, and they have expanded the study of ethics in existing courses. Typically, topics include fairness in hiring, employment, and promotions; ethical issues in multinational business; ethical issues arising from technology; economic justice; environmental ethics; and ecology.

RESPONSES OF GOVERNMENTS

Governments endeavor to protect consumers and the environment and to influence the ethical behavior of business firms in various ways. For example, governments enact legislation and create programs to ensure and encourage ethical behavior. The Federal Sentencing Guidelines provide an incentive for corporations to act more ethically. Under this mandate, when an employee violates a law in the course of their employment, a firm can reduce its possible liability if it can show that it took action to develop moral guidelines for its employees. It can have its potential penalties reduced by millions of dollars. This federal mandate has motivated companies to develop codes of conduct, to appoint high-level personnel (often called *corporate ethics officers*) to oversee compliance and to establish ethics auditing and monitoring systems, and to enforce discipline throughout the firm. Legislators reasoned that if firms integrate ethics into their structure in this way, employees will be less likely to break the law for the company's benefit and that companies that have taken positive steps to integrate ethics should not be penalized as harshly as those that have not. The guidelines are a response to the public's desire to hold companies to a higher standard and to impose on white-collar criminals penalties heavier than those previously imposed.

Even the operation of government itself is monitored and regulated. The U.S. Office of Government Ethics, for example, is concerned with the following topics: conflicting financial interests, misuse of position, financial disclosure, impartiality in performing official duties, and other areas of concern. On an international level, federal and state governments require that U.S. firms perform ethically in global markets. For example, the Foreign Corrupt Practices Act prohibits American firms from bribing foreign officials. In addition, diplomatic activities aim to protect American firms from corrupt practices in other countries (see Chapter 36).

RESPONSES OF TRADE AND PROFESSIONAL ASSOCIATIONS

Trade associations develop guidelines for ethical business practices for their diverse memberships. For example, the Direct Marketing Association (DMA) provides self-regulatory standards of conduct for some of the following activities: telephone marketing, sweepstakes, fund-raising, marketing to children, and the collection and use of marketing data. Similarly, many professionals, such as attorneys, are now required annually to successfully complete a minimum number of ethics courses as part of continuing education requirements to maintain their licenses.

2.5 WAYS TO ENSURE ETHICAL PRACTICES

Despite the efforts of the aforementioned groups–businesses, educational institutions, governments, and trade and professional associations–unethical practices persist. Businesses concerned with ethics usually focus on their corporate responsibility and the development of codes of conduct. Unethical behavior frequently results in unfavorable public relations, loss of consumer goodwill and confidence, and poor employee morale. The threat of legal prosecution and penalties does not eliminate all unethical practices. Sometimes, the driving force for reform may be the individual whistleblower.

CORPORATE RESPONSIBILITY

The actions of corporations that are intended to demonstrate their wish to behave responsibly take many forms and are conducted under the banner of corporate responsibility. In some cases, the corporation will "adopt" a nearby school and provide equipment and expert personnel to teach particular skills. In other cases, the firm might construct a park, donate funds to a local symphony orchestra, provide scholarships to a university, or repackage its products to be more environmentally friendly. In some instances, these actions are little more than thinly veiled public relations efforts to enhance the image of the corporation. In other instances, however, corporate actions reflect a moral and ethical concern with social problems and a sincere effort to improve society.

Many states have enacted statutes that allow for profit corporations to include social and environmental benefits into the mission that boards of directors must consider in making decisions. These corporations are known as Benefit Corporations or B Corporations.

Critics of corporate social action, however, question whether it is appropriate to commit corporate resources to socially desirable goals. It might be better, they suggest, to maximize earnings for shareholders, who could then use the higher earnings to advance society if they so desire. It is interesting to note that in many states, charitable contributions by corporations are legal, while political contributions are not.

CODES OF ETHICS

Despite a few glaring lapses, many companies today understand the need to maintain ethical standards in their dealings with customers, suppliers, and employees. To do this, some firms or industries establish a code of ethics, sometimes called a *credo* or a values statement, that sets down the principles of ethical behavior expected of personnel in various situations (see Figure 2.1). For example, a firm or industry may place a dollar limit on the value of gifts that may be accepted from suppliers doing business with the firm. A code makes clear that the company expects its personnel to recognize the ethical dimensions of corporate policies and actions.

code of ethics
A set of rules that a company or other group adopts to express principles of ethical behavior that are expected of its personnel.

Many firms expect employees to strictly follow codes. Some even require employees to sign contracts annually, mandating that they adhere to ethical standards and complete ethics training and education. In such organizations, senior executives will be held to the highest standards for professional and ethical behavior so as to set a benchmark for the firm's stakeholders. A stakeholder is a person or group who may be affected by a firm's actions or decisions, such as employees, owners, shareholders, and customers. Managers should consider relevant stakeholders when establishing codes or engaging in ethical decision making.

stakeholders
People or groups who may be affected by a firm's actions or decisions.

OUR PEOPLE We act with integrity. We treat each other with fairness and respect.
OUR CONSUMERS We delight our consumers with safe, high-quality, great-tasting foods.
OUR MARKETPLACE We compete vigorously and with integrity. We partner with those who demonstrate our values.
OUR INVESTORS We are a preferred investment because we deliver the present while creating the future.
OUR COMMUNITIES We use natural resources responsibly and support our communities.

FIGURE 2.1 Kellogg Company's Global Code of Ethics Principles

Source: Kellogg Company's Global Code of Ethics https://www.kelloggcompany.com/content/dam/kellogg-company/files/KGlobalCodeofEthics.pdf

EXAMPLE 2.6

▶ Hewlett-Packard's (HP's) board of directors agreed to request the resignation of company CEO Mark Hurd after discovering he was responsible for engaging in activities considered inappropriate by the company's standards of business conduct. HP's board remained steadfast in upholding the company's ethical and professional standards regardless of the fact that Hurd not only was chairperson and company CEO but also was partially responsible for a company turnaround.

While the areas covered in codes vary from one firm or industry to another, a general list of topics typically includes the following:

- Fundamental honesty and adherence to the law.
- Product safety and quality.
- Health and safety in the workplace.
- Possible conflicts of interest.
- Employment practices.
- Fairness in selling and marketing practices.
- Financial reporting.
- Supplier relationships.
- Pricing, billing, and contracting.
- Trading in securities and using insider information.
- Payments to obtain business.

WHISTLEBLOWING

Our language has a number of derogatory words to describe people who disclose information about wrongdoing. Such terms as *stool pigeon, stoolie, fink, snitch, rat,* and *tattletale* suggest that our society does not regard such behavior highly. But despite society's disdain for informers, certain individuals have been so outraged by unethical behavior that they have risked widespread condemnation and loss of their jobs to reveal information about the activity. These people are usually termed *whistleblowers.*

whistleblower
An employee who discloses to the government, media, or upper management that the company is involved in wrongful or illegal activities.

Typically, a whistleblower is a person who reveals to a governmental authority, or to news media, confidential information concerning some wrongdoing or conduct that they regard as unethical and/or illegal. The information may have come to them in the course of employment or in other ways. The whistleblower may be a secretary, for example, who knows that his or her boss is cheating customers or the company or an engineer who knows that a product is unsafe and that purchasers of the product could be injured or killed. Authorities may respond by prosecuting the company. The media may publicize the wrongdoing, which can be equally damaging to a firm. In addition to illegal and fraudulent activities, employees are also now exposing other misconduct, such as conflicts of interest, sexual harassment, and discrimination.

The whistleblower, too, may be confronted with an ethical dilemma. Often the choice is between remaining silent or revealing information that could result in adverse effects on the firm that may cause many coworkers to lose their jobs.

It is not surprising that retaliation is frequently the result of speaking out. The whistleblower is often regarded as an outcast to the organization or to peers, is often passed over for promotions and raises, and may even be subject to physical attacks to their person or property.

The federal government and many states have statutes that protect whistleblowers from retaliation. Still, with the possible exception of certain individuals who may have a personal grudge, the usual motivation behind whistleblowing is the outrage to a person's sense of ethics.

The federal government has now enacted programs to encourage whistleblowing by providing financial incentives for doing so. For example, the Securities and Exchange Commission, in an effort to enhance its reputation, has established a program to reward whistleblowers with a percentage of penalties imposed. The Internal Revenue Service also has a similar program to reward the reporting of illegal tax activities.

INTEGRATION OF ETHICS INTO BUSINESS AND GOVERNMENT

In the abstract, there is agreement that business should be conducted in ways that will not harm the consumer or the environment. What is the most effective way to achieve this? The corporation may indeed adhere to the highest ethical practices, but a new chief executive officer (CEO) or board of directors may discontinue those practices if they reduce profits or otherwise adversely affect the firm. Further government regulation could ensure compliance with ethical standards, but such an arrangement might require a costly and oppressive bureaucracy. The ideal is for responsible individuals, industry organizations, and watchdog groups to encourage corporations and governments to reach mutually agreed-upon ethical practices.

Air traffic control whistleblower Anne Whiteman was threatened and harassed after reporting air traffic controllers allowing planes to fly in air space less than 1,000 feet apart at the Dallas–Fort Worth Airport, an illegal and dangerous practice.
Novikov Aleksey/Shutterstock

CHAPTER SUMMARY

2.1 Examples of how ethics in our world have negatively affected business practices include investors acting on insider information, accounting scandals, investment fraud, businesses polluting our natural habitat, and individuals acting unethically in the development of medical and electronic technology. The expansion of global markets also raises some ethical predicaments for business professionals.

2.2 Morals are concerned with an individual person's beliefs as to right and wrong. Ethics is about the standards and principles for the behavior of individuals within a society. Values are beliefs or standards considered worthwhile.

2.3 Legal mandates are imposed on individuals or groups by authorities or governments. In contrast, ethical considerations generally spring from within individuals or organizations. However, ethical beliefs are the foundation of many of our laws.

2.4 Business firms respond to ethical concerns by acts of corporate responsibility and the formulation of codes of ethics, or credos. Educational institutions offer courses and workshops and expand their existing programs. Governments enact legislation and create programs to protect consumers and the environment and to ensure ethical behavior of business firms and the government itself. Trade and professional associations develop guidelines for business and professional members.

2.5 Some ways business can ensure ethical practices include integrating corporate codes of ethics and relying on whistleblowers. Corporate codes of ethics vary from one firm or industry to another. Whistleblowing is the exposing of an unethical situation to an authority or the media.

CHAPTER TWO ASSESSMENT

MATCHING LEGAL TERMS

Match each of the numbered definitions with the correct term in the following list.

a. code of ethics
b. stakeholder
c. ethics
d. morals
e. corporate responsibility
f. values
g. whistleblower

1. An individual person's beliefs as to what is right and wrong. **1.** _____

2. The standards and principles society has adopted as a guide for the behavior of individuals within a society. **2.** _____

3. The beliefs or standards considered worthwhile by an orderly society. **3.** _____

4. People or groups who may be affected by a firm's actions or decisions. **4.** _____

5. The actions of a business demonstrating its wish to behave in a socially correct manner. **5.** _____

6. A document that sets down a firm's principles of the ethical behavior expected of its employees. **6.** _____

7. A person who reveals confidential information concerning some wrongdoing or unethical behavior. **7.** _____

TRUE/FALSE QUIZ

Indicate whether each of the following statements is true or false.

8. Unethical behavior has not been a problem in society until recent times. **8.** _____

9. Generally, what is unethical is also illegal. **9.** _____

10. The term *values* relates to the price of merchandise on sale. **10.** _____

11. Although ethical principles have influenced many laws, the laws themselves are usually more precise. **11.** _____

12. A whistleblower is a person who calls attention to illegal or unethical behavior. **12.** _____

13. A corporate code of ethics might be called a set of guidelines for the ethical behavior expected of employees. **13.** _____

MULTIPLE CHOICE QUIZ

Indicate which of the following answers is correct from the choices following each question.

14. Individual and societal beliefs are (a) ethics (b) laws (c) morals (d) values. **14.** _____

15. The standards that underlie an individual or society's beliefs are (a) ethics (b) laws (c) morals (d) values. **15.** _____

16. Standards that govern behavior but are not enforceable in court are (a) ethics (b) laws (c) morals (d) values. **16.** _____

17. Requirements of behavior enforceable in court are (a) ethics (b) laws (c) morals (d) values. **17.** _____

18. Ethical reasoning based on consequences of actions is known as (a) consequential-based reasoning (b) outcome-based reasoning (c) duty-based reasoning (d) responsive reasoning. **18.** _____

19. Ethical reasoning based on creating the most good for the most people is known as (a) consequential-based reasoning (b) outcome-based reasoning (c) duty-based reasoning (d) responsive reasoning. **19.** _____

20. Corporate officers tasked with overseeing ethics compliance are usually known as (a) chief executives (b) corporate ethics officers (c) corporate values champions (d) corporate discipline officers. **20.** _____

21. An employee who discloses employer wrongful or illegal activities may be offered protection as (a) a protected witness (b) at-will employee (c) whistleblower (d) a directed witness. **21.** _____

DISCUSSION QUESTIONS

Answer the following questions and discuss them in class.

22. Describe the two broad categories of ethical reasoning, including the similarities and differences between the two.

_____

_____

23. Identify some typical issues for people who are ethically concerned with the environment.

_____

_____

24. Discuss and provide examples of values that are highly regarded in our society.

25. Suggest several unfavorable consequences facing a business firm that consistently engages in unethical practices.

26. Discuss the relationship between ethics and the law.

27. Discuss several responses by businesses to ethical issues.

THINKING CRITICALLY ABOUT THE LAW

Answer the following questions, which require you to think critically about the legal principles that you learned in this chapter.

28. Whistleblowing A person who blows the whistle on some unethical practice in a firm is often treated as an outcast by his or her coworkers. Why does this occur? Does this mean that the coworkers are less ethical?

29. Codes of Ethics A number of firms accused of unethical behavior had established codes of ethics, or credos, and formal employee orientation programs. It might seem that these efforts had little influence on the practices of the firms. Critique the practice of establishing codes of ethics, and suggest ways that their use could be made more effective.

30. Corporate Responsibility Critics of corporate social action question whether it is appropriate to commit corporate resources to socially desirable goals. It might be better, they suggest, to maximize earnings for shareholders, who could then use the higher earnings to advance society if they so desire. Critique the arguments of those who advocate direct corporate action to achieve social goals versus the views of those who oppose such action.

31. Responses of Governments to Ethical Issues Analyze and critique some current activities of government relating to ethics in business.

____

____

32. A Question of Ethics The corporate culture exerts a major influence on the ethical behavior of every employee and executive in the firm. Since it is recognized that management largely determines the corporate culture, recommend steps management might take to establish a culture that will instill reasonable standards of ethical behavior for *everyone* in the firm.

____

____

CASE QUESTIONS

Study each of the following cases. Answer the questions that follow with Yes or No.

33. Whistleblowing Ayer, an engineer with product development responsibilities, was confronted with an ethical dilemma. He knew that a product being manufactured by the firm was unsafe for consumer use as a result of cost cutting. He also believed that if he complained to management or to a government body concerned with product safety, he would probably be fired.

a. If Ayer did nothing, would he still have made an ethical decision? **a.** _____

b. If Ayer did nothing because he was concerned that if he complained and manufacturing was suspended many workers would lose their jobs, would he have made an ethical decision? **b.** _____

c. Assume Ayer considered blowing the whistle on the firm by releasing information to the newspapers and television networks. Is it likely that such action would have any effect on the firm or on Ayer? **c.** _____

34. Avoiding Regulation Maas owns a company that manufactures children's toys. The Consumer Product Safety Commission develops a regulation that requires companies to label any toys containing certain types of plastics together with a notice of the health dangers of those plastics. The regulation is set to take effect in 90 days. Maas calls a meeting and orders that all shipments pending be sent out as soon as possible and that any orders pending be completed in advance of the 90-day deadline in order to avoid compliance as long as possible.

a. Is the decision by Maas illegal? **a.** _____

b. Is the decision by Maas unethical? **b.** _____

c. Would there be a business justification for this decision? **c.** _____

35. Ethical Decisions Lackowitz, a college student, was concerned about a final examination. During previous examinations in the same course, he had seen other students cheat and obtain good grades. If he failed the course, he would need to repeat it and pay additional tuition. Also, if he had to repeat the course, his graduation would be delayed one semester, as would his entry into the full-time job market. The financial considerations were of great concern to him.

a. Would Lackowitz be justified in cheating on the examination? **a.** _____

b. Could a decision by Lackowitz to inform the instructor about the cheating that he had seen on previous examinations represent an ethical decision? **b.** _____

CASE ANALYSIS

Study each of the following cases carefully. Briefly state the principle of law and your decision.

36. Deception Siwek took his new Buick to his dealer for minor repairs. While the car was in the dealer's repair shop, the dealer informed Siwek that the car was equipped with a Chevrolet engine. The standard engine for a car of the model and year in question was a 2.4-liter 4-cylinder manufactured by the Buick division of General Motors. Before the introduction of the year's models, the manufacturer determined that there would not be enough engines built to equip all the Buick models manufactured. For this reason, it was decided to install Chevrolet engines in some Buick cars without disclosing the practice to the buyers. Siwek complained to the Illinois attorney general, who filed a class-action suit against General Motors, charging that GM deceived consumers by not informing them of the engine switch.

Ethical and/or Legal Principle:

____

____

Decision:

____

____

37. Ethical Responsibility Quinly and her husband, customers at Greenway Supermarkets, purchased several pounds of filet mignon and checked out their purchases at the newly installed self-scanners. The price listed on the packages of meat totaled $38; however, when Quinly swiped the packages through the self-scanner, it indicated a price of only $6. Quinly believed that she should inform the management at the supermarket that the computer in the self-scanner had been incorrectly programmed with respect to the price of this product. However, Quinly's husband argued that because the store would be legally obligated to charge the lower price, it was not necessary to call attention to the error. Is Quinly correct in her belief that the ethical course of action is to inform the store?

Ethical and/or Legal Principle:

____

____

Decision:

____

____

38. Ethical Violation Stotts was employed as a technician in the engineering department of Raytron Corporation. All the engineers on staff were required to sign agreements that they would not accept employment with another company in the industry within three years of leaving Raytron. Technicians, who had limited access to company secrets, were not required to sign such agreements. After working at Raytron for about two years, Stotts realized that he was deeply involved in development and had access to the same data as the engineers did. Stotts actively sought a position with Raytron's primary competitor and was hired by Watani Engineering. Because he did not have an engineering degree, he assumed that he had been hired because of his knowledge of Raytron's trade secrets. Did Stotts violate legal or ethical dictates?

Ethical and/or Legal Principle:

Decision:

LEGAL RESEARCH

Complete the following activities. Share your findings with the class.

39. Working in Teams One of the important functions of corporate executives is to develop and implement ethical policies for their companies. In groups of four or five, imagine that you are the executives of a major corporation charged with developing a corporate code of ethics. What are some of the issues you would want to address? Create a list and share them with the class.

40. Using Technology Using the Internet and search engines, find information about the Securities and Exchange Commission's program to reward individuals who blow the whistle on securities fraud. Report on the program itself as well as the responses to the program.

chapter 3
Criminal Law

LEARNING OUTCOMES

After studying this chapter and completing the assessment, you will be able to

3.1 Define *crime* and distinguish between crimes and torts.

3.2 Identify the three major classifications of crimes.

3.3 Discuss several common crimes of particular concern to business and employees.

LEGAL terms

crime	burning to defraud
tort	larceny
treason	robbery
felony	burglary
misdemeanor	bribery
white-collar crime	false pretenses
RICO	forgery
securities fraud	perjury
Ponzi scheme	embezzlement
arson	extortion

CRIMINAL LAW

"Good people do not need laws to tell them to act responsibly, while bad people will find a way around the laws."

Plato, Greek philosopher

167/Richard Nowitz/Ocean/CORBIS

3.1 CRIME

The law assures each person certain rights and assigns each person certain duties. As was discussed in Chapter 1, the law enforcement authorities of federal, state, and local governments enforce specific laws called *statutes.* Violation of certain statutes that are designed to protect society at large is a crime. In contrast, a private wrong that causes injury to person, property, or reputation is called a tort.

crime
An offense against the public at large punishable by the official governing body of a nation or state.

tort
A private wrong that injures another person's physical well-being, property, or reputation.

It is important to note that a certain action can be both a crime and a tort. For example, a person who operates an automobile recklessly or negligently and causes injury to another, or damages their property, has committed both the crime of reckless driving and the tort of negligence. The reckless driver can be prosecuted by the appropriate law enforcement authorities for the crime and also can be sued for the tort in a civil court by the person whose property was damaged or who was injured. Chapter 4 is devoted to torts and how they may relate to both personal and business life.

At times, a corporation may be held criminally liable for the actions or omissions of its employees. In general, if a criminal offense is punishable by imprisonment, the corporation is not held liable; instead, courts usually punish corporations by requiring that they pay fines. However, it must be noted that, when corporations do pay these fines, it is the shareholders who are ultimately the ones being punished.

Certain actions can be both a crime and a tort.
Halfdark/Getty Images

While statutory law determines what is and what is not a crime, many statutes reflect legal principles derived from common law. What makes a particular act, or failure to act, a crime? Why is a certain act, or failure to act, a crime in one state and not in another? Why is a certain act, or failure to act, a crime one day and not the next? These questions can all be answered by one statement: An act, or failure to act, is a crime because the governing statutes say it is. Of course, a high degree of uniformity has emerged among states, so it is uncommon for a particular act to be legal in one state and illegal in another. Also, legislatures attempt to reflect the public interest and will enact legislation that makes a certain act a crime if there is sufficient demand.

In other instances, also reflecting changing public sentiments, legislatures and courts may decide that a particular act previously considered a crime should no longer be viewed as a violation of the law. For example, laws concerning reproductive rights, LGBTQ status, and drug use have been modified considerably in recent years. Similarly, a legislature may repeal statutes, thus making an act legal when it previously had been a crime.

3.2 CLASSIFICATION OF CRIMES

Crimes are classified into three groups according to the seriousness of the offense:

- Treason
- Felony
- Misdemeanor

TREASON

treason
The levying of war against the United States, or the giving of aid and comfort to the nation's enemies.

Treason is a major crime defined by the Constitution of the United States as follows: "Treason against the United States shall consist only in levying War against them, or in adhering to their Enemies, giving them Aid and Comfort."

FELONY

felony
A crime punishable by death or imprisonment in a federal or state prison for a term exceeding one year.

A felony is a serious crime against society, such as murder, arson, larceny, bribery, and embezzlement. It may be punished by execution, by a prison sentence of more than a year, or by a fine.

EXAMPLE 3.1

▶ Flogg was an employee of a firm that manufactured expensive electronic equipment. Due to a delay, a truckload of equipment was held at the shipping dock over a three-day weekend. Flogg stole the truck and its contents, intending to drive to another state, sell the equipment, and fly to another country. Unluckily for him, he was caught 75 miles away and ultimately charged with grand larceny, a felony.

MISDEMEANOR

misdemeanor
A less serious crime that is generally punishable by a fine and/or a prison sentence of not more than one year.

A misdemeanor is a less serious offense than a felony. It is usually punished by a fine and/or imprisonment for no more than one year. Examples of misdemeanors include certain traffic offenses, thefts of small amounts of money, use of illegal measuring devices, and other relatively minor infractions of statutes.

EXAMPLE 3.2

▶ Centerport had a local ordinance that prohibited door-to-door sales without a permit. Dowe, without obtaining the permit, began calling on homeowners in the town and trying to sell home repairs. When a resident objected, the local police issued Dowe a misdemeanor citation—similar to a traffic ticket—that required him to appear in court, pay a fine, and avoid similar actions until the permit was issued.

Federal law and the laws of the states determine the classification and largely specify the punishment for crimes that are committed. It is important to note that some crimes violate both federal and state laws. (For examples of federal and state crimes, see Figures 3.1 and 3.2.)

- Aircraft hijacking
- Aiming a laser pointer at an aircraft
- Art theft from a museum
- Assassination or attempted assassination of the president or vice president
- Bank robbery
- Carjacking
- Computer crimes
- Counterfeiting
- Crimes committed on federal property or on Indian reservations
- Damaging or destroying public mailboxes
- Electoral fraud
- Federal hate crimes
- Insider trading (see Chapter 31)
- Illegal wiretapping
- Immigration offenses
- Kidnapping
- Mail fraud
- Possession of certain weapons
- Tax evasion
- Violations of the Patriot Act

FIGURE 3.1 Federal Felony and Misdemeanor Crimes

- Arson
- Assault/battery
- Bribery
- Burglary
- Corruption
- Criminal trespass
- Driving while under the influence
- Embezzlement
- Extortion
- False pretenses
- Forgery
- Fraud
- Homicide
- Illegal possession or sale of drugs
- Kidnapping
- Larceny
- Perjury
- Rape
- Robbery
- Stalking

FIGURE 3.2 State Felony and Misdemeanor Crimes

3.3 CRIMES IN THE BUSINESS WORLD

Many people associate crime with criminals and gangsters as they are portrayed on television and in the movies. Crimes, however, are not always committed in the sensational style of blazing guns and wild car chases. Often the site of a business crime is the well-appointed office of a corporate executive, their private club, or a nearby bar where employees meet after work.

WHITE-COLLAR CRIME

white-collar crime
A term used to describe various crimes that typically do not involve force or violence committed by and against businesses.

White-collar crime is the term used to describe various crimes that typically do not involve force or violence committed by and against businesses. Originally white-collar crime related only to nonviolent crimes against businesses, usually committed by their own employees. The most common white-collar crime was the theft of an employer's funds by employees with access to such funds (embezzlement). In recent years, however, this unofficial category of illegal activity has been applied to nonviolent crimes committed *by* business firms as well as *against* business firms. In this newer, broader application, white-collar crime covers a wide range of crimes, including stock swindles, frauds against insurance companies, credit card fraud, income tax evasion, cyberspace fraud and theft of computer programs, agreements with competitors to fix prices, and others. Depending on its seriousness, a white-collar crime can be either a felony or a misdemeanor and can violate federal or state law.

RICO
One of the most successful laws used to combat white-collar crime, RICO prohibits an organization's employees from engaging in a pattern of racketeering activity.

The Racketeer Influenced and Corrupt Organizations Act of 1970, also known as RICO, is one of the most successful laws used to combat white-collar crime. Originally created to restrict the entry of organized crime into legitimate businesses, RICO prohibits an organization's employees from engaging in a pattern of racketeering activity. Some examples of the wide variety of crimes considered to be racketeering activities are securities fraud, mail fraud, wire fraud, bribery, acts of violence, and embezzlement from pension funds. Under the RICO act, it is easier to both prosecute corrupt organizations and seize assets obtained through corruption. In addition, under RICO, a person who suffers damages to their business or property may sue for treble damages, an amount equal to three times actual damages.

SECURITIES FRAUD

securities fraud
A fraud that occurs when a person or company provides false information to potential investors to influence their decisions to buy or sell securities.

Securities fraud occurs when a person or company, such as a stockbroker or investment firm, provides false information to potential investors to influence their decisions to buy or sell securities. In addition, securities fraud encompasses theft of an investor's assets, stock trading based on nonpublic information (see "insider trading" as discussed in Chapter 31), and the wrongful manipulation of financial statements.

EXAMPLE 3.3

▶ Updike, the chief executive officer of Coast-to-Coast Airlines, knew that FlyToday Airlines intended to purchase all outstanding shares of Coast-to-Coast Airlines at a higher price than its current market value. Using insider information, Updike bought as much stock in Coast-to-Coast Airlines as he could afford and resold it to FlyToday Airlines at a huge profit. If discovered, Updike could be charged with the crime of insider trading.

Ponzi scheme
A type of securities fraud in which large gains are promised to investors, but in reality, newer investments are used to provide a return on older investments.

A Ponzi scheme is a type of securities fraud in which large gains are promised to investors; but in reality, newer investments are used to provide a return on older investments. These schemes inevitably collapse over time as older investments eventually become too large to cover with new investments. For more information on Ponzi schemes, visit http://www.sec.gov/answers/ponzi.htm.

EXAMPLE 3.4

▶ In 2008 Bernard Madoff, former chairman of NASDAQ and owner of an investment firm with more than 4,000 clients, was charged with securities fraud for orchestrating one of the most massive Ponzi schemes to date. Madoff's Ponzi scheme operated for years by promising steady gains to investors during all economic climates; however, the scheme failed when Madoff was unable to meet increased demands for withdrawals resulting from investor uncertainty in the stock market. In the end, total losses to Madoff's investors, including charity organizations, pension funds, celebrities, and average investors, totaled more than $20 billion. The court found Madoff guilty of securities fraud and, because of the egregious nature of his corrupt acts, sentenced him to serve 150 years in a federal prison. Subsequently, Peter Madoff, the chief compliance officer and younger brother of Bernard Madoff, admitted his role in the scheme and pleaded guilty to conspiracy and falsifying records. Sentenced to 10 years in prison, he was the eighth person to plead guilty.

ARSON

The crime of arson is the willful or malicious act of causing the burning of property belonging to another person. Some states have broadened the definition of arson to include the burning of a house by its owner and the destruction of property by other means, such as by explosion. Aside from the few persons who start fires for irrational reasons, most instances of arson are profit related. When the motivation is profit, the arsonist is usually trying to collect money from an insurance company for a building that they own. Most states have statutes that provide for the punishment of persons who burn their own property with the aim of collecting insurance money. Such statutes establish a special category of crime called burning to defraud. To combat these practices, the insurance industry has developed very sophisticated investigation techniques and has an impressive record of assisting in successful prosecutions.

Arson is the willful or malicious act of causing the burning of property belonging to another person.
TFoxFoto/Shutterstock

arson
The willful or malicious act of causing the burning of another's property.

burning to defraud
A special category of crime providing for the punishment of persons who burn their own property with the aim of collecting insurance money.

EXAMPLE 3.5

▶ Filkins, the owner of a clothing manufacturing firm, was losing money because of unexpected fashion changes. A large inventory of clothing had accumulated before it became apparent that little of it would ever be sold. Desperate, Filkins hired an arsonist to set the building on fire one night when Filkins had an unshakable alibi. The building, inventory, and equipment were insured. Insurance investigators and the fire marshal found evidence of arson and caught the criminal, who identified Filkins as the person who had hired him. The insurance company refused to pay for the loss, and Filkins and the arsonist were both charged with the crime of arson.

larceny
The act of taking and carrying away the personal property of another without the right to do so.

robbery
The taking of property in the possession of another person against that person's will and under threat of bodily harm.

burglary
The illegal entering of another person's premises for the purpose of committing a crime.

LARCENY/ROBBERY/BURGLARY

Larceny is a broad term that includes most forms of theft—that is, robbery, hijacking, embezzlement, and shoplifting. Larceny is often classified as petty (small) or grand (large), depending upon the value of the stolen property. It is important to distinguish among the various types of larceny. Robbery is defined as the taking of property in the possession of another person against that person's will and under threat of bodily harm—as in the case of a holdup. *Hijacking* is stealing from a vehicle in transit or the vehicle itself, and *shoplifting* is stealing merchandise from a retail store. Burglary is the illegal entering of another person's premises for the purpose of committing a crime.

EXAMPLE 3.6

Jelkin Electronics was in the business of selling and repairing computers. One morning, as he opened for business, the manager discovered that a rear window had been broken, obviously to gain entry during the night, and a number of laptops and tablets had been stolen. The owner immediately called his insurance agent and learned, to his dismay, that his policy covered robbery, but not burglary. The firm suffered the complete loss of the stolen property.

Bribery consists of giving or taking money or property of value with the intent of influencing someone in the performance of their duty.
2007 Getty Images, Inc

bribery
The act of offering, giving, receiving, or soliciting something of value to influence official action or the discharge of a public duty.

BRIBERY

The crime of bribery consists of giving or taking money or property of value with the intent of influencing someone (usually a public official) in the performance of their duty. Some states have enacted laws that also make it a crime to bribe someone other than a public official, such as a purchasing agent employed by a business firm. Both the giver of the bribe and the receiver can be charged with bribery.

EXAMPLE 3.7

Rodriguez was employed as a secretary at Balasen Corporation. She had access to enormous amounts of confidential information, including sales projections, short- and long-range plans, and product development plans. Turner, an executive with a competing firm, initially came to know Rodriguez socially and after a short time recognized the value of the personal contact. An agreement resulted whereby Rodriguez turned over to Turner electronic files containing many confidential documents in exchange for a cash sum. If discovered, both parties could be charged with bribery.

FALSE PRETENSES

The term false pretenses (fraud) describes a broad category of crimes that involve activities intended to deceive others by making false claims or to obtain goods by using false pretenses. A number of federal and state statutes govern activities that might be considered false pretenses.

false pretenses
A broad category of crimes that involves activities intended to deceive others or to obtain goods by making false claims.

EXAMPLE 3.8

▶ Rollings operated a small catering and take-out food service. He could see that his business was headed for failure unless he installed additional equipment to increase productivity. For this he needed a bank loan, but he was afraid that he did not own sufficient assets to qualify for the loan. As a result, when Rollings applied for the loan, he claimed under false pretenses that he owned certain equipment that he was actually renting from a restaurant supply company.

A person who makes false statements to a bank for the purpose of obtaining a loan could be prosecuted under the appropriate statute. In Example 3.8, there were no actual "goods," but the bank had extended credit and the credit could be considered a "good."

Another example of the crime of using false pretenses would be a person who continues to purchase goods with a canceled credit card after having been notified of its cancellation.

FORGERY

The crime of forgery consists of wrongfully making or altering the writings of another with the intent to defraud. Forgery could include falsifying a signature on a check or the endorsement (the signature on the reverse side of the check). The act of signing another person's name to a credit card charge slip without permission is also considered forgery. The common practice of a secretary signing a boss's name to letters, however, could hardly be considered forgery because the secretary signs the letters with the authorization of their boss and with the boss's express or implied consent.

forgery
The false making or alteration of a writing with the intent to defraud.

EXAMPLE 3.9

▶ Corcoran was employed as a gas station attendant. One day he noticed that a regular customer, Cosolino, kept a number of oil company credit cards in a wallet in the glove compartment of his car. When Cosolino left his car for repair, Corcoran stole one of the cards and began using it to charge gasoline, tires, and other items at a service station in another town, signing Cosolino's name each time. When he was caught, Corcoran was charged with forgery and other crimes.

PERJURY

The crime of perjury consists of intentionally giving false oral or written statements under oath in a judicial proceeding after having sworn to tell the truth. In some instances, giving false information on a government form is also considered perjury.

perjury
The crime of intentionally giving false oral or written statements under oath in a judicial proceeding after having sworn to tell the truth.

EXAMPLE 3.10

▶ Danvers, a former government official, was called to testify before a congressional committee regarding his activities after leaving government service that might have been in violation of the law. Under oath, he intentionally lied about the extent of these activities. Investigation revealed the untruths in his testimony, and he was charged with and convicted of perjury.

EMBEZZLEMENT

embezzlement
The wrongful taking of money or other property that has been entrusted to a person as a part of his or her job.

The crime of embezzlement may be defined as the wrongful taking of money or other property that has been entrusted to a person as a part of their employment. Some jobs, such as accountant, cashier, and bank teller, generally provide more opportunity for embezzlement than other jobs where the employee has little contact with money. The use of computers in business has led to some ingenious schemes for embezzling.

EXAMPLE 3.11

▶ Bingham was employed as a computer programmer at the headquarters of a bank. He secretly programmed the computer so that interest earned on depositors' accounts would be split: Only part of the payment would go to the depositor's account, while a small amount would be placed in an account that Bingham had set up to receive the payments. When he was caught, Bingham was charged with embezzlement.

EXTORTION

extortion
The act of taking or demanding money or other property from someone by using force, threats of force, or economic harm.

The crime of extortion is the act of taking or demanding money or other property from someone by using force, threats of force, or economic harm. The difference between extortion and bribery is that in bribery both parties are willing participants, whereas in extortion one person is willing and the other is unwilling.

Returning to the case of Rodriguez and Turner, discussed in Example 3.7 to illustrate bribery, if Rodriguez had been unwilling to disclose the confidential information and if Turner had threatened to break her legs or burn down her house, the crime would be extortion.

Certain individuals have seized the opportunity for illegal gain by using stolen or counterfeit credit cards.
Adam Crowley/Photodisc/Getty Images

OTHER BUSINESS-RELATED CRIMES

The number of crimes that involve businesses continues to grow as changes in business practices and technology offer new opportunities for wrongdoers to benefit from illegal or questionable activities.

Credit Card Fraud Credit cards provide cardholders with many conveniences, but certain individuals have seized the opportunity for illegal gain by using stolen or counterfeit credit cards.

Frequently, persons with knowledge of computers access the credit card numbers of consumers who have made purchases on the Internet and use these credit card numbers without authorization. In addition, the practice of obtaining credit cards under false pretenses continues to plague banks, credit card issuers, and consumers.

Identity Theft Identity theft occurs when an unscrupulous individual steals the name and personal information of someone else by stealing private mail, by obtaining personal data on the Internet, or by soliciting personal information from an unwitting victim over the telephone. The person stealing another's identity does so in order to obtain credit cards and other types of loans with no intention of ever repaying these. It is, therefore, as important to protect one's identity as it is to protect one's credit cards.

CHAPTER SUMMARY

3.1 A crime is a violation of a specific statute. A tort is a private wrong that causes injury to another person's physical well-being, property, or reputation.

3.2 The three classifications of crimes, based on their perceived seriousness, are (a) treason, (b) felonies, and (c) misdemeanors. Criminal conduct may violate either federal or state laws.

3.3 Many crimes are particularly important to businesses and employees, including the following: white-collar crime, securities fraud, arson, burning to defraud, larceny, robbery, hijacking, shoplifting, burglary, bribery, false pretenses, forgery, perjury, embezzlement, extortion, credit card fraud, and identity theft.

CHAPTER THREE ASSESSMENT

MATCHING LEGAL TERMS

Match each of the numbered definitions with the correct term in the following list.

a. arson
b. bribery
c. burglary
d. extortion
e. felony
f. forgery
g. misdemeanor
h. perjury
i. Ponzi scheme
j. white-collar crime

1. A classification of serious crimes such as murder or arson. **1.** _____

2. A classification of less serious crimes such as certain traffic offenses. **2.** _____

3. An act of willful or malicious burning of another's property. **3.** _____

4. The giving or taking of money or property with the intent of influencing, or being influenced, in the performance of an official duty. **4.** _____

5. Wrongfully making or altering the writing of another with the intent to defraud. 5. _____

6. The taking of someone's property against that person's will under threat of bodily harm. 6. _____

7. An unofficial category of crime that generally does not involve force or violence. 7. _____

8. Breaking into and entering another person's property with the intent of committing a felony or stealing property of value. 8. _____

9. A type of securities fraud in which large gains are promised to investors, but in reality, newer investments are used to provide a return on older investments. 9. _____

10. Making false oral or written statements under oath. 10. _____

TRUE/FALSE QUIZ

Indicate whether each of the following statements is true or false.

11. The purpose of criminal law is to compensate injured parties for their losses. 11. _____

12. If a person's reckless driving results in an automobile accident, he or she can be charged with both a tort and a crime. 12. _____

13. Shoplifting is the term that describes the theft of merchandise from retail stores. 13. _____

14. When employees with access to a firm's money, such as accountants, cashiers and bank tellers, wrongfully divert money to themselves or to others, they are usually charged with burglary. 14. _____

15. A person who profits from the sale of publicly traded stock as a result of using non-public information can be charged with violations of federal law. 15. _____

16. The crime of perjury is limited to the false swearing under oath before a judge in a federal court. 16. _____

MULTIPLE CHOICE QUIZ

Indicate the correct answer from the choices after each question:

17. Criminal laws are enforced (prosecuted) by (a) only private individuals (b) only government officials (c) both private individuals and government officials (d) neither private individuals nor government officials. 17. _____

18. The crime of reckless driving is most equivalent to the tort of (a) arson (b) battery (c) negligence (d) defamation. 18. _____

19. The crime of giving aid and comfort to the nation's enemies is (a) treason (b) arson (c) larceny (d) felony. **19.** _____

20. A felony is (a) less serious than a misdemeanor (b) the same as a misdemeanor (c) more serious than a misdemeanor (d) more serious than treason. **20.** _____

21. Punishments for a misdemeanor usually include (a) fines and imprisonment more than one year (b) only imprisonment for more than one year (c) death (d) fines and imprisonment less than one year. **21.** _____

22. An example of a violation of the Racketeer Influenced and Corrupt Organizations Act of 1970 (RICO) is (a) arson by one individual (b) wire fraud among several individuals (c) fraud by a business (d) treason. **22.** _____

23. The difference between robbery and burglary is (a) both involve taking of property, but robbery includes threat of bodily harm (b) that there is no difference between the two (c) both involve taking of property, but burglary includes threat of bodily harm (d) both involve threat of bodily harm, but only burglary requires taking of property. **23.** _____

24. The crime of perjury is an intentional false statement in which circumstance? (a) at a business meeting (b) at a speech made to business professionals (c) in a court proceeding (d) in a paid advertisement. **24.** _____

25. The crime of embezzlement occurs (a) in any theft of property (b) in any theft of property from any business (c) in any theft of property from a business where the embezzler is an employee (d) only in thefts of property from the government. **25.** _____

26. The theft of a victim's personal information for the purpose of illegally obtaining loans is (a) identify theft (b) personality theft (c) lending theft (d) informational theft. **26.** _____

DISCUSSION QUESTIONS

Answer the following questions and discuss them in class.

27. What is the difference between a tort and a crime?

____

____

28. What are the three major classifications of crimes?

____

____

29. What are some crimes that are particularly applicable to business?

___

___

30. What are some acts that were previously considered crimes but are no longer viewed as violations of the law?

___

___

31. What are some examples of federal crimes?

___

___

32. What are some common examples of white-collar crime?

___

___

THINKING CRITICALLY ABOUT THE LAW

Answer the following questions, which require you to think critically about the legal principles that you learned in this chapter.

33. White-Collar Crime Why do some highly paid business executives engage in illegal practices such as insider trading? What would you recommend to reduce the incidence of such practices?

___

___

34. Burning to Defraud What would be the effect on the insurance business and the economy if there were no "burning to defraud" statutes?

___

___

35. Embezzlement Has the use of computers in business increased or reduced the incidence of embezzlement?

___

___

36. Extortion What is the difference between extortion and bribery?

___

___

37. False Pretenses What is the intent of someone who is said to engage in activities called "false pretenses"?

____

____

38. A Question of Ethics Do you think that a U.S. citizen who disagrees with U.S. foreign policy against one of its enemies should be charged with treason for donating money to that enemy's war efforts against the United States? Why or why not?

____

____

CASE QUESTIONS

Study each of the cases. Answer the questions that follow with Yes or No.

39. Arson Williamson owned and operated a restaurant named Plum Pudding. His restaurant had a difficult time competing with Green Apple Snack Shoppe, located across the street. It seemed that whenever Plum Pudding offered a new special price on a particular meal, its competitor met the price and offered some other inducement as well. As a last desperate effort to remain in business, Williamson hired a "torch" to set fire to the Green Apple. Just as the hired criminal had finished his work, he was apprehended by an off-duty police officer. The hired "torch" admitted his guilt and implicated Williamson.

a. Would Williamson be charged with arson? **a.** ______

b. Would the hired "torch" be charged with arson? **b.** ______

c. Is it likely that Green Apple's insurance would pay for the damage? **c.** ______

d. Is this an example of the crime of extortion? **d.** ______

40. False Pretenses Zaks, the owner of a hairstyling salon, Locks Unlimited, applied for a bank loan to buy new hair dryers and other equipment she felt were needed to attract new customers. To enhance her chances of getting the loan, she told the bank that she owned considerable equipment and furniture, although most of the equipment and furnishings in the shop were actually rented.

a. If Zaks's deception were discovered, is it likely that she could be charged with false pretenses? **a.** ______

b. If the bank accepted the false statements at face value, did the bank perform responsibly? **b.** ______

c. Could Zaks be charged with extortion? **c.** ______

d. Could the banker be charged with bribery? **d.** ______

41. Bribery Gelfis owned and operated Welltech, a janitorial service company that provided services to a number of city and state agencies. Eager to expand his firm and increase his profits, he approached Biondi, the director of purchasing for a state agency, and offered to sell Biondi stock in Welltech at a greatly reduced price.

It was clear to both Gelfis and Biondi that Biondi would be expected to award the janitorial services contract to Welltech.

a. If the arrangement were completed, could Gelfis be charged with bribery? **a.** _____

b. Could Gelfis be charged with burglary? **b.** _____

c. Could Gelfis be charged with extortion? **c.** _____

CASE ANALYSIS

Study each of the following cases carefully. Briefly state the principle of law and your decision.

42. Credit Card Fraud Buckley, a worker in a restaurant, stole a credit card from the coat of its owner with the intention of using it to charge goods. He purchased some merchandise at a retail store and paid for these goods by presenting the stolen credit card to the salesperson and signing the name of the person whose name appeared on the card. Was Buckley guilty of a crime? [*Buckley v. Indiana,* 322 N.E.2d 113 (Indiana)]

Principle of Law:

Decision:

43. Criminal Law DeCoster and his son, owners of a large egg production company, negligently sold eggs contaminated by salmonella poisoning, causing illness to 1,939 people, according to an estimate by the U.S. Centers for Disease Control and Prevention. According to estimates by some officials, however, the actual number of persons affected amounted to as many as 56,000. Are DeCoster and his son subject to criminal liability and jail sentences, even though their conduct was only negligent and not intentional? [*United States v. DeCoster,* No. 15-1890 (8th Circuit, 2016)]

Principle of Law:

Decision:

44. Insider Trading Franken, president of Monarch Pharmaceuticals Incorporated, was one of only three persons who knew that one of the firm's experimental drugs had just been approved by the federal government. The drug had been found to cure several serious diseases. As soon as news of the approval became public, Franken reasoned, the price of the firm's stock would increase substantially. He arranged with a friend to buy thousands of shares of the company's stock, hoping to sell at a profit after the price increased as a result of the good news. Can Franken be prosecuted for his actions?

Principle of Law:

____

____

Decision:

____

____

45. Forgery Searle, office manager of Entro Products, had access to the firm's checks to be used in paying for office supplies. However, Searle was not authorized to sign them. Each time he wanted to pay invoices, Searle had to have the firm's president sign them. After some months, he was able to copy the president's signature. He had invoices printed for a nonexistent company, and periodically he made out checks to the fake company and signed the president's signature. Ultimately his wrongdoings were discovered. Is it likely Searle will be prosecuted for his crime?

Principle of Law:

____

____

Decision:

____

____

LEGAL RESEARCH

Complete the following activities. Share your findings with the class.

46. Working in Teams Small and medium-sized businesses are often concerned with crimes that could affect the firm. In teams of three or four, interview one or several business owners or managers and ask them to briefly describe the kinds of crimes they are concerned about and the steps they take to minimize the risk of crime.

____

____

47. Using Technology Using the Internet and search engines, investigate common internal business crimes committed by employees.

____

____

chapter 4
Tort Law

LEARNING OUTCOMES

After studying this chapter and completing the assessment, you will be able to

4.1 Explain the nature of torts and identify some common torts.

4.2 Describe defamation.

4.3 Explain the differences between libel and slander.

4.4 Explain the two common defenses to charges of defamation.

4.5 Define nuisance and the types of nuisance charges.

4.6 Describe conversion and explain its main purpose.

4.7 Define *negligence* and distinguish between the different types of negligence.

4.8 Explain the legal concept of liability and provide examples.

LEGAL terms

- defamation
- libel
- slander
- trade libel
- nuisance
- conversion
- negligence
- reasonable person
- vicarious negligence
- negligence *per se*
- contributory negligence
- comparative negligence
- assumption of risk
- liable
- vicarious liability
- strict liability

TORT LAW

"Truth is generally the best vindication against slander."

Abraham Lincoln, 16th president of the United States

Hisham Ibrahim/Photodisc/Getty Images

4.1 THE NATURE OF TORTS

Chapter 3 defined a crime as a violation of the rights of society as a whole, whether an individual is the victim of the crime or there is no identifiable wronged party. A tort, in contrast to a crime, holds a defendant liable for injury to an identifiable individual or business that has been wronged either intentionally or by negligence. For example, when the crime of larceny has been committed and the victim can be identified, then both a crime has been committed and the victim of the larceny has suffered the tort of conversion (the wrongful taking of property). The law of torts does not deal with duties imposed by contract but is concerned only with the violation of private rights related to person, property, or reputation.

Whether acting as an individual or as an employee, a person has a responsibility to consider the rights of others. The common torts discussed in this chapter all have some direct or indirect bearing on an individual's personal life and on how they perform their job. These common torts include defamation, nuisance, conversion, and negligence.

4.2 DEFAMATION

defamation
The harming of a person's reputation and good name by the communication of a false statement.

Defamation is the harming of a person's reputation and good name by the communication of a false statement. For an act to be considered defamatory, it is necessary to show that the statement was made in such a way that others hear or read it. To call someone a thief to the person's face may be an insult, but it is not defamation. A defamatory statement usually holds a person up to hatred, ridicule, or contempt or causes a person's esteem, respect, or social position to be diminished. Defamation also involves some suggestion of disgrace, and it tends to generate negative feelings about the person who suffers the defamation. For a statement to be defamatory, it must be addressed to a third party.

Occasionally more than one party may be guilty of spreading a defamatory statement. For example, suppose a newspaper reporter includes a previously published defamatory statement on a website. The reporter, along with the party who originally created the false statement, may be found guilty of defamation.

The charge of defamation has been separated into two torts: libel and slander.

4.3 LIBEL AND SLANDER

libel
The spreading of damaging statements in written form, including pictures, cartoons, and effigies.

Generally, libel is the spreading of damaging statements in written form–including pictures, cartoons, and effigies (likenesses). Defamation on radio, television, and websites is also considered libel.

slander
The spreading of damaging words or ideas about a person, directly or indirectly, in all other forms not considered libel.

Slander is the spreading of damaging words or ideas about a person, directly or indirectly, in all other forms not considered libel. Of course the most common form of slander involves spoken words, but slander also can be committed by means of gestures and actions.

Many libel cases involve defamatory statements published in books, newspapers, magazines, and on websites.
Ingram Publishing/SuperStock

CHARACTERISTICS OF LIBEL

Although many libel cases involve defamatory statements published in books, newspapers, magazines, and on websites, the possibility of libel also exists in business and personal letters, emails, memos, and catalogs. The libel need not be direct. Subtle suggestion or implication is enough to bring about legal charges. For example, there have been cases in which the use of quotation marks has been interpreted as giving a libelous meaning to otherwise harmless words.

EXAMPLE 4.1

▶ Jesse, a sales manager, wrote an email to their supervisor stating that an employer was taking another "sick" day.

By placing the quotation marks around the word *sick,* Jesse suggested that the employee was not really sick and was possibly violating company policy. The important point in this case is that it is not so much the exact wording of the statement that matters, but rather how others–including a jury–might reasonably interpret the statement.

The previous illustration may not seem very damaging, given today's more liberal standards of social behavior, but the same principle can apply to other situations. Suppose that a supervisor had written an email stating, "I don't know what became of the laptop computer, but you might want to check with Fred Chaffee; he has been known to 'borrow' things before."

Another example of how a statement might be interpreted as damaging a person's reputation can be seen in Example 4.2, in which no statement was made, but the implication was damaging nevertheless.

EXAMPLE 4.2

▶ The First National County Bank noticed shortages of money and asked its employees to submit to polygraph (lie detector) tests. One employee, Baxter, was unable to pass the test, and the bonding company refused to renew his bond (a form of insurance that protects a firm from losses due to employee dishonesty). The local newspaper learned of the problems at the bank and interviewed the president, who mentioned that some employees were no longer working because the insurance company would not issue bonds for them. When the newspaper printed the story, Baxter sued the bank, charging libel.

Even though the newspaper account did not mention Baxter by name, he charged that people who knew him and knew that he was no longer working at the bank would assume that he had been involved in the shortages of money.

Most cases of libel are not quite as unusual as those previously described. Many problems simply involve thoughtless written remarks or unfounded gossip. Other problems arise when employers make negative statements when providing references for employees.

EXAMPLE 4.3

▶ Evans and her secretary did not get along well. When the secretary resigned to take a job with another firm, Evans was happy to see her leave. The secretary's new employer sent a routine inquiry form to Evans to verify the secretary's claims of prior employment. The form provided spaces in which to answer routine questions and also a section for other comments. Evans, who still disliked her former secretary and intended to damage her reputation, added "untrustworthy and dishonest." The new employer discharged the secretary and pointed to Evans's comment as the reason. The secretary brought suit against Evans, charging libel.

In recent years, the threat of libel suits by former employees who are unhappy with the references given by former employers has gotten so serious that many firms refuse to respond to any inquiry about former workers—even those who have good records.

CHARACTERISTICS OF SLANDER

Slander is the term that describes almost all defamation that cannot be classified as libel. Slander includes spoken words, gestures, actions, and even omissions. Most cases of slander involve thoughtless statements that reflect on another person's good name and reputation. Because oral statements, unless recorded, cannot be reproduced as evidence, some people tend to speak carelessly about others without realizing that anyone hearing a slanderous statement can be called upon later to testify to having heard it.

EXAMPLE 4.4

▶ Feely, a sales manager, was speaking with a group of employees and customers at a convention when the name of a former salesperson, Tummer, came up. Feely said that Tummer was incompetent and had cheated on his expense account, even though this had never been proven. One of those in the group reported the statement to Tummer and agreed to swear to the fact that Feely had made the statement. Tummer brought suit, charging slander.

The tort of slander does not require a directly defamatory statement. Gestures and actions can sometimes be equally damaging. Consider Example 4.5, in which no defamatory words were spoken.

EXAMPLE 4.5

▶ Mason entered a variety store, examined various articles of merchandise, and then left the store. Conant, the store manager, suspecting that Mason had stolen something, followed her into the street, where—in full view of several bystanders—he ordered her to stop. He then searched her and examined her handbag. Finding nothing, he released her and returned to the store. Mason believed that Conant, by his actions and gestures, had falsely accused her of being a thief. She brought suit for damages to her reputation, charging slander.

Although the store manager did not actually call the customer a thief, by his actions he implied as much. Cautious businesspersons, given a similar situation, would quietly ask the shopper to return to the store and consent to a search in the privacy of the manager's office. Obviously, the damages that result from a slanderous statement are influenced by the number of people who hear it. Many people are careful to avoid making such statements publicly before large groups. However, making a defamatory statement to even a single person might still provide the basis for legal action.

EXAMPLE 4.6

Hamm, the sales manager of Linn Products, dictated an angry memo to Pennington, one of her salespersons. In the memo she called Pennington a "thief," among other things. Shortly thereafter, Pennington left the employ of Linn Products and brought suit, charging slander. Hamm argued that she had dictated a confidential memo, without sending copies to third parties, and that she had not damaged Pennington's reputation because the defamatory words had not been heard or seen by anyone else. Pennington claimed that Hamm had dictated the memo to a secretary and, in so doing, had slandered him. The court decided that Hamm had indeed slandered Pennington.

TRADE LIBEL

trade libel
Defamation that deals with an individual's title to property or to the quality or conduct of a business.

In conducting business, a firm and its owners have the right to remain free from false and malicious statements by others that may cause a loss or damage to the reputation of the firm, the owners, the products produced, or the merchandise carried or manufactured by the firm. The tort of trade libel is similar to traditional defamation but deals with an individual's title to property or to the quality or conduct of a business.

EXAMPLE 4.7

Philo posted a message to several suppliers on social media, claiming that his competitor, Willit, was about to file for bankruptcy and go out of business. The statements were without foundation because Willit's business was prosperous, and there was no likelihood of a bankruptcy. Because such an untrue statement could damage his business, Willit could sue Philo, charging trade libel.

HUMOR AND SLANDER

It might seem that a quick apology and a "sorry, just kidding" might be enough to avoid some charges of slander, but consider Example 4.8, where the subject of a seemingly harmless remark did not think it was funny.

EXAMPLE 4.8

A radio station was sued as a result of its broadcast of a listener call-in program that invited listeners to nominate a person or a business for the title of "dodo of the day." A listener, who identified herself only as "Bonnie," called to nominate her insurance agent, Lawrence Faro, as the "dodo of the day." She claimed that after she consulted him about a damaged windshield, he advised her to throw a brick through her windshield to make the claim large enough that the insurance company would pay it. Faro denied knowing a customer named Bonnie and sued the radio station for defamation.

4.4 DEFENSES TO DEFAMATION

There are two common defenses to charges of defamation: (1) truth and (2) privilege. If a defamatory statement can be proved to be true, the person who claims that he or she was defamed cannot recover damages. However, a person engaged in business should still be careful because it is often expensive to go to court in order to prove the truth of a statement. The expense can be avoided by being cautious in the first place.

Similarly, if the person accused of defamation had a special privilege in making the defamatory statement, such as an attorney in a court proceeding who accuses a witness of lying, the defamed person cannot recover damages.

nuisance
An unlawful interference with the enjoyment of life or property.

The law gives everyone the right to enjoy their land without unreasonable interference from others.
Image Source/Getty Images

4.5 NUISANCE

An unlawful interference with the enjoyment of life or property constitutes a nuisance. The law gives everyone the right to enjoy their land without unreasonable interference from others. A person who acts in a way that denies this right to a specific person or persons has created a *private nuisance.* A *public nuisance,* by comparison, affects the community or the general public. Creating a nuisance does not mean taking another's property—only detracting from the enjoyment of it. A person can be charged with creating a private nuisance by causing loud noises, creating foul odors, shining bright lights, or diverting a stream.

EXAMPLE 4.9

▶ Springs Manufacturing Company had operated a small factory in the town of Burlingame for many years and was regarded as a responsible firm that created no problems for the community. It even employed 30 townspeople. In an effort to expand the company's business, management decided to begin making a line of goods that required a fairly noisy stamping process. The families in the immediate area complained loudly about the noise. Management took the position that the noise was the price the community had to pay for the economic benefits of having the plant located there.

Example 4.9 illustrates the tort of nuisance. It also illustrates the tough choices people must sometimes make between seeking relief from a nuisance and having to do without some offsetting benefit. The law recognizes that when people live together in a society such as ours, not all people can have their own way. The benefits to one person must be balanced against the inconvenience to another.

4.6 CONVERSION

conversion
The wrongful exercise of dominion and control over another's personal property.

The law gives each person the right to own and use personal property without interference from others. When this right is denied or abridged by another, the wrongdoer is said to have committed the tort of conversion. This tort can involve a wrongful taking, a wrongful detention, or an illegal assumption of ownership. Conversion may involve removal, damage, destruction, or unauthorized use of another person's property. A shoplifter commits the crime of larceny as well as the tort of conversion. Note, however, that unlike larceny, conversion can occur without intent. For example, if a student accidentally takes a friend's laptop computer under the mistaken assumption that it is their own, the student has committed the tort of conversion–regardless of the student's lack of intent. A lawsuit charging a person with conversion provides the victim with the means of collecting money damages from someone who steals personal property. It is one thing to have a dishonest employee arrested, found guilty of the crime of larceny, and punished; but a criminal action does not return the stolen goods or money. A tort action for conversion is one way to help replace the money or property.

EXAMPLE 4.10

▶ Clemente sees Quinn's lawnmower in Quinn's front yard. Clemente takes the lawnmower, intending to return it after mowing his yard, but does not notify Quinn that he has borrowed the mower. While mowing his yard, the mower engine catches on fire damaging the mower. Quinn could sue Clemente for the damages charging Clemente with conversion.

4.7 NEGLIGENCE

negligence
The failure to exercise necessary care to protect others from unreasonable risk of harm.

The tort of negligence is the failure to exercise reasonable care necessary to protect others from risk of harm. Negligence cases cover a broad group of lawsuits such as automobile accidents and customer "slip and fall" cases. Other negligence lawsuits have charged professionals such as doctors, dentists, nurses, pharmacists, lawyers, and accountants with malpractice (a term that is used in cases involving the negligence of professionals–see Chapter 35). Homeowners have been sued for negligence for injuries that have occurred on their property. Corporations have been sued for negligent design or manufacture of products that cause injury (see Chapter 34).

To avoid legal action either as an individual or as an employee, each person must exercise reasonable care and good judgment to avoid causing injury to others. Even so, good judgment and care will not prevent all accidents. It is also important to carry adequate insurance coverage for protection against the financial losses that can result from being adjudged liable for the tort of negligence.

EXAMPLE 4.11

▶ Jensen, employed as a truck driver, was driving a new light truck at 40 miles per hour on a mild day when a tire blew out. As a result, his truck collided with another vehicle and caused both extensive damage to the other vehicle and injury to the driver.

While it is difficult to predict how a jury would decide this case, most reasonable persons would say that Jensen was not negligent. But suppose that Jensen was driving at 70 miles per hour, the tires were worn, the day and pavement were hot, and the truck was heavily loaded. In that case, most people would say that Jensen was negligent. It is not just a particular act that constitutes negligence but the circumstances that surround it.

UNAVOIDABLE ACCIDENT

In theory, most accidents are avoidable. Jensen, the truck driver, could have avoided the accident by simply not driving the truck at all—or by not getting out of bed that morning. But the concept of unavoidable accident is intended to focus attention on whether an accident could have been avoided if the person alleged to be responsible had acted reasonably.

THE "REASONABLE PERSON"

The law provides certain ways by which juries can determine if a person has acted negligently. One of these ways is the doctrine of the "reasonable person of ordinary prudence," a completely fictitious individual who is assumed to have the judgment and skill one would expect from a person with the strengths and limitations of the person whose behavior is being judged. While there is no standard reasonable person, a jury is asked to determine how the mythical person would have behaved under the same or similar circumstances. Obviously, one reason the law has kept this imaginary individual alive is to prevent jurors from judging a defendant in terms of how they themselves would have behaved.

reasonable person
A completely fictitious individual who is assumed to have the judgment and skill one would expect from a person with the strengths and limitations of the person whose behavior is being judged.

KINDS OF NEGLIGENCE

The legal concept of negligence is not quite so simple as deciding if the driver of an automobile was driving negligently. Many cases are far more complex, particularly when the law must decide if one or more third parties also can be held responsible for the negligence.

Vicarious Negligence The term *vicarious* as used in the law means essentially the same as when it is used generally—that is, to describe an act performed by one person as a substitute for another. Vicarious negligence, therefore, means charging a negligent act of one person to another.

vicarious negligence
Charging a negligent act of one person to another.

EXAMPLE 4.12

▶ Christensen rented a house from Hoover. After a few months, a dispute developed about the amount of rent owed. Hoover obtained a court order to recover possession of the house. Because Christensen was out of town at the time, Hoover hired a local moving and storage company to remove and store the renter's possessions. After Christensen paid the rent owed, Hoover told the storage company to release Christensen's possessions. Unfortunately, some items were damaged and still others were missing. Christensen sued, and after the trial in favor of Hoover, the Colorado State Supreme Court held on appeal that Hoover was vicariously responsible for the loss that occurred while the goods were in the hands of the moving company. [*Christensen v. Hoover*, 643 P.2d 525 (Colo. 1982)]

In many cases that involve the negligence of an employee, the employer is held responsible, provided the employee was performing the tasks they were hired to do. (The practical reason is that the employer usually has the money or insurance to settle the suit. There is little to gain from a judgment against an employee who does not have the financial resources to pay the damages.)

negligence *per se*
Negligence *per se* occurs when a defendant in a case of negligence has violated a law that was enacted in order to prevent the type of injury that occurred.

Negligence *Per Se* Negligence *per se*, which translates to "negligence in or of itself," occurs when a defendant in a case of negligence has violated a law that was enacted in order to prevent the type of injury that occurred. For example, if a defendant, while driving their vehicle while intoxicated, strikes another vehicle, they may be found liable of negligence *per se*.

contributory negligence
A legal defense that involves the failure of an injured party to be careful enough to ensure personal safety.

Contributory Negligence The previous paragraphs described the concept of negligence. Contributory negligence is not an accusation but rather a legal defense by the party who is charged with negligence. In effect, the defendant admits to being negligent but argues that the plaintiff was negligent as well and that the plaintiff's negligence contributed to their own injuries. Another term for this principle is *contributory fault.* Under the doctrine of contributory negligence, the injured party would not be able to sue successfully if they were partly responsible, even in a minor way. Note the case in Example 4.13, involving Alvis and Ribar, in which the trial court rejected Alvis's suit because of his contributory negligence.

EXAMPLE 4.13

▶ Alvis was injured while riding in a car driven by Ribar. The car had crashed into a metal barrel anchoring an intersection stop sign at the site of some highway construction. Alvis sued Ribar, the county, and a contractor. The suit was dismissed in the trial court because of contributory negligence; apparently there was some evidence of carelessness on Alvis's part as well (he may not have been wearing his seatbelt). But when the appeal reached the Supreme Court of Illinois, it saw injustice in denying any damage to Alvis simply because he had contributed to his injuries. The Supreme Court sent the case back to the trial court to let a jury decide the extent to which Alvis had contributed to the accident and to proportion damages accordingly. [*Alvis v. Ribar*, 85 Ill. 2d 1, 421 N.E.2d 886 (Ill. 1981)]

comparative negligence
A form of negligence that requires the court to assign damages according to the degree of fault of each party.

Comparative Negligence Many legislatures and courts have now replaced the doctrine of contributory negligence with the doctrine of comparative negligence. Under this latter doctrine, the injured party bringing the lawsuit is not prevented from recovering damages even if they were partly at fault. The jury determines how much the plaintiff was at fault and reduces the verdict by that amount. For example, if the plaintiff was found to be 10 percent negligent, they would get an award 10 percent less than the full damages as determined by the jury.

Only five states apply pure contributory negligence; only three states apply pure comparative negligence; the remaining states apply a mixture of the two.

assumption of risk
A defense in a case of negligence in which the defendant demonstrates that the plaintiff voluntarily assumed the risk associated with the dangerous condition caused by the defendant.

Negligence and Assumption of Risk Sometimes an injured party in a case of negligence assumes the risk as a result of their actions. Assumption of risk is a defense raised by the defendant in a case of negligence in which the defendant demonstrates that the plaintiff voluntarily assumed the risk associated with the dangerous condition caused by the defendant. Often parties voluntarily agree to assume the risk associated with dangerous conditions because the advantageous outcomes involved with such exceed the hazards; thus, the defendant will not be liable for negligence. Consider Example 4.14.

EXAMPLE 4.14

▶ Singh, the owner of a sailboat, contacted O'Shea to inquire about renting a boat slip. O'Shea informed Singh that the only boat slip available was one that was accessible only by walking a rocky and steep trail, but that if Singh were willing to sign a rental agreement in which she assumed the risk for any injuries that might result from using the unkept trail, O'Shea would lower the rent substantially. Because Singh enjoyed hiking and could greatly benefit from the monetary savings involved with renting this particular boat slip, Singh signed the rental agreement. Because Singh assumed the risk, the court would not find O'Shea liable for negligence should Singh injure herself while using the access trail.

4.8 LIABILITY

When a person has been judged to be responsible for a loss, they are said to be liable (not to be confused with *libel,* covered earlier in this chapter). In most lawsuits, the court must decide if the defendant is liable for the damages as charged. In some instances, the law shields certain persons. In other instances, liability is automatically assumed.

liable
Being judged legally responsible.

EXAMPLE 4.15

▶ Wimpers was in the business of renting power tools. Woo rented a power saw from him that lacked a standard safety guard. While using the saw, Woo cut off two fingers. Wimpers might be charged with negligence (carelessness) for having rented the tool without the guard. Because of the negligence, he would be held liable (responsible) for the injuries and the payment of damages.

It would be easy to state that all liability results from negligence and all negligence creates liability, but this is not the case. There are instances in which a person is liable even though no negligence has been proved.

VICARIOUS LIABILITY

In some cases, the law holds persons liable for the acts of others, such as when an employer is held responsible for the acts of employees or when a general contractor is held responsible for acts of a subcontractor. The term for this shifting of responsibility is vicarious liability, and it is related to vicarious negligence, discussed earlier.

vicarious liability
The concept of laying responsibility or blame upon one person for the actions of another.

STRICT LIABILITY

Certain events cause death or injury to others even when no negligence exists. Under a doctrine known as strict liability, people may be liable for injuries to others whether or not they have exercised reasonable care. Examples include damage caused by inherently dangerous activities, events, or animals and might involve domestic pets, fire, water, explosives, or dangerous chemicals.

strict liability
The doctrine under which persons may be liable for injuries to others whether or not they have been negligent or committed an intentional tort. This establishes liability without the necessity of proving fault.

EXAMPLE 4.16

The Helfer Construction Company was building a highway and found it necessary to use explosives to blast away some rock formations. Employees of the firm were well trained and careful in their work. Despite their care, however, some rock fragments damaged a nearby house. The owner of the house sued the construction company for the damages. Helfer raised the defense that the homeowner could not show negligence on the part of the company. Judgment was entered for the homeowner because, under the doctrine of strict liability, it was not necessary to show negligence, only that the damage occurred.

The broad range of injuries suffered by employees on the job is another example of strict liability. Workers' compensation laws limit the amount of money employees may recover from their employers for most work-related injuries and illnesses; however, the employer and the firm's insurance company cannot avoid payment by claiming that the employee contributed to their own injury or illness or that they assumed the risks of the job (see Chapter 33).

In recent years, the doctrine of strict liability also has been applied to cases involving injury or death caused by manufactured products, such as machinery—even if the injured

A manufacturer of saws may be liable under the doctrine of strict liability. Stevecoleimages/E+/Getty Images

person misused the product. Some courts believe that the manufacturer found liable for a product that causes harm is in a better position than the injured person to absorb the costs associated with this injury. Typically, the manufacturer's insurance company will pay the damages, and the manufacturer will pass the cost of insurance to all users of the product (see Chapter 34).

A purchaser who is injured by a product has a cause of action by demonstrating merely that (1) the product was defective, (2) the defect was the cause of the injury, and (3) the defect caused the product to be unreasonably dangerous. Strict liability has been recognized and applied in approximately two-thirds of the states in this country.

EXAMPLE 4.17

▸ Greenman purchased a power saw for use in his home workshop. He was using the saw when a sliver of wood flew out of the machine and caused him to suffer serious eye injuries. Greenman sued the manufacturer of the machine. The court ruled that the manufacturer was liable under the doctrine of strict liability.

Proponents of strict liability claim that eliminating the need to prove negligence on the part of the manufacturer will encourage manufacturers and sellers to be more concerned with producing safer products. Others argue that the application of strict liability will inhibit the development of new products because of the fear of product liability lawsuits and the high cost of product liability insurance.

CHAPTER SUMMARY

4.1 A tort is a violation of the personal, property, or reputational rights of an identifiable individual or business that has been wronged either intentionally or by negligence. Common torts include the following: defamation, nuisance, conversion, and negligence.

4.2 Defamation is the harming of a person's reputation and good name by the communication of a false statement.

4.3 Libel is the spreading of damaging statements in written form, which include pictures, cartoons, effigies, and any type of media communication. Slander is spreading damaging words or ideas about a person, directly or indirectly, in all other forms not considered libel.

4.4 Two common defenses to claims of defamation are (1) truth and (2) privilege.

4.5 Nuisance is an unlawful interference with the enjoyment of life or property. There are two types of nuisance charges in the U.S. system: private and public. A private nuisance occurs when a person acts in a way that denies the right of enjoyment to a specific person or persons. A public nuisance occurs when an entire community or the general public is denied enjoyment as a result of an act.

4.6 Conversion is a wrongful act against a person's right to own and use personal property. This act can include removal, damage, destruction, or unauthorized use of another person's property. A tort action for conversion is one way to help replace the money or property the victim lost.

4.7 Negligence is the failure to exercise reasonable care to protect others from risk of harm. Types of negligence include vicarious negligence, negligence *per se,* contributory negligence, comparative negligence, and negligence as a result of assumption of risk.

4.8 The legal concept of liability involves judging a party legally responsible for a loss or wrong. Examples include being found liable for any of the torts mentioned in this chapter, including defamation, nuisance, conversion, or negligence.

CHAPTER FOUR ASSESSMENT

MATCHING LEGAL TERMS

Match each of the numbered definitions with the correct term in the following list.

a. conversion
b. contributory negligence
c. defamation
d. liability
e. libel
f. negligence
g. nuisance
h. slander
i. tort
j. vicarious liability

1. A broad category of violations of the rights of individuals. **1.** _____

2. False written or spoken statements that harm a person's reputation. **2.** _____

3. Actions that unreasonably deny someone the enjoyment of their land. **3.** _____

4. False written statements that harm a person's reputation or good name. **4.** _____

5. Actions that physically remove or destroy the personal property of others. **5.** _____

6. False spoken statements or actions that damage a person's reputation or good name. **6.** _____

7. Carelessness that results in injury to another person or their property. **7.** _____

8. The state or condition of being responsible for wrong or injury. **8.** _____

9. The shifting of responsibility from one person to another. **9.** _____

10. A concept that states that one person partially caused their own injuries. **10.** _____

TRUE/FALSE QUIZ

Indicate whether each of the following statements is true or false.

11. A tort is a violation of the rights of a particular person. **11.** _____

12. Defamation includes both libel and slander. **12.** _____

13. The tort of libel is concerned with injury to a person's reputation caused by false statements that are used in testimony in court. **13.** _____

14. Liability is the state of being responsible for a wrong or injury. **14.** _____

15. The tort of conversion is concerned with acts that deny a person the possession of their property. **15.** _____

16. The "reasonable person" doctrine is concerned with the appeal to a jury to assume how a person would behave under the best conditions . **16.** _____

MULTIPLE CHOICE QUIZ

Answer the following using the choices provided.

17. A tort is a violation of private rights related to (a) person only (b) person or property (c) person, property, or reputation (d) reputation only. **17.** _____

18. The crime of larceny is often related to the tort of (a) battery (b) negligence (c) defamation (d) conversion. **18.** _____

19. In a defamation suit, a plaintiff alleges harm to (a) person (b) reputation (c) commerce (d) property. **19.** _____

20. Libel requires that false damaging statements are made (a) in written form (b) in oral or written form (c) in oral form (d) in neither written nor oral form. **20.** _____

21. Defenses to defamation include (a) truth only (b) privilege only (c) truth and privilege (d) neither truth nor privilege. **21.** _____

22. Nuisance that denies enjoyment to a community is (a) public nuisance (b) community nuisance (c) cumulative private nuisance (d) private nuisance. **22.** _____

23. One defense to a tort claim when the plaintiff is aware of the dangers of an activity and is injured from that activity is (a) negligence per se (b) contributory negligence (c) comparative negligence (d) assumption of risk. **23.** _____

24. A person responsible for a loss in a tort lawsuit is referred to as (a) liable (b) guilty (c) libel (d) not guilty. **24.** _____

25. The charging of a negligent act of one person to another not directly involved in the act is known as (a) negligence per se (b) vicarious negligence (c) comparative negligence (d) contributory negligence. **25.** _____

26. The doctrine that assigns liability regardless of the level of care is (a) absolute liability (b) negligence (c) inherent care (d) strict liability. **26.** _____

DISCUSSION QUESTIONS

Answer the following questions and discuss them in class.

27. Identify several common torts and explain how each might be committed in a business environment.

28. Explain the legal concept of liability and provide examples.

29. Compare contributory negligence with comparative negligence and provide examples of each.

30. Explain vicarious liability and provide an example.

31. Explain strict liability and provide an example.

THINKING CRITICALLY ABOUT THE LAW

Answer the following questions, which require you to think critically about the legal principles that you learned in this chapter.

32. Defamation Why is it that public figures find it difficult to successfully sue a publication for libel, whereas private persons have a better chance? Should public figures be required to accept libelous accusations as the price of fame?

33. Trade Libel The law protects businesses against defamatory statements or writings just as it does for individuals. Should there be a different standard for businesses that would permit a firm to attack a competitor?

34. Private Nuisance The law gives a person the right to enjoy their land without unreasonable interference from others. If a person plays loud music on their property and a neighbor charges them with creating a public nuisance, where does the music player's constitutional right to free expression end, and where does the neighbor's right to be free of a private nuisance begin? How should a court decide?

____

____

35. Conversion If a person suffers a loss of their property as a result of the criminal wrongdoing of another, would it matter whether the thief (wrongdoer) is charged by the victim with the crime of larceny or the tort of conversion?

____

____

36. A Question of Ethics Do you believe it is unethical to exaggerate the extent of injuries suffered in an automobile accident resulting from another driver's negligent driving in an effort to increase the amount of a financial settlement that will be paid by an insurance company?

____

____

CASE QUESTIONS

Study each of the following cases. Answer the questions that follow with Yes or No.

37. Libel and Slander Goldman, an ex-convict, was employed in the accounting department of Rogers Products Incorporated. None of his coworkers was aware of his previous conviction and imprisonment, although the president of the firm and Ruiz, the human resources manager, knew of it. During an office party, Goldman and Ruiz became involved in an argument, and Ruiz shouted, "You're an ex-con and a jailbird. We'd be better off without you here."

a. Would Goldman have a basis for a suit for libel? **a.** _____

b. Would Goldman have a basis for slander? **b.** _____

c. Did Ruiz violate the professional ethics of his position? **c.** _____

38. Negligence The Sock 'n' Rock Music Store was located in a small shopping mall. In an effort to attract additional customers, the manager of the store installed an outdoor loudspeaker and played rock music at high volume. Nearby stores in the shopping mall objected, claiming that the loud music drove their customers away.

a. Does Sock 'n' Rock have the right to use the rented property as it pleases? **a.** _____

b. Do the other stores in the mall have a basis for suit, charging private or public nuisance? **b.** _____

c. Do the other stores in the mall have a basis for suit, charging conversion? **c.** _____

d. Would a court order preventing the loud music seem to be a good remedy? **d.** _____

39. Negligence Leffingwell engaged the Bartwell Tree Removal Service to cut down and remove a diseased tree from her property. When the work began, it was a calm day. As the work progressed, however, a high wind arose and blew a portion of the tree onto a neighbor's car, causing considerable damage. The neighbor brought suit against Bartwell, charging negligence.

a. Does it seem likely that the accident could have been prevented? **a.** _____

b. Could the owner of the car be charged with negligence for parking his car in a place where it could be damaged by the falling tree? **b.** _____

c. Would the neighbor have a sound basis upon which to sue for damages? **c.** _____

d. Do the circumstances seem to support a defense Bartwell might make claiming that this was an unavoidable accident? **d.** _____

40. Conversion Pratt, a stock-car racing driver, had entered a race to be held several months later. Two days before the race, he left his racing car at a shop to have some last-minute adjustments made. When Pratt went to pick up the car before the race, the shop owner refused to release it until Pratt paid for work that had been done two years earlier on another car. Pratt could not raise the money in time and was unable to participate in the race. As a result, he had to forfeit the $75 fee he had paid to enter.

a. Does it seem that the repair shop acted responsibly? **a.** _____

b. Could Pratt bring suit, charging conversion? **b.** _____

c. Could Pratt bring suit against the repair shop to recover his $75 entry fee? **c.** _____

d. Could Pratt have the shop owner arrested for larceny? **d.** _____

CASE ANALYSIS

Study each of the following cases carefully. Briefly state the principle of law and your decision.

41. Defamation At a special meeting, the board of directors of Family Federal Savings & Loan Association asked Newton, its president, manager, and director, to resign. He did so. Shortly thereafter, a reporter for the *Oregon Statesman* talked about Newton's resignation with one of the directors. The very next day, the paper published an article that stated, "The board of directors of the six-branch Family Federal Savings & Loan Association has forced Thomas Newton out of his position as the association's president, charging that he is 'administratively incapable.'" Newton thereupon sued the association and its individual directors for defamation. When a jury awarded him damages, the directors appealed on the ground that the quoted language was not capable of a defamatory meaning. Will the directors succeed in overturning the judgment? [*Newton v. Family FS&L Association,* 616 P.2d 1213 (Oregon)]

Principle of Law:

____

____

Decision:

42. **Conversion** Rensch left two diamond rings for cleaning at Riddle's Mall in Rapid City, South Dakota. Riddle's had advertised free ring cleaning to the public. When Rensch returned for the rings, he found that a clerk had mistakenly given them to another customer. They were never recovered, and Rensch ultimately sued Riddle. What tort was involved in this case? Is it likely that the court will find for Rensch? [*Rensch v. Riddle's Diamonds of Rapid City,* 393 N.W.2d 269 S.D. (South Dakota)]

Principle of Law:

Decision:

43. **Trade Libel** Robin Williams, famous entertainer and comedian, gave a performance at a San Francisco nightclub, The Great American Music Hall. As part of his comedy routine, he disparaged a particular brand of wine, Rege, by suggesting that it would be a great success if it were directed toward a particular minority group. The discussion of the wine also included certain obscene and vulgar expressions. It seemed that the Rege wine was the target of Williams's jokes. Video and audiotapes were made of the performance and were distributed by the recording company, Polygram Records. Rege brought suit, claiming trade libel. What would be the probable outcome of this suit? Did the fact that the alleged libel took place during a comedy routine alter the case? [*Polygram Records v. Superior Court,* 170 Cal. App. 3d 543 (California)]

Principle of Law:

Decision:

44. **Defamation** Fortrell, an aide in a child care center, was particularly concerned about the behavior of a certain child who frequently fought with and teased other children at the center. LaRena, the mother of one of the children who had been a victim of the troublesome child, was at the center one day, and Fortrell explained that the behavior of the problem child was caused by his mother, Yung, who was herself unbalanced and unfit to have custody of the child. What Fortrell did not know was

that LaRena was a friend of Yung and reported the conversation to her. Yung sued Fortrell, charging defamation. Will Yung succeed in a defamation suit?

Principle of Law:

Decision:

LEGAL RESEARCH

Complete the following activities. Share your findings with the class.

45. Working in Teams In teams of three or four, interview several property/casualty insurance agents or claims adjusters (as distinguished from life or health insurance personnel) to learn more about claims filed against small businesses for negligence or other torts. Ask what steps or measures might have been taken to avoid the commission of the tort.

46. Using Technology Using the Internet and search engines, investigate a case involving negligence.

chapter 5 Constitutional Law

LEARNING OUTCOMES

After studying this chapter and completing the assessment, you will be able to

5.1 Explain the difference between express and implied powers, describe the process used to amend the U.S. Constitution, and explain judicial review and the doctrine of preemption.

5.2 Discuss the main provisions of the commerce clause, the full faith and credit clause, and the supremacy clause.

5.3 Describe three provisions of the First Amendment.

5.4 Discuss the current state of constitutional law with respect to the Second Amendment.

5.5 Describe the requirement of probable cause under the Fourth Amendment.

5.6 Identify and explain four protections provided by the Fifth Amendment.

5.7 Provide examples of cases that are addressed by the Eighth Amendment.

5.8 Explain the due process and equal protection clauses of the Fourteenth Amendment.

5.9 Discuss how the Internal Revenue Service administers the collection of income taxes pursuant to the Sixteenth Amendment.

CONSTITUTIONAL LAW

"A constitution, as important as it is, will mean nothing unless the people are yearning for liberty and freedom.."

Ruth Bader Ginsburg, U.S. Supreme Court Justice

Tetra Images/CORBIS

LEGAL terms

- express powers
- implied powers
- Bill of Rights
- judicial review
- doctrine of preemption
- commerce clause
- full faith and credit clause
- supremacy clause
- probable cause
- procedural due process
- substantive due process
- rational basis
- intermediate scrutiny
- strict scrutiny

5.1 THE UNITED STATES CONSTITUTION

Every federal statute enacted by Congress, every state statute enacted by state legislatures, every ordinance and code enacted by local municipalities, every administrative law and decision, and every court decision in every case in every jurisdiction–each of these must be consistent with the United States Constitution. This document, although relatively brief (see Appendix), forms the basis for all American law. This chapter describes several provisions of the Constitution and explains the various ways in which these provisions impact individuals and businesses in the United States.

CONSTITUTIONAL POWERS

Both the federal government and the 50 states' governments have the power to regulate the people who reside within their jurisdictions; and, in addition to the federal Constitution, each state has its own state constitution. This system of government is known as *federalism.* In addition, within the federal government, there are three distinct branches, forming a *separation of powers.* These concepts are discussed in more depth in Chapter 6.

The federal Constitution and state constitutions confer two types of powers on the governments of which they are a part:

express powers
Those that are specifically stated in the federal Constitution.

implied powers
Those that have arisen as a result of interpretation of the express powers by the courts.

- Express powers are those that are specifically stated. For example, the federal Constitution grants the federal government the explicit powers to raise an army and to impose taxes.
- Implied powers are those that have arisen as a result of interpretation of the express powers by the courts. For example, the federal Constitution gives Congress the implied power to create an agency to explore outer space–something not even imagined by the individuals who wrote the Constitution.

CONSTITUTIONAL AMENDMENTS

Although the drafters of the Constitution were persons of vision, they could not, of course, foresee the changing needs of our country and its people in the many years that were to follow. The Constitution has been amended, or changed, 27 times, and it will probably continue to be amended. Amending the Constitution is an onerous process. Each amendment must be proposed by a two-thirds vote of Congress and ratified, or approved, by the legislatures of three-fourths of our 50 states. It is also possible for an amendment to be initiated by the states. The first 10 amendments are referred to as the Bill of Rights.

bill of rights
The first 10 amendments of the U.S. Constitution.

JUDICIAL REVIEW

Both federal and state courts have the power to determine whether laws enacted by legislatures or decisions made by lower courts violate the provisions of the Constitution. If a court decides that a law is contrary to the Constitution, the law can be declared unconstitutional and therefore invalid. The process of deciding if a law is contrary to the Constitution is known as judicial review.

judicial review
The process of deciding if a law is contrary to the Constitution.

THE DOCTRINE OF PREEMPTION

doctrine of preemption
A principle that states that when certain state or local laws are inconsistent with the federal law, the federal law must be followed.

There are several instances in which the Constitution expressly or implicitly provides that Congress has the power to pass legislation. Frequently states and municipalities pass legislation in one or more of these areas, as well. If a state or local law is inconsistent with the federal law, the state or local law may be declared unconstitutional, and the federal law must be followed. This is known as the doctrine of preemption–that is, the federal law preempts, or supersedes, the state law. However, this doctrine applies only in instances where the law in question pertains to a power that the Constitution has expressly or implicitly granted to Congress.

EXAMPLE 5.1

▶ Congress enacted the Airline Deregulation Act in 1978, which eliminated the government's price regulation of airfares. In this case, states are preempted from enacting laws that would regulate or affect prices for airline services.

5.2 THE COMMERCE CLAUSE, THE FULL FAITH AND CREDIT CLAUSE, AND THE SUPREMACY CLAUSE

The Constitution is divided into major divisions, called *articles;* subdivisions, called *sections;* and in some cases sub-subdivisions, called *clauses.* This chapter addresses three of these particular clauses that have a specific impact on businesses. These clauses are referred to as the commerce clause, the full faith and credit clause, and the supremacy clause.

ARTICLE 1, SECTION 8, CLAUSE 3: THE COMMERCE CLAUSE

The **commerce clause** reads as follows: "The Congress shall have Power . . . to regulate Commerce with foreign Nations, and among the several States, and with the Indian Tribes."

commerce clause
A provision of the Constitution that grants Congress the power to regulate trade with foreign nations, and among the several states, and with the Indian tribes.

This clause grants Congress the power to regulate commerce among states in order to prevent the restriction of trade activity. Courts have held that the term *commerce,* as used in the Constitution, is defined as the movement or exchange of persons, goods, or information between states.

The commerce clause creates one of the most fundamental powers in the Constitution. Some judges and legal scholars take a broad and expansive view of this clause and make the claim that Congress has the power to regulate many business activities that would otherwise be left to state legislatures. In fact, nearly all business regulation at the federal level is based on the commerce clause. Others, however, are *strict constructionists.* These individuals maintain that many of the matters that Congress now legislates would be more appropriately left to the states. The commerce clause generates a great deal of intensive legal and political debate; it forms the basis for the division of power between the federal and the state governments, and even among the three branches of the federal government (see Chapter 1).

EXAMPLE 5.2

▶ A number of small, out-of-state wineries challenged Michigan and New York state laws that allowed only in-state wineries to sell directly to consumers. The out-of-state wineries claimed that under the laws, they were unable to compete effectively with the in-state wineries; they incurred additional expenses associated with selling their product solely through retailers. Because the state laws restricted commerce between states, the U.S. Supreme Court held that the laws violated the commerce clause of the Constitution. [*Granholm v. Heald,* 544 U.S. 460]

ARTICLE IV, SECTION 1: THE FULL FAITH AND CREDIT CLAUSE

full faith and credit clause
A provision of the Constitution that mandates that each state respect and enforce both the judgments awarded by courts in other states and the statutes and case law of other states.

The full faith and credit clause reads as follows: "Full Faith and Credit shall be given in each State to the public Acts, Records, and judicial Proceedings of every other State."

This clause mandates that each state respect and enforce both the judgments awarded by courts in other states, and the statutes and case law of other states (see Chapter 1). The Supreme Court has made a distinction in the level of the respect that must be given. A great deal of respect must be given to the judgments awarded by courts in other states; however, a lower level of respect must be given to another state's statutes and case law.

ARTICLE VI, CLAUSE 2: THE SUPREMACY CLAUSE

supremacy clause
A provision of the Constitution that requires state judges to follow federal law in the event of a conflict with state law.

The supremacy clause reads as follows: "This Constitution . . . the Laws of the United States . . . and all treaties made . . . shall be the supreme law of the land; and the judges in every state shall be bound thereby. . ."

This clause, closely tied to the doctrine of preemption, requires state judges to follow federal law in the event of a conflict with state law. According to the supremacy clause, a Supreme Court ruling that involves a constitutional issue is binding on state courts. For instance, in Example 5.2, Michigan and New York state courts must comply with the Supreme Court ruling pertaining to the invalidity of the laws affecting out-of-state wineries. Note that the supremacy clause also requires states to recognize the provisions of U.S. treaties over any conflicting state regulations.

5.3 THE FIRST AMENDMENT

The First Amendment reads as follows: "Congress shall make no law respecting an establishment of religion, or prohibiting the free exercise thereof; or abridging the freedom of speech, or of the press; or the right of the people peaceably to assemble, and to petition the Government for a redress of grievances." There are several parts to this amendment, three of which are discussed in the following paragraphs.

The First Amendment protects freedom of religion.
Rob Melnychuk/Getty Images

THE ESTABLISHMENT AND FREE EXERCISE CLAUSES RELATING TO RELIGION

The First Amendment right to freedom of religion is divided into two interconnected pieces, referred to as the *establishment clause* and the *free exercise* clause. The establishment clause makes it unconstitutional for government to recognize a single national religion or even to create policies or practices that favor one religion over another. The free exercise clause requires that government not interfere with an individual's practicing the religion of their choice.

While the nature of court decisions relating to both of these clauses has changed significantly over time, in general, the current view is that a law is constitutionally permissible provided that it does not unduly burden the practice of religion unless there is a compelling interest. For example, if a specific religion were to encourage the practice of polygamy—that is, simultaneously being married to two or more people—a state might successfully argue that it has a compelling interest in disallowing this practice by passing a law against the crime of bigamy.

FREEDOM OF SPEECH

The First Amendment's freedom of speech clause gives Americans a fundamental right. While individuals certainly have the right to freedom of political or religious speech, this right should be guarded most zealously when the speech is unpopular, upsetting, ignorant, or even anger-provoking. Thus speech that is sexist, racist, ageist, or otherwise offensive is also protected. Similarly, the act of burning the American flag is considered protected speech, and laws prohibiting such acts are unconstitutional.

All speech, however, is not protected under the First Amendment. The following are examples of speech that may constitutionally be limited or silenced: speech that incites imminent danger; child pornography; speech that is legally obscene; speech that threatens physical harm; speech that is defamatory, including both slander and libel (see Chapter 4); interference with works protected by trademark, patent, or copyright law (see Chapter 28); and commercial speech such as deceptive advertising (see Chapter 31). (See Figure 5.1).

EXAMPLE 5.3

- Weissenberg, a student at a university, had a disagreement with Heit, one of his classmates, regarding a local sporting team. Weissenberg became so enraged that he posted deceptive information on social media alleging that Heit had been convicted of shoplifting. He also threatened to do physical harm to Heit if she responded to his post. When Weissenberg was charged by the authorities with making threats, he claimed that his speech was protected by the First Amendment. Weissenberg's tirade is not protected because his speech is both defamatory and threatens physical harm.

- Speech that incites imminent danger
- Child pornography
- Speech that is legally obscene
- Speech that threatens physical harm
- Speech that is defamatory
- Interference with works protected by trademark, patent, or copyright law
- Commercial speech

FIGURE 5.1 Examples of Speech That May Constitutionally Be Limited or Silenced

The First Amendment gives Americans freedom of speech, but not all speech is protected under this amendment.
John Flournoy/McGraw Hill

FREEDOM OF THE PRESS

It would certainly be unconstitutional for a state or municipality to pass a law limiting what a journalist could write or say about a political candidate or issue. However, not all laws pertaining to the news media are unconstitutional. For example, it is constitutionally acceptable for government to tax newspapers. In addition, the question of whether or not a journalist or a newspaper may be sued for defamation is the subject of Example 5.4.

EXAMPLE 5.4

Sullivan, a police commissioner in Montgomery, Alabama, filed a libel suit against *The New York Times* for publishing allegedly inaccurate information about the Montgomery police department. In overturning a lower court's decision on First Amendment grounds, the Supreme Court held that debate on public issues would be inhibited if public officials could sue for inaccuracies that were made by mistake. The ruling made it more difficult for public officials to bring libel charges against the press because these officials now need to prove that a harmful untruth was printed either maliciously or with a reckless disregard for the truth. [*New York Times v. Sullivan,* 376 U.S. 254]

5.4 THE SECOND AMENDMENT

The Second Amendment reads as follows: "A well regulated Militia, being necessary to the security of a free State, the right of the people to keep and bear Arms, shall not be infringed."

There are several issues associated with this amendment. The first is what is meant by the term to "keep and bear arms." Generally this term has been interpreted to mean "to carry firearms." In addition, much debate has centered on the question of whether the term applies only to military use of arms versus arms held by private citizens. Although some compelling arguments suggest that the term to "keep and bear arms" applies only to the military use of arms, most courts now agree that this right also applies to private citizens.

The right to bear arms is not unlimited, however. Some 21st-century weapons were never imagined by the framers of the Constitution. Once again, interpreting the Constitution is a matter of drawing a line between what is and what is not permissible, balancing rights versus responsibilities.

EXAMPLE 5.5

McDonald, a 76-year-old resident of Chicago, claimed the city's 1982 ban on handguns left him prey to street gangs. In a landmark decision, the Supreme Court held that the right of an individual to "keep and bear arms" protected by the Second Amendment applies to states and ruled that the ban was unconstitutional. However, the opinion also reaffirmed that certain laws are permissible under the Second Amendment, such as those that prohibit the possession of firearms by felons or persons with mental illness; those forbidding the carrying of firearms in sensitive places, such as government buildings and schools; or those imposing conditions and qualifications on the commercial sale of arms. [*McDonald v. Chicago,* 130 S. Ct. 3020]

5.5 THE FOURTH AMENDMENT

The Fourth Amendment reads as follows: "The right of the people to be secure in their persons, houses, papers, and effects, against unreasonable searches and seizures, shall not be violated, and no Warrants shall issue, but upon probable cause, supported by Oath or affirmation, and particularly describing the place to be searched, and the persons or things to be seized."

The Fourth Amendment requires that police officers and other government officials (but not private citizens) must have probable cause to be able to conduct a personal or property search. Probable cause may be defined as a reasonable belief that a prudent police officer must have that a suspect has committed, is committing, or is about to commit a crime, thereby giving the officer the authority to conduct a search. All other unreasonable searches and seizures are unconstitutional and invalid. The Supreme Court has ruled that a search occurs only when a person expects privacy in the thing searched, and society believes that expectation is reasonable.

probable cause
A reasonable belief that a prudent police officer must have that a suspect has committed, is committing, or is about to commit a crime, thereby giving the officer the authority to conduct a search.

Examples of unreasonable searches and seizures include a detention of longer than 48 hours after a criminal arrest, a nonconsensual extraction of blood, and the gathering of fingerprint and DNA evidence in certain circumstances. However, stops of motorists at sobriety checkpoints to investigate possible instances of driving under the influence are not considered unreasonable and are permissible under the Fourth Amendment.

EXAMPLE 5.6

▶ Concerned that police officers were using their text pagers mostly for personal messages, a police chief decided to read some of them. He discovered that most of the messages sent by one officer were personal in nature. Some of these messages were sent to an ex-wife, others to a female friend. During a one-month period, the chief found that the officer had sent or received 456 messages, but only 57 were work related. After learning that his messages had been read, the officer sued both the chief and the city, claiming that this action violated the Fourth Amendment. The Supreme Court ruled that public employees have only a limited privacy expectation when using a text pager supplied by the police department, and because the search by the police chief was motivated by a legitimate work-related purpose and because it was not excessive in scope, the search was reasonable. [*City of Ontario v. Quon,* 130 S. Ct. 2619]

5.6 THE FIFTH AMENDMENT

The Fifth Amendment reads, in part, as follows: "No person shall . . . be subject for the same offence to be twice put in jeopardy of life or limb; nor shall be compelled in any criminal case to be a witness against himself, nor be deprived of life, liberty, or property, without due process of law; nor shall private property be taken for public use, without just compensation."

This passage contains four distinct protections from governmental actions:

1. *Double jeopardy:* The Fifth Amendment does not allow a court to try a criminal defendant more than once for the same offense, whether the first trial has ended in an acquittal or a conviction.

EXAMPLE 5.7

O. J. Simpson, a celebrity and former professional football player, was found not guilty and acquitted in criminal court for the murders of Nicole Brown Simpson and Ronald Goldman. He was subsequently sued for damages in civil court and found liable. Because the first case was criminal but the second civil, there was no double jeopardy, and the judgment in the civil case did not violate the Fifth Amendment.

2. *Self-incrimination:* The Fifth Amendment gives individuals the right to refuse to divulge information that could later be used against them in a criminal proceeding. This right to refuse applies to any federal or state legal proceeding, whether criminal, civil, judicial, or administrative.
3. *Due process:* The Fifth Amendment requires that all persons be granted both procedural and substantive due process. Procedural due process mandates that all persons affected by a legal proceeding receive notice of its subject matter, time, and place and that these proceedings be conducted by a judge who is fair and impartial. Substantive due process mandates that government not unreasonably interfere with an individual's life, liberty, or property rights.
4. *Eminent domain:* The Fifth Amendment permits the government to take private property, both real and personal, for a public purpose so long as the owner receives just compensation (see Chapter 24).

procedural due process
A constitutional mandate that all persons affected by a legal proceeding receive notice of its subject matter, time, and place and that these proceedings be conducted by a judge who is fair and impartial.

substantive due process
A constitutional mandate that government not unreasonably interfere with an individual's life, liberty, or property rights.

5.7 THE EIGHTH AMENDMENT

The Eighth Amendment reads as follows: "Excessive bail shall not be required, nor excessive fines imposed, nor cruel and unusual punishments inflicted."

The Eighth Amendment restricts both the severity and the types of punishments that may be imposed by federal and state governments. The Supreme Court has ruled that punishments must be proportionate to the crime committed. The following are examples of punishments prohibited under the Eighth Amendment:

- A person convicted of armed robbery is sentenced to death.
- A person convicted of shoplifting is sentenced to life in prison.
- A minor is sentenced to life in prison for stealing a car.
- A person convicted of assault and battery is sentenced to death.
- A person convicted of any crime is sentenced to being burned at the stake.

In addition, the Supreme Court has found that certain barbarous types of punishment, such as burning at the stake, are prohibited regardless of the type of crime committed.

In addition, the Eighth Amendment mandates that people accused or convicted of crimes are not to be subject to excessive bail. The Supreme Court has found that bail is reasonable when it is not substantially greater than the amount required to guarantee the suspected criminal's appearance in court. However, the Supreme Court has ruled that in extreme cases a court may deny bail altogether.

Finally, the Eighth Amendment prevents the government from imposing an unjustly harsh fine on a person convicted of a crime. If a fine is found to be grossly disproportionate to the crime committed, the fine may be overturned.

EXAMPLE 5.8

- Lyle Austin was indicted on four counts of violating South Dakota's drug laws. Austin ultimately pleaded guilty to one count of possessing cocaine with intent to distribute and was sentenced by the state court to seven years' imprisonment. The federal prosecutor then filed an additional lawsuit in federal court, requesting that the court require Austin to forfeit both his mobile home and auto body shop. Austin argued that the forfeiture of these properties would violate the Eighth Amendment. The federal court ruled that forcing Austin to transfer his property to the government under these circumstances did not constitute an excessive fine and thus was not in violation of the Eighth Amendment. [*Austin v. United States,* 509 U.S. 602]

5.8 THE FOURTEENTH AMENDMENT

The Fourteenth Amendment reads, in part, as follows: "No State shall . . . deprive any person of life, liberty, or property, without due process of law; nor deny to any person within its jurisdiction the equal protection of the laws."

While the first 10 amendments, the Bill of Rights, apply to actions of the federal government, the Fourteenth Amendment applies directly to the 50 states. Just as it is impermissible for the federal government to deny an individual either substantive or procedural due process under the Fifth Amendment, it is also unconstitutional for a state to deny an individual due process.

EXAMPLE 5.9

- Miranda confessed to a crime during police questioning without knowing he had a right to have an attorney present. Based on his confession, Miranda was convicted. The Supreme Court overturned the conviction, ruling that the due process clause of the Fourteenth Amendment requires that criminal suspects be warned of their rights before they are questioned by police. These rights are the right to remain silent; the right to have an attorney present during questioning; and, if the suspect cannot afford an attorney, the right to have one appointed by the state. The police must also warn suspects that any statements they make may be used against them in a court of law. These are now known as the Miranda warnings. Miranda was re-tried without using the illegal confession as evidence and was nonetheless convicted a second time. [*Miranda v. Arizona,* 384 U.S. 436]

The Fourteenth Amendment also provides that when states pass laws, they must treat all individuals equally. Laws that do not treat all people equally are unconstitutional unless the state can demonstrate the following:

- If the law places restrictions on economic or property interests, or if the law discriminates on a basis other than race, sex, national origin, and related categories, the state must show that the law passes the rational basis test. The rational basis test is a standard that measures whether the legislature had a reasonable, and not an arbitrary, basis for enacting a particular statute.

rational basis
A test that measures whether the legislature had a reasonable, and not an arbitrary, basis for enacting a particular statute.

intermediate scrutiny
A test that measures whether a particular statute is substantially related to an important government objective.

strict scrutiny
A test that measures whether the legislature had a compelling interest for enacting a particular statute.

- If the law discriminates on the basis of sex, or if the law restricts commercial speech, the state must demonstrate that the law passes the intermediate scrutiny test. The intermediate scrutiny test is a standard that measures whether a particular statute is substantially related to an important government objective.
- If the law discriminates on the basis of race or national origin, or if the law infringes on a fundamental constitutional right, the state must show that the law passes the strict scrutiny test. The strict scrutiny test is a standard that measures whether the legislature had a compelling interest for enacting a particular statute.

EXAMPLE 5.10

- The U.S. Supreme Court, while addressing numerous appeals from lower courts in various states, ruled that the Fourteenth Amendment requires a state to license a marriage between two people of the same sex, and to recognize a marriage between two people of the same sex when their marriage was lawfully licensed and performed out-of-state. [*Obergefell v. Hodges*, 576 U.S. (2015).]

5.9 THE SIXTEENTH AMENDMENT

The Sixteenth Amendment reads as follows: "The Congress shall have power to lay and collect taxes on incomes, from whatever source derived, without apportionment among the several States, and without regard to any census or enumeration."

Prior to the passage of the Sixteenth Amendment, there were a series of conflicting court decisions regarding the federal government's right to levy an income tax. The Sixteenth Amendment granted the federal government the power to impose and collect a tax on individuals' incomes. The government exercised this power immediately and, by doing so, created a substantial source of revenue.

The Internal Revenue Service (IRS) is a federal agency (see Chapter 6) established by Congress and tasked with administering and collecting federal income tax under the Sixteenth Amendment. The IRS creates and enforces tax laws and improves taxpayers' understanding of these laws. To learn more about the IRS, visit www.irs.gov.

CHAPTER SUMMARY

5.1 Express powers are those that are specifically stated in the federal Constitution; implied powers are those that have arisen as a result of interpretation of the express powers by the courts. Each constitutional amendment must be proposed by a two-thirds vote of Congress and ratified, or approved, by the legislatures of three-fourths of the 50 states. The process of deciding if a law is contrary to the Constitution is known as judicial review. The doctrine of preemption is a principle that states that when state or local laws are inconsistent with a federal law, the federal law must be followed.

5.2 The commerce clause grants Congress the power to regulate trade with "foreign nations, and among the several states, and with the Indian tribes." The full faith and credit clause mandates that each state respect and enforce other states' court judgments, statutes, and case law. The supremacy clause requires state judges to follow federal law in the event of a conflict with state law.

5.3 The First Amendment's establishment clause makes it unconstitutional for government to recognize a single national religion or to favor one religion over another; its free exercise clause requires that government not interfere with individual religious practice. The First Amendment's freedom of speech clause gives individuals the right to freedom of political or religious speech. The First Amendment's freedom of the press clause allows journalists to write or say whatever they wish about political candidates and issues.

5.4 Under the Second Amendment, the term to "keep and bear arms" has been interpreted to mean "to carry firearms." Most courts now agree that the right to bear arms applies to private citizens. The right to bear arms is not unlimited, however.

5.5 The Fourth Amendment requires that police officers and other government officials (but not private citizens) must have probable cause to conduct a personal or property search.

5.6 Four protections provided by the Fifth Amendment include double jeopardy, self-incrimination, due process, and eminent domain.

5.7 The Eighth Amendment restricts both the severity and the types of punishments that may be imposed by federal and state governments.

5.8 Just as it is impermissible for the federal government to deny an individual either substantive or procedural due process under the Fifth Amendment, it is also unconstitutional for a state to deny an individual due process under the Fourteenth Amendment. This amendment also provides that state laws must treat all individuals equally unless the state can demonstrate that a law passes the rational basis test, the intermediate scrutiny test, or the strict scrutiny test.

5.9 The Internal Revenue Service is a federal agency established by Congress and tasked with administering and collecting federal income tax under the Sixteenth Amendment. The IRS creates and enforces tax laws and improves taxpayers' understanding of the laws.

CHAPTER FIVE ASSESSMENT

MATCHING LEGAL TERMS

Match each of the numbered definitions with the correct term in the following list.

a. commerce clause
b. doctrine of preemption
c. Eighth Amendment
d. express powers
e. Fifth Amendment
f. First Amendment
g. Fourth Amendment
h. full faith and credit clause
i. implied powers
j. judicial review
k. probable cause
l. procedural due process
m. rational basis test
n. strict scrutiny test
o. substantive due process

1. Rights specifically granted to Congress by the federal Constitution. **1.** _____

2. A provision of the Constitution that mandates that each state respect and enforce both the judgments awarded by courts in other states, and the statutes and case law of other states. **2.** _____

3. A provision of the Constitution that requires that police officers and other government officials must have probable cause to conduct a personal or property search. **3.** _____

4. Rights granted to Congress that have arisen as a result of interpretation of the express powers by the courts. **4.** _____

5. A reasonable belief that a prudent police officer must have that a suspect has committed, is committing, or is about to commit a crime, thereby giving the officer the authority to conduct a search. **5.** _____

6. A provision of the Constitution that restricts both the severity and the types of punishments that may be imposed by federal and state governments. **6.** _____

7. The process of deciding if a law is contrary to the Constitution. **7.** _____

8. A constitutional mandate that all persons affected by a legal proceeding receive notice of its subject matter, time, and place and that these proceedings be conducted by a judge who is fair and impartial. **8.** _____

9. A test that measures whether the legislature had a compelling interest for enacting a particular statute. **9.** _____

10. A principle that states that when certain state or local laws are inconsistent with the federal law, the federal law must be followed. **10.** _____

11. A constitutional mandate that government not unreasonably interfere with an individual's life, liberty, or property rights. **11.** _____

12. A provision of the Constitution that provides for freedom of religion, freedom of speech, and freedom of the press. **12.** _____

13. A provision of the Constitution that grants Congress the power to regulate trade with "foreign nations, and among the several states, and with the Indian tribes." **13.** _____

14. A test that measures whether the legislature had a reasonable, and not arbitrary, basis for enacting a particular statute. **14.** _____

15. A provision of the Constitution that relates to double jeopardy, self-incrimination, due process, and eminent domain. **15.** _____

TRUE/FALSE QUIZ

Indicate whether each of the following statements is true or false.

16. The federal Constitution has been amended more than 100 times. **16.** _____

17. The First Amendment's right to freedom of religion is divided into two interconnected pieces, referred to as the enterprise clause and the free exercise clause. **17.** _____

18. The Supreme Court has ruled that the term "to keep and bear arms" applies only to the military use of arms. **18.** _____

19. The Supreme Court has ruled that a Fourth Amendment search only occurs when a person expects privacy in the thing searched and society believes that expectation is reasonable. **19.** _____

20. The Fifth Amendment does not allow a court to try a criminal defendant more than once for the same offense unless the first trial has ended in an acquittal. **20.** _____

21. The Eighth Amendment mandates that people accused or convicted of crimes are not to be subject to excessive bail. **21.** _____

22. While it is impermissible for the federal government to deny an individual due process under the Fifth Amendment, it is not unconstitutional for a state to deny an individual due process. **22.** _____

23. The Sixteenth Amendment granted the federal government power to impose and collect a tax on individuals' incomes. **23.** _____

MULTIPLE CHOICE QUIZ

Indicate the correct answer to each question using the choices after each question.

24. Amendment of the U.S. Constitution requires (a) two thirds vote of Congress only (b) approval of three fourths of the states only (c) both two thirds vote of Congress and approval of three fourths of states (d) neither approval of Congress nor approval of the states. **24.** _____

25. Under the doctrine of preemption, when a state law is inconsistent with a federal law (a) federal law must be applied (b) state law must be applied (c) both federal law and state law must be applied (d) neither state law nor federal law can be applied. **25.** _____

26. Federal regulation of business activities is most often based on which of the following constitutional provisions (a) full faith and credit clause (b) Supremacy clause (c) Commerce clause (d) Preemption doctrine. **26.** _____

27. The First Amendment free exercise clause (a) prohibits establishment of a national religion (b) prohibits government interference with individual religious practice (c) requires individual religious practice (d) requires establishment of a national religion. **27.** _____

28. The Second Amendment gives the right (a) only for state militias to carry firearms (b) only for federal militias to carry firearms (c) only for private citizens to carry firearms (d) for both militias and private citizens to carry firearms. **28.** _____

29. The Fourth Amendment prohibition against unreasonable search and seizure (a) allows government searches only with probable cause (b) never allows government searches (c) allows government searches with or without probable cause (d) does not apply to government searches. **29.** _____

30. The Fifth Amendment protections include (a) only double jeopardy (b) only due process (c) due process and double jeopardy (d) due process, double jeopardy, and eminent domain. **30.** _____

31. The Fifth Amendment protection against self-incrimination (a) requires a citizen to testify in their own criminal trial (b) does not require that a citizen testify in their own criminal trial (c) requires that a citizen incriminate other defendants in a criminal trial (d) prohibits citizens from incriminating other defendants in a criminal trial. **31.** _____

32. Constitutional due process under the U.S. Constitution (a) includes due process at both the federal and state levels (b) includes due process at neither the federal nor the state levels (c) includes due process only at the federal level (d) includes due process only at the state level. **32.** _____

33. The Sixteenth Amendment providing the federal government authority to collect income tax is administered by (a) state taxing authorities (b) the Department of Commerce (c) the Internal Revenue Service (d) the U.S. Congress. **33.** _____

DISCUSSION QUESTIONS

Answer the following questions and discuss them in class.

34. Describe the process used to amend the Constitution.

35. Provide some examples of speech that may constitutionally be limited or silenced.

36. Provide some examples of laws that are permissible under the Second Amendment.

37. Provide some examples of unreasonable searches and seizures.

38. Describe the circumstances under which a law must pass the rational basis test and the strict scrutiny test.

39. Provide some examples of cases covered under the Eighth Amendment.

THINKING CRITICALLY ABOUT THE LAW

Answer the following questions, which require you to think critically about the legal principles that you learned in this chapter.

40. Full Faith and Credit Clause Why is it important that each state respect and enforce both the judgments awarded by courts in other states, and the statutes and case law of other states?

____

____

41. First Amendment Should speech that is sexist, racist, ageist, or otherwise offensive be protected under the First Amendment?

____

____

42. Second Amendment Should the right to bear arms be limited to the military use of arms, or should this right also apply to private citizens?

____

____

43. Eighth Amendment Should the death penalty be considered cruel and unusual punishment, thus violating the Eighth Amendment?

____

____

44. A Question of Ethics Is it ethical for a state legislature to pass a law for the sole purpose of testing its constitutionality?

____

____

CASE QUESTIONS

Study each of the following cases. Answer the questions that follow with Yes or No.

45. First Amendment The town of Homesdale passes an ordinance that requires all retail establishments to remain closed on Christmas Day. Several groups sue, arguing that the ordinance is unconstitutional.

a. Does the ordinance violate the First Amendment of the Constitution? **a.** _____

b. Does the ordinance violate the full faith and credit clause of the Constitution? **b.** _____

c. Would your answer to either of the previous two questions be different if you learned that over 95 percent of Homesdale's population approves of this ordinance? **c.** _____

46. Second Amendment The town of Ericton is considering passing an ordinance that would severely restrict the possession and carrying of firearms.

a. May the ordinance prohibit the possession of firearms by felons? **a.** _____

b. May the ordinance prohibit the possession of firearms by persons with mental illness? **b.** _____

c. May the ordinance prohibit the carrying of firearms in sensitive places, such as government buildings and schools? **c.** _____

47. Eighth Amendment In an effort to stem the rising usage of illegal drugs, the town of Zhemville passes an ordinance that mandates that all people found guilty of possessing illegal drugs be flogged.

a. Does the ordinance violate the Eighth Amendment of the Constitution? **a.** _____

b. Does the ordinance violate the commerce clause of the Constitution? **b.** _____

c. Would the ordinance violate the Eighth Amendment of the Constitution if the punishment applied only to people selling, rather than simply possessing, illegal drugs? **c.** _____

CASE ANALYSIS

Study each of the following cases carefully. Briefly state the principle of law and your decision.

48. Fourth Amendment Katz was convicted in federal court under an indictment charging him with transmitting wagering information by telephone from Los Angeles to Miami and Boston, in violation of a federal statute prohibiting gambling. At the trial, the federal prosecutor was permitted, over the objections of Katz's attorney, to introduce evidence of Katz's telephone conversations. These telephone conversations had been overheard by agents of the Federal Bureau of Investigations (FBI). The agents had attached an electronic listening and recording device to the outside of the public telephone booth from which Katz had placed his calls. Did the FBI violate the Fourth Amendment by listening to Katz's telephone conversations? [*Katz v. United States,* 389 US 347 (California)]

Principle of Law:

____

____

Decision:

____

____

49. Eighth Amendment While in the custody of the New Castle Youth Development Center (YDC), 17-year-old Betts suffered a tragic spinal cord injury while attempting to make a tackle during a football game. Following the injury, Betts sued YDC and several of its staff members, claiming that his injury resulted from a violation of his Eighth Amendment rights. Was Betts subjected to cruel and unusual punishment while playing football? [*Betts v. New Castle Youth Development Center,* 2009 U.S. District Court (Pennsylvania)]

Principle of Law:

Decision:

50. Sixteenth Amendment The IRS filed a lawsuit against Stern to collect unpaid income taxes, penalties, and interest that had amassed over 10 years. In response, Stern petitioned the court to disallow the IRS from collecting his tax debt, arguing that discrepancies existed between the Constitution and certain Supreme Court cases. Was Stern required to pay federal income taxes pursuant to the Sixteenth Amendment? [*In Re: Peter Kay Stern, Petitioner,* 114 F.3d 1177 (North Carolina)]

Principle of Law:

Decision:

LEGAL RESEARCH

Complete the following activities. Share your findings with the class.

51. Working in Teams In teams of three or four, visit the offices of local college and city newspapers. Ask the reporters and writers to explain the processes they use to verify the truth and accuracy of their reports and articles.

52. Using Technology Using the Internet and search engines, investigate blogs that contain political speech. Make a listing of statements and explain why the speech is protected under the First Amendment.

chapter **6**

Administrative Law

LEARNING OUTCOMES

After studying this chapter and completing the assessment, you will be able to

6.1 Describe the purpose of administrative agencies.

6.2 Discuss the organization of governments and define the specific duties of the three branches of government.

6.3 List and provide examples of the functions of administrative agencies.

6.4 Explain why and how an administrative agency is formed.

6.5 Explain the similarities and differences between administrative agencies and governments.

6.6 Discuss criticism of administrative agencies.

LEGAL terms

- administrative agency
- legislative branch
- executive branch
- judicial branch
- subpoena
- administrative hearing

ADMINISTRATIVE LAW

"The only two things that scare me are God and the IRS."

Dr. Dre, rapper, record producer, entrepreneur, and actor

Chip Somodevilla/Getty Images

6.1 ADMINISTRATIVE AGENCIES

Administrative agencies were introduced in Chapter 1, where the point was made that they affect nearly every individual, business firm, and organization in the country. An administrative agency is a governmental body responsible for the control and supervision of a particular activity or area of public interest. Our society is extraordinarily complex, and no legislature can pass laws specific enough to ensure that all objectives are achieved under all circumstances.

administrative agency
A governmental body responsible for the control and supervision of a particular activity or area of public interest.

Legislatures lack the time and expertise to make the necessary rules to govern the operations of complex areas of our social and economic life, such as energy, taxation, transportation, environmental pollution, employee safety, and communication. Neither do legislatures have the time or expertise to supervise the many details of these complex areas on a daily basis. As a result, legislatures delegate these responsibilities to administrative agencies, or regulators. These agencies exist at all levels of government: federal, state, and local. Some of the more important agencies are shown in Table 6.1.

TABLE 6.1A Examples of Federal Administrative Agencies

FEDERAL AGENCIES	PURPOSE AND AREA OF REGULATION
Consumer Financial Protection Bureau (CFPB)	Protects consumers with respect to financial products and services.
Consumer Product Safety Commission (CPSC)	Establishes safety standards for products.
Equal Employment Opportunity Commission (EEOC)	Protects employees from illegal discrimination.
Environmental Protection Agency (EPA)	Regulates activities that affect the environment.
Federal Communications Commission (FCC)	Regulates radio and television communications.
Federal Trade Commission (FTC)	Regulates antitrust, deceptive advertising, and fair trade practices.
Internal Revenue Service (IRS)	Establishes rules on tax matters and supervises collection of taxes.
Nuclear Regulatory Commission (NRC)	Establishes standards and oversees uses of nuclear energy.
Occupational Safety and Health Administration (OSHA)	Regulates safety and health in the nation's workplaces.
Securities and Exchange Commission (SEC)	Regulates operations of financial markets.

TABLE 6.1B Examples of State Administrative Agencies

STATE AGENCIES	PURPOSE AND AREA OF REGULATION
Alcoholic Beverage Control Board	Issues licenses to sell liquor.
Department of Insurance	Licenses agents and companies; monitors financial soundness of companies.
Public Service Commission	Regulates the provision of electrical power, gas, and water.
Workers' Compensation Board	Regulates payments made to injured workers.

TABLE 6.1C Examples of Local Administrative Agencies

LOCAL AGENCIES	PURPOSE AND AREA OF REGULATION
Board of Education	Operates local schools.
Board of Health	Inspects food establishments.
Consumer Protection Agency	Regulates businesses; protects consumers' interests.
Department of Weights and Measures	Checks accuracy of scales and other measuring devices.

The legislative branch of the federal government.
Amanda Clement/Getty Images, Inc.

When a legislature passes a particular law, it often stresses general objectives and guidelines. At the same time, it may create an administrative agency to establish specific rules to be followed by those affected by the law. When the agency is established, the legislature usually specifies the purpose and the powers of the agency, and the actions the agency may take in carrying out the intentions of the law. Administrative agencies have various names, including boards, commissions, and departments. In many respects, administrative agencies are like governments within a government because they combine all three governmental functions: legislative, executive, and judicial.

6.2 ORGANIZATION OF GOVERNMENTS

To appreciate the similarity of administrative agencies and governments, it will be valuable to review the traditional constitutional governments that operate at the federal, state, and local levels.

Each level of government has three branches: legislative, executive, and judicial. Each branch has specific duties and powers. The organization of administrative agencies often resembles the organization of governments.

LEGISLATIVE BRANCH OF GOVERNMENT

legislative branch
The branch of a government body that consists of elected representatives who have the responsibility for passing laws that represent the will of the people.

The **legislative branch** at all levels of government consists of elected representatives who have the responsibility for passing laws that represent the will of the people.

At the federal level, there are two houses of Congress: the House of Representatives and the Senate. At the state level, the legislative branch is often called the general assembly; like the federal Congress, it consists of two houses (except in Nebraska). At the local level, the legislative branch is often called a city council or given a similar name.

EXECUTIVE BRANCH OF GOVERNMENT

executive branch
The branch of a government body that consists of an elected executive, including his or her appointed staff.

The **executive branch** at all levels of government ensures that all enacted legislation is enforced. At the federal level, the executive branch is headed by the president; at the state level, the executive is the governor; and at the local level, the executive is the mayor, county executive, or someone with a similar title.

JUDICIAL BRANCH OF GOVERNMENT

judicial branch
The branch of a government body that determines if there have been violations of the law and interprets the law if there are questions about what the law means in particular situations.

The **judicial branch** of government determines if there have been violations of the law. It also interprets the law if there are questions about what the law means in particular situations.

At the federal level, there are district courts, appeals courts, and the U.S. Supreme Court. Each state also has several levels of courts: trial courts, appeals courts, and a supreme court. At the local level, there are municipal courts, justice-of-the-peace courts, and magistrate courts.

6.3 FUNCTIONS OF ADMINISTRATIVE AGENCIES

Administrative agencies have been created for a variety of purposes and to fulfill diverse functions. These functions include regulating conduct, satisfying government requirements, disbursing benefits, and providing goods and services.

REGULATING CONDUCT

Often an agency regulates such economic matters as price, entry into a particular geographical area, or entry into a particular kind of business.

EXAMPLE 6.1

▶ Yamoto, a recent college graduate who had majored in insurance and worked part-time for an insurance agency, decided to start his own insurance agency. He learned that before he could enter this kind of business, he would have to pass an examination to test his knowledge of insurance and related law and be licensed by the state insurance department. State insurance regulations require insurance agents to be licensed to make certain that persons in this position are competent to perform their duties and to serve the people who rely on them.

FULFILLING GOVERNMENT REQUIREMENTS

Administrative agencies exist at all levels of government–for example, to collect taxes and to raise revenues through various licensing laws. At the federal level, one of these agencies is the Internal Revenue Service (IRS), which collects taxes needed to operate the federal government (see Chapter 5).

DISBURSING BENEFITS

A number of governmental agencies distribute subsidies and benefits of various kinds to farmers, persons in need of public assistance, students, individuals who are unemployed, and senior citizens.

PROVIDING GOODS AND SERVICES

Although the United States is largely a capitalist country, in which the private sector provides most of the goods and services needed by the people, many believe that certain essential services cannot be efficiently provided by the private sector. Some governments at all levels provide goods and services, such as electricity, water, highway maintenance, hospital care, and public housing.

6.4 WHY AND HOW AN ADMINISTRATIVE AGENCY IS FORMED

For illustration, suppose that the consumers in a mythical, medium-sized city called Legis have problems with local businesses. Merchants are cheating customers, scales in stores are inaccurate, businesses that promise to provide certain services do not provide them, advertising is often false and misleading, and auto repair shops overcharge and perform poor-quality work. In short, the consumers in the imaginary city of Legis are having trouble coping with the abuses of the businesses in their community.

As might be expected, many consumers have complained to their elected representatives on the city council. When the need for a change became apparent, the city council decided to pass a consumer protection law. The law required that all businesses in the city of Legis be licensed and also stated that it would be unlawful for businesses to engage in "false advertising, deception, or the employment of unqualified workers to perform auto repair work."

Now let us examine a few aspects of the Legis consumer protection law. The law as passed does not define just what will be considered deceptive. For example, would a furniture store's newspaper advertisement be deceptive if it announced a Presidents' Day sale but failed to mention that the sale would be in effect at its downtown store only and not at its branch stores? Would the advertisement be deceptive if it failed to mention that quantities of certain items were significantly limited? The city council cannot legislate answers to these questions and many more like them. If it tried, it would be tied up for months or years because the legislators have neither the time nor the expertise to cope with these kinds of problems.

Many cities pass laws requiring that all businesses be licensed.

The city council knew that the goals of the consumer protection law would not be met by merely licensing businesses unless someone developed answers to such specific questions. Consequently, the law also established a consumer protection agency. The new agency would be headed by a director with the authority to (1) hire experts in various fields to clarify and enforce the law and assist in the formulation of agency rules and regulations, (2) license businesses operating in the city of Legis, and (3) establish rules and regulations that businesses will need to follow to maintain their licenses. In addition to establishing the consumer protection agency (CPA), the law required that all businesses would have to be licensed to operate within the city of Legis.

After the law had been passed, the mayor, with the approval of the city council, hired Savus, a qualified consumer affairs person, to be the head of the CPA. Of course, the CPA–like any government entity–needs money to operate. The city council, therefore, appropriated a certain amount of money that the CPA could use to hire the necessary people, rent office space, pay telephone bills, and so on. The director, Savus, hired experts to develop rules and regulations governing advertising, auto repair shops, and other kinds of businesses.

However, what good would it do for the people of Legis to establish an agency staffed with experts and to make rules and regulations covering the operations of particular businesses if there were no way to enforce the rules? Unfortunately, people do not always obey rules and laws simply because they have been enacted.

There must be some authority to ensure that people will obey the rules. In response, statutes have been enacted to grant administrative agencies the power to investigate potential violations of rules or statutes. Accordingly, Savus also hired a group of inspectors to check the accuracy of scales, others to check the truthfulness of newspaper advertising, and so on.

Carrying the example a bit further, suppose that an inspector from the CPA finds that a scale in a supermarket is inaccurate and customers are being overcharged. The inspector notifies the store manager of the condition, but the manager, knowing that the inspector does not have the power of a police officer, points to the door and says, "Get out." What happens next? The inspector would probably report back to the CPA director, informing her that the scale in the store is inaccurate and in violation of rules established by the CPA. The director would likely issue the merchant a subpoena, or an order requiring the recipient to appear at a hearing to provide testimony. To comply with the subpoena, the merchant must attend the hearing at the specified time and place to answer the inspector's complaint. An administrative hearing conducted by an administrative agency is in some respects like an informal court trial but without a jury. If the merchant refuses to appear, their license can be revoked. The CPA director would then notify the regular court prosecutor that the business is operating without the required license—a violation of the law that established the agency. The court could then order the business closed.

subpoena
An order requiring the recipient to appear at a legal proceeding to provide testimony.

administrative hearing
A trial-like judicial proceeding, without a jury, in which an administrative agency rules on matters of the law that the agency is charged with enforcing.

6.5 SIMILARITIES AND DIFFERENCES BETWEEN ADMINISTRATIVE AGENCIES AND GOVERNMENTS

Earlier in this chapter, we reviewed the three branches of federal, state, and local government—that is, executive, legislative, and judicial. We pointed out that administrative agencies often carry out all three functions. Let us go back to the city of Legis and look at the CPA to see the comparisons between administrative agencies and governments.

SIMILARITIES

There are several significant similarities between administrative agencies and governments.

Executive Function The executive function of the CPA is performed by the CPA director, Savus, together with her staff of experts, inspectors, and others. The executive function of the CPA includes the daily operations of the agency and the establishment of general policies and objectives.

Legislative Function The rules and regulations established by the CPA resemble the laws passed by a legislature and have the force of law. This is the legislative function of the administrative agency.

Judicial Function The activity of the CPA in holding hearings and requiring compliance with its decisions has an effect similar to the decisions made in a regular court of law. This activity is the judicial function of the administrative agency.

DIFFERENCES

While administrative agencies are very much like the three levels of government—federal, state, and local—they also differ in some important respects.

Executive Function At all three levels of government, the voter has the opportunity to vote the executive into and out of office. Voters elect the president, the governor, and the mayor.

Usually, however, voters do not elect the administrator of a regulatory agency. For the most part, the voter has little control over the activities of an administrative agency.

There are two general patterns in the executive organization of an administrative agency. In some agencies, the executive is appointed by and serves at the discretion of the elected executive of the government–the president, the governor, or the mayor–subject to approval by the legislature. At the federal level, examples include the people who head the Department of Transportation, the Department of the Interior, and the Department of Commerce. These executives can be removed from office either with or without cause. In other cases, Congress has created agencies outside the executive branch that are headed by groups or individuals, such as boards or commissions appointed by Congress. Such boards or commissions carry out the executive function of the agency. Once appointed to their multiyear terms, members may not be removed by the president without cause. Examples include appointees of the Federal Trade Commission (FTC) and the Securities and Exchange Commission (SEC).

Legislative Function At one time, there was debate about whether a legislature could delegate to an administrative agency some of the lawmaking authority that some people believed should remain with the legislature. This issue was resolved, and the notion of administrative agencies functioning in a lawmaking role is now widely accepted.

Legislatures frequently delegate some of their lawmaking authority to administrative agencies.
Kitt Cooper-Smith/Alamy

Rules and regulations are established by the agency, not by elected representatives. However, the law requires federal agencies to submit all new rules and regulations to Congress for review. After review, if Congress finds a new rule or regulation to be unjust, Congress can override it. Again, the voter does not have direct control over the legislative function of the administrative agency.

Administrators are usually appointed by the executive with the advice and consent of the legislature. This practice gives the public, through its legislatures, at least some indirect control over the operations of administrative agencies. After administrators have been approved, however, it is generally very difficult to remove them. If the people do not like the way the agency is being run, their only recourse is to bring pressure on the executive or legislative branch to change the agency or to remove the administrator. It is important to note that Congress has the power to dissolve or alter federal agencies; for example, Congress can enact legislation to reduce an administrative agency's funds or its powers.

Judicial Function The hearings conducted by an administrative agency do not provide for a jury, and the procedures are not as formal as a regular court hearing. Moreover, unlike the judge in a court trial, the "judge" at an administrative agency hearing is not entirely impartial because they are determining whether a person or firm has complied with the agency's own rules rather than with statutes enacted by the legislature. There was early debate over whether a legislature could delegate to an administrative agency the authority to function as judge in certain matters. This question was largely settled in the case of *Crowell v. Benson,* 285 U.S. 22 (1932), in which the Supreme Court decided that an administrative agency does have such authority.

The determinations reached at a hearing conducted by an administrative agency can be appealed through the regular court system. As a practical matter, the courts seldom reverse the decisions of the agency unless it can be shown that the agency has clearly abused its authority.

To determine whether an administrative agency has abused its authority, the courts are guided by the statutes that established the agency and by the Constitution of the United States and the constitutions of individual states.

6.6 CRITICISM OF ADMINISTRATIVE AGENCIES

A number of critics allege that certain administrative agencies have been "captured" by the enterprises they were created to regulate. Because of the economic benefits or burdens that administrative agencies can bestow on a firm or an industry, those regulated have a powerful incentive to secure favorable rulings. In many cases, the need for specialized expertise in a given area can usually come only from the industry being regulated. The insurance industry, for example, is highly complex, and many of the people who have the expertise needed to perform as effective regulators are, or have been, employed by the industry. Some have suggested that the heads of administrative agencies be elected by popular vote, as are some insurance commissioners. However, having these individuals elected would not mean that they would not be influenced as time passed, or that they would not use their positions to further their own economic or political ambitions.

CHAPTER SUMMARY

6.1 Legislatures have neither the time nor the expertise to make the necessary rules to govern the operations of complex areas of our social and economic life. Legislatures also lack the time and expertise to supervise the many details of these complex areas on a day-to-day basis. Consequently, legislatures delegate these responsibilities to administrative agencies. There are numerous federal, state, and local administrative agencies. Table 6.1 provides examples of these agencies. A typical administrative agency is a consumer protection agency, which licenses firms, formulates agency regulations, and clarifies and enforces the laws.

6.2 Each level of government has three branches: legislative, executive, and judicial. Each branch has specific duties and powers. The organization of administrative agencies often resembles the organization of governments. The legislative branch consists of elected representatives who have the responsibility for passing laws that represent the will of the people. The executive branch ensures that all enacted legislation is enforced. The judicial branch determines if there have been violations of the law and interprets the law if there are any questions about what the law means in particular situations.

6.3 The functions of administrative agencies are regulating conduct in areas such as economic matters and entry into a particular location or industry; fulfilling government requirements such as collecting taxes and raising revenues through various licensing laws; disbursing benefits to agencies or persons; and providing goods and services such as water, highway maintenance, and public housing.

6.4 The law may establish an administrative agency to protect members of the public who have trouble coping with the abuses of businesses in their communities. Administrative agencies may be headed by a director with the authority to (1) hire experts in various fields to clarify and enforce the law and assist in the formulation of agency rules and regulations, (2) license businesses in the city in which they operate, and (3) establish rules and regulations that businesses will need to follow to maintain their licenses.

6.5 Each level of government has three branches: legislative, executive, and judicial. Each branch has specific duties and powers. The organization of administrative agencies often resembles the organization of governments. However, at all three levels of government, the voter has the opportunity to vote the executive into and out of office. In contrast, voters do not elect the administrator of a regulatory agency. For the most part, voters have little control over the activities of an administrative agency.

6.6 Critics allege that administrative agencies are too closely aligned with the enterprises they were created to regulate. In many cases, the need for specialized expertise in a given area can come only from the industry being regulated. Some have suggested that the heads of administrative agencies be elected by popular vote.

CHAPTER SIX ASSESSMENT

MATCHING LEGAL TERMS

Match each of the numbered definitions with the correct term in the following list.

a. administrative agency
b. executive branch
c. administrative hearing
d. judicial branch
e. legislative branch

1. A branch of government headed by the president, a governor, or a mayor. **1.** _____

2. A branch of government with responsibility for enacting legislation. **2.** _____

3. An organization that has executive, legislative, and judicial functions. **3.** _____

4. A branch of government with responsibility for deciding cases brought before it. **4.** _____

5. An activity conducted by an administrative agency to receive complaints and to make decisions as to the guilt or innocence of parties charged. **5.** _____

TRUE/FALSE QUIZ

Indicate whether each of the following statements is true or false.

6. Each level of government has three branches: executive, legislative, and judicial. 6. _____

7. The executive branch of government sees that all enacted legislation is enforced. 7. _____

8. The judicial branch of government determines if there have been violations of law. 8. _____

9. The hearings conducted by administrative agencies customarily include trial by jury. 9. _____

10. The sole purpose of administrative agencies is to regulate business firms. 10. _____

11. There is no recourse from the decisions made at an administrative agency hearing. 11. _____

12. Administrative agencies are found at local, state, and federal levels of government. 12. _____

13. In most cases, the individual voter has direct control over administrative agencies. 13. _____

14. The courts often reverse the decisions of administrative agencies. 14. _____

MULTIPLE CHOICE QUIZ

Indicate the correct answer from the choices after each question.

15. The branches of the U.S. government are (a) legislative, administrative, and judicial (b) executive, legislative, and judicial (c) legislative and executive (d) legislative and judicial. 15. _____

16. The branch of government tasked with passing laws is (a) judicial (b) administrative (c) legislative (d) executive. 16. _____

17. The branch of government tasked with interpreting laws is (a) judicial (b) administrative (c) legislative (d) executive. 17. _____

18. The branch of government tasked with enforcing laws is (a) judicial (b) administrative (c) legislative (d) executive. 18. _____

19. Which of the following is *not* a function of an administrative agency? (a) Regulate conduct (b) Disburse benefits (c) Enact statutory law (d) Provide services. 19. _____

20. Administrative agencies are created by (a) the legislative branch (b) the judicial branch (c) the executive branch (d) the administrative branch. 20. _____

21. Administrative rules and regulations resemble (a) decisions made in a court of law (b) decisions made by the executive branch (c) laws passed by a legislature (d) guidance given by a consultant. **21.** _____

22. An order to appear at a judicial proceeding is known as (a) a regulation (b) administrative hearing (c) *res judicata* (d) subpoena. **22.** _____

23. A judicial proceeding conducted by an administrative agency is known as (a) an administrative hearing (b) a circuit court hearing (c) an executive hearing (d) a legislative hearing. **23.** _____

24. A common criticism of administrative agencies is that they are (a) too influenced by the businesses that they regulate (b) not influenced enough by the businesses that they regulate (c) not influenced at all by the businesses that they regulate (d) staffed by people voted in by the businesses that they regulate. **24.** _____

DISCUSSION QUESTIONS

Answer the following questions and discuss them in class.

25. Explain the similarities and differences between administrative agencies and governments.

26. Using examples, describe the operation of a typical administrative agency.

27. Name at least three administrative agencies at each level of government: federal, state, and local.

28. Discuss criticism of administrative agencies.

29. Explain why legislatures establish regulatory agencies.

THINKING CRITICALLY ABOUT THE LAW

Answer the following questions, which require you to think critically about the legal principles that you learned in this chapter.

30. Operation of Administrative Agencies Compare and contrast the operation of a government body with the operation of an administrative agency.

____

____

31. Judicial Function of an Administrative Agency Compare the procedure followed by an individual appearing as a defendant in a court of law to the procedure followed by an individual charged with a violation of a regulation appearing at a hearing of an administrative agency.

____

____

32. Criticism of Administrative Agencies Discuss some current criticism of administrative agencies and evaluate the validity of this view.

____

____

33. Impact of Administrative Agencies Individuals as well as businesses are affected by actions of administrative agencies in different ways. Select a particular agency and discuss how the agency affects individuals and businesses.

____

____

34. A Question of Ethics Analyze and discuss recourses available to citizens who believe that an executive of an administrative agency is behaving unethically.

____

____

CASE QUESTIONS

Study each of the following cases. Answer the questions that follow with Yes or No.

35. Government Regulations For three years, Patterson operated a small restaurant and enjoyed a growing business. His customers were pleased with the food and service. One day an inspector from the city's board of health visited the restaurant to inspect the sanitary conditions in the kitchen. The inspector informed Patterson that he would have to install a tile floor to replace the wooden one in the kitchen because the wooden floor permitted the growth of disease-carrying insects and was, therefore, a health hazard.

a. Does the board of health have the authority to force Patterson to make the alteration? **a.** ______

b. Can Patterson appeal the order to a regular court with jurisdiction in the city? **b.** _____

c. Can the board of health close the restaurant if Patterson refuses to comply with the order? **c.** _____

d. Does it appear that the board of health is acting in the interest of the people of the community? **d.** _____

36. Government Permits Billings lived in a community that required a building permit before any major alterations could be made to residential property. Billings refused to obtain the permit and proceeded to build a garage on her property.

a. Can the city agency responsible for enforcing the law issue an order to stop the construction? **a.** _____

b. Does it seem likely that the legislation requiring a building permit was intended to prevent construction? **b.** _____

c. Does it seem likely that an appeal to a regular court would be successful? **c.** _____

d. If Billings constructed the garage on her property without obtaining the permit but met all the requirements of the appropriate building codes in her city, could the administrative agency require that it be torn down? **d.** _____

37. Regulatory Agencies Technology Unlimited operated a small factory that employed 100 workers. The company manufactured special measuring devices that were sold throughout the world to the aircraft industry.

a. Would federal regulatory agencies have control over any of the operations of Technology Unlimited? **a.** _____

b. Would state regulatory agencies have control over any of the operations of Technology Unlimited? **b.** _____

c. Would local regulatory agencies have control over any of the operations of Technology Unlimited? **c.** _____

CASE ANALYSIS

Study each of the following cases carefully. Briefly state the principle of law and your decision.

38. State Agencies The law in a particular state provided that the commissioner of insurance had the authority to approve or not approve the rates charged consumers for automobile insurance. The managers of a particular insurance company believed that the services they provided their policyholders were superior to those offered by other companies, and they should be allowed to charge higher rates than those approved by the commissioner for all companies licensed to sell insurance in the state. At a hearing held in response to the company's request for permission to charge the higher rates, the commissioner considered the request. Does it appear likely that the decisions of the state insurance commissioner will be binding on the company?

Principle of Law:

____

____

Decision:

39. **Administrative Hearings** An inspector from the department of weights and measures in a particular city made a routine examination of the gasoline pumps at a service station to check their accuracy. The inspector found that one pump delivered only 4.5 gallons when the meter showed 5 gallons. The inspector sealed the pump and had a subpoena issued, ordering the station owner to report to a hearing to be held the following day. The hearing would be conducted by the commissioner of the department of weights and measures. The operator of the service station claimed that the commissioner lacked authority to compel him to appear at the hearing. Does the commissioner have authority to regulate the operation of the service station?

Principle of Law:

Decision:

40. **Local Agencies** English was an employee of the city of Long Beach, California. His fitness to perform his duties was brought into question by an administrative agency of the city that customarily held hearings where such decisions were made. English was not notified of the hearing. Despite the fact that English was not present, the agency decided that he was unfit to continue his employment. English appealed the decision on the grounds that he was not present at the hearing and that the commission had acted improperly. Does it appear that the administrative agency acted properly in making a decision affecting a person's employment without his being present? [*English v. City of Long Beach,* 217 P.2d 22 (California)]

Principle of Law:

Decision:

41. **Codes** The New York City charter authorizes the board of health to adopt a health code and to take other appropriate steps to ensure the health of the citizens of the city. The charter states that the code "shall have the force and effect of law." The board took action to provide for the fluoridation of the public water supply. Paduano objected to the plan and brought suit to prevent the water treatment, claiming that the action was discriminatory because it benefited only children and the

dental health of children could be achieved in other ways. Is it likely that Paduano would succeed in his action? [*Paduano v. City of New York,* 257 N.Y.S.2d 531 (New York)]

Principle of Law:

Decision:

LEGAL RESEARCH

Complete the following activities. Share your findings with the class.

42. Working in Teams Working in teams of three or four, interview officials or supervisors of some department or agency of municipal government–such as the department of weights and measures or board of health. The following are topics that might be included in the interview: the purposes of the agency, how the agency's performance is evaluated, and by whom. Report your findings to the class.

43. Using Technology Using the Internet and search engines, locate the website of one of the administrative agencies that affect the lives of individuals and businesses in your community. Identify the kinds of services provided to the community.

PART 2

Contracts

Stockbyte/Getty Images

chapter 7 Introduction to Contracts

LEARNING OUTCOMES

After studying this chapter and completing the assessment, you will be able to

7.1 Describe the nature of a contract.

7.2 Identify the sources of contract law and distinguish between agreements and contracts.

7.3 Explain the purpose of a contract.

7.4 Identify the six elements of an enforceable contract.

7.5 Distinguish among the different kinds of contracts, including oral and written, express and implied, formal and simple, and entire and divisible.

7.6 Explain the status of contracts and differentiate between executory and executed contracts.

7.7 Distinguish among valid, void, and voidable contracts.

7.8 Explain the concept of smart contracts and cryptocurrency.

terms

LEGAL

- contract
- tangible personal property
- offer
- offeror
- offeree
- acceptance
- mutual agreement
- consideration
- competent
- legality of purpose
- proper form
- oral contract
- written contract
- express contract
- implied contract
- formal contract
- simple contract
- entire contract
- divisible contract
- executory contract
- executed contract
- valid contract
- void contract
- voidable contract
- smart contract
- cryptocurrency

INTRODUCTION TO CONTRACTS

"Only free men can negotiate; prisoners cannot enter into contracts."

Nelson Mandela, social activist, statesman, and former president of South Africa

John Lund/Drew Kelly/Blend Images LLC

7.1 THE NATURE OF A CONTRACT

A contract is a legally enforceable agreement that is created when two or more competent parties agree to perform, or to avoid performing, certain acts that they have a legal right to do and that meet certain legal requirements. The Uniform Commercial Code (UCC) defines a contract as "the total legal obligation which results from the parties' agreement as affected by the Uniform Commercial Code or any other applicable rules of law."*

This chapter introduces the six elements of a contract and discusses enforceability of contracts. Later chapters will examine each of these six elements in greater detail.

contract
A legally enforceable agreement that is created when two or more competent parties agree to perform, or to avoid performing, certain acts that they have a legal right to do and that meet certain legal requirements.

7.2 SOURCES OF CONTRACT LAW

The part of the UCC* that is relevant to contract law is Article 2. However, Article 2 applies only to transactions in goods or other tangible personal property. Tangible personal property can be defined as personal property that can be moved, such as a vehicle, kitchen table, or cell phone. Common law, on the other hand, is the source of contract law regarding the sale of fixed assets, services, or intangibles.

tangible personal property
Personal property that can be moved.

AGREEMENTS THAT RESULT IN CONTRACTS

All contracts are agreements, but not all agreements are contracts. The reason is that agreements very often deal with personal or social matters that cannot be enforced by law. If an agreement imposes a legal obligation, an enforceable contract results; if it imposes only a social or moral obligation, however, it is not a contract and is not legally enforceable.

EXAMPLE 7.1

▶ Allen, an executive secretary, agreed to meet Kobayashi, a college friend from the firm's accounting department, at noon to share a ride to a company-training seminar. Allen failed to keep the appointment, and Kobayashi, who waited an hour for her, missed the seminar. She had no legal course of action against Allen because the agreement was based on a social, rather than a legal, relationship.

7.3 PURPOSE OF A CONTRACT

Contracts may be created for any number of reasons. They may relate, for example, to the sale of merchandise or services, to employment, or to the transfer of ownership of land (real property) or personal property such as a sailboat. A contract also may be extended and revised as needed to reflect the wishes of the parties. An engineer, for example, might enter into a contract with an assistant, who might agree to provide research help. Later the two might broaden the contract to form a partnership; finally, they might extend their contractual relationship to actually manufacturing and selling the products they develop.

*The Uniform Commercial Code (UCC) is a joint project between the National Conference of Commissioners on Uniform State Laws (NCCUSL) and the American Law Institute (ALI).

offer
A proposal made by one party (the offeror) to another person (the offeree) that indicates a willingness to enter into a contract.

offeror
The person making a proposal.

offeree
The person to whom a proposal is made.

acceptance
An indication made by the offeree that he or she agrees to be bound by the terms of the offer.

mutual agreement
The state of mind that exists between an offeror and an offeree when a valid offer has been accepted and the parties know what the terms are and have agreed to be bound by them. Mutual agreement is also known as "a meeting of the minds."

consideration
The promise to give up something of value that a party to a contract has a legal right to keep, or to do something that the party is not otherwise legally required to do.

competent
Being mentally capable of understanding the terms of a contract.

legality of purpose
The requirement that the intent of a contract be legal for the contract to be enforceable.

proper form
The requirement that the form of a contract be correct for the terms of the contract to be enforceable.

7.4 ELEMENTS OF AN ENFORCEABLE CONTRACT

To be legally enforceable, a contract must contain six elements: (1) offer and acceptance, (2) mutual agreement, (3) consideration, (4) competent parties, (5) legality of purpose, and (6) proper form. If one of these elements is missing, the courts will usually refuse to enforce the contract. Each of these elements will be addressed in this chapter.

OFFER AND ACCEPTANCE

An offer is a proposal made by one party, the offeror, to another party, the offeree, that indicates a willingness to enter into a contract. An acceptance is an indication made by the offeree that they agree to be bound by the terms of the offer.

MUTUAL AGREEMENT

The parties to a contract must have a clear understanding of what they are undertaking. The contract must show mutual agreement, sometimes referred to as a *meeting of the minds.*

CONSIDERATION

Each party to a contract must promise either to give up something of value that they have a legal right to keep, or to do something that they are not otherwise legally required to do. This exchange of promises or value is called consideration. If only one party promises something, such as paying a certain amount of money, and the other party promises nothing, then the agreement lacks consideration. Exceptions to the general rule will be discussed in Chapter 10.

COMPETENT PARTIES

The parties to a contract must be competent–that is, be capable of understanding what they are doing. They must be of legal age and normal mentality. The functioning of a party's mind must not be impaired by injury, mental disease, or the influence of drugs or alcohol.

LEGALITY OF PURPOSE

The intent of the contract must not violate the law. It must have legality of purpose. The courts will not enforce a contract to do something that violates the law (see Example 7.12).

PROPER FORM

Certain contracts, such as those involving the sale of personal property for $500 or more or those that cannot be fulfilled within a year, must be in writing to be enforceable. Other kinds of contracts must not only be in writing but must also follow a prescribed form, such as containing the signatures of the parties. These requirements for contracts are known as proper form.

These essential elements of a contract will be discussed in more detail in later chapters. At this point it is necessary only to remember that an agreement, to be legally enforceable, must contain these six elements.

EXAMPLE 7.2

▶ Rossetti offered to sell his grand piano to Bray for $2,000. Bray agreed to buy it at that price, and the two parties put their agreement in writing. Both Rossetti and Bray were legally competent to enter into a contract. They came to a mutual agreement about the terms of the transaction. Rossetti promised to give up his grand piano in return for Bray's promise to pay $2,000 for it. This was the consideration given by Rossetti and by Bray. Because the agreement involved more than $500, the written contract fulfilled the requirement of proper form. And of course the sale of a grand piano was perfectly legal. Because the agreement satisfied the six elements, a legally enforceable contract resulted.

7.5 KINDS OF CONTRACTS

Contracts may be classified in several ways, depending on the manner in which they are created, expressed, or performed. Thus, a contract may be either oral or written, it may be express or implied, it may be formal or simple, and it may be entire or divisible.

ORAL CONTRACTS

Most contracts in business and in private life are simple, unwritten agreements that result from conversation between the parties involved. Even a telephone conversation can result in an enforceable oral contract. An oral contract is one that is not in writing or signed by the parties. That is, it is a real contract created entirely by the conversation of the parties. A person who discusses the terms of a purchase with a salesperson, pays cash for it, and takes the item with him or her is making an oral contract. A person makes many such contracts in a day, and yet each of these simple transactions contains all the elements of a contract.

oral contract
An agreement that is not in writing or signed by the parties.

written contract
An agreement that is reduced to writing on a permanent surface.

A written contract can be simply a handwritten note.
Stockbyte/Getty Images

WRITTEN CONTRACTS

A written contract is one that is reduced to writing on a permanent surface. Although an oral contract may be just as binding as a written contract, it is advisable to put a contract in writing if the transaction is important or complicated, if the contract involves a large amount of money, or if the contract will extend over a long period of time. Thus, a contract calling for the construction of a building, the installation of expensive machinery, or the payment of a large sum of money for household furnishings should be in writing to protect the parties involved and to prevent a later disagreement over the terms.

The law does not specify any particular form or language to be used. It is sufficient that the parties clearly express themselves in understandable language.

A written contract can be simply a handwritten note, a printed statement or letter, an email, a text, or any other memorandum containing the terms of the agreement, as long as it is signed by the party or parties who wish to be bound by the agreement. Some important agreements are not even called contracts, although in fact they are; they may be called simply a "memorandum of agreement" or other such term.

EXAMPLE 7.3

▶ Ward, an editor with a publishing company, had frequent dealings with Michalski, an author with whom the company had a binding contract. During personal meetings and telephone conversations while working together on a book manuscript, a number of agreements concerning matters that were not covered in the existing contract were made. Wishing to strengthen the existing contract and make it more specific, Ward sent Michalski an email with an attached letter that began, "The purpose of this letter is to reduce to writing the substance of our several discussions in which we agreed. . . ." At this point the letter confirmed all the points that needed clarification. The letter concluded with, "if the above reflects our agreements, please electronically sign and date this letter in the place indicated and email it back to me at your earliest convenience." At the bottom of the letter, there was the following:

▶ Accepted and agreed to: Date:

The purpose of this simple business letter was to reduce the possibilities of later disagreement. In the event of a dispute involving an oral contract, the parties must depend on circumstances, or on the testimony of witnesses, to determine the rights of the parties. The problem, of course, is that memories fade, and even witnesses cannot be relied on to recall exactly what was said. With a written contract, these particular problems are eliminated.

EXPRESS CONTRACTS

express contract
A contract that explicitly states the agreement of the parties, either orally or in writing.

A contract that specifically states the agreement of the parties, either orally or in writing, is called an express contract. The term is used to distinguish such contracts from others in which the meaning or the intention of the parties is inferred from their actions.

IMPLIED CONTRACTS

implied contract
A contract that does not explicitly state the agreement of the parties but in which the terms of the agreement can be inferred from the conduct of the parties, the customs of the trade, or the conditions or circumstances.

Certain business and personal transactions are neither oral nor written but are, nevertheless, legally binding. The terms of these agreements are understood from the actions or conduct of the parties, from the customs of the trade, or from the conditions or circumstances, rather than from oral or written words. A transaction of this kind is considered an implied contract. Thus, an implied contract results when a customer asks a merchant to deliver an article to their home with no mention of payment. The buyer implies that they will pay the market price of the article when it is delivered or when the bill is presented.

EXAMPLE 7.4

▶ Levy entered a retail office supply store, ordered a printer, and left instructions that it was to be delivered to his office. The price of the printer, when payment was to be made, and the exact time of delivery were not discussed.

Example 7.4 provides an illustration of an implied contract. Three implied agreements are involved: (1) that the market price of the printer will be paid, (2) that payment will be made on delivery or when it is customary to make payment (depending on the usual relationship of the merchant and the customer or the customs of the business), and (3) that delivery will be made within a reasonable time.

An implied contract results when a person accepts goods or services that cannot reasonably be considered a gift. A person who stands idly by while another confers an unrequested benefit implies a promise to pay a reasonable amount for the benefit. Such a promise of payment, however, is not implied if goods were delivered or the services rendered during the absence of, and without the knowledge of, the recipient.

EXAMPLE 7.5

▶ Cushing drove his car into Jerseyland Auto and asked for a regular tune-up. While he waited for the work to be done, he noticed a second service attendant begin to install a new battery, which he had not ordered. Obviously a mistake had been made, but when it came time to pay his bill, he was charged only for the tune-up and not the battery. When the mistake was discovered the next day, Jerseyland Auto sent Cushing a bill. Cushing will have to pay for the battery. A person who accepts or uses goods not intended for themselves has an implied obligation to pay the reasonable value for these goods.

FORMAL CONTRACTS

A formal contract, or specialty contract, is a written contract under seal. The seal on a formal contract may consist of simply the word *Seal* or *L.S.* (which means *locus sigilli,* the place of the seal), a scroll, a wafer, or an impression on the paper. Four ways in which a seal may appear are shown in Figure 7.1. Today only a few contracts, such as bonds, mortgages, and deeds conveying title to real estate, are required to have a seal. Many states have stopped using the seal entirely.

formal contract
A specialty contract that is written and under seal.

SIMPLE CONTRACTS

A contract that is not formal, whether it is written, oral, or implied, is called a simple contract. That is, a simple contract is an informal contract made without seal—even though the subject matter of the contract may be extremely complex and may involve huge amounts of money.

simple contract
An informal contract made without seal—even though the subject matter of the contract may be extremely complex and may involve huge amounts of money.

EXAMPLE 7.6

▶ The laws of a certain state require that every real estate mortgage be in writing and under seal. A mortgage bond was made in this state on the prescribed form by a home owner who printed the letters *L.S.* opposite the signature and thereby fulfilled the legal requirement that the mortgage bond be under seal. A seal may consist of any design adopted for that purpose.

FIGURE 7.1 Four Ways of Indicating a Seal

ENTIRE CONTRACTS

entire contract
An agreement that is made up of two or more parts, in which each part is dependent upon the others.

An entire contract, or indivisible contract, has two or more parts. Each part is dependent upon the others for satisfactory performance. Such a contract must be completely performed. The law of sales specifically states that "unless otherwise agreed, all goods called for by a contract for sale must be tendered [offered] in a single delivery and payment is due only on such tender."

EXAMPLE 7.7

Kibbi Real Estate had planned to move into new offices and ordered 20 new desks and accompanying chairs from Belmont Office Supply. On the delivery date, Belmont delivered only the desks and explained that the manufacturer of the chairs had been experiencing labor difficulties. Belmont, however, demanded immediate payment for the desks. The order for the desks and chairs is an entire contract because these items are usually ordered in sets, and the desks are of little use without the chairs. Kibbi Real Estate is not required to pay for the desks until the chairs are delivered.

DIVISIBLE CONTRACTS

divisible contract
An agreement that is made up of two or more parts, each part being independent of the others.

A divisible contract is one that is made up of two or more parts, each part being independent of the others. In the case of a contract for the sale of goods, a party to such a contract must be paid upon request for any part of the contract performed as agreed, even though the entire contract is not performed. The law of sales provides that "where the circumstances give either party to a contract for sale the right to make or demand delivery in lots, the price, if it can be apportioned, may be demanded for each lot."

EXAMPLE 7.8

Schiff, a dealer in playground equipment, placed an order with Play and Grow Company for five playground swings and three freestanding slides. Play and Grow delivered the swings but, because of a shortage of materials, could not deliver the slides until three months later. Schiff must accept and pay for the swings even though the slides were not sent with the swings because the swings can be used without the slides (unlike the previous case, in which the chairs were needed to use the desks).

7.6 STATUS OF CONTRACTS

Where computers, but not accompanying printers, were installed, the contract is considered executory.
Royalty Free/CORBIS

Contracts frequently have a long life. At any particular time, a contract may be awaiting the first act of the parties to execute its terms, in the process of completion, or completed.

EXECUTORY CONTRACTS

executory contract
An agreement in which some future act or obligation remains to be performed under its terms.

An executory contract is one in which some future act or obligation remains to be performed under its terms. A contract is completely executory if no part of it has been performed. It is partly executory if some parts have been performed and some have yet to be performed. If an article is ordered and delivered but not yet paid for, for example, the contact is executory since it is completed on the part of the seller but not completed on the part of the buyer.

EXAMPLE 7.9

▶ Tran signed an agreement with French's Technology Company for the installation of an office computer network. The computers were installed, but because of a shortage of the new models of laser printers covered by the contract, the printers were not installed. The part of the contract dealing with the computers and connecting cables was completed, but the part concerned with the printers was still not completed. The contract is, therefore, executory.

EXECUTED CONTRACTS

A contract in which all of the terms of the agreement have been fully performed by both parties is an executed contract. An executed contract is not really a contract at all. It is more a record of an agreement that has been completed in all respects by all the parties.

executed contract
A record of an agreement that has been completed in all respects by all the parties.

EXAMPLE 7.10

▶ Lee, an employed secretary, signed a contract with an employment agency that agreed to find him a new position as an executive secretary. He agreed to pay the agency 50 percent of his first month's salary. The agency found him a position with a brokerage firm, and a month later Lee sent the agency a check for 50 percent of his first month's salary, as he had agreed to do. The contract is now executed, with no part uncompleted.

7.7 ENFORCEABILITY OF CONTRACTS

It is important to determine whether a contract is valid, void, or voidable because not all contracts can be enforced.

VALID CONTRACTS

The vast majority of contracts entered into in any business day are valid. A valid contract is an agreement resulting in an obligation that is legally enforceable. It meets all the requirements of a contract because all six essential elements are present.

valid contract
An agreement resulting in an obligation that is legally enforceable.

EXAMPLE 7.11

▶ Gorbea, the owner of a computer supply company, agreed in writing with Bretz's Sign Company to pay $800 to have a specific sign erected on her property within 30 days. Bretz's Sign Company constructed and installed the sign within the specified time, and Gorbea sent the company $800. All the essential elements of a legal contract are present in this case.

Offer and Acceptance Gorbea offered Bretz's Sign Company $800 to erect a specific sign within 30 days. Bretz's Sign Company indicated its acceptance of the offer by signing the contract.

Mutual Agreement There was no confusion regarding the amount, the specifications, or the time limits for completion of the transaction. There was, in effect, a meeting of the minds.

Consideration Gorbea promised to pay $800, and Bretz's Sign Company promised to build and install the sign.

void contract
A contract that is not enforceable from the beginning because it lacks one of the requirements of a valid contract.

Competent Parties Gorbea and Bretz's Sign Company are competent to enter into a legal contract.

Legality of Purpose The sale and installation of the sign are legal acts. There are no indications of violations of local codes or ordinances.

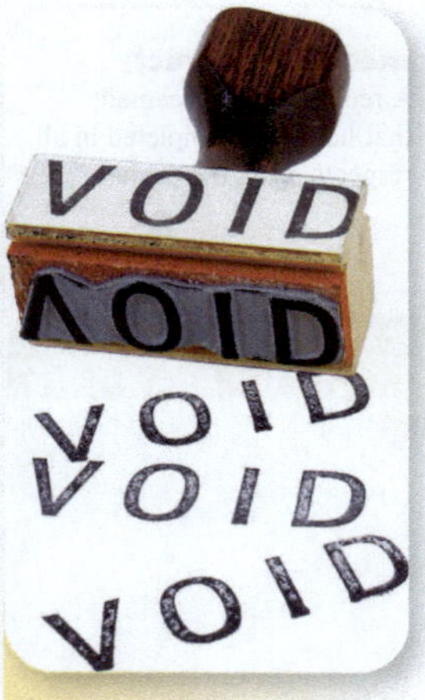

An agreement that lacks one or more of the essential elements of a contract is a void contract.
Comstock Images/Alamy Stock Photo

Proper Form The contract concerned the sale of a sign for an amount over $500, and it was in written form.

Now consider the six elements again. If Gorbea offered Bretz's Sign Company $800, and Bretz said it would charge $900, there would be no acceptance of the offer. If Gorbea thought she was getting a revolving electric sign and Bretz's Sign Company thought she wanted a simple electrically lighted sign, there would not be mutual agreement. If Gorbea did not agree to pay for the sign, consideration would be lacking. If Gorbea were a minor, she would not have the authority to make a binding contract; that is, she would not have been a competent party. If local zoning regulations prohibited the type of sign Gorbea wanted, the contract would not have been for a legal purpose. The UCC* requires that contracts for the sale of goods for $500 or more be in writing. If this agreement were not in writing, it would not be enforceable because it would lack proper form.

VOID CONTRACTS

An agreement that lacks one or more of the essential elements of a contract is a void contract from the very beginning. That is, it is not a true contract at all and is therefore unenforceable.

EXAMPLE 7.12

Hritzik operated a clothing manufacturing firm and entered into an agreement with an unlawful enterprise that offered to bring undocumented immigrants into the country to work for Hritzik. When the first truckload of immigrants arrived, a number were seriously ill, rendering them unfit to work. Hritzik wanted healthy workers and refused to pay the agreed-upon price. The enterprise wanted its money. Neither Hritzik nor the importer would have access to any legal remedy because their agreement violated federal immigration laws and was void from the very beginning: It lacked one of the essential elements of a contract—legality of purpose.

*The Uniform Commercial Code (UCC) is a joint project between the National Conference of Commissioners on Uniform State Laws (NCCUSL) and the American Law Institute (ALI).

VOIDABLE CONTRACTS

An agreement that may be rejected by one of the parties for a legally acceptable reason is a voidable contract. Such a contract is valid and enforceable unless and until it is rejected by the party who has the right to withdraw. Thus, in a contract between a minor and an adult, the adult must perform his or her part of the agreement, unless and until the minor decides to withdraw from the contract.

voidable contract
An agreement that can be rejected by one of the parties for a legally acceptable reason.

EXAMPLE 7.13

▶ Braun, a 16-year-old minor, agreed with Main Street Used Cars to purchase a certain automobile. The dealership must perform as agreed, but Braun, who is not legally a competent party, can withdraw from this voidable contract.

Suppose that Braun was an adult who agreed to buy a certain automobile only if it were repainted blue. Assume also that because of an error the automobile was repainted green. Braun can withdraw from the contract because the seller failed to perform according to the terms of the contract. The contract is voidable at Braun's option. If the color green is not acceptable to Braun, she can withdraw from the contract, or she can insist that the car be repainted blue, or she can accept the car as is but with some settlement, such as a lower price than that to which she originally agreed.

7.8 SMART CONTRACTS

A smart contract is a fully digital enforceable agreement. The full substance of the agreement is actually digitally written into the lines of code across a network that can be accessed, but not modified, by the parties to the contract. The technology that accommodates this is known as distributed ledger technology, better known to some as blockchain.

smart contract
An agreement using blockchain technology in which the terms are digitally written into the lines of code across a network that can be accessed, but not modified, by the parties to the contract.

Distributed ledger technology is a platform that uses decentralized nodes with multiple sources to validate each aspect of a transaction. Thus, each aspect of a smart contract is divided into a transaction that must be validated on the platform. Because of the nature of the technology, no intervention outside of the platform is allowed with a smart contract, and all coded transactions in the contract are automatically verified on the platform, resulting in a self-enforcing contract.

There are several advantages to smart contracts. First, they do not require the use of a middleman, who may or may not be trustworthy, to connect the parties to an agreement. Second, they allow the parties to digitally transfer money, shares of stock, property, or other assets quickly, simply, accurately, and safely. Third, they are less expensive to enter into since they do not require attorneys or third parties. Fourth, smart contracts are said to be immutable–that is, they cannot be changed by any one of the parties. Because of these and other advantages, governments, banks, accounting firms, and insurance companies are increasingly utilizing smart contracts to conduct their business dealings.

However, there are also limitations to smart contracts. First, they are not available for all types of contracts. If the contract has any transaction that requires validation that is not possible on the platform, the contract cannot exist on the platform. An example would be an employment contract with compensation dependent on a manager's performance appraisal. Second, the platform cannot determine if all elements of the contract are present, particularly mutual agreement, competent parties, or legal purpose. Third, because these contracts are self-executing, court systems are not able to intervene in the executory stage as they would with a traditional contract.

cryptocurrency
A digitally encrypted currency not connected with any country's central banking system.

When parties to a smart contract wish to exchange money, they use a form of money referred to as a cryptocurrency, which is currency encrypted digitally into the blockchain platform so as to prevent unauthorized access. Unlike the U.S. dollar, which is controlled through monetary policy established by the Federal Reserve System, cryptocurrencies are not connected with any country's central banking system. A cryptocurrency can be transferred from person to person without third-party interference.

CHAPTER SUMMARY

7.1 A contract is a legally enforceable agreement.

7.2 The sources of contract law appear in Article 2 of the UCC* and common law. All contracts are agreements, but not all agreements are contracts. In some cases, agreements are of a social nature and are not enforceable by law.

7.3 Contracts may be created for any number of reasons. They may relate, for example, to the sale of merchandise or services, to employment, or to the transfer of ownership of land (real property) or personal property.

7.4 The six elements of an enforceable contract are (1) offer and acceptance, (2) mutual agreement, (3) consideration, (4) competent parties, (5) legality of purpose, and (6) proper form.

7.5 An oral contract is one that is legally enforceable and is created entirely by the conversation of the parties. A written contract is one that is reduced to writing in a permanent form.

Express contracts specifically state the agreement of the parties, either orally or in writing. Implied contracts are agreements, the terms of which are inferred from the conduct of the parties, the customs of the trade, or the circumstances.

A formal contract, or specialty contract, is a written contract under seal. A simple contract is an informal contract made without seal—even though the subject matter of the contract is extremely complex.

An entire contract has two or more parts, each dependent upon the others for satisfactory performance. A divisible contract is one that consists of two or more parts, each part being independent of the others.

7.6 Contracts frequently have a long life. At any particular time, a contract may be awaiting the first act of the parties to execute its terms, in the process of completion, or completed. An executory contract is one in which some future act or obligation remains to be performed under its terms. An executed contract is one in which the terms of the agreement have been fully performed by both parties.

7.7 Valid contracts are agreements resulting in obligations that are legally enforceable. Void contracts are agreements that lack one or more of the essential elements of a contract. Voidable contracts are agreements that may be rejected by one of the parties for a legally acceptable reason.

7.8 A smart contract is an agreement using blockchain technology in which the terms are digitally written into the lines of code across a network that can be accessed, but not modified, by the parties to the contract. Cryptocurrency is digitally encrypted currency not connected with any country's central banking system.

*The Uniform Commercial Code (UCC) is a joint project between the National Conference of Commissioners on Uniform State Laws (NCCUSL) and the American Law Institute (ALI).

CHAPTER SEVEN ASSESSMENT

MATCHING LEGAL TERMS

Match each of the numbered definitions with the correct term in the following list.

a. competent party
b. consideration
c. divisible contract
d. entire, or indivisible, contract
e. executed contract
f. executory contract
g. express contract
h. formal contract
i. implied contract
j. legality of purpose
k. mutual agreement
l. smart contract
m. proper form
n. voidable contract
o. void contract

1. A "meeting of the minds" regarding the rights and obligations of the parties to a contract. **1.** _____

2. A person who is of legal age and normal mentality. **2.** _____

3. The promises exchanged by parties to a contract. **3.** _____

4. An agreement using blockchain technology in which the terms are digitally written into the lines of code. **4.** _____

5. A contract that is understood from the acts or conduct of the parties. **5.** _____

6. A written contract that bears a seal. **6.** _____

7. A contract with several unrelated parts, each of which can stand alone. **7.** _____

8. The requirement that a contract cannot violate the law. **8.** _____

9. A contract with several related parts, each dependent on the other parts for satisfactory performance. **9.** _____

10. A contract whose meaning is not determined by the conduct of the parties. **10.** _____

11. A contract that has not yet been completed by both parties. **11.** _____

12. A contract that allows the incompetent party to withdraw. **12.** _____

13. A contract that has been fully completed by both parties. **13.** _____

14. A contract that lacks an essential element and hence was never legally a contract. **14.** _____

15. A requirement for contracts for the sale of goods for $500 or more. **15.** _____

TRUE/FALSE QUIZ

Indicate whether each of the following statements is true or false.

16. All agreements between two competent parties are contracts. **16.** _____

17. Written contracts must be handwritten to be legally enforceable. **17.** _____

18. Entire contracts are those composed of several related parts. 18. _____

19. To be legally enforceable, contracts must be in writing. 19. _____

20. The terms of express contracts are specifically stated. 20. _____

21. A contract is considered executed as soon as all parties have performed their obligations stated in the terms. 21. _____

MULTIPLE CHOICE QUIZ

Indicate the correct answer by choosing from the choices following each question.

22. Which of the following is *not* required for a contract to be legally enforceable? (a) Mutual agreement (b) In Writing (c) Competent Parties (d) Legal purpose. 22. _____

23. A contract that does not require a seal is known as (a) a formal contract (b) an express a contract (c) a simple contract (d) an implied contract. 23. _____

24. A contract that has been fully performed is (a) an executed contract (b) an executory contract (c) a void contract (d) a voidable contract. 24. _____

25. A contract that is still in the process of being performed is (a) an executed contract (b) an executory contract (c) a void contract (d) a voidable contract. 25. _____

26. A contract that is rejected by a party under the legal age to contract is known as (a) an executed contract (b) an executory contract (c) a void contract (d) a voidable contract. 26. _____

27. Which of the following is the common requirement of all contracts? (a) That it is legally enforceable (b) That it is socially enforceable (c) That it is morally enforceable (d) That it is both socially and morally enforceable. 27. _____

28. A contract based only on a conversation between the parties is (a) a simple contract (b) a formal contract (c) an oral contract (d) a void contract. 28. _____

29. One advantage of a smart contract is (a) that it is self-executing (b) that it can be used for any purpose (c) that it still can use dollars as currency (d) that the execution of the contract can be stopped at any time. 29. _____

30. One disadvantage of a smart contract is (a) that it can be changed by either of the parties in the executory stage (b) that it can use dollars as currency (c) that it cannot be used for all purposes (d) that it is self-executing. 30. _____

31. A smart contract requiring currency exchange must use (a) dollars (b) euros (c) cryptocurrency (d) no currency. 31. _____

DISCUSSION QUESTIONS

Answer the following questions and discuss them in class.

32. Provide examples of typical offers and acceptances.

33. Parties to a contract must have a clear understanding of what they are undertaking–a meeting of the minds. Provide an example of two parties who have reached such a clear understanding.

34. Provide an example of a contracting party offering consideration by doing something that they are not legally required to do.

35. The law requires that the parties be competent to enter into a contract. Give an example of a party who lacks competence.

36. The law requires that the purpose of a contract must be legal. Provide an example of a contract that would not be enforceable because it lacks legality of purpose.

37. Provide an example of an agreement that would need to be in writing to be enforceable.

THINKING CRITICALLY ABOUT THE LAW

Answer the following questions, which require you to think critically about the legal principles that you learned in this chapter.

38. **Competent Parties** The law allows a minor to withdraw from a contract simply because they are a minor, whereas the other party is bound if the minor wishes to carry out the contract. Do you think the law is fair in such instances?

39. Implied Contracts Certain business and personal transactions are neither oral nor written but are nevertheless legally binding. The terms of these agreements are understood from the actions or conduct of the parties, from the customs of the trade, or from the conditions or circumstances rather than from oral or written words. Do you think implied contracts should be enforceable?

40. Legality of Purpose Some contracts freely entered into by the parties involve activities that have been made illegal by state or federal statutes. Because they are illegal, these contracts are unenforceable. Examples are wagering agreements or lending money at high rates of interest (usury). Do you believe that legislatures should interfere with the free will of contracting parties?

41. Proper Form For many years the law has required that certain kinds of contracts, such as those involving $500 or more, be in writing to be enforceable. Should the amount of $500 be increased to reflect the effects of inflation?

42. A Question of Ethics Do you think it is unethical for an underage person who looks much older to enter into a contract with another person who in good faith expects the underage party to fulfill the terms of the contract?

CASE QUESTIONS

Study each of the following cases. Indicate whether the contract is executed, executory, or neither and whether it is valid, voidable, or void.

43. Status of Contract Knoll and Kalichuk signed an agreement for the sale of Knoll's sailboat. The agreement was complete in all respects, including the provision of time and place of delivery, sale price, and accessories included. On the date agreed for the exchange of payment and delivery of the boat, Knoll informed Kalichuk that he had changed his mind and decided not to sell.

a. Executed Executory Neither **a.** _____

b. Valid Voidable Void **b.** _____

44. Status of Contract Arslantian, a suburban homeowner who was involved in a major landscaping project, offered to pay Manley, a county employee, 50 percent of the market price for certain shrubbery belonging to the county parks commission if Manley would deliver it to a meeting place in a shopping mall.

a. Executed	Executory	Neither	**a.** _____
b. Valid	Voidable	Void	**b.** _____

Study the following case. Answer the questions that follow.

45. Elements of Contract Fiscus, age 23, entered into an oral contract with Badger, a 30-year-old bricklayer, for the construction of a backyard barbecue for a fee of $300. The work was completed in two weeks, as agreed.

a. Is there an offer and an acceptance? **a.** _____

b. Is this a valid contract? **b.** _____

c. Are the parties competent? **c.** _____

d. Name the parties. **d.** _____

e. Is the purpose of the contract legal? **e.** _____

f. What is the purpose? **f.** _____

g. Is there consideration present? **g.** _____

h. What is the consideration? **h.** _____

i. Is there mutual agreement? **i.** _____

j. Explain the purpose of the contract. **j.** _____

CASE ANALYSIS

Study each of the following cases carefully. Briefly state the principle of law and your decision.

46. Elements of Contract Esposito hired Excel Construction Company to repair a porch roof for $625 while she was out of town on vacation. All terms of the agreement were specified in a written contract, but the agreement failed to specify whether it was the front or rear porch that needed repair. When Esposito returned, she discovered that Excel had repaired the rear porch roof. She refused to pay, claiming that she wanted the front porch roof repaired. Were all essential elements of a contract present, and will Esposito be required to pay for the work that was done?

Principle of Law:

____

____

Decision:

____

____

47. Consideration William Storey Sr. promised his nephew, William Storey II, that he would pay him $5,000 if his nephew avoided drinking, using tobacco, swearing, and playing cards and billiards for money until he became 21 years old. The nephew agreed to the offer and kept his part of the bargain. At the age of 21, he wrote to his uncle and asked for the $5,000. The uncle acknowledged the promise, praised his nephew for keeping his part of the bargain, but did not pay the money at that time. A short time later, the uncle died. The executor of his estate refused to pay the nephew, claiming that the contract was invalid due to the lack of consideration. Was the nephew's promise to avoid drinking, using tobacco, swearing, and playing cards and billiards for money until he became 21 legal consideration? [*Hamer v. Sidway,* 27 N.E. 256 (New York)]

Principle of Law:

____

____

Decision:

____

____

48. Proper Form Hodge, a 54-year-old employee of a bank, discussed his job and future with Tilley, president of Evans Financial Corporation and his employer. They agreed orally on a number of matters, including job title and location. After eight months on the new job, Tilley became dissatisfied with Hodge's work and discharged him. Hodge immediately sued, claiming that the oral agreement provided for employment until he retired at age 65. Does the length of time needed to fulfill the contract have a bearing on the enforceability of the contract? [*Hodge v. Evans Financial Corp.,* 778 F.2d 794 (District of Columbia)]

Principle of Law:

____

____

Decision:

____

____

49. Divisible or Entire Contract Grogan, a marketing consultant, was hired by Kreger Bottling Company to conduct market research into the taste preferences of consumers in a major city. Before he concluded the project, he was asked to take on the additional task of analyzing the appeal of various shapes of bottles that Kreger was considering for a new line of soft drinks. When the taste test was finished, but before the second project was completed, Grogan submitted his bill for the taste test.

Kreger refused to pay until the bottle test was completed. Does Grogan have a basis for demanding payment for the portion of the work done?

Principle of Law:

____

____

Decision:

____

____

LEGAL RESEARCH

Complete the following activities. Share your findings with the class.

50. Working in Teams In teams of three or four, interview several small businesses to learn some of the steps businesspersons routinely follow to avoid problems involving contracts.

____

____

51. Using Technology Visit the Ethereum site (www.ethereum.org) and find the steps on that site to create a smart contract.

____

____

chapter 8
Offer and Acceptance

LEARNING OUTCOMES

After studying this chapter and completing the assessment, you will be able to

8.1 Identify the first step in reaching agreement and forming a valid contract.

8.2 Explain and provide examples of the three requirements for a valid offer.

8.3 Distinguish among bids, advertisements, and public offers, and describe how each relates to offer and acceptance.

8.4 Explain and provide examples of the two requirements for a valid acceptance.

8.5 Identify the five ways in which an offer may be terminated.

LEGAL terms

- request for proposal
- invitation to trade
- public offer
- mailbox rule
- counteroffer
- termination by lapse of time
- revocation
- rejection
- option contract

OFFER AND ACCEPTANCE

"I'm gonna make him an offer he can't refuse."

Don Vito Corleone, from the movie *The Godfather*

Ryan McVay/Getty Images

8.1 REACHING AGREEMENT

Chapter 7 discussed the six elements of an enforceable contract. The first of these essential elements is offer and acceptance. For a contract to be valid, there must be a proposal that is both offered by the offeror and accepted by the offeree. This chapter addresses the characteristics of offers and acceptances, and describes the ways in which offers are terminated. Smart contracts, discussed in Chapter 7, require valid offer and acceptance by the parties before the contract is coded and entered into the blockchain platform.

8.2 REQUIREMENTS FOR A VALID OFFER

For an offer to be valid, it must be (1) definite and certain, (2) communicated to the offeree, and (3) made with a serious intention that the offeror will be bound by it.

AN OFFER MUST BE DEFINITE AND CERTAIN

To be definite and certain, an offer should specify all the terms and conditions of the contract. Later disagreement can be avoided if the offer is made as specific as possible. Under the Uniform Commercial Code (UCC), however, the omission of one or more essential terms does not necessarily make the offer invalid as long as the contract contains sufficient information to suggest that the parties intended to enter into a contract (UCC 2-204).*

According to the UCC, uncertainty with respect to specific terms does not necessarily invalidate a contract. For example, when an offer of sale does not specify a price, it is assumed that the parties intended "a reasonable price at the time set for delivery" (UCC 2-305). Moreover, uncertainty regarding place of delivery, time for shipment, and time for payment does not always invalidate a contract (UCC 2-308, 309, 310). Of course a court resolution of a dispute that arises from uncertainty about contract terms is a difficult way to do business. As a general rule, if an offer is to be definite and certain, it should cover the same points as a good news story: who, what, when, where, and how much.*

AN OFFER MUST BE COMMUNICATED

An offeror can make the offer known to the offeree in various ways. The usual means of communication are generally used, including oral communication (in person or by telephone, television, or radio) and written communication (letters, fax, email, websites, or other written forms). Making an offer and having it accepted are such common events in today's business world that people in business frequently use a printed or electronic purchase order upon which the terms of the offer are shown. Purchase orders are usually considered to be offers to buy. In these cases, the buyer of the goods is the offeror and the seller is the offeree. Communication also may be implied by the actions of the parties.

*The Uniform Commercial Code (UCC) is a joint project between the National Conference of Commissioners on Uniform State Laws (NCCUSL) and the American Law Institute (ALI).

EXAMPLE 8.1

▶ Ellenby, an executive secretary, entered the Metro Stationery store, where he frequently purchased office supplies for his employer. He selected a box of ballpoint pens and several boxes of envelopes and showed them to the owner, who was busy with another customer at the time. The owner nodded and smiled, and the secretary departed from the store. By his action, the executive secretary made an implied offer. The owner of the store, by her conduct, implied that she had accepted the offer and that she would add the charges for his purchases to the employer's account.

AN OFFER MUST INTEND AN ENFORCEABLE OBLIGATION

Offers made in anger or jest, or those made under severe emotional strain, are obviously not made with the intent of entering into a valid, enforceable agreement. The lack of serious intent must, however, be apparent to a reasonable person.

EXAMPLE 8.2

▶ Clayton, a retired executive, was outraged at the amount of a repair bill for his one-year-old car, which was worth about $32,000. He screamed that repair bills were costing him more than the car was worth. He said, "I'll sell this bucket of bolts to anyone for $500." One of the mechanics who heard this quickly offered Clayton five $100 bills. It is doubtful that the mechanic could enforce the sale because a lack of serious intent would be apparent to a reasonable person.

8.3 BIDS, ADVERTISING, AND PUBLIC OFFERS

The requirement of offer and acceptance is usually fairly straightforward in contracts involving just two or perhaps a few parties. However, the issue gets complicated when there is little or no direct contact between the parties, as in the case of bidding, advertising, and public offers.

BIDS AND ESTIMATES

A call for a bid or estimate for materials to be furnished or work to be done is not considered an offer, but rather a request for an offer or an invitation to negotiate that can be accepted or rejected by the person calling for the bid. Such an announcement or solicitation is often called a request for proposal (RFP). Many cities and states that wish to enter into a contract with private firms or individuals for the performance of work or the purchase of goods or services require that the lowest bid be accepted. The main purposes of such a regulation are to ensure that the purchaser gets the most economical price and to prevent dishonesty in the form of bribery and kickbacks.

request for proposal (RFP)
A request for an offer or an invitation to negotiate that can be accepted or rejected by the person calling for a bid.

Note that in Example 8.3, if the board of education's call for bids was considered an offer, and the bids were considered acceptances, then a valid contract would result when the first bid was submitted. Instead, the call for bids or proposals was regarded as a solicitation of offers, and thus the proposals submitted were deemed offers.

EXAMPLE 8.3

▶ The board of education of a particular city decided to incorporate a new technology course in its vocational program. Because the course was highly specialized, it was believed that experts would be needed to prepare the new curriculum. Requests for proposals were sent to experts in technology education, and an announcement was published in publications that normally reach specialists in that field.

ADVERTISING

Sometimes goods are advertised in a newspaper at an incorrect price.
Thinglass/Shutterstock

invitation to trade
An announcement published for the purpose of creating interest and attracting a response by many people. It is not considered a valid offer because it does not contain sufficient words of commitment to sell.

An advertisement, such as one that appears every day on television or radio, in a newspaper or a magazine, or on a website, is generally regarded as an invitation to trade, or an invitation to make an offer, rather than a valid offer because it does not contain sufficient words of commitment to sell. Sometimes goods are advertised in a newspaper or in a circular at an incorrect price. If the error is the fault of the merchant, they will be required to honor the lower price. Even if the error is not their fault, the merchant may decide to sell the goods as advertised even though this may not be profitable. The reason is usually that the merchant believes it is a good business decision to sell at the advertised price in order to retain public goodwill. Goodwill is worth more than whatever the merchant would gain by enforcing their legal rights. If the error is the fault of the newspaper or publisher of the circular, the merchant may be able to recoup their losses from the publication.

If, however, an advertisement contains a positive promise and a positive statement of what the advertiser expects in return, the courts will usually hold that the advertisement is an offer. This is especially true if the word *offer* is used in the advertisement.

EXAMPLE 8.4

▶ Surplus Store ran an advertisement in a Minneapolis newspaper that read, "SATURDAY 9 A.M. 2 BRAND NEW PASTEL MINK 3-SKIN SCARFS SELLING FOR $89.50. OUT THEY GO SATURDAY. EACH $1.00. 1 BLACK LAPIN STOLE, BEAUTIFUL, WORTH $139.50 . . . $1.00 FIRST COME, FIRST SERVED." Lefkowitz was the first to present himself on Saturday and demanded the lapin stole for $1.00. Surplus Store refused to sell it to him because of a "house rule" that the offer was intended for women only. Lefkowitz sued and was awarded $138.50. The court held that the words "First come, first served" created a language of promise that is ordinarily lacking in advertisements. [*Lefkowitz v. Great Minneapolis Surplus Store,* 86 N.W.2d 689 (Minnesota)]

PUBLIC OFFERS

When an advertisement offers a reward for information that might lead to the arrest of a criminal or for the return of a lost article, it is regarded as a general offer to the public at large. Acceptance of a public offer by anyone, as indicated by the performance of the act, results in an enforceable contract.

public offer
A general offer to the public at large.

EXAMPLE 8.5

Jamison lost an expensive pedigreed dog while at a park. He placed an advertisement in the *Daily Journal*, offering a $500 reward for the dog's return. This public offer is valid, even though it is directed to thousands of readers, only one of whom could accept it.

The number of persons reached by an advertisement has no bearing on the validity of the offer. The purpose of such an advertisement is to reach a person of unknown identity with whom a valid contract can be made.

8.4 REQUIREMENTS FOR A VALID ACCEPTANCE

In order for an acceptance of an offer to be valid, (1) it must be communicated to the offeror, and (2) it must be unconditional.

AN ACCEPTANCE MUST BE COMMUNICATED

It is important to determine how an acceptance may be communicated and when such acceptance becomes effective.

Method of Communication Any of the usual forms of communication, such as telephone, letter, email, text message, and others, may be used in accepting an offer, unless the offer specifies a certain form of communication, such as "Reply by registered mail," "Reply by return mail," or "Reply by email." The UCC states, "An offer to make a contract shall be construed as inviting acceptance in any manner and by any medium reasonable in the circumstances."*

When an Acceptance Becomes Effective The general rule is that an acceptance becomes effective when the parties so intend. The offer may explicitly state whether an acceptance is effective when it is sent by the offeree or when it is received by the offeror. If the offer is silent as to the time the acceptance is effective, the mailbox rule (also known as the *postal acceptance rule*) states that an acceptance sent via the postal system or by courier is effective when sent. However, an acceptance communicated by telephone message or voicemail is effective when received. State law varies on whether an acceptance sent via email, fax, or text message is effective when sent or when received.

mailbox rule
A rule that states that an acceptance sent via the postal system or by courier is effective when sent.

*The Uniform Commercial Code (UCC) is a joint project between the National Conference of Commissioners on Uniform State Laws (NCCUSL) and the American Law Institute (ALI).

EXAMPLE 8.6

▶ Smigel, a Minnesota supplier of oil drilling supplies, sent several of his customers who were located in various parts of the country a letter offering to sell surplus inventory of certain drilling bits for a relatively low price. The offer stated, "Reply by certified mail." On May 14 Chontos sent a certified letter accepting the offer. The letter was received by Smigel on May 17. On May 16 Lukin sent an email message accepting the offer. The email was received the same day, May 16. Smigel must sell his stock to Chontos even though Lukin's acceptance was received first because Chontos used Smigel's specified medium of communication for his acceptance.

Silence as Acceptance In general, a person cannot be compelled to speak or to write in order to avoid a binding agreement and is under no obligation to reply to an offer. However, silence may indicate assent to an offer when both parties agree beforehand that this is to be the means of acceptance.

EXAMPLE 8.7

▶ In a letter to Westerly Dry Cleaners, Central Solvent, a regular supplier, offered to sell a newly formulated cleaning solvent and stated that it would consider the offer accepted if Westerly did not respond within 10 days. Westerly did not respond, and the solvent was shipped. Central billed Westerly for the solvent and shipping charges. Westerly refused to pay and demanded that the solvent be removed from its premises. Central claimed that Westerly's silence indicated acceptance of the offer. A court would hold that Westerly's silence is not considered an acceptance because Central cannot require the firm to speak.

However, suppose that Westerly and Central had previously agreed that Westerly's failure to turn down Central's written offer for the sale of goods would result in a valid, enforceable contract. In this instance, both parties would have agreed that silence was to be the manner of acceptance. The UCC provides that a "contract for the sale of goods may be made in any manner sufficient to show agreement, including conduct by both parties which recognizes the existence of such a contract."*

AN ACCEPTANCE MUST BE UNCONDITIONAL

A counteroffer—that is, a conditional, or qualified, acceptance of an offer—is generally interpreted as a rejection and is not binding on the parties.

counteroffer
A response to an offer in which the terms and conditions of the original offer are changed.

EXAMPLE 8.8

▶ Churchill, the owner of an apple orchard, signed a contract in February to sell the land to Czek but reserved the right to recover the apples when they ripened in the fall. Czek signed the contract but crossed out the words that pertained to the recovery of the apples. In this case there was no contract because Czek did not accept Churchill's offer and his act of crossing out the words constituted a counteroffer.

*The Uniform Commercial Code (UCC) is a joint project between the National Conference of Commissioners on Uniform State Laws (NCCUSL) and the American Law Institute (ALI).

In a contract, an owner of an apple orchard might reserve the right to recover the apples when they ripen.
Photo by Scott Bauer, USDA-ARS

The general rule of contract provides that the acceptance of an offer must be the same as the offer and that if there are any material (important) differences between the offer and the acceptance, the acceptance is regarded as a rejection of the offer. The UCC provides an exception to this rule and states that, between merchants, "a definite and reasonable expression of acceptance or a written confirmation which is sent within a reasonable time operates as an acceptance even though it states terms additional to or different from those offered or agreed upon, unless acceptance is expressly made conditional on assent to the additional or different terms."*

The UCC also provides that "additional (or different) terms are to be construed as proposals for addition to the contract, and between merchants, become part of the contract . . . unless the offer expressly limits acceptance to the terms of the offer, they materially alter it; or notification of objection to them . . . is given within a reasonable time after (they) are received."*

EXAMPLE 8.9

Wayfar Printers ordered a drum of printing ink from Barlette & Co. On its order, Wayfar stated that delivery must be made by June 1. When Barlette accepted the order, it included the statement "impossible to ship before June 15." The acknowledgment also stated that "if these terms are not acceptable, buyer must notify the seller at once." Wayfar did not complain about the later delivery date. Barlette's acceptance was valid even though it stated terms different from those offered. The UCC states that the different terms become a part of the contract between merchants unless the alterations are material. At times, disagreements can result as to whether or not such different terms are important.

8.5 TERMINATION OF AN OFFER

Offers are terminated by (1) lapse of time, (2) revocation, (3) rejection, (4) death or incapacity, and (5) destruction or illegality.

TERMINATION BY LAPSE OF TIME

termination by lapse of time
When an opportunity to form a contract ends because the offeree fails to accept an offer within the time specified.

When the offeree fails to accept an offer within the time specified, the opportunity to form a contract ends because of a termination by lapse of time. When no definite time for acceptance is stated in an offer, it terminates after a reasonable time has passed. What is considered a reasonable time can vary according to the circumstances.

*The Uniform Commercial Code (UCC) is a joint project between the National Conference of Commissioners on Uniform State Laws (NCCUSL) and the American Law Institute (ALI).

EXAMPLE 8.10

▶ In the early spring, Wilkerson, a wholesaler of sporting goods, offered several dozen of a popular brand of tennis racquets at a specified price to Sportique Stores. Three months later, the store accepted the offer and demanded delivery. Obviously an offer to sell seasonal goods, such as tennis racquets, has a short life and must be accepted long before the passage of three months.

TERMINATION BY REVOCATION

An offer that has been neither accepted nor rejected by the offeree can be revoked, or withdrawn, by the offeror. The offeror may communicate the revocation to the offeree in either spoken or written words. The UCC provides, however, that any written offer by a merchant to buy or sell goods that states that the offer will be held open for a specified time period cannot be revoked during this time period or, if no time period is specified, until a reasonable time has elapsed. An offer that includes specific time limits expires automatically when the time is up unless the offeror chooses to extend the offer (UCC 2-309).*

revocation
The calling back of an offer by the offeror before the offer has been accepted or rejected.

EXAMPLE 8.11

▶ Armstrong owned a painting with an appraised value of nearly $100,000. Hoping to sell the work, he placed it in the hands of Westport Galleries for an agreed-upon period of three months for sale at $80,000. After three months, no sale had been arranged. Armstrong took back possession of the painting and turned it over to another gallery.

TERMINATION BY REJECTION

A direct, unqualified rejection, or a refusal to accept, terminates an offer. The offer, once rejected by the offeree, cannot be revived or made into a counteroffer once the communication of the rejection has been received by the offeror. If the offeror acknowledges the rejection but restates the offer, the offeree still has the opportunity to accept, or reject, or make a counteroffer.

rejection
The express or implied refusal by an offeree to accept an offer.

A direct, unqualified rejection terminates an offer.
E. Audras/PhotoAlto

Just as a qualified acknowledgment of the rejection of an offer serves to keep an offer alive, a qualified rejection may have a similar effect. Suppose, in Example 8.12, Fishkin had said, "Although I'd like to buy your car, I'm pretty sure I won't accept your offer; but I'd like to think about it for a week." The qualified rejection was, in fact, not really a rejection at all.

*The Uniform Commercial Code (UCC) is a joint project between the National Conference of Commissioners on Uniform State Laws (NCCUSL) and the American Law Institute (ALI).

EXAMPLE 8.12

Kenna (the offeror) offered to sell his antique car to Fishkin (the offeree) for $40,000. Fishkin sent an email message to Kenna saying, "You know how much I'd like to buy the car, but I simply cannot afford it at this time." Kenna acknowledged Fishkin's rejection of the offer by saying, "I received your note rejecting my offer, but if you want to think about it for another month or two, I'll keep the offer open." By his acknowledgment of Fishkin's rejection and restatement of the offer, Kenna has allowed Fishkin an opportunity to accept the restated offer at a later date.

TERMINATION BY DEATH OR INCAPACITY

Mutual agreement cannot occur if either the offeror or the offeree dies or becomes incompetent. Therefore, an offer is immediately terminated as a result of the death or legal incapacity of either the offeror or the offeree. However, if either the offeror or the offeree is bound by an option contract, the surviving party may still be obligated to the contract. An option contract is one that has a provision to keep an offer open for a certain period of time. In the event of death, the estate of the deceased would be responsible to carry out the provisions of a contract that includes an option.

option contract
A contract that has a provision to keep an offer open for a certain period of time.

TERMINATION BY DESTRUCTION OR ILLEGALITY

If the subject matter of a contract is destroyed or declared illegal after the offer has been made but before it has been accepted, the contract is terminated.

EXAMPLE 8.13

Gipson offered to sell Ramirez her boat for $8,000. While the boat was docked, a storm damaged the boat, causing it to sink. Because the boat was destroyed, the offer was terminated.

CHAPTER SUMMARY

8.1 The first step in reaching agreement and forming a valid contract is that there must be a proposal that is both offered by the offeror and accepted by the offeree.

8.2 For an offer to be valid, it must be (a) definite and certain, (b) communicated to the offeree, and (c) made with a serious intention that the offeror will be bound by it. One example would be a salesperson offering a potential buyer an item in a store, putting the terms of sale in clear writing, and signing the document before handing it to the potential buyer for their consideration.

8.3 A call for bids or estimates is not considered an offer, but rather a request for an offer or an invitation to negotiate that can be accepted or rejected by the person calling for the bid. To determine whether an advertisement is an invitation to trade or a valid offer, one should carefully examine whether the wording in the advertisement contains sufficient words to demonstrate a commitment to sell. If it contains a positive promise and positive statement of what the advertiser expects in return, the courts will usually hold that the advertisement is an offer. When an advertisement offers a reward for information, it is regarded as a general offer to the public at large, and acceptance of a public offer by anyone results in an enforceable contract.

8.4 A valid acceptance of an offer must be (a) communicated to the offeror and (b) unconditional. An example would be when a buyer informs a seller that the buyer will accept the seller's offer to sell a copy of the daily newspaper for $1.

8.5 An offer can be terminated by (a) lapse of time, (b) revocation, (c) rejection, (d) death or incapacity, or (e) destruction or illegality.

CHAPTER EIGHT ASSESSMENT

MATCHING LEGAL TERMS

Match each of the numbered definitions with the correct term in the following list.

a. acceptance
b. counteroffer
c. invitation to trade
d. lapse of time
e. mailbox rule
f. offeree
g. offeror
h. public offer
i. request for a proposal
j. revocation

1. A new and different response to an offer. **1.** _____

2. A principle that states that an acceptance sent via the postal system or by courier is effective when sent. **2.** _____

3. Agreement to a proposal or an offer. **3.** _____

4. A call for a bid or estimate for materials to be furnished or work to be done. **4.** _____

5. The prevailing legal view of a newspaper advertisement. **5.** _____

6. The offeror's rescinding of an offer that has never been accepted by the offeree. **6.** _____

7. The party to whom an offer is made. **7.** _____

8. The reason for termination of an offer that has not been accepted by the offeree within the time limits specified. **8.** _____

9. An offer to large groups of people, only one of whom can accept. **9.** _____

10. The person who makes an offer. **10.** _____

TRUE/FALSE QUIZ

Indicate whether each of the following statements is true or false.

11. In order for an offer to be valid, it must be definite and certain. **11.** _____

12. In order for an acceptance to be valid, it must be communicated to the offeror. **12.** _____

13. Requests for proposals and announcements asking for bids or estimates are usually considered legally binding offers. 13. _____

14. A newspaper advertisement of goods for sale is usually considered an invitation to trade. 14. _____

15. A direct, unqualified rejection terminates an offer. 15. _____

16. An offer that includes a specific time limit expires automatically when the time is up unless the offeror chooses to extend the time. 16. _____

MULTIPLE CHOICE QUIZ

Indicate the correct answer from the choices following the question.

17. In order for an offer to be valid it must be (a) communicated (b) definite (c) made with serious intent (d) all of the above (e) a and b only. 17. _____

18. An advertisement is usually (a) an offer (b) an acceptance (c) an invitation to trade (d) none of the above. 18. _____

19. A city seeking an estimate from multiple contractors to perform specific work is known as (a) an offer (b) an acceptance (c) a public offer (d) a request for proposal. 19. _____

20. In order for an acceptance to be valid, it must be (a) communicated (b) unconditional (c) both a and b (d) neither a nor b. 20. _____

21. When a reply changes any important term in the offer, it is (a) a counteroffer that requires acceptance from the other party (b) an acceptance on its own (c) a counteroffer that the other party cannot accept (d) none of the above. 21. _____

22. A smart contract (a) does not require offer and acceptance (b) requires offer and acceptance only after the contract begins (c) requires offer and acceptance before the contract begins (d) requires only an offer. 22. _____

23. An offer may be communicated (a) only in writing (b) only in person (c) in writing or in person (d) in writing, in person, or by other means of written or oral communication. 23. _____

24. When an offeree refuses to accept an offer, the offer (a) terminates by lapse of time (b) terminates by rejection (c) terminates due to incapacity (d) terminates due to illegality. 24. _____

25. When an offeree fails to answer by the deadline stated in the offer, the offer (a) terminates by lapse of time (b) terminates by revocation (c) terminates due to incapacity (d) terminates due to illegality. 25. _____

26. When an offeror decides to terminate an offer before acceptance, the offeror has terminated (a) by lapse of time (b) by revocation (c) by rejection (d) by argument of illegality. 26. _____

DISCUSSION QUESTIONS

Answer the following questions and discuss them in class.

27. What are some circumstances that can lead to uncertainty in offers and acceptances, and how can they be avoided?

____

____

28. What are some advantages of written offers and acceptances over spoken ones?

____

____

29. Under what circumstances might a specific time be crucial to a transaction that would justify limiting the time for an offer or acceptance?

____

____

30. When a definite time for acceptance has not been set, when does the acceptance time terminate?

____

____

31. Explain the three requirements of a valid offer.

____

____

32. Explain the two requirements of a valid acceptance.

____

____

THINKING CRITICALLY ABOUT THE LAW

Answer the following questions, which require you to think critically about the legal principles that you learned in this chapter.

33. Offer Why are newspaper advertisements not considered valid offers?

____

____

34. Acceptance Describe the circumstances under which silence on the part of an offeree will be a valid acceptance. Does this seem reasonable and fair?

____

____

35. Counteroffer Why does the law interpret a counteroffer that is a conditional or qualified acceptance as a rejection of the offer and not binding on the parties?

____

____

36. Termination of an Offer If an offer is rejected, should the offeree have the right to negotiate before the offer is considered terminated?

____

____

37. A Question of Ethics Is it appropriate for a city or state official to accept a bid for the performance of work or the purchase of goods or services that is higher than others, even if there are no laws requiring that officials accept the lowest bid?

____

____

CASE QUESTIONS

Study each of the following cases. Answer the questions that follow with Yes or No.

38. Definite and Certain Offer Neto learned that Quan, his neighbor, intended to sell his powerboat. Neto texted Quan stating that he wanted to buy the boat, and he would pay a "fair price." A few days later, Quan sold the boat to someone else for a higher price than Neto would have been willing to pay.

a. Does Neto have a legal course of action against Quan? **a.** _____

b. Is there anything illegal about this case? **b.** _____

c. Can Quan safely ignore Neto's offer because it lacked certainty and definiteness? **c.** _____

d. If Neto had specified a price he was willing to pay, would Quan have been obligated to accept it? **d.** _____

39. Silence as Acceptance Kallinteris opened a travel agency in her small town. She then received an email message from a local office supply company, with which she had no prior dealings, wishing her luck with her new business and advising her that she would soon be receiving $250 worth of office supply items, such as file folders, pens, printer cartridges, and so on, unless she informed the company that she did not want these items. Kallinteris did not respond to the email message and received the supplies a few days later.

a. Does Kallinteris's silence constitute an acceptance of the terms of the agreement? **a.** _____

b. Does a valid contract between Kallinteris and the office supply company exist? **b.** _____

c. If Kallinteris uses the supplies, will she be required to pay for them? **c.** _____

40. Termination of an Offer Redmond offered to sell Goosen her used car for $6,000. Goosen could not make up his mind and, finally, after five months, told Redmond that he would accept her offer.

a. Goosen can accept Redmond's offer even though five months have passed. **a.** _____

b. Goosen cannot accept Redmond's offer due to the doctrine of revocation. **b.** _____

c. Redmond could have required that the offer be accepted within three days. **c.** _____

d. Goosen's statement after five months that he wanted to purchase the car for $6,000 is an offer by him that may be accepted by Redmond if she so chooses. **d.** _____

CASE ANALYSIS

Study each of the following cases carefully. Briefly state the principle of law and your decision.

41. Bids and Estimates Fletcher-Harlee Corp., a general contractor, solicited bids from subcontractors on various aspects of a building project for which it intended to compete. In response, Pote Concrete Contractors Inc. submitted a written price quotation for providing the concrete for the project. Pote, however, indicated that its price quotation was for informational purposes only. Did Pote's bid constitute a valid offer? [*Fletcher-Harlee Corp. v. Pote Concrete Contractors, Inc.,* 2007 U.S. App. LEXIS 7808 (New Jersey)]

Principle of Law:

____

____

Decision:

____

____

42. Counteroffer Browne offered to sell Houlihan his recently purchased 50-inch plasma screen television set for $400. Houlihan sent Browne an email message accepting the offer but asked if she could pay Browne in four equal monthly installments of $100 each. Browne did not acknowledge Houlihan's email and instead later sold the television set to Drew for $450. Houlihan then purchased a new set for $500 and sued Browne for $100, the difference in price. Did Houlihan and Browne have a valid contract, and will Houlihan be able to recover $100 from Browne?

Principle of Law:

____

____

Decision:

43. Silence as Acceptance Bell Microproducts Inc. mailed McGurn an offer of employment that stated that if McGurn was terminated without cause during the first 12 months of employment, he would receive a severance package worth $120,000. McGurn crossed out the number *12,* replaced it with the number *24,* and signed the contract. Bell did not acknowledge the change that had been made to the contract and hired the applicant. McGurn was terminated without cause 13 months later. Did Bell's silence as to McGurn's counteroffer amount to an acceptance? [*McGurn v. Bell Microproducts, Inc.,* 284 F.3d 86 (Massachusetts).]

Principle of Law:

Decision:

44. Valid Offer Sanderson Mart ran an advertisement in the *Daily Tribune* that stated, "Special offer to our customers–3/8-inch Electric Hand Drills, Saturday only–$14.99, only 100 in stock, while they last! Be here when we open for the bargain of the year!" Cruz arrived at the store at 8:00 a.m. when the store opened. The salesperson refused to sell him an electric drill, claiming that he had only two in stock and those were already set aside for another customer–and besides, the advertisement was not really a binding offer. Will Sanderson be required to sell the electric drill for the advertised price?

Principle of Law:

Decision:

LEGAL RESEARCH

Complete the following activities. Share your findings with the class.

45. Working in Teams In teams of three or four, interview a local retailer and ask him or her how, when planning and writing advertising copy, he or she avoids wording that might cause a reader to regard the ad as a definite offer, instead of simply an advertisement.

____

____

46. Using Technology Using the Internet and search engines, locate websites that offer goods and services for sale and that specify time periods during which such offers must be accepted.

____

____

chapter 9

Mutual Agreement

LEARNING OUTCOMES

After studying this chapter and completing the assessment, you will be able to

9.1 List seven ways in which a lack of a meeting of the minds may cause defective agreements.

9.2 Identify the elements of fraud.

9.3 Explain misrepresentation and how it differs from fraud.

9.4 Explain the concept of mistake in the eyes of the law.

9.5 Define *undue influence* and explain its impact upon the validity of a contract.

9.6 Describe duress and the forms that it may take.

9.7 Define *contracts of adhesion* and describe the conditions under which these contracts are voidable.

9.8 Define *unconscionable contracts.*

LEGAL terms

- fraud
- puffing
- misrepresentation
- mistake
- undue influence
- duress
- contract of adhesion
- unconscionable contract

MUTUAL AGREEMENT

"Make fair agreements and stick to them."

Confucius, renowned Chinese teacher, philosopher, and political theorist

Jupiterimages/Getty Images

9.1 DEFECTIVE AGREEMENTS

In Chapter 7, the six elements of an enforceable contract were discussed. Potential problems with achieving a meeting of the minds, the second of these essential elements, are discussed in this chapter.

Genuineness, or reality, of agreement is said to be present in a contract when there is a true meeting of the minds of the parties. If there is any misunderstanding or if any force or deception is used by either party to obtain the necessary agreement of the other party, the contract is voidable and may be disaffirmed at the option of the injured party. A voidable contract results if agreement of either party is obtained by fraud, misrepresentation, mistake, undue influence, or duress, or if the contract is one of adhesion or is unconscionable. Each of these terms will be explained in this chapter.

Depending on the type of defect, one or both parties to the contract can raise the issue during the executory stage of the contract to void the contract based on lack of mutual agreement. However, one should note that this argument is not available during the executory stage of a smart contract, since neither the parties nor a court of law can prevent the execution of the terms of a smart contract on the blockchain platform.

9.2 FRAUD

Fraud is the intentional misstatement or nondisclosure of a material fact made by one party in an attempt to influence the actions of another party. It does not matter how the fraud is committed. It may be by spoken or written words or by acts or conduct. Regardless of how the fraud is committed, the party who relies on the misstatement or nondisclosure must suffer a loss as a result of the act.

fraud
The intentional misstatement or nondisclosure of a material (essential) fact made by one party in an attempt to influence the actions of another party.

In order to prove a fraud case, a plaintiff must demonstrate five elements:

1. A misstatement or nondisclosure of a material fact.
2. Knowledge of its falsity or reckless disregard of its truth.
3. Intent to cause the other party to enter into the agreement.
4. Reliance by the injured party.
5. Harm to the injured party (financial, physical, or both).

EXAMPLE 9.1

▶ Eppers went to Micro New Age Computer Store to buy a personal computer, so he could process his large collection of digital photos. Donaldson, the owner of the store, quickly sensed that Eppers did not know much about computers and also recognized that Eppers was unfamiliar with how much memory would be necessary to run most available photo-processing software packages. In response to Eppers's questions about the memory of a particular model, Donaldson assured him that the model would accommodate any software on the market and any likely to be developed in the foreseeable future. Eppers, relying on Donaldson's assurances, bought the model that was recommended. To his dismay, Eppers quickly discovered that the memory was inadequate for many popular photo-processing software programs.

The law allows for a certain amount of "sales talk," or puffing, that is not considered fraudulent.
Graham Oliver/Getty Images

Now reexamine the case:

1. Was there a misstatement or nondisclosure of a material fact? Yes, the misstatement was of a material fact. Memory capacity is a vital part of computer equipment.
2. Was the misstatement made intentionally or recklessly? Yes, Donaldson either knew, or should have known, that the memory was inadequate for many programs.
3. Was the misstatement made with intent to deceive Eppers? Yes, Donaldson knew that the memory was important to Eppers.
4. Did Eppers rely on Donaldson's statements and act on them? Yes, Eppers bought the computer that Donaldson recommended.
5. Did Eppers suffer a loss as a result of his reliance on the false statements? Yes, Eppers would need to increase memory at an added cost in order to use the computer as he had intended.

puffing
A general expression of opinion, typically in a sales context, that is used to persuade a prospective purchaser to buy. It does not constitute a misrepresentation of material text.

It is important to recognize the difference between a fraudulent statement and a salesperson's puffing, which is considered a mere expression of opinion. Most salespeople use persuasive statements in an effort to induce a prospective purchaser to buy. In Example 9.1, assume Donaldson also used statements such as "This machine is the best buy in town" and "This computer is as good as the well-known brands." In the eyes of the law, these statements are merely "dealer's talk" and are not considered misstatements of material facts. Puffing refers to generalities and, at times, is directed toward the five senses (the suit looks great, the cola tastes crisp and fresh, the facial tissues feel soft).

Intentional concealment or intentional nondisclosure of material facts (deliberately hiding important information) is just as fraudulent as making false statements. Suppose that, in Example 9.1, Donaldson did not comment on the adequacy of the computer memory but knew from Eppers's comments that he intended to use it with a particular brand of software, and Donaldson knew, or should have known, that the computer sold to Eppers was not adequate. Because Eppers relied on Donaldson's information, it appears that Donaldson was guilty of intentional concealment or intentional nondisclosure. In order to avoid a case of fraud, a seller must disclose pertinent facts that a buyer might not inquire about or notice during a reasonable inspection.

9.3 MISREPRESENTATION

misrepresentation
A misstatement of a material fact that results in inducing another to enter into an agreement to their injury.

Misrepresentation is the unintentional misstatement or nondisclosure of a material fact that results in inducing another to enter into an agreement to their loss. (Remember that when the misstatement is made knowingly or recklessly, it is, as previously discussed, fraud.)

It is important to note the distinction between fraud and misrepresentation because the remedy is different. An injured party who can successfully prove fraud may have the contract canceled and bring suit for damages. If the party can prove only misrepresentation, the contract can be canceled, but the injured party cannot sue for additional damages.

EXAMPLE 9.2

▶ Arnold hired BluWater Pool Company to build a swimming pool in his backyard. It was only after construction had begun that Arnold learned from a neighbor that local zoning ordinances prohibited backyard swimming pools in the community. The salesperson for BluWater admitted that he had been thinking about another community where no prohibitions existed. Arnold may void the contract, but he may not seek additional damages because BluWater's misrepresentation was unintentional and not fraudulent.

9.4 MISTAKE

In the eyes of the law, a **mistake** is a belief that is not in accord with the facts. Mistakes relating to contracts may be concerned with the nature of the subject matter or the quality of the subject matter. Obviously not every erroneous idea or notion is a mistake, and the law makes it clear that the mistaken belief must concern an existing fact and not a belief about what might happen in the future. Court decisions involving mistakes are often complex, and the courts attempt to determine whether the mistake was "unilateral" (i.e., made by only one party) or whether the mistake was "mutual" (i.e., made by both parties). For a contract to be dissolved because of a mistake, the law usually requires that both parties be a part of the misunderstanding–that is, the mistake must be mutual.

mistake
A belief that is not in accord with the facts.

EXAMPLE 9.3

▶ Chin, a collector of rare paintings, offered to sell a particular Picasso painting (catalog number 1401) to Kovacs for $14,000. When it came time to exchange the painting for the money, it was obvious that Kovacs was expecting a different Picasso (catalog number 1410) and not the catalog number 1401 that Chin had expected to sell. Chin also was surprised because he thought Kovacs wanted to buy catalog number 1401. The contract can be canceled by either party because this was a mutual mistake.

9.5 UNDUE INFLUENCE

Sometimes a person has the power to control the actions of another because of a special or confidential relationship to that person. Such relationships are sometimes found between employer and employee, physician or nurse and patient, teacher and student, attorney and client, and so on. When someone uses this power improperly to their personal advantage, **undue influence** is said to exist. A contract resulting from the use of undue influence is voidable at the option of the party wrongfully influenced.

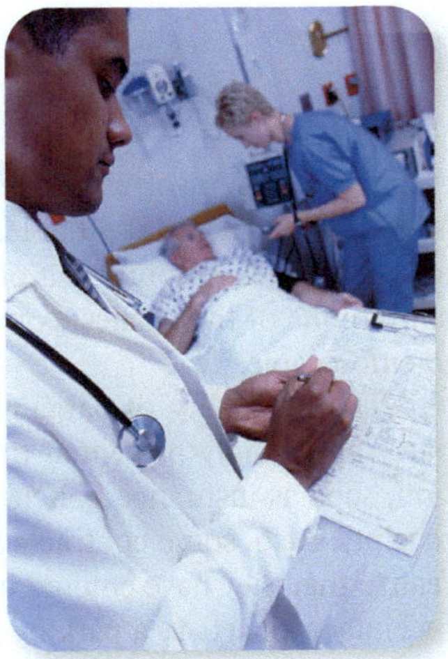

A physician may have the power to control the actions of their patients because of a special or confidential relationship.
Stockbyte/Getty Images

undue influence
The improper use of excessive pressure by the dominant member of a confidential relationship to convince the weaker party to enter a contract that greatly benefits the dominant party.

EXAMPLE 9.4

Hsu, a professor of electrical engineering, was working with a foreign student, Placido, on a new ceramic compound in the field of superconductivity. Hsu encouraged his student to continue his research and said that he would undertake to secure the patent on the new compound in both names. Placido was suspicious about the arrangement suggested by Hsu but recognized Hsu's influence over him. Once the patent was issued, Placido realized that it was his work and inventiveness that had resulted in the new compound—and not that of his professor. In this case, the court would likely find that the relationship between professor and student resulted in undue influence.

9.6 DURESS

duress
The act of applying unlawful or improper pressure or influence to a person to gain their agreement to a contract.

Duress is the act of applying unlawful or improper pressure or influence to a person in order to gain their agreement to a contract. Such pressure can take the form of a threat of bodily harm to an individual or to their family or the threat of serious loss or damage to their property. When threats are used to force someone to enter into a contract, the agreement may be dissolved by the injured party.

EXAMPLE 9.5

Brent, the owner of a small trucking company, called on Goodwin, president of Goodwin Manufacturing Company, to sell his company's trucking services. As they concluded their conversation, Brent indicated that it would be a good idea to agree to hire Brent's company to handle Goodwin's trucking needs because other companies that did not utilize Brent's company's services often experienced unexpected fires. Brent's message was clearly a threat, and Goodwin agreed to sign the contract for trucking services. The contract is voidable and could be rescinded by Goodwin because of the duress applied by Brent.

contract of adhesion
A contract drawn by one party that must be accepted as is on a take-it-or-leave-it basis.

9.7 CONTRACTS OF ADHESION

An admission ticket may be a contract of adhesion.
Jupiterimages/Brand X Pictures/Alamy

A contract that involves parties who have unequal bargaining power is known as a contract of adhesion. These take-it-or-leave-it contracts are quite common and are normally enforceable. But when enforcement of an otherwise legal contract will result in a significant hardship to one of the parties, courts have considered such agreements to be so unfair as to be unenforceable.

The inequality of bargaining power can exist in contracts that are prepared by one party and simply presented to the other without the opportunity for meaningful negotiation, such as insurance policies or the disclaimers printed on ticket stubs and dry cleaning receipts. Also, some contracts have become so routine that one of the parties may not even realize that they have entered into a contract—an example would be checkroom and luggage receipts or tickets to a parking garage or a theater.

EXAMPLE 9.6

▶ Lorenz brought several expensive shirts to a laundry service for cleaning. A note on the receipt he was given indicated that the establishment was not responsible for goods left over 30 days. Lorenz attempted to pick up his shirts 35 days later and was told that, under the terms of the contract, he was not entitled to their return. The "30-day" clause would be a contract of adhesion, and Lorenz would be entitled to get back his apparel.

9.8 UNCONSCIONABLE CONTRACTS

A contract that is regarded as shockingly unjust or unfair is said to be an unconscionable contract. While courts have long been reluctant to uphold these, more recently the UCC has made such contracts even less likely to be enforced. The Code states, "If the court as a matter of law finds the contract or any clause of the contract to have been unconscionable at the time it was made, the court may refuse to enforce the contract, or it may enforce the remainder of the contract without the unconscionable clause, or it may so limit the application of any unconscionable clause as to avoid any unconscionable result."*

unconscionable contract A contract that is so one-sided that it is oppressive and gives unfair advantage to one of the parties.

When the UCC was written, it was intended that the unconscionable clause would apply only to sales of goods. In recent years, however, virtually the only successful use of unconscionability under the Code has been made by consumers in various kinds of contracts involving such acts as making home improvements, opening a checking account, leasing a gasoline filling station, and leasing an apartment. For example, the UCC has been cited to cancel contracts where one party has written agreements in such a way as to take an obvious unfair advantage of another party who lacked familiarity with the English language.

EXAMPLE 9.7

▶ The sales representative for Frostifresh Corporation sold a freezer to Reynoso, who spoke little English. The salesperson neither translated nor explained the contract, but told Reynoso that the freezer would cost nothing because he would receive a bonus of $25 for each sale made to his friends. The total price of the freezer, made with periodic payments, would have been more than $1,100. The cash price would have been $900, and the wholesale price to the company was $348. The court ruled that the contract was unconscionable and awarded the company a reasonable profit, service and finance charges, and its own cost of $348. [*Frostifresh Corp. v. Reynoso,* 274 N.Y.S.2d 757 (Dist. Ct. 1966), *rev'd on other grounds,* 281 N.Y.S.2d 964 (Sup. Ct. App. Term 1967)]

*The Uniform Commercial Code (UCC) is a joint project between the National Conference of Commissioners on Uniform State Laws (NCCUSL) and the American Law Institute (ALI).

CHAPTER SUMMARY

9.1 Seven ways in which a lack of a meeting of the minds may interfere with the legal enforcement of agreements include cases involving (a) fraud, (b) misrepresentation, (c) mistake, (d) undue influence, (e) duress, (f) contracts of adhesion, and (g) unconscionable contracts.

9.2 Fraud (a) is a misstatement or nondisclosure of a material fact, (b) is made with knowledge of its falsity or with reckless disregard of its truth, (c) is made with the intention of causing the other party to enter into the agreement, (d) is relied on by the injured party, and (e) results in loss to the injured party.

9.3 Misrepresentation (a) is the unintentional misstatement or nondisclosure of a material fact, (b) results in inducing another to enter into an agreement, and (c) results in loss to the injured party.

9.4 A mistake is a belief that is not in accord with the facts. Mistakes relating to contracts may be concerned with the nature of the subject matter or the quality of the subject matter.

9.5 Undue influence is the improper use of power to control the actions of another because of a special or confidential relationship to that person. A contract resulting from the use of undue influence is voidable at the option of the party wrongfully influenced.

9.6 Duress is the act of applying unlawful or improper pressure or influence to a person in order to gain their agreement to a contract. Such pressure can take the form of a threat of bodily harm to an individual or to their family or the threat of serious loss or damage to their property.

9.7 Contracts of adhesion are contracts that involve parties who have unequal bargaining power. When enforcement of an otherwise legal contract will result in a significant hardship to one of the parties, courts have considered such agreements to be so unfair as to be unenforceable.

9.8 Unconscionable contracts are contracts that are regarded as shockingly unjust or unfair.

CHAPTER NINE ASSESSMENT

MATCHING LEGAL TERMS

Match each of the numbered definitions with the correct term in the following list.

a. contract of adhesion
b. duress
c. fraud
d. intentional concealment
e. misrepresentation
f. mistake
g. mutual agreement
h. puffing
i. unconscionable contract
j. undue influence

1. A contract regarded as shockingly unfair and unjust. **1.** _____

2. Domination of a person's will by force or by threat of force or injury. **2.** _____

3. A contract characterized by unequal bargaining power of the parties. **3.** _____

4. A "meeting of the minds." **4.** _____

5. Intentional misstatement of a material fact. **5.** _____

6. Purposely not disclosing material facts to a contracting party. **6.** _____

7. The power to control the actions of another that results from a special or confidential relationship. **7.** _____

8. Unintentional misstatement of a material fact. **8.** _____

9. A belief not in accord with the facts that may be concerned with the nature of the subject matter or the quality of the subject matter. **9.** _____

10. A mere expression of opinion. **10.** _____

TRUE/FALSE QUIZ

Indicate whether each of the following statements is true or false.

11. Intentional concealment of material facts is just as fraudulent as making false statements. **11.** _____

12. When threats are used to force someone to enter into a contract, the agreement may be dissolved by either party. **12.** _____

13. The distinction between fraud and misrepresentation is important because the remedies available to an injured party are different. **13.** _____

14. For a contract to be dissolved because of a mistake, the law usually requires that the mistake be mutual. **14.** _____

15. A contract of adhesion is characterized by unequal bargaining power of the parties. **15.** _____

16. A contract considered shockingly unjust or unfair is an unconscionable contract. **16.** _____

MULTIPLE CHOICE QUIZ

Indicate the correct answer from the choices following each question.

17. Which of the following would *not* invalidate a contract due to mutual agreement? (a) Duress (b) Lack of written document (c) Mistake (d) Contract of adhesion. **17.** _____

18. A contract lacking mutual agreement is (a) voidable at the option of the injured party (b) automatically void (c) neither void nor voidable (d) both void and voidable. **18.** _____

19. Fraud requires (a) written words presented as fact (b) either spoken or written words presented as fact (c) neither spoken nor written words (d) only an opinion by either party. **19.** _____

20. Fraud occurs when a party (a) intentionally misrepresents facts (b) unintentionally misrepresents facts (c) intentionally mispresents an opinion (d) none of the above. **20.** _____

21. Misrepresentation occurs when a party (a) intentionally misrepresents facts (b) unintentionally misrepresents facts (c) intentionally misrepresents an opinion (d) none of the above. **21.** _____

22. Both fraud and misrepresentation require (a) that the statements at issue be in writing (b) that the statements be intentional (c) that the statements result in loss to the injured party (d) none of the above. **22.** _____

23. When arguing that a contract should be voided due to mistake, the courts generally require that (a) only one party has been mistaken (b) neither party has been mistaken (c) both parties have been mistaken (d) none of the above. **23.** _____

24. An example of a contract involving undue influence would be (a) between two friends (b) between salespeople at different firms (c) between physician and patient (d) between executives at different firms. **24.** _____

25. An example of duress would be (a) threat of physical force (b) threat to a family member (c) threat of damage to property (d) all of the above. **25.** _____

26. An example of a contract of adhesion would be (a) a contract for laundry services that disclaims liability for damage (b) a contract to purchase goods for a business (c) a preprinted contract for insurance (d) a and c. **26.** _____

DISCUSSION QUESTIONS

Answer the following questions and discuss them in class.

27. List five elements an injured party must prove in order to claim fraud.

28. Explain the distinction between fraud and misrepresentation.

29. Explain the UCC provision relating to when a contract is unconscionable.

30. What are some examples of duress?

31. Persuasive statements based on a salesperson's opinion are referred to as puffing. Provide examples of typical sales situations in which puffing is used.

32. What are some examples of undue influence?

THINKING CRITICALLY ABOUT THE LAW

Answer the following questions, which require you to think critically about the legal principles that you learned in this chapter.

33. Material Fact How should a court decide whether a particular term in a contract is material?

34. Mistake Why does the law provide that a mistake must be mutual, and not unilateral, in order for a contract to be voidable?

35. Undue Influence versus Duress When does an abuse of power to control the actions of another because of a special or confidential relationship go beyond undue influence and become duress?

36. Unconscionable Contracts What criteria should a court use in determining whether a contract is shockingly unjust or unfair and thus unconscionable?

37. A Question of Ethics Is the failure to disclose material facts or information to a prospective buyer fair and ethical?

CASE QUESTIONS

Study each of the following cases. Answer the questions that follow with Yes or No.

38. Undue Influence Guss, a professor at a small college, offered to sell his five-year-old car to Kantrowitz, a student in one of his classes. The price Guss asked was well above market value. Kantrowitz accepted Guss's offer without even test-driving the car.

a. Is the contract between Guss and Kantrowitz voidable by either Guss or Kantrowitz? **a.** _____

b. Is the contract between Guss and Kantrowitz voidable only by Guss? **b.** _____

c. Is this a contract of adhesion? **c.** _____

d. Is this an example of misrepresentation? **d.** _____

39. Intentional Concealment Gortino, while trying to sell his house to Gawlas, was asked if he had ever seen or suspected termites in the house. Gortino replied that he had not and that the house was sound. Several months after Gawlas had purchased the house, she learned from neighbors that Gortino had paid for soil treatment to eliminate termites.

a. Can the contract for sale be canceled because of fraud? **a.** _____

b. Was there a misstatement of a material fact? **b.** _____

c. Did Gawlas suffer a loss as a result of Gortino's actions? **c.** _____

d. Can Gawlas sue for damages? **d.** _____

40. Voidable Contract Gallagher Restaurant Supply was in the business of leasing equipment to small restaurants. Quezada, the operator of a small diner, leased a coffeemaker from Gallagher. It was only after the contract had been signed that Quezada learned that similar lease agreements with other restaurants were far less costly. Also, the agreement between the parties provided for an accelerated payment of the entire balance if Quezada failed to perform any condition of the lease, "no matter how trivial the condition may be." In addition, Gallagher would be entitled to take back the coffeemaker and collect a 20 percent penalty.

a. Is this an example of a contract signed under duress? **a.** _____

b. Is it likely that a court would enforce this contract? **b.** _____

c. Is this an example of a void contract? **c.** _____

d. Is this an example of a voidable contract? **d.** _____

CASE ANALYSIS

Study each of the following cases carefully. Briefly state the principle of law and your decision.

41. Mutual Mistake Brooking agreed to sell a tract of land to Dover Pool & Racquet Club Inc. on which Dover planned to build a swim and tennis club. Neither party to the contract knew that just before the contract was signed, the local zoning board of the town in which the land was located published a notice of public hearings on a proposal to amend the zoning in a way that would have prevented Dover from using the land as it had planned to do. Will this contract be enforced? [*Dover Pool & Racquet Club, Inc. v. Brooking,* 322 N.E.2d 168 (Massachusetts)]

Principle of Law:

____

____

Decision:

____

____

42. Contract of Adhesion Weaver, a high school dropout, leased a gas station from American Oil Company and signed a standard agreement prepared by the oil company's lawyers. The lease (contract) contained a clause in fine print that provided that the oil company would not be liable for any injury occurring on the premises regardless of fault. No one representing the oil company called Weaver's attention to the clause or explained it to him. In addition, the lease provided that Weaver would have to pay American Oil for any loss or damages, even if they resulted from the oil company's negligence. An employee of the oil company spilled gasoline on Weaver and his assistant, causing them to be burned and injured. The oil company brought an action seeking to be relieved of liability for the injury and to have Weaver held liable for any damages to the assistant. Will the contract provision for Weaver being held liable be enforced? [*Weaver v. American Oil Co.,* 276 N.E.2d 144 (Indiana)]

Principle of Law:

____

____

Decision:

____

____

43. Misrepresentation Malina, the owner of an old, multistory factory building, offered to lease the building to Larson, a manufacturer. Larson wanted to know whether the construction of the floors was strong enough to support the heavy machinery he planned to install. Malina assured him that the floors would support any machinery brought into the building. After the lease was signed, Larson's engineer studied the construction and reported that the floors would hold only half of the machinery that Larson planned to install. Is Larson bound by the lease?

Principle of Law:

____

____

Decision:

____

____

44. Fraud Power-Sports wished to obtain Harley-Davidson's permission to purchase a motorcycle dealership. Power-Sports provided written and oral statements about its business model, and based upon these statements, Harley-Davidson approved the purchase. Later Harley-Davidson learned that Power-Sports was operating in a manner inconsistent with its statements about its business model. Harley-Davidson sued for damages. Will Harley-Davidson be successful in its lawsuit against Power-Sports? [*Harley-Davidson Motor Company v. Power-Sports, Inc.*, 319 F.3d 973 (Wisconsin)]

Principle of Law:

Decision:

LEGAL RESEARCH

Complete the following activities. Share your findings with the class.

45. Working in Teams In teams of three or four, visit local dry cleaning establishments, movie theaters, or parking garages. Ask them to allow you to view their receipts, and identify terms that might be viewed as contracts of adhesion.

46. Using Technology Using the Internet and search engines, investigate "unconscionable contracts"; then, with additional research, find examples of existing legislation in several jurisdictions that concern such contracts. Share your findings with the class.

chapter 10
Consideration

LEARNING OUTCOMES

After studying this chapter and completing the assessment, you will be able to

10.1 Explain consideration and define *forbearance*.

10.2 Identify and explain the three essential characteristics of valid consideration.

10.3 Describe the kinds of valid consideration, including (a) a promise for a promise, (b) a promise of forbearance, and (c) a pledge or subscription.

10.4 Discuss the situations in which the UCC dispenses with the requirement of consideration in contracts to sell goods.

10.5 Define the term *general release*.

10.6 Identify five kinds of agreements that lack consideration.

CONSIDERATION

"The law 'an eye for an eye' makes the whole world blind."

Mahatma Gandhi, respected spiritual and political Indian leader

Jim Arbogast/Getty Images

LEGAL terms

- forbearance
- promisor
- promisee
- pledge
- general release
- barren promise
- preexisting duty
- gratuitous promise
- illusory promise
- moral consideration
- past consideration

10.1 THE NATURE OF CONSIDERATION

forbearance
The promise to refrain from doing something that a party has a legal right to do.

promisor
In the making of a contract, the party who makes a promise.

promisee
In the making of a contract, the party to whom a promise is made.

Consideration was defined in Chapter 7 as the promises exchanged by the parties to a contract: to give up something of value they have a legal right to keep, such as money or property; to do something they are not otherwise legally required to do, such as performing a service; or to refrain from an action. The promise to refrain from doing something that a party has a legal right to do, or the promise of inaction, is known as forbearance.

Consideration in a contract may be more than just the promises exchanged by the parties; it may include the actual benefit gained and the detriment suffered by them. A party who makes a promise, the promisor, may make a promise to pay a sum of money to another party, the promisee, for the performance of a certain act.

EXAMPLE 10.1

Pollard promised to pay his 19-year-old nephew $3,000 on his 22nd birthday if he refrained from smoking cigarettes until he graduated from Northern State College.

This contract is legal and illustrates the promise of forbearance as consideration. Although it seems unlikely that Pollard would break his promise or that his nephew would bring suit to collect, it is possible. For example, if Pollard were to die before his nephew's 22nd birthday, the executors of his estate might not wish to pay, and the nephew might want to sue to collect.

EXAMPLE 10.2

Lund, a homeowner, promised to pay $600 to Carposi to install a new Wi-Fi network on Lund's property. In this example, Lund (the promisor) made a promise to pay a sum of money to Carposi (the promisee) for the performance of a certain act. The consideration of the promisor is the money ($600), and the consideration of the promisee is the performance of the act (installing the Wi-Fi network).

10.2 CHARACTERISTICS OF VALID CONSIDERATION

There are three essential characteristics of valid consideration: (1) legality, (2) adequacy, and (3) the possibility of performance.

LEGALITY OF CONSIDERATION

If the contract in Example 10.1 required the nephew to obey all traffic laws, it would not be enforceable because the nephew is legally required to obey these laws anyway. Also, a valid contract does not exist if the consideration is a promise to perform an illegal act or to avoid performing an act that is legally required to be performed.

ADEQUACY OF CONSIDERATION

Traditionally, the courts generally made no attempt to judge whether or not the exchange of promises in a contract was fair–that is, whether there was adequacy of consideration. The law assumed that, as long as no undue pressure was brought to bear, the parties were free to reject a proposed unfair contract. In recent times, however, society has recognized some of the problems associated with contractual relationships in which the unrestricted bargaining power of one party gives them an unfair advantage when dealing with another party who lacks the economic power or the education to enter into contracts on an equal footing.

In an attempt to level the playing field, many consumer protection statutes have been passed. The notions of unconscionable contracts (contracts that are shockingly unfair and unjust) and contracts of adhesion (contracts in which the parties have unequal bargaining power) are now widely applied. These concepts were discussed in Chapter 9.

POSSIBILITY OF PERFORMANCE

A legally enforceable contract cannot be based on a promise that is impossible to fulfill. However, a party who promises to do something that is merely difficult to perform, or poses unforeseen expenses, is still bound by the terms of the contract.

EXAMPLE 10.3

▶ Hicky operated a small processing plant that added certain finishing processes to other companies' partially manufactured products. Hicky bid successfully on a job to spray-paint assembled products. Subsequently, Hicky learned that local safety regulations required that spray-painting be done in ventilated paint booths, which Hicky's plant did not have. His choices narrowed down to (1) installing the required booths at great expense, (2) paying considerably higher insurance premiums and fines for violating the regulations, or (3) outsourcing the spray-painting job at additional expense to another company that could meet the ventilation requirements. For all three alternatives, Hicky would lose money on the spray-painting contract. Because the contract is valid and enforceable, if Hicky chose to break the agreement, he would be subject to suit for breach of contract.

10.3 KINDS OF VALID CONSIDERATION

Consideration required in an enforceable contract can take various forms: exchange of promises, forbearance, and pledges or subscriptions.

A PROMISE FOR A PROMISE

As indicated earlier in this chapter, the most common form of valid consideration is the promise of money by one party for the promise of an act by another. Example 10.1, discussed earlier, illustrates this point. It should be noted that the mere promise to act is usually deemed valid consideration. Whether or not the promise is actually carried out is another matter, having to do with the execution of the contract terms and, specifically, with the issue of performance by the parties. The law provides certain remedies to a wronged party where there is partial performance or nonperformance of a promised act (discussed in Chapter 15). A promise of an act by one party in exchange for the promise of an act by another is also considered valid consideration. In other words, the exchange of money is not a requirement.

EXAMPLE 10.4

Carleo promised to repair Mills's car if Mills painted one of Carleo's rooms. The exchange of promises would be considered valid consideration even though no money actually changed hands.

A PROMISE OF FORBEARANCE

Valid consideration is not necessarily either the performance of an act or the payment of money. One party to a contract may, for a variety of reasons, wish to exchange their promise to pay money for a promise of inaction from the other party. Many contracts in which part of the consideration is forbearance involve agreements not to compete (to be discussed in greater detail in Chapter 28). Notice that in Example 10.5, part of the consideration is a promise not to act.

EXAMPLE 10.5

Kim agreed to purchase a fruit and vegetable business from Rosen for a certain price if Rosen promised to refrain from opening another fruit and vegetable business in the same town for three years. In this case, Kim's consideration was his promise to pay the agreed selling price for Rosen's business. Rosen's consideration was her promise to (1) transfer the business to Kim and (2) avoid opening a similar business in the same town for three years (forbearance).

Charitable organizations frequently raise money by asking for pledges.
David Gould/Photographer's Choice RF/Getty Images

pledge
A promise to donate money to a church, temple, mosque, hospital, college, cultural institution, or other charitable organization.

A PLEDGE OR SUBSCRIPTION

Churches, temples, mosques, hospitals, colleges, cultural institutions, charitable organizations, and other groups frequently raise money by asking for a pledge or subscription (a promise to donate money). Are these pledges enforceable? What is the consideration? What benefit is gained by the person making the pledge? Because these pledges are usually for some worthy cause, the courts have generally held that they are enforceable. Some courts have held that the consideration given by the charitable institution is the promise to use the money for the purpose for which it was donated. Other courts have held that the consideration is the promises of all the other parties who have donated to the same cause. Still other courts hold that, if the charitable institution has made commitments to spend the money as a result of relying on the promises, the subscriptions are enforceable. Despite their right to sue for donations promised but never paid, very few charitable organizations sue donors because suing could affect their ability to raise future contributions.

10.4 CONSIDERATION AND THE UNIFORM COMMERCIAL CODE

In some cases that involve contracts to sell goods, the Uniform Commercial Code (UCC) dispenses with the requirement of consideration in certain contracts that involve any of the following:

- A merchant's written firm offer that provides that the contract is irrevocable.
- A written discharge of a claim for an alleged breach of contract.
- Modifications of existing contracts (UCC 2-209).

EXAMPLE 10.6

- Sullivan and Baker agreed that Sullivan would sell 5,000 imported shirts to Baker at a certain price to be delivered by May 15. Sullivan learned that he would be unable to meet the delivery date because of transportation delays. He contacted Baker, who agreed to an extension of the time of delivery. Later, Baker had a change of heart and demanded that the goods be delivered by the original date. Under the UCC, Baker is bound by the agreed modification even though Sullivan gave no additional consideration for the extension of the delivery date.

10.5 GENERAL RELEASE

Statutes in many states have permitted a person who has a claim against another to give up, or release, their claim without an exchange of consideration by making a written statement to that effect. The UCC provides that "any claim or right arising out of an alleged breach can be discharged in whole or in part without consideration by a written waiver or renunciation signed and delivered by the aggrieved party" (UCC 2A-107).* Such a written agreement is called a general release. Figure 10.1 is an illustration of a general release.

general release
A written agreement in which an aggrieved party can discharge in whole or in part a claim resulting from an alleged breach of contract.

General Release

July 1, 20–

The Conway Resort Hotel hereby releases Mary Jacobson from all obligations on her account as of this date.

Conway Resort Hotel

Frank Conway

FIGURE 10.1 General Release

*The Uniform Commercial Code (UCC) is a joint project between the National Conference of Commissioners on Uniform State Laws (NCCUSL) and the American Law Institute (ALI).

A general release may be regarded as valid consideration if the parties so intend. In such cases, the general release would be viewed as forbearance.

In some states, a general release is supported by consideration only where the original claim that is being released is not regarded by the courts as frivolous—that is, the plaintiff would have had almost no chance of success had the case gone to court. If the original claim is deemed frivolous, there is no forbearance because, in effect, the releasing party is not giving up anything.

10.6 AGREEMENTS THAT LACK CONSIDERATION

barren promise
A promise to pay an existing debt or to obey the law, or a similar promise of something already owed.

preexisting duty
An obligation that a party is already bound to by law or by some other agreement. The party may not use this as consideration in a new contract.

Certain agreements are not enforceable because they lack consideration.

BARREN PROMISES

A promise to do something that one is already required to do either by law or by contract represents no additional sacrifice and is not valid consideration. A promise to pay an existing debt or to obey the law, or a similar promise, is called a barren promise, and the obligation to perform acts already required is known as a preexisting duty.

EXAMPLE 10.7

The First State Bank was robbed of more than $300,000 by three armed men. The local bankers' association advertised a reward of $10,000 for the arrest and conviction of each bank robber. In time, all three robbers were convicted. Claims to the reward were made by a number of people, including employees of the bank and the police officers who arrested the robbers. The court ruled that neither the bank employees nor the police were able to collect the reward because they already had a preexisting duty to aid in the capture of the criminals. Another police officer from another county, who had no duty to assist in this case, was allowed to collect the reward.

GRATUITOUS PROMISES

gratuitous promise
A promise that does not require some benefit in return.

A person who makes a promise without requiring some benefit in return has made a gratuitous promise. Agreements based on such one-sided promises are generally not enforceable. A promise to give a gift is a gratuitous promise—that is, one that is made without receiving anything in return. Because there is no consideration, the promise is not binding. Once a promised gift is presented or delivered, however, the transfer of ownership is complete and consideration is not required (see Chapter 24).

EXAMPLE 10.8

Taylor and Ryan were good friends and golfing enthusiasts. Taylor promised Ryan that when he returned from a golf competition, he would give Ryan the clubs he used in the match. During the competition, he learned the resale value of the clubs was greater than he had originally thought, and he changed his mind. Taylor is under no obligation to fulfill the promise because there was no consideration—that is, it was a gratuitous promise.

ILLUSORY PROMISES

An illusory promise consists of an indefinite, open-ended statement purporting to be an agreement. An illusory promise is neither consideration nor an enforceable agreement. A person who makes an illusory promise never commits to a specific or absolute act. For example, a contractor who is purchasing lumber and tells a lumberyard associate, "If your lumber is high quality, I will buy all of the lumber I need from you," is making an illusory promise.

A gratuitous promise to give golf clubs to another is generally not enforceable.
Mike Flippo/Shutterstock

illusory promise
One that consists of an indefinite, open-ended statement purporting to be an agreement.

AGREEMENTS SUPPORTED BY MORAL CONSIDERATION

A person is not legally bound to do what they may feel obligated to do because of love, friendship, honor, sympathy, conscience, or some other moral consideration. Some courts, however, will justify the enforcement of some contracts, even though there is no consideration, by stating that there was "moral consideration." A further explanation is that the enforcement of certain contracts is socially beneficial.

moral consideration
Something that a person is not legally bound to do but that they may feel bound to do because of love, friendship, honor, sympathy, conscience, or other reason.

EXAMPLE 10.9

- Gerber, the owner of Nail Style, a fingernail styling salon, had many financial obligations to suppliers, as well as to the landlord of the building where the salon was located. When the firm failed and Gerber declared bankruptcy, he was legally, but perhaps not morally, relieved of his obligations to pay his creditors. Gerber made a gratuitous promise, based on his own values, to pay the now-forgiven debts from future earnings. Many courts would agree that the promise is enforceable even though there was no consideration.

AGREEMENTS SUPPORTED BY PAST CONSIDERATION

Past consideration is a promise to repay someone for a benefit after it has been received. Such a promise is generally not valid consideration and is considered a gratuitous promise, except in cases such as those described in the discussion of moral consideration.

past consideration
A promise to repay someone for a benefit after it has been received.

EXAMPLE 10.10

- George Welt promised Frank Welt, his younger brother, that he would give him a round-trip ticket to Paris if Frank graduated from a particular college. Frank graduated as agreed, and George gave him the plane ticket. When Frank realized how expensive the ticket was, he promised to pay George one-half of the round-trip fare. Frank later changed his mind and decided not to keep his promise. Frank will not be legally held to his promise because it was based on past consideration.

CHAPTER SUMMARY

10.1 Consideration is the promises exchanged by the parties to a contract: to give up something of value they have a legal right to keep, to do something they are not otherwise legally required to do, or to refrain from an action. The promise to refrain from doing something that a party has a legal right to do, or the promise of inaction, is known as forbearance.

10.2 The three essential characteristics of valid consideration are legality, adequacy, and the possibility of performance.

10.3 Consideration can be based on a promise being exchanged for another promise. It also can be based on forbearance, a party's promise not to do something they have a legal right to do. A third kind of valid consideration is a pledge or subscription (a promise to make a donation).

10.4 The UCC dispenses with the requirement of consideration in contracts to sell goods in the following situations: (a) a merchant's written firm offer that provides that the contract is irrevocable, (b) a written discharge of a claim for an alleged breach of contract, and (c) modifications of existing contracts.

10.5 A person who has a claim against another may give up, or release, their claim without an exchange of consideration by making a written statement to that effect.

10.6 Five kinds of agreements that lack consideration are (a) barren promises, (b) gratuitous promises, (c) illusory promises, (d) agreements supported by moral consideration, and (e) agreements supported by past consideration.

CHAPTER TEN ASSESSMENT

MATCHING LEGAL TERMS

Match each of the numbered definitions with the correct term in the following list.

a. barren promise
b. consideration
c. forbearance
d. gratuitous promise
e. general release
f. moral consideration
g. past consideration
h. pledge or subscription
i. preexisting duty
j. promisee

1. The benefit received and the loss suffered by parties to a contract. **1.** _____

2. A demand of the conscience based on love, friendship, honor, or sympathy. **2.** _____

3. A promise to do what one is already required to do. **3.** _____

4. An offer to confer a benefit on someone without requiring a sacrifice in return. **4.** _____

5. A promise to contribute to a charitable organization. **5.** _____

6. An obligation to perform actions that are already required. 6. _____

7. An offer to pay for a benefit that has already been received. 7. _____

8. The act of refraining from exercising a legal right. 8. _____

9. A written agreement to give up a claim or settle a debt for less than the amount demanded. 9. _____

10. The party to an agreement who receives a promise. 10. _____

TRUE/FALSE QUIZ

Indicate whether each of the following statements is true or false.

11. Consideration is one of the elements of a contract. 11. _____

12. A promise of inaction, or forbearance, can be valid consideration. 12. _____

13. Pledges and subscriptions are never legally enforceable because they lack the element of consideration. 13. _____

14. A contract in which consideration is based on a promise that is impossible to fulfill cannot be enforced. 14. _____

15. An offer to pay for a benefit after it has been received is enforceable. 15. _____

16. An agreement based on an illusory promise is enforceable if the purpose of the agreement is legal. 16. _____

17. A general release allows for the discharge of debt because it is viewed as forbearance, a form of consideration. 17. _____

18. Past consideration is a promise to repay someone for a benefit after it has been received. 18. _____

MULTIPLE CHOICE QUIZ

Indicate the correct answer from the choices that follow the question.

19. Which of the following is *not* a requirement of valid consideration? (a) In writing (b) Legal (c) Adequate (d) Possible to perform 19. _____

20. A general release is an example of a contract with which type of consideration? (a) Mutual promise of performance (b) A pledge (c) A promise of forbearance (d) A subscription 20. _____

21. A promise to donate money to a charity is (a) a mutual promise of performance (b) a pledge (c) a promise of forbearance (d) a barren promise. 21. _____

22. A promise to paint a house in exchange for a promise to fix a car is (a) a mutual promise of performance (b) a pledge (c) a promise of forbearance (d) a subscription. 22. _____

23. A promise to avoid violating the law in return for payment is void consideration as a (a) barren promise (b) gratuitous promise (c) illusory promise (d) moral promise. **23.** _____

24. A promise of a gift without any expectation in return is void consideration as a (a) barren promise (b) gratuitous promise (c) illusory promise (d) moral promise. **24.** _____

25. A promise to purchase unspecified amounts of a produce would be void consideration as a (a) barren promise (b) gratuitous promise (c) illusory promise (d) moral promise. **25.** _____

26. A promise to pay additional expenses after a contract has been made is an example of (a) barren promise (b) moral consideration (c) past consideration (d) illusory promise. **26.** _____

27. Which of the following valid contracts does not require consideration under the Uniform Commercial Code? (a) Agreement between a merchant and a new customer to purchase goods (b) Written discharge of a claim for alleged breach of contract (c) Agreement between merchants for purchase of business (d) Agreement between consumers for purchase of goods **27.** _____

DISCUSSION QUESTIONS

Answer the following questions and discuss them in class.

28. Explain how forbearance can satisfy the requirements of consideration.

29. Explain the three characteristics of valid consideration, and provide an example of an agreement having these characteristics.

30. Describe the position generally held by the courts on the matter of adequacy of consideration.

31. Identify five kinds of agreements that lack consideration.

32. Why are courts reluctant to rule on the adequacy of consideration?

33. In some contractual relationships, the bargaining power of one party gives them an unfair advantage when dealing with another who might lack the economic power or the education to enter into contracts on an equal footing. What has the law done in an attempt to level the playing field in such cases?

THINKING CRITICALLY ABOUT THE LAW

Answer the following questions, which require you to think critically about the legal principles that you learned in this chapter.

34. Forms of Consideration Critique the various exchanges of promises that are legally regarded as acceptable consideration. Your analysis should concentrate on whether each type of consideration facilitates or hinders the execution of a contract.

35. Invalid Consideration Because valid consideration is an exchange of promises, it is obvious that a promise to commit an illegal act is not valid consideration. Describe a promise to commit an illegal act that is not legally acceptable.

36. Consideration—A Promise for a Promise The most common form of valid consideration is the promise of money by one party for the promise of an act by another. Why is a mere promise deemed adequate in the eyes of the law when consideration based on completed actions might result in fewer disputes?

37. Consideration—Forbearance Valid consideration is not necessarily either the performance of an act or the payment of money. One party to a contract, for a variety of reasons, may wish to exchange their promise to pay money for a promise of inaction from the other party. Because promises of inaction are often difficult to verify, should promises of forbearance be legally acceptable?

38. A Question of Ethics Agreements between parties of unequal bargaining power are known as contracts of adhesion. For example, an apartment owner presented a tenant with a lease renewal that contained additional and burdensome provisions. The tenant, finding it difficult to move, was forced to accept the lease despite the hardship. Beyond the legal aspects of a contract of adhesion, what are the ethical dimensions to consider in this example?

CASE QUESTIONS

Study each of the following cases. Answer the questions that follow with Yes or No.

39. Adequacy of Consideration Duggan inherited some nondescript furniture, including an old desk that he sold to Andersen for $50. A short time later he learned that the desk was an antique worth about $500. Duggan brought suit to recover $450, the difference between the sale price and what the desk was really worth.

a. Will Duggan succeed in this suit? **a.** _____

b. Is the contract between Duggan and Andersen unconscionable? **b.** _____

c. Is the contract void because of the inadequacy of consideration? **c.** _____

40. Forbearance Helfrich, in a barroom brawl, broke Grady's arm. Grady brought suit against Helfrich for damages. Before the case came to trial, Helfrich offered to give Grady an $800 note, payable in 30 days, as full settlement for all claims Grady had against Helfrich. Grady accepted this offer. When the note came due, Helfrich refused to pay, claiming that there was no exchange of benefits and no consideration.

a. Is Helfrich correct in his claim that consideration was lacking? **a.** _____

b. Could Grady's action in dropping the suit be regarded as consideration? **b.** _____

c. Is forbearance a form of consideration? **c.** _____

41. Acceptable Consideration Alfieri, a hunting enthusiast, frequently shot birds in his own and his neighbor's backyard in violation of a city ordinance that prohibited guns being discharged within the city limits. The neighbor offered to pay Alfieri $200 if he would refrain from shooting birds for one year. At the end of the year, the neighbor refused to pay, claiming that there was no consideration.

a. Will Alfieri succeed in collecting the $200? **a.** _____

b. Is there consideration present in this agreement? **b.** _____

c. Is a barren promise acceptable consideration? **c.** _____

CASE ANALYSIS

Study each of the following cases carefully. Briefly state the principle of law and your decision.

42. Unconscionable Contract Jackson, a widow who was desperate for money, sold land to her brother, Seymour, for $275. Later Seymour found valuable timber on the land and sold some of it for $2,353. When Jackson realized that the property was worth much more than she had originally thought, she offered to return the sales price with interest. Seymour refused. Jackson sued, claiming fraud—that her brother, upon whom she relied for the management of her affairs, had misrepresented the value of the land. The initial court decision favored Seymour, and the decision was appealed. Is it likely that the court will invalidate the sale of the property? [*Jackson v. Seymour,* 71 S.E.2d 181 (Virginia)]

Principle of Law:

____

____

Decision:

____

____

43. Specificity of Consideration Forrer was an employee of Sears for many years. He eventually left because of health problems and began operating a farm. Sears persuaded Forrer to return to work on a part-time basis, and about one month later promised permanent employment if Forrer gave up the farm and returned to work full-time. Forrer did so, but four months later he was discharged without cause. Forrer sued for damages, lost the case in the trial court, and appealed. Will Forrer be successful in his complaint against Sears? What consideration was promised by Forrer and Sears? [*Forrer v. Sears, Roebuck & Co.,* 153 N.W.2d 587 (Wisconsin)]

Principle of Law:

____

____

Decision:

____

____

44. Gratuitous Consideration The plaintiff, Jo Laverne Alden, was the mother of Ginger Alden, a former fiancée of the late Elvis Presley, a renowned singer and wealthy man. Presley was generous with the Alden family, even after his relationship with Alden ended. Presley offered to pay the remaining mortgage debt on Jo Alden's home. Presley died suddenly before he could pay off the mortgage debt for Alden. The attorney for Presley's estate refused to pay the mortgage. Is the attorney for the estate correct? Why or why not? [*Alden v. Presley,* 637 S.W. 2d 862 (Tennesee)]

45. Validity of Consideration Maitland ran a fund-raiser for Arbor College, soliciting contributions for the college's building program. Hamill Manufacturing pledged a contribution to the program. When the company did not pay, Maitland sued. Hamill claimed there was no consideration. Will Maitland be successful in the suit?

Principle of Law:

Decision:

LEGAL RESEARCH

Complete the following activities. Share your findings with the class.

46. Working in Teams In teams of three or four, interview officials of religious organizations, hospitals, colleges, cultural and charitable institutions, or any group that raises money by asking for pledges or subscriptions (a promise to donate money). What is the rate of success collecting on these pledges? Have the officials ever attempted to enforce collection by legal means?

47. Using Technology Using the Internet and search engines, investigate federal, state, and local laws relating to unconscionable contracts.

chapter 11 Competent Parties

LEARNING OUTCOMES

After studying this chapter and completing the assessment, you will be able to

11.1 Explain what is meant by contractual capacity and define *competent parties.*

11.2 Discuss minors' contracts and how the age of majority impacts the legality of contracts.

11.3 Describe the operation of the law as it relates to liability for a minor's torts and crimes.

11.4 Assess the legal status of contracts made by persons who are incompetent.

COMPETENT PARTIES

"I started a restaurant business at the age of 19 as a waitress. I loved the atmosphere and the comraderie of the restaurant business. I loved not having to go into an office. I loved making people happy."

Anne Burrell, American chef and television personality

Purestock/SuperStock

LEGAL terms

competent party	disaffirmance
contractual capacity	necessaries
minor	ratified
age of majority	emancipation
coming of age rule	abandonment
birthday rule	incompetent

11.1 THE CAPACITY TO CONTRACT

competent party
A person of legal age and at least normal mentality who is considered by law to be capable of understanding the meaning of a contract and is permitted to enter into a valid contract.

contractual capacity
The ability to make a valid contract.

minor
A person who has not yet reached the age of majority.

Parties to a contract must be competent in both age and mentality. A competent party is a person of legal age and at least normal mentality who is considered by law to be capable of understanding the meaning of a contract. A competent party is said to have contractual capacity–that is, the ability to make a valid contract.

A person who has not yet reached the age of majority is considered a minor, or an infant, in the eyes of the law. Minors and persons with mental illness or intellectual disabilities are usually considered incompetent and lacking in contractual capacity. As a result, they cannot make legally binding contracts, although they are not denied the opportunity to benefit from their legal rights. The responsibility of determining whether a person is competent to contract rests on everyone who enters into a contract with such a person.

11.2 MINORS' CONTRACTS

age of majority
The age at which a person is legally recognized as an adult and is bound by the terms of his their contract.

coming of age rule
In common law, the view that a person's legal birthday is 12:01 a.m. of the day before their actual birthday.

birthday rule
The modern view that a person attains a given age on the anniversary date of their birth.

disaffirmance
In contract law, to indicate by a statement or act an intent not to live up to the terms of a contract.

necessaries
Goods and services that are essential to a minor's health and welfare.

The law has always tried to protect young people from adults who might try to take advantage of them. Until individuals reach what is known as legal age, or the age of majority, they are not legally required to carry out most of their contracts (such contracts are voidable, as discussed in Chapter 7). The legal age of majority varies from state to state. In most states it is 18, while in others it is 19 or 21.

Exactly when does a person reach the age of majority? According to the interesting coming of age rule in common law, a person's legal birthday is 12:01 a.m. of the day before their actual birthday (see *Mason,* 66 N.C. at 637). Thus, a person who celebrates their 18th birthday on April 26, for example, in a state where the age of majority is 18, would become an adult–and legally competent–at 12:01 a.m. on April 25. However, under the modern birthday rule, a person attains a given age on the anniversary date of their birth.

AVOIDANCE OF MINORS' CONTRACTS

In contracts between a minor and a competent person, only the minor has the privilege of disaffirmance, or avoidance of the contract; the competent party is bound. However, in contracts for necessaries, such as food, shelter, clothing, employment, and medical care, in many states the minor is bound as well. Also, in general, a minor may not disaffirm a contract for the sale or purchase of real estate.

EXAMPLE 11.1

Blevins, a 45-year-old automobile dealer, agreed to sell Alvarez, a minor, a used car for $3,800. Before the car was delivered, Blevins received a higher offer from another person and attempted to cancel the contract with Alvarez on the grounds that the buyer was a minor. The law permits Alvarez to cancel, or disaffirm, the contract but not Blevins, who is considered a competent party.

RATIFICATION OF MINORS' CONTRACTS

A minor who purchases a used car may disaffirm the contract.
LWA/Dann Tardif/Blend Images LLC

In most cases, whether the contract has not yet been performed (an executory contract) or has been fully performed (an executed contract), the minor may disaffirm the contract if they wish. However, once the minor reaches the legal age of majority, the contract may either be ratified (i.e., agreed to) or disaffirmed within a reasonable time. A contract involving a minor can be ratified by an act that shows that the minor party intends to live up to the terms of the contract. Furthermore, if a reasonable period passes after a minor reaches legal age and they have said nothing about disaffirming the contract, it is considered ratified in the eyes of the law. In this sense, silence or inaction is the basis for a voidable contract becoming a valid, enforceable contract through ratification.

ratified
An approval of a contract made by a minor after reaching majority.

When a contract is ratified, the entire contract must be ratified, not merely a part of it. Suppose, for example, that the contract involved personal property and had already been performed before the minor reached legal age. In this situation, many states would hold that the minor could either return all (but not part) of the property or money received or demand the return of all (but not part) of the money or property, at any time either before reaching the age of majority or within a reasonable time thereafter.

DISAFFIRMANCE OF MINORS' CONTRACTS

An individual may disaffirm a contract–that is, state their intention either orally or in writing not to honor a contract that had been made before reaching legal age. Disaffirmance may be done before reaching the legal age or within a reasonable time after reaching the age of majority. The exact time will vary depending on the nature of the contract and current legislation. Disaffirmance, like ratification, may be implied by the acts of the person who has reached legal age and wishes to disaffirm. Disaffirmance might be implied, for example, by failing to make an installment payment. Figure 11.1 shows a sample letter of disaffirmance.

EXAMPLE 11.2

▶ Gibbon, age 17, sold her pickup truck to Deng for $4,800. Shortly after completing the transaction, Gibbon realized that in her eagerness to sell her truck, she had priced it considerably below market value. She then demanded the return of her truck and offered to refund the $4,800 purchase price to Deng. A court would permit Gibbon to disaffirm the contract and get back her truck if she returned the $4,800 to Deng.

Letter of Disaffirmance

3356 Fifth Street
Anytown, USA
October 1, 20–

Seller's address

Electronics World
4321 First Street
Anytown, USA

Salutation

Minor's name and address

To Whom It May Concern:

The purpose of this letter is to notify you that I, Anthony Romeo, of 3356 Fifth Street, Anytown, USA, hereby disaffirm the contract entered into between you and me on September 1, 20–, at Electronics World, 4321 First Street, for the purchase of one Gold Bond digital surround sound system with a retail price of $475.

Date and place of contracting

On the date the contract was executed, I was seventeen years of age, a minor under the laws of this state. I am now eighteen years of age.

I hereby demand the return of all consideration received by you from me under the contract, amounting to $475.

Time and place to return consideration

I will return the sound system to your store address at 10:00 a.m. on Thursday, October 15.

Thank you for your understanding in this matter.

Sincerely,
Anthony Romeo
Anthony Romeo

FIGURE 11.1 Sample Letter of Disaffirmance

If, however, in Example 11.2, the situation were reversed–that is, Deng, the adult, had sold the truck to Gibbon, the minor, and wanted to cancel the sale–he could not do so if Gibbon were unwilling to cancel the contract.

In some states the minor may avoid the contract even if they falsely represented themselves as being of age. The minor may then, however, be subject to criminal prosecution on the charge of fraud as well as civil liability (damages) for the tort of deceit.

MINORS' ENFORCEABLE CONTRACTS

The law that protects minors from their contractual commitments is not intended to deny them the opportunity to enter into contracts for necessaries that are not provided by their parents or a guardian. Of course, the nature of the contract must bear some relationship to the minor's individual needs and to their social and financial status. As a result of a minor's emancipation, they assume many of the rights and obligations of a person of legal age. Emancipation could result from marriage or from voluntary separation of a minor from their parents or guardians in order to assume adult responsibilities, such as financial independence. Emancipated minors are generally liable for necessaries purchased for themselves or supplied to a spouse, just as if they were adults.

The law regards actions on the part of the minor that result in emancipation as abandonment–that is, a surrender of the special protection given to minors by the law.

emancipation
In contract law, the condition that exists when minors are no longer under the control of their parents and are responsible for their contracts.

abandonment
In contract law, the condition that exists when a minor has left home and given up all rights to parental support.

EXAMPLE 11.3

- Eakins was 17 years old and married. A doctor sued him to recover the cost of medical care and surgery provided to him. Eakins did not have medical insurance. The court would hold that Eakins was responsible for the necessaries the doctor provided to him.

If a merchant brings suit to collect payment for merchandise furnished to a minor, the merchant must show that the articles of merchandise are necessaries and that the minor did not already have an adequate supply.

EXAMPLE 11.4

- Pineapple Plantation Clothing Store brought suit to recover the cost of clothing sold to Bautista, who was a minor and had refused to pay for the clothing. Bautista already had an ample wardrobe. The store could not recover the cost of the goods because Bautista already had an adequate supply; therefore, the purchases from Pineapple were not necessaries, even though Pineapple had no way of knowing this fact.

A minor is liable only for the reasonable value of necessaries purchased by them. If the contract price is more than the sum that the minor should have been charged, they can be held responsible only for the lower amount. If the minor has already paid the amount called for in the contract, they can recover the amount that was overcharged.

EXAMPLE 11.5

- For several years, a druggist charged Matos, a minor, $250 for medication that she needed each month for a chronic disease. The price was three times the price normally charged to other purchasers. In this case, a court would enable Matos to recover the amount that she was overcharged.

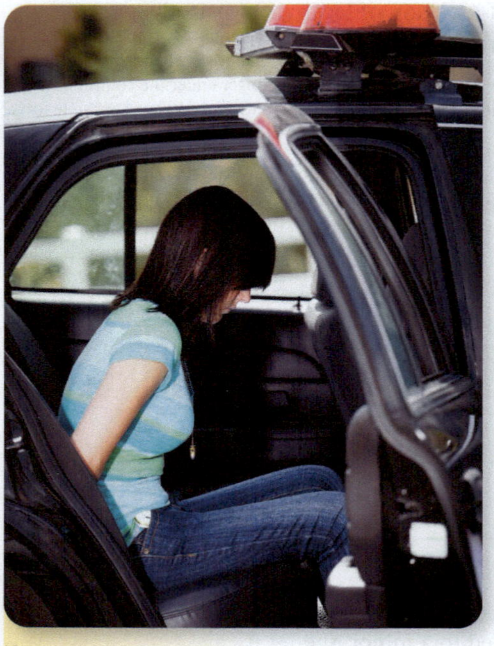

Minors are not protected against their own wrongdoing.
RichLegg/E+/Getty Images

With the passing years and the growing independence of young people, the courts have recognized that, in many instances, minors need relatively little protection from the consequences of their youthful decisions. In some cases, the courts have held that contracts made by minors who are nearly adults or that deal with a business are enforceable contracts.

11.3 LIABILITY FOR MINORS' TORTS AND CRIMES

The law does not protect anyone, even a minor, who has committed a tort or a crime. Minors are protected against their own inexperience but not against their own wrongdoing. If a minor injures another person or damages another person's property, they may be liable for such injuries or damages and may be prosecuted by the state in a criminal action. A minor may be held liable for money damages in a tort action when they destroy property, appropriates it for themselves or for another, causes another person to suffer a money loss through their negligence, or persuades another person to break a contract. A minor also can be held liable if they make damaging statements in writing (the tort of libel) or orally (the tort of slander).

EXAMPLE 11.6

McDonnell, who was 17, looked much older because of his large size and full beard. When the merchant asked McDonnell's age, he claimed that he was 18, the age of majority in his state. He bought an MP3 player for $80. After using the player for six months, McDonnell brought it back to the dealer and demanded the return of his money.

In most states, the dealer would have to return the money to McDonnell even though he did not know that he was dealing with a minor. The minor, despite the false representation of his age, may avoid the contract. The dealer, however, may sue him for the tort of fraud and attempt to recover any damages that the dealer suffered. In many states, when a minor disaffirms a contract and returns the goods, they can be held liable for damages to the goods.

In most states, parents are not held liable for torts committed by their children; however, if a child causes damage due to a lack of parental supervision, the parent may be held liable for any damages caused by the unsupervised child.

11.4 CONTRACTS OF THE MENTALLY INCOMPETENT

incompetent
Being unable to make binding contracts due to having an unsound mind and being unable to safeguard one's own interests and affairs.

Persons of unsound mind are considered incompetent to make binding contracts because they are assumed to lack the mental capacity to safeguard their own affairs. Consequently, most of their contracts are considered voidable and cannot be enforced against them if they do not carry them out.

A person with mental illness may sometimes have lucid periods during which they can exercise sound judgment. If the person entered into a contract during a lucid interval and the other party can prove it, such person will be held to the contract. The cause of the incompetence does not matter. For example, the cause might be bipolar disorder, Alzheimer's disease, brain injury, drugs, or alcohol.

Persons with mental incompetence are liable for the reasonable value of necessaries that they buy, unless they can return them. For all other contracts, the person with mental incompetence can recover their money or property, but the other party's consideration must be returned if possible.

EXAMPLE 11.7

▶ Friedman, an aged recluse, lived alone and had in years past engaged Cullman, a local handyman, to perform various maintenance jobs around their house such as lawn cutting, painting, and minor repairs. Shortly before their death, Friedman had engaged Cullman to make some plumbing repairs. After their death, the administrator of Friedman's estate attempted to avoid paying Cullman's bill, claiming that Friedman was mentally incompetent when they ordered the plumbing repairs. A court would probably require the estate to pay the reasonable value of the repairs.

A contract with a person who has been declared mentally incompetent by the courts is void even if the party who contracted with the incompetent individual did not know this fact. When a court classifies a person as mentally incompetent, it appoints a legal guardian to handle their affairs. Any contracts the incompetent person makes thereafter, including contracts that have been made during lucid periods, are considered void, not simply voidable. Nevertheless, if a person who has been declared mentally incompetent by the courts purchases necessaries, most courts will hold the legal guardian liable for their reasonable value.

CONTRACTS OF PERSONS AFFECTED BY DRUGS OR ALCOHOL

If a person makes a contract while so intoxicated by alcohol or impaired by drug use that they are unable to understand the nature and effect of the contract, it is voidable at their option. The law considers the person with impairment to have been mentally incompetent at the time the contract was made, and thus they are not bound by it. However, if the party, when no longer impaired, and within a reasonable time, chooses to carry out the contract, it has been ratified. If the contract is for necessaries, they must pay their reasonable value.

EXAMPLE 11.8

▶ Fogel, while intoxicated, bought a parka from Plymouth Army-Navy Store on credit. When billed, he refused to pay for the garment, claiming that he was so intoxicated at the time he bought it that he did not know what he was doing. If Fogel could not return the parka, he would be required to pay for it because it would be considered a necessary.

If a contract does not involve necessaries, the person who wishes to disaffirm it on the grounds that they were intoxicated or affected by drugs when the contract was made must either return the other party's consideration or prove that they lost possession of it while still impaired. Obviously, if the person disposed of the other party's consideration after returning to normal, the law would not permit disaffirmance of the contract because the contract had been ratified by the intoxicated person after regaining the power to contract.

CHAPTER SUMMARY

11.1 Contractual capacity is the ability to make a valid contract. A competent party is a person of legal age and at least normal mentality who is considered by law to be capable of understanding the meaning of a contract.

11.2 Until individuals reach what is known as legal age, or the age of majority, they are not legally required to carry out most of their contracts. The age of majority is the age at which a person can make binding contracts. Until a person reaches the age of majority, they are not legally required to carry out most of their contracts because such contracts are voidable. Once the minor reaches the legal age of majority, the contract must be either ratified or disaffirmed within a reasonable time.

11.3 The law does not protect minors who have committed a tort or crime. A minor is held responsible for injury to other persons, damaged property, and damaging statements. In many states, even if a minor disaffirms a contract and returns the goods, they can be held liable for any damages to the goods.

11.4 If a person enters into a contract while so impaired that they are unable to understand the nature and effect of the contract, then the contract is voidable at their option.

CHAPTER ELEVEN ASSESSMENT

MATCHING LEGAL TERMS

Match each of the numbered definitions with the correct term in the following list.

a. abandonment
b. age of majority
c. contractual capacity
d. competent party
e. disaffirmance
f. emancipation
g. incompetence
h. minor
i. necessaries
j. ratification

1. Items considered essential for a person's well-being, such as food, shelter, clothing, medical care, and employment. **1.** _____

2. Affirming, or agreeing to, the terms of a contract entered into previously. **2.** _____

3. A person who has not yet reached the age of majority. **3.** _____

4. The state of a minor who has married and/or left home that renders the minor responsible for their contracts. **4.** _____

5. The act of canceling a voidable contract. **5.** _____

6. Legal incapacity to make a binding contract. **6.** _____

7. Statutory legal age. **7.** _____

8. A person of legal age and normal mentality who is capable of understanding the meaning of a contract. 8. _____

9. The ability of a party to make a contract. 9. _____

10. A minor's surrender of the special protection given to him or her by the law. 10. _____

TRUE/FALSE QUIZ

Indicate whether each of the following statements is true or false.

11. An emancipated minor's contracts for necessaries are valid. 11. _____

12. A contract with a minor can be ratified by either party. 12. _____

13. Upon reaching legal age, a minor must ratify earlier completed contracts in writing. 13. _____

14. Contracts made while a person is intoxicated are voidable by either party. 14. _____

15. A person who is of legal age and at least normal mentality is considered a competent party. 15. _____

16. In some states, a minor may avoid a contract even if they falsely represented themselves as of legal age. 16. _____

17. A contract ratification must apply to the entire contract. 17. _____

MULTIPLE CHOICE QUIZ

Indicate the correct answer from the choices following the question.

18. Which of the following is most likely to be a competent party to a contract? (a) A 19-year-old who has taken strong sedatives (b) A 26-year-old undergoing a psychotic episode of mental illness (c) An 18-year-old diagnosed with depression (d) A 75-year-old in advanced stage of dementia 18. _____

19. The standard for legal competence is (a) understanding all of the ramifications of signing a contract (b) understanding the meaning of a contract (c) understanding every word of the contract (d) understanding all stages of the court process for enforcement of a contract. 19. _____

20. A person living in a state that uses the coming of age rule becomes legally competent (a) on the 18th anniversary of their birth (b) on the 21st anniversary of their birth (c) the day before the 18th anniversary of their birth (d) the day before the 21st anniversary of their birth. 20. _____

21. A person living in a state that uses the birthday rule becomes legally competent (a) on the 18th anniversary of their birth (b) on the 21st anniversary of their birth (c) the day before the 18th anniversary of their birth (d) the day before the 21st anniversary of their birth. 21. _____

22. In a contract between a minor and a competent party for goods that are not necessaries (a) both parties may disaffirm the contract (b) neither party may disaffirm the contract (c) only the competent party may disaffirm the contract (d) only the minor may disaffirm the contract. **22.** _____

23. Which of the following is *not* a necessity? (a) Food (b) Health care (c) Electronics (d) Clothing **23.** _____

24. Ratification is (a) failure to disaffirm in a reasonable time after reaching majority (b) positive agreement to the contract after reaching majority (c) silence about the agreement for a reasonable time after reaching majority (d) all of the above. **24.** _____

25. A minor who negligently causes an accident (a) is not liable for a contracted settlement for damages (b) is not liable for the accident at all (c) is liable for a contracted settlement for damages (d) none of the above. **25.** _____

26. A person impaired by drugs or alcohol when entering into a contract and unable to understand the nature and effect of the contract (a) may not disaffirm the contract (b) may disaffirm the contract on their own (c) may only disaffirm the contract with the permission of the other party (d) none of the above. **26.** _____

27. A party to a contract with episodic mental illness is (a) always legally incompetent (b) legally incompetent only during episodes rendering them unable to understand the legal nature of the contract (c) never legally incompetent (d) none of the above. **27.** _____

DISCUSSION QUESTIONS

Answer the following questions and discuss them in class.

28. Discuss what is meant by "age of majority" and how it affects the legal status of minors entering into contracts.

____

____

29. How is a contract with a minor affected by the minor's ratification of the contract?

____

____

30. A minor is held legally responsible if they injure another person or another person's property. Would it make a difference if the injury were accidental?

____

____

31. A minor purchased a desk, computer, and printer–all on sale. If the minor later attempted to purchase only the computer, the salesperson could legally refuse to limit the sale to the one item on the grounds of the buyer's minority. In this example, what is the legal principle regarding partial ratification of the minor's contract?

32. A 17-year-old dancer signed a contract for a season with a ballet company. After rehearsals and two performances, the dancer received a better offer from another company. Could she terminate the contract? Why or why not?

33. Contracts made by persons with mental incompetence are generally voidable. Are there any exceptions? If yes, explain.

THINKING CRITICALLY ABOUT THE LAW

Answer the following questions, which require you to think critically about the legal principles that you learned in this chapter.

34. Age of Majority The minimum age required under the law for obtaining a driver's license is usually lower than the age for drinking or voting. What is the rationale for this?

35. Minors' Contracts Is it fair that minors' contracts are voidable, whereas those of adults are legally binding?

36. Contracts of Emancipated Minors The contracts of emancipated minors are usually considered legally binding. Give an example to illustrate why this is necessary.

37. Contracts of Persons Who Are Mentally Incompetent If a contract is made by a responsible adult who later becomes mentally incompetent, is the contract enforceable by either party?

____

____

38. A Question of Ethics Is it fair and ethical for a minor to take advantage of the protection accorded by the law to breach a contract made with a person who believed the minor to have reached the age of majority?

____

____

CASE QUESTIONS

Study each of the following cases. Answer the questions that follow with Yes or No.

39. Minors' Contracts Nguyen, who was 17 years old, purchased a used boat, agreeing to pay for it in monthly installments over a two-year period. During the next six months, she made 6 of the 24 payments she had agreed to make. The day before she celebrated her 18th birthday, she made the seventh payment. One month later, instead of making the regularly scheduled payment, she attempted to disaffirm the contract, claiming that she was a minor when she made the contract. (Nguyen lived in a state where the age of majority is 18.)

a. Did Nguyen's first six payments indicate her ratification? **a.** _____

b. Is this a contract for necessaries?

c. Did the seventh payment serve to ratify the contract? **c.** _____

d. Is it likely that Nguyen will be successful in her attempt to disaffirm the contract? **d.** _____

40. Voidable Contract Caroli, who was 17 years old, signed an agreement to buy a used ornamental rug from Egan for $150. While Caroli was on his way to pick up the rug, Egan got an offer for $250 from someone else. When Caroli arrived with the money to complete the transaction, Egan told him he was unwilling to go through with the agreement because Caroli was a minor.

a. Can Egan cancel the contract? **a.** _____

b. Is this a voidable contract? **b.** _____

c. Can Caroli cancel the contract? **c.** _____

d. If Egan sells the rug to Caroli, can Caroli later return the rug? **d.** _____

41. Contracts of Persons Who Are Mentally Incompetent Jena, who had been declared mentally incompetent by the courts, purchased a high-powered sports car for $66,000. Because he made the purchase during a lucid interval, his condition was not evident to the seller. Jena drove the car for several months; subsequently, he returned it to the seller and claimed that his mental condition permitted him to avoid the contract.

a. Was Jena's contract valid at the time of purchase? a. _____

b. Did Jena's continued use of the car constitute ratification? b. _____

c. Can the seller claim that the contract was valid because the car was a necessary? c. _____

d. Will Jena be successful in avoiding the contract? d. _____

CASE ANALYSIS

Study each of the following cases carefully. Briefly state the principle of law and your decision.

42. Contracts of Persons Who Are Mentally Incompetent Staples, following extensive injuries in an automobile accident, was declared mentally incompetent. He imagined himself to be in command of a large army engaged in protecting the country against an invasion. He ordered several large tents, sleeping bags, and other military supplies from a firm that specialized in selling such goods. When he failed to pay for the goods, the firm attempted to seize Staples's bank deposits and his disability pension. Will the military supply firm be successful in its attempt to secure payment?

Principle of Law:

____

____

Decision:

____

____

43. Contracts of Emancipated Minors Doran, a young man of 17, married a 17-year-old woman. After the wedding they moved to another city, where they both found work and began to buy furniture and appliances. When they realized that they had been unwise in some of their purchases, they attempted to rescind the contracts, claiming they were minors. Will the Dorans be successful in avoiding the contracts?

Principle of Law:

____

____

Decision:

____

____

44. Contracts of Persons Who Are Mentally Incompetent Ortelere, a retired teacher, had built up a substantial amount of funds in her retirement plan before she retired because of "involutional psychosis" (a form of mental illness). She had previously specified that a lowered monthly retirement benefit would be paid to her so that her husband would get some benefit from the retirement plan if she died before he did. After her mental problems began, she changed her payout plan and borrowed from the pension fund. As a consequence of the changes she made, her husband lost his rights to benefits. Two months after she made the changes, she died. The husband sued to reverse the changes his wife had made, claiming that she was not of sound mind when she made them. Will the changes in the plan be voided? [*Ortelere v. Teachers' Retirement Board,* 250 N.E.2d 460 (Wisconsin)]

Principle of Law:

Decision:

LEGAL RESEARCH

Complete the following activities. Share your findings with the class.

45. Working in Teams In teams of three or four, interview several retailers of home appliances or furnishings to determine how they ascertain the age of customers who wish to enter into an installment contract for purchases.

46. Using Technology Using the Internet and search engines, compare the age of majority provisions in several states. Also, determine the differences in the legal ages required for various activities, such as marriage, driving, voting, and military service.

chapter 12
Legal Purpose of Contracts

LEARNING OUTCOMES

After studying this chapter and completing the assessment, you will be able to

12.1 Discuss legality of purpose in relation to public interest and classify illegal agreements into three major categories.

12.2 Identify four kinds of agreements that violate statutes.

12.3 Identify five kinds of agreements that violate public policy.

12.4 Explain the provisions of two major laws governing illegal restraint of trade: the Sherman Antitrust Act and the Robinson-Patman Act.

12.5 Discuss four instances where restraints of trade are legally enforceable.

LEGAL PURPOSE OF CONTRACTS

"When the President does it, that means that it's not illegal."

Richard M. Nixon, 37th president of the United States

in-future/iStock/Getty Images

LEGAL terms

- blue laws
- Sunday agreement
- gambling agreement
- interest
- usury
- unlicensed transaction
- champerty
- exculpatory clause
- restraint of trade
- monopoly power
- Sherman Antitrust Act
- Robinson-Patman Act
- government-granted franchise
- franchisor
- franchisee

12.1 LEGALITY AND THE PUBLIC INTEREST

As discussed in Chapter 7, legality of purpose is one of the essential elements of an enforceable contract. Although the parties to a contract are legally competent and have reached mutual agreement, the law still requires that the purpose of the agreement be legal and not contrary to the public interest.

CLASSIFICATION OF ILLEGAL AGREEMENTS

There are three broad classifications of illegal agreements: (1) agreements that are contrary to the common law, (2) agreements that have been declared illegal by statute, and (3) agreements the courts have found to be against the security or welfare of the general public.

EFFECT OF ILLEGALITY

An agreement with an illegal purpose is usually void and unenforceable. However, if the contract is divisible—that is, if it has several unrelated parts—and if one or more parts have a legal purpose, then those components are enforceable. However, the part or parts that have an illegal purpose are not enforceable.

EXAMPLE 12.1

Revak contracted with Sunnyside Home Remodelers to make some major repairs and to add a room to one side of her house. After Sunnyside began the work, it was discovered that if the room were added to the house, Revak would be in violation of local zoning ordinances. If the agreement had specified one price for all the work, the contract would be unenforceable. If the estimate and contract were sufficiently detailed, then the part of the agreement that covered the remodeling would be enforceable and the part involving the added room would be unenforceable.

12.2 AGREEMENTS IN VIOLATION OF STATUTES

Agreements that violate government statutes are not enforceable by the courts. Examples of such agreements include (1) agreements made on Sundays or legal holidays, (2) gambling and wagering agreements, (3) usurious agreements, and (4) unlicensed transactions.

AGREEMENTS MADE ON SUNDAYS OR LEGAL HOLIDAYS

blue laws
State statutes and local ordinances that regulate the creation and performance of certain types of contracts on Sundays and legal holidays.

Sunday agreement
A contract made on a Sunday; in a small number of jurisdictions, such contracts are invalid unless they are ratified on a weekday.

Some state statutes and local ordinances, referred to as blue laws, regulate the creation and performance of certain types of contracts on Sundays and legal holidays. Many of these restrictions originate in religious customs and practices. In recent years, there has been a steady decline in the number of activities that are prohibited on Sundays and holidays.

In a small number of jurisdictions, a contract that is made on a Sunday but is to be carried out on a weekday is invalid. In some states, a Sunday agreement must be ratified on a weekday. The contract is considered ratified if it is performed on a weekday or if the terms are restated on a weekday. Contracts made on a legal holiday can generally be performed on the next business day following the holiday. Examples of contracts that might be made on a Sunday or on a legal holiday and ratified on a weekday are contracts involving the payment of a note, the delivery of merchandise, and the repair of equipment.

GAMBLING AND WAGERING AGREEMENTS

All states have legislation that regulates gambling.
Steve Allen/Brand X Pictures/Jupiterimages

All states have legislation that regulates gambling—that is, risking money or something of value on the uncertain outcome of a future event. A gambling agreement is one in which performance by one party depends on the occurrence of an uncertain event. Many states permit betting on certain kinds of races and sports, as well as table games. Most states permit state-run lotteries. Where gambling agreements are permitted, the state closely regulates the nature of the betting and usually derives considerable revenue from it. For example, even in a state that permits betting on horse races, the bets must be placed with state-approved outlets, such as racetracks or off-track betting facilities operated or regulated by the state. Other bets in these states are illegal unless approved by state law and are, therefore, as unenforceable as they would be in a state that permits no gambling at all. (Examples of illegal gambling would include typical office basketball and football pools.) In some states, gambling on Native American reservations is legal, and laws relating to online gambling vary from state to state.

gambling agreement
An agreement in which performance by one party depends on the occurrence of an uncertain event.

EXAMPLE 12.2

▶ In a state that permits betting on horse races only at racetracks and at off-track betting facilities, Cohen bet his friend, Hermann, that a certain horse would win a particular race. The horse lost, but Cohen refused to pay. This bet is unenforceable because it was made privately without compliance with the betting regulations established by the state.

USURIOUS AGREEMENTS

Interest is the charge for the use of borrowed money, generally expressed as an annual percentage of the amount of the loan (principal). A majority of states have laws that regulate interest charges. If a loan is made at an interest rate higher than that allowed by state law, the lender is guilty of usury, which is defined as charging interest higher than the law permits. Such usurious agreements are illegal and void. In some states, usury laws do not apply to transactions between corporations. In many states, the usury statutes apply to retail installment credit sales and credit card transactions. Most states have varying usury rates, depending on the kind of loan.

interest
The charge for using borrowed money, generally expressed as an annual percentage of the amount of the loan (principal).

usury
Charging interest higher than the law permits.

EXAMPLE 12.3

▶ Nunez purchased a refrigerator from a local appliance dealer. Because he did not have a credit record, he agreed to pay the dealer $100 down and $100 per month for one year from the date of purchase. There were no other benefits to Nunez, such as delivery or an investigation of his credit. The price for a cash transaction would have been only $800. When Nunez computed how much it was costing him to finance the purchase through the dealer, he refused to make anymore payments, claiming that the rate of interest was illegal. A court would likely rule that the interest charge was usurious.

UNLICENSED TRANSACTIONS

To protect the public, most states require persons engaged in certain businesses, professions, and occupations to be licensed. The requirements for a license usually include paying an annual fee and passing an examination—written, oral, or both—to ensure competence. Persons in licensed professions and occupations include doctors, dentists, lawyers, nurses, certified public accountants, pharmacists, plumbers, barbers, and teachers. An agreement with a person who does not have the required license is an unlicensed transaction and is generally illegal if the purpose of the statute is regulatory and enforcement of the licensing requirements is clearly in the public interest.

unlicensed transaction
An agreement with a person who does not have a required license.

EXAMPLE 12.4

▶ Joblin, a foreign-trained doctor with years of experience in his own country, was working in a hospital until he could take the required examinations and be licensed to practice in the United States. He also maintained a small practice in his home and provided for some of the medical needs of people in his neighborhood. One patient ran up a large bill and finally refused to pay. Because Joblin was not licensed when he performed these medical services, he has no legal way to collect his fee.

Unlike Example 12.4, however, if the purpose of the licensing requirement is solely to raise revenue for the jurisdiction and not to ensure competence, the absence of a license does not make the agreement void.

12.3 AGREEMENTS AGAINST PUBLIC POLICY

Some agreements are unenforceable because they are contrary to the interests of the public. Examples include agreements that (1) obstruct or pervert justice, (2) restrain marriage, (3) interfere with public service, (4) defraud creditors and other persons, or (5) contain exculpatory clauses.

AGREEMENTS THAT OBSTRUCT OR PERVERT JUSTICE

Among the kinds of agreements that obstruct or pervert justice are the following: (1) an agreement to conceal a crime or not to prosecute a criminal—such as a thief if they return the stolen property; (2) an agreement to encourage a lawsuit in which one or more of the parties have no legitimate interest, called champerty; (3) an agreement to give false testimony or to suppress evidence; (4) an agreement to bribe a juror or a court official; and (5) an agreement to refrain from testifying as a witness in a legal action.

champerty
An agreement to encourage a lawsuit in which one or more of the parties have no legitimate interest.

EXAMPLE 12.5

▶ Blasky, an investor and speculator, agreed to pay a percentage of his profits on stock trading to Gillian, who had access to confidential information. When the scheme was uncovered and Blasky was charged with violating federal securities regulations, he offered $10,000 to Gillian if Gillian would deny knowing about or being involved in Blasky's illegal activities. The contract was clearly unenforceable because it was an agreement to give false testimony.

In Example 12.5, even if the money was paid, neither side could sue the other. A court will not touch an illegal contract even if one party is out the money or service. Courts require that parties to a lawsuit have *clean hands,* meaning that they are not using illegal acts as the basis for their lawsuits.

AGREEMENTS THAT RESTRAIN MARRIAGE

Agreements in restraint of marriage are void. For example, a person's promise to pay money to their child on the condition that the child never marries would not be enforceable. If the child agreed to this arrangement and avoided marrying, they could not enforce the agreement.

EXAMPLE 12.6

▶ Heath, a lonely widower, wished his only daughter not to marry and offered her $200,000 if she remained single. The agreement would not be enforceable, and neither the father nor his daughter would be obligated to honor the agreement.

AGREEMENTS THAT INTERFERE WITH PUBLIC SERVICE

Agreements that attempt to bribe or interfere with public officials, obtain political preference in appointments to office, pay an officer for signing a pardon, require one of the parties to the agreement to break a law, or influence a lawmaking body for personal gain are examples of agreements that are illegal because they interfere with public service.

Some very clever schemes have been used to influence public officials. These may include giving "no-show" or "no-work" jobs to relatives of political officials, making contributions to political campaigns, and offering "vacations" as bribes. Public officials, and those who attempt to influence them, are exposed and prosecuted every year. Often these activities do not involve specific contracts but are, nevertheless, illegal.

An agreement to wrongfully use one's influence is illegal and unenforceable.
James Lauritz/Photodisc/Getty Images

EXAMPLE 12.7

Furth, a government official, used his influence with the parking violations bureau to ensure that a particular firm received a contract for parking meters without competitive bidding. The manufacturer of the meters agreed to employ the official as a consultant when he left office. The agreement was clearly illegal and unenforceable.

AGREEMENTS TO DEFRAUD CREDITORS AND OTHER PERSONS

Because agreements to defraud lack the element of legality of purpose, they are void and unenforceable. An example of an agreement to defraud another person might be an agreement to sell or give away property with the intention of defrauding creditors in anticipation of bankruptcy. Consider Example 12.8.

EXAMPLE 12.8

Lachman, who had been operating a retail store at a loss for several years, agreed to sell his brother-in-law inventory worth $100,000 for the modest sum of $1,000, with the understanding that after bankruptcy proceedings were concluded and his creditors were satisfied, the property would be returned to him. An agreement such as this is void and unenforceable.

EXCULPATORY CLAUSES

exculpatory clause
A statement in a contract that releases one party from liability resulting from their own negligence throughout the performance of a contract.

An exculpatory clause is a statement in a contract that releases one party from liability resulting from their own negligence throughout the performance of the contract. Exculpatory clauses are contrary to public policy; one party is protected from the consequences of their own negligence or willful actions, while the other party is not allowed to recover their losses. Exculpatory clauses are illegal when used by companies in a business directly related to the public interest, such as banks, public utilities, and transportation providers. It is logical that such businesses should be held accountable for their actions because they impact the safety and well-being of the public they serve.

EXAMPLE 12.9

Wang entered into a contract with Valenti Construction Company to erect an outdoor deck for the sum of $8,000. Attorneys for Valenti Construction placed a clause in the contract that stated that the company would not be liable for any injuries that resulted due to the negligence of the company's workers. Such an exculpatory clause is illegal because it violates public policy.

12.4 ILLEGAL RESTRAINTS OF TRADE

Competition in public sales and in bidding for contracts is essential in our market-oriented economy because the competition of a free market encourages lower prices, improved products, and better service. Unless specifically permitted by law, agreements to suppress or eliminate competition are illegal and unenforceable. These kinds of agreements are said to be in restraint of trade.

restraint of trade
A limitation on the full exercise of doing business with others.

Monopoly power is the term used to describe a situation in which one or more people or firms have sufficient market share, or power, to control prices in the market in a particular area or for a certain product. A monopoly is illegal because it results in a restraint of trade.

monopoly power
A situation in which one or more people or firms control the market in a particular area or for a particular product.

SHERMAN ANTITRUST ACT

In 1890 Congress passed the *Federal Antitrust Act,* also known as the Sherman Antitrust Act. This law and several amendments to it are still vigorously enforced against large and small businesses. It forbids certain agreements that tend to unreasonably inhibit competition, fix prices, allocate territories, or limit production. Persons or businesses found guilty of such practices are liable to punishment by heavy fines and imprisonment, and the contracts will be judged to be void. While the act does not prohibit firms from growing large as a result of producing good products and utilizing effective management, if a firm's size allows it to dominate a market, the federal government can require it to be split into smaller businesses. Similar antitrust statutes have been passed by most states to prohibit local anticompetitive practices.

Sherman Antitrust Act
A federal statute that forbids certain agreements that tend to unreasonably inhibit competition, fix prices, allocate territories, or limit production.

EXAMPLE 12.10

▶ The two pharmacies in the village of Wagonwheels agreed between themselves that they would each serve a particular section of the town and would charge the same low prices for certain prescription medicines. The purpose of the agreement was to create a monopoly and discourage competition from any new store that might wish to open in the town. This agreement would be found to be in restraint of trade and a violation of state law.

ROBINSON-PATMAN ACT

The Robinson-Patman Act of 1936, which amended earlier antitrust legislation, makes it unlawful to discriminate, directly or indirectly, in matters involving product pricing, advertising, and promotion. It specifically prohibits sellers from discriminating among different purchasers of goods of like grade and quality under certain conditions. The purpose of the act is to ensure that no one customer has an advantage over others. A seller of goods can, however, legally charge a certain customer a lower price if the seller can prove that the lower price is a result of savings due to large-quantity sales to that customer. The act does not force a large buyer to give up the advantages resulting from greater efficiency but rather puts a limit on the use of the economic power that often results from large size.

Robinson-Patman Act
A federal statute that makes it unlawful to discriminate, directly or indirectly, in matters involving product pricing, advertising, and promotion.

EXAMPLE 12.11

▶ Meadowbrook Fuel is a large national company that markets fuel oil in the city of Westerville. The company has little competition within the city limits and, because of this competitive advantage, sells fuel oil at a price much higher than it does in the rural areas surrounding Westerville, where numerous competitors are located. Meadowbrook would be in violation of the Robinson-Patman Act for such discriminatory pricing practices.

12.5 LEGAL RESTRAINTS OF TRADE

Although federal and state legislation and many court decisions encourage competition, there are times when agreements in restraint of trade are in the public interest and are legally enforceable.

Trade secrets, trademarks, patents, copyrights, and agreements not to compete are legally enforceable and are discussed in Chapter 28.

GOVERNMENT-GRANTED MONOPOLIES

government-granted franchise
A legal monopoly in which a state or federal government grants a person or firm a license to conduct a specific business, usually an essential service.

A government-granted franchise is another form of legal monopoly in which a state or the federal government grants a firm or person a license to conduct a specific—usually essential—business such as a bus line, railroad, electric power company, natural gas company, and TV cable service. Such franchises are granted because it is in the public interest to limit the number of companies operating in an area if those companies provide a necessary service. These legal monopolies (sometimes called *natural monopolies*) are subject to a greater degree of regulation than other businesses and are responsible to administrative agencies, boards, or public service commissions.

An example of a private franchise.
Jill Braaten/McGraw-Hill Education

PRIVATE FRANCHISES

A government-granted franchise should not be confused with a private franchise, which is a special kind of business organization involving a contractual relationship between a franchisor (the parent company) and a franchisee (the independent firm). In a private franchise, the contractual relationship provides that the franchisor will supply certain services, such as management consulting, to the franchisee and will allow the franchisee to use the franchisor's name, join with others in national advertising, and secure other benefits. The private franchise is a form of business organization that is usually used in industries such as fast-food chains, motels, automobile dealerships, and gasoline service stations.

franchisor
The parent firm in a franchise agreement.

franchisee
The independent company in a franchise agreement.

ZONING REGULATIONS

A community may designate certain areas as zones for such uses as light industrial, industrial, commercial, and residential. While zoning regulations are intended to provide security for the citizens of a community, they also may act as legal restraints of trade because they restrict where and how businesses may operate.

ENVIRONMENTAL AND SAFETY REGULATIONS

Federal and state legislatures have enacted statutes to protect the health and welfare of the general population from the effects of pollution of the atmosphere and bodies of water. Safety regulations protect the health and welfare of the general population of a community, customers, and employees. Like zoning regulations, safety and environmental regulations (discussed in Chapters 33 and 37) also serve as legal restraints of trade because they place limits and restrictions on how a firm may operate.

CHAPTER SUMMARY

12.1 Although the parties to a contract are legally competent and have reached mutual agreement, the law still requires that the purpose of the agreement be legal and not contrary to the public interest. The three major categories of illegal agreements are (a) agreements that are contrary to the common law, (b) agreements that have been declared illegal by statute, and (c) agreements that have been found by the courts to be against the security or welfare of the general public.

12.2 Four kinds of agreements that violate statutes are (a) agreements made on Sundays or legal holidays, (b) gambling and wagering agreements, (c) usurious agreements, and (d) unlicensed transactions.

12.3 Five kinds of agreements that violate public policy are those that (a) obstruct or pervert justice, (b) restrain marriage, (c) interfere with public service, (d) defraud creditors and other persons, and (e) contain exculpatory clauses.

12.4 The Sherman Antitrust Act forbids agreements that tend to unreasonably lessen competition, fix prices, allocate territories, or limit production. The Robinson-Patman Act makes it unlawful to discriminate, directly or indirectly, in matters involving product pricing, advertising, and promotion.

12.5 Restraints of trade are legally enforceable in the following instances: (a) government-granted franchises, legal monopolies in which a state or the federal government grants a person or firm a license to conduct a specific—usually essential—business; (b) private franchises, special kinds of business organizations involving contractual relationships between franchisors and franchisees; (c) zoning regulations, legal restraints of trade that restrict where and how businesses may operate; and (d) environmental and safety regulations, statutes to protect the health and welfare of the general population.

CHAPTER TWELVE ASSESSMENT

MATCHING LEGAL TERMS

Match each of the numbered definitions with the correct term in the following list.

a. champerty
b. exculpatory clause
c. franchisor
d. gambling agreement
e. government-granted franchise
f. interest
g. monopoly power
h. restraint of trade
i. unlicensed transaction
j. usury

1. An agreement based on the uncertain outcome of some future event. **1.** _____

2. The practice of charging a higher interest rate than that permitted by law. **2.** _____

3. An agreement with a person who is required to have, but lacks, the approval of the state to practice their business, profession, or occupation. **3.** _____

4. An agreement by a person to encourage or support a lawsuit in which they have no legitimate interest. 4. _____

5. The ability to control the market in a particular area or for a certain product. 5. _____

6. A legal monopoly granted to a firm or person to conduct a specific business such as a railroad or electric company. 6. _____

7. Actions or agreements intended to suppress or eliminate competition. 7. _____

8. A statement in a contract that releases one party from liability resulting from their own negligence throughout the performance of a contract. 8. _____

9. The charge for the use of borrowed money. 9. _____

10. A government or parent firm that grants a monopoly to another. 10. _____

TRUE/FALSE QUIZ

Indicate whether each of the following statements is true or false.

11. An agreement to perform an illegal act is void and unenforceable. 11. _____

12. All states prohibit all forms of gambling. 12. _____

13. Agreements that require the performance of acts against public policy are void. 13. _____

14. Agreements that restrain marriage are valid if both parties agree to all provisions. 14. _____

15. The government will always prosecute companies that wield monopoly power because competition is always deemed in the public's best interest. 15. _____

16. Zoning regulations also may act as legal restraints of trade because they restrict where and how businesses may operate. 16. _____

MULTIPLE CHOICE QUIZ

Indicate the correct answer from the choices following the question.

17. A contract that has an illegal purpose is (a) void (b) voidable (c) enforceable (d) valid. 17. _____

18. Which of the following is not an illegal agreement? (a) Agreement contrary to common law (b) Agreement contract to common purpose (c) Agreement contrary to statute (d) Agreement contrary to security or welfare of the general public 18. _____

19. An unlicensed contractor enters into a construction contract even though the state where they operate requires licensure. In this case, the contract is (a) illegal as contrary to common law (b) not illegal (c) illegal as contrary to statute (d) illegal as contrary to common purpose. 19. _____

20. An agreement to encourage a party with no legitimate interest to bring a lawsuit is (a) illegal as contrary to common law (b) not illegal (c) illegal as contrary to public policy (d) illegal as contrary to common purpose. **20.** _____

21. Monopoly power is defined as (a) the power to control prices in a given market (b) 100 percent market share of a given market (c) 50 percent market share of a given market (d) any power in a given market. **21.** _____

22. An example of an illegal agreement in restraint of trade would be (a) a franchise agreement that gives a business exclusive right to operate the franchise (b) an agreement between an electric utility and the government to provide exclusive services in an area (c) an agreement between two businesses to not lower prices below a certain amount in a given market (d) none of these agreements are illegal. **22.** _____

DISCUSSION QUESTIONS

Answer the following questions and discuss them in class.

23. Explain the enforceability of divisible contracts in which some parts have a legal purpose while other parts have an illegal purpose.

____

____

24. Provide an example of an agreement that has been made illegal by statute.

____

____

25. Is an illegal agreement enforceable? Why or why not?

____

____

26. Why are contracts made with individuals who are required to be licensed, but are not, usually unenforceable?

____

____

27. Legislation intended to protect the natural environment can have unexpected consequences and may serve as a disincentive to business. Explain.

____

____

28. How does society benefit from the actions of governments granting monopolies for such services as electric power service and railroads?

____

____

THINKING CRITICALLY ABOUT THE LAW

Answer the following questions, which require you to think critically about the legal principles that you learned in this chapter.

29. Illegal Agreements Certain kinds of agreements, such as gambling agreements, are illegal or highly regulated. What do you believe is the primary motivation for such prohibitions?

30. Licensing Most states require people engaged in certain professions or businesses to be licensed. How do licensing requirements protect the public?

31. Environmental Protection Enforcement of laws that are intended to protect the environment sometimes has unforeseen economic effects, such as plant closings and unemployment. How should society attempt to balance environmental and economic issues?

32. Competition Various federal and state laws are intended to encourage competition. Analyze and report on the benefits of competition to society.

33. Restraint of Trade Zoning regulations have the effect of restraining trade because they limit the activities of certain kinds of businesses. Explain how society benefits from such limitations.

34. A Question of Ethics The Robinson-Patman Act prohibits price discrimination. What were the ethical considerations that motivated the passage of this federal statute?

CASE QUESTIONS

Study each of the following cases. Answer the questions that follow with Yes or No.

35. Gambling Agreements Pickens was one of a group of four army veterans who met once a month to play poker. On one occasion, Pickens lost more than $5,000 and refused to pay, claiming that gambling debts are uncollectible. The winner claimed that because the state had legalized off-track betting and had begun a lottery, gambling debts were now legal and collectible.

a. Does the existence of state-approved gambling affect the legality of other forms of gambling? **a.** _____

b. Can the winner of the gambling activity legally collect his winnings? **b.** _____

36. Unlicensed Transactions Rogan, who had worked for eight years as an electrician's helper, tried several times to pass the state-required electrician's test, but he failed each time. Still, he felt that he knew enough about his trade that he could perform the work of an electrician and accepted several jobs that required a fully licensed electrician. Nooney hired Rogan to install the wiring in a room addition. Just as Rogan was beginning work, Nooney learned that Rogan did not have a valid electrician's license and canceled the contract. Rogan claimed that he should be paid anyway because he turned down other employment elsewhere to accept Nooney's work.

a. Is the contract between Nooney and Rogan enforceable? **a.** _____

b. Does it seem that Rogan should be paid for the work he and Nooney agreed he would do? **b.** _____

c. Is Nooney partly to blame because he failed to ask to see Rogan's license? **c.** _____

CASE ANALYSIS

Study each of the following cases carefully. Briefly state the principle of law and your decision.

37. Usurious Agreements Alfino borrowed money from Yakutsk and agreed in writing to pay a rate of interest higher than that allowed by local law. Later, when Alfino was called upon to pay, he refused, claiming that the agreement was void because of the usurious rate. Yakutsk, the lender, sued to collect. Yakutsk agreed to accept the legal rate of interest and felt he was entitled to collect the debt. Alfino believed that the entire debt was void because of the illegality of the original agreement. In view of Yakutsk's willingness to accept the legal rate of interest, can Alfino be compelled to pay? [*Yakutsk v. Alfino,* 349 N.Y.S.2d 718 (New York)]

Principle of Law:

____

____

Decision:

____

____

38. Price Discrimination Morton Salt Company, a large producer of table salt, had an established price scale for its product based on the quantity of salt ordered in a 12-month period. Thus, a firm that ordered a substantial quantity of salt paid less per package than a store that ordered a smaller quantity. Acting in response to complaints from small firms, the Federal Trade Commission investigated and determined that the lowest price offered by Morton Salt Company, although available to all customers, was practical only for five national customers who purchased in sufficiently large quantities to benefit from the lowest prices established. Would the alleged price discrimination be covered under the Robinson-Patman Act? [*FTC v. Morton Salt Co.*, 334 U.S. 37]

Principle of Law:

____

____

Decision:

____

____

39. Illegal Agreement Jason decided to declare bankruptcy because his financial situation was desperate and his only property was a nearly new car worth about $24,000. In an attempt to conceal the value of his property, he sold the car to his friend Dane for $2,000. He planned to buy the car back from Dane when the bankruptcy proceedings were concluded. Is the sale of the car a valid contract? Why or why not?

Principle of Law:

____

____

Decision:

____

____

LEGAL RESEARCH

Complete the following activities. Share your findings with the class.

40. Working in Teams In teams of three or four, interview several owners or managers of small businesses. Ask these individuals whether there are legal obstacles that make it more difficult for their businesses to earn a profit.

____

____

41. Using Technology Use the Internet and search engines to investigate the Sherman Antitrust Act and the Robinson-Patman Act and the various prosecutions under each.

____

____

chapter 13 Form of Contracts

LEARNING OUTCOMES

After studying this chapter and completing the assessment, you will be able to

13.1 Describe the requirement of proper form of contracts and name instances when contracts (a) should not be in writing, (b) should be in writing, and (c) must be in writing.

13.2 Explain how the parol evidence rule affects the addition of supplementary provisions to a written contract.

13.3 Discuss the Statute of Frauds.

13.4 Identify the six types of contracts that the Statute of Frauds requires to be in writing.

13.5 Specify items of information that must be included in a written contract to satisfy the Statute of Frauds.

FORM OF CONTRACTS

"Do you have a record contract? I have a recording agreement. What's the difference? One is an agreement and one is a contract! I am a man who deals by ear."

Bob Marley, Jamaican singer, songwriter, and musician

Design Pics

LEGAL terms

- parol evidence rule
- Statute of Frauds
- executor
- administrator
- guaranty
- antenuptial or prenuptial agreement
- auction sale
- memorandum

13.1 THE REQUIREMENT OF PROPER FORM

The essential elements of a valid contract were introduced in Chapter 7. These requirements are (1) offer and acceptance, (2) mutual agreement, (3) consideration, (4) competent parties, (5) legality of purpose, and (6) proper form. Following the introduction of the essential elements, several chapters were devoted to the first five elements. In this chapter, the final element, proper form, is covered.

WHEN CONTRACTS SHOULD BE IN WRITING

The element of proper form requires that certain contracts must be in writing to be enforceable. However, not all contracts should be in writing because many of them are so routine that reducing them to writing would be a waste of time and effort. For example, a written contract is not needed when one is taking a bus ride, purchasing groceries, or ordering a meal in a restaurant. Some contracts *should* be in writing to protect against later disagreement, such as a contract for the purchase of a television. Still others *must* be in writing because the law requires such for the contract to be enforceable.

13.2 THE PAROL EVIDENCE RULE

parol evidence rule
The rule that any spoken or written words in conflict with what the written contract states cannot be introduced as evidence in a court of law.

The word *parol* (not to be confused with the word *parole*) as used in the parol evidence rule simply means "speech" or "words." Parol evidence refers to any supplementary evidence or conditions, written or oral, that a party wants to add to a written contract. The parol evidence rule states that any spoken or written words that are in conflict with what the written contract states cannot be introduced as evidence in a court of law.

There are numerous exceptions to the parol evidence rule. Perhaps the most common exception occurs when oral evidence serves to clear up an ambiguous part of an agreement. Accordingly, oral evidence introduced after a contract is signed is legally accepted if it clarifies some point in the written agreement. The Uniform Commercial Code (UCC) specifically states that the terms of a written contract may not be changed by evidence of any prior agreement but may be explained or supplemented (UCC 2-202).

Some other exceptions to the parol evidence rule apply to (1) incomplete contracts, (2) contracts that contain obvious printed errors, (3) contracts that are partly written and partly oral, (4) voidable contracts, and (5) subsequent oral modification of contracts. In all of these instances, the court may rule that oral evidence is admissible.

EXAMPLE 13.1

When Wlodyka signed a purchase agreement for a small garden tractor, the salesperson orally assured her that several attachments came with the purchase. However, when the tractor was delivered, the attachments were not included. The seller has no legal obligation to furnish the attachments if their inclusion was not specified in the original purchase agreement. If Wlodyka decides to sue the seller, the court will probably refuse to allow her to introduce testimony regarding the oral statements.

In Example 13.1, if the purchase agreement had included a reference such as "and attachments," oral evidence could have legally been introduced later to identify the specific attachments that were required to be included. In a minority of states, however, even consistent oral statements may not be introduced into evidence if a contract is in writing.

EXAMPLE 13.2

- Albano purchased an automobile from McSweyn for $5,000. Not wishing to inform his wife of the real purchase price, Albano asked that the written contract state that the purchase price was only $2,000. McSweyn agreed to this change. When Albano later discovered that the odometer had been modified, he sued for the return of his $5,000. Albano will be allowed to collect only $2,000, the amount specified in the written contract.

13.3 THE STATUTE OF FRAUDS

Like the parol evidence rule, the **Statute of Frauds** is a confusing name for an important legal principle. The name is taken from the English law of 1677 called "An Act for Prevention of Frauds and Perjuries." The law specifies that certain kinds of agreements must be in writing to be enforceable. While there is some variation in its interpretation, most states agree on the main principle of the statute.

Statute of Frauds
A law requiring certain contracts to be in writing to be enforceable.

It is important to note that the Statute of Frauds does not prohibit a person from legally entering into oral contracts for certain kinds of agreements; it only specifies that certain contracts must be in writing to be enforceable. The Statute of Frauds applies only to executory contracts–that is, contracts that have yet to be performed. However, once a contract has been completed, it cannot be canceled merely because it was not in writing–even though it should have been.

13.4 TYPES OF CONTRACTS THAT MUST BE IN WRITING

The Statute of Frauds specifies six types of contracts that must be in writing to be legally enforceable:

- Agreements by an executor or administrator to pay the debts of a deceased person.
- Agreements to answer for the debts of another.
- Agreements that cannot be completed in less than one year.
- Agreements made in contemplation of marriage.
- Agreements to sell any interest in real property.
- Agreements to sell personal property for $500 or more.

executor
A personal representative named in a will to handle matters involving the estate of a deceased person.

administrator
A personal representative named by the court to perform as the executor would in instances in which the deceased person has not left a will.

AGREEMENTS BY AN EXECUTOR OR ADMINISTRATOR TO PAY THE DEBTS OF A DECEASED PERSON

The law recognizes that there are often many unsettled matters that need to be resolved when a person dies. As will be explained in Chapter 27, an executor is a personal representative named in a will to handle matters involving the estate of the deceased person. An administrator is a personal representative named by the court to perform as the executor would in instances in which the deceased person has not left a will. Either an executor or an administrator has legal authority to arrange for the distribution of the assets of a deceased person, and in such a position may be inclined to promise to pay debts of the deceased personally. The Statute of Frauds requires that such a promise must be in writing to be enforceable.

EXAMPLE 13.3

▶ Dellner was named executor in his father's will. After his father's death, Dellner was attempting to close the estate when a creditor demanded immediate payment of an old debt of $4,000. To avoid embarrassment for other members of the family, Dellner orally advised the creditor that he would pay the debt personally. Such a promise is not enforceable because it is not in writing.

guaranty
A promise to pay the debts or settle the wrongdoings of another if he or she does not make settlement personally.

AGREEMENTS TO ANSWER FOR THE DEBTS OF ANOTHER

A guaranty, or promise, to pay the debts or settle the wrongdoings of another if they do not make settlement personally is not enforceable unless it is written.

EXAMPLE 13.4

▶ Mata, the president of Callin Products Inc., orally promised to pay the corporation's debts from his own resources in an effort to calm several persistent creditors. Under the Statute of Frauds, Mata's promise is not enforceable because it is not in writing.

An oral promise to pay the debts of another is enforceable in some states, however, if the promise is not dependent on the inability or unwillingness of the other party to pay them.

AGREEMENTS THAT CANNOT BE COMPLETED IN LESS THAN ONE YEAR

A contract that obviously cannot be completed within one year must be in writing. If the life of the contract is indefinite and there is a possibility of it being completed within a year, it need not be in writing.

EXAMPLE 13.5

▶ Rizzi, a building contractor constructing a condominium, orally agreed with a food service company to deliver coffee and lunch to the workers on the job until the construction was completed. Six months later, Rizzi canceled the contract. When the food service company complained, Rizzi said that the contract could not possibly have been completed within a year because the schedule called for completion of the condominium in 18 months. Because it was impossible to complete the contract within a year, it must have been in writing to be enforceable.

In Example 13.5, if the building had been scheduled for completion in 9 months but took 14 months because of delays, then the contract would not need to have been in writing to be enforceable.

An exchange of promises made by persons planning to marry is known as a prenuptial agreement.
zimmytws/123RF

AGREEMENTS MADE IN CONTEMPLATION OF MARRIAGE

An exchange of promises made by persons planning to marry is known as an antenuptial agreement, sometimes referred to as a prenuptial agreement. Such a contract is enforceable only if it is reduced to writing before the marriage takes place. This law applies to agreements by the parties to accept additional obligations not ordinarily included in the marriage contract.

antenuptial or prenuptial agreement
An exchange of promises made by persons planning to marry.

EXAMPLE 13.6

▶ Kennedy inherited a computer retail store worth several hundred thousand dollars. To ensure that her fiancé was not interested solely in her wealth, she asked him to agree, in writing and before their marriage, that all rights to this property would be hers alone. This agreement, made in contemplation of marriage, is a valid, enforceable contract.

It should be noted that antenuptial agreements often include a provision whereby they expire after a long period of time. Also, antenuptial agreements relating to custody of children in the event of divorce or separation are unenforceable; courts decide custody issues because the welfare of the child is always paramount.

AGREEMENTS TO SELL ANY INTEREST IN REAL PROPERTY

Real property, often called *real estate,* is land and items permanently attached to the land, such as buildings or trees (all other property is considered *personal property*). All contracts to sell real property or any interest in it must be in writing to be enforceable.

There is an exception to the written requirement for contracts to sell real property. This occurs when there has been partial performance of an oral agreement, thus proving the existence of the contract. Let us assume, for example, that the buyer of real property has made significant improvements to the property; paid all, or a portion of, the purchase price; or taken possession of the property. In such a case, a court might rule that partial performance is substantial enough to prove that the contract is enforceable even though it was not in writing.

EXAMPLE 13.7

▶ Abdula agreed to sell a portion of his property to his neighbor, Sasaki. Because they had known each other for many years, they agreed orally on the terms of the contract. When Abdula realized that the property had increased in value over the years, he changed his mind. Sasaki would have no legal recourse because a contract for the sale of any interest in real property must be in writing.

AGREEMENTS TO SELL PERSONAL PROPERTY FOR $500 OR MORE

The English law of 1677 that served as the basis for the Statute of Frauds provided that a contract of sale for more than 10 pounds sterling had to be in writing. This early law has found its way into today's UCC as a requirement that sales of personal property for $500 or more must be in writing (UCC 2-201). (It should be noted that several states have increased this amount in recent years.) The UCC also has other requirements for written contracts, which are discussed in later chapters.

auction sale
A sale in which goods are sold to the highest bidder.

EXAMPLE 13.8

▶ Suard, the owner of a clothing store, orally agreed to buy a made-to-order display case for $1,200 from Island Fixtures, a manufacturer of display and exhibit equipment. Because of a long-standing relationship between the parties to the contract, neither one demanded that the agreement be in writing. Although either Suard or Island Fixtures could back out of the deal, in most instances, they would not because they value their reputations in the community. Legally, however, the contract is unenforceable.

All contracts to sell real property or any interest in it must be in writing to be enforceable.
Phillip Spears/Getty Images

There are several exceptions to this requirement. Partial or full payment to the seller renders the contract enforceable because it shows the serious intent of the buyer, just as much as a written agreement does.

In Example 13.8, if Suard paid part of the sale price to Island Fixtures at the time of the agreement, both parties would be bound to the contract. Acceptance by the buyer or attempted delivery by the seller of the goods or part of them also indicates the serious intent of the parties and renders the oral contract enforceable.

In auction sales, in which goods are sold to the highest bidder, the sale is completed at the fall of the hammer. The notation in the auctioneer's book, initialed by the buyer, is sufficient to meet the requirements for written contracts. In the case of auction bids made by telephone from another city, the bidder is required to sign an agreement in which they agree to be bound by the telephone bids made. In the case of an online sale, the web page or email is generally regarded as the writing that satisfies the Statute of Frauds (see Chapter 31).

13.5 INFORMATION INCLUDED IN A WRITTEN CONTRACT

Most important contracts are printed and signed by hand by the parties to the agreement. A signature may include any symbol used by a contracting party intending to authenticate a written agreement. This can include, for example, a firm's logo or a purchase order. A valid agreement can be entirely handwritten as long as it is legible. It may even be a series of letters, emails, or text messages among several persons. It can be written on almost any surface with any material that makes a discernible mark, such as pen, pencil, or crayon. (Electronically produced and signed contracts, including smart contracts, will be covered in Chapter 31.)

To satisfy the Statute of Frauds, a written contract or agreement, sometimes called a **memorandum**, must contain the following information (see Figure 13.1):

memorandum A written contract or agreement.

1. The names of the parties.
2. The purpose of the agreement.
3. A description of the consideration promised.
4. The date and place where the contract was made.
5. The signatures of the parties.

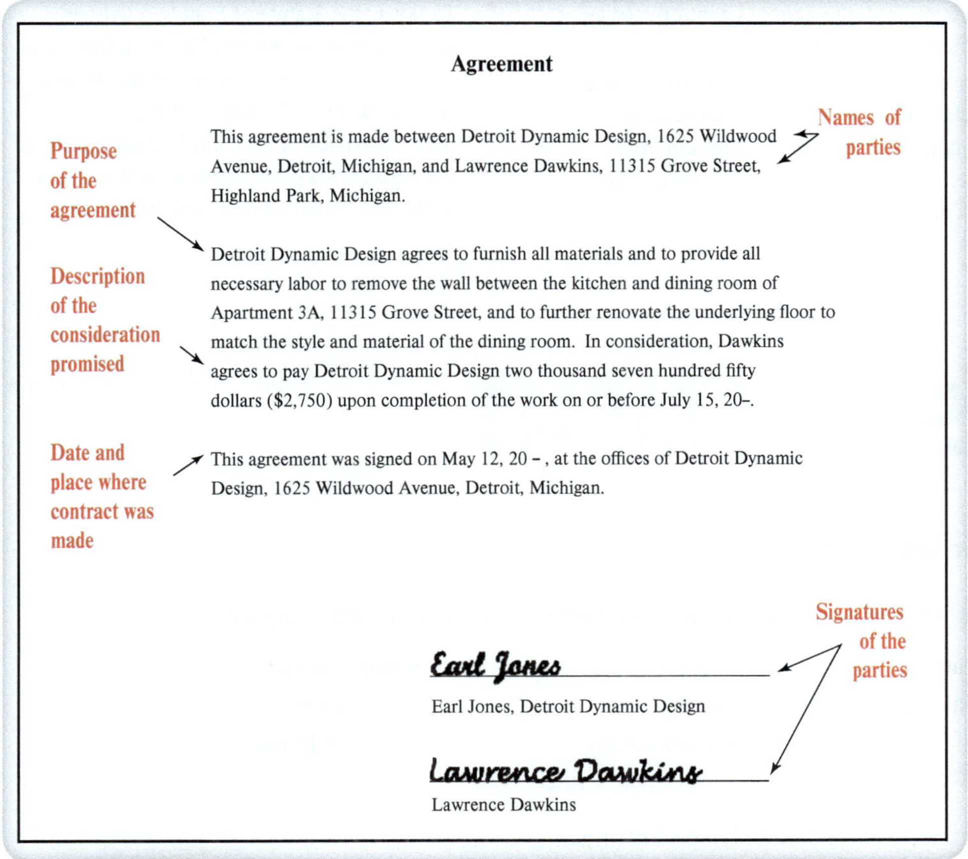
Agreement

This agreement is made between Detroit Dynamic Design, 1625 Wildwood Avenue, Detroit, Michigan, and Lawrence Dawkins, 11315 Grove Street, Highland Park, Michigan.

Detroit Dynamic Design agrees to furnish all materials and to provide all necessary labor to remove the wall between the kitchen and dining room of Apartment 3A, 11315 Grove Street, and to further renovate the underlying floor to match the style and material of the dining room. In consideration, Dawkins agrees to pay Detroit Dynamic Design two thousand seven hundred fifty dollars ($2,750) upon completion of the work on or before July 15, 20–.

This agreement was signed on May 12, 20 – , at the offices of Detroit Dynamic Design, 1625 Wildwood Avenue, Detroit, Michigan.

Earl Jones
Earl Jones, Detroit Dynamic Design

Lawrence Dawkins
Lawrence Dawkins

FIGURE 13.1 A Written Contract, or Agreement, Containing Information Sufficient to Satisfy the Statute of Frauds

In addition, written contracts frequently contain the following information:

1. Warranties provided by the seller.
2. An agreement to be bound by the laws of a specific state.
3. An acknowledgment that the buyer has inspected the goods or has waived their right to such inspection.
4. The form of acceptable payment (cash, certified check, cryptocurrency, etc.).

CHAPTER SUMMARY

13.1 Routine contracts *should not* be in writing because it would be a waste of time and effort. Some contracts *should* be in writing to protect against later disagreement. Still other contracts *must* be in writing because the law requires such for the contract to be enforceable.

13.2 The parol evidence rule states that any spoken or written words in conflict with what the written contract states cannot be introduced as evidence in a court of law.

13.3 The Statute of Frauds is a law requiring certain contracts to be in writing to be enforceable. It does not, however, prohibit a person from legally entering into oral contracts for certain kinds of agreements.

13.4 Contracts that must be in writing to be legally enforceable include agreements (a) by an executor or administrator to pay the debts of a deceased person, (b) to answer for the debts of another, (c) that cannot be completed in less than a year, (d) made in contemplation of marriage, (e) to sell any interest in real property, and (f) to sell personal property for $500 or more.

13.5 To satisfy the Statute of Frauds, a written contract must include the following five items of information: (a) the names of the parties, (b) the purpose of the agreement, (c) a description of the consideration promised, (d) the date and place where the contract was made, and (e) the signatures of the parties.

CHAPTER THIRTEEN ASSESSMENT

MATCHING LEGAL TERMS

Match each of the numbered definitions with the correct term in the following list.

a. administrator
b. antenuptial or prenuptial agreement
c. auctioneer
d. executor
e. guaranty
f. memorandum
g. parol evidence rule
h. personal property
i. real property
j. Statute of Frauds

1. The law that requires certain types of contracts to be in writing. 1. _____
2. Property other than land and items permanently attached to it. 2. _____

3. The point of law that prevents oral changes to a written contract from being legally enforceable. 3. _____

4. A written contract or agreement. 4. _____

5. The personal representative appointed by a court to distribute the assets of the estate of the deceased. 5. _____

6. Land and items that are permanently attached to it. 6. _____

7. The personal representative named in a will to distribute the assets of the estate of the deceased. 7. _____

8. A promise to pay the debts or settle the wrongdoings of another. 8. _____

9. A person who conducts sales of articles in which individuals bid against one another. 9. _____

10. A contract containing promises made by persons planning to marry. 10. _____

TRUE/FALSE QUIZ

Indicate whether each of the following statements is true or false.

11. Some types of contracts must be in writing to be enforceable. 11. _____

12. The parol evidence rule affects the enforceability of contracts that include oral or written changes in the terms of an existing contract. 12. _____

13. The Statute of Frauds specifies that certain kinds of contracts must be in writing. 13. _____

14. Oral or written evidence cannot legally be introduced to explain unclear portions of a contract. 14. _____

15. A valid contract can be entirely handwritten. 15. _____

16. An agreement that cannot be completed within six months must be in writing. 16. _____

17. An agreement for the sale of personal property for over $500 must be in writing to be enforceable. 17. _____

18. An agreement for the sale of real estate must be in writing to be enforceable. 18. _____

MULTIPLE CHOICE QUIZ

Please indicate the correct answer from the choices following each question.

19. Which of the following contracts must be in writing? (a) Contract to repair porch for $250 (b) Contract for employment for term of two years (c) Contract to write advertisement for $400 (d) Contract to do three months of lawn work for total of $450 19. _____

20. The requirement for certain contracts to be in writing stems from which law? (a) Parol evidence rule (b) Res judicata (c) Statute of Frauds (d) Promissory estoppel **20.** ____

21. A contract to loan money includes the term that the interest rate will be calculated based on the current U.S. Treasury rate at any given time. In this case, (a) the contract may incorporate the outside evidence under the parol evidence rule (b) the contract may not incorporate the evidence under the parol evidence rule (c) the contract may incorporate the evidence under the Statute of Frauds (d) the contract may not incorporate the evidence under the Statute of Frauds. **21.** ____

22. Which of the following contracts should be in writing? (a) Contract to repair porch for $250 (b) Contract to write advertisement for $400 (c) Both a and b (d) Neither a nor b **22.** ____

23. Which of the following contracts must be in writing? (a) Contract to repair porch for $250 (b) Contract to write advertisement for $400 (c) Both a and b (d) Neither a nor b **23.** ____

24. A contract between two parties must include which of the following information in order to be in valid form? (a) The address of each party to the contract (b) The age of the parties to the contract (c) The place where the contract is being made (d) The Social Security numbers of the parties to the contract **24.** ____

DISCUSSION QUESTIONS

Answer the following questions and discuss them in class.

25. What are the chief provisions of the Statute of Frauds? Can you suggest other agreements that also should be in writing?

______

______

26. What is the minimum dollar amount specified in the Uniform Commercial Code as a requirement for written contracts for the sale of personal property? Should this amount be greater?

______

______

27. In auction sales, how is the legal requirement for a written contract satisfied? What problems might arise from this arrangement?

______

______

28. Why do you think an antenuptial agreement dealing with the custody of children would not be enforceable?

29. Why does the Statute of Frauds apply only to executory contracts—that is, contracts that have yet to be performed?

THINKING CRITICALLY ABOUT THE LAW

Answer the following questions, which require you to think critically about the legal principles that you learned in this chapter.

30. Parol Evidence Rule Even though the parol evidence rule prohibits any oral amendments to a contract, try to envision circumstances when this rule might be unreasonable.

31. Statute of Frauds Under the Statute of Frauds, an oral promise to take on the debts of another is enforceable in some states. Can you think of any other activities that might be legally acceptable despite the fact that they are not in writing?

32. Personal Property A buyer places a deposit on an item valued at more than $500 but later wishes to cancel the order. Arguing that there is no written contract, could the buyer expect a refund of the deposit?

33. Statute of Frauds Why must a contract that obviously cannot be completed within one year be in writing?

34. A Question of Ethics A person dies without leaving a will. The administrator of the estate refuses to pay the deceased's debts on the grounds that there is no written evidence of the obligation. Comment on the ethics of this situation.

CASE QUESTIONS

Study each of the following cases. Answer the questions that follow with Yes or No.

35. Statute of Frauds Coursey orally agreed to sell three acres of land to Oulette for $8,000. After Oulette had paid the $8,000 and the transfer had been officially recorded, Coursey received an offer of $9,000 for the land from another prospective buyer. Hoping to set aside the first transaction so that he could accept the second, higher, offer, Coursey attempted to cancel the sale to Oulette on the grounds that the Statute of Frauds required a written contract.

a. Does the fact that there is evidence (the recording of the sale) indicate Coursey's agreement to the terms of the sale? **a.** _____

b. Will Coursey succeed in canceling the contract of sale? **b.** _____

c. Is the contract enforceable? **c.** _____

36. Statute of Frauds Garcia, an independent computer consultant, was orally engaged by the Eastern Institute of Management, a publisher of management newsletters, to set up an office computer network that included needs assessment, employee training, and a desktop publishing system. The plan envisioned at least 18 months of work. Three months after he began work, Eastern paid Garcia for the work he had done and discharged him in order to hire another consultant, who appeared to have wider experience and greater expertise.

a. Can Eastern Institute legally cancel this agreement? **a.** _____

b. If the work could have been done in six months, would the oral contract have been legally enforceable? **b.** _____

37. Parol Evidence Rule Safran, the owner of an automobile repair shop, placed an order for an engine diagnostic machine from the Mountain Range Equipment Company. The salesperson, Rubinstein, orally assured Safran that a number of test programs for both gasoline and diesel engines would be included as part of the order. When the machine was delivered, the test programs were not included. When the buyer protested, Rubinstein claimed that Safran was mistaken and must have been thinking about another special offer the firm was running.

a. Are the oral promises Rubinstein made that supplement the written contract of sale enforceable? **a.** _____

b. Is it likely that Safran will gain legal satisfaction? **b.** _____

c. Does the parol evidence rule allow introduction of oral revisions to a contract? **c.** _____

CASE ANALYSIS

Study each of the following cases carefully. Briefly state the principle of law and your decision.

38. Statute of Frauds Anderson was seriously injured in a traffic accident. Anderson's daughter called a doctor, Lawrence, and told him to "give my father the best care you can give him, and I'll pay whatever you charge." The doctor provided the care, but the father died before the bill was paid. Lawrence attempted to collect for his services from the father's estate. The executor of the estate refused to pay. Lawrence then attempted to collect from the daughter who had guaranteed payment. Is the daughter legally responsible for the debts of her father if the agreement was not in writing? [*Lawrence v. Anderson,* 184 A. 689 (Vermont)]

Principle of Law:

____

____

Decision:

____

____

39. Parol Evidence Rule Dennison agreed to purchase land from Harden with the understanding that the land contained fruit trees. To prove that there were fruit trees on the property, Harden provided nursery reports stating that Pacific Gold peach trees were growing on the land. When Dennison discovered that the land contained valueless, shrubby trees and only a few of the fruit trees he had been expecting, he sued, charging breach of contract. At the trial, Dennison wanted to introduce the nursery reports as parol evidence to clarify the meaning of the "fruit trees" referred to in the contract. Harden resisted having the nursery report introduced to clarify the contract. Was Dennison successful in his attempt to clarify the contract by adding the term *fruit trees,* or did Dennison get what he agreed to buy? [*Dennison v. Harden,* 186 P.2d 908 (Washington)]

Principle of Law:

____

____

Decision:

____

____

40. Contract Essentials Marti, the owner of an expensive sports car, agreed in writing to sell the car to Berini. Because both parties recognized that some necessary engine repairs were needed, their contract did not specify the sales price, intending to determine the cost of repairs first. The cost of repairs was later determined and the final price settled, but the price was never included in the contract. Is this an enforceable contract?

Principle of Law:

____

____

Decision:

____

____

41. Statute of Frauds Phung orally agreed to sell a thoroughbred horse to Presti for $60,000. When Presti sent a check in payment, Phung told him that he intended to hold the check for a month for tax purposes. Phung retained possession of the horse. While the check remained uncashed, a disagreement arose between Phung and Presti. Phung announced that he would not go through with the transaction and that, because the contract was oral, it was unenforceable. Presti claimed that his sending of the check was payment and this action made the oral contract valid and enforceable. Phung denied accepting payment. Is Presti's claim, that sending the check made the contract enforceable, valid?

Principle of Law:

Decision:

LEGAL RESEARCH

Complete the following activities. Share your findings with the class.

42. Working in Teams There are numerous risks in the preparation of contracts. Some must be written as specified by the Statute of Frauds, while others need not be. In teams of three or four, interview owners or managers of several small businesses and ask about the procedures followed to minimize these risks.

43. Using Technology Using the Internet and search engines, investigate the parol evidence rule and the Statute of Frauds in two states. Compare and contrast the rules in the two states.

chapter 14
Operation of Contracts

LEARNING OUTCOMES

After studying this chapter and completing the assessment, you will be able to

14.1 Identify two instances in which a contract may involve third parties.

14.2 Distinguish between a third-party beneficiary and an incidental beneficiary and outline the rights of each.

14.3 Interpret the legal concept of assignment of rights.

14.4 Identify three kinds of contracts that may not be assigned.

14.5 Explain the legal concept of delegation of duties.

14.6 Provide examples of contracts that may be assigned by a court of law.

14.7 Discuss novation and how it differs from assignment.

OPERATION OF CONTRACTS

"When three persons are together, two of them must not whisper to each other, without letting the third hear; because it would hurt him."

The prophet Muhammad, founder of the religion of Islam

Ariel Skelley/Blend Images/Getty Images

LEGAL terms

- third-party beneficiary
- incidental beneficiary
- assignment
- assignor
- assignee
- guarantor
- personal-service contract
- delegation
- bankruptcy
- novation

14.1 CONTRACTS INVOLVING THIRD PARTIES

In the previous chapters about contracts, only contracts between two parties were discussed. The reason is that normally only the two parties to a contract have rights and duties under it. However, there are two important exceptions to this rule: (1) when the purpose of a contract is to benefit a third party and (2) when rights or duties that arise from a contract are legally transferred to a third party.

14.2 RIGHTS OF THIRD PARTIES

Third parties to a contract are those who are in some way affected by it but who are not one of the parties to the contract. There are two ways in which third parties can be affected by a contract: if they are either (1) third-party beneficiaries or (2) incidental beneficiaries.

THIRD-PARTY BENEFICIARIES

third-party beneficiary
A person who is not a party to a contract but is intended by the contracting parties to benefit as a consequence of a contract.

A third-party beneficiary to a contract has a legal right to the benefits resulting from the contract only if it is the intent of the contracting parties to benefit the third party. A life insurance policy is an example of a third-party contract, and the beneficiary named in the insurance policy is legally a third-party beneficiary.

EXAMPLE 14.1

Hamomoto contracted with an artist, Frey, to create a painting of his family's farmhouse for $1,000. The artist was informed that the painting was to be presented to Hamomoto's son as a birthday gift. Just before the painting was finished, Hamomoto died. Frey learned that she could sell the painting through an art gallery for an amount in excess of $10,000. She offered to return to Hamomoto's son the portion of the fee that his father had already paid, but the son insisted that Frey fulfill the terms of the contract. The son, who is not one of the contracting parties, is a third-party beneficiary and is entitled to receive the painting.

INCIDENTAL BENEFICIARIES

incidental beneficiary
A person who will benefit as an indirect consequence of a contract, although that was not the intent of the contracting parties.

An incidental beneficiary is one who may benefit as an indirect consequence of a contract, although that was not the intent of the contracting parties. That is, the purpose of the contract is not to confer a benefit to a third party, but a third party does, in fact, benefit from it. Such parties have no rights in the contract, regardless of the size of their gain or benefit.

EXAMPLE 14.2

Sceneview Development Company entered into a contract with Soula Realtors to construct a marina and condominium on the shore of a lake. Philbus owned property adjacent to the planned development. Knowing that the value of his property was about to be greatly enhanced, Philbus began developing his own property and planned to open a number of stores and a restaurant to serve the people who would be attracted to the Sceneview Development. However, because of financial difficulties, Sceneview requested, and Soula Realtors agreed, to cancel their contract. Philbus suffered a loss as a consequence of Sceneview's cancellation, but because he is an incidental beneficiary, he has no rights in the contract and no legal course of action.

14.3 ASSIGNMENT OF RIGHTS

In most states, the law permits a party to a contract to assign rights–that is, to transfer them to a third party and permit the third party to receive the benefits of the contract. This change of a contract is known as an assignment. The person who transfers their rights is known as the assignor; the third party to whom the rights are transferred is known as the assignee. A party to an existing contract may also appoint a third person to perform contractual duties; this appointment is referred to as a delegation (discussed later in this chapter).

A party may transfer their rights by assignment and their duties by delegation, subject to several restraints (e.g., prohibition by law and personal-service contracts). It is important to note that the term *duties* means tasks and performance, not responsibilities. A person who agrees in a contract to perform a particular task may generally delegate this task to someone else but is still responsible for getting it done. Consider Example 14.3, in which Higgins transfers his duty to Randall but is still responsible for making certain that the duty is met.

assignment
The transfer of a contract right to a third party who can receive the benefits of the contract.

assignor
The person who transfers his or her rights in an assignment.

assignee
The third party to whom rights are transferred in an assignment.

EXAMPLE 14.3

▶ Higgins, a professor of finance, agreed to conduct a financial planning workshop for Randall, the president of a local club of retirees, for a fee of $1,200. Before conducting the workshop, Higgins assigned his right to the $1,200 to the Holiday Villa Motel, where he had held a number of workshops and to whom he owed $1,500. Holiday Villa was eager to agree to this arrangement because it was concerned about Higgins's ability to pay his bill. When the workshop was finished, Randall simply paid the $1,200 to Holiday Villa instead of to Higgins. Higgins is the assignor and Holiday Villa is the assignee.

FORM OF ASSIGNMENT

In general, an assignment may be either written or oral. However, if the original contract is required to be in writing under the Statute of Frauds, the assignment also must be in writing. Obviously it makes good sense to put important assignments in writing, whether or not required by the Statute of Frauds (see Chapter 13).

NOTICE OF ASSIGNMENT

A party to a contract will not be obligated by an assignment made by the other party without his or her knowledge until notified. In Example 14.3, it is the responsibility of the assignee, Holiday Villa, to notify the other party to the contract, Randall, of the assignment. The burden of investigating claims of assignment then falls on the party notified of the assignment (Randall). After a party (Randall) has received a notice of an assignment, they may demand a reasonable time to investigate its validity.

Parties to a contract must give notice of assignment.
Yuri Arcurs/Cutcaster

RIGHTS THAT MAY BE TRANSFERRED

Most rights are assignable, except in cases in which the obligations of the parties would be significantly altered. Suppose that, in the case of Professor Higgins's financial planning workshop, Randall contracted with Higgins, but then the retirees vetoed the idea of the workshop altogether–because most of them had modest incomes and little interest in financial planning.

Assume also that, to salvage some value from the workshop to which she was already committed, Randall attempted to assign her right to have the workshop conducted to a local group of bankers. It is likely that this assignment would not be acceptable to Higgins because he would be required to significantly modify his presentation. Usually, contracts for personal services are neither assignable nor delegable.

THE ASSIGNOR'S GUARANTY

guarantor
The party who guarantees the promises assigned.

The assignor of a contract right becomes a guarantor–that is, one who guarantees the promises assigned. The Uniform Commercial Code (UCC) states, "No delegation of performance relieves the party delegating of any duty to perform or any liability for breach" (UCC 2-210).*

EXAMPLE 14.4

Von Berg, a residential homeowner, entered into a contract with Rountree Construction to have a driveway installed. Before construction began, Von Berg learned that a proposed local zoning regulation would no longer allow concrete driveways on her street. Rather than breach her contract with Rountree Construction, Von Berg assigned her rights to have the driveway installed to Levi, a friend who owned a similar home nearby. If Rountree Construction installed a substandard driveway for Levi, Von Berg, the original assignor of the contract right to have the driveway installed, would be responsible to Levi for Rountree's failure to perform properly.

14.4 CONTRACTS THAT MAY NOT BE ASSIGNED

Three types of contracts may not be assigned: (1) contracts that include assignment restrictions, (2) contracts for which assignments are prohibited by law or public policy, and (3) contracts that require personal services.

CONTRACTS THAT INCLUDE ASSIGNMENT RESTRICTIONS

When parties to a contract include in the contract itself a specific provision forbidding assignment, both parties are prevented from assigning their rights or delegating their duties. A contract also may prohibit just one party from assigning or delegating.

CONTRACTS FOR WHICH ASSIGNMENTS ARE PROHIBITED BY LAW OR PUBLIC POLICY

Various state and federal statutes have been enacted to prohibit the assignment of certain contracts. For example, members of the armed services are prohibited from assigning

*The Uniform Commercial Code (UCC) is a joint project between the National Conference of Commissioners on Uniform State Laws (NCCUSL) and the American Law Institute (ALI).

their pay, and many state and local governments prohibit the assignment of salaries of public officials.

CONTRACTS THAT REQUIRE PERSONAL SERVICES

A personal-service contract is one in which services that require a unique skill, talent, ability, and so forth are provided by a specific person. In such a case, the party who hires the specific person to perform certain duties has a substantial interest in having only the hired person perform.

personal-service contract A contract in which services that require a unique skill, talent, ability, and so forth are provided by a specific person.

Personal-service contracts may not be assigned. For example, artists, musicians, photographers, and athletes are hired because of their special personal skills, and consequently, their services under a contract may not be delegated to anyone else. In most cases, an employment contract is considered a personal-service contract and may not be assigned.

EXAMPLE 14.5

▶ Janik, vice president of marketing for Maximal Products, hired Papandreau, an inspirational speaker, to address her annual meeting of salespeople. Because of a last-minute scheduling problem, Papandreau canceled her appearance but offered to send her brother to speak in her place. Janik refused the offer, claiming that Papandreau was well-known and the salespeople were expecting her unique inspirational message. Should this case reach a courtroom, a court would find in favor of Janik.

14.5 DELEGATION OF DUTIES

delegation The appointment of a third party by a party to an existing contract to perform contractual duties that do not involve unique skills, talents, abilities, and so on.

Just as a party's rights in a contract can be assigned to another party, a party's duties can be transferred to a third party if the duties do not involve unique skills or abilities. This transfer is known as a delegation of duties. Even employment contracts may be assigned if there is

Because athletes are hired for their special personal skills, their services under a contract may not be delegated to anyone else.
Imac/Alamy Stock Photo

no relationship of trust or confidence, or any other circumstance that would create a materially greater burden on the party whose services are being assigned.

EXAMPLE 14.6

Rensal Services had a three-year employment contract with Kopelek, an accountant. After Kopelek had been employed for only three months, Rensal Services was sold to Pacific Accountants and Kopelek's contract was assigned to Pacific. Kopelek refused to work for Pacific, claiming that he had a special relationship with Rensal and the working atmosphere was "almost family." The duties assigned to him by Pacific were substantially the same as before the sale of Rensal. Consequently, the assignment of Kopelek's contract would be legally enforceable.

14.6 ASSIGNMENT AND DELEGATION BY LAW

Rights or duties under a contract may be assigned by a court of law when a contracting party dies or becomes bankrupt.

DEATH OF A CONTRACTING PARTY

When a party to a contract dies, all contractual rights are assigned to the administrator or executor of the estate. All rights to the collection of money, to demands for performance, and to the sale or purchase of real or personal property are assigned by law immediately upon the party's death. This assignment does not include personal-service contracts of the deceased that are not delegable because of the unique skills of the deceased.

EXAMPLE 14.7

Zarb, a composer, agreed in writing to sell an original musical score to Olney, a music promoter, for $65,000. One week before the completed score was to be delivered and payment made, Olney was killed in an accident. Meanwhile, Zarb got an offer of $75,000 for the score from a different promoter and as a result stood to gain from not completing the transaction with Olney. The right to purchase the music, however, was assigned by law to Olney's executor, and Zarb must complete the transaction.

In Example 14.7, if, instead of Olney, Zarb had been killed in the accident, neither Olney nor Zarb's executor would have any rights or duties under the contract, which was for Zarb's personal services.

bankruptcy
The legal state that occurs when a debtor is insolvent, is in default, and is unable to fulfill their obligations to pay back their creditors.

BANKRUPTCY OF A CONTRACTING PARTY

The laws dealing with bankruptcy provide that the assets and contracts of a bankrupt (legally recognized as unable to pay legitimate debts) person or business be assigned to the trustee in bankruptcy. The trustee is then empowered to sell the assets and exercise contract rights for the benefit of the creditors of the bankrupt person or firm (see Chapter 21).

14.7 NOVATION

When all parties to a contract agree to a significant change in the contract, the change is called a novation. Such a change actually creates a new contract that is simply based on the earlier one. A novation differs from an assignment in the following ways:

novation
A situation in which all parties to a contract agree to a significant change to a contract.

- A novation requires mutual consent of all parties (the original parties to the agreement and any new third parties) just as does a new contract. However, an assignment can be made without the mutual consent of both contracting parties.
- A novation transfers all rights and obligations in a contract, but an assignment transfers only the rights of the assignor and leaves the assignor with the duty of fulfilling their obligations under the contract.

As a result, a party to a contract who assigns their rights or delegates their duties to a third party is never free from the contract until it is completely executed. In contrast, if the third party enters the contract as a result of a novation, the party whose rights or duties are assumed is completely relieved of any obligations.

EXAMPLE 14.8

- Fortesi and Yellen entered into a contract in which Fortesi agreed to build a garage on Yellen's property. Later they and Zink agreed that Zink would perform Fortesi's obligations, with Yellen expressly releasing Fortesi from the original contract. This is a novation, and Fortesi's obligations are now discharged.

CHAPTER SUMMARY

14.1 A contract may involve more than two parties (a) when the purpose of a contract is to benefit a third party and (b) when rights or duties that arise from a contract are legally transferred to a third party.

14.2 A third-party beneficiary to a contract has a legal right to the benefits resulting from the contract only if the contracting parties intend to benefit the third party. An incidental beneficiary is one who may benefit as an indirect consequence of a contract, although that was not the intent of the contracting parties. An incidental party has no rights in the contract.

14.3 An assignment occurs when a party to a contract transfers their rights under the contract to a third party and permits the third party to receive the benefits of the contract.

14.4 Three types of contracts that may not be assigned include (a) contracts that include assignment restrictions, (b) contracts for which assignments are prohibited by law or public policy, and (c) contracts that require personal service.

14.5 A delegation of duties obliges a third party to carry out the tasks and performance under the terms of the contract, provided they do not involve unique skills or abilities.

14.6 A court can assign rights and duties under a contract when a contracting party dies or becomes bankrupt.

14.7 A novation occurs when parties to a contract agree to a significant change in the contract. A novation differs from an assignment because (a) unlike an assignment, it requires the mutual consent of all parties, and (b) a novation transfers all rights and obligations in a contract, but an assignment transfers only the rights of the assignor and still leaves the assignor with the duty of fulfilling their obligations under the contract.

CHAPTER FOURTEEN ASSESSMENT

MATCHING LEGAL TERMS

Match each of the numbered definitions with the correct term in the following list.

a. assignee
b. assignment
c. assignor
d. bankrupt
e. delegation
f. guarantor
g. incidental beneficiary
h. novation
i. personal-service contract
j. third-party beneficiary

1. A significant change in a contract that is made with the mutual consent of all parties. 1. _____
2. The transfer of duties to a third party by a party to a contract. 2. _____
3. A party who would benefit from the performance of a contract, but for whom the contract is not created. 3. _____
4. An outside party for whose benefit a contract is made by other parties. 4. _____
5. A party to a contract who transfers their rights to a third party. 5. _____
6. A contract in which services that require a unique skill, talent, ability, or the like are provided by a specific person. 6. _____
7. The state of a person or firm recognized to be unable to pay obligations. 7. _____
8. An outside party to whom contract rights are transferred. 8. _____
9. The transfer of contract rights by one of the parties. 9. _____
10. An assignor who guarantees or stands behind an assignment. 10. _____

TRUE/FALSE QUIZ

Indicate whether each of the following statements is true or false.

11. A third-party beneficiary has the legal right to receive the benefits of a contract if it is the intent of the contract to benefit the third party. 11. _____
12. The law in most states permits the assignment of most contract rights to a third party. 12. _____
13. The assignment of certain contracts is prohibited by law. 13. _____
14. Contracts for personal services may be assigned if there is no agreement to the contrary. 14. _____
15. Services of artists, musicians, photographers, and athletes can be delegated. 15. _____

16. Once a person completes a contractual duty, they no longer have responsibility under the contract. **16.** _____

17. A novation is a special kind of assignment in which none of the parties to the contract are required to agree to its terms. **17.** _____

MULTIPLE CHOICE QUIZ

Indicate the correct answer from the choices following each question.

18. The two categories of third parties to a contract are legally known as (a) original contractors and third party beneficiaries (b) third party contractors and incidental contractors (c) original beneficiaries and incidental beneficiaries (d) third party beneficiaries and incidental beneficiaries. **18.** _____

19. A named beneficiary to a life insurance contract is a (a) third party beneficiary (b) incidental beneficiary (c) original beneficiary (d) original contractor. **19.** _____

20. The difference between a third-party beneficiary and an incidental beneficiary is (a) only the incidental beneficiary can enforce the terms of the contract (b) there is no difference and both can enforce the terms of the contract (c) only the third-party beneficiary can enforce the terms of the contract (d) there is no difference and neither can enforce the terms of the contract. **20.** _____

21. When performance of duties under a contract are assigned, the assignor (a) is no longer liable for performance (b) must pay the assignee additional compensation (c) only the assignor is liable for performance (d) both the assignor and the assignee are liable for performance **21.** _____

22. Which of the following is an example of a contract that cannot be assigned? (a) Contract for residential house construction (b) Contract for catering services at a wedding (c) Contract for a musician to perform a concert (d) Contract for transportation services **22.** _____

23. Which of the following is an example of assignment by law? (a) Assignment to collect contractual payment from a party's estate after death of that party (b) Assignment to collect money from a third party before death of the original party (c) Assignment to collect money from a collection agency (d) None of the above **23.** _____

24. A novation differs from an assignment in that (a) there is no difference between the two (b) the novation creates a new contract but the original parties remain liable for performance, together with all new parties (c) the original parties are no longer liable because there is a new contract (d) all of the above. **24.** _____

25. A novation requires (a) significant change to the terms of the original contract (b) mutual consent of the parties (c) transfer of all rights and obligations under the contract (d) all of the above. **25.** _____

DISCUSSION QUESTIONS

Answer the following questions and discuss them in class.

26. Distinguish between a third-party beneficiary and an incidental beneficiary.

27. Explain the legal concept of assignment of contracts, and provide an example of a contract that is assignable.

28. Distinguish between the assignment of rights and delegation of duties.

29. Identify the three kinds of contracts that cannot be assigned.

30. Describe the circumstances in which a court might assign rights or duties under a contract.

31. Discuss novation and explain how it differs from assignment.

THINKING CRITICALLY ABOUT THE LAW

Answer the following questions, which require you to think critically about the legal principles that you learned in this chapter.

32. Third-Party Beneficiary Do you think a third-party beneficiary should be required to sign a contract as one of the parties involved?

33. Incidental Beneficiary Should an incidental beneficiary to a contract have any legal recourse if the contract is terminated?

____

____

34. Personal-Service Contract Under what circumstances could the duties under a personal-service contract be delegated?

____

____

35. Novation What are some advantages of using a novation over a contract assignment?

____

____

36. A Question of Ethics Under the law, a bankrupt person is allowed to retain certain property–including his or her residence. Is it ethical for a bankrupt person to use the law to avoid payment on their legitimate debts and still retain some, often valuable, property?

____

____

CASE QUESTIONS

Study each of the following cases. Answer the questions that follow with Yes or No.

37. Performance Liability Chang, a florist, contracted with Torres to provide delivery services in the local community. Torres discovered that his vehicles did not have the equipment to handle the work well, so he asked Chang if another delivery service, Rush Truk, would be acceptable to him. After some meetings with Torres and Rush Truk, Chang agreed to the change in delivery services.

a. Is Torres responsible for the performance of Rush Truk? **a.** ______

b. Is this a valid assignment? **b.** ______

c. Is this an example of a novation? **c.** ______

38. Beneficiary Benefits Becker, a college student, recognized that she was financially very dependent upon her widowed mother's financial support while she was in college. To protect against the risk of financial loss in the event of her mother's death, Becker persuaded her mother to take out an insurance policy naming her as the beneficiary.

a. Is Becker an incidental beneficiary? **a.** ______

b. Is Becker a third-party beneficiary? **b.** ______

c. In the event of the mother's death, would Becker's college be deemed to be a third-party beneficiary? **c.** ______

39. Contractual Rights Westerfield contracted with Bradley Building Company for the construction of a ranch house as a wedding gift for his daughter. Before construction began, Westerfield died and Bradley announced that he would not build the house. Westerfield's daughter brought suit in her own name to compel Bradley to build the house as it had contracted to do.

a. Does the daughter have any rights in the contract between her father and Bradley Construction Company? **a.** _____

b. Can the daughter, a third-party beneficiary, seek to have the court force Bradley Construction Company to construct the house or to pay damages to the daughter? **b.** _____

40. Contract Assignment Rodrigos, the leader of a rock-and-roll group, agreed to provide music for the annual Park College Marketing Club dinner dance. On the night of the dinner dance, however, another, very amateurish group showed up and said that Rodrigos had assigned the contract to them and that they would play the engagement.

a. Is a person who hires an outside entertainer required to accept the services of a substitute if it is impossible for the original party to perform? **a.** _____

b. Are all contracts assignable? **b.** _____

c. Can contracts for personal services be assigned? **c.** _____

CASE ANALYSIS

Study each of the following cases carefully. Briefly state the principle of law and your decision.

41. Assignable Contracts A restaurant, Pizza of Gaithersburg Inc. (PG), agreed with Virginia Coffee Service (VCS) to have vending machines installed in PG's restaurants. The contract was to run for one year and was automatically renewable unless PG gave 30 days' notice. One year later, VCS was sold to Macke Company, including the contract with PG. PG canceled the contract because of the change of ownership. Macke sued PG, claiming that VCS had delegated the duties to Macke and it was performing the duties previously done by VCS. PG claimed that the contract it had with VCS was a personal-service contract and was therefore not assignable. Does Macke Company have a valid argument? [*Macke Co. v. Pizza of Gaithersburg, Inc.*, 270 A.2d 645 (Maryland)]

Principle of Law:

____

____

Decision:

____

____

42. Third-Party Beneficiaries The employees of Powder Power Tools Corp. were represented by a labor union that had negotiated an agreement covering pay rates. A number of employees did not receive the higher rates of pay specified in the union contract. Springer, an employee, brought suit on behalf of those employees who did not receive the higher pay, claiming that they were third-party beneficiaries of the contract. The employer claimed that Springer could not sue because he was not a party to the contract. Is it likely that Springer will be successful in his suit? [*Springer v. Powder Power Tool Corp.,* 348 P.2d 1112 (Oregon)]

Principle of Law:

____

____

Decision:

____

____

43. Lost Benefits Birmingham Automotive Supply Company entered into a contract with the Excel Construction Company to build a chain-link fence around the property of the auto supply company. Included in the contract was a provision that the fence must be manufactured by Tornado Fence Company. Excel used another brand of fence, and Tornado sued Excel for the loss suffered, claiming that it was a third-party beneficiary to the contract. Will Tornado be successful in its claim of loss suffered?

Principle of Law:

____

____

Decision:

____

____

44. Death of a Contracting Party Weintraub wished to donate a music rehearsal room to Northern College, from which she had graduated. She hired Hazelton, an architect who specialized in acoustics, to design the room. Shortly after the agreement was made, Weintraub died. Hazelton refused to begin work, claiming that his contract was made with Weintraub. Can the college compel Hazelton to complete the work he agreed to do for Weintraub?

Principle of Law:

____

____

Decision:

____

____

LEGAL RESEARCH

Complete the following activities. Share your findings with the class.

45. Working in Teams Working in teams of three or four, interview the owners or managers of small businesses to determine whether they typically are impacted by contract assignments.

46. Using Technology Using the Internet and search engines, investigate typical state regulations or legislation that govern the assignment of certain contracts. What are some types of contracts that are typically controlled?

chapter 15
Discharge of Contracts

LEARNING OUTCOMES

After studying this chapter and completing the assessment, you will be able to

15.1 Identify seven ways in which a contract may be terminated.

15.2 Discuss termination of a contract by agreement.

15.3 Explain the three types of termination by performance.

15.4 Explain termination by impossibility of performance.

15.5 Describe when termination by alteration occurs.

15.6 Identify the circumstances under which a contract would be terminated by operation of law.

15.7 Provide examples of contracts terminated by breach.

15.8 Explain how contracts can be terminated to protect consumers.

15.9 Discuss the remedies for breach of contract and provide examples of situations that would be appropriate for each remedy.

DISCHARGE OF CONTRACTS

"It ain't over 'til it's over."

Yogi Berra, baseball Hall-of-Famer who played for the New York Yankees

Brian A Jackson/Shutterstock

LEGAL terms

- substantial performance
- tender of performance
- tender of goods
- tender of payment
- impossibility of performance
- frustration of purpose
- material alteration
- breach of contract
- anticipatory breach
- mitigate
- promissory note
- punitive damages
- liquidated damages clause
- specific performance
- restraining order
- injunction

15.1 TERMINATION OF CONTRACTS

Earlier chapters described the formation and operation of contracts. This chapter is concerned with the termination, or end, of contracts.

Contracts may be terminated by (1) agreement, (2) performance, (3) impossibility of performance, (4) alteration, (5) operation of law, (6) breach, and (7) laws and regulations protecting the consumer.

15.2 TERMINATION BY AGREEMENT

A contract may provide for its termination after a certain period of time or upon the occurrence of a certain event.

EXAMPLE 15.1

▶ Office Products agreed to act as a local distributor for the Comet Cell Phone Company for a period of five years. The agreement required Office Products to sell cellular telephones, maintain an inventory of telephone accessories and other supplies, and provide repairs. In this case, the termination was provided for in the contract.

Suppose that after only two years, Office Products found that the distributorship agreement was unprofitable and also that Comet was somewhat disappointed in Office Products' performance. If both firms agreed that cancellation of the contract was the best course of action, the contract could be terminated by mutual agreement even though the original contract did not provide for termination after two years. If, however, only one party was dissatisfied with the contract, both parties would be bound by the terms of the agreement until the specified five years had passed.

Occasionally, instead of agreeing to cancel a contract, both parties may agree to substitute a new contract in place of the original in order to maintain a working relationship. In such a case, the original contract is immediately terminated upon substitution of the new contract.

15.3 TERMINATION BY PERFORMANCE

Complete and satisfactory performance of the terms of a contract will bring about termination. When a contract is fulfilled, there is no need to provide for contract termination.

EXAMPLE 15.2

▶ The Soft Sound Recording Studio agreed to record several radio commercials for Sachley Advertising Agency. When the work was completed on schedule and payment was made, the contract was considered terminated by performance.

SUBSTANTIAL PERFORMANCE

Substantial performance occurs when a party to a contract, in good faith, executes all of the promised terms and conditions of the contract with the exception of minor details that do not materially affect the intent of their agreement. In Example 15.2, if the contract had been largely completed and only small details remained unfinished, then the contract would have been considered substantially performed. Suppose the commercials were completed and the only unfinished work consisted of mailing the recordings to radio stations. Soft Sound would have substantially performed the contract and would be entitled to payment according to the terms of the contract, less the cost of the mailing.

substantial performance When a party to a contract, in good faith, executes all of the promised terms and conditions of the contract with the exception of minor details that do not affect the real intent of their agreement.

If an important part of a contract is not performed within the period of time specified, the agreement may be canceled, but the omission of a small detail entitles the injured party to claim only a proportionate reduction in the payment. Some states provide for a remedy only in the event of a material breach and do not proportion the award.

PERFORMANCE BY PAYMENT OF MONEY

Contracts that require the payment of money are not complete until the amount agreed upon has been paid. If the agreement provides that payment may be made by check, as many payments are, payment by check is considered conditional and subject to collection in cash. A party to a contract who pays by check is not relieved of the obligation for payment under the contract until the cash has been paid by the bank on which the check is drawn.

TENDER AND ITS EFFECT

A tender of performance is an offer to perform and is considered evidence of a party's willingness to fulfill the terms of a contract. If a tender of performance of an act is refused, the person making the offer is relieved of the obligation to perform and may sue the other party for breach of contract.

tender of performance An offer to perform that is considered evidence of a party's willingness to fulfill the terms of a contract.

EXAMPLE 15.3

- Sunset Realty contracted with Clean Sweep to purchase janitorial services, including carpet cleaning, window washing, and general cleaning services. When personnel from Clean Sweep arrived for their evening's work, the manager of Sunset advised them that they would not be needed because a staff meeting was being held in the offices. Clean Sweep made a tender of performance, so although Sunset did not use the services, they were obligated to pay under the contract.

A tender of goods is an offer to provide the goods agreed upon and is considered evidence of a party's willingness to fulfill the terms of a contract. As is true for a tender of performance, if a tender of goods is refused, the person making the offer of goods is relieved of the obligation to provide the goods and may sue the other party for breach of contract.

tender of goods An offer to provide the goods agreed upon that is considered evidence of a party's willingness to fulfill the terms of a contract.

Finally, a tender of payment is an offer of money in payment of an obligation and is considered evidence of a party's willingness to fulfill the terms of a contract. If a tender of payment is refused by the creditor, the debt is not canceled, but penalties and interest cannot be charged beyond the date on which the offer of payment was made.

tender of payment A money offer of payment of an obligation.

Certain requirements must be met for tender of money or performance to be valid.

First, tender must be made as specified in the contract. If the contract specifies that payment or performance be made at a certain time or place, or to a particular person, these conditions must be met.

EXAMPLE 15.4

▶ Phin ordered a truckload of Christmas trees from Spruce Tree Company to be delivered to his used car lot on December 5. Because bad weather in Canada and Vermont affected the cutting schedule, the trees were not delivered until December 15. Phin refused delivery, claiming that he had already lost a considerable amount of business he had hoped to get, and he had dismissed the two college students he had hired to sell the trees. Phin had the right to refuse the tender because Spruce Tree failed to meet the conditions of the contract.

The mention of money in a contract implies payment in cash.
ptnphoto/Shutterstock

Second, when tender of payment is made, it must be for the exact amount. The mention of money in a contract implies payment in cash. Although checks are used in most business transactions, the seller has the right to refuse such a payment and to insist on cash.

Third, if the contract calls for the delivery of specific goods, only the tender of these particular goods will satisfy the contract.

15.4 TERMINATION BY IMPOSSIBILITY OF PERFORMANCE

impossibility of performance
When unforeseen circumstances make it impossible to fulfill the terms of a contract; in these cases, the contract is considered void.

Unforeseen circumstances may make it impossible to fulfill the terms of a contract as originally agreed. In a case of impossibility of performance, the contract is considered void and the parties are discharged.

EXAMPLE 15.5

▶ Solvey Brick Company, a manufacturer of standard building bricks used in construction, had a contract to supply several hundred thousand bricks to Ramon Construction. While the contract did not specify the source of the bricks, Solvey assumed that the bricks would be from its own plant. As Solvey was preparing to manufacture the bricks, the plant burned down. Solvey could buy the same type of bricks from another manufacturer and supply them to Ramon at a loss. Most courts would rule that the subject matter was standard bricks, not specific bricks from Solvey's own production facilities, and would not excuse Solvey from its contractual obligations. There was no impossibility of performance.

In Example 15.5, Solvey would be required to perform, even at a loss. In fact, a business can protect against the risk of loss resulting from such an event by purchasing insurance.

The Uniform Commercial Code (UCC) makes a special provision for failure to perform when the goods under contract are destroyed. If the contract covers goods that have been identified (such as a particular article of merchandise), and if the goods are destroyed without fault of either party, the contract is canceled. If the seller's source of supply or means of production creates only a partial inability to perform, the seller may tender only a portion of the goods under contract. Also, if the loss is only partial, the buyer may demand the right to inspect the damaged goods in order to decide whether to reject them or to accept them in their damaged state and claim an allowance for the damages.

PERSONAL-SERVICE CONTRACTS

Death or disabling illness of a party to a contract also may render the contract impossible to perform if it can be shown that the contract calls for a special skill or talent possessed by the deceased or ill person. Such personal-service contracts were discussed in Chapter 14.

EXAMPLE 15.6

▶ Iverson, a concert pianist, had a contract to perform at a summer music festival. Before the concert, she was stricken with a paralytic stroke and was unable to perform. Because this was a personal-service contract, she was excused from the contract.

On the other hand, a personal-service contract that does not call for a special skill or talent possessed by the deceased or ill person does not excuse performance.

EXAMPLE 15.7

▶ Jackanski, a house painter, had been hired to paint Rollins's colonial-style house. He had already begun work when he fell from a ladder and broke his back. The period of convalescence was estimated at one year. Jackanski is still responsible for painting the house because the skill required is not unique. The court would probably rule that Jackanski could assign the work to another painter—even though the cost might result in a loss to Jackanski.

FRUSTRATION OF PURPOSE

Closely related to impossibility is the doctrine of frustration of purpose. Where both parties know the purpose of a contract and, through no fault of either party, the reason for the contract no longer exists, the contract is terminated.

frustration of purpose
A doctrine that states that where both parties know the purpose of a contract and, through no fault of either party, the reason for the contract no longer exists, the contract is terminated.

EXAMPLE 15.8

▶ Gould contracted with Foxen Limo Services for a chauffeur-driven limousine to a nearby city to view game 7 of the World Series. Both parties knew that the purpose of the trip was to attend the baseball game. The series ended four games to two in game 6, and game 7 was never played. Because the purpose of the ride was frustrated and because Gould likely would no longer want to use the limousine company's services, he can terminate the contract.

15.5 TERMINATION BY ALTERATION

material alteration
A deliberate change or alteration of an important element in a written contract that affects the rights or obligations of the parties.

A deliberate change or alteration of an important element in a written contract that affects the rights or obligations of the parties is known as a material alteration and results in termination of the contract.

EXAMPLE 15.9

▶ Perry agreed to buy a vacant lot from Serio for $28,600. When the parties were to close the transaction, it was discovered that the contract to purchase had been changed by Serio to $38,600. Her illegal act of changing the contract not only terminated the contract, but also made Serio subject to criminal prosecution for the crime of forgery.

15.6 TERMINATION BY OPERATION OF LAW

If a law or regulation makes the performance of a contract illegal, the contract is void from the beginning. In fact, there is no contract. If, however, a law is passed *after* the parties enter into a contract that makes performance illegal, the contract is terminated by operation of law.

EXAMPLE 15.10

▶ Burlington, a dealer in shrubbery and trees, agreed with DaVall, a grower in a foreign country, to import several hundred decorative shrubs. To prevent the spread of a plant disease, the U.S. Department of Agriculture enforced a newly created embargo on this variety of shrub and refused to allow the shipment into the country. The parties are released from the agreement because of termination by operation of law.

Laws and regulations that increase the cost of performance, however, do not absolve the parties from their contractual obligations.

Suppose, in Example 15.10, that a new regulation had been passed that required special packaging for imported plants and that this packaging increased the total cost of the plants. In this case, the seller would not be relieved of her obligations, even if the added cost meant that she would lose money on the transaction.

15.7 TERMINATION BY BREACH OF CONTRACT

breach of contract
When a party to a contract refuses to perform as required by the contract or performs in an unsatisfactory manner.

A breach of contract occurs when a party to a contract refuses to perform as required by the contract or performs in an unsatisfactory manner. There are three common ways in which contracts are breached:

- Anticipatory breach, sometimes referred to as anticipatory repudiation.
- Breach resulting from a deliberate or negligent act.
- Failure to perform an obligation.

ANTICIPATORY BREACH

A party who announces an intention to break a contract is said to create an anticipatory breach. They have given notice of intention to break the contract even before being required to perform. Court decisions have allowed the injured party to bring suit for damages at the time of the announcement and have not required the party to wait until the time for performance has passed.

anticipatory breach
When a party to a contract announces their intention to break the contract in the future.

EXAMPLE 15.11

Zikmund, an actor, had agreed to appear in a supporting role in a play scheduled to open on February 1. On December 1, she announced that she would not be available because she had been given a starring role in a motion picture. The producer has a right to initiate a suit on December 1 for anticipatory breach without waiting for the time the contract was to start.

When one party has received notice from the other party of intent to breach, they cannot continue with the performance of the work or service covered by the contract; doing so would only increase the amount of damages. When a party breaches a contract, the injured party has the duty to mitigate, or lessen, the amount of damages.

mitigate
The obligation of the injured party to protect the other party from any unnecessary damages.

EXAMPLE 15.12

Ebersol hired Weston Restorers to restore a 1936 Chevrolet to classic car condition. While Weston was still ordering and manufacturing needed parts, Ebersol announced that he had changed his mind and intended to breach the contract. Weston cannot continue restoring the car and later sue for a greater amount than if he had stopped work at the time when Ebersol breached. He can sue only for damages suffered up to the time he was notified of the anticipatory breach.

The law regarding anticipatory breach does not apply to promises to pay money at some future date. A person who renounces an obligation to pay on a promissory note (a written promise to pay a specified sum of money) cannot be sued until after the due date of the first payment on the note, even if such person announces their intention to breach before the first payment is due.

The law regarding anticipatory breach does not apply to promises to pay money at some future date.
Stockbakery/Shutterstock

promissory note
A written note or letter in which one person promises to pay a certain amount of money to another at a definite time.

BREACH RESULTING FROM A DELIBERATE OR NEGLIGENT ACT

A contract is breached if one party deliberately or negligently stands in the way of performance. For example, if a party who has agreed to sell certain perishable foods negligently allows them to become damaged by freezing, they have breached the contract.

EXAMPLE 15.13

▶ Herrera hired Kotley to conduct marketing research at a shopping mall. They agreed that Kotley would interview shoppers selected at random and conduct a survey using a questionnaire. Before the interviews began, Herrera changed his mind and destroyed the questionnaires. The contract was breached by Herrera's deliberate act. Herrera is subject to Kotley's suit for damages—the agreed fee to be paid to Kotley.

FAILURE TO PERFORM AN OBLIGATION

A party who fails to perform contractual obligations, within the time specified or within a reasonable time, has breached the contract. The breach occurs whether the party has completely or partially failed to perform. In the case of complete failure, the contract is terminated. Partial failure to perform may require the nonbreaching party to pay for the work that has already been completed. However, suppose that in Example 15.13, Kotley did have access to the questionnaires but conducted only half the number he had agreed to do. In this situation, it is doubtful that partial work (a survey with only half the responses) would have much, if any, value to Herrera.

15.8 TERMINATION TO PROTECT A CONSUMER

To protect consumers against their own impulsiveness and various questionable sales techniques, a number of federal, state, and local laws and regulations allow consumers to terminate a contract under certain conditions.

For example, a Federal Trade Commission (FTC) regulation gives the consumer a "cooling off" period of three days and the right to cancel contracts for either goods or services made in the consumer's home and to receive a full refund. The cooling off rule requires that the salesperson explain the cancellation rights at the time of the sale and provide the consumer with a cancellation form.

Similarly, the federal Truth in Lending Act states that a borrower may cancel a contract for any type of personal loan within three days of entering into the contract.

15.9 REMEDIES FOR BREACH OF CONTRACT

Each party to a contract has the right to expect complete and satisfactory performance. When such performance is not made, the injured party may sue to recover *compensatory damages,* a sum of money that will compensate for their loss. In all such claims for damages, the injured party must determine the damage in terms of money, and the court will determine if the claim is fair and adequate. Compensatory damages are intended to return the injured party to the same position they were in before the contract was breached.

EXAMPLE 15.14

▶ Namsang was to be married, and he and his fiancée planned a large reception. After inspecting several restaurants and catering halls, they reached an agreement with Portsmith Villa for the use of the facilities and for the food and beverage service. A week before the event, Portsmith canceled the contract, claiming that they had overlooked an earlier commitment. Namsang found alternative facilities but for a fee $1,300 higher. After the event, Namsang sued for damages of $1,300—the difference between the contract price and the higher fee he had to pay as a result of Portsmith's breach. A court would likely rule in Namsang's favor for $1,300.

Occasionally a court may award *consequential damages* to a plaintiff. Consequential damages are monetary compensation for losses resulting from the special circumstances of a plaintiff that are foreseeable by both parties to a contract. Suppose a contractor breaches a contract by not completing the renovations to a business on time. In this example, the special circumstance is that the business cannot operate while the renovation is taking place. In such a case, a court may award consequential damages to the business to compensate for revenues lost as a result of the business remaining closed.

A court may also award *nominal damages* to a plaintiff in a case where they incurred no actual monetary damages as a result of a breach of contract on the part of a defendant. Nominal damages are small monetary awards, typically $1, that serve to indicate that a plaintiff was wronged by a defendant.

PUNITIVE DAMAGES

It should be noted that, in addition to the previously described damages, a court may also decide to award punitive damages. Punitive damages are used to punish a defendant for wrongful conduct that is willful, malicious, or fraudulent in order to deter him or her and others from engaging in the same type of conduct again in the future. However, it must be pointed out that punitive damages are rarely awarded in breach of contract cases and are granted in only a very small number of cases–for example, when the defendant commits a fraud while breaching the contract or when an insurance company acts in bad faith.

punitive damages
Damages used to punish a defendant for wrongful conduct that is willful, malicious, or fraudulent in order to deter them and others from engaging in the same type of conduct again or in the future.

LIQUIDATED DAMAGES CLAUSE

At times, the parties include a statement right in their contract wherein damages are explicitly set in the event one of the parties breaches the agreement. Such a statement is called a liquidated damages clause. Courts will generally enforce liquidated damages clauses provided the damages specified are closely related to the actual damages. Courts will usually not enforce these if the specified damages amounts are viewed as a penalty or forfeiture–that is, an amount much greater than the actual measure of damages.

liquidated damages clause
A statement wherein damages are explicitly set in the event one of the parties breaches an agreement.

SPECIFIC PERFORMANCE

Sometimes a judgment of money damages will not really repay an injured party for a breach of contract. In some cases, the injured party may sue for specific performance–that is, a court order directing a person to perform as they agreed to do. To obtain an order of specific performance, the injured party asks the court to order the other party to do what they promised to do. For example, if a contract is made for the sale of some unique item, such as an antique, an original painting, or real estate, the buyer can bring an action for specific performance if the seller attempts to breach the contract. A court order for specific performance serves as a remedy in cases in which an award of money damages for a breach of contract cannot adequately compensate the injured party.

specific performance
A court order directing a person to perform—or not perform—as they agreed to do in a contract.

Courts almost never order specific performance of a contract for personal services, partly because it is difficult to ensure the performance of someone who is being forced to work after a dispute, in that any loyalty or normal relationship is nearly impossible to achieve. Also, courts do not wish to impose what might be viewed as involuntary servitude.

An order for specific performance may be obtained not only in cases of breach of contract for the sale of unique goods or real estate, but also in cases where the purchaser is not able to obtain the goods called for by the contract elsewhere.

EXAMPLE 15.15

Resol bought and remodeled a restaurant and named it the Packard Roadster. He contracted with Timmons, a collector of classic cars, to purchase a 1932 Packard for $47,000, which he planned to display in the front window of the restaurant. He also registered the restaurant name, had signs made, and ran advertising announcing the grand opening. Sensing an opportunity to sell the vehicle to another buyer for a higher price, Timmons attempted to cancel the contract. Because Resol could not obtain the vehicle elsewhere, he sought an action of specific performance that required Timmons to sell the car as Timmons had agreed to do. Because the product is unique, the court would likely grant the decree of specific performance that Resol requested.

restraining order
A court order prohibiting the performance of a certain act. In some states, a restraining order is temporary.

injunction
A permanent court order prohibiting the performance of a certain act.

RESTRAINING ORDER OR INJUNCTION

Whereas a decree of specific performance is a court order requiring the performance of a certain act, a restraining order, or injunction, is a court order prohibiting the performance of a certain act. In some states, a restraining order is temporary and an injunction is permanent.

EXAMPLE 15.16

Segal sold a heavily wooded parcel of land to Hargett, who claimed that he wanted to use it as a hunting preserve. Hargett agreed to refrain from cutting the trees down for a period of 15 years. One year after the sale, Hargett decided to build a shopping mall on the property, which would require cutting down the trees. Segal began legal action but was concerned that the trees would be destroyed by the time the case was heard. She therefore sought a temporary restraining order to stop all work at the site until the case could be heard.

If, as a result of the legal action taken by Segal, it was found that Hargett had indeed violated his contract, the court could replace the temporary restraining order with a permanent injunction. That would bar Hargett from cutting the trees down for the period specified by the contract. If Hargett failed to obey either the temporary restraining order or the permanent injunction, his actions could result in his being found to be in contempt of court. He could then be fined or even imprisoned.

CHAPTER SUMMARY

15.1 Contracts may be terminated by (a) agreement, (b) performance, (c) impossibility of performance, (d) alteration, (e) operation of law, (f) breach, and (g) laws and regulations protecting the consumer.

15.2 A contract can be terminated by agreement if both parties agree that it should end.

15.3 The three types of termination by performance are (a) substantial performance, in which the contract has been largely completed and only small details remain; (b) performance by payment of money, in which the agreed-upon payment has been paid; and (c) tender of performance, in which there has been an offer to pay the required sum or to perform the required acts.

15.4 Contracts can be terminated by impossibility of performance when unforeseen circumstances make it impossible to fulfill the terms of a contract as originally agreed.

15.5 Termination by alteration occurs when an important element in a written contract that affects the rights or obligations of the parties is changed.

15.6 A contract can be terminated by operation of law if a law passed after the parties entered into a contract makes performance illegal.

15.7 Contracts terminated by breach occur when a party to a contract refuses to perform as required by the contract or performs in an unsatisfactory manner. Three common ways in which contracts are breached are by (a) anticipatory breach, (b) a deliberate or negligent act, and (c) failure to perform an obligation.

15.8 Some contracts can be terminated to protect consumers because the law hopes to protect them against their own impulsiveness, questionable sales techniques, and similar problems.

15.9 The remedy of specific performance is a court order that a person perform as they agreed to do. The remedies of restraining order and injunction are court orders that prohibit performance of a certain act.

CHAPTER FIFTEEN ASSESSMENT

MATCHING LEGAL TERMS

Match each of the numbered definitions with the correct term in the following list.

a. anticipatory breach
b. impossibility of performance
c. material alteration
d. mitigation
e. promissory note
f. specific performance
g. restraining order or injunction
h. substantial performance
i. punitive damages
j. tender of performance

1. A written promise to pay a specified sum of money. 1. _____
2. The completion of a contract except for some small details. 2. _____
3. A change of an important term in a contract that affects the rights or obligations of the parties. 3. _____
4. An offer to perform acts required by a contract. 4. _____
5. An award used to punish a defendant for wrongful conduct that is willful, malicious, or fraudulent. 5. _____
6. Inability to fulfill the terms of a contract due to unforeseen circumstances. 6. _____
7. Cancellation of a contract due to an announcement of intention to breach prior to the time performance is due. 7. _____
8. A court decree that prohibits the performance of a certain act. 8. _____
9. A court order that directs that a certain act be carried out. 9. _____
10. The duty of an injured party to lessen the amount of damages. 10. _____

TRUE/FALSE QUIZ

Indicate whether each of the following statements is true or false.

11. A contract can be terminated in accordance with provisions in the contract itself. 11. _____
12. Complete and satisfactory performance of a contract will bring about its termination. 12. _____
13. A contract must be completely performed in all its details in order to be considered terminated. 13. _____
14. Death or disabling illness of a party terminates the contract if such requires the particular skill or talent of the contracting party. 14. _____
15. A deliberate material alteration of a contract that affects the rights or obligations of the parties is cause for termination of the contract. 15. _____
16. A party to a contract is released from their obligations if a law is passed that increases the cost of performing the contract. 16. _____
17. A contract is breached if one party deliberately or negligently stands in the way of satisfactory performance. 17. _____
18. When one party to a contract receives notice of the other party's intent to breach, they may continue with the performance of work or service covered under the contract, complete such work or service, and then sue for the entire amount of damages. 18. _____

MULTIPLE CHOICE QUIZ

Indicate the correct answer from the choices following each question.

19. A contract that ends based on a date set in the contract terms is an example of (a) termination by alteration (b) termination by operation of law (c) termination by agreement (d) termination by breach. **19.** _____

20. A contract to deliver specifically identified goods ends when those goods are destroyed before delivery. This contract termination is an example of (a) termination by alteration (b) termination by impossibility of performance (c) termination by operation of law (d) termination by breach. **20.** _____

21. A contract for performance of services is considered terminated by performance when (a) there is complete performance of all duties (b) there is substantial performance of all duties (c) there is either complete performance of all duties or substantial performance of all duties (d) there is neither substantial performance of all duties nor complete performance of all duties. **21.** _____

22. Termination by alteration occurs (a) when there is any change to the contract terms (b) when either party states that change has occurred (c) when there is a material change to the contract terms (d) when there is no change to the contract terms. **22.** _____

23. Which of the following would *not* be considered termination by breach? (a) One party announces that they will not be able to perform obligations under the contract before the contract term ends. (b) One party is negligent in performing their duties. (c) One party fails to perform obligations altogether. (d) One party to a contract dies unexpectedly. **23.** _____

24. When one party announces that they are not able to perform service obligations under the contract before the contract term ends, the other party (a) must attempt to mitigate damages (b) is not obligated to mitigate damages (c) may not collect any damages under the contract (d) none of the above. **24.** _____

25. A contract termination resulting from a party cancelling after 24 hours to consider the terms is most likely a (a) termination by breach (b) termination by alteration (c) termination due to impossibility of performance (d) termination to protect a consumer. **25.** _____

26. Compensatory damages for breach of contract can include (a) consequential damages foreseeable by the parties (b) damages resulting directly from the breach (c) nominal damages to indicate wrongdoing (d) all of the above. **26.** _____

27. An employment agreement requires an employee to pay a specified amount of money as damages if they leave employment before the end of the agreement term. In this case, the damages are (a) liquidated damages that can be imposed if they are not punitive (b) liquidated damages that can be imposed under any circumstances (c) liquidated damages that can never be imposed under any circumstances (d) all of the above. 27. ______

28. Courts rarely impose specific performance as a remedy in personal-service contracts because (a) the order is difficult to enforce (b) the order would be viewed as involuntary servitude (c) the court does not have authority to order specific performance (d) the court does not have jurisdiction over personal-service contracts. 28. ______

DISCUSSION QUESTIONS

Answer the following questions and discuss them in class.

29. Discuss termination of a contract by agreement.

______

______

30. Explain how a contract is terminated by performance.

______

______

31. Provide an example of a contract terminated by impossibility of performance.

______

______

32. Explain how a contract might be terminated by breach.

______

______

33. Explain how a contract might be terminated to protect a consumer.

______

______

34. Discuss the remedies of specific performance and injunction.

______

______

THINKING CRITICALLY ABOUT THE LAW

Answer the following questions, which require you to think critically about the legal principles that you learned in this chapter.

35. Termination by Performance Contract termination by performance seems so final. Do you think that the parties to a contract should be given an opportunity to change their minds if circumstances change after the required performance? Why or why not?

36. Termination by Impossibility of Performance At times, one of the parties to a contract terminated by impossibility of performance suffers some injury or loss as a result. Should the law recognize this possibility and provide some form of redress?

37. Termination by Breach The law provides a remedy for a party injured by the breach of a contract. But the usual remedy, a lawsuit that awards money damages, does not always give the injured party the level of redress appropriate to the situation. What other remedies are available, and how effective are they?

38. Personal-Service Contracts Death or disabling illness of a party to a personal-service contract requiring a special skill or talent terminates the contract. How would a concert promoter, who had sold tickets and rented a hall, protect against a loss that would likely result from the termination of a contract with a renowned pianist?

39. A Question of Ethics To protect consumers against their own impulsiveness and various questionable sales techniques, a number of federal, state, and local laws and regulations allow consumers to terminate a contract under certain conditions. Is it ethical for a consumer to take advantage of this protection when their own good judgment should have suggested avoidance of the contract?

CASE QUESTIONS

Study each of the following cases. Answer the questions that follow with Yes or No.

40. Termination to Protect a Consumer Bushek signed a contract with Aluminum Window Products Company to replace the windows and wooden window frames of his house with new ones made of aluminum. The salesperson asked Bushek to sign a "routine form" to help ensure that credit would be granted. The following day he read the "routine form" and discovered that he had, in fact, pledged the entire house as security, and if he defaulted on payments, the house could be taken from him.

a. Is the contract Bushek signed legal? **a.** _____

b. Does Bushek have the right to cancel the contract? **b.** _____

c. If Bushek decides to cancel the contract, is he liable for damages? **c.** _____

41. Substantial Performance Central City Garage Builders contracted with Morgan for the construction of a two-car garage and an attached greenhouse of similar size. The garage was built on schedule, but, because of a shortage of special materials, it appeared that the construction of the greenhouse would be delayed for several months. Central City requested payment for the entire contract.

a. Does Central City have a legitimate claim that it had performed substantially? **a.** _____

b. Can Central City claim that it was prevented from completing the project because of impossibility of performance? **b.** _____

c. Would Central City have a right to request payment for the portion of the contract that was completed? **c.** _____

42. Revoked Contract Scher, a homeowner, purchased a vacuum cleaner from a door-to-door salesperson. When the salesperson demonstrated the machine in her home, it seemed to work quite effectively. After signing the contract, she checked several business rating websites and learned that the company was noted for its deceptive practices and that the demonstration machine was specially constructed and not the same type as the one a consumer gets.

a. Does Scher have the opportunity to terminate the contract? **a.** _____

b. Was the contract Scher signed a valid one? **b.** _____

c. Is the contract voidable? **c.** _____

43. Termination by Breach Chiu agreed to sell his custom-built sailboat to Graham for $60,000. Before delivery, Chiu received another offer for $68,000 and wrote to Graham that he had decided not to sell his boat after all.

a. Can Graham obtain a decree of specific performance? **a.** _____

b. Would a suit for money damages completely satisfy Graham? **b.** _____

c. Can Chiu avoid Graham's suit by claiming that he was merely selling to the highest bidder? **c.** _____

CASE ANALYSIS

Study each of the following cases carefully. Briefly state the principle of law and your decision.

44. Impossibility of Performance Bunge, a grain dealer, contracted with Recker, a farmer, to purchase 10,000 bushels of soybeans at $3.35 per bushel. The contract did not specify where the beans were to have been grown, except that they were to be grown in the United States. As a result of crop failure, Recker was unable to deliver the beans, even with several extensions of the deadline. Finally, Recker admitted that he could not deliver, claiming impossibility of performance. In the meantime, the market price had increased from $3.35, the agreed price, to $5.50 at the time agreed for delivery. Bunge sued for the difference between $3.35 and the market price at the time agreed for delivery. Will Recker be excused from his contractual obligations, or should he be held responsible for delivering as agreed? [*Bunge Corp. v. Recker,* 519 F.2d 449 (8th Cir.)]

Principle of Law:

____

____

Decision:

____

____

45. Termination by Agreement Laclede Gas Company purchased propane gas from Amoco Oil Company and sold it to various residential subdivisions. After the contract had been in operation for some time, Amoco refused to supply any more gas. Laclede was unable to find another supplier willing to enter into a long-term contract such as Laclede had with Amoco. Management of Laclede felt that money damages would not provide a reasonable settlement. What would be a reasonable resolution of Laclede's problem? [*Laclede Gas Co. v. Amoco Oil Co.,* 522 F.2d 33 (8th Cir.)]

Principle of Law:

____

____

Decision:

____

____

46. Termination by Performance Blackburn, a painting contractor, agreed in writing to paint DeSoto's house for a certain price. After the house was painted, DeSoto asked Blackburn to paint his garage. Blackburn had other painting jobs scheduled and refused the additional work. DeSoto felt that his offer of additional work was entitled to higher priority. Is DeSoto correct that the completed contract should entitle him to a higher priority?

Principle of Law:

Decision:

47. Termination by Breach Dahl, the owner of a machine shop, agreed to manufacture 22 valves for $460 each for Capobianco. When six valves were finished and shipped, Capobianco advised Dahl of his intention to cancel the contract. Dahl went on to build the remaining valves according to the contract. Will Dahl be successful in his suit for the entire amount?

Principle of Law:

Decision:

LEGAL RESEARCH

Complete the following activities. Share your findings with the class.

48. Working in Teams In teams of three or four, interview owners or managers of small businesses to learn some typical contracts in which the firms have been involved and how they were terminated.

49. Using Technology Using the Internet and search engines, investigate the Federal Trade Commission's website to learn when contracts may be terminated to protect the consumer.

PART 3

Sales, Agency, and Business Organizations

Frank and Helena/Cultura/Getty Images

chapter 16
Transfer of Title

LEARNING OUTCOMES

After studying this chapter and completing the assessment, you will be able to

16.1 Explain how title and certificate of title relate to the concept of ownership.

16.2 Distinguish between the two main types of property and indicate which one is subject to the law of sales.

16.3 Describe how title passes and discuss how bills of sale, bills of lading, and warehouse receipts are involved in the passing of title.

16.4 Explain when title to goods passes.

16.5 Define the term *conditional sales* and identify the two types of conditions found in contracts for conditional sales.

16.6 Explain the law governing title to lost or stolen goods.

16.7 Define the principle of estoppel and provide examples of how this principle is applied in various situations.

16.8 Discuss sales by persons with possession of, but not title to, goods.

16.9 Describe the passage of title to fungible goods.

LEGAL terms

- title
- bill of sale
- bill of lading
- straight bill of lading
- order bill of lading
- warehouse receipt
- nonnegotiable warehouse receipt
- negotiable warehouse receipt
- conditional sale
- conditions precedent
- conditions subsequent
- estoppel
- remote party
- wrongful possession
- fungible goods

TRANSFER OF TITLE

"Is it not lawful for me to do what I will with mine own?"

The Bible, Matthew 20:15

Radius Images/Getty Images

16.1 TITLE

Many business transactions that involve disputes are like a game of musical chairs. The person who is left standing when the music stops is the one who loses. Similarly, legal disputes often involve the determination of who holds title when a loss occurs.

Prior to the adoption of the Uniform Commercial Code (UCC), the concept of title was crucial in determining the rights and responsibilities of the parties to a contract and, perhaps even more important, who bore the risk of loss. The UCC has reduced the significance of title, concentrating instead on the law of sales transactions as described in Chapter 17.

THE RIGHT OF OWNERSHIP

The concept of private property is one of the foundations of our economic and social system. The laws of our country recognize the right of individuals to own property.

title
Ownership and the right to possess something.

Title, as it relates to property, is intangible—you cannot see it or feel it. The person who has title to property (the owner) also has the right to possess it unless, of course, the person has given up the right to possess the property by, for example, renting it to someone else. Thus if you own something—a house, a car, a suit—you have title to it and the right to sell it. Moreover, a person who has title to a property also has the right to encumber it, or offer it as collateral for a debt.

When you sell something, you sell not only the property but also the intangible right of ownership called *title*. The automobile *certificate of title,* used in many states, is not title, but rather proof of title. Sometimes an exchange of letters or a department store bill of sale can be used as proof of ownership (title).

16.2 KINDS OF PROPERTY

The two main classifications of property are real property and personal property (introduced in Chapter 13).

REAL PROPERTY

Real property, sometimes referred to as real estate, is land and all articles permanently attached to it, such as buildings and trees.

PERSONAL PROPERTY

Personal property is all property other than real property, such as automobiles, clothing, and computers. Personal property can be tangible—that is, it can be seen and touched, like the examples just cited; or it can be intangible, such as patents, copyrights, or ownership in a corporation, which cannot be seen or touched. Only personal property—tangible or intangible—is affected by the law of sales and the UCC. Real property is governed by a separate branch of law, to be covered in Chapter 24. Sales of services do not involve either real or personal property; and contracts for such services are considered ordinary contracts.

16.3 HOW TITLE PASSES

There are a variety of ways in which title can pass. Involved in the passage of title are the legal concepts of bill of sale, bill of lading, and warehouse receipt.

BILL OF SALE

bill of sale
A written statement that the seller is passing ownership to the buyer.

A bill of sale is simply a written statement that the seller is passing ownership to the buyer. The bill of sale need not be an elaborate legal document–a handwritten note is just as effective. Similarly, a bill of sale can be created by a digital record, such as a series of email exchanges. The important thing to remember is that the description of the goods should be as complete as possible. For example, if you bought a computer from a neighbor, a simple note describing the goods involved in the transaction as "a computer" would probably be adequate. However, if the note included a more complete description, such as "one Apple MacBook Pro, 13 inch: 2.66 GHz, Serial No. 175274," you would be further protected from a claim of ownership by another person. A bill of sale does not guarantee that a valid title is being transferred; it only transfers the rights or ownership of the transferor.

BILL OF LADING

bill of lading
A receipt for goods to be shipped, acknowledging that such goods have been received and indicating agreement that the goods will be transported to the destination specified.

straight bill of lading
A nonnegotiable receipt for goods to be shipped, acknowledging that such goods have been received and indicating agreement that the goods will be transported to the destination specified.

order bill of lading
A receipt for goods to be shipped that is negotiable and is proof of title that can be used to transfer title from one person to another.

A bill of lading is a receipt for goods to be shipped, acknowledging that such goods have been received and indicating agreement that the goods will be transported to the destination specified. The bill of lading is prepared by the common carrier, such as a trucking firm, a railroad, or an ocean liner, that has agreed by contract to transport the goods by land or water. In the case of goods shipped by air, an *airbill* is prepared. One copy of the document is signed by the common carrier–when the carrier accepts the goods for shipment.

There are two kinds of bills of lading. The most common is a straight bill of lading, which is simply a receipt but is not negotiable. An order bill of lading, in addition to being a receipt, is negotiable; that is, the order bill of lading is proof of title and can be used to transfer title from one person to another. Such a negotiable order bill of lading can be used to ensure that the carrier will not deliver the goods until the receiver surrenders the original copy of the order bill of lading to the carrier. Because it would be nearly impossible for anyone to possess the original order bill of lading without the shipper's agreeing to it, such a document is proof of ownership. Bills of lading are covered by Article 7 of the UCC.

EXAMPLE 16.1

Global Art Importer in New York agreed, through a series of email messages, to sell 15 expensive paintings to an art gallery in Peoria, Illinois. Global Art received an order bill of lading from the trucking line, turned over the shipment, and notified the Peoria art gallery that the paintings were being shipped. The shipper gave the original order bill of lading to its bank, which in turn sent it to a cooperating bank in Peoria. The Peoria art gallery was instructed by email to pay the agreed-upon sales price for the merchandise to the Peoria bank in order to obtain the original copy of the order bill of lading. When the Peoria art gallery paid the money to the bank, it was given the original order bill of lading, which it then surrendered to the trucking firm upon delivery of the artwork.

WAREHOUSE RECEIPT

A warehouse receipt is much like a bill of lading except the goods involved are not being transported but merely stored. There are two kinds of warehouse receipts. A nonnegotiable warehouse receipt is like a straight bill of lading—it is simply a receipt for the goods to be stored. A negotiable warehouse receipt, like the negotiable order bill of lading, requires that the original copy be presented to the warehouser before the goods will be surrendered to someone claiming them. Also, like an order bill of lading, a negotiable warehouse receipt is proof of ownership.

Suppose that, in Example 16.1, the purchaser of the artwork was located in the same community as the manufacturer. The transaction would be similar to the one in the preceding case. The warehouser would play the same role as the trucking line, but a cooperating bank would probably not be involved in the transaction.

A warehouse receipt is used for goods that are being stored.
Alistair Berg/Photodisc/ Getty Images

16.4 WHEN TITLE PASSES

Title to goods passes when the parties intend for it to pass. In the event that the intent of the parties is not clear, title passes at the moment when they unconditionally agree to sell specific goods that are in a deliverable state. The issue of timing of title transfer can be particularly important in determining which party to the transaction bears the risk of loss. The party deemed to have title at the time of loss will bear the risk of loss, even if that party does not have possession of the goods at the time.

warehouse receipt
Much like a bill of lading except the goods are not being shipped but merely stored.

nonnegotiable warehouse receipt
A receipt for the goods to be stored.

negotiable warehouse receipt
Proof of ownership that can be used to transfer title from one person to another.

INTENT

Since, in the eyes of the law, title passes when the parties intend it to pass, how does a party prove what they intended? Suppose that a person bought a boat and arranged to pick it up the following day. Before the buyer had a chance to pick it up, the boat was destroyed by fire. Quite likely, the seller would claim that they intended title to pass at the time of the transaction, thus insisting that the buyer bear the loss. The buyer, on the other hand, would probably say that they intended title to pass when they picked up the boat, arguing that the seller should bear the loss. To minimize the number of such disagreements, certain rules for determining the intent of the parties have been established.

EXAMPLE 16.2

▶ Castelli agreed to purchase Piak's car for $18,000. They both agreed that Castelli would return the following day with license plates and take delivery of the vehicle. In the eyes of the law, title passed at the time of agreement, even though the parties may have taken a few minutes to complete the necessary written documents, such as a bill of sale and the check for payment of the car.

SPECIFIC TIME

Although it may take some time to complete the documents that signify the passing of title, title itself passes in a single instant. While both parties are free to create a contract that stipulates precisely when the transfer of title passes, the law does provide guidelines as to when this occurs.

16.5 CONDITIONAL SALES

conditional sale
A sale with contract provisions that specify conditions that must be met by one of the parties.

A conditional sale is one with contract provisions that specify conditions that must be met by one of the parties. The two types of conditions found in contracts for conditional sales are conditions precedent and conditions subsequent.

CONDITIONS PRECEDENT

conditions precedent
Conditions in a sales contract that must be met before title passes.

When a sales contract provides that specific conditions must be met before title passes, the agreement contains conditions precedent.

Suppose that in Example 16.2, Castelli agreed to purchase Piak's car if Piak had new tires installed. Title would pass when the tires were installed. If anything had happened to the car before the tires were installed, Piak would bear the loss.

CONDITIONS SUBSEQUENT

conditions subsequent
Conditions in a sales contract that must be met after title has passed.

When a sales contract provides that specific conditions must be met after title has passed, it is said to contain conditions subsequent. A right-of-return provision in a sales contract is an example of a condition subsequent that gives the buyer the right to *revest,* or transfer back, title to the seller if the buyer is not satisfied after making the purchase.

Returning to the case of Castelli and Piak in Example 16.2, suppose that the parties agreed that Castelli would purchase the car but would have the right to return it to Piak if it did not have enough power to pull a travel trailer that Castelli had ordered. Whether the car would be adequate for this purpose would not be known until the trailer was delivered. If the sales contract included this condition and upon delivery of the trailer it was discovered that the car did not have enough power, Piak would be obliged to take the car back and title would be revested to her.

16.6 LOST AND STOLEN GOODS

When a person possesses an item, ownership is presumed, but it is possible to have possession of goods without having title, just as it is possible to have title without having possession.

A person who finds an article has good title against anyone except the true owner. Anyone who buys an article from someone who has found it must be prepared to surrender the article to the true owner. However, it is often difficult to prove ownership of a lost article. Local police departments and insurance agents' associations have mounted campaigns to help people identify their property with the use of a tool that engraves identifying information on property. They also have encouraged persons to retain receipts with model and serial numbers of valuable personal property.

EXAMPLE 16.3

▶ Fortuna, while on a business trip, left a laptop computer in an airline waiting room, where it was found by Moreno. Because the computer had a serial number that matched the one on her bill of sale, Fortuna was able to prove ownership and recover her property.

A thief has no title to goods they have stolen and, therefore, cannot pass title to anyone else. The real owner of stolen goods has not passed title to anyone, and even an innocent purchaser who bought the stolen items in good faith would have to return them to the original owner.

16.7 TRANSFER OF TITLE BY ESTOPPEL

Under certain circumstances, it is possible for title to goods to be passed by a nonowner who does not have title. In these cases, title is said to pass by estoppel. Estoppel is a legal bar to the use of contradictory words or acts in asserting a claim against another. As the concept of estoppel is used in discussions of title, the titleholder is estopped—legally prevented—from claiming ownership of the property as a result of certain actions taken by the titleholder. UCC 2-202 and UCC 2-403 deal with the rights of persons who acquire questionable title.

estoppel
A legal bar to using contradictory words or acts in asserting a claim against another.

For title to pass by estoppel, the purchaser must be able to prove the following:

1. The purchase was made in good faith. That is, the buyer believed the seller to be the real owner or one appointed to act for the real owner.
2. The purchase was made from one in rightful possession.
3. Value was given by the buyer for that which they now claim ownership under the principle of estoppel.

EXAMPLES OF ESTOPPEL

The following are examples of how the principle of estoppel is applied.

Transfer of Money or Commercial Paper Made Out to Bearer When the owner of cash or commercial paper, such as a check, makes it payable to bearer, who then gives it to a third person, the original owner cannot demand the return of the money from a third party to whom it was given in exchange for something of value (see Chapter 22).

EXAMPLE 16.4

▶ Schultz gave his brother-in-law, Robb, $150 cash and asked him to buy a DVD player because Robb could use his employee discount. Instead, Robb bought himself a suit. Schultz cannot demand the return of the cash from the person who sold the suit.

Transfer of Property to a Seller Dealing in the Same Type of Goods When the owner of goods entrusts property to a person who sells the same type of goods and that person sells the property to an innocent third party, the owner is estopped from recovering the goods from the third party.

EXAMPLE 16.5

▶ Unger left an electric lawnmower at a garden shop for repair and service, and the owner of the shop inadvertently sold the mower to another customer. Unger would be estopped from recovering the mower from the purchaser, an innocent third party. Unger can, however, sue the owner of the garden shop for the value of the mower.

Transfer of Property to a Seller Permitted to Appear as the Real Owner If the owner of property gives possession of it to a second party and allows that person to act as the real owner, the rightful owner cannot recover the property if the second party sells the property to an innocent third party.

Suppose that Unger, in Example 16.5, borrowed a lawnmower from his neighbor to use while his own was being repaired. Without permission, Unger then sold the borrowed mower to a gardener who was working on his lawn. The neighbor would be estopped from recovering the lawnmower from the gardener. However, the neighbor could bring legal action against Unger.

Transfer of Proof of Ownership to an Unauthorized Seller If the owner of goods entrusts proof of ownership to someone in possession of the goods, the goods cannot be recovered by the true owner from an innocent purchaser.

Returning again to Example 16.5 regarding Unger and the lawnmower, suppose that the neighbor who loaned the mower to Unger also gave him the bill of sale (proof of ownership). If Unger then sold the mower to another neighbor, the rightful owner would be estopped from recovering the mower from the innocent purchaser because Unger, the unauthorized seller, had proof of ownership.

remote party
A person with the right to make legitimate sales as a representative of the owner of the goods, although he or she is not a titleholder.

wrongful possession
When property, such as stolen goods, is transferred without permission of the owner.

16.8 SALES BY PERSONS HAVING POSSESSION

There are instances when individuals have possession of goods, but not title to them, and sell these goods to third persons.

A salesperson in a grocery store is known as a remote party.
Ariel Skelley/Digital Vision/Blend Images/Getty Images

SALES BY PERSONS HAVING RIGHTFUL POSSESSION

A salesperson in a retail store, service station, restaurant, and so on is known as a remote party. Such individuals have the right to make legitimate sales as representatives of the owner of the goods, although they themselves are not titleholders. A salesperson has the express or implied permission of the titleholder of the merchandise to sell it. Agents acting on behalf of principals can pass title without holding title themselves (see Chapter 19).

SALES BY PERSONS HAVING WRONGFUL POSSESSION

Unlike the situations described previously, in which possession of goods was transferred with the permission of the owner, situations of wrongful possession occur when property, such as stolen goods, is transferred without permission of the owner. The titleholder, or rightful owner, of stolen goods is never estopped. That is, they are never prevented from exercising a claim to the goods, even if the person in possession of them is an innocent purchaser of the property.

EXAMPLE 16.6

▶ Brilley, a shipping clerk employed by Rexeer Auto Parts, stole an automobile engine and sold it to a friend, Petras. After Rexeer Auto discharged Brilley, the owners suspected that Petras had possession of the stolen engine, which they could prove was their property by its serial number. With the aid of the police, they recovered the stolen engine. Even if Petras had sold the engine to Jones, who sold it to Smith, Rexeer Auto could recover the property at any point when it could be found because Rexeer Auto never lost title to it.

16.9 TRANSFER OF TITLE TO FUNGIBLE GOODS

fungible goods Goods that are generally sold by weight or measure.

Fungible goods are those that are generally sold by weight or measure. Examples include wheat, sugar, flour, gasoline, and oil. A unit of such goods is like any other unit. Consequently, 1,000 gallons of No. 2 fuel oil in a storage tank that holds many thousands of gallons are exactly like all the other gallons of No. 2 oil in the tank. Nevertheless, it is important to determine when title to such fungible goods passes. Generally, the following rules apply:

- If goods are ordered and the building, tank, storage yard, or grain elevator from which they are to come is not specified, this general rule of title passing applies: Title passes when the goods become ascertained–that is, when they become clearly identifiable. As a result, when a person simply orders 1,000 gallons of No. 2 fuel oil, title passes when the 1,000 gallons are delivered or at least separated from the larger mass.
- If a buyer orders a specific quantity of fungible goods from a specific mass–for example, if the preceding order for fuel oil specified that it be from "Hunters Point Storage Yard"–title passes at once, even before the portion ordered is separated from the rest. In the eyes of the law, the buyer acquires immediate title to an undivided share of the specific mass because the units of oil are all the same and no selection is necessary to identify the particular units that the buyer is purchasing.

EXAMPLE 16.7

▶ Rural Cannery received an order from Fisk Supermarkets for 1,000 cases of canned peas bearing the Fisk label. The cannery normally packaged such goods for many supermarkets and had an abundant supply of canned peas. After it received this order, the cannery began placing Fisk labels on cans of peas. Title to the canned peas passed to Fisk when the labels were affixed to the cans.

CHAPTER SUMMARY

16.1 Title, as it relates to property, is intangible. It represents ownership and the right to possess something, unless that right has been given up.

16.2 Real property is land and all articles permanently attached to it, such as buildings and trees. Personal property is all kinds of property other than real property. Only personal property is governed by the law of sales.

16.3 There are a variety of ways in which title can pass. A bill of sale is a written statement that the seller is passing ownership to the buyer. A bill of lading is a receipt for goods to be shipped, acknowledging that such goods have been received and indicating agreement that the goods will be transported to the destination specified. A warehouse receipt is like a bill of lading except the goods involved are not being transported but merely stored.

16.4 Title to goods passes when the parties intend for it to pass. In the event that the intent of the parties is not clear, title passes at the moment when they unconditionally agree to sell specific goods that are in a deliverable state.

16.5 A conditional sale is one with contract provisions that specify conditions that must be met by one of the parties. The two types of conditions found in contracts for conditional sales are conditions precedent and conditions subsequent. Conditions precedent are those that must be met before title passes. Conditions subsequent are those that must be met after title passes.

16.6 A person without good title to goods cannot transfer title, except in cases of transfer of title by estoppel. Someone who finds lost goods has title to them against anyone but the true owner. A thief has no title to goods that they have stolen and, consequently, cannot pass title, even to innocent purchasers.

16.7 Estoppel is a legal bar to using contradictory words or acts in asserting a claim against another. Examples of estoppel include transfer of money or commercial paper made out to the bearer, transfer of property to a seller dealing in the same type of goods, transfer of property to a seller permitted to appear as the real owner, and transfer of proof of ownership to an unauthorized seller.

16.8 Persons having rightful possession of goods have the right to make legitimate sales as representatives of the owners of the goods, although they are not titleholders. Persons having wrongful possession of goods have no right to make sales, and the titleholders of these goods are never estopped.

16.9 Title to fungible goods passes when the goods become clearly identifiable. In cases in which a specific quantity is ordered from a specific mass, title passes at once, even before the portion ordered is separated.

CHAPTER SIXTEEN ASSESSMENT

MATCHING LEGAL TERMS

Match each of the numbered definitions with the correct term in the following list.

a. bill of sale
b. certificate of title
c. condition subsequent
d. condition precedent
e. estoppel
f. fungible goods
g. order bill of lading
h. personal property
i. real property
j. remote party
k. straight bill of lading
l. warehouse receipt

1. A common carrier's nonnegotiable receipt for goods accepted for shipment. 1. _____
2. A written statement that the seller is passing, or transferring, ownership to a buyer. 2. _____
3. A carrier's receipt for goods accepted for shipment that ensures that the goods will not be delivered unless the original bill of lading is surrendered. 3. _____
4. A provision in a contract that requires the performance of a specific act before title passes. 4. _____
5. A salesperson authorized to sell merchandise for a merchant. 5. _____
6. Land and articles permanently attached to it. 6. _____
7. A provision in a contract that requires the performance of a specific act after title passes. 7. _____
8. A legal bar to the use of contradictory words or acts in asserting a claim against another. 8. _____
9. Goods generally sold by weight or measure, such as grain or gasoline, where each unit is like all others. 9. _____
10. A document that is proof of ownership. 10. _____
11. Possessions other than real property, such as jewelry. 11. _____
12. Evidence of ownership provided by a storage facility. 12. _____

TRUE/FALSE QUIZ

13. A bill of sale must be prepared on a specific legal form. 13. _____
14. Personal property is land and anything attached to it. 14. _____
15. The general rule of law regarding the passing of title is that title passes when the parties intend it to pass. 15. _____
16. Estoppel is a legal principle that can prevent an owner from recovering their own property under certain circumstances. 16. _____
17. Conditions precedent are required acts that must be performed before title passes. 17. _____
18. Title to goods can never pass to another without the consent of the owner. 18. _____
19. Conditions subsequent are required acts that must be performed after a contract is signed. 19. _____
20. The owner of personal property cannot recover it from an innocent third party who purchased it from a seller in possession of the property and who was entrusted with proof of ownership by the real owner. 20. _____

MULTIPLE CHOICE QUIZ

Please choose the correct answer from the choices following each question.

21. Trees planted in a residential yard are (a) personal property (b) conditional property (c) fungible property (d) real property. **21.** _____

22. Trees sold at a retail nursery to be planted in a residential yard are (a) personal property (b) conditional property (c) fungible property (d) real property. **22.** _____

23. A seller agrees to sell goods to a buyer with the bill of sale stating that title will transfer to buyer on December 1. Due to a supply chain problem, the goods are not shipped until December 3. The goods are destroyed in transit on December 4. Who bears the risk of loss of these goods? (a) Buyer only (b) Seller only (c) Both buyer and seller (d) Neither buyer nor seller **23.** _____

24. A seller agrees to sell goods to a buyer but gives the buyer the right to return the goods by December 31 if not satisfied. The buyer possesses the goods on December 29 when they are destroyed. Who bears the risk of loss of these goods? (a) Buyer only (b) Seller only (c) Both buyer and seller (d) Neither buyer nor seller **24.** _____

25. The owner of goods leaves the goods at a repair shop for service. The repair shop also sells the same type of goods. A customer sees the goods for repair and, thinking they are for sale, asks to purchase them. The repair shop owner agrees. In this case, (a) the customer cannot keep the goods because they did not get title in the sale (b) the customer can keep the goods because they did get title in the sale (c) the customer can keep the goods but will not get title in the sale (d) the customer cannot keep the goods even though they got title in the sale. **25.** _____

26. Goods are stolen from an owner and sold to a retail store. A customer in the store purchases the goods from the store. In this case, (a) the customer cannot keep the goods because they did not get title in the sale (b) the customer can keep the goods because they did get title in the sale (c) the customer can keep the goods but will not get title in the sale (d) the customer cannot keep the goods even though they got title in the sale. **26.** _____

DISCUSSION QUESTIONS

Answer the following questions and discuss them in class.

27. Distinguish between real and personal property and indicate which is subject to the law of sales.

_____

_____

28. Explain how title and certificate of title relate to ownership.

29. Explain how title passes and discuss how bills of sale, bills of lading, and warehouse receipts are involved in the passing of title.

30. Explain the law governing title to lost or stolen goods and sales by persons having wrongful possession of goods.

31. Discuss the principle of estoppel and provide examples of how this principle is applied in various situations.

32. Explain the passage of title to fungible goods.

THINKING CRITICALLY ABOUT THE LAW

Answer the following questions, which require you to think critically about the legal principles that you learned in this chapter.

33. Title An important application of the concept of title relates to who is holding title when a loss occurs. Are there other ways of determining who should bear a loss in a business transaction?

34. Conditions Precedent A contract stipulates that certain conditions must be met before title can pass. A seller might wish to hasten the passage of title to minimize the risk of loss and the cost of insurance to indemnify such losses. Consider a typical sales transaction and suggest steps a seller might take to accelerate title transfer.

35. **Estoppel** It seems that passage of title by estoppel might deny the rights of an innocent though inattentive property owner. Should a legitimate titleholder lose title because of their inattention?

____

____

36. **Remote Parties** How can a buyer in a store know whether they are dealing with a titleholder or a remote party? Does it make a difference? Generally, whom does a buyer hold responsible for problems?

____

____

37. **A Question of Ethics** Is it ethical for a person who is not a titleholder to act as one who has title to goods, thereby misleading a prospective buyer?

____

____

CASE QUESTIONS

Study each of the following cases. Answer the questions that follow with Yes or No.

38. **Passage of Title** Crowley, a building contractor, ordered 500 bags of cement from Litvak Building Supply. It was agreed that Litvak would deliver to a building site, and title would pass when delivery was made. Before the bags of cement could be loaded on a delivery truck, a train derailment destroyed much of the supply company's inventory.

    a. Must Crowley bear the loss and recover damages from the railroad? **a.** _____

    b. Is the requirement of delivery to a building site a condition precedent? **b.** _____

    c. Did title to the bags of cement pass at the time the order was placed? **c.** _____

39. **Estoppel** Hollander purchased a computer from a pawnshop for use in his real estate office. Several weeks later, Diem, one of Hollander's customers, mentioned that the computer looked familiar and asked if he could examine it. After checking the underside of the machine, he pointed to his Social Security number, which had been engraved on the metal frame by his insurance agent. Diem demanded the return of the computer, claiming that it had been stolen from him and that he could produce the original sales slip.

    a. Can Diem legally recover the computer if he could prove that it had been stolen? **a.** _____

    b. Can a rightful owner be estopped from recovering his or her property from an innocent purchaser? **b.** _____

    c. Could the pawnshop have given good title to Hollander? **c.** _____

40. Condition Precedent Fallon agreed in writing to purchase a used truck from Moonlit Motors with the understanding that a snowplow attachment would be added. When Fallon attempted to take delivery of the truck, he found that the plow attachment had not been added. He refused to accept delivery. Moonlit protested that the plow attachment was being shipped from Minnesota and that it would be installed when it arrived. Moonlit demanded that Fallon accept the truck.

a. Can Fallon legally refuse to accept the truck? **a.** _____

b. Is this an example of a condition precedent? **b.** _____

c. Is the contract enforceable? **c.** _____

41. Certificate of Title Forell, a resident of Des Moines, purchased a nearly new Buick automobile from a seller in Cleveland for the unusually low price of $4,000. The seller explained that he was in town to take delivery of another automobile that he had just inherited from his late father. The seller produced a certificate of title. After Forell had possession of the Buick for several months, he sold it to Bates for $3,800. After Bates had driven the car for two months, he was stopped by the police for a minor traffic violation. When the police routinely checked the vehicle identification number through their computer, it was discovered that the car had been stolen from Santiago in Cleveland and that the certificate of title was forged. When Santiago learned that his car had been located, he claimed ownership.

a. Will Santiago be able to recover his automobile? **a.** _____

b. Will the certificate of title Forell obtained from the out-of-town seller entitle him to ownership? **b.** _____

c. Was Forell a good-faith purchaser? **c.** _____

CASE ANALYSIS

Study each of the following cases carefully. Briefly state the principle of law and your decision.

42. Title to Stolen Goods Alttarbi was on a group vacation tour when he discovered that his camcorder was not where he had left it on the tour bus. Later on the tour, Alttarbi noticed another vacationer, Carlsen, with a similar camcorder. When Carlsen was confronted, he claimed that he had found the camcorder at one of the tour bus stops. When Alttarbi produced a bill of sale with a serial number that matched the one on the disputed camcorder, Carlsen refused to surrender it, claiming that since he had found it, it was his. Will Alttarbi be able to regain possession of his lost camcorder?

Principle of Law:

____

____

Decision:

____

____

43. Remote Party Kiang, a sales representative working for Prat's Appliances, sold a refrigerator to Pogany. After several weeks, Pogany changed her mind and wanted to repudiate the sales contract. Her argument was that a valid contract did not exist because Kiang did not possess title to the refrigerator and therefore could not convey title to her. Will Pogany be allowed to repudiate the sales contract?

Principle of Law:

Decision:

44. Passage of Title Hughes purchased a new Lincoln Continental automobile from Al Greene Inc., an authorized new car dealership. On the day of the sale, Hughes made a cash down payment and signed a purchase contract and an application for the title certificate. The understanding was that Hughes would take immediate possession of the car and return in a few days for new-car preparation and the installation of a CB radio. On the way home from the dealer, Hughes wrecked the car. The certificate of title had not yet been issued by the state. The buyer, Hughes, claimed that title had not yet passed because the title certificate had not yet been issued. Who must bear the loss? [*Hughes v. Al Greene, Inc.,* 418 N.E.2d 1355 (Ohio)]

Principle of Law:

Decision:

LEGAL RESEARCH

Complete the following activities. Share your findings with the class.

45. Working in Teams In teams of three or four, interview a variety of local businesses to determine how they transfer title for the sale of goods. Some types of businesses would include equipment retailers, automobile dealerships, and pet stores.

46. Using Technology A bill of sale, bill of lading, or warehouse receipt must be in writing. Find (or create) a digital example of these documents.

chapter 17
Sales

LEARNING OUTCOMES

After studying this chapter and completing the assessment, you will be able to

17.1 Discuss the concept of title in relation to the law of sales.

17.2 Distinguish between a contract for sale and a contract to sell.

17.3 Identify the classifications of sales contracts, including oral, written, express, and implied.

17.4 Discuss the difference between entire and divisible contracts.

17.5 Describe the special requirements of contracts for labor and materials.

17.6 Discuss trial periods and returns.

17.7 Discuss auction sales, conditional sales, and consignment sales.

17.8 Discuss how the delivery of shipments affects the passage of title, and how FOB shipping point and FOB destination differ.

17.9 Explain both sellers' and buyers' remedies for breach of sales contracts.

SALES

"Shopping online is the greatest invention of life."

Kim Kardashian, reality TV star

LEGAL terms

- contract for sale
- existing goods
- future goods
- contract to sell
- contract for labor and materials
- contract for sale with the right of return
- sale on approval
- sale or return
- auction without reserve
- auction with reserve
- conditional sales contract
- FOB shipping point
- FOB destination
- stoppage in transit
- specific performance
- replevin
- cover

17.1 THE LAW OF SALES

Because the law of sales affects so many individuals and businesses, Article 2 of the Uniform Commercial Code (UCC) is quite comprehensive. Article 2, however, does not include investment securities (covered by Article 8 of the UCC), real estate, or services. Contracts for services are considered ordinary contracts and are not covered by the UCC. UCC Article 2 only covers the sale of "goods," defined as tangible, moveable personal property.

In the case of transactions that involve both goods and services, courts look to the predominant portion of the contract to determine whether it is a sales contract for goods or a services contract for repairs, which incidentally includes the parts necessary to make the repairs.

The term *title,* introduced in Chapter 16, as used in contracts for sale, refers to ownership. Consequently, having title to something usually means having the right to possess it. However, there are important exceptions. For example, if *A* leases *B* an automobile, *B* has the right to possess the vehicle, but *A* retains ownership. The concept of title is important in the law of sales. Equally important are the remedies for *breach of contract*–that is, breaking a contract.

17.2 CONTRACTS FOR SALE VERSUS CONTRACTS TO SELL

contract for sale
A legally enforceable agreement that has as its purpose the immediate transfer of title to personal property in return for consideration.

A contract for sale is a legally enforceable agreement that has as its purpose the immediate transfer of title to personal property in return for consideration. The contract may be for a present sale of goods or for a sale of future goods–goods that are not yet in existence or manufactured. A sale, according to the UCC, is the passing of title from the seller to the buyer for a price (UCC 2-106). Payment for goods can be in the form of money, or goods, or in the performance of services (UCC 2-304).

EXAMPLE 17.1

Jesup agreed to sell an amateur radio transmitter to Moncada for $750. Moncada paid the agreed price, and Jesup gave him the equipment.

This is an executed contract for sale, and title (ownership) to the transmitter passed when the money was paid to Jesup. If Moncada, after purchasing the transmitter, left it with Jesup for a day while he arranged delivery and it was damaged, destroyed, or stolen during that time, the loss would be borne by Moncada.

existing goods
Goods that physically exist and are owned by the seller at the time of sale.

future goods
Goods that do not exist at the time of the sales transaction but are expected to come into the possession of the seller.

Suppose that, in Example 17.1, the parties had agreed that the sale of the radio equipment would be completed when Moncada had passed his FCC amateur's examination. The transaction would be viewed as an agreement in which both parties intended title to pass when Moncada passed the examination. If anything happened to the equipment in the interim, Jesup would suffer the loss.

Goods that physically exist and are owned by the seller at the time of sale are considered existing goods. Goods that do not exist at the time of the sales transaction but are expected to come into the possession of the seller are considered future goods. Examples of such future goods include growing crops and timber, unborn livestock and pets, and goods not yet manufactured. An agreement to sell future goods is considered a contract to sell, in contrast to a contract for sale. The distinction between existing and future goods is important because a person cannot sell goods to which they do not hold title.

contract to sell
An agreement to sell future goods.

EXAMPLE 17.2

Kierman paid a $500 deposit to Mondrus, a breeder of pedigree dogs, who agreed to sell Kierman a male puppy from the next litter of his prize terrier for $1,200. Before the terrier gave birth to the expected litter, it was killed in a fire that destroyed the kennel. Kierman demanded the return of his deposit, claiming that title to the puppy did not pass until delivery was made. Mondrus demanded the balance of the agreed price of $1,200, claiming that the unborn puppy belonged to Kierman from the time of their agreement.

The courts have heard many such cases, and in almost every one, they have held that title to such future goods remains with the seller. In Example 17.2, Kierman would get back his deposit and Mondrus would bear the loss.

In a contract to sell unharvested wheat, title remains with the seller.
mihalec/Shutterstock

17.3 ORAL, WRITTEN, EXPRESS, AND IMPLIED CONTRACTS

As is true for all contracts, sales contracts may be oral or written and express or implied. As pointed out in Chapter 13, contracts for $500 or more must be in writing to be enforceable (UCC 2-201). The complete agreement need not be in writing, but there must be some evidence of the intention of the parties. The contract also must be signed by the affected parties.

17.4 ENTIRE AND DIVISIBLE SALES CONTRACTS

Entire and divisible contracts were introduced in Chapter 7, and examples were provided to show the difference between them. The significance of the distinction between entire and divisible sales contracts can be seen in numerous business transactions.

EXAMPLE 17.3

Management Mode, a publisher of newsletters, decided to switch from using an outside typesetter to internal desktop publishing to save the cost of typesetting and to speed up its operation. The firm ordered personal computers from Compu-Writ for each of its editors and writers, appropriate word-processing software, desktop publishing software, in-house training software, and laser printers. Delivery of the equipment and software was scheduled to be made within 30 days of placing the order. However, delivery of the laser printers was delayed for two months.

Because all the components are interdependent and were included in the same order–an entire contract–payment for the contract would not be required until the whole order was filled. Payment for the portion of the order delivered–the computers–would not be due when they were delivered. On the other hand, if the computers and the printers were ordered for separate offices–a divisible contract–payment for the computers would be due when delivery was made, even though delivery of the printers was delayed for two months.

17.5 CONTRACTS FOR LABOR AND MATERIALS

contract for labor and materials
A sales contract for goods of special design, construction, or manufacture.

A sales contract for goods of special design, construction, or manufacture is neither a contract for sale nor a contract to sell. Such a contract is considered a contract for labor and materials. A contract for labor and materials, even though it involves $500 or more, need not always be in writing to be enforceable. This is an exception to the UCC requirement that contracts of $500 or more be in writing. The UCC provides that "if the goods are to be specially manufactured for the buyer and are not suitable for sale to others,"* the requirement of a written contract does not necessarily apply [UCC 2-201(3)]. The contract will not be binding if the buyer repudiates (cancels) the oral contract and the seller receives the notice before they have made either a substantial beginning in manufacturing the goods or commitments for their procurement. If, however, the seller has begun manufacture or made a commitment, the cancellation is not effective.*

EXAMPLE 17.4

Little Lucy's Bakery orally contracted with Foremost Conveyor Company for the design and construction of a special conveyor system to be installed in the shipping room of the bakery. After the conveyor was designed, built, and ready to be installed, Little Lucy's hired a new manager. The new manager canceled the order, claiming that it was invalid because it was not in writing. Foremost Conveyor can recover damages from the bakery for breach of contract because the cancellation was received after work on the conveyor system had begun.

17.6 TRIAL PERIODS AND RETURNS

While a merchant might prefer to sell for cash with no return privilege, if the seller's competitors are willing to allow prospective customers a trial period or the right of return, the seller also must do so in order to remain competitive. In these kinds of selling arrangements, it is important to determine who owns and has title to the merchandise while it is in the prospective buyer's possession, in the event of loss or damage.

*The Uniform Commercial Code (UCC) is a joint project between the National Conference of Commissioners on Uniform State Laws (NCCUSL) and the American Law Institute (ALI).

CONTRACT FOR SALE WITH RIGHT OF RETURN

Certain kinds of goods are frequently sold on a trial basis. Because a sales brochure or demonstration may not persuade a businessperson that a certain office machine will be an asset to the business, a short trial period during which the buyer can use the machine is often arranged. A contract for sale with the right of return gives the buyer both title to the goods and the opportunity to return them to the seller at a later time.

contract for sale with the right of return
A contract for the sale of goods that gives the buyer both title to the goods and the opportunity to return them to the seller at a later time.

SALE ON APPROVAL

When a contract provides for the sale of goods subject to the buyer's approval, the transaction is a sale on approval. The goods remain the property of the seller until the buyer has expressed approval of the goods. Title and risk of loss remain with the seller. The buyer may indicate approval orally or in writing, or by retaining the goods for more than a reasonable time.

sale on approval
A contract for the sale of goods subject to the buyer's approval.

EXAMPLE 17.5

▶ The sales representative of Scrub 'n' Clean Equipment was attempting to persuade the manager of River Rock Car Wash to install a new type of car wash brush. The cost of the brushes and uncertainty about their effectiveness made the car wash manager hesitant to make a commitment to buy until he had the opportunity to try the equipment. The sales representative agreed to let the car wash use four brushes for two months on approval.

Both parties in this case agreed to a sale on approval. After using the brushes for a month or two, the car wash manager could agree to purchase them, and at such time, title would pass to the car wash. It is not wise for a potential buyer to let the trial period slip by on the assumption that the seller does not mind or that the buyer is getting something for nothing. The buyer must notify the seller of their decision to return the goods, if that is the intention, within the time agreed upon for trial of the goods or within a reasonable time if no time has been agreed upon. If notification is not given during that period, the user's continued, prolonged use of the goods on approval could be interpreted as implied consent to buy, and the user could be held responsible for the goods and be obligated to pay for them.

SALE OR RETURN

Most goods sold by reputable merchants can be returned for a variety of reasons unless the sale is clearly identified as final or the circumstances of the return are unreasonable. Very often a merchant will agree to a sale or return—that is, an agreement whereby the seller will accept the return of goods at the request of the buyer in order to maintain goodwill rather than because the seller is legally obliged to accept the returned goods. The sale of goods can be made with the understanding that the purchaser takes title to the goods but has the right to return them within a specified or reasonable time. In such cases, the purchaser must assume all the obligations of ownership while the goods are in their possession.

sale or return
An agreement whereby the seller will accept the return of goods at the request of the buyer to maintain goodwill, rather than because the seller is legally obliged to accept the returned goods.

Suppose that in Example 17.5, the manager of River Rock Car Wash was sure that the new brushes were what he wanted and needed. Suppose also that the funds were available for the planned purchase of the brushes and that a purchase order for the brushes was issued. If the brushes did not prove satisfactory, the manager could probably still return them. The major distinction between this example and the previous one is that in this instance, title to the brushes is in the hands of the purchaser, who would be held responsible for loss or damage of the equipment. Not only would the parties to the agreement have an interest in who held title, but the insurance carriers for the car wash as well as the supplier, Scrub 'n Clean, would also have an interest in who held title.

17.7 OTHER KINDS OF SALES

A bidder's offer is accepted when the auctioneer lets the hammer fall.
Sean Justice/CORBIS

Two additional kinds of sales are auction sales and conditional sales.

AUCTION SALES

Auction sales were introduced in Chapter 13. At an auction sale, the buyer is the party making the offer, or bid. The seller is the owner of the goods, who has engaged an auctioneer to gather bids from interested parties with the intent of selling to the highest bidder. The bidder's offer is accepted when the auctioneer says, "Going once, twice, three times, sold!" and at the same time lets the hammer fall. A bidder may retract a bid at any time before the hammer falls, and such retraction does not revive any previous bid. If a bid is made while the hammer is falling, the auctioneer may use their discretion to reopen the bidding or declare the goods sold under the bid made as the hammer was falling [UCC 2-328(2)].

There have been reported instances of expensive pieces of property being sold at auction for a pittance simply because no one offered a higher bid. This possibility occurs only at an auction without reserve—one at which the goods must be sold to the highest bidder and may not be withdrawn after bidding has begun. An auction with reserve gives the auctioneer the right to withdraw the goods at any time before announcing completion of the sale if reasonable bids are not made. If a *reserve amount* has been established, it is announced by the auctioneer before bidding begins or is disclosed in posters or catalogs listing the goods to be auctioned. Auction sales are with reserve unless otherwise specified [UCC 2-328(3)].

auction without reserve
One at which the goods must be sold to the highest bidder and may not be withdrawn after bidding has begun.

auction with reserve
One that gives the auctioneer the right to withdraw the goods at any time before announcing completion of the sale if reasonable bids are not made.

The legal requirement that sales of personal property for $500 or more be in writing is satisfied by the notations made in the auctioneer's sales book. In the case of telephone bids made from distant branches of the auction house, the bidder must sign an agreement in advance that sets out the conditions under which they agree to pay any accepted bid.

Online auctions are conducted on the Internet; but unlike live auctions during which a buyer can inspect goods to be auctioned, bidders in an online auction rely on the reputation of the seller, photographs that display the goods, and email. Items offered for sale can be offered with a reserve so that the sale price must be equal to or greater than the reserve.

CONDITIONAL SALES

Some sales contracts include conditions that must be met either before or after the sale is completed. In most instances, the conditions deal with arrangements for payment. A conditional sales contract is one way of selling merchandise with the condition that title will remain with the seller until the purchase price has been paid. The buyer cannot legally resell goods purchased this way because title has not passed; a person cannot sell goods to which they have no title. The seller can *repossess* the goods (take back property through judicial action) if the buyer does not pay in the time agreed.

conditional sales contract
A sales contract that includes conditions that must be met either before or after the sale is completed.

CONSIGNMENT SALES

A consignment sale occurs when a seller (a consignor) entrusts goods to a merchant (a consignee) who acts under contract as the seller's agent to sell the goods in exchange for a small fee.

17.8 DELIVERY

Many transactions require shipment of the goods purchased. However, shipping goods is not without risk. While goods are in transit, there is a distinct possibility that damage may occur. Any number of unfortunate events may transpire; for example, shifting cargo can cause damage to fragile items; a natural disaster, like a flood or tornado, can destroy or damage goods; a shipper can even lose the goods. Generally, a prudent party will make certain that goods are insured against these types of losses; but in order to do so, the party must have an insurable interest in the goods. An insurable interest is the right to insure goods against any potential loss. Sellers have an *insurable interest* in the goods as long they have title to them, whereas buyers are allowed to insure goods even before they obtain title to them [UCC 2-501(1)].

The manner in which the goods are shipped affects the passing of title. Title to goods that are shipped by private carrier or delivered by the seller passes at the time of delivery to the buyer. If the buyer arranges for delivery, title passes when the buyer, or their agent, picks up the goods. However, in the case of goods that are shipped by *common carrier*–someone who is in the business of transporting goods (or persons), whether by rail, truck, plane, or any other mode of transportation–title passes to the purchaser according to the conditions that follow.

SALES FOB SHIPPING POINT

The abbreviation *FOB* means "free on board." When goods are sold FOB shipping point, title to the goods passes from the seller to the buyer when the carrier receives the shipment, and it is understood that the buyer will pay the transportation charges. From that point, the goods belong to the buyer, and in the event of loss or damage, the buyer must attempt to recover any loss from the carrier. Further, the buyer is responsible for paying the seller for the merchandise even if they never receive it (UCC 2-319).

FOB shipping point
Title to goods passes from the seller to the buyer when the carrier receives the shipment, and it is understood that the buyer will pay the transportation charges.

SALES FOB DESTINATION

Title to goods shipped FOB destination passes when the goods are delivered to the buyer. In the event of their loss or damage en route, the seller must attempt to recover any loss from the carrier. In such a case, the cost of transporting the goods is paid to the carrier by the seller but is usually included in the buyer's invoice or is billed to the buyer separately.

FOB destination
Title passes from the seller to the buyer when the goods are delivered to the buyer.

This method of shipment offers the buyer an advantage. For example, in case of a lost or damaged shipment, the buyer can quickly call the seller and arrange for a duplicate shipment. The buyer's money is not tied up in goods not received, and the buyer is spared the inconvenience of filing a claim with the carrier.

17.9 REMEDIES FOR BREACH OF SALES CONTRACTS

The law provides a number of remedies to protect the buyer and the seller in disputes involving sales contracts. It is important to note that remedies are available for only a limited time. The UCC provides a *statute of limitations*–that is, a time limit after which the usual legal remedies are no longer available. The UCC provides that in the absence of negligence or fraud (for which there may be different statutes of limitations), legal action to remedy a breach of sales contract must be started within four years from the breach (UCC 2-725).

SELLERS' REMEDIES

A seller has a number of remedies at law, depending on the circumstances of the case. The most common circumstances are discussed here.

When the Buyer Refuses to Accept Delivery of the Goods When the buyer refuses to accept delivery of the goods, the seller may do one of the following:

1. Store the goods for the buyer and sue to recover the sales price if the goods are not readily resalable to another customer (UCC 2-704).
2. Resell the goods immediately if they are perishable or if their market value might depreciate rapidly. Also, the seller can sue the buyer for the difference between the price the goods brought in the resale and the price the buyer had agreed to pay for them plus incidental damages (UCC 2-706).
3. Retain the goods and sue the buyer for the difference between the contract price and the market price at the time the buyer refused to honor the contract (UCC 2-706).

EXAMPLE 17.6

Georgio placed an order with Med-Lab Manufacturing Company for specially designed medical laboratory testing equipment. When the equipment was ready for shipment, Georgio notified Med-Lab of her intention to cancel the order. Med-Lab has the right to hold the equipment for Georgio and sue for the agreed-upon purchase price.

If the equipment was not of special design and could be sold to others, Med-Lab could return the equipment to stock for sale to others and sue Georgio for damages resulting from Georgio's breach. In this case, the damages would be limited to the profit Med-Lab would have made on the sale if there had been no breach.

When the Buyer Refuses to Pay the Purchase Price When the buyer refuses to pay the purchase price, the seller may do one of the following:

1. If the seller still has possession of the goods, they can resell them after a reasonable period and sue for any damages incurred.
2. If the merchandise has already been delivered to the buyer, they can sue for the purchase price.

EXAMPLE 17.7

Molstad bought a laser printer from Computer Cosmos Company, agreeing to pay cash for it. Computer Cosmos insisted on retaining possession of the printer until the invoice amount was paid in full. When Molstad failed to pay within the agreed-upon time, Computer Cosmos sold the printer to Fishman at a lower price because of a general lowering of prices that took place between the time Molstad agreed to buy and the time it was sold to Fishman. Computer Cosmos sued Molstad for the difference between the price Molstad had agreed to pay and the price paid by Fishman. Computer Cosmos was successful in its efforts to recover this difference.

When the Buyer Is Insolvent Sometimes, after goods have been shipped to the buyer but before actual delivery has been made by the carrier, the seller learns that the buyer is *insolvent*–that is, the buyer no longer has sufficient assets to pay their debts.

When the buyer is insolvent, the UCC provides the seller with the right of stoppage in transit. Stoppage in transit is the right of an unpaid seller to stop goods in transit and order the carrier to hold them for the seller. This right to interrupt the shipment of goods to the buyer exists for both FOB shipping point sales and FOB destination sales (UCC 2-705).

To exercise this right of stoppage in transit, the seller must satisfy the common carrier that the buyer is insolvent. If the seller's information proves unfounded, both the seller and the carrier are subject to suit for damages. For this reason, the carrier should require the seller by contract to accept full responsibility for any loss that it may suffer as a result of a suit by the purchaser.

To exercise the right of stoppage in transit, the seller must satisfy the common carrier that the buyer is insolvent.
Comstock Images/Alamy

EXAMPLE 17.8

An order of books was en route to Readers' Haven bookstore, timed to arrive in time for a well-promoted author's book-signing party. The seller, Words in Print, notified the carrier not to deliver the books, claiming that it had received information from a reliable source that the buyer, Readers' Haven, was insolvent. Later it was revealed that the information was in error. Both the publisher and the carrier are subject to Readers' Haven's suit for damages.

BUYERS' REMEDIES

The UCC provides a buyer with certain remedies depending on the specific circumstances (UCC 2-711).

stoppage in transit
When the buyer is insolvent, the right of an unpaid seller to stop goods in transit and order the carrier to hold them for the seller.

When the Wrong Quantity Is Delivered Should the seller deliver the incorrect quantity of the goods ordered, the buyer has several options. If a smaller quantity of merchandise is delivered than was ordered, the buyer may either reject delivery and sue for damages or accept the quantity delivered and sue for damages, which would be calculated as the lost profits that would have resulted from the sale of the undelivered portion. If a larger quantity of goods is delivered than was ordered, the buyer may reject the entire shipment, accept only what was ordered and reject the rest, or accept the entire shipment and pay for the additional items at the contract price.

EXAMPLE 17.9

Woodbury Way, an appliance store, ordered 100 microwave ovens from an importer. By mistake, the importer shipped 200. Woodbury Way was delighted to learn that he had an unexpected bargain because the wholesaler's price was going to be increased as a result of changes in the foreign exchange rate. The buyer has the right to keep the entire shipment and pay for all 200 microwaves at the contract price.

When the Goods Are Not as Ordered In the event that the seller delivers goods that are not as specified in the contract, the buyer may revoke the contract and return the goods that are substantially different from those that were ordered. If the goods have already been paid for, the buyer may demand a refund of the purchase price and, in most states, sue for damages for breach of warranty, a legally binding guarantee (see Chapter 18). Alternatively, the buyer may keep the goods and sue for damages for any loss resulting from the seller's breach of contract. If the goods are of a higher quality than what was ordered, the buyer has the option of either rejecting the order or keeping the order and paying the contract price.

EXAMPLE 17.10

Susuki purchased and paid for a standby electric generator for emergency use at his factory. The seller assured Susuki that the generator would produce enough power to keep his essential operations going during a power failure. When the generator was tested, however, it failed to produce sufficient power. Susuki could demand and obtain a refund. In this instance, Susuki probably could not show that he had sustained additional damages, so a lawsuit would be unlikely.

When the Seller Fails to Deliver the Goods When title has passed to the buyer for goods the seller has failed to deliver, the buyer has the following remedies:

1. The buyer can sue for damages by bringing a tort action charging conversion. As explained in Chapter 4, conversion is a tort that results when a person has unlawfully assumed ownership of property that belongs to another. The amount of damages sought would be the value of the goods at the time of the seller's failure to deliver.
2. If the goods are unique, such as a one-of-a-kind work of art, and the buyer wants the particular goods that are specified in the contract, the buyer can seek a court order of specific performance. Such an order requires the seller to deliver the goods specified in the contract or face being held in contempt of court (UCC 2-716) (see Chapter 15).
3. Another remedy available to a buyer who wishes to obtain goods that are rightfully theirs, rather than money damages, is to sue to obtain them by bringing an action of replevin—an action to recover possession of specific goods wrongfully taken or detained by another (UCC 2-716). In such an action, the court will order the sheriff to seize the goods and deliver them to the buyer.
4. The UCC also permits a buyer to cover—that is, to buy similar goods elsewhere to substitute for those not delivered by the seller. If the buyer chooses to cover, they may demand from the seller, as damages, the difference between the cost of cover (what they paid for the replacement goods) and the contract price, plus any incidental expenses, less expenses saved as a result of the seller's breach (UCC 2-712).

specific performance
A court order directing a person to perform—or not perform—as they agreed to do in a contract.

replevin
An action to recover possession of specific goods wrongfully taken or detained by another.

cover
When the seller fails to deliver the goods, the right of a buyer to buy similar goods elsewhere to substitute for those not delivered by the seller.

EXAMPLE 17.11

▶ Andrews, a retail electronics dealer, purchased and paid for 60 netbooks of an advanced design from a wholesaler. The netbooks were in stock, and delivery was promised. Clearly title had passed. Because of a sharp increase in the manufacturer's prices, the wholesaler refused to deliver the devices as agreed in the contract. Andrews can sue the distributor for the difference between the contract price and the higher market price at the time of the wholesaler's refusal to deliver. If she is seeking money damages, her suit will be an action for conversion. Alternatively, if the devices are in short supply and she is more interested in getting the netbooks than in a money settlement, she can seek an order of specific performance. Or she can institute an action of replevin for delivery of the netbooks. If the netbooks are available elsewhere at a higher price, she could cover by buying them at the higher price and then suing the wholesaler for the difference between the contract price and the price of the cover. The suit also could seek repayment of expenses such as the additional cost of transportation from a distant seller.

If title has not yet passed to the buyer, their remedy when the seller refuses to deliver at the time and place stated in the contract is a suit for breach of contract. The amount of damages would be the difference between the contract price and the market price at the time delivery was refused. The UCC also permits recovery of other damages that the buyer can prove, less any expenses saved as a result of the seller's breach (UCC 2-713).

EXAMPLE 17.12

▶ Ho, the owner of a business school, ordered 30 computers from Latimer, a supplier of office equipment, at a price of $875 each. A week before the time agreed for delivery, Latimer got an order for 30 of the same kind of computers from an insurance company that had relocated to the city. The second buyer agreed to pay a price of $1,150 each. Sensing an opportunity to increase his profit, Latimer refused to fill Ho's order. While it would be difficult to determine the amount of damages, Ho could sue for foreseeable damages that might include the lost tuition that would have been paid by students who would have enrolled in the school if the computers had been delivered as promised.

CHAPTER SUMMARY

17.1 The term *title,* as it is used in contracts for sale, refers to ownership. Having title to something usually means having the right to possess it.

17.2 A contract for sale is a legally enforceable agreement that has as its purpose the immediate transfer of title to personal property in return for consideration. A contract to sell is an agreement to sell future goods.

17.3 Sales contracts may be oral or written and express or implied.

17.4 An entire contract is one in which all of the components of the agreement are included in the same order; a divisible contract is one in which components of an agreement are in separate orders.

17.5 A contract for labor and materials is a sales contract for goods of special design, construction, or manufacture. These contracts need not always be in writing, and they can be canceled before a substantial beginning or commitment to procurement has been made.

17.6 If a seller's competitors are willing to allow prospective customers a trial period or the right of return, the seller also must do so in order to remain competitive. A contract for sale with the right of return is an agreement that gives the buyer both title to the goods and an opportunity to return them to the seller at a later time. A contract for sale on approval is one in which the goods remain the property of the seller until the buyer has expressed approval of the goods.

17.7 An auction sale is one in which the buyer is the party making the offer, or bid. A conditional sale is one in which certain conditions must be met before or after the sale is completed. A consignment sale occurs when a seller (a consignor) entrusts goods to a merchant (a consignee) who acts under contract as the seller's agent to sell the goods in exchange for a small fee.

17.8 In sales FOB shipping point, title to the goods passes from the seller to the buyer when the carrier receives shipment, and it is understood that the buyer will pay the transportation charges. In sales FOB destination, title to goods passes when the goods are delivered to the buyer.

17.9 Sellers' remedies and buyers' remedies for breach of a sales contract depend on the circumstances. The UCC provides a statute of limitations in which legal action for breach of contract must be started. A seller may seek damages when the buyer refuses to accept delivery of the goods, when the buyer refuses to pay the purchase price, or when the buyer is insolvent. A buyer may seek damages when the wrong quantity is delivered, when the goods are not as ordered, or when the seller fails to deliver the goods.

CHAPTER SEVENTEEN ASSESSMENT

MATCHING LEGAL TERMS

Match each of the numbered definitions with the correct term in the following list.

a. conditional sales contract
b. contract for labor and materials
c. contract to sell
d. insolvency
e. reserve amount
f. sale on approval
g. sale or return
h. title
i. statute of limitations
j. stoppage in transit

1. Ownership of goods. **1.** _____

2. A contract for the sale of goods of special design, construction, or manufacture. **2.** _____

3. A contract for sale that gives the buyer the title to goods and the opportunity of returning them to the seller at a later time. **3.** _____

4. A sales agreement whereby the seller retains title and the buyer can return the goods. **4.** _____

5. An agreement for the sale of future goods. **5.** _____

6. An amount used in auction sales that specifies the lowest acceptable bid. **6.** _____

7. A sales agreement whereby the seller retains title until the buyer pays for the goods. 7. _____

8. A time limit after which legal remedies are no longer possible. 8. _____

9. A state in which a person is unable to pay their debts. 9. _____

10. The right of an unpaid seller to stop goods in transit and order the carrier to hold them for the seller. 10. _____

TRUE/FALSE QUIZ

Indicate whether each of the following statements is true or false.

11. Contracts for sale can be oral or written, express or implied. 11. _____

12. In most cases of the sale of future goods, title remains with the seller until the goods are in a deliverable state. 12. _____

13. A contract for the sale of various, unrelated articles is considered a divisible contract. 13. _____

14. A contract for labor and materials must always be in writing, regardless of the amount of money involved. 14. _____

15. When goods are sold on approval, the buyer has title during the trial period. 15. _____

16. The buyer of goods sold on approval can indicate their consent to keep the goods by retaining them for longer than the agreed time or a reasonable time. 16. _____

17. The notations in an auctioneer's book of sales of more than $500 satisfies the requirements of the Uniform Commercial Code that such contracts be in writing to be enforceable. 17. _____

18. Title to goods shipped FOB shipping point remains with the seller until delivery is made to the buyer. 18. _____

19. The buyer of goods that have been shipped FOB destination must bear the loss if the goods are lost or damaged in transit. 19. _____

MULTIPLE CHOICE QUIZ

20. A seller agrees to sell a buyer goods that will be ready for delivery in six months. This contract is a (a) contract of purchase (b) contract for sale (c) contract for future purchase (d) contract to sell. 20. _____

21. A seller agrees to sell a buyer a set of golf clubs, a tennis racket, and an autographed baseball and they signed a contract for the sale, but noted that the orders for these goods were "separate." The seller is able to deliver the golf clubs and the tennis racket, but is unable to deliver the

autographed baseball and cancels that order. In this case, (a) the buyer must pay for only the golf clubs (b) the buyer must pay for the golf clubs and the tennis rackets (c) the buyer must pay for the golf clubs, the tennis racket, and the autographed baseball (d) the buyer does not have to pay for any of the items. **21.** _____

22. A buyer contracts with a seller to manufacture and deliver specialized equipment for their business. The buyer and seller do not execute a written contract but agree to terms over the phone. The seller begins work on the equipment and notifies the seller that the equipment is "80% complete" and will be ready for delivery in a week. The buyer replies that they no longer want the equipment. In this case, (a) the buyer has canceled the contract and is not liable for the purchase (b) the contract was never valid because it was not in writing (c) the seller has invited cancellation of the contract with the notice (d) the buyer is liable for the purchase because the manufacture is substantially complete. **22.** _____

23. A seller contracts with a buyer to sell goods "on approval." The buyer keeps the goods for two months and then notifies the seller that they would like to return the goods. The seller had sent an invoice at the end of the first month, but the buyer had not paid. In this case, (a) the buyer did not return the goods in a reasonable amount of time and cannot return the goods (b) the buyer can return the goods at any time (c) the buyer can keep the goods but does not have to pay for them (d) the buyer must return the goods and pay for the goods. **23.** _____

24. A seller and buyer agree to ship goods "FOB shipping point." While in transit the goods are destroyed. Who bears the risk of loss? (a) Both the seller and the buyer (b) Neither the seller nor the buyer (c) Only the seller (d) Only the buyer **24.** _____

25. A seller and buyer agree to ship goods "FOB destination." While in transit the goods are destroyed. Who bears the risk of loss? (a) Both the seller and the buyer (b) Neither the seller nor the buyer (c) Only the seller (d) Only the buyer **25.** _____

26. A seller and buyer agree to the purchase and delivery of goods. The buyer refuses to accept delivery. In this case, the seller may (a) resell the goods to another buyer and sue buyer for the difference in price (b) resell the goods to another buyer but may not sue the buyer for the difference in price (c) destroy the goods and sue the buyer for the entire price (d) force the buyer to accept the goods. **26.** _____

27. A seller and buyer agree to the purchase and delivery of a specific quantity of goods. The seller delivers the order with an additional 15 units. In this case, the buyer may (a) reject the shipment (b) accept only what was ordered and reject the rest (c) accept the entire shipment (d) all of the above. **27.** _____

DISCUSSION QUESTIONS

Answer the following questions and discuss them in class.

28. How can a contract for future goods provide price flexibility for the seller and, at the same time, provide predictability to the buyer?

____

____

29. Why is it important to determine when title passes?

____

____

30. A contract for sale with the right of return gives the buyer both title to the goods and the opportunity to return the goods to the seller at a later time. What are the benefits to the seller of this type of sales transaction?

____

____

31. When a contract provides for the sale of goods subject to the buyer's approval, the transaction is a sale on approval. What are the benefits to the buyer of this type of sales transaction?

____

____

32. Discuss advantages and disadvantages to both sellers and buyers of shipping FOB destination and FOB shipping point.

____

____

33. Explain both sellers' and buyers' remedies for breach of contract.

____

____

THINKING CRITICALLY ABOUT THE LAW

Answer the following questions, which require you to think critically about the legal principles that you learned in this chapter.

34. Contract for Labor and Materials A contract for labor and materials need not be in writing, even if it is over $500. Does the buyer of the labor and materials enjoy the same level of legal protection as if the contract were in writing?

____

____

35. Definition of Goods Should the definition of *goods* include license to use software?

36. Internet Auction Compare and contrast online auctions with actual live auctions.

37. Sellers' Remedies How might a seller avoid pitfalls in selling to unknown buyers?

38. Buyers' Remedies How might a buyer avoid pitfalls in buying from unknown sellers?

39. A Question of Ethics Is it fair for a buyer to ask a seller to hold merchandise while the buyer shops for a better price?

CASE QUESTIONS

Study each of the following cases. Answer the questions that follow with Yes or No.

40. Contract for Labor and Materials Rios furnished Stern, a carpenter, with a set of sketches for a cabinet she wanted to built. They orally agreed on a price of $1,000, the type of wood to be used, and the delivery date. Before Stern had begun work or obtained the necessary materials, Rios canceled the agreement, saying that she planned to move to another apartment and would not need the cabinet.

a. Was this a contract for sale? **a.** _____

b. Was this a contract for labor and materials? **b.** _____

c. Was this a contract to sell? **c.** _____

d. Will Stern be successful in a suit for damages? **d.** _____

41. Divisible or Entire Contracts Miro, the owner of a supermarket, contracted with Market Supply Company for one complete checkout counter, including a cash register. After the counter was installed, but before the cash register was delivered, Market Supply Company demanded payment for the checkout counter. Miro refused to pay, claiming that he had contracted for a complete checkout counter, including the cash register, and he would pay when the cash register was installed.

a. Was this a sales contract? **a.** _____

b. Was this a divisible contract? **b.** _____

c. Was this an entire contract? **c.** _____

d. Does Market Supply have grounds for suit to collect for the portion of the order that was delivered? **d.** _____

42. Contract for Labor and Materials Galen, a purchasing agent for Ziff Construction Company, agreed orally with Houk Lumber to purchase 800 double-hung vinyl windows. The agreed price was $40,000. When Ziff Construction lost its financial backing, it had to cancel its plans for the houses it had planned to build. Houk sued to collect the purchase price.

a. Was this a contract for sale? **a.** _____

b. Was this a contract for labor and materials? **b.** _____

c. Did the contract meet the Uniform Commercial Code requirement of writing? **c.** _____

d. Is it likely that Houk would win the lawsuit? **d.** _____

43. Sales Contracts Eamons offered to sell his sailboat, complete with boat trailer, to Fitzgerald for $12,000. Fitzgerald agreed to the offer, gave Eamons a deposit of $500, and said that he would pay the balance when he came back with his car to pick up the boat and trailer. While Fitzgerald was away, the boat caught fire and was destroyed.

a. Was this a contract for sale? **a.** _____

b. Did the parties intend title to pass when Fitzgerald picked up the boat? **b.** _____

c. Must Eamons bear the loss? **c.** _____

d. Was this a contract to sell? **d.** _____

CASE ANALYSIS

Study each of the following cases carefully. Briefly state the principle of law and your decision.

44. Substitute Goods Gagne made a good living selling snacks, hamburgers, and refreshments at athletic events. He placed a written order with Pacific Container Company for 4,000 Styrofoam containers to be used to package hamburgers. Gagne requested that delivery be made three days before the last big football game of the season, and Pacific promised to meet the date. Two days before the game, the order still had not been delivered. In desperation, Gagne ordered 4,000 similar containers from another firm. When his order from Pacific finally arrived, Gagne refused to accept delivery or to pay for it. Pacific Container sued to collect the purchase price. Is Pacific likely to collect?

Principle of Law:

Decision:

45. Auction Sales Bundeson, a farmer, attended an auction of used farm equipment and successfully bid $1,600 for a tractor. When he returned home, he learned that a real estate developer was eager to buy his farm and build a shopping center on the property. Bundeson agreed to sell his farm, but then realized that he would not need the tractor he had just purchased and that it would be to his advantage to avoid the sale. He notified the auctioneer that he would not go through with the sale because the Uniform Commercial Code required a written contract for personal property sales of $500 or more. Will Bundeson succeed in avoiding the contract?

Principle of Law:

Decision:

46. Contract for Services Gates entered into a contract with Mennonite Deaconess Home & Hospital for the installation of a new, "one-ply roofing system." The work was to be done by an installer chosen by Mennonite but approved by Gates. When the work was nearly complete, but before Gates had approved the work, the hospital paid the installer 90 percent of the balance due. After inspection, Gates did not approve, and in addition, the roof leaked and had to be replaced at the hospital's expense. The hospital claimed that Gates was responsible for the quality of the work. Gates claimed that he could not be held accountable because service contracts are not covered by the Uniform Commercial Code. Did the contract involve goods or services, and will Gates be held responsible? [*Mennonite Deaconess Home & Hospital Inc. v. Gates Engineering Co.*, 363 N.W.2d 155 (Nebraska)]

Principle of Law:

Decision:

LEGAL RESEARCH

Complete the following activities. Share your findings with the class.

47. Working in Teams In teams of three or four, interview owners or managers of small businesses to determine how their sales contracts address returns, delivery, and remedies for breach.

48. Using Technology Using the Internet and search engines, investigate online auctions to determine the operating rules of the various sites.

chapter 18 Warranties

LEARNING OUTCOMES

After studying this chapter and completing the assessment, you will be able to

18.1 Identify the various provisions of the law that protect consumers and third parties who suffer physical injuries or financial losses.

18.2 Explain the term *warranty* and distinguish between express and implied warranties.

18.3 Identify the four kinds of express warranties.

18.4 Identify the three kinds of implied warranties.

18.5 Explain the provisions of the Magnuson-Moss Warranty Act.

LEGAL terms

- warranty
- express warranty
- implied warranty
- custom of the marketplace
- disclaimer
- implied warranty of merchantability
- merchant
- implied warranty of fitness for a particular purpose
- Magnuson-Moss Warranty Act
- interstate commerce
- full warranty
- limited warranty
- lemon laws

WARRANTIES

"You spent seventy-two dollars getting your hair done? You wasted your money!"

Judge Judy Sheindlin, lawyer, judge, and TV personality

Photodisc/Getty Images

18.1 PROTECTING CONSUMERS AND THIRD PARTIES

A seller or manufacturer has a significant legal responsibility to buyers and users of goods and services, as well as to third parties. These obligations are covered by the law of sales, contract law, the Uniform Commercial Code (UCC), and tort law. Together, these various provisions of the law provide remedies to buyers and users of goods and services, and to third parties, who suffer physical injuries or financial losses. Two important aspects of the law protecting buyers and users concern warranties and product liability.

Warranties, covered by the law of sales, contract law, and the UCC, provide consumers with remedies when goods that they purchase are not or do not perform as expected. Warranties are addressed in this chapter. Product liability, on the other hand, covered by tort law, provides consumers and users with remedies when they are injured or suffer property damage as a result of defective goods. Product liability is discussed in Chapter 34.

18.2 THE LAW OF WARRANTIES

A warranty, as the term is used in the UCC, is a guarantee or promise made by the manufacturer or seller that the goods offered really are what they are claimed to be, or that the goods are what a reasonable person has a right to expect. As discussed in greater detail in this chapter, one warranty that is recognized by the UCC is an express warranty—that is, explicit, specifically stated promises (UCC 2-313). Another recognized warranty is an implied warranty, which is a guarantee suggested or inferred from known facts and circumstances (UCC 2-312 to 2-315).

Like many other areas of the law, rights and obligations are all subject to the courts' applications and interpretations of the law. In addition, the law is always changing as new legislation is passed and as the courts make decisions that break new ground, sometimes overruling decisions made in earlier, similar cases.

While the law dealing with warranties is intended to protect the general public, it often has the effect of limiting the seller's obligations and responsibilities. For example, a warranty for an appliance might state that the manufacturer will replace it if it fails during the first 90 days. While this promise may appear to be a benefit to the buyer, it also relieves the manufacturer of any obligation if the appliance fails after 90 days.

At times, a manufacturer or seller issues statements limiting a warranty to provide less protection than the law requires. While such statements may discourage an unknowledgeable buyer from legal action, they do not have the force of law, and the manufacturer or seller is still responsible for breach of warranty.

warranty
A guarantee or promise made by the manufacturer or seller that the goods or services offered really are what they claim to be, or that goods or services are what a reasonable person has a right to expect.

express warranty
An explicit, specifically stated promise.

implied warranty
A guarantee suggested or inferred from known facts and circumstances.

EXAMPLE 18.1

▶ Prist purchased a DVR device from JM Electronics for $90. The warranty to which Prist agreed covered parts, but not labor, in cases where repairs became necessary during the first 180 days after the sale. When the DVR device ceased functioning properly after only two months, Prist learned that she would be responsible for $120, the labor portion of the repair bill. Prist recognized that she would be better-off just purchasing a new DVR device and that her warranty did not afford her any real protection.

18.3 EXPRESS WARRANTIES

Express warranties can be made in many ways, both orally and in writing, including by promise, description, sample, or model. They also can be made before or after a sale. However, not everything that a salesperson communicates can be construed as a warranty, and sometimes salespeople can disclaim express warranties.

EXPRESS WARRANTY BY PROMISE

custom of the marketplace What a warranty usually means in similar transactions.

An *express warranty* is an explicit, definite promise by the seller that the goods will have certain characteristics. An express warranty that is made by the seller to the buyer and becomes part of the basis of the agreement creates an explicit warranty that the goods will be as promised. If a written warranty is vague and indefinite, the court may apply the custom of the marketplace, or what such a warranty usually means in similar transactions [UCC 2-313(1)(a)].

The UCC requirement that the warranty be part of the basis of the agreement has been interpreted to mean that the buyer must have relied on the promise and did not dismiss it as puffing, or sales talk (see Chapter 9).

It is not required that a seller make a specific written or oral statement of warranty for an express warranty to exist. Actions of the seller also may be considered express warranties. While opinions given by the seller to the buyer are not express warranties, statements of fact are warranties.

EXAMPLE 18.2

Sickler purchases an emerald ring from Bixby Jewelers for $10,000. Bixby provides Sickler with a written appraisal that states, "The emerald stone is Natural AAA," which is the highest rating for color in emerald gemstones. In this case, Bixby is not issuing an opinion, but a statement of fact that will be considered a legally enforceable warranty.

A sample or model that is made part of the basis of the bargain creates an express warranty that the goods will conform to the sample or model. Pixtal/age fotostock

EXPRESS WARRANTY BY DESCRIPTION, SAMPLE, OR MODEL

The UCC states that "any description of goods which is made part of the basis of the bargain creates an express warranty that the goods shall conform to the description" [UCC 2-313(1)(b)]. A manufacturer of electric wire, for example, that accepts orders for No. 8 electric wire would be held to have warranted that the wire shipped will in fact be No. 8.

The UCC also states that any sample or model that "is made part of the basis of the bargain creates an express warranty that the whole of the goods will conform to the sample" or model [UCC 2-313(1)(c)]. A buyer may refuse delivered goods if the goods are not the same as described by the seller or do not conform to the sample or model used by the seller to effect the sale.

EXAMPLE 18.3

▶ Clawson Appliance had on display a General Electric microwave oven Model JE 1590. Prospective buyers were encouraged to examine the appliance, take measurements, and make note of technical specifications. By using a display model as the basis for the sale, Clawson warranted that any of the same model oven it sold would be substantially the same as the one on display.

THE TIMING OF THE EXPRESS WARRANTY

While most express warranties are made before or during a sales transaction, written or oral statements issued by the seller after the transaction has been completed also can be interpreted as express warranties. Marketers recognize the uneasiness that many buyers experience after having made a buying decision. "Did I make the right decision?" "Should I have purchased the Ford instead of the Acura?" In an effort to reduce this uneasiness, sellers often send out mailings to assure buyers that they did indeed make a wise purchase. These statements, subsequent to the sale, also can be regarded as express warranties.

THE EFFECT OF SELLERS' "PUFFING"

The UCC states that "it is not necessary to the creation of an express warranty that the seller uses formal words such as 'warrant' or 'guarantee' or that the seller has a specific intention to make a warranty, but an affirmation merely of the value of the goods or a statement purporting to be merely the seller's opinion or commendation of the goods does not create a warranty" [UCC 2-313(2)]. Consequently, puffing, however sincere and persuasive this sales talk may be, does not constitute a warranty. This is true even if the buyer relies on such statements.

EXAMPLE 18.4

▶ A salesperson in an appliance store told a customer that the washing machine she was considering "is the best in the world and will be trouble-free for many years to come." Such a statement is considered a mere expression of opinion. Because the statement is mere puffing, it does not form the basis of a warranty and, therefore, would be unenforceable.

Only when statements of fact about quality of merchandise, construction, price, durability, performance, effectiveness, and safety are made part of the contract and later prove false may the buyer bring action against the seller for breach of express warranty.

DISCLAIMERS OF EXPRESS WARRANTIES

In an effort to limit the effect of express warranties, some sellers put specific limitations in the warranty. Such a denial or repudiation in an express warranty is known as a disclaimer and serves to limit the effectiveness of a warranty. Suppose, for example, that a manufacturer claims a pump will deliver a certain number of gallons of water per minute. A disclaimer may say, "Warranty does not cover applications where water must be pumped into storage tanks."

disclaimer
A denial or repudiation in an express warranty that places specific limitations in the warranty.

Another example of a disclaimer is when oral warranties are given and then followed by a written document containing a disclaimer. This might happen when a salesperson is attempting to be persuasive and promises more orally than the firm is willing to promise in writing. Remember that the *parol evidence rule* would prevent a court from considering such oral statements that were inconsistent in the written document (see Chapter 13).

18.4 IMPLIED WARRANTIES

In addition to the provisions dealing with express warranties, the UCC also makes specific references to implied warranties, which are those warranties not made explicitly but that a buyer might reasonably expect a seller to honor. Implied warranties can relate to either the title or the quality of goods.

TITLE

The UCC provides that "the title conveyed shall be good, and its transfer rightful; and the goods shall be delivered free from any security interest or other lien or encumbrance of which the buyer at the time of contracting has no knowledge" [UCC 2-312(1)(a)(b)]. This simply means the seller promises that

1. They are the real owner of the goods offered for sale.
2. The seller has the right to sell the goods.
3. There are no claims or liens of any kind against the goods that might later cause the seller to lose title to someone else who might claim ownership or an interest in the goods.

EXAMPLE 18.5

Futaba bought a used car from Jalik, a college friend, for $4,800. A short time later, a local bank notified Futaba that Jalik owed $700 to the bank, he had used the car as security for the loan, and the indebtedness was recorded at the appropriate county office. As a result, the bank had an interest in the car. Futaba may sue his former friend for his loss on the grounds that the implied warranty of title had been breached.

QUALITY

The law recognizes two types of implied warranties of quality: (1) warranties of merchantability, which are given solely by merchants; and (2) warranties of fitness for a particular purpose, which apply more generally to merchants as well as to others.

implied warranty of merchantability
The law's assumption that goods sold by a merchant/seller are fit to be sold and are adequate for the ordinary purposes for which such goods are sold.

merchant
An individual who deals in goods of the kind being sold in the ordinary course of business or who presents himself or herself as having the skills or knowledge relating to the goods.

Implied Warranty of Merchantability The law assumes that the goods sold by a merchant/seller are fit to be sold or resold, and therefore carry an implied warranty of merchantability. A merchant is anyone who deals in goods of the kind being sold in the ordinary course of business or who presents himself or herself as having the skills or knowledge relating to the goods [UCC 2-104(1)]. The UCC provides that when a merchant sells goods, they warrant that the goods will:

1. Pass without objection in the trade under the contract description.
2. In the case of fungible goods, be of fair average quality within the description.
3. Be fit for the ordinary purposes for which such goods are used.

4. Run, within the variations permitted by the agreement, of even kind, quality, and quantity within each unit and among all units involved.
5. Be adequately contained, packaged, and labeled as the agreement may require.
6. Conform to the promise or affirmations of fact made on the container or label if any [UCC 2-314(2)].

The implied warranty of merchantability is probably the most important warranty the law provides from the viewpoint of the buyer. It imposes a general duty upon the merchant/seller to furnish goods that are at least of minimum acceptable quality.

EXAMPLE 18.6

▶ Dos Santos entered a diner and ordered a piece of apple pie. She finds a coin in the pie. Because this is a foreign substance that would not normally be part of any of the ingredients, the diner has breached the implied warranty of merchantability.

Implied Warranty of Fitness for a Particular Purpose If a seller, at the time of making a contract, knows or has reason to know any particular purpose for which the goods are required and that the buyer is relying on the seller's skill or judgment in selecting or furnishing suitable goods, there is an implied warranty of fitness for a particular purpose (sometimes referred to as *fitness of purpose*). That is, the goods must be fit for the intended purpose (UCC 2-315).

implied warranty of fitness for a particular purpose
The law's assumption that goods are fit for their intended use.

EXAMPLE 18.7

▶ Business Printers Inc. informed its supplier that it was seeking a new high-speed press that would be suitable for printing high-quality, four-color brochures. Bonhomme, the manufacturer's representative, thinking more of his commission than the needs of his customer, recommended a particular press. When the press was delivered and installed, Business Printers discovered that it printed only in black. Clearly, Bonhomme violated the manufacturer's implied warranty of fitness of purpose.

It must be noted, however, that an implied warranty of fitness exists even if the buyer does not expressly inform the seller of their intended use of the merchandise. To recover for breach of the implied warranty of fitness of purpose, a buyer must prove that (1) the seller knew or had reason to know the buyer's purpose, (2) the seller knew or had reason to know that the buyer was relying on the seller's skill or judgment, and (3) the buyer did rely on the seller's skill or judgment.

DISCLAIMERS OF IMPLIED WARRANTIES

The two important implied warranties of merchantability and of fitness for a particular purpose may be disclaimed in several ways. The UCC provides specific rules that must be followed by a seller who wants to avoid the responsibility of these implied warranties. A disclaimer of the warranty of merchantability must mention the word *merchantability.* If the disclaimer is in writing, it must be conspicuous; that is, it cannot be buried in the fine print of the contract (UCC 2-316). In fact, most states require a specific type size or mandate that the disclaimer must be in bold print.

Disclaimers of the warranty of fitness for a particular purpose must be in writing and must be conspicuous. Such warranties are excluded by the use of expressions such as "as is" or "with all faults" or other language that would call the buyer's attention to the exclusion of this implied warranty (UCC 2-316).

The court may refuse to enforce unconscionable disclaimers, just as it may refuse to enforce unconscionable contracts as discussed in Chapter 9 (UCC-302). *Unconscionable disclaimers* are ones that are inconspicuous, oppressive, or unfair.

EXAMPLE 18.8

Hao went to an electronics store to shop for a new television. A salesperson at the store told Hao that all new televisions include a 12-month warranty. Hao purchased the set and received the receipt when the television was delivered. Hao hung the television on the wall of her living room and enjoyed it until it stopped working two months later. When Hao made a claim with the store based on the implied warranty of merchantability, the salesperson refused to honor the warranty, pointing out that the receipt contained a disclaimer stating that the warranty was void if the television was installed on a wall. Because Hao had not read the disclaimer on the receipt, and because the disclaimer seems unfair, a court will likely find the disclaimer to be unconscionable and thus unenforceable.

18.5 MAGNUSON-MOSS WARRANTY LEGISLATION

Magnuson-Moss Warranty Act
A federal statute that addresses many different kinds of abuses to consumers relating to warranties.

Even with the protection provided by the UCC, consumers were not always protected adequately. The federal Magnuson-Moss Warranty Act addresses many different kinds of abuses to consumers relating to warranties.

PROVISIONS OF MAGNUSON-MOSS

interstate commerce
Trade between two or more states.

The Magnuson-Moss Warranty Act applies only when written warranties are made voluntarily on consumer products that cost more than $15. Under the act, a seller or manufacturer must clearly disclose the details of such warranties to the consumer prior to the purchase of a warranted product. In addition, the act requires that such warranties must be labeled as either "full" or "limited." The act applies only to purchases by consumers of tangible personal property normally used for personal, family, or household purposes, not to commercial or industrial transactions. Because it is a federal statute, the act affects only warranties on products that are sold in interstate commerce–that is, trade between two or more states.

The type of warranty to which the act applies is much more narrowly defined than is an express warranty under the UCC. Specifically, warranties covered by the act are (1) any written statement of fact made by a seller to a purchaser relating to the quality or performance of a product and stating that the product is free of defects or that it will meet a specified level of performance over a period of time, or (2) a written promise to "refund, repair, replace, or take other action" if a product fails to meet written specifications.

Obviously, express warranties that are not in writing, such as those created by verbal description or by sample, continue to be governed solely by the UCC, even though a consumer transaction is involved.

DISTINCTION BETWEEN FULL AND LIMITED WARRANTY

The Magnuson-Moss Act makes a distinction between a *full warranty* and a *limited warranty.*

Full Warranty A full warranty promises that a defective product will be repaired without charge within a reasonable time after a complaint has been made. If the product cannot be repaired within a reasonable time, the consumer may receive either a replacement product or a refund of the purchase price. The consumer is not required to do anything unreasonable, such as ship a heavy product back to the factory, to obtain warranty service. In addition, a full warranty applies to anyone who owns the product during the warranty period, not just the original buyer. No time limitation can be placed on a full warranty.

full warranty
The promise that a defective product will be repaired without charge and within a reasonable time after a complaint has been made.

Limited Warranty A written warranty that does not meet the minimum requirements of a full warranty must be designated as a limited warranty. If only a time limitation distinguishes a limited warranty from a full warranty, then the act permits the seller to indicate this fact by such language as "full 12-month warranty."

For additional information regarding the Magnuson-Moss Warranty Act, visit https://www.ftc.gov/tips-advice/business-center/guidance/businesspersons-guide-federal-warranty-law#Magnuson-Moss.

limited warranty
A written warranty that does not meet the minimum requirements of a full warranty.

REMEDIES

Generally, a consumer who has suffered damages due to a violation of the provisions of the Magnuson-Moss Warranty Act may sue for breach of warranty in state court. If, however, a large number of consumers are injured by the same seller, a *class action lawsuit,* which is a lawsuit collectively filed by many individuals, may be brought against the seller in federal court. In either situation, consumers can recover court costs and attorney's fees if they win the case.

lemon laws
Statutes that provide remedies to consumers for products such as automobiles that repeatedly fail to meet certain standards of quality and performance.

LEMON LAWS

The Magnuson-Moss Warranty Act is sometimes referred to as the *federal lemon law*. In addition to federal law, consumers are also protected by lemon laws enacted by the individual states. Lemon laws are statutes that provide remedies to consumers for products such as automobiles that repeatedly fail to meet certain standards of quality and performance. Lemon laws vary greatly from state to state and may not necessarily cover used or leased products. "Lemon law" is the common nickname for these laws, but each state has different names for its laws and acts. For additional information about state lemon laws, visit https://www.bbb.org/autoline/bbb-auto-line-state-laws/.

Lemon laws are statutes that provide remedies to consumers for products such as automobiles that repeatedly fail to meet certain standards of quality and performance.
Beverley Lu Latter/Alamy Images

CHAPTER SUMMARY

18.1 Consumers and third parties are protected by the law of sales, contract law, the UCC, and tort law. Together, these various provisions of the law provide remedies to buyers and users of goods and services and to third parties who suffer physical injuries or financial losses.

18.2 A warranty is a guarantee made by a manufacturer or a seller that the goods offered for sale are what they are claimed to be or that the goods are what a reasonable person has a right to expect. An express warranty is explicitly stated, whereas an implied warranty is suggested or inferred from known facts and circumstances.

18.3 Express warranties can be made both orally and in writing, by promise, description, sample, or model.

18.4 Implied warranties include that of ownership when title is passed and of merchantability and fitness for a particular purpose in contracts for the sale of goods.

18.5 The Magnuson-Moss Warranty Act addresses many different kinds of abuses to consumers relating to warranties.

CHAPTER EIGHTEEN ASSESSMENT

MATCHING LEGAL TERMS

Match each of the numbered definitions with the correct term in the following list.

a. disclaimer
b. express warranty
c. full warranty
d. implied warranty
e. limited warranty
f. product liability
g. custom of the marketplace
h. warranty of fitness for a particular purpose
i. warranty of merchantability
j. warranty of title

1. A warranty provided by law for the protection of the buyer and not specifically included in the agreement. **1.** _____

2. An implied warranty that goods are suitable for the specific purpose for which they are sold. **2.** _____

3. What a vague or ambiguous warranty usually means in similar transactions. **3.** _____

4. A denial or repudiation of an express warranty made at the time of sale. **4.** _____

5. An implied warranty that the seller actually owns the goods sold. **5.** _____

6. Law that provides consumers and users with remedies when they are injured or suffer property damage as a result of defective goods. **6.** _____

7. An implied warranty that goods sold are fit for the ordinary purpose for which they are intended. **7.** _____

8. A written or oral promise or statement regarding goods sold. 8. _____

9. Under the Magnuson-Moss Act, a warranty that requires a seller to repair or replace a defective product without charge within a reasonable time. 9. _____

10. Under the Magnuson-Moss Act, the designation that must be used if a warranty does not meet the minimum requirements. 10. _____

TRUE/FALSE QUIZ

Indicate whether each of the following statements is true or false.

11. Warranties are promises or statements made by manufacturers or sellers. 11. _____

12. While the law dealing with warranties is intended to protect the general public, it often has the effect of limiting the seller's obligations and responsibilities. 12. _____

13. Sales talk, or puffing, is considered a warranty. 13. _____

14. The implied warranty of merchantability means that all merchants warrant their goods to be of the highest quality. 14. _____

15. There is an implied warranty of title with the sale of merchandise that means the seller actually owns the goods. 15. _____

16. The sale of food involves the implied warranty of merchantability. 16. _____

17. An implied warranty of fitness may exist even if the buyer does not make their intended use of the merchandise known to the seller. 17. _____

MULTIPLE CHOICE QUIZ

Indicate the correct answer from the choices following each question.

18. A seller promises to a buyer that the seller will repair the goods sold "free of charge" for two years following purchase. This promise is (a) puffing and not a warranty (b) an implied warranty of merchantability (c) implied warranty of fitness for a particular purpose (d) express warranty. 18. _____

19. A restaurant serves soup to a customer. That soup is subject to (a) an express warranty (b) an implied warranty of merchantability (c) implied warranty of fitness for a particular purpose (d) no warranty. 19. _____

20. A seller shows a buyer a sample of goods and the buyer agrees to purchase units of those same goods. In this case, the seller has made (a) no warranty (b) implied warranty of merchantability (c) express warranty (d) implied warranty of title. 20. _____

21. A buyer contacts a seller and explains that they need a piece of equipment to make brochures. The seller sends information on a piece of equipment and the buyer buys that equipment. In this case, the seller has made

(a) no warranty (b) express warranty for repair (c) express warranty of specific quality (d) implied warranty of fitness for a particular purpose. **21.** ______

22. A seller includes the statement "goods are sold as is." In this case the seller has (a) created an express warranty (b) disclaimed the implied warranty of merchantability (c) disclaimed the implied warranty of fitness for a particular purpose (d) neither created a warranty nor disclaimed a warranty. **22.** ______

DISCUSSION QUESTIONS

Answer the following questions and discuss them in class.

23. Explain the term *warranty* and distinguish between express and implied warranties.

24. Provide examples of four kinds of express warranties and three kinds of implied warranties.

25. Explain disclaimers of implied warranties and the requirements for them to be legally valid.

26. Explain the provisions of the Magnuson-Moss Warranty Act.

27. Explain the effect of warranties offered after a transaction has been completed.

THINKING CRITICALLY ABOUT THE LAW

Answer the following questions, which require you to think critically about the legal principles that you learned in this chapter.

28. Custom of the Marketplace In the case of a vague or indefinite written warranty, how can a court determine what such a warranty usually means in similar transactions?

29. Disclaimers What is the primary objective of warranty disclaimers?

____

____

30. Disclaimers Should the law distinguish between a reasonable basis for a warranty disclaimer and one that attempts to substantially negate the warranty?

____

____

31. Oral Warranties How would the law distinguish between oral statements of warranty and puffing?

____

____

32. A Question of Ethics Can it be ethically justified for a manufacturer to sell a product with a warranty less than the law requires?

____

____

CASE QUESTIONS

Study each of the following cases. Answer the questions that follow with Yes or No.

33. Warranty Buynoski, the operator of a restaurant, served a dinner to Costas. Costas had nearly finished her soup when she found several metal chips in the bottom of her bowl. When Costas showed the chips to Buynoski, the restaurant owner was very apologetic and offered not to charge for the meal. Costas, still angry at the risk to which she had been exposed, said, "I'll see you in court!"

a. Does Costas have a case involving a warranty? **a.** _____

b. Had Buynoski offered an express warranty? **b.** _____

c. Could Costas claim an implied warranty of fitness of purpose? **c.** _____

34. Disclaimer Liang was about to purchase an air-conditioning unit for her apartment at a closeout sale at Center City Appliance. The salesperson assured her that the unit was large enough to cool the apartment she described. The price was right, but she was nervous when the salesperson said, "Remember that you're taking this unit 'as is.'" When she found that the unit would not cool the apartment, she returned to the store, where she claimed that the unit had been sold with an implied warranty of fitness for a particular purpose. The salesperson reminded her that he had said "as is."

a. Can the oral disclaimer void the implied warranty of fitness for a particular purpose? **a.** _____

b. Is there an implied warranty still in effect? **b.** _____

c. Is Liang reasonable in her demand? **c.** _____

35. Warranty Pathek sold a pair of skis to Whelan, making no specific warranties or promises of any kind other than letting Whelan examine and try them. In fact, Pathek did not own the skis; he had only rented them. When the true owner claimed them, Whelan demanded his money back. Pathek defended his actions by stating that he had made no warranty of any kind.

a. Did Pathek give an implied warranty of title? **a.** _____

b. Will Whelan be able to recover his money? **b.** _____

c. Did Pathek give an express warranty of any kind? **c.** _____

CASE ANALYSIS

Study each of the following cases carefully. Briefly state the principle of law and your decision.

36. Warranty Walters bought a power lawnmower. Attached to the engine was a tag that read in part, "For 90 days from purchase date Power Engine Company will replace for the original purchaser, free of charge, any part or parts found, upon examination at any factory authorized dealer, to be defective under normal use and service." Two weeks after purchase, the starter mechanism broke, and Walters returned her machine to the factory authorized dealer. Can the dealer be compelled to repair the mower?

Principle of Law:

____

____

Decision:

____

____

37. Warranty Adano Restaurant Supply, which sells only to commercial customers, sold 200 plastic dishes to Airport Diner. When the owner of the diner attempted to wash the dishes in the dishwasher, they were distorted by the heat. Airport Diner claimed that there was an implied warranty of fitness for a particular purpose because most restaurants used the same type of dishwasher it did. When the owner bought the dishes from Adano, he assumed that they could be washed with the equipment in his restaurant. Does Airport Diner have a legal remedy?

Principle of Law:

____

____

Decision:

____

____

38. Disclaimer Ferguson contracted to buy a quantity of knitting yarn. After receipt he cut it and knitted it into sweaters. At this point, he discovered color variations from one piece to another. Ferguson refused to pay the agreed price, claiming that the yarn had been sold with a warranty of merchantability. The seller, Wilson Trading Corporation, sued to collect the contract price and pointed out that the sales contract provided that "no claims . . . shall be allowed if made after weaving, knitting, or processing, or more than ten days after receipt of shipment." Ferguson viewed the time-limit clause as modifying the warranty of merchantability, which was stated explicitly elsewhere in the contract, and that the disclaimer was in conflict with the warranty. Will the disclaimer be viewed as negating the warranty? [*Wilson Trading Corp. v. David Ferguson, Ltd.,* 244 N.E.2d 685 (New York)]

Principle of Law:

____

____

Decision:

____

____

LEGAL RESEARCH

Complete the following activities. Share your findings with the class.

39. Working in Teams In teams of three or four, visit an appliance retailer. Check the warranties on various products to find out their duration, disclaimers, and any other related information. What safety information is included?

____

____

40. Using Technology Using the Internet and search engines, find examples of warranties that are covered by the Magnuson-Moss Warranty Act. Evaluate whether the warranty is a full or limited warranty and whether it meets the standards required by that act.

____

____

chapter 19 Agency

LEARNING OUTCOMES

After studying this chapter and completing the assessment, you will be able to

19.1 Describe the principal–agent relationship.

19.2 Classify the two major kinds of agents.

19.3 Discuss the four ways in which an agency may be created.

19.4 Explain the various forms of an agent's authority.

19.5 Describe the duties of (a) an agent to a principal, (b) a principal to an agent, (c) a principal and third party to each other, and (d) an agent and third party to each other, in light of whether the principal is disclosed, partially disclosed, or undisclosed.

19.6 Explain how an agency may be terminated.

19.7 Differentiate between the principal–agent and employer–employee relationship.

LEGAL terms

- agent
- principal
- contract of agency
- general agent
- special agent
- power of attorney
- attorney in fact
- durable power of attorney
- agency by ratification
- agency by necessity
- agency by operation of law
- express authority
- implied authority
- apparent authority
- gratuitous agent
- irrevocable agency

AGENCY

"Hell hath no fury like a hustler with a literary agent."

Frank Sinatra, singer, actor, producer, and director

BananaStock/Age Fotostock

19.1 PRINCIPAL–AGENT RELATIONSHIPS

It is often necessary or desirable for a person or firm to be represented by another in business or personal dealings with third parties. This relationship is called a principal–agent relationship. The person who represents another is known as the agent. The person the agent represents or for whom they perform duties is called the principal. An agreement between a principal and an agent by which the agent is vested with authority to represent the principal is known as a contract of agency. The law of agency is governed primarily by state law.

agent
A person authorized to act on behalf of another and subject to the other's control in dealing with third parties.

principal
A person who authorizes an agent to act on their behalf and subject to their control.

contract of agency
An agreement between a principal and an agent by which the agent is vested with authority to represent the principal.

Many, but not all, employees act as agents of their employers. Often, an agent is not specifically referred to as an agent, and similarly, some people or firms referred to as agents or as an agency are not really agents at all. For example, an automobile dealership may be referred to as an agency when the dealer is simply a retailer selling a product made by a manufacturer. As a result, it is important to distinguish between an agency relationship and other forms of relationships.

WHO MAY APPOINT AN AGENT

Any competent party (a person or a corporation) who has the legal right to perform an act may delegate their performance to another by appointing an agent. Certain acts of a personal character, however, such as voting, serving on juries, rendering professional services, and holding public office, may not be delegated to others.

A minor who has appointed an agent may avoid the contract of agency in some states, just as they may avoid other kinds of contracts, as discussed in Chapter 11. In some instances, courts have held that minors who operate businesses are bound by the contracts they make. So, too, is a minor who operates a business and whose agent enters into contracts with third parties.

EXAMPLE 19.1

▶ Diego, a minor who owned an automobile repair shop, employed Fenstermacher, an adult, as head mechanic. Fenstermacher contracted with Mid-City Auto Supply for the purchase of needed supplies and equipment. When the order was delivered, Diego refused to accept it. In some states, Diego has a right to avoid the contract, just as if he had entered into the contract himself.

WHO MAY BE APPOINTED AS AN AGENT

Anyone who is legally competent to act for themself may serve as an agent for another. Minors and others who lack the capacity to enter into contracts on their own (discussed in Chapter 11) may still be considered competent to represent other persons as agents if they are capable of properly carrying out the duties of an agency relationship. Additionally, an organization, such as a partnership or corporation, may act as an agent (see Chapter 20).

EXAMPLE 19.2

▶ Jutson, a minor, was employed by Quong as a buyer in the young men's department of a retail clothing store. Jutson's duties included making contracts with third parties in the name of his employer. Jutson's contracts are binding on Quong because of the legal relationship of principal and agent that exists between them. Jutson is expected to exercise good judgment and discretion in making contracts for his employer, just as any other agent would be.

19.2 CLASSES OF AGENTS

Agents are usually classified according to the nature of their relationship with their principals.

GENERAL AGENT

general agent
A person authorized to assume complete charge of their principal's business or who is entrusted with general authority to act for the principal in all business-related matters.

A general agent is a person authorized to assume complete charge of their principal's business or who is entrusted with general authority to act for the principal in all business-related matters.

SPECIAL AGENT

special agent
A person delegated to act only in a particular transaction, under definite instructions, and with specific limits on the scope of their authority.

A special agent is a person delegated to act only in a particular transaction, under definite instructions, and with specific limits on the scope of their authority. Examples of special agents are real estate firms that have been given authority to manage the property of an owner; lawyers who have been given authority to manage the financial affairs of a client; and auctioneers who have been given authority to represent a seller. Typically, the average real estate broker is not acting as an agent if their responsibility is limited to locating a buyer or seller of real property.

19.3 CREATION OF AGENCY

An agency may be created by agreement, ratification, necessity, or operation of law.

AGENCY BY AGREEMENT

The most common method of creating an agency is by contract or agreement. A contract of agency usually states the rights and duties of the principal and the agent, the duration of the agency, and any other agreements made between the parties. Generally, an agency contract may be either oral or written and either express or implied. The requirements of the Statute of Frauds (discussed in Chapter 13) concerning the kinds of contracts that must be in writing also apply to contracts of agency. For example, a contract appointing an agent must be in writing if the appointment is to extend beyond a year.

power of attorney
An instrument in writing by which one person, as principal, appoints another person as agent and confers the authority to perform certain specified acts on behalf of the principal.

attorney in fact
The person appointed as agent when the power of attorney is exercised.

durable power of attorney
A document that appoints an individual as an agent with authority to make decisions on behalf of the principal in the event that the principal becomes incompetent.

The legal document that formally creates an agency is called a power of attorney. The precise legal term for the person appointed as agent is attorney in fact. If, for example, Nancy Williams, an agent, signs documents on behalf of Susan McGowan, her principal, the signature is "Susan McGowan, by Nancy Williams, her attorney in fact."

A principal must be competent in order to appoint an agent. In the event a principal becomes incompetent after an agent has been appointed, the power of attorney may be invalidated. A principal should execute a document known as a durable power of attorney if they intend for the agent's authority to act on their behalf to remain intact in the event the principal becomes incompetent. Alternatively, a durable power of attorney can be used to give an attorney in fact authority to act on behalf of the principal only in the event the principal becomes incompetent. Often, durable power of attorneys are used in health care situations (see Chapter 38).

EXAMPLE 19.3

▶ Ogle, the owner of a gift shop, expected to be out of the country for several months on a buying trip to Asia. Although she employed several salespeople, Ogle did not trust any of them to run the business during her absence. She appointed Gross, her brother-in-law, as an agent, by power of attorney, and gave him the authority to hire and discharge employees, renew the lease on her store, set prices, purchase merchandise, and perform other such duties as necessary. The relationship between Ogle and Gross is that of principal and agent, created by power of attorney.

AGENCY BY RATIFICATION

An agency by ratification results when a principal (1) approves an unauthorized act performed by an agent or (2) approves an act done in the principal's name by an unauthorized person. The ratification must apply to the entire act; a principal cannot accept the benefits of such a transaction and refuse to accept the obligations that are a part of it. Ratification occurs after the fact, while authorization (in an agency by agreement) occurs before the fact.

agency by ratification
An agency that results when a principal approves an unauthorized act performed by an agent or approves an act done in the principal's name by an unauthorized person.

EXAMPLE 19.4

▶ Geiser purchased a camera on behalf of a friend, Jacinto, without his knowledge or consent. Geiser asked the dealer to hold the camera until directed to deliver it. When Jacinto learned of the purchase, he could have canceled the purchase. Instead, he notified the dealer to send the camera immediately. By this act, Jacinto ratified the unauthorized purchase. Therefore, Jacinto cannot later refuse to accept and pay for the camera. Jacinto's responsibility dates from the time of the original transaction with Geiser, not from the time of ratification. Jacinto is bound by the contract just as if Geiser had possessed full authority to make it.

AGENCY BY NECESSITY

An agency by necessity is created when circumstances make such an agency necessary. Although a family relationship does not normally give members of a family the right to act as agents for one another, the law in some states recognizes an agency by necessity when one spouse fails to support the other spouse or their minor children. In these states, the spouse—acting as agent for the other spouse—may purchase necessities for themself and their children, even against the will of the nonsupporting spouse, and thereby make the other spouse responsible for payment. Similarly, a minor may purchase necessities if their parent fails to provide these.

agency by necessity
An agency that is created when circumstances make such an agency necessary.

A court may appoint a guardian ad litem, with the authority to purchase whatever necessities the parent has failed to provide.
Ronnie Kaufman/Blend Images LLC

AGENCY BY OPERATION OF LAW

An agency by operation of law is created when a court finds the need for an agency to achieve a desired social policy. For example, a child's parent may not be providing the child with certain necessities of life. In this case, a court may appoint an agent, called a *guardian ad litem,* with the authority to purchase whatever necessities the parent has failed to provide. Under such a court-directed agency, the parent would be bound by reasonable contracts made by the agent.

agency by operation of law
An agency that is created when a court finds the need for an agency to achieve a desired social policy.

19.4 AUTHORITY OF AN AGENT

An agent may perform only those acts that have been authorized by the principal or court. If an agent exceeds the authority, they can become personally liable unless the unauthorized act was reasonably assumed by a third party to be within the powers delegated to the agent. Just as third parties can be justified in assuming that an agent has certain authority, so, too, an agent can be justified in assuming that they have certain authority not specifically stated in the contract of agency. While the courts have an interest in protecting the property and the interests of the principal, they also have an interest in protecting the property and interests of third parties who may have had good reason to rely on the apparent authority of the agent.

The authority of an agent can be express, implied, or apparent.

EXPRESS OR IMPLIED AUTHORITY

express authority
An agent's authority that the principal voluntarily and specifically sets forth as oral or written instructions in an agency agreement.

implied authority
The authority an agent reasonably assumes they has that relates to the express authority granted by the principal.

The authority of an agent to perform the duties that are specifically stated in the contract of agency is known as express authority—that is, the authority that has actually been given by the principal, either orally or in writing.

Authority also can be implied by the agency relationship. Implied authority is the authority an agent reasonably assumes they have that relates to the express authority granted by the principal. If, for example, the agency agreement gives the agent the express authority to purchase goods for the principal, the agent has implied authority to purchase the goods using the principal's credit. It is easy to confuse implied authority with apparent authority, discussed in the following paragraph. Remember that implied authority is the relationship between principal and agent in which the principal implies the authority. This authority is sometimes called incidental authority. For example, if *A* appoints *B* as his agent and asks *B* to purchase a car for him, *B* has the implied authority to fill the tank with gasoline.

APPARENT AUTHORITY

apparent authority
The authority that a third party may reasonably assume an agent possesses, despite the fact that the agent does not actually possess such authority.

Apparent authority is the authority that a third party may reasonably assume an agent possesses, despite the fact that the agent does not actually possess such authority. It would be reasonable, for example, for a third party to assume that a retail store manager has the authority to set prices, hire salespeople, and purchase merchandise because the customs of the business usually give store managers this kind of authority. On the other hand, it would be unreasonable for the owner of a multistory building to assume that a store manager had the authority to sign a 20-year lease.

EXAMPLE 19.5

Kertz, the assistant manager of the sporting goods department of a large store, offered customers a 25 percent reduction on the prices of all merchandise in her department during an end-of-season sale, despite the fact that authority to change prices was limited by the store to managers. Because customers (third parties) would be reasonable in assuming that Kertz had authority to reduce prices, the store is bound to these customers under the doctrine of apparent authority.

AGENT'S TORTS AND CRIMES

A principal is liable for the torts and crimes of the agent if they are committed at the direction of the principal or while the agent is performing authorized duties during the ordinary course of the agency. Thus, if an agent makes a fraudulent statement in a contract within the scope of their authority, the principal is responsible. In such a case, the third party may either cancel the contract with the principal and recover compensation for losses sustained or affirm the contract and sue the principal for any monetary damages. Whether an agent commits a tort or crime willfully, recklessly, or negligently, the fact of the principal's liability is the same. Both the principal and the agent may be held liable for an agent's torts or crimes committed while the agent is acting within the scope of their authority.

EXAMPLE 19.6

▶ Mamnani, acting as a sales agent in an electronics store owned by Fischer, purchased, and intended to resell, merchandise that Mamnani knew to be stolen. If Fischer knew of the nature of the merchandise, both Mamnani (the agent) and Fischer (the principal) would be subject to criminal prosecution. On the other hand, if only Mamnani knew that the merchandise was stolen, Fischer would not be subject to prosecution because purchasing and selling stolen merchandise was not within the scope of Mamnani's authority.

19.5 DUTIES OF AGENTS, PRINCIPALS, AND THIRD PARTIES

When an agency is created, three parties are affected—the agent, the principal, and the third party. Each of these parties has duties to one another. We now turn our attention to these rights and obligations.

DUTIES OF AGENT TO PRINCIPAL

There are several duties that an agent owes to a principal:

- An agent must obey all the principal's reasonable and lawful orders and instructions within the scope of the agency contract.
- An agent may not perform any act that would betray the principal's trust.
- An agent may not act for two parties to a contract without the consent of both.
- An agent may not buy their own property for the principal, sell the principal's property to themself, or compete with the principal in any way, without the principal's knowledge and consent.
- An agent must possess the qualifications needed to carry out the work of the agency as agreed.
- An agent is liable for losses to the principal resulting from the agent's incompetence.
- An agent must keep accurate accounts of their transactions conducted as part of the agency agreement.
- An agent must remit to the principal all profits from contracts made by the agent unless other provisions are made in the agency agreement.

EXAMPLE 19.7

Basso, a sales representative employed by Gilman Products, was authorized to enter into contracts for the installation of burglar alarms. Her responsibilities included negotiating prices for the complete installation and arranging for local workers to install the alarms. General guidelines were established for the usual prices of the equipment sold and the fees to be paid for the installation. On the sale of a system to Ballwin, Basso correctly gauged Ballwin's urgent need for the alarm and his high income. The price quoted was considerably higher than usual for an installation of this kind. Basso was also fortunate in locating a maintenance worker who was willing to do the work for much less than the usual rate. While there was a very substantial profit because of the higher sales price and the lower installation cost, the higher profits all belong to Gilman Products (the principal).

DUTIES OF PRINCIPAL TO AGENT

There are several duties that a principal owes to an agent:

- A principal must pay the agent the compensation agreed to in the contract.
- If a person acts as an agent for more than one party with their knowledge, the agent is entitled to receive compensation from each principal.
- A principal must reimburse the agent for any money advanced by the agent in carrying out the principal's instructions and for debts legally paid to third parties on behalf of the principal.
- A principal must reimburse the agent for any loss or damage suffered by the agent in the legitimate performance of duties.

In all cases where an agent is owed money by the principal and is in possession of the principal's property or goods, the agent may place a lien and refuse to surrender the property or goods to the principal until payment has been made.

gratuitous agent
One who acts on behalf of a principal without being paid.

Although the majority of agents are paid, it is not necessary for an agent to receive compensation for their services in order for an agency relationship to exist. A gratuitous agent is one who acts on behalf of a principal without being paid. One should note, however, that gratuitous agents are held to a lower level of liability than paid agents.

EXAMPLE 19.8

Hillman was employed as a sales representative for the Common Merchandise Company. As part of his agreement with the company, he received a salary, commission, and traveling expenses. The automobile that Hillman used was supplied by the company. While on a business trip, Hillman finished his work early and took a side trip to visit friends 75 miles off his normal route. A hit-and-run driver damaged the car through no fault of Hillman. It cost $1,500 to have the damages repaired. The company need not reimburse Hillman for the repairs because the cost of these was an expense unrelated to the discharge of his duties and not in the ordinary course of the agency.

DUTIES OF PRINCIPAL AND THIRD PARTY TO EACH OTHER

A principal is responsible to third parties for all agreements made by the agent on behalf of the principal if the agent acted within the scope of their authority.
Cathy Yeulet/iStockphoto/Getty Images

A principal is responsible to a third party for all agreements made by the agent on behalf of the principal if the agent acted within the scope of their authority, either express or implied. If, however, the agreement was not authorized by the principal, and if it was apparently (or obviously) outside the scope of the agent's employment, the principal is not liable. The third party is liable to the principal on all lawful contracts made by their agent.

EXAMPLE 19.9

▶ Masoudi, a distributor, whose business was limited to the sale of computers, employed Kavulich as a sales representative in a certain territory. Even though Masoudi did not accept trade-ins, Kavulich offered Sciamenti an arrangement whereby Kavulich would exchange a laptop computer for Sciamenti's used photocopy machine. If Kavulich, after taking possession of Sciamenti's photocopy machine, refused to surrender the laptop computer, Sciamenti could not require Masoudi to give it to him. There would be no apparent authority because Sciamenti should have suspected that Kavulich's offer was beyond the scope of his actual (express or implied) or apparent authority.

DUTIES OF AGENT AND THIRD PARTY TO EACH OTHER

The relationship between an agent and a third party, and whether an agent can be held personally responsible, are influenced by a number of factors.

Disclosed Principal When the agent informs the third party that they are acting on behalf of another, and makes the third party aware of the identity of the principal, the principal is known as a *disclosed principal.* For example, when an agent signs a contract "Louise Smith, by Susan Jacobs, Agent" or merely signs the principal's name, they are acting on behalf of a disclosed principal.

Because the third party knows of the agency and knows the identity of the principal, the agent cannot be held personally responsible as long as the agent acts within the scope of their actual authority.

Partially Disclosed Principal When the agent informs the third party that they are acting on behalf of another, but the identity of the principal is unknown to the third party, the principal is known as a *partially disclosed principal.* For example, when the agent signs their own name and the title "Agent," they are acting on behalf of a partially disclosed principal.

Because the third party does not know the identity of the principal, the agent can be held personally responsible to the third party. If the agent acts with authority (either actual or apparent), and the third party later learns of the identity of the principal, the third party may also hold the principal liable.

Undisclosed Principal When the agent does not inform the third party that they are acting on behalf of another person, the unidentified principal is known as an *undisclosed principal.*

Once again, because the third party does not know the identity of the principal, the agent can be held personally responsible to the third party. Similarly, if the agent acts with authority (either actual or apparent), and the third party later learns of the fact of the agency and the identity of the principal, the third party may also hold the principal liable.

EXAMPLE 19.10

Watanabe, as agent for Bangor Supply, purchased 500 bags of Portland cement from Northwest Cement without disclosing his agent status. After shipment, Watanabe attempted to cancel the order. Northwest Cement can sue Watanabe because he became a party to the contract when he neglected to disclose his principal during his dealings with Northwest. If Northwest Cement learned later that Watanabe was an agent for Bangor, Northwest might choose to sue Bangor instead, or it could sue both Bangor and Watanabe.

19.6 TERMINATION OF AGENCY

Agency is a type of contract and, like other contracts, may be terminated by agreement, by performance, or by operation of law.

An agency contract is terminated by an act of the parties when (1) the principal and the agent have mutually agreed on termination, (2) the principal has dismissed the agent, (3) the agent has given up the position, or (4) the purpose of the agency relationship is fulfilled.

If an agency exists "at will," the principal has the right to revoke the agency agreement and discharge the agent for a reason, such as incompetence, disloyalty, or similar shortcomings, or for no reason at all.

A principal who dismisses an agent must give notice of the termination of the agency to all third parties who are accustomed to doing business with the agent or who have knowledge of the appointment. Failure to do so will render the principal liable on any further contracts made by the agent in the principal's name because the agent would still have apparent authority in the eyes of third parties until they have been notified.

irrevocable agency
An agency contract that cannot be terminated by a principal in which the agent has an interest in the subject matter of the agency in addition to the remuneration that they receive for services.

A principal may not revoke an agency contract if the agent has an interest in the subject matter of the agency in addition to the remuneration (e.g., salary, commissions) that they receive for services. Such a contract is an irrevocable agency, or an *agency coupled with an interest.* An agency agreement that authorizes an agent to sell specific property, deduct commissions, and apply the proceeds toward an outstanding debt that the principal owes the agent is an example of an irrevocable agency. Similarly, partners who have a shared interest in a business are agents for each other and cannot dismiss each other (see Chapter 20).

EXAMPLE 19.11

A manufacturer of office machines offered Irving a three-year exclusive agency to sell a new model of fax machines. Irving accepted the offer and paid the agreed-upon price of $25,000. The manufacturer/principal cannot revoke the agreement until the end of the three-year period. This contract is an example of an agency coupled with an interest.

With the exception of an agency coupled with an interest, the death of either party terminates the agency contract immediately. The agency relationship also may be terminated by insanity, illness, impossibility of performance, disloyalty, or bankruptcy.

19.7 DIFFERENCES BETWEEN PRINCIPAL-AGENT AND EMPLOYER-EMPLOYEE RELATIONSHIPS

The legal principles governing the relationship of principal and agent and of employer and employee are, in many respects, the same. The main difference between principal-agent and employer-employee relationships is an employer's power to control the activities of a non-agent employee. Whereas an agency agreement brings about a relationship between a principal and a third party that results in a contract, an employee who is not also an agent has no such rights or powers. An employee acts under the employer's direction and is subject to the employer's control.

The employer controls not only what shall be done by the employee, but also how it shall be done. If, however, an employee is required to perform duties for the employer that necessitate the exercise of judgment and discretion and that result in the establishment of a contractual relationship between the employer and a third party, then the employee has the status of an agent even without a formal contract of agency.

EXAMPLE 19.12

▶ Stein operated an automobile repair shop and frequently sent a senior mechanic, Lopez, to the local auto parts distributor to purchase parts needed for repairs. The cost of the parts was charged to Stein's account, which he paid periodically.

In Example 19.12, Lopez is clearly an employee. Lopez is also Stein's agent, with authority to enter into contracts for the purchase of parts on behalf of the repair shop. If Lopez bought parts for his own use without Stein's permission, the parts distributor could still collect from Stein because an employer is responsible for the acts of employees performed within the scope of the employee's duties and because the parts distributor would reasonably believe that Lopez had an agent's authority. If Stein had directed Lopez to negotiate an agreement for a quantity discount on parts with the supplier for future purchases, Lopez would be an agent with actual express authority to enter into such an agreement.

Some employees are agents; some are not. Some agents are also employees, and some are not. The two relationships are judged independently.

CHAPTER SUMMARY

19.1 The person who represents another is known as the agent. The person whom the agent represents is called the principal. An agreement between a principal and an agent by which the agent is vested with authority to represent the principal is known as a contract of agency.

19.2 The major kinds of agents are general agents, persons authorized to assume complete charge of their principal's business, and special agents, persons delegated to act only in particular transactions.

19.3 An agency can be created by agreement, ratification, necessity, or operation of law.

19.4 Authority can be express, implied, or apparent. Express authority is the authority of an agent to perform the duties that are specifically stated in the contract of agency. Implied authority is the authority an agent reasonably assumes they have that relates to the express authority granted by the principal. Apparent authority is the authority that a third party may reasonably assume an agent possesses, despite the fact that the agent does not actually possess such authority.

19.5 (a) An agent has a duty to obey all of the principal's reasonable and lawful orders and instructions within the scope of the agency contract. (b) A principal must pay the agent the compensation agreed upon in the contract, must reimburse the agent for any money advanced by the agent in carrying out the principal's instructions and for debts legally paid to third parties, and must reimburse the agent for any loss or damages suffered by the agent in the legitimate performance of duties. (c) A principal is responsible to a third party for all agreements made by the agent on behalf of the principal if the agent acted within the scope of their authority, either express or implied. (d) In the case of a disclosed principal, an agent cannot be held personally responsible to a third party as long as the agent acts within the scope of their actual authority. In the case of a partially disclosed or undisclosed principal, an agent can be held personally responsible to the third party.

19.6 Agency can be terminated by agreement, performance, operation of law, or fulfillment of the agency's purpose. Specific reasons may include death, insanity, illness, impossibility of performance, or bankruptcy.

19.7 The main difference between principal-agent and employer-employee relationships is an employer's power to control the activities of a non-agent employee.

CHAPTER NINETEEN ASSESSMENT

MATCHING LEGAL TERMS

Match each of the numbered definitions with the correct term in the following list.

a. agent	**f.** express authority	**k.** partially disclosed principal
b. agency by necessity	**g.** contract of agency	**l.** power of attorney
c. agency by ratification	**h.** disclosed principal	**m.** principal
d. apparent authority	**i.** implied authority	**n.** undisclosed principal
e. attorney in fact	**j.** irrevocable agency	

1. The party in an agency contract who represents another. **1.** _____

2. A principal whose existence and identity are not known to third parties. **2.** _____

3. The name given to a legal document that formally creates an agency. **3.** _____

4. The party in an agency contract who delegates power to another. **4.** _____

5. An agreement between a principal and an agent in which the agent is vested with authority to represent the principal. **5.** _____

6. An agency coupled with an interest. 6. _____

7. The authority possessed by an agent that may be reasonably assumed by a third party. 7. _____

8. The authority possessed by an agent that is specifically stated in the agency contract. 8. _____

9. A principal who is known to third parties. 9. _____

10. The precise legal term for an agent. 10. _____

11. The agency that results when a person approves an unauthorized act done in the principal's name by a person who had no authority to act as agent. 11. _____

12. The agency that results when a person fails to support their spouse or minor children. 12. _____

13. The authority an agent reasonably assumes they have that relates to the express authority granted by the principal. 13. _____

14. A principal whose identity is not known to a third party who knows they are dealing with an agent. 14. _____

TRUE/FALSE QUIZ

Indicate whether each of the following statements is true or false.

15. A general agent is a person authorized to assume complete charge of their principal's business. 15. _____

16. A competent party may delegate their service on a jury to another by appointing an agent. 16. _____

17. An agent is reasonable in assuming that they have the authority that is related to the responsibilities covered in the contract of agency. 17. _____

18. An agent is liable to the principal for any losses that result from the agent's neglect or incompetence. 18. _____

19. A principal is liable for an agent's torts and crimes if they were committed in the ordinary course of the agent's performance of authorized duties. 19. _____

20. An agent representing a partially disclosed principal becomes a party to the contract. 20. _____

21. In a contract between an agent and a third party, the agent can be held responsible to the third party if the identity of the principal is not disclosed. 21. _____

22. An employee who performs only mechanical acts under the employer's direction and is subject to the employer's control is still legally an agent. 22. _____

23. Acts of an employee while performing duties of employment are considered the acts of the employer. 23. _____

24. If an agency exists "at will," the principal has the right to revoke the agency agreement and discharge the agent, provided such discharge is for a good reason. 24. _____

MULTIPLE CHOICE QUIZ

Please indicate the correct answer from the choices after each question.

25. One party contracts with another to act on their behalf in purchasing a building. In this case, the contract has created (a) apparent agency (b) implied agency (c) no agency (d) express agency. 25. _____

26. One party (Principal) has consistently used another party (Agent) to purchase real estate in a certain community. Since that agent is well known for acting on behalf of the principal, a seller approaches the agent to purchase their property for the principal. The second party agrees. In this case, the second party has (a) apparent agency (b) implied agency (c) real agency (d) express agency. 26. _____

27. In the previous question, the transaction on behalf of the principal requires (a) that the principal sign an agreement with the agent for the transaction (b) that the principal ratify the transaction (c) nothing to be effective (d) that a statute be passed to be effective. 27. _____

28. A principal contracts with an agent to perform transactions on their behalf, but requests that the agent not disclose the agency agreement to any other parties. In this case, (a) the principal is liable for any claims related to the agent transactions (b) both the principal and the agent are liable for claims related to the agent transactions (c) the principal is not liable for any claims related to the agent transactions (d) neither the principal nor the agent are liable for claims related to the agent transactions. 28. _____

29. An agent purchases a piece of property for their principal under the terms of an agency agreement. The principal is not aware that the real property is owned by the agent's spouse and the price is 20 percent above market rate. In this case, the agent (a) has violated the duty to account for all transactions (b) has not violated any duties (c) has violated the duty of self dealing (d) has violated the duty to act with competence. 29. _____

DISCUSSION QUESTIONS

Answer the following questions and discuss them in class.

30. Identify the parties to an agency agreement and describe the relationship of the parties.

31. Classify the two major kinds of agents and discuss the four ways in which an agency may be created.

32. Differentiate among disclosed principal, partially disclosed principal, and undisclosed principal.

33. Explain how an agency may be terminated.

34. Differentiate between the principal-agent and employer-employee relationships.

35. Distinguish among express, implied, and apparent authority.

THINKING CRITICALLY ABOUT THE LAW

Answer the following questions, which require you to think critically about the legal principles that you learned in this chapter.

36. **Agency** It is often difficult for a third party to distinguish between an agent and an employee. Are there times when it is important to distinguish between the two? Should there be a clear identification system established?

37. **Agent's Liability** A principal is liable for the torts and crimes committed by an agent if they are performing authorized duties. To what extent should the agent also be liable?

38. **Undisclosed Principal** Does it seem likely that a third party would be suspicious if an agent disclosed the existence but not the identity of their principal?

39. Employees as Agents Does it place an unnecessary burden on a third party to determine whether they are dealing with an employee who has the authority of an agent?

____

____

40. A Question of Ethics In some states, an agent's contracts may be voided if they are acting for a principal who is a minor. Is this fair to a third party with whom the contract is signed?

____

____

CASE QUESTIONS

Study each of the following cases. Answer the questions that follow with Yes or No.

41. Authority of an Agent Peterman, a resident of Florida, sold a home in California to Oliveras. Peterman hired Fogelman, an attorney-at-law, to represent her at the real estate closing and provided Fogelman with a contract of agency, giving Fogelman the authority to sell the home. At the closing, Fogelman also agreed to sell Oliveras an expensive piano owned by Peterman that was still in the home.

a. Does Fogelman have implied authority to sell the piano? **a.** _____

b. Does Fogelman have apparent authority to sell the piano? **b.** _____

c. Is Fogelman a special agent? **c.** _____

d. Is Fogelman an attorney in fact? **d.** _____

42. Apparent Authority A shipper asked a truck driver to deliver a shipment of chemicals and to protect them from freezing while en route. The driver assured the shipper that the chemicals would be carried in heated trucks. When the shipper learned that the shipment had been damaged in transit by freezing, she demanded payment from the trucking company.

a. Did the truck driver have any authority to assure the shipper that the chemicals would be protected from freezing? **a.** _____

b. Would the trucking company be responsible for the damaged chemicals? **b.** _____

c. Did the truck driver have apparent authority? **c.** _____

d. Was the truck driver acting as an agent? **d.** _____

43. Agency by Necessity The Chalmers family lived in poverty. Despite their destitute condition, Mrs. Chalmers bought several articles of jewelry for herself and an expensive painting for their home. When the retailer attempted to collect payment, Mr. Chalmers refused to pay. The merchant claimed that Mrs. Chalmers was acting as an agent for Mr. Chalmers.

a. Is this an example of agency by necessity? **a.** _____

b. Is this an example of agency by ratification? **b.** _____

c. Will the retailer succeed in collecting from Mr. Chalmers? **c.** _____

d. Does the law recognize agency by necessity when a spouse makes essential purchases? **d.** _____

CASE ANALYSIS

Study each of the following cases carefully. Briefly state the principle of law and your decision.

44. Responsibility of Employer Franklyn, a clerical employee of Woodbury Manufacturing Company, told Buron that he was an agent of the company and made a contract on behalf of Woodbury. Later Woodbury repudiated the contract and claimed that Franklyn had no authority to enter into a contract. Buron then sued Franklyn, who claimed that he thought he had the authority. Will Buron succeed in her suit?

Principle of Law:

____

____

Decision:

____

____

45. Undisclosed Principal Ferrara made a contract with Perret without informing her that he was acting on behalf of National Steel Wire Company. Ferrara had actual express authority, as provided in his contract of agency with National. The contract was breached and Perret sued National. National claimed that Perret could not sue because her contract was with Ferrara and not with National. Will Perret be successful in her suit against National?

Principle of Law:

____

____

Decision:

____

____

46. Agency Washington purchased an automobile from Courtesy Motor Sales, a Ford automobile dealer. After the car was delivered, she discovered that the car she thought was new was, in fact, used and that the odometer had been turned back to conceal the mileage. Washington sued Courtesy and named Ford Motor Company in the suit on the grounds that Courtesy was acting as an agent for the manufacturer. Will Washington succeed in her suit against Ford Motor? [*Washington v. Courtesy Motor Sales, Inc.*, 199 N.E.2d 263 (Illinois)]

Principle of Law:

____

____

Decision:

47. Agency Blodgett, while walking on a public sidewalk, was injured when a large piece of wood fell from a construction job at the offices of Olympic Savings and Loan Association. The construction work was being done by Drury Construction Company. Blodgett sued both Olympic and Drury, claiming that Drury was an agent for Olympic. Olympic denied both responsibility for the injury and the existence of an agency relationship with Drury. Will Blodgett succeed in her suit against Olympic? [*Blodgett v. Olympic Savings and Loan Association,* 646 P.2d 139 (Washington)]

Principle of Law:

Decision:

LEGAL RESEARCH

Complete the following activities. Share your findings with the class.

48. Working in Teams In teams of three or four, interview managers of small real estate agencies. Discuss with these managers the nature of the agent's relationship with the principal, including agent's authority and other matters.

49. Using Technology Using the Internet and search engines, investigate "contract of agency" and identify key terms in such a contract.

chapter 20 Business Organizations

LEARNING OUTCOMES

After studying this chapter and completing the assessment, you will be able to

20.1 Identify the business organizational forms available in the United States whose purpose is to earn a profit.

20.2 Define *sole proprietorship* and discuss its advantages and disadvantages.

20.3 Define *partnership* and discuss the advantages and disadvantages of organizing as a partnership, as well as the advantages and disadvantages of being a limited partner.

20.4 Explain the major characteristics of a corporation.

20.5 Describe limited liability companies.

20.6 Identify organizational forms that are not business entities.

BUSINESS ORGANIZATIONS

"Forty for you, sixty for me. And equal partners we will be."

Joan Rivers, television personality, comedian, writer, film director, and actress

ColorBlind Images/Blend Images LLC

LEGAL terms

- sole proprietorship
- unlimited liability
- partnership
- winding-up period
- joint venture
- joint and several liability
- limited partnership
- limited liability
- corporation
- articles of incorporation
- bylaws
- quorum
- subchapter S corporation
- proxy
- fiduciary responsibility
- duty of loyalty
- duty of care
- limited liability company (LLC)

20.1 ORGANIZATIONAL FORMS

Many people in the United States have an entrepreneurial spirit that encourages them to pursue the "American dream" of owning and operating their own business. However, there are numerous responsibilities and decisions that come with accomplishing this objective. Questions such as "Should I begin the business by myself, or share authority with others?" "How can I obtain enough money to keep the business afloat and profitable?" and "Will I have personal responsibility for the debts of the business, and how can I protect myself from creditors and others?" will be addressed in this chapter.

There are several different types of organizational forms that may be selected for a business structure. The organizational forms that are emphasized in this chapter are those that are available to firms that are in business to make a profit for their owners, as distinct from those organizations whose existence is primarily to benefit society.

Businesses are generally structured as one of the following: (1) sole proprietorship, (2) partnership, (3) corporation, or (4) limited liability company. While different states have variations on these forms, the descriptions and discussion that follow generally apply to all businesses in the United States.

sole proprietorship
A business owned and operated by one person.

unlimited liability
Legal exposure in which an owner of a business is personally liable for all of the debts and obligations of the business.

20.2 SOLE PROPRIETORSHIP

A sole proprietorship is a business owned and operated by one person. The great majority of small businesses in the United States are organized as sole proprietorships.

A sole proprietorship is a business owned and operated by one person.
Ingram Publishing/SuperStock

ADVANTAGES OF A SOLE PROPRIETORSHIP

A person wishing to open a business may elect to organize as a sole proprietorship because these are extremely easy to form. Generally, all the entrepreneur needs to do is obtain a general business license from their local municipality, allowing them to conduct business in the community. Another advantage to a sole proprietorship is that the owner has complete authority, within the boundaries of the law, for the running of the business and does not need to report to any other person. They can be creative and entrepreneurial, and all profits generated will flow directly to the owner. The owner pays income taxes on earned profits at their personal rate (although there are some special rules regarding the deductibility of certain expenses). Just as it is quite easy to begin a business as a sole proprietorship, it is also easy to dissolve the business in the event the owner wishes to do so.

DISADVANTAGES OF A SOLE PROPRIETORSHIP

The major disadvantage of a sole proprietorship is the fact that the owner of the establishment has unlimited liability, which means that the owner is personally liable for all of the legal debts and obligations of the business. By having unlimited liability, the owner places their assets at risk, whether these assets are personal or business related. Obviously, this is a major consideration and the owner needs to carefully weigh this risk. Accordingly, the owner should consider purchasing liability and other appropriate insurance coverage.

A second disadvantage of a sole proprietorship is the difficulty the owner faces in raising money to finance the operations of the business. Because the owner is managing the business alone, they cannot turn to other owners to provide additional funds, should this become necessary to maintain the stability or growth of the company. The owner is often limited to borrowing from creditors who will charge the owner interest and demand repayment of the principal, whether the firm makes a profit or not. Similarly, because the owner is on their own, it is often difficult for a sole proprietorship to attract trustworthy employees.

EXAMPLE 20.1

▶ Milotin decided to open his own store, offering ink refills for printer cartridges to local companies. Between his own savings and some borrowing, Milotin believed he had sufficient financing to keep the store as a going concern for two years. Not wishing to share profits or management with any other person, Milotin formed a sole proprietorship; obtained a general business license; purchased liability, fire, and theft insurance; and opened for business.

20.3 PARTNERSHIP

A **partnership** is a business owned and operated by two or more persons. The shares of the partners might be equal, or they might vary according to an agreement between or among the partners. This would be true for either profits or losses, and it is not even necessary that profits and losses be shared in the same percentages. Similarly, partners, by agreement with one another, share responsibility for managing the affairs of the business.

partnership
A business owned and operated by two or more persons.

Dissolution of a partnership is governed by the partnership contract and usually occurs due to (1) the death or disability of one of the partners, (2) the expulsion of one of the partners (at times for cause, and at other times for no cause), (3) illegality of the partnership's business, (4) the retirement of one of the partners, or (5) the bankruptcy of the business. Dissolution is followed by a **winding-up period**, during which there is an orderly liquidation of the partnership assets.

winding-up period
The time after dissolution of a partnership during which there is an orderly liquidation of the partnership assets.

At times, individuals become partners for only a short period of time, or for only a single project. This activity is defined as a **joint venture**.

joint venture
An activity in which individuals become partners for only a short period of time or for only a single project.

The Uniform Partnership Act (UPA), which governs partnerships, has been adopted by the majority of states.

ADVANTAGES OF A PARTNERSHIP

Each partner has the right to share in the profits of the business. While the partnership itself does not pay federal income taxes, it does complete an informational tax return, wherein it reports profits or losses to the government and how these profits or losses have been apportioned between or among the partners. Each partner is then required to pay income taxes on those profits (or is entitled to deduct those losses) that have been apportioned to them.

Just as each partner has a right to share in the profits of the company, each partner also has a right to share in the value of the firm's assets; that is, all business assets are owned jointly by all partners.

Like a sole proprietorship, a partnership is fairly easy to form, and the owners have complete authority for the running of the business.

DISADVANTAGES OF A PARTNERSHIP

joint and several liability
Legal exposure such that a person with a claim against a general partnership can elect to sue either all of the partners together or any individual partner whom they choose.

As is true for a sole proprietorship, the major disadvantage of a partnership is the fact that each partner has unlimited liability for all legal obligations and debts of the business. Recall from Chapter 19 that each partner is an agent for all other partners, and that when a partner acts with either actual or apparent authority, all other partners become liable for their acts. In addition, partners have joint and several liability, which means that a person with a claim against the partnership can elect to sue either all of the partners together or any individual partner whom they choose.

EXAMPLE 20.2

Petrillo and Patel co-owned a bakery in the form of an equal general partnership. The two of them agreed that Petrillo, who worked the morning hours by himself, would be responsible for cleaning the sidewalk in front of the store. After a heavy snowstorm, Petrillo failed to remove the ice, and Weissman, a pedestrian, slipped, sustaining a compound fracture to her leg. Weissman elected to sue only Patel because he lived in the same town as she. Patel would be found liable to Weissman and could recoup his financial losses only by suing his partner, Petrillo.

Example 20.2 illustrates clearly just how risky a business organized as a partnership can be to a partner, especially as they are responsible for all authorized or ratified acts by any other partner. Once again, it is extremely important for partnerships to have ample liability and other forms of insurance.

Another disadvantage of the partnership form is the fact that there may be times when partners disagree on how the business should be run. Whether relating to day-to-day operations or major strategic undertakings, sharing authority at times can be difficult when partners are of different minds.

LIMITED PARTNERSHIP

limited partnership
A business in which there are one or more general partners and one or more limited partners.

limited liability
Legal exposure in which an owner of a business is not personally liable for all of the debts and obligations of the business.

A limited partnership is a business in which there are one or more general partners (with rights and obligations as described previously) and one or more limited partners. Limited partnerships receive the same tax treatment as all partnerships. Also, as with all partnerships, authority, dissolution, and so forth are governed by the partnership contract.

Advantage of Being a Limited Partner The limited partner is attracted to the limited partnership because it provides them with limited liability: Their personal liability for all of the legal debts and obligations of the business is limited to their investment in the business.

EXAMPLE 20.3

Jefferson and Aaron were general partners in a business that purchased old homes, remodeled them, and sold them at a profit. Because they needed a large amount of additional financing, they approached Shah, encouraging her to join their partnership. Shah knew very little about the business but saw this as an opportunity for investment. Shah provided a large sum of cash and became a limited partner, thus protecting her personal assets from creditors of the partnership.

Disadvantage of Being a Limited Partner While the limited partner does not have the disadvantage of unlimited liability, they are not able to participate in the overall management of the business, lest they be deemed by the courts to be a general partner and lose their limited liability.

In Example 20.3, if Shah were to become actively involved with the remodeling of the homes, a court might well determine that she was a general partner, and her liability could be construed to be unlimited.

LIMITED LIABILITY PARTNERSHIP

A limited liability partnership (LLP) is a type of partnership commonly used by professionals who are in business together. LLPs were created in order to shield a partner's personal assets from a third party's claim of negligence against another partner. Generally in an LLP, all partners have limited liability for other partners' negligence.

20.4 CORPORATION

A corporation is a business formed as a separate legal entity. Individuals can start a corporation by applying for a charter in one of the 50 states. Corporations are owned by *shareholders,* who purchase shares of stock in the corporation. In order to sell these shares to the general public, it is often necessary that documentation be filed by the corporation with the Securities and Exchange Commission (SEC) (see Chapter 31).

corporation
A business formed as a separate legal entity.

articles of incorporation
A document that lists the general powers of a corporation.

bylaws
A document that provides rules for the meetings of a corporation.

quorum
The minimum number of shares necessary to be present at a corporate meeting in order for action to be taken.

The corporation drafts articles of incorporation that list the general powers of the company. The company usually has bylaws, which provide rules for the meetings of the corporation. A corporation's owners are shareholders whose ownership interests are represented by shares of stock in the corporation. A quorum, the minimum number of shares necessary to be present at a meeting, is required for action to be taken.

A corporation is considered a kind of *legal person,* and courts have granted corporations constitutional rights similar to those granted individuals and other organizations, such as freedom of speech, due process of law, and freedom from unreasonable searches and seizures. While, in general, corporations may freely give charitable contributions, political contributions are strictly regulated.

Some states require corporations to have a *corporate seal,* which must be affixed to contracts and other legal documents. Corporations also have a special *tax identification number,* similar to an individual's Social Security number, that identifies them on tax returns, bank records, and other official documents. Generally, corporations are said to *exist in perpetuity:* They continue to live on unless some formal action is taken to discontinue the business.

A corporation is a business formed as a separate legal entity.
Andrew Resek/McGraw-Hill Education

ADVANTAGES OF A CORPORATION

The major advantage of a corporation is the fact of limited liability to shareholders for claims against the business. Courts are extremely hesitant to *pierce the corporate veil;* that is, the law assigns responsibility for corporate obligations to shareholders only under very unusual circumstances. For example, the court may hold corporate shareholders liable if the corporation is set up specifically to defraud the public.

EXAMPLE 20.4

▶ Bonnice inherited a large sum of money and wished to invest a portion of the funds in the stock market. Through a broker, she purchased shares of common stock in several corporations whose shares were duly registered with the SEC and traded publicly. Bonnice's personal assets are shielded from creditors, and her risk is limited to the money she invested in the stock market.

Another advantage to a corporation is the ease with which the company can raise capital. A corporation can obtain additional financing by issuing and selling new shares of stock in the company, without the necessity of altering its organizational form.

DISADVANTAGES OF A CORPORATION

The major disadvantage of a corporation is the fact that the corporation is required to pay separate income taxes at a special corporate rate for any year during which a profit is earned. At the time profits are distributed to shareholders, these may be subject to an additional tax, depending on applicable tax regulations.

A second disadvantage to a corporation is the expense associated with forming and maintaining the company. Corporations are required to keep updated minutes of meetings, provide detailed financial statements to creditors and investors, prepare complex tax returns, among other requirements.

SUBCHAPTER S CORPORATION

subchapter S corporation
A corporation that is taxed as a partnership.

A subchapter S corporation is a corporation for all purposes as explained previously but with the advantage of being taxed as a partnership. In order to qualify as a subchapter S corporation, the company must comply with tax regulations, such as the restriction that there be a limited number of shareholders, among other requirements.

CORPORATE DIRECTORS AND OFFICERS

proxy
A legal document that transfers the right to vote in a corporate election to another person.

While the shareholders own the corporation, they do not directly manage the activities of the firm. Shareholders vote for *directors,* members of a board who are responsible for managing the overall strategy and operations of the firm over the long term. Frequently, shareholders who cannot attend meetings of the corporation nonetheless vote for directors by signing a proxy, a legal document that transfers the right to vote in a corporate election to another person (remember that, as was explained in Chapter 14, it is not permitted to transfer the right to vote in a political election to another person).

Directors do not involve themselves in the day-to-day operations of the corporation. Rather, directors appoint *officers,* who exercise control over the normal, routine matters that arise on a daily basis. These officers could include a president, vice presidents, a comptroller, and others.

FIDUCIARY RESPONSIBILITY

fiduciary responsibility
A legal requirement that a person will exercise their authority while working under a duty of loyalty and a duty of care.

Directors and officers have a fiduciary responsibility to the company in which they hold their positions. Fiduciary (from the Latin word for "faith") responsibility means that directors and officers will exercise their authority while working under a duty of loyalty and a duty of care.

Shareholders vote for directors, who are responsible for managing the overall strategy and operations of the firm over the long term.
moodboard/SuperStock

Duty of Loyalty The duty of loyalty means that a director has a legal and ethical obligation to administer to the affairs of the corporation with personal integrity, honesty, and candor. Directors are, for example, prohibited from advancing their own personal or outside business interests at the expense of the corporation. Neither can directors use their authority to assist persons outside the corporation when such action would harm the firm.

duty of loyalty
A legal and ethical obligation placed upon a director to administer to the affairs of the corporation with personal integrity, honesty, and candor.

EXAMPLE 20.5

- Lennox, a senior partner in a law firm, also served on the board of directors for a large manufacturing corporation. When the company decided to purchase a new warehouse, Lennox convinced the board of directors to hire his law firm to handle the transaction for an exorbitant fee. Lennox has breached his duty of loyalty and violated both his legal and ethical responsibilities.

Duty of Care The duty of care means that a director has a legal and ethical obligation to act diligently and prudently in conducting the affairs of the corporation. A director is responsible for selecting, monitoring, and evaluating competent management. They must promote and advance the policies and strategic initiatives of the firm, while at all times making certain that the implementation of these policies and strategies adheres to principles of law and safety. When a director considers a corporate matter, they must make a decision only after fully informed, meaningful deliberation. Most states impose a rule that requires a director to make judgments only as an ordinarily prudent person would make in the best interests of the corporation.

duty of care
A legal and ethical obligation placed upon a director to act diligently and prudently in conducting the affairs of the corporation.

EXAMPLE 20.6

Nagy serves on the board of directors for a large software company. Nagy's position on the board requires that she oversee the company's investment portfolio. Nagy enjoys the prestige of serving on this board; however, she frequently fails to review the financial statements provided by the company's accountants or trends taking place in the stock market. As a result, the company's investments perform extremely poorly. By her failure to exercise due care, Nagy is violating both her legal and ethical responsibilities.

20.5 LIMITED LIABILITY COMPANY

limited liability company (LLC)
A relatively new organizational form available in most states that provides all of the owners with limited liability.

A limited liability company (LLC) is an organizational form separate and distinct from a corporation currently recognized by all 50 states. Laws governing the formation of LLCs vary from state to state. Thus, it is important to follow the precise requirements of the applicable state law when organizing an LLC. Generally, to organize an LLC, members (owners) draft an operating agreement that governs the business in important matters, such as how the LLC will be managed, the members' rights and responsibilities, and how the LLC is to be dissolved. An LLC is taxed as a partnership for federal tax purposes (state laws vary in terms of state tax treatment). The members of the LLC act as a *management team;* that is, they share in the overall control of the business.

ADVANTAGES OF A LIMITED LIABILITY COMPANY

The LLC provides all members with limited liability, while allowing them to participate in the management of the business. In addition, since the LLC is treated in the same manner as a partnership by the IRS, members can avoid double taxation of earnings. Finally, because it is generally a small company, in most states it is quite easy to form. Figure 20.1 provides an overview of the relative advantages of the different organizational forms discussed in this chapter.

	Sole Proprietorship	Partnership	Limited Partnership	Limited Liability Partnership	Corporation	Subchapter S Corporation	Limited Liability Company
Ease of Formation	Yes	Yes	Yes	Yes	No	No	Yes
Tax Advantages	Yes	Yes	Yes	Yes	No	Yes	Yes
Limited Liability	No	No	Yes	Yes	Yes	Yes	Yes
Owner's Ability to Manage	Yes	Yes	Yes/No	Yes	No	No	Yes
Ease of Raising Capital	No	No	No	No	Yes	Yes	No
Separate Legal Entity	No	No	No	No	Yes	Yes	Yes

FIGURE 20.1 Organizational Forms

DISADVANTAGES OF A LIMITED LIABILITY COMPANY

As is true for all small firms, the members of an LLC frequently have difficulty in raising additional funds to expand or maintain the business. Furthermore, as was true for partnerships, there may be times when members of the management team disagree on how the business should be run.

20.6 OTHER ORGANIZATIONAL FORMS

The organizational forms discussed in this chapter are those whose purpose is to earn profits. It must be noted that there are several other organizational forms that exist in the United States whose purpose is to aid society. Many states have adopted laws that allow for-profit corporations to elect to become benefit (or B) corporations. These B corporations may include items other than profit for shareholders as motivations for corporate priorities. All states also have organizational firms referred to as *not-for-profits* including charitable organizations as well as others, such as universities, political parties, labor unions (discussed in Chapter 33), social clubs, and others.

CHAPTER SUMMARY

20.1 For-profit businesses are generally organized as one of the following forms: (1) sole proprietorship, (2) partnership, (3) corporation, or (4) limited liability company.

20.2 A sole proprietorship is a business owned and operated by one person. Advantages to organizing as a sole proprietorship include (a) the business is easy to form, (b) the owner has complete authority for the running of the business, (c) all profits generated flow directly to the owner, and (d) the business is easy to dissolve. Disadvantages of organizing as a sole proprietorship include (a) the owner has unlimited liability and (b) the owner faces difficulty in raising money to finance the operations of the business.

20.3 A partnership is a business owned and operated by two or more persons. Advantages to organizing as a partnership include (a) each partner has the right to share in the profits of the business and (b) each partner has a right to share in the value of the firm's assets. Disadvantages of organizing as a partnership include (a) each partner has unlimited liability for all legal obligations and debts of the business and (b) partners have joint and several liability. The advantage of being a limited partner is that they are provided with limited liability. The disadvantage of being a limited partner is that they are not able to participate in the overall management of the business, lest they be deemed by the courts to be a general partner. Limited liability partnerships were created in order to shield a partner's personal assets from a third party's claim of negligence against another partner.

20.4 A corporation is a business formed as a separate legal entity, a kind of legal person. Corporations are owned by shareholders, who purchase shares of stock in the corporation. A corporation drafts articles of incorporation, which list the general powers of the company, and bylaws, which provide rules for the meetings of the corporation. Generally, corporations exist in perpetuity.

20.5 A limited liability company (LLC), which provides all of the owners with limited liability, is taxed as a partnership for federal tax purposes. The owners of the LLC act as a management team; that is, they share in the overall control of the business.

20.6 Organizational forms that are not business entities are not-for-profits that include universities, political parties, labor unions, social clubs, and others. In some states, for-profit corporations may also elect to become benefit (or B) corporations.

CHAPTER TWENTY ASSESSMENT

MATCHING LEGAL TERMS

Match each of the numbered definitions with the correct term in the following list.

- **a.** articles of incorporation
- **b.** corporation
- **c.** duty of care
- **d.** duty of loyalty
- **e.** partnership
- **f.** joint venture
- **g.** limited liability company
- **h.** limited partnership
- **i.** sole proprietorship
- **j.** subchapter S corporation

1. An organizational form other than a corporation available in most states that provides all of the owners with limited liability. **1.** _____

2. A legal and ethical obligation placed upon a director to administer the affairs of the corporation with personal integrity, honesty, and candor. **2.** _____

3. A business formed as a separate legal entity. **3.** _____

4. A business owned and operated by one person. **4.** _____

5. A business owned and operated by two or more persons. **5.** _____

6. A legal document that lists the general powers of a corporation. **6.** _____

7. A type of corporation that is taxed as a partnership. **7.** _____

8. A legal and ethical obligation placed upon a director to act diligently and prudently in conducting the affairs of the corporation. **8.** _____

9. A business in which there are one or more general partners and one or more limited partners. **9.** _____

10. An activity in which individuals become partners for only a short period of time, or for only a single project. **10.** _____

TRUE/FALSE QUIZ

Indicate whether each of the following statements is true or false.

11. The great majority of small businesses in the United States are organized as limited liability companies. **11.** _____

12. The major disadvantage of a sole proprietorship is the fact that the owner of the establishment has unlimited liability. **12.** _____

13. A disadvantage of a sole proprietorship is the difficulty the owner faces in raising money to finance the operations of the business. **13.** _____

14. In a partnership, the shares of the partners might be equal, or they might vary according to an agreement between or among the partners. **14.** _____

15. In a partnership, it is necessary that profits and losses be shared in the same percentages. **15.** _____

16. While a partnership itself does not pay federal income taxes, it does complete an informational tax return. **16.** _____

17. A limited partner is allowed to participate in the overall management of the business, and at the same time maintain limited liability. **17.** _____

18. A corporation usually has bylaws, which provide rules for the meetings of the corporation. **18.** _____

19. Corporations may freely give both charitable contributions and political contributions. **19.** _____

20. Corporations continue to live on unless some formal action is taken to discontinue the business. **20.** _____

21. The shareholders who own the corporation directly manage the activities of the firm. **21.** _____

MULTIPLE CHOICE QUIZ

22. An individual wants to open a business in the most inexpensive, easiest way possible. In this case, the individual should choose which form of organization? (a) General partnership (b) Limited partnership (c) Corporation (d) Sole proprietorship **22.** _____

23. A group of individuals want to open a business and all be active in the management of the business. They are not concerned with liability for claims against the business but are concerned about keeping formation costs low. In this case, the group should choose which form of organization? (a) General partnership (b) Limited partnership (c) Corporation (d) Sole proprietorship **23.** _____

24. A group of individuals want to open a business, but are concerned about their personal liability for claims against the business. However, they all would like to have some activity in the management of the business. In this case, the group should choose which form of organization? (a) General partnership (b) Limited partnership (c) Corporation (d) Sole proprietorship **24.** _____

25. A group of individuals want to open a business, are concerned about liability, all want to be involved in the business, but also want to minimize tax liability. In this case, the group should choose which form of organization to achieve all these goals? (a) Limited partnership (b) Limited liability company (c) Corporation (d) General partnership **25.** _____

26. A, B, and C operate their business as a general partnership but do not have a partnership agreement. They are sued for a large claim against the business, and A is concerned because they have more personal assets at risk. In this case, which is the most correct answer to A's concerns? (a) A, B, and C are all liable for the claims equally. (b) A, B, and C are not liable at all for the claims. (c) The plaintiff must choose only one of the partners to sue. (d) A, B, and C are all liable, and A may be 100 percent liable for the claims. **26.** _____

27. Shareholders of a corporation have decided that they would like to prioritize environmental impact in all decisions made by the corporation. In order to ensure this prioritization by the board but still operate the business, which of the following is the best option for this corporation? (a) Amend the corporation to be a B corporation. (b) Do nothing and stay as a C corporation. (c) Reform as a not-for-profit corporation. (d) Elect to become a subchapter S corporation. **27.** _____

28. A director of a corporation proposes that A be retained as the new accountant for the firm, not disclosing to the board that A is the director's brother and is paying A a "finder's fee" for obtaining the appointment. In this case, (a) A has violated the standard of care required of directors (b) A has not violated any standard of care (c) A has violated the duty of loyalty required of directors (d) A has violated the standard of care and the duty of loyalty required of directors. **28.** _____

DISCUSSION QUESTIONS

Answer the following questions and discuss them in class.

29. Identify the four forms in which businesses are generally organized.

_____

_____

30. Name four advantages and two disadvantages of organizing as a sole proprietorship.

_____

_____

31. Identify two advantages and two disadvantages of organizing as a partnership.

32. Explain the differences between a limited partnership and other partnerships.

33. Differentiate among corporate shareholders, directors, and officers.

34. Explain both the duty of loyalty and the duty of care as these pertain to corporate directors and officers.

THINKING CRITICALLY ABOUT THE LAW

Answer the following questions, which require you to think critically about the legal principles that you learned in this chapter.

35. Limited Partnership Is it fair that in a limited partnership, the limited partner enjoys limited liability while the general partner faces unlimited liability?

36. Limited Liability Persons who face unlimited liability (such as sole proprietors and partners) are allowed to purchase insurance to protect themselves from creditors and others. Should the law allow insurance to be used for this purpose?

37. Sole Proprietorship How can a sole proprietor attract employees who are trustworthy?

38. Corporation Corporations have been granted freedom of speech, freedom from unreasonable searches and seizure, and due process of law. Does it make sense that a legal (as opposed to natural) person has these rights?

39. A Question of Ethics Is it ethical for a broker or a financial adviser to earn commissions from investments of corporations of which the broker or financial adviser is also a director?

____

____

CASE QUESTIONS

Study each of the following cases. Answer the questions that follow with Yes or No.

40. Sole Proprietorship Horvath opened a small convenience store, organizing the business as a sole proprietorship. Because she was concerned that she would not have sufficient financing, she borrowed $20,000 from Blaum, her brother-in-law. When the business began earning profits, Horvath spent these monies on personal items. When her accountant completed her tax return, Horvath was informed that she owed a great deal of money to the government.

a. Is Horvath required to pay taxes herself on the profits from the store? **a.** _____

b. Is Blaum required to pay taxes himself on the profits from the store? **b.** _____

c. Can Blaum legally demand that he be allowed to manage the business's financial matters in the future? **c.** _____

41. Authority of General Partners Felagi and MacWilliams agreed to open a restaurant selling pizza and sandwiches. The business was organized as a partnership, with each partner owning 50 percent and sharing profits and losses equally. The two partners also agreed that each would have actual authority to spend up to $500 for purchases relating to the restaurant without the prior approval of the other partner. Salespersons of a nearby automobile dealership regularly ate lunch in the restaurant and came to know that Felagi was an owner of the establishment. Felagi, without consulting MacWilliams, then signed a contract to purchase a $17,000 vehicle in the partnership's name. MacWilliams later learned of the transaction and refused to honor the contract.

a. Can the automobile dealership sue the partnership to enforce the contract? **a.** _____

b. Can the automobile dealership elect to sue only Felagi to enforce the contract? **b.** _____

c. Can the automobile dealership elect to sue only MacWilliams to enforce the contract? **c.** _____

d. Does Felagi have apparent authority to bind the partnership? **d.** _____

42. Fiduciary Duty Olav, a retired banker, served on the board of directors for a nationally prominent charitable organization. The local chapter of the charity discussed plans to purchase and relocate to a new building across town. Olav approached Mansfield, a close friend, and the two of them quickly closed on a deal for the new building, purchasing it for $1.2 million and placing title in Mansfield's name only. When the matter later came before the board of the charitable organization,

Olav encouraged the organization to make an offer of $1.6 million to Mansfield. Olav did not disclose to the board that he would share in the profits of the sale.

a. Is Olav violating his fiduciary duty? **a.** _____

b. Is Olav violating his duty of loyalty? **b.** _____

c. Is Mansfield violating his fiduciary duty? **c.** _____

d. Is this an example of a proxy dispute? **d.** _____

CASE ANALYSIS

Study each of the following cases carefully. Briefly state the principle of law and your decision.

43. Liability of Shareholders Holley and Holley, an interracial couple, alleged that they were the victims of discrimination in housing as a result of actions by Crank, an employee of Triad Inc. The Holleys sued Meyer, the sole shareholder, the president, and a broker of Triad. Meyer argued that he was not personally responsible for the actions of either Triad or its employee, Crank. Will the Holleys be successful in their efforts to hold Meyer personally responsible? [*Meyer v. Holley,* 537 U.S. 280 (2003).]

Principle of Law:

____

____

Decision:

____

____

44. Organization's Constitutional Rights Dale, an assistant scoutmaster for the Boy Scouts, lost his position when the organization learned that he was gay. Dale contended that he was the victim of discrimination, while the Boy Scouts argued that they were exercising their First Amendment right of freedom of expression. Does the organization have First Amendment rights, or will Dale be successful in his suit against the Boy Scouts? [*Dale v. Boy Scouts of America,* 160 N.J. 562, 734 A.2d 1196 (2000)]

Principle of Law:

____

____

Decision:

____

____

45. Partnership Shares Melvin and his brother, Russell Ballantyne, formed an oral partnership, which started out as a farming operation but grew into oil and gas exploration. Russell was in charge of the farming operation, while Melvin was in charge of the oil and gas exploration. In practice, and by mutual agreement, the brothers withdrew profits from the partnership that were attributable to each of their respective business pursuits and paid the expenses related to each of their respective activities. In other words, Melvin kept the oil and gas income and paid those expenses, while Russell did the same with the farm income and expenses. However, for tax purposes, Melvin and Russell each reported 50 percent of the partnership's total income, gains, losses, deductions, and credits on their individual federal tax returns. When Melvin died, the partnership automatically dissolved and family relations also took a turn for the worse. A dispute later arose regarding tax liability, and it was the contention of the Internal Revenue Service that there should be a 50–50 split with respect to tax treatment and distribution of the assets from the farming operation. Russell argued that he alone was entitled to the benefits from the farming operation. Is Russell correct in his contention that he alone should be entitled to the benefits from the partnership? [*Estate of Melvin W. Ballantyne, Deceased* (T.C.M. (CCH) 2002-160) (2003)]

Principle of Law:

Decision:

LEGAL RESEARCH

Complete the following activities. Share your findings with the class.

46. Working in Teams In teams of three or four, interview owners of small businesses in your city or town. Ask them to explain why they chose their particular business organizational form.

47. Using Technology Using the Internet and search engines, investigate the tax rules relating to the organizational forms discussed in the chapter.

chapter 21 Creditor's Rights and Bankruptcy

LEARNING OUTCOMES

After studying this chapter and completing the assessment, you will be able to

21.1 Explain the conditions under which individuals and businesses become insolvent and default on their loans.

21.2 Explain the state laws governing creditors rights.

21.3 Distinguish between a voluntary filing and an involuntary filing in bankruptcy.

21.4 Explain the provisions and applications of Chapter 7 of the federal bankruptcy law.

21.5 Explain the provisions and applications of Chapter 13 of the federal bankruptcy law.

21.6 Explain the major applications of Chapters 9, 11, 12, and 15 of the federal bankruptcy law.

BANKRUPTCY

"Bankruptcy is about financial death and financial rebirth. Bankruptcy is the great American story rewritten."

Elizabeth Warren, United States Senator

narvikk/E+/Getty Images

LEGAL terms

- debtor
- creditor
- preferential payment
- insolvency
- default
- bankruptcy
- voluntary filing
- Bankruptcy Abuse Prevention and Consumer Protection Act
- means test
- straight or liquidation bankruptcy
- reorganization bankruptcy
- secured debt
- fraudulent transfer
- security interest
- perfection of security interests
- involuntary filing
- liquidation
- priority debts

21.1 INSOLVENCY AND DEFAULT

debtor
An individual or business that owes money.

creditor
An individual or business to which money is owed.

insolvency
The state that occurs when an individual's or business's liabilities exceed assets.

default
The state in which a debtor fails to meet one or more financial obligations to their creditors.

Unfortunately, there are times when individuals or businesses face significant financial challenges that cannot be overcome, no matter how responsible these individuals are or how competently these businesses are run. This situation might occur for a variety of reasons: a serious downturn in the economy, significant mismanagement of financial assets, a series of poor investment decisions, a personal tragedy, a failure of health, or the like. An individual or business that owes money is said to be a debtor; an individual or business to which money is owed is said to be a creditor. People familiar with good accounting practices recognize that assets (the value of the property an individual or business owns) should exceed liabilities (the value of what an individual or business owes). On the other hand, insolvency occurs when an individual's or business's liabilities exceed assets.

Unless the insolvent individual or business can quickly correct the problem, insolvency often leads to default, wherein the debtor fails to meet one or more financial obligations to their creditors. When this occurs, it becomes important to protect, at least in part, the interests of the creditors who otherwise would not receive most, or even any, of the money they are rightfully owed.

State Laws govern how creditors can secure their positions in the event that debtors default on financial positions. Collateral is the term used to define debtor assets that the debtor agrees the creditor may seize in the event of a default. In particular, Article 9 of the Uniform Commercial Code governs the process of securing collateral and the priority of claims in the event of default.

bankruptcy
The legal state that occurs when a debtor is insolvent, is in default, and is unable to fulfill their obligations to pay back their creditors.

Bankruptcy is the federal process that applies when a debtor is insolvent, is in default, and is unable to fulfill their obligations to pay back their creditors and meets all requirements for bankruptcy proceedings. In most instances, when bankruptcy is filed, the debtor's assets are sold and the money is distributed among the debtor's creditors to pay the debt that is owed.

Under federal law, bankruptcy filings must not be made in bad faith–that is, for the sole purpose of defrauding a creditor. In addition, it is illegal for a debtor to knowingly conceal property or to falsify records; both crimes are punishable by fines or imprisonment.

This chapter explains a few of the many provisions of the law that pertains to creditors rights and to bankruptcy.

21.2 CREDITOR'S RIGHTS

security interest
Interest created under state law to ensure that specific personal property assets are collateral for debt.

As indicated in the previous section, UCC Article 9 sets forth the state law governing the rights of creditors to personal property collateral. These state laws outline steps to create the right of the creditor to seize collateral in the event of debtor default and governs the priority of claims when multiple creditors have claims on the same collateral.

Personal property becomes collateral for a debt when the creditor creates a security interest in that property. A security interest is created by execution of a contract between the debtor and creditor known as a security agreement.

EXAMPLE 21.1

Kachov has just opened a restaurant and is seeking financing from First Bank. First Bank agrees to lend Kachov money for working capital but wants to use his restaurant kitchen equipment as collateral. Kachov and First Bank enter into a security agreement in which Kachov agrees to give First Bank a security interest in his restaurant kitchen equipment.

What happens when there are multiple security interests in the same collateral? The priority of claims among the competing creditors is determined by another step in the process: perfection of security interests.

perfection of security interests
Process to ensure priority of claims against specific collateral.

Under UCC Article 9, perfection can occur in three ways:

1. Control of goods applies to currency and negotiable instruments. Because only one creditor can have possession, or control, of these types of property at any given time, the law ensures that multiple creditors cannot have perfected interests in currency and negotiable instruments at the same time.
2. Automatic perfection is obtained through a purchase money security interest. This method of perfection is available to merchants selling goods to ensure priority if they offer financing for the purchase of goods.
3. Filing a financing statement perfects a security interest for general creditors in personal property not meeting the requirements of the previous categories. The financing statement is a public document filed with a county or state authority designated by state law and includes, among other things, names of the debtor and creditor, the date of filing, and the description of the collateral.

If a debtor defaults and there are multiple claims on the same collateral, the priority is as follows:

1. Secured interests have priority over unsecured interests.
2. Among secured claims, perfected claims have priority over unperfected claims.
3. With multiple perfected claims, priority is generally determined by the date of filing of the financing statement. However, a purchase money security interest (automatic perfection) will have priority over any filed perfection.

EXAMPLE 21.2

Matamoris owns a landscaping business and over several months has sought financing as his business geared up for the busy season. He obtained loans from several creditors, all of whom used his landscaping equipment as collateral: Financing Plus filed a financing statement on February 1, 2019; County Bank filed on March 20, 2019; and Lenders Plus filed on April 23, 2019. Among these three creditors having a security interest in the same collateral, Financing Plus would have first priority in making a claim against the collateral if the debtor were to default on his loan.

21.3 THE LAW OF BANKRUPTCY

Bankruptcy filings are governed by Congress under Article 1, Section 8 of the U.S. Constitution. This section gives Congress the power "to establish . . . uniform laws on the subject of bankruptcies throughout the United States." As a result, Congress passed the *Bankruptcy Code* in 1978 under Title 11 of the U.S. Code. It is important to recognize that bankruptcies are governed under both federal and state laws, which vary greatly. Therefore, both debtors and creditors must be acquainted with the provisions of both sets of laws.

voluntary filing
A form of bankruptcy that occurs when the debtor themself files a bankruptcy petition.

involuntary filing
A form of bankruptcy that occurs when creditors pressure a debtor to file.

Bankruptcy filings can either be voluntary or involuntary. A voluntary filing occurs when the debtor themself files a bankruptcy petition; an involuntary filing occurs when creditors pressure the debtor to file. Bankruptcy cases are administered by the U.S. Bankruptcy Courts, which are part of the district courts of the United States (see Chapter 1).

Bankruptcy law is divided into *chapters,* which is where they appear in the federal bankruptcy law. While all the chapters relating to bankruptcy law are important, select chapters will be discussed in the following sections. For additional information regarding federal bankruptcy law, visit: http://www.uscourts.gov/FederalCourts/Bankruptcy.aspx.

Bankruptcy Abuse Prevention and Consumer Protection Act of 2005
A federal law that instituted strict rules and eligibility requirements for debtors filing for bankruptcy.

Providing the most significant changes to bankruptcy law in nearly 30 years, the Bankruptcy Abuse Prevention and Consumer Protection Act was passed in 2005. This federal law instituted strict rules and eligibility requirements for debtors filing for bankruptcy. Among the many provisions in the law were the application of a new means test and the requirement of debtor education and credit counseling.

means test
A complex formula that measures an individual's income relative to the median income of the people in the state where they reside.

The Bankruptcy Abuse Prevention and Consumer Protection Act provides that debtors filing for bankruptcy under Chapter 7 must meet a means test. The means test uses a complex formula that measures an individual's income relative to the median income of the people in the state where they reside. The Bankruptcy Abuse Prevention and Consumer Protection Act in effect allows the bankruptcy court to disallow a petition for a Chapter 7 bankruptcy if the individual filing for bankruptcy earns an income that is too high to meet the standards of the means test. In such a case, the debtor might be required to file under a different chapter of the bankruptcy law. For more information about means testing, visit www.justice.gov/ust/eo/bapcpa/meanstesting.htm.

In addition to the means test, the Bankruptcy Abuse Prevention and Consumer Protection Act requires that a debtor who wishes to file under any chapter of the bankruptcy law must, unless exempt, receive individual or group credit counseling from an approved, not-for-profit, individual or group budget or credit counseling agency. The debtor must obtain a certificate from this agency outlining the assistance in budgeting that the debtor received. The counseling must be performed by telephone or online within 180 days prior to the bankruptcy filing. For a listing of approved agencies, visit www.usdoj.gov/ust.

21.4 CHAPTER 7 OF THE FEDERAL BANKRUPTCY LAW

liquidation
A process in which assets are sold to obtain cash.

straight or liquidation bankruptcy
The name given to a Chapter 7 bankruptcy, in which a trustee collects the debtor's nonexempt property, sells it, and dispenses the proceeds.

The most common type of bankruptcy filed by individuals and businesses is Chapter 7. After a petition for bankruptcy is filed, a trustee, usually an attorney-at-law who is experienced in handling bankruptcy cases, is appointed. The assets of the debtor then go through a process called liquidation, in which the assets are sold to obtain cash. Chapter 7 bankruptcy is sometimes referred to as straight or liquidation bankruptcy. The trustee divides the assets into those that are exempt (i.e., those that are protected from the creditors) and those that are nonexempt (i.e., those that are not afforded such protection). Examples of exempt property under federal law (up to a specified dollar limit) include the debtor's interest in real property used as a residence; one motor vehicle; household furnishings, appliances, books, pets, and musical instruments; jewelry; trade tools; individual retirement accounts (IRAs); life insurance contracts; and prescription health aids. Unless specifically exempted under federal or state law, all other property is nonexempt. Figure 21.1 shows examples of property exempt under federal law.

In addition to determining assets subject to exemption, the court will also use the means test (described in 21.3: The Law of Bankruptcy previously) to ensure that the debtor is entitled to the protection of Chapter 7 bankruptcy. The following is an example of an application of the means test.

- Real property used as a residence
- One motor vehicle
- Household furnishings
- Appliances
- Books
- Pets
- Musical instruments
- Jewelry
- Trade tools
- Life insurance contracts
- Individual retirement accounts
- Prescription health aids

FIGURE 21.1 Examples of Exempt Property under Federal Law (up to a Specified Dollar Limit)

EXAMPLE 21.3

▶ Morris, a highly paid vice president at a large oil company, overextended herself by making too many personal purchases using credit cards, and she found herself unable to pay her numerous credit card bills. Despite discontinuing making purchases on her credit cards, she noticed that her debt nonetheless continued to grow due to the cards' onerous interest and penalty charges. When she finally recognized the importance of personal fiscal responsibility and wished to be debtfree, she filed for bankruptcy under Chapter 7. After Morris underwent a means test, it was determined that her high income made her ineligible to file under this chapter.

After the Court has determined that the petitioner meets the means test and the trustee has determined which of the debtor's property is exempt and which is nonexempt, they collect the debtor's nonexempt property, sell it, and dispense the proceeds in a fair manner to protect the interests of the creditors to the fullest extent possible. The trustee is responsible for monitoring the claims of these creditors to be certain that all these claims are proper and legally enforceable.

Like the state law process of determining priority of creditor claims, the trustee also distinguishes between the debts that are secured versus those that are unsecured. A secured debt is a loan for which a specific asset is used as collateral, or pledged. Examples of secured loans are mortgages, which are secured by the real property (the land and the home), and automobile loans, which are frequently secured by the vehicles that have been purchased.

secured debt
A loan for which a specific asset is used as collateral.

Two types of actions by the debtor are prohibited under bankruptcy law. The first is a preferential payment, in which the debtor gives favorable treatment to one creditor over another. The second is a fraudulent transfer, in which the debtor sells property for an amount far below its market value, thus depriving creditors of the fair value had the property been liquidated by the trustee. A contract that is entered into by the debtor that includes either a preferential payment or a fraudulent transfer is illegal and, therefore, as described in Chapter 12, void.

preferential payment
A transfer of funds in which the debtor gives favorable treatment to one creditor over another.

fraudulent transfer
A transaction in which the debtor sells property for an amount far below its market value.

EXAMPLE 21.4

▶ Trung owned a valuable racehorse worth more than $100,000. After a series of poor investment decisions, she became insolvent and realized that she was about to default on her numerous loans. Trung decided to petition the court for Chapter 7 bankruptcy. Prior to the petition, she entered into a contract to sell the racehorse to her cousin for $500. Recognizing that this was a fraudulent transfer, the court held that the contract was void and ordered the racehorse turned over to the trustee. Trung then claimed that the racehorse was really a pet and thus was exempt property. The court rejected this argument as well. The trustee sold the horse for its market value and turned the proceeds over to Trung's creditors.

Under Chapter 7, a record of bankruptcy may remain in your credit report for up to 10 years—which might make creditors reluctant to extend funds.
George Doyle/Getty Images

At the conclusion of the process prescribed by Chapter 7, most or all of the debtor's debts are *discharged,* meaning they cease to exist and do not survive the bankruptcy. Examples of debts that are discharged are credit card bills, medical bills, and lawsuit judgments. However, bankruptcy law provides that some debts survive the bankruptcy. Examples of debts that are not discharged are student loans, unless repaying them would constitute an extreme hardship to the debtor and their dependents; debts of more than $550 to any one creditor for luxuries borrowed within 90 days before filing; back alimony and child support; cash advances of more than $825 taken within 70 days before filing; most tax debts; and debts resulting from an incident in which the debtor kills or injures someone while they are driving under the influence of drugs or alcohol. Figure 21.2 gives examples of debts that may not be discharged in bankruptcy.

EXAMPLE 21.5

McAndrew ran up numerous credit card charges and owed a significant amount of money on his student loans. When he lost his job, he petitioned the court for Chapter 7 bankruptcy. McAndrew's credit card debts were discharged, but the debt relating to the student loans survived the bankruptcy. McAndrew must still pay back these loans.

In Example 21.5, it is important to note that although McAndrew's credit card debts were discharged, a record of his bankruptcy may remain in McAndrew's credit report for up to 10 years–which might make creditors reluctant to extend funds to him during that period. However, some creditors may choose to provide financing to an individual who has recently received a bankruptcy discharge because, in general, a debtor may not file a Chapter 7 bankruptcy if they have received a bankruptcy discharge in the last eight years.

- Student loans
- Certain debts for luxuries
- Back alimony and child support
- Certain cash advances
- Most tax debts
- Certain debts resulting from driving under the influence

FIGURE 21.2 Examples of Debts That Are Not Discharged

21.5 CHAPTER 13 OF THE FEDERAL BANKRUPTCY LAW

Under the provisions of Chapter 13 of the federal bankruptcy law, the debtor retains their property but agrees to pay back all or a portion of their debts on an interest-free basis over a period spanning from three to five years. This is quite different from the provisions of Chapter 7, in which the debtor surrenders their assets to a trustee. Due to this difference, Chapter 13 bankruptcy is sometimes referred to as a reorganization bankruptcy.

reorganization bankruptcy The name given to a Chapter 13 bankruptcy, in which the debtor agrees to pay back all or a portion of their debts over a period of from three to five years.

Chapter 13 proceedings are initiated voluntarily, unlike Chapter 7 proceedings, which can be initiated either voluntarily or involuntarily. To be eligible to file for Chapter 13 bankruptcy, a debtor must be able to demonstrate that they have an income that is sufficient to pay off their debts within the prescribed period and that the amount of debt that is currently owed does not exceed the specified limits of $1,010,650 for secured debts and $336,900 for unsecured debts. Note that the Bankruptcy Abuse Prevention and Consumer Protection Act also applies to Chapter 13 and requires that the debtor receive the same prefiling counseling as is required under Chapter 7.

Under Chapter 13, certain debts are considered to be priority debts. Priority debts are deemed to be sufficiently important that they must be paid in full. Examples of priority debts include certain tax obligations, alimony and child support, and wages owed to employees. Furthermore, the reorganization plan must include regular payments on secured debts such as a home mortgage or automobile loan.

priority debts Debts deemed sufficiently important under Chapter 13 of the bankruptcy law that they must be paid in full.

EXAMPLE 21.6

- Polumbo incurred a significant amount of expenses on behalf of her mother, who had serious health issues. Although occupying a relatively high-paying position at her company, Polumbo has now fallen behind on the monthly mortgage payments for her home, which is valued at approximately $350,000. She is quite concerned that the mortgage company will bring a legal action against her and that she will lose her home due to foreclosure. She decides to file for Chapter 13 bankruptcy to stop her creditors from repossessing her home. Because her home is not valued over $1,010,650 and because she earns an income, Polumbo is put on a strict four-year repayment plan and is allowed to keep her home as long as she abides by the rules set forth in the reorganization plan.

Under Chapter 13, once the repayment plan is satisfied, all remaining debts that are eligible for discharge are discharged. The debtor must, however, first demonstrate to the bankruptcy court that they are current on alimony and child support obligations and that they have completed a second budget counseling course with an agency approved by the U.S. trustee. This second counseling course does not replace, but is in addition to, the prefiling counseling course described earlier in this chapter. For a listing of approved agencies at the trustee's website, visit www.usdoj.gov/ust.

Finally, it is important to point out that some debtors prefer Chapter 13 to Chapter 7 because Chapter 13 allows the debtor to retain nonexempt property.

21.6 CHAPTERS 9, 11, 12, AND 15 OF THE FEDERAL BANKRUPTCY LAW

In addition to Chapter 7, the federal bankruptcy law contains several other chapters that might apply to individuals or businesses that become insolvent and default on their debts. Several of these other chapters are discussed in the following paragraphs.

CHAPTER 9

Chapter 9 bankruptcy involves the adjustment of debts for a municipality. The purpose of this chapter is to provide a municipality with a debt repayment plan, rather than to require the liquidation of municipal assets. A *municipality* in the bankruptcy code is defined as a political subdivision or public agency or instrumentality of a state, including cities, towns, villages, counties, taxing districts, municipal authorities, and school districts.

CHAPTER 11

While partnerships, sole proprietorships, and individuals all may file for Chapter 11 bankruptcy, this chapter is most commonly used by corporations. In a Chapter 11 bankruptcy, the debtor proposes a reorganization plan in order to pay back creditors over time. Daily business decisions continue to be made and implemented by management, but major decisions must be approved by the bankruptcy court.

EXAMPLE 21.7

Saarsgard Motor Corporation, a publicly traded automobile manufacturer, finds that it is unable to pay its debts but wishes to remain in business. It files for Chapter 11 bankruptcy. The company is forced to restructure its business with the approval of the bankruptcy court and work out a plan to become profitable once again. Saarsgard will continue to be able to conduct its normal business operations and to sell its stocks and bonds to members of the public.

EXAMPLE 21.8

Adelphia Communications Corporation announced that, due to stiff competition in the telecom industry, it was necessary for the company to file for Chapter 11 bankruptcy protection. The decision to file for Chapter 11, rather than Chapter 7 bankruptcy, was made in order to provide the company enough time to secure the sale of a large portion of company assets to other companies in the telecom industry. Under Chapter 7 bankruptcy, Adelphia shareholders and creditors may have fared worse; the immediate liquidation of company assets could have resulted in far greater losses.

Some individuals elect to file bankruptcy under Chapter 11, rather than Chapter 13, because they have high levels of debt—levels that are greater than the debt limits specified by Chapter 13.

CHAPTER 12

During the 1980s, a serious economic downturn in the agricultural sector prompted Congress to amend the bankruptcy code to provide distressed farmers a more favorable alternative to a Chapter 7 bankruptcy proceeding. As a result, Chapter 12 bankruptcy was specifically created to adjust the debts of family farmers or fishers who earn an annual income. Under a Chapter 12 bankruptcy, a plan is created to ensure that these debtors repay their debt over a period spanning from three to five years. The family farmer or fisher can be an individual, corporation, or partnership. Both the dollar amount and the percentage of total debt are subject to limits prescribed by the bankruptcy statute. For more information, visit: http://www.uscourts.gov/FederalCourts/Bankruptcy/BankruptcyBasics/Chapter12.aspx.

EXAMPLE 21.9

▶ Alessi, who works full-time as a highly paid executive at a local manufacturing company, supplements his income by growing corn on his farm. Alessi now finds that he is facing financial trouble due to ongoing problems in the corn industry, as well as several large purchases he made to satisfy his personal desires. He decides to file for Chapter 12 bankruptcy to help pay his debts but is rejected because only 40 percent of his income is generated from farming activities. Alessi will need to find an alternative way to address his financial predicament.

CHAPTER 15

Added to the Bankruptcy Code by the Bankruptcy Abuse Prevention and Consumer Protection Act, Chapter 15 provides a framework for bankruptcy cases when foreign countries are involved. The purpose of this chapter is to promote cooperation between the U.S. courts and those of foreign countries in bankruptcy cases by providing a process whereby foreign companies can get jurisdiction over U.S. cases and access to legal documents (see Chapter 36).

Chapter 12 bankruptcy was specifically created to adjust the debts of family farmers or fishers who earn an annual income.
Uppercut RF/Getty Images

EXAMPLE 21.10

Kelly, a U.S. citizen, owed a significant amount of money to Conti Motors, an Italian company, for an expensive sports car that Kelly had purchased and imported several years earlier. Kelly had numerous debts, became insolvent, and sought protection under U.S. bankruptcy laws. Conti Motors used Chapter 15 to request the federal bankruptcy court both to issue a subpoena to Kelly and an order to turn over his assets.

CHAPTER SUMMARY

21.1 Insolvency occurs when a individual's or business's liabilities exceed assets. Insolvency often leads to default, wherein the debtor fails to meet one or more financial obligations to their creditors.

21.2 State laws (UCC Article 9) set for the process for creating a creditor's security interest in personal property and in perfecting that interest, which creates the system for prioritizing the security interests for multiple creditors in the same personal property.

21.3 Bankruptcy filings are governed by Congress under the U.S. Constitution. A voluntary filing occurs when the debtor themself files a bankruptcy petition; an involuntary filing occurs when creditors pressure the debtor to file.

21.4 In a Chapter 7 bankruptcy, the assets of the debtor are liquidated to obtain cash. The trustee divides the assets by whether they are exempt or not. The trustee collects the debtor's nonexempt property, sells it, and dispenses the proceeds in a fair manner to protect the interests of creditors. At the conclusion of this process, most or all of the debtor's debts are discharged and do not survive the bankruptcy.

21.5 Under Chapter 13 of the federal bankruptcy law, the debtor retains their property but agrees to pay back all or a portion of their debts interest-free over a period spanning from three to five years.

21.6 Chapter 9 bankruptcy involves the adjustment of debts for a municipality. In a Chapter 11 bankruptcy, the debtor proposes a reorganization plan to pay back creditors over time. Chapter 12 bankruptcy was specifically created to adjust the debts of family farmers or fishers who earn an annual income. Chapter 15 bankruptcy involves ancillary and other cross-border cases.

CHAPTER TWENTY-ONE ASSESSMENT

MATCHING LEGAL TERMS

Match each of the numbered definitions with the correct term in the following list.

a. assets
b. bankruptcy
c. creditor
d. debtor
e. default
f. insolvency
g. involuntary filing
h. liabilities
i. liquidation
j. means test
k. perfection
l. reorganization bankruptcy
m. secured debt
n. straight bankruptcy
o. voluntary filing

1. A form of bankruptcy in which the debtor agrees to pay back all or a portion of their debts over a period spanning from three to five years. **1.** _____
2. A complex formula that measures an individual's income relative to the median income of the people in the state where they reside. **2.** _____
3. A form of bankruptcy that occurs when creditors pressure a debtor to file. **3.** _____
4. The legal state that occurs when a debtor is insolvent, is in default, and is unable to fulfill their obligations to pay back their creditors. **4.** _____
5. An individual or business that owes money. **5.** _____
6. The process under state law of creating a priority interest in collateral. **6.** _____
7. The value of the property an individual business owns. **7.** _____
8. An individual or business to which money is owed. **8.** _____
9. A form of bankruptcy that occurs when the debtor files a bankruptcy petition on their own. **9.** _____
10. A debt for which a specific asset is used as collateral. **10.** _____
11. The value of what an individual or business owes. **11.** _____
12. A form of bankruptcy in which a trustee collects the debtor's nonexempt property, sells it, and dispenses the proceeds. **12.** _____
13. The state that occurs when an individual's or business's liabilities exceed assets. **13.** _____
14. A process in which assets are sold to obtain cash. **14.** _____
15. The state in which a debtor fails to meet one or more financial obligations to their creditors. **15.** _____

TRUE/FALSE QUIZ

Indicate whether each of the following statements is true or false.

16. Persons familiar with good accounting practices recognize that assets should never exceed liabilities. **16.** _____
17. In most instances, when bankruptcy is filed, the debtor's assets are sold and the money is distributed among the debtor's creditors to pay the debt that is owed. **17.** _____
18. Bankruptcies are governed under both federal and state law. **18.** _____
19. All bankruptcy filings are involuntary. **19.** _____
20. Chapter 9 bankruptcy is sometimes referred to as straight or liquidation bankruptcy. **20.** _____
21. Chapter 13 bankruptcy is sometimes referred to as reorganization bankruptcy. **21.** _____
22. A bankruptcy court may disallow a petition for a Chapter 7 bankruptcy if the individual does not meet the standards of the means test. **22.** _____

23. All debtors wishing to file for bankruptcy must receive individual or group credit counseling from an approved, not-for-profit, individual or group budget, or credit counseling agency. **23.** _____

24. In a Chapter 11 bankruptcy, all daily business decisions must be made and implemented by the bankruptcy court. **24.** _____

25. Chapter 12 bankruptcy was specifically created to adjust the debts of family farmers or fishers who earn an annual income. **25.** _____

MULTIPLE CHOICE QUIZ

Please indicate the correct answer from the choices following each question.

26. Bank A lends money to a customer on October 1 and files their security interest on November 1. Bank B lends money to a customer on October 15 but files their security interest on October 16. Assuming the banks have the same assets as collateral, (a) Bank A has priority claim to the collateral because they were the first to loan money (b) neither Bank A nor Bank B have priority claim to the collateral (c) Bank B has priority claim to the collateral because they were first to file (d) Bank A and Bank B must divide the collateral equally. **26.** _____

27. A company becomes insolvent and has no chance of making the business succeed in the future. The company should file for which type of bankruptcy? (a) Chapter 7 (b) Chapter 9 (c) Chapter 13 (d) Chapter 11 **27.** _____

28. A company becomes insolvent due to the failure of their largest customer but has confidence that they can rebuild the business. The company should file for which type of bankruptcy? (a) Chapter 7 (b) Chapter 9 (c) Chapter 13 (d) Chapter 11 **28.** _____

29. An individual with a well-paying job becomes insolvent after spending too much on credit card debt. This individual should file for which type of bankruptcy? (a) Chapter 7 (b) Chapter 9 (c) Chapter 13 (d) Chapter 11 **29.** _____

DISCUSSION QUESTIONS

Answer the following questions and discuss them in class.

30. List some examples of exempt property under Chapter 7 of the federal bankruptcy law.

31. Describe the two types of actions by the debtor prohibited under bankruptcy law that were discussed in this chapter.

32. List some examples of debts that are not discharged under a Chapter 7 bankruptcy.

33. Explain the debtor education and credit counseling requirement under the Bankruptcy Abuse Prevention and Consumer Protection Act.

34. Explain the process of creating and perfecting a security interest under state law.

35. Describe the process used in a Chapter 11 bankruptcy.

THINKING CRITICALLY ABOUT THE LAW

Answer the following questions, which require you to think critically about the legal principles that you learned in this chapter.

36. Exempt Property Why is some property considered exempt under Chapter 7 of the federal bankruptcy law?

37. Debtor Education and Credit Counseling Why does the law require a debtor to receive individual or group credit counseling prior to be allowed to file for bankruptcy?

38. Chapter 13 Why are certain debts considered to be priority debts under Chapter 13 of the federal bankruptcy law?

39. A Question of Ethics Is it ethical for an individual to purchase numerous items on credit when they know that bankruptcy is available as an option in the event of a default?

CASE QUESTIONS

Study each of the following cases. Answer the questions that follow with Yes or No.

40. Perfection of Security Interest Milbank Enterprises decided to purchase equipment for its printing business from Lee Equipment. On April 1, Lee Equipment agreed that Milbank could finance the purchase by paying Lee in equal monthly installments over a period of two years. Two months after buying the equipment, Milbank needed to borrow money for working capital from Capital Bank. Capital Bank secured the debt using Milbank's printing equipment as collateral, filing a financing statement on July 1. Subsequently, Milbank needed more money for working capital and borrowed money from Easy Times Credit. Easy Times Credit also filed a financing statement listing the printing equipment as collateral on September 1.

a. Do Capital Bank and Easy Times Credit have perfected security interests? **a.** _____

b. Does Lee Equipment have a perfected security interest? **b.** _____

c. If Milbank defaults, would Capital Bank have first priority to seize the printing equipment? **c.** _____

41. Exempt Property Chen had numerous debts from credit card bills, a home mortgage, and a loan resulting for a second automobile purchased on credit. He filed for bankruptcy under Chapter 7. Chen's assets, in addition to his two automobiles, included a home, some rare coins, a pet pedigree dog, and a baby grand piano.

a. Is the second automobile exempt property? **a.** _____

b. Are both the dog and the piano exempt property? **b.** _____

c. Are the rare coins exempt property? **c.** _____

d. Is the home exempt property? **d.** _____

42. Chapter 11 Travel Junction, a corporation, encounters financial difficulties and files for bankruptcy under Chapter 11. The bankruptcy court approves a reorganization plan to pay back creditors over time and begins monitoring the activities of the business.

a. Must Travel Junction receive prior approval from the bankruptcy court to purchase three new desks for the office? **a.** _____

b. Must Travel Junction receive prior approval from the bankruptcy court to purchase two new computers for the office? **b.** _____

c. Must Travel Junction receive prior approval from the bankruptcy court to purchase a new building with 12 rental apartments? **c.** _____

43. Chapter 13 Brown earned a significant income as a pilot for a major airline. Despite this high income, Brown ran into serious financial difficulties when she invested in a business owned by her brother that failed. Brown filed for bankruptcy under Chapter 13 to gain some time to get her financial affairs back in order.

a. Will Brown need to receive individual credit counseling prior to being allowed to file for bankruptcy? **a.** _____

b. Must Brown demonstrate to the bankruptcy court that the amount of debt that she owes is less than $1,010,650 for secured debts and $336,900 for unsecured debts? b. _____

c. Must Brown complete a second budget counseling course after the bankruptcy court approves the reorganization plan? c. _____

CASE ANALYSIS

Study each of the following cases carefully. Briefly state the principle of law and your decision.

44. Bad Faith A mere eight days after it was formally incorporated as a business, Schaefer Salt Recovery Inc. (SSR) filed a petition under Chapter 11 of the bankruptcy code. SSR's only assets were mortgages on three properties on which foreclosure actions brought by Segal were pending in court. SSR's vice president and attorney, Khoudary, advised Segal's attorney that the foreclosure actions could not be enforced as a result of the filing. Presumably this was one of the reasons Khoudary advised Segal's attorney that "Segal was skunked." Segal moved to dismiss the Chapter 11 petition for cause, arguing that the petition had been filed for the sole purpose of frustrating Segal's efforts to conclude the pending foreclosure actions. Did SSR act in bad faith by filing the petition for bankruptcy, and will Segal be successful in foreclosing on the mortgages? [*In Re: Schaefer Salt Recovery, Inc.*, U.S. Third Circuit, Docket No. 06-4574 (New Jersey)]

Principle of Law:

_____

_____

Decision:

_____

_____

45. Discharged Debts Jensen was involved in a motor vehicle accident with Boyer. Jensen brought suit against Boyer, alleging that her negligence caused the accident. Boyer then brought a countersuit against Jensen, claiming that it was actually Jensen's negligence that caused the accident. Jensen subsequently filed for bankruptcy protection. The bankruptcy court issued a discharge, and Jensen filed a motion to dismiss Boyer's lawsuit due to the bankruptcy discharge. Are lawsuit judgments discharged in a bankruptcy, and will Jensen be successful in having Boyer's claim against him discharged? [*Boyer v. Jensen*, California Court of Appeal, Docket No. B174899 (California)]

Principle of Law:

_____

_____

Decision:

_____

_____

46. Chapter 11 Following months in which Chrysler experienced deepening losses and received billions in bailout funds from the federal government, the company, now referred to as Old Chrysler, filed a bankruptcy petition under Chapter 11. The filing unsuccessfully sought additional government bailout funds for a restructuring, but the bankruptcy court ultimately settled on a transaction in which most of Old Chrysler's operating assets would be transferred to New Chrysler in exchange for $2 billion in cash and other consideration. In addition, Fiat, another automobile manufacturer, agreed to provide New Chrysler with certain fuel-efficient vehicle platforms, access to its worldwide distribution system, and new management that was experienced in turning around a failing auto company. Financing for the sale would come from the U.S. Troubled Asset Relief Program (TARP) and from Export Development Canada. The United Auto Workers union, the U.S. Treasury, and Export Development Canada would own the New Chrysler. Fiat, for its contributions, would immediately own 20 percent of the equity with rights to acquire more. Numerous groups appealed, seeking to stop the Chapter 11 bankruptcy from proceeding. Does it seem likely that the appeals court will support the settlement reached in the bankruptcy court? [*In Re: Chrysler LLC, et al.,* U.S. Second Circuit, Docket No. 09-2311-bk (New York)]

Principle of Law:

____

____

Decision:

____

____

LEGAL RESEARCH

Complete the following activities. Share your findings with the class.

47. Working in Teams In teams of three or four, list some events that might occur in the course of an individual's life or a business's transactions that could result in insolvency, default, and bankruptcy.

____

____

48. Using Technology Using the Internet and search engines, investigate individuals and businesses that have declared bankruptcy, and determine under which chapter(s) these bankruptcies filed. Speculate about the reasons for the bankruptcies and the selection of the particular chapter(s). What types of economic conditions would lead an individual or business to select a particular chapter?

____

____

PART 4

Commercial Paper

22. Introduction to Commercial Paper

23. Transfer and Discharge of Commercial Paper

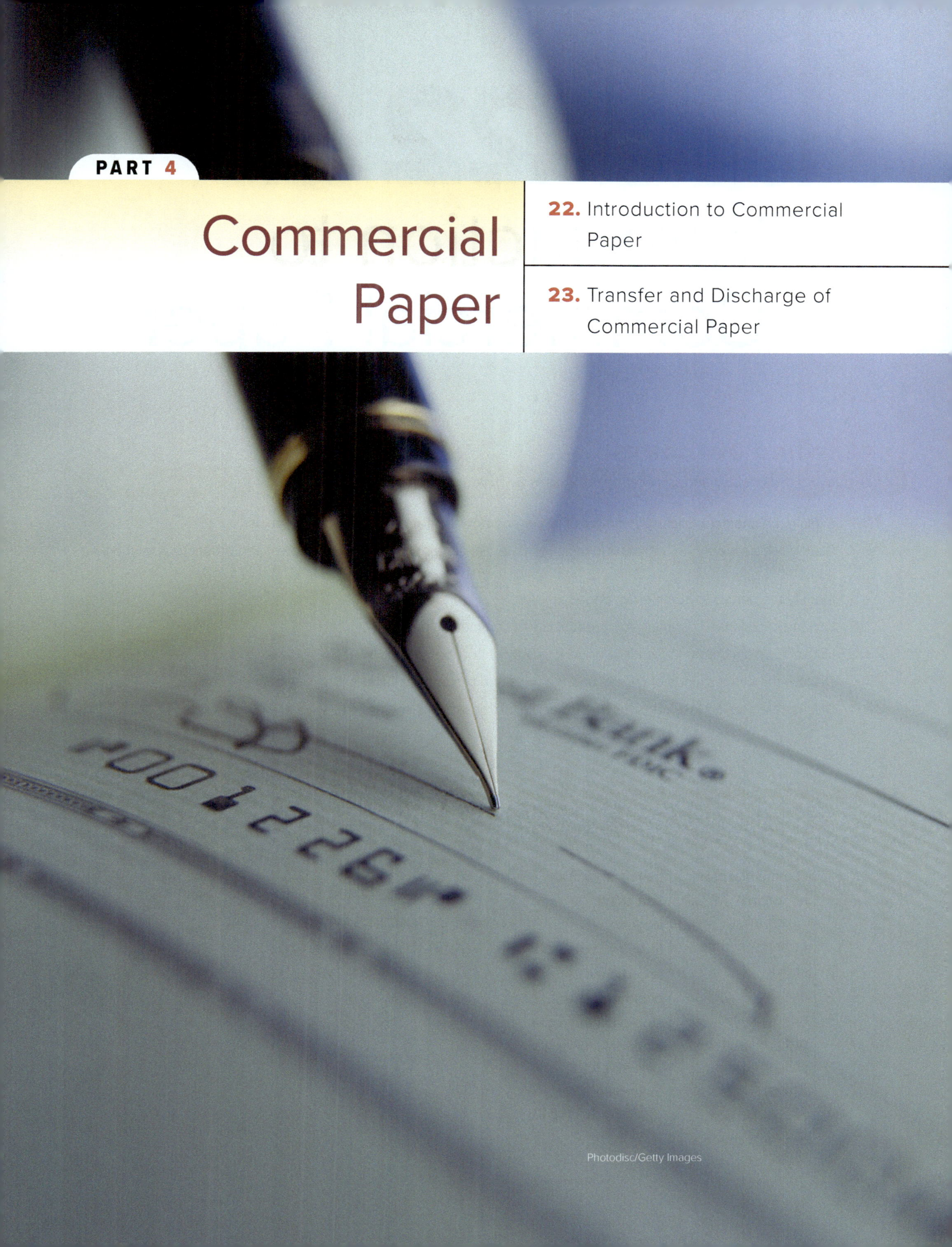

Photodisc/Getty Images

chapter 22
Introduction to Commercial Paper

LEARNING OUTCOMES

After studying this chapter and completing the assessment, you will be able to

22.1 Explain the characteristics of commercial paper and how it differs from ordinary contracts.

22.2 Distinguish between the two basic kinds of commercial paper: promises to pay (notes) and orders to pay (checks and drafts).

22.3 Identify the parties to commercial paper.

22.4 List and explain the essentials for negotiability of commercial paper.

22.5 List and explain the nonessentials for negotiability of commercial paper.

22.6 Discuss the various kinds of checks and the rules and procedures for stopping payment on a check.

22.7 Discuss electronic funds transfers and other digital transactions and provide several examples of these.

LEGAL terms

- commercial paper
- negotiable instrument
- promissory note
- check
- draft
- negotiability
- order instrument
- stale check
- Check 21
- certified check
- cashier's check
- traveler's check
- bad check
- forgery
- forged check
- raised check
- postdated check
- stop-payment order
- electronic funds transfer (EFT)
- Electronic Funds Transfer Act (EFTA) of 1978

INTRODUCTION TO COMMERCIAL PAPER

"The most pain I feel—and my accountants will tell you this—is every time I write a check to the IRS."

Oprah Winfrey, TV host, producer, and entrepreneur

Digital Vision/Getty Images

22.1 CHARACTERISTICS OF COMMERCIAL PAPER

Commercial paper is a term widely used in law to describe a number of legally binding and commercially acceptable documents, such as notes, checks, and drafts, that are used to transfer money from one person to another. These documents are negotiable–that is, they are freely transferable–and they circulate throughout our commercial system almost as readily as cash. Commercial paper is sometimes referred to as negotiable instruments. A negotiable instrument is an unconditional written promise to pay, or pay to the order of another party, a certain sum of money on demand or at a definite time. Negotiable instruments are highly trusted and play an important role in everyday individual and business transactions.

commercial paper
A number of legally binding and commercially acceptable documents that are used to transfer money from one person to another.

negotiable instrument
An unconditional written promise to pay, or pay to the order of another party, a certain sum of money on demand or at a definite time.

Commercial paper (negotiable instruments) forms the basis of contracts, but it differs from ordinary contracts in two important ways: presumption of consideration and assignability.

PRESUMPTION OF CONSIDERATION

The law presumes that commercial paper is issued for value–that is, for consideration. A party to a simple contract who is seeking to enforce the promise contained in the agreement must prove that they gave consideration; however, a party to commercial paper who is trying to collect payment does not. Instead the person trying to avoid payment must prove that they received no consideration.

NEGOTIABILITY VERSUS ASSIGNABILITY

As described in Chapter 14, ordinary contracts usually may be assigned; but the assignee, or the person to whom rights are transferred, may receive only those rights held by the person making the assignment (the assignor) at the time of the transfer. In addition, the person who has acquired assigned rights to a contract must notify the other party to the contract of the assignment. These conditions do not apply to commercial paper that is being negotiated (transferred). The person to whom commercial paper is transferred may acquire a better right to it than the person who made the transfer. For example, if commercial paper that has been found or stolen is sold (transferred) to an innocent person for value, that person becomes the legal owner with title enforceable even against the rightful owner–unlike the innocent purchaser of found or stolen jewelry, who does not acquire title. In addition, in some cases the person receiving the instrument can receive money on the instrument when the transferring person could not.

22.2 KINDS OF COMMERCIAL PAPER

There are many different kinds of commercial paper. The two basic types of commercial paper are promises to pay (notes) and orders to pay (checks and drafts).

PROMISES TO PAY

A promissory note is, as the name suggests, a written note or letter in which one person promises to pay a certain amount of money to another at a definite time. A simple promissory note would be one saying, "I, John Jones, promise to pay to the order of Frieda Smith $100 in 60 days from the date this note is issued." If Frieda Smith should need the $100 before the 60 days have passed, she could take this written promise to a bank or to another person and, if the bank or other person felt that John Jones would keep his promise, Smith could then transfer, or negotiate, her interest in the promise to the bank, or to the other person, in exchange for $100.

promissory note
A written note or letter in which one person promises to pay a certain amount of money to another at a definite time.

Smith would then have the money she needed without having to wait for it, and the bank or the other person would be entitled to receive Jones's $100 at the time promised.

ORDERS TO PAY

There are situations in which a person orders another individual to pay a definite sum of money. This form of commercial paper includes checks (in which a bank is ordered) and drafts (in which a third party is ordered).

check
A written order drawn on a bank by a depositor that requests the bank to pay, on demand and unconditionally, a definite sum of money to the bearer of the check or to the order of a specified person.

Checks A check is a written order drawn on a bank by a depositor that requests the bank to pay, on demand and unconditionally, a definite sum of money to the bearer of the check or to the order of a specified person. Consider a check for $50 from Frieda Smith to John Jones simply as a letter from Smith to her bank saying, "Dear Ms. Banker: You are in possession of some of my money, and I now wish you to pay $50 of it to John Jones." The banker would ask Jones to prove his identity; ask Jones to sign his name on the back of the check–that is, to endorse it–as an indication that he is receiving the $50; and then pay Jones the $50 as directed by Smith. Additional discussion of endorsements is presented in Chapter 23.

draft
An unconditional written order to a person instructing them to pay money to another, third person.

Drafts Whereas a check is a letter to a bank instructing it to pay money to a certain person, a draft, or *bill of exchange,* is an unconditional written order to a person instructing them to pay money to another, third person. Drafts are often used in certain kinds of businesses.

EXAMPLE 22.1

▶ Bayoumi traveled for extended periods and, not wanting to delay payments to utility companies during his absences, authorized his attorney to make periodic payments of specified amounts. Bayoumi used drafts to accomplish this objective.

THE MEANING OF "PAY TO THE ORDER OF"

If the check from Frieda Smith to John Jones was worded, "Pay to John Jones. . .," the banker could not do otherwise. But if the check said, "Pay to the order of John Jones. . .," it would mean, "Pay this money to John Jones or do whatever else he wants you to do with it." These few key words, "Pay to the order of," give commercial paper negotiability, or the ability to be transferred freely from one person to another and be accepted as readily as cash. As a result, Jones can tell the banker, "I don't really want the money Smith is telling you to give me. I want you to pay it to Brown instead."

negotiability
The ability to be transferred freely from one person to another and be accepted as readily as cash.

An item of commercial paper containing the key words of negotiability, "pay to the order of," or their equivalent, is an order instrument. Notes, drafts, and checks are all examples of order instruments.

order instrument
An item of commercial paper that contains the key words of negotiability, "pay to the order of," or their equivalent.

22.3 PARTIES TO COMMERCIAL PAPER

The parties involved in a promissory note have particular names. The person who makes the promise is called the *maker.* If the maker has someone else add their name to the promise to strengthen it, the other person is known as the *comaker.* The person to whom the promise is made is the *payee.*

Similarly, the parties involved in a draft or a check have particular names. The person who draws or creates the check or draft is called the *drawer.* The person who receives the money is called the *payee.* The person who is ordered to pay the money is called the *drawee* (in the case of a check, the drawee is a bank). Whoever is in possession of commercial paper is called the *holder.* Some holders are called *holders in due course,* to be covered in Chapter 23. The holder can be the payee, the drawee, or the drawer, but obviously only one of these parties can be the holder at one time.

22.4 ESSENTIALS FOR NEGOTIABILITY OF COMMERCIAL PAPER

To be negotiable under the Uniform Commercial Code (UCC), commercial paper must conform to the following requirements [UCC 3-104(1)].

IT MUST BE IN WRITING AND SIGNED BY THE MAKER OR DRAWER

Commercial paper may be handwritten, printed, or written by any other means that will make a mark. The signature may be written either at the bottom or in the body of the instrument, as, "I, Fred Allan, promise to pay . . ." [UCC 1-201(46)].

The device used in writing a note does not affect its negotiability. Anything that will make a mark is satisfactory.

EXAMPLE 22.2

▶ Forgue offered Aiello a $500 note in payment for merchandise she had purchased. The note specified payment within 30 days. Aiello refused to accept the note because of the fact that it was written in red ink, incorrectly assuming that it was not enforceable.

Only the person who writes their name on a note as the maker, or on a check or draft as the drawer, is liable for it. The liability is the same even if the person signs a trade name or an assumed name. Thus, in a note bearing the signature "Charles Lamb, Agent for Clark Insurance Company," Lamb is personally liable. The phrase "Agent for Clark Insurance Company" merely describes Lamb. If the note were signed "Clark Insurance Company, by Charles Lamb, Agent," the company would be liable. Lamb would have clearly indicated that he had signed for his employer (see Chapter 19).

IT MUST CONTAIN AN UNCONDITIONAL PROMISE OR ORDER TO PAY A DEFINITE SUM IN MONEY

The promise in a note, or the order in a check or draft, must be unconditional. Statements requiring that certain things be done or that specific events take place before payment make the instrument a simple contract rather than commercial paper. Contrary to popular opinion, an IOU is not a promise to pay; it is merely an acknowledgment of a debt.

EXAMPLE 22.3

Spiegelgras received a note from an individual who owed him money. The note contained the statement, "Payment to be made from my income tax refund check." This note was not negotiable because payment depended on the Internal Revenue Service agreeing that a refund was due. In case of a lawsuit, this instrument would be considered a simple contract. Suppose that, instead of the provision about the tax refund, the note contained the statement, "This note is in payment of purchases made in January." This latter statement would not affect the negotiability of the note because it does not in any way limit, restrict, or condition payment.

Commercial paper must be payable in money–any money that has a known or established value. An instrument payable in a foreign currency is negotiable.

IT MUST BE PAYABLE ON DEMAND OR AT A DEFINITE TIME

Commercial paper must be payable on demand or at some definite time. A note payable "on or before July 1, 20- -," or "one month after sight," or "on presentation" is negotiable because the time of payment is certain.

An instrument payable "within 60 days after death [of a named person]" is not payable at a definite time and is not negotiable. A promise to pay when a person marries or when they reaches a certain age is not a promise to pay at a definite time because the person might never marry or might die before reaching the specified age. In such instances, the instruments are nonnegotiable.

IT MUST BE PAYABLE TO ORDER, TO BEARER, OR TO CASH

Unless an instrument contains words of negotiability such as "payable to bearer" or "payable to the order of" or "payable to cash," it is not negotiable.

A DRAFT OR CHECK MUST NAME OR INDICATE THE DRAWEE WITH REASONABLE CERTAINTY

The person who is expected to pay a draft or check must be named or otherwise indicated in the instrument with reasonable certainty for the instrument to be considered negotiable.

22.5 NONESSENTIALS FOR NEGOTIABILITY OF COMMERCIAL PAPER

Certain items may be omitted from commercial paper without affecting its negotiability. Because consideration is presumed, the words "for value received" are not needed. Also, the consideration or value given by the maker or the drawer need not be specified.

If the date of a note, check, or draft is not indicated, the holder may write in the date when the instrument was issued without affecting its negotiability. If this date is not known, the date when the paper was received is considered the date of issue. Commercial paper may be *antedated* (dated previously) or *postdated* (dated ahead).

The place of business or home of a maker of a note is presumed to be where the instrument was drawn or where it is payable if this information is not given on the paper.

In a note, draft, or check, if the amount payable expressed in figures differs from the sum stated in words, the amount expressed in words is considered the true one. If the sum stated in words is not also expressed in figures, this omission does not affect negotiability.

The numbering of (or the failure to number) commercial paper does not affect its negotiability.

22.6 CHECKS

The check is used more than any other instrument of credit as a means of making payment, both to settle debts and to pay for purchases.

Checks need not be made out on the printed forms supplied by banks. Any writing that includes the essential elements of negotiability is considered a valid check when signed and delivered by the drawer. However, many banks today prefer that the encoded routing number assigned a drawer (depositor) be shown on every check written by them. For proper processing through computers and other electronic machinery, these numbers are recommended, although they are not legally necessary. Figure 22.1 shows an example of a check.

RELATIONSHIP BETWEEN BANK AND DEPOSITOR

A check provides a safe means of transferring money and serves as a receipt when paid and canceled by the bank. It may circulate through several persons, banks, and organizations. The bank must honor a check when it is properly drawn against the money the drawer has on deposit or the bank will be liable to the drawer for damages.

PAYMENT OF CHECKS

Checks are always payable on demand. The UCC provides that, with respect to the liability of the drawer, a reasonable length of time for presentation for payment is 30 days after the date appearing on the check or after issue (the date the check is actually written), whichever is later. A bank may pay a check presented more than 30 days after its date, but it is not required to do so. A check presented more than six months after its date is known as a stale check (UCC 4-404). Stale checks will not be honored by banks.

stale check
A check presented more than six months after its date.

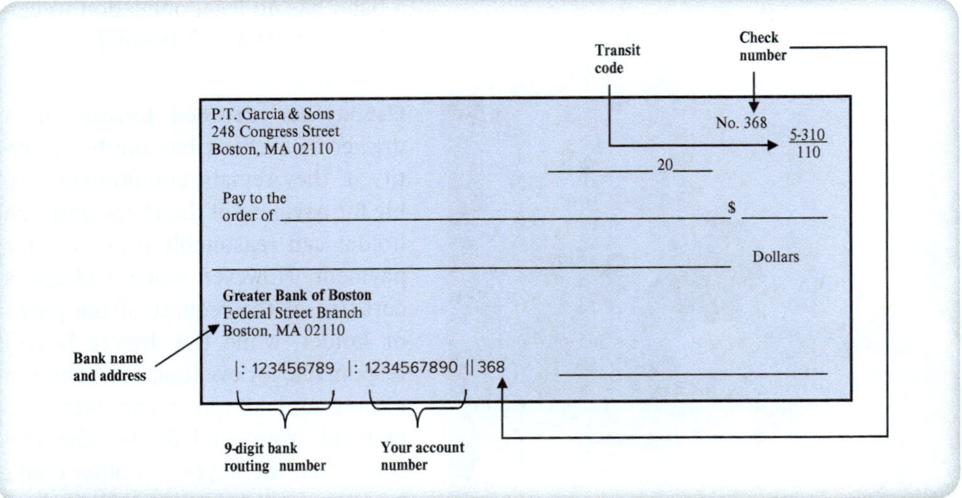

FIGURE 22.1 Example of a Check

EXAMPLE 22.4

▶ Shuster received a check from Cavanagh and immediately presented it to her bank for payment. Cavanagh's bank, for reasons of its own, refused to honor the check, although Cavanagh had sufficient funds on deposit to cover it. Cavanagh can sue her bank for any damages that she may have sustained as a result of the bank's refusal to cash her check.

THE CHECK CLEARING FOR THE 21ST CENTURY ACT

Check 21
The term commonly used to refer to the Check Clearing for the 21st Century Act, a federal law revolutionizing the manner in which checks are handled by banks.

The *Check Clearing for the 21st Century Act,* a federal law commonly known as Check 21, became effective in 2004. The law revolutionized the manner in which checks are handled by banks. In the past, banks physically transported checks between the drawee bank and the bank in which they were deposited. Check handling was inefficient, costly, and time-consuming. Check 21 created efficiency in check handling by allowing banks to create digital substitutes of checks to be handled electronically, thereby removing paper checks from the process.

Under Check 21, banks provide checking account customers with copies of the digital check substitutes rather than the original canceled checks. Also, the drawer must be certain funds are immediately available in their account to cover a check. Electronic check transfers occur almost instantaneously.

CERTIFIED CHECKS

certified check
A check that the bank has promised to pay when it is presented for payment.

A merchant who sells goods to a person whose credit standing is not known may request the customer to make payment by certified check, a check that the bank has promised to pay when it is presented for payment. If the drawer's funds on deposit are sufficient to cover the amount of the check, the teller or cashier will write or stamp across the face of the check the word "certified" and the date. The teller will then sign their name and title and make an entry in the depositor's account indicating that the depositor's balance has been reduced by the amount of the check. While actual cash is not set aside for the payment of the check, a notation of the transaction is made on the depositor's record. The bank assumes absolute liability for payment. It should be noted that under the UCC, unless otherwise agreed by contract, a bank has no legal obligation to certify a check [UCC 3-409(d)].

Checks are always payable on demand.
Image Source

Liability for Certified Checks If a drawer of a check has the bank certify it, they remain conditionally liable for payment of the check until the holder can reasonably present it for payment. However, when a check is certified at the request of the payee or holder, while the drawee is still responsible for eventual payment, the drawer and all prior endorsers are released from all liability. The reason is that the payee or holder could have requested payment instead of certification.

EXAMPLE 22.5

▶ Sherwin asked her bank to ***stop payment*** (a service offered by banks whereby a depositor can have the bank refuse to pay a depositor's check when it is presented for payment by a holder) on a check that she had certified. The bank refused to stop payment, even though the check had not yet been presented for payment.

In Example 22.5, the bank was justified in refusing to honor Sherwin's request. By certifying the check, the bank had assumed absolute liability for its payment. Certification assures the payee or any subsequent holder that the check is genuine and that the bank will honor the check when it is presented for payment.

There is no time limit for the presentation of a certified check for payment. The bank must honor it whenever the holder demands payment.

CASHIER'S CHECKS

A cashier's check, sometimes called an *official check,* a *teller's check,* or a *bank check,* is issued by the cashier or other designated officer of a bank and drawn against bank funds. A depositor may request such a check when, for example, they intend to use it to pay for merchandise from an out-of-town dealer who will not accept a personal check.

cashier's check
A check issued by a cashier or other designated officer of a bank and drawn against bank funds.

A cashier's check is made payable either to the depositor who purchases it from the bank or to the person who is to cash it. If the check is made payable to the depositor, they endorse it to the person to whom it is being transferred.

The UCC provides for recovery of a lost, stolen, or destroyed certified or cashier's check. If such an event occurs, either the payee or the person who purchased the check may request a full refund from the bank. According to UCC 3-312, if a claim is made for recovery of a cashier's check and that check is not presented for payment within 90 days after the check was made (or 90 days after acceptance of a certified check), the bank will generally issue a refund. If the bank does issue a full refund to either party, it is released from all liability regarding the certified or cashier's check.

TRAVELER'S CHECKS

A traveler's check is a certified check issued in a denomination of $20 or more by certain banks, travel agencies, and financial services companies. The issuer usually charges the purchaser of traveler's checks a fixed rate, perhaps 1 percent, to issue them.

traveler's check
A certified check, useful when traveling in foreign countries, that is issued in denominations of $10 or more by certain banks, travel agencies, and financial services companies.

For persons who are traveling, especially in foreign countries, traveler's checks are a safe form in which to carry money because anyone finding or stealing them would have difficulty using them. Only the purchaser who signed the checks when they bought them may negotiate them. They are convenient because they are accepted almost all over the world.

To cash a traveler's check, the purchaser countersigns it in the presence of the person who is converting it into cash or accepting it in payment of a purchase. However, with the growing availability of ATMs and the widespread acceptance of credit cards in foreign countries, the use of traveler's checks has declined greatly in recent years.

MONEY ORDERS

A money order is similar in form to a personal check and may be purchased at a bank or other third-party location. Because the funds are prepaid, much like a cashier's check, a money order is considered a more trusted method of payment than a personal check. A money order, however, is limited in maximum face value. The person who purchases a money order fills in the name of the payee, signs it as the drawer, and retains the receipt.

BAD CHECKS

bad check
A check against a bank in which the drawer has insufficient funds on deposit to cover the check or no funds at all.

forgery
The false making or alteration of a writing with the intent to defraud.

A bad check is one against a bank in which the drawer has insufficient funds on deposit to cover the check or no funds at all. Most states have statutes making a person who issues a check drawn on a bank in which they have no account guilty of the criminal offense of larceny. In some states, it is a criminal offense for a person to intentionally issue a check drawn on a bank in which that person has an account but has insufficient funds on deposit. The law in most states allows the drawer of a check a specified number of days, usually 5 or 10, to deposit funds to cover the check without incurring criminal liability.

In some states, it is a criminal offense for a person to intentionally issue a check drawn on an account with insufficient funds.
Janis Christie/Getty Images

FORGED AND RAISED CHECKS

Forgery is the act of fraudulently making or altering a note, check, draft, or some other document, causing the financial loss of another. Both the intent to defraud and the creation of a liability must be proved in order for an act to constitute forgery. A person who commits a forgery is guilty of a crime. A forged check, one signed by a person other than the drawer, and a raised check, one on which the amount has been raised by the payee or bearer, are two of the most common types of forgery.

forged check
A check that is signed by a person other than the drawer.

raised check
A check on which the amount has been raised by the payee or bearer.

Liability for Forged Checks A depositor who opens a checking account with a bank must fill out a signature card and leave it on file with the bank. The bank is then assumed to know the depositor's signature and is liable if it pays any checks on which the drawer's signature has been forged. Currently, many banks are transferring signature cards to electronic databases to allow for quick and efficient verification of signatures at all branch locations. The depositor has the responsibility of notifying the bank of a forgery within a reasonable time (or a period set by statute) after receiving their monthly statement and canceled checks (although many banks have discontinued the practice of returning the actual paper copies of checks). Failure to notify the bank in a timely manner releases the bank from liability.

Because the bank alone has the opportunity to inspect a check at the time of payment, it is liable if it pays a raised check unless the drawer, through carelessness, wrote the check in such a way that it could easily be altered. Although the drawer was careless, if the bank could have readily detected the alteration, it may still be held liable.

Courts have repeatedly held that when a check is drawn in such a careless and incomplete manner that a material alteration can easily be made without the check looking suspect, the drawer has prepared the way for forgery and is liable if it is committed.

EXAMPLE 22.6

▶ On April 15, LaRosa mailed her federal income tax forms with a check payable to the "Internal Revenue Service." She wisely did not make the check payable to "IRS." She recognized that, in the event her check became lost or stolen, "IRS" could easily be altered to "MRS" followed by the finder's or thief's surname.

POSTDATED CHECKS

postdated check
One that is dated later than the date on which the check is written.

A postdated check is one that is dated later than the date on which the check is written. A person may write a postdated check when insufficient funds are in the bank at the time the check is drawn, but the person expects to deposit sufficient funds to cover it by the date on the check. A person also may postdate a check for self-protection when some act is to be completed by the payee before the date of the check. Such a check has the effect of a promissory note at the time it is drawn. It is a mere promise to pay, at a future date, the amount specified. A postdated check may not be cashed by the payee before the date shown on the check.

By accepting a postdated check, the payee agrees not to cash it before the date indicated. However, it is important to note that a bank may honor an otherwise properly payable postdated check before its date unless the drawer has given the bank reasonable notice of the postdating [UCC 4-401]. To avoid a payee cashing a check prior to the date indicated, the drawer must notify their bank of the postdating, thus placing the bank on formal notice. If the bank cashes the postdated check after receiving formal notification of the postdated check, the bank can be held liable for any losses incurred by the drawer as a result of the premature payment.

EXAMPLE 22.7

▸ Iamani expected to travel to several foreign countries. Before leaving, he gave his college-bound son a number of postdated checks, one dated for each month of the college semester. The arrangement provided a monthly allowance without the risks associated with making one lump payment.

STOPPING PAYMENT ON CHECKS

A stop-payment order is an instruction a depositor gives to their bank not to pay a particular check. The notice can be given at any time before a check is presented for payment. If the bank does not do as requested by the drawer and cashes the check, it is liable to the depositor for the amount paid. A small charge is usually made by the bank for the service of carrying out a stop-payment order [UCC 4-403(a)].

stop-payment order
An instruction a depositor gives to their bank not to pay a particular check.

If the drawer of a check dies before the check is paid, the bank may, nevertheless, honor it. The UCC provides that the death of the drawer of a check does not revoke the authority of the bank to accept, pay, or collect an item or to account for proceeds of its collection until the bank learns of the death and has a reasonable opportunity to act. Even with knowledge of the depositor's death, a bank may pay or certify checks drawn on it before the death and for 10 days thereafter unless ordered to stop payment by a person claiming an interest in the account [UCC 4-405 (a)].

22.7 ELECTRONIC FUNDS TRANSFER SYSTEMS AND DIGITAL TRANSACTIONS

In past years it was said that the use of commercial paper would result in a "cashless" society. There is now speculation that the use of electronic funds transfers may result in a "checkless" society. Electronic funds transfer (EFT) refers to a variety of electronic applications for handling money, including peer-to-peer digital transactions using applications such as Venmo or Google Pay.

electronic funds transfer (EFT)
A variety of electronic applications for handling money.

APPLICATIONS OF ELECTRONIC FUNDS TRANSFER SYSTEMS

EFT systems offer a variety of convenient and useful applications, including ATMs, point-of-sale systems, direct deposit and withdrawal, and peer-to-peer digital transactions that allow access to a bank account, to name a few.

An ATM performs many of the functions that a teller in a bank does.
Keith Brofsky/Getty Images

Automated Teller Machines An *automated teller machine (ATM)* performs many functions that tellers in banks do. Typically, a depositor will activate the machine by inserting a plastic card encoded with information to be read by the machine, identify themself by entering a personal identification number (PIN), and choose from a menu of bank transactions. The customer can make inquiries about the status of the account, withdraw cash, make deposits, and transfer funds from one account to another. The usefulness of the customer's identification card is further enhanced when banks are linked by networks that connect different banks into a local, national, or international system. For example, a traveler in California can insert a plastic card into a Los Angeles bank's ATM and withdraw cash and have the withdrawal charged to their bank account in New York.

Banks in foreign countries are similarly linked with U.S. banks, and it is possible for a traveler in London, Paris, Rome, or Hong Kong to use an ATM to withdraw local currencies and have the amount charged to their account at the prevailing rate of exchange.

Point-of-Sale Systems A *point-of-sale system* allows a consumer to transfer funds from a bank account to the merchant's bank account to pay for merchandise purchased. The terminal is located at the merchant's place of business.

Direct Deposits and Withdrawals The electronic movement of funds from one bank account to another has many useful applications, such as when an employee authorizes an employer to deposit their wages to the employee's bank account electronically instead of paying them by cash or check.

Digital Applications Recently, a variety of applications have entered the market allowing users to digitally transfer funds in a peer-to-peer network. Examples of these applications include Venmo, Google Pay, Apple Pay, and Zelle, among others. While some transactions may use funds in the application account, many transactions rely on electronic funds transfers from financial institutions.

Other Applications of EFT Most banks provide customers with the use of an online portal through which they can access information about their accounts, transfer funds from one account to another, and authorize the bank to pay regular bills. Alternatively, bank customers may use pay-by-phone systems to telephone their bank's computer and authorize payment of certain bills and transfer funds to other accounts or to third parties.

The transfer of funds between banks is still another application of EFT. Although this has some usefulness to individual customers, it has far-reaching effects on the worldwide banking system. Because of the speed with which it processes financial settlements, EFT facilitates international trade.

Electronic Funds Transfer Act (EFTA) of 1978
A federal statute that makes it an offense to use any device that is part of an electronic transfer mechanism to steal money, goods, or services or to alter data, interrupt wire transmissions, or use stolen codes or passwords, when the purpose of such activity is to obtain something of value unlawfully.

THE ELECTRONIC FUNDS TRANSFER ACT

The most comprehensive federal legislation in this area is the Electronic Funds Transfer Act (EFTA) of 1978. The act establishes the rights, responsibilities, and liabilities of consumers in dealings with financial institutions. Because the purpose of the act is consumer protection, it does not govern transfers among financial institutions or among businesses.

The EFTA covers transactions that involve financial institutions, such as banks, and does not currently regulate transactions that are solely within a digital application, such as Venmo. However, the EFTA protections do cover transactions in a digital application that involve any transaction with a financial institution such as a bank. Thus, if a digital application draws money from a user's bank account as part of a transaction within the app, EFTA will regulate that transaction.

The EFTA limits consumer liability to $50 if the consumer notifies a card issuer within two days of learning that a card has been lost or stolen. If the customer fails to notify the issuer within two days, the consumer's liability increases to $500.

The EFTA also requires the institution to provide written receipts each time an ATM is used and monthly statements on which electronic transactions are shown.

CHAPTER SUMMARY

22.1 *Commercial paper* is a term widely used in law to describe a number of legally binding and commercially acceptable documents, such as notes, checks, and drafts, that are used to transfer money from one person to another. Commercial paper consists of contracts but differs from ordinary contracts in two ways: the presumption of consideration and assignability.

22.2 Promises to pay consist of a written note or letter in which one person promises to pay a certain amount of money to another at a definite time. Orders to pay typically use an expression such as "pay to the order of" and give commercial paper negotiability.

22.3 The parties involved in a promissory note include the maker, the comaker, and the payee. The parties involved in a draft or a check include the drawer, the payee, the drawee, the holder, and the holder in due course.

22.4 For commercial paper to be negotiable, it must be in writing and signed by the maker or drawer, contain an unconditional promise or order to pay a definite sum of money, be payable on demand or at a definite time, and be payable to order or to bearer; a draft must name or indicate the drawee with reasonable certainty.

22.5 Nonessentials for negotiability include the words "for value received" or specific mention of the consideration or its value (because consideration is assumed). Indicating dates, specifying the place of business or home of the maker of the note, and numbering the commercial paper are all nonessential to negotiability.

22.6 A certified check is a check that the bank has promised to pay when it is presented for payment. A cashier's check is issued by the cashier or other designated officer of a bank and drawn against bank funds. A traveler's check is a certified check issued in a denomination of $20 or more by certain banks, travel agencies, and financial services companies. A depositor at a bank can place a stop-payment order by giving the bank an instruction not to pay a particular check.

22.7 Electronic funds transfer systems offer convenient and useful electronic money-handling applications, including automated teller machines, point-of-sale systems, digital applications, direct deposit and withdrawals, among others.

CHAPTER TWENTY-TWO ASSESSMENT

MATCHING LEGAL TERMS

Match each of the numbered definitions with the correct term in the following list.

a. bad check	**f.** drawee	**k.** payee
b. draft or bill of exchange	**g.** drawer	**l.** postdated check
c. cashier's check	**h.** holder	**m.** promissory note
d. certified check	**i.** maker	**n.** raised check
e. check	**j.** negotiability	**o.** stop-payment order

1. A person who is in possession of commercial paper. **1.** _____
2. An instrument that is essentially a depositor's order to their bank to pay money to a party named on the instrument. **2.** _____
3. A characteristic of a credit instrument that allows its transfer from one party to another. **3.** _____
4. A type of commercial paper that is essentially a written promise to pay money to a designated party. **4.** _____
5. The party to commercial paper who makes a promise to pay. **5.** _____
6. The party to commercial paper who is designated as the one to receive payment. **6.** _____
7. The party to a draft against whom it is drawn. **7.** _____
8. The party who draws a draft against another. **8.** _____
9. A check drawn against an account with insufficient funds or against a bank in which the drawer has no funds. **9.** _____
10. A check that bears a date later than the date on which the check was written. **10.** _____
11. A check for which the bank ensures that the drawer has sufficient funds to make payment. **11.** _____
12. A notice to a bank requesting that a certain check not be paid. **12.** _____
13. A check drawn against a bank's own funds. **13.** _____
14. An unconditional written order from one party to another directing them to pay a certain sum to a third party. **14.** _____
15. A check on which the amount has been altered to increase it. **15.** _____

TRUE/FALSE QUIZ

Indicate whether each of the following statements is true or false.

16. A subsequent holder of commercial paper can have no greater rights than the original holder. **16.** _____

17. The words "pay to the order of" are required for an instrument to have negotiability. **17.** _____

18. A stale check is one that is presented six months or more after it was written or issued. **18.** _____

19. The main purpose of a certified check is to ensure that funds are on deposit to cover the check. **19.** _____

20. A bank can refuse to honor a depositor's check even if it is properly drawn and there are sufficient funds on deposit. **20.** _____

21. A postdated check is one that is written subsequent to the date appearing on the instrument. **21.** _____

22. The Uniform Commercial Code provides that a reasonable length of time for demand for payment of a check is one year. **22.** _____

MULTIPLE CHOICE QUIZ

Indicate the correct answer from the choices after each question.

23. Negotiable instruments differ from contracts because negotiable instruments (a) do not require offer and acceptance (b) presume consideration exists (c) presume competent parties (d) do not require proper form. **23.** _____

24. A promissory note documenting a debt is (a) not commercial paper (b) an order to pay, which is commercial paper (c) a promise to pay, which is commercial paper (d) a draft, which is commercial paper. **24.** _____

25. Which of the following is not a requirement for negotiability? (a) Typewritten document (b) Document signed by the maker (c) Unconditional (d) Payable on demand or at a definite time **25.** _____

26. Commercial paper that promises to pay the holder "when and if the maker wins the lottery" is (a) not negotiable because the terms are illegal (b) negotiable (c) not negotiable because it is conditional (d) not negotiable because it is a promise to pay. **26.** _____

27. The traditional instrument for transferring money in a bank account from the drawer to a drawee is a (a) check (b) promissory note (c) stock (d) traveler's check. **27.** _____

28. When a customer timely notifies their bank of a forged signature on one of their checks made payable to an innocent payee, (a) the customer is liable for the check payment (b) the bank is liable for the check payment (c) both the customer and the bank are liable for the check payment (d) neither the bank nor the customer are liable for the check payment. **28.** _____

29. Digital peer-to-peer transactions using apps such as Venmo (a) are never subject to EFTA regulation (b) are always subject to EFTA regulation (c) are subject to EFTA regulation when the transaction accesses a financial institution account (d) are subject to EFTA regulation when they are more than $500. **29.** _____

DISCUSSION QUESTIONS

Answer the following questions and discuss them in class.

30. Explain the two ways in which commercial paper differs from ordinary contracts.

31. Discuss the major differences between the two basic kinds of commercial paper: promises to pay (notes) and orders to pay (checks and drafts).

32. If a checkbook is stolen and checks are written by the thief and cashed, who bears the loss?

33. Discuss the law and liability as applied to bad checks and to forged, raised, and materially altered checks.

34. Discuss circumstances that might require stopping payment on a check.

35. What are the benefits and drawbacks to the consumer of using electronic funds transfer systems, digital applications, automated teller machines, and point-of-sale systems?

THINKING CRITICALLY ABOUT THE LAW

Answer the following questions, which require you to think critically about the legal principles that you learned in this chapter.

36. Financial and Banking System The complexity of the financial and banking system is a bit staggering. What might be done to simplify the system for consumers?

____

____

37. Traveler's Checks Issuers of traveler's checks encourage buyers to retain unused checks as a form of "emergency fund." Given other methods of accessing funds, are traveler's checks still relevant?

____

____

38. Postdated Checks Should the practice of writing postdated checks be illegal?

____

____

39. A Question of Ethics The practice of floating provides an opportunity to "borrow" interest-free by cashing a check for which there are inadequate funds on deposit. If the check writer makes a deposit to cover the check in time to avoid a "bounced check" charge, is this practice ethical?

____

____

40. Digital Applications Should digital applications such as Venmo be regulated as an electronic funds transfer? Why or why not?

____

____

CASE QUESTIONS

Study each of the following cases. Answer the questions that follow with Yes or No.

41. Safety of Funds Bolena sold some valuable jewelry to McGovern, whom she had never met before. She was concerned about whether McGovern's check was good and whether there were sufficient funds on deposit in McGovern's account to cover it.

a. Would a certified check relieve Bolena's concern? **a.** _____

b. Would a cashier's check relieve Bolena's concern? **b.** _____

c. Would McGovern's promissory note give greater security? **c.** _____

42. Parties to a Check Neville had a checking account at her local bank. She wrote out a check to Shin, a maintenance worker, in payment for services he had provided.

a. Is Neville the drawee? **a.** _____

b. Is Shin the drawee? **b.** _____

c. Is her bank the drawee? **c.** _____

43. Safety of Traveler's Funds Hausen was planning an extensive trip to Europe and wanted to avoid carrying large sums of cash.

a. Would you advise Hausen to carry certified checks? **a.** _____

b. Would you advise Hausen to carry traveler's checks? **b.** _____

c. Would you advise Hausen to charge his purchases to his credit card? **c.** _____

44. Postdated Checks Tandy wanted to issue a check in payment of her rent, due June 1, before leaving on a vacation trip on May 15, but she did not have sufficient funds on deposit in her checking account. Her employer automatically deposits her paycheck to her bank on the last day of each month.

a. Should Tandy issue an antedated check? **a.** _____

b. Should Tandy issue a postdated check? **b.** _____

c. Should Tandy borrow money from the bank to pay the rent? **c.** _____

CASE ANALYSIS

Study each of the following cases carefully. Briefly state the principle of law and your decision.

45. Negotiablity of Note Grove Hotel hired Fortas, an electrical contractor, and paid him with a promissory note for $3,400. The note stated that it was "with interest at prevailing bank rates." Did the stipulation about interest rates affect the negotiability of the note?

Principle of Law:

____

____

Decision:

____

____

46. Postdated Check Graver gave Srau a postdated check for $2,000 as a deposit on a sailboat as acceptance of Srau's offer to sell the boat. Later, after Srau sold the boat to someone else, he claimed that the check was not really part of a binding contract because it was postdated and thus created a qualified acceptance. Did postdating the check affect its negotiability?

Principle of Law:

Decision:

47. Refusal to Pay Draft Higgins was a used car dealer. He purchased a Corvette, giving the seller a draft drawn by him on the First State Bank of Albertville in the amount of $8,115. This draft was later presented by the seller to the bank for payment. Meanwhile, Higgins sold the car to Holsonback, who paid with a draft on the Albertville National Bank in the amount of $8,225. When the Albertville National Bank requested Holsonback to pay the draft, he refused, claiming that there was a problem with the certificate of title. The issue was raised as to whether, under the Uniform Commercial Code, negotiable instruments can be issued conditionally. Did Holsonback have the right to withhold payment on the draft because of the problem with the certificate of title? [*Holsonback v. First State Bank,* 394 So. 2d 381 (Alabama)]

Principle of Law:

Decision:

48. Negotiable Instruments After Balkus died intestate, included among Balkus's possessions were bank deposit slips for a savings account owned by him. On each deposit slip was a handwritten notation, "Payable to Ann Balkus Vesley [Balkus's sister] on P.O.D. the full amount and other deposits." Each slip was dated and signed by Balkus. His sister claimed that she was entitled to the money because "P.O.D." meant "payable on death," the deposits were negotiable instruments, and she was a holder in due course. Are the deposit slips negotiable instruments under the Uniform Commercial Code? [*Estate of Balkus,* 381 N.W.2d 593 (Wisconsin)]

Principle of Law:

Decision:

LEGAL RESEARCH

Complete the following activities. Share your findings with the class.

49. Working in Teams Working in teams of three or four, interview personnel at your local bank to check liability for lost or stolen bank-issued ATM, credit, and debit cards.

50. Using Technology Using the Internet and search engines, investigate legal safeguards to protect electronic transfer of funds.

chapter 23 Transfer and Discharge of Commercial Paper

LEARNING OUTCOMES

After studying this chapter and completing the assessment, you will be able to

23.1 Identify the purpose of endorsing commercial paper.

23.2 Describe the four kinds of endorsements.

23.3 Explain the obligations, warranties, and discharge of endorsers and specify the five warranties assumed to exist in endorsements.

23.4 Describe the four requirements that qualify a person as a holder in due course.

23.5 Distinguish between personal and real defenses against payment of commercial paper and list the types of defenses in each case.

23.6 Explain when presentment of commercial paper occurs.

23.7 Describe when commercial paper is deemed dishonored.

TRANSFER AND DISCHARGE OF COMMERCIAL PAPER

"By the way, lunch is on me. I just cashed my Nana's birthday checks."

Jerry Seinfeld, from the TV series *Seinfeld*

James Lauritz/Getty Images

LEGAL terms

- endorsement
- endorser
- endorsee
- blank endorsement
- bearer instrument
- special endorsement
- restrictive endorsement
- qualified endorsement
- without recourse
- holder in due course
- personal defense
- real defense
- counterclaim
- material alteration
- presentment
- dishonored

23.1 ENDORSING COMMERCIAL PAPER

One of the valuable characteristics of commercial paper in our personal and business lives is the ease with which it can be transferred from one person to another and the ease with which final settlements can be made. This chapter considers the various legal principles and procedures that are used to transfer and discharge commercial paper.

endorsement
When the holder of commercial paper signs their name, with or without words, on the back of an instrument to transfer ownership to another.

When the holder of commercial paper signs their name, with or without other words, on the back of the instrument, this writing is referred to as an endorsement. The effect of an endorsement is to transfer ownership of commercial paper to another. When the transferee (the person to whom the instrument is transferred) receives the endorsed instrument, that person becomes the new holder, or owner, of it. This is what is meant when we say that a paper has been negotiated. In this way, commercial paper takes the place of money for the payment of debts and purchase of goods and services.

EXAMPLE 23.1

Hatfield received a check from a customer that read in part, "Pay to the order of Harriet Hatfield.. . ." Hatfield signed her name on the back of the check and gave it to Tai. By so doing she transferred (negotiated) the check to Tai, who then became the holder, or owner, of the check.

endorser
The person who signs their name to a negotiable instrument.

endorsee
The person to whom a negotiable instrument is transferred.

The endorser of an instrument is the person who signs their name on it; the endorsee is the person to whom the instrument is transferred.

Commercial paper is usually endorsed on the back. The endorsement may be written by hand, printed, or even stamped. To be valid, the endorsement must be written for the entire amount stated in the instrument. Attempting to transfer only part of the face value of the negotiable instrument by endorsement invalidates the negotiation.

EXAMPLE 23.2

Canaan used a check that he had received as a birthday gift to pay for purchases at a retail store. He endorsed the check by printing his name in green ink on the back of it. The merchant refused to accept it, claiming that the endorsement should have been script-written in black or blue ink. The merchant was incorrect. The check was properly endorsed. The intent to transfer ownership was indicated by Canaan's signature. The fact that the signature was printed and in green ink did not affect its validity.

23.2 KINDS OF ENDORSEMENTS

Any of the following endorsements may be used in transferring commercial paper. The choice of endorsement will depend on the purpose of the transfer. Figure 23.1 shows an example of a blank endorsement of commercial paper.

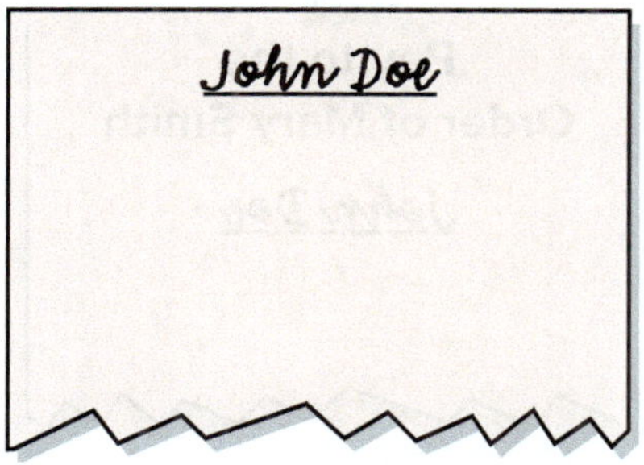

FIGURE 23.1 Example of a Blank Endorsement

BLANK ENDORSEMENT

A blank endorsement is an endorsement where the name of the payee is written by the payee on the back of a negotiable instrument. According to the Uniform Commercial Code (UCC), an instrument endorsed in blank is payable to anyone who is in possession of it; it is called a bearer instrument.

blank endorsement An endorsement in which the name of the payee is written by the payee on the back of a negotiable instrument.

bearer instrument An instrument that is payable to anyone who is in possession of it.

Technically, an instrument made payable to bearer is negotiable by delivery only; that is, the bearer is not required to endorse it. As a practical matter, however, banks require the bearer of such an instrument to sign it on the reverse side for purposes of identification.

The UCC also provides that "where an instrument is made payable to a person under a misspelled name or one other than his own, he may endorse in that name or his own or both; but signature in both names may be required by a person paying or giving value for the instrument" (UCC 3-204).

EXAMPLE 23.3

- Newson received a check with a blank endorsement from a customer. Because of the blank endorsement, the check is a bearer instrument. Newson can negotiate it merely by delivery. But in all probability, anyone accepting the check from Newson would insist that she endorse it as well. The transferee would require this endorsement so that if the check proved to be bad and the bank refused to honor it, Newson would have to pay.

SPECIAL ENDORSEMENT

A special endorsement, or *full endorsement,* is one in which the payee specifies the person to whom, or to whose order, it is to be paid. The instrument can be further negotiated only when it has been endorsed by the specified person. Figure 23.2 shows an example of a special endorsement of commercial paper.

special endorsement An endorsement in which the payee specifies the person to whom, or to whose order, it is to be paid.

EXAMPLE 23.4

- Porenta requested that a friend, Hartley, cash a dividend check for her. Hartley gave Porenta the money and accepted her check, which Porenta had endorsed in blank. Hartley had just moved to another city and decided to use the check to open a new account at a local bank. To protect himself in case he lost the check before he could open the account, he wrote over Porenta's signature endorsement, "Pay to the order of Thomas Hartley." He had the right to do so and was probably acting prudently.

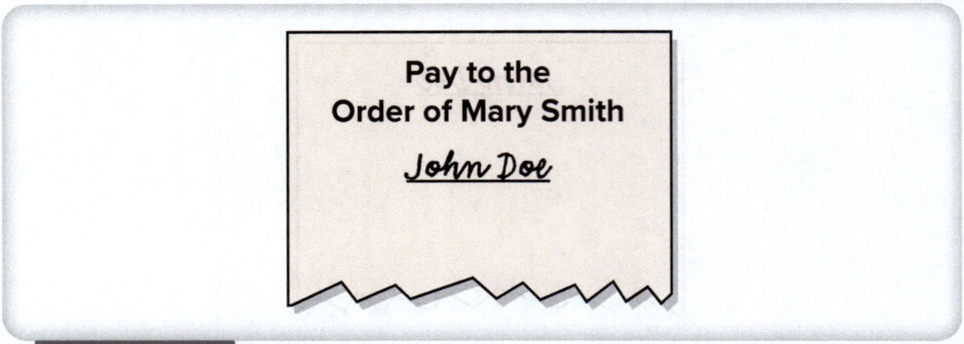

FIGURE 23.2 Example of a Special Endorsement

The UCC specifically provides that the holder of an instrument may convert a blank endorsement into a full endorsement by writing "Pay to the order of [transferee's or holder's name]" over the endorser's signature (UCC 3-205). In Example 23.4, Hartley is the endorsee (transferee) and Porenta is the endorser (transferor).

RESTRICTIVE ENDORSEMENT

restrictive endorsement An endorsement with a signature to which words have been added restricting further endorsement of the instrument.

A restrictive endorsement is a signature to which words have been added restricting the further endorsement of the instrument. According to the UCC, however, a restrictive endorsement does not prevent further transfer or negotiation of the instrument. The holder has the rights of any purchaser of commercial paper except that they must do with the instrument as the endorsement directs (UCC 3-206).

The phrases "For deposit only" and "Pay to [endorser's bank] for deposit only" are examples of restrictive endorsements that are often used when deposits are sent to a bank by messenger or by mail. "Pay Herbert Fredericks only" and "Pay Herbert Fredericks, for collection" are other examples of restrictive endorsements. Figures 23.3 and 23.4 show examples of restrictive endorsement and qualified endorsement, respectively.

EXAMPLE 23.5

While on vacation, Leonard received a check in payment of a debt. Because it would be several weeks before she could deposit it personally in her bank, she endorsed it "For deposit only—Patricia Leonard" and mailed it to the bank. If the check should be lost in the mail or stolen, it could not be cashed by the holder.

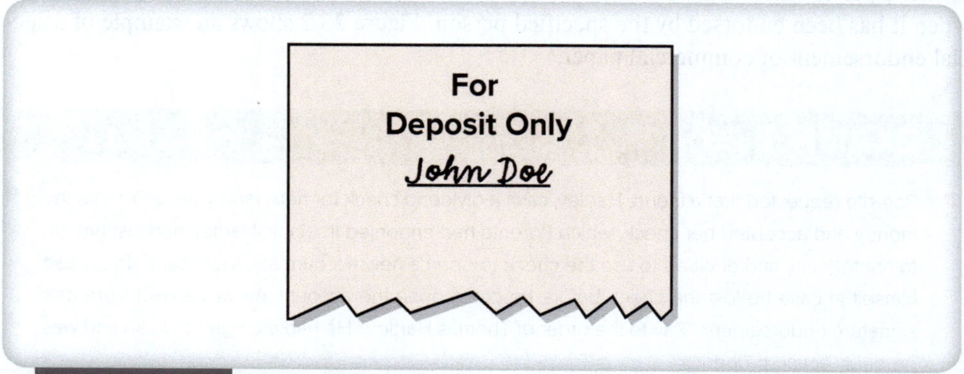

FIGURE 23.3 Example of a Restrictive Endorsement

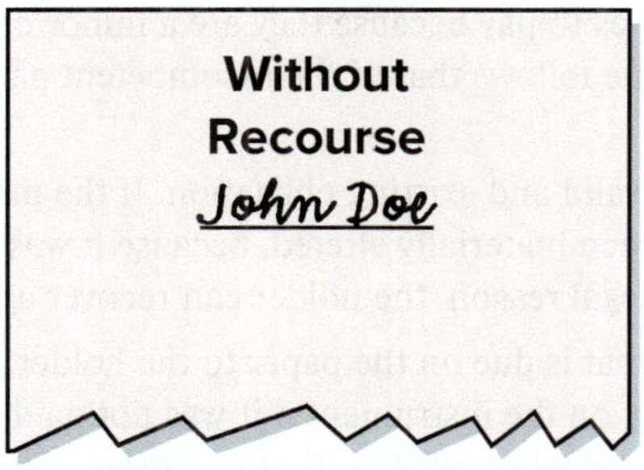

FIGURE 23.4 Example of a Qualified Endorsement

QUALIFIED ENDORSEMENT

In the case of a **qualified endorsement**, the endorser avoids liability for payment even if the maker or drawer defaults on the instrument. A qualified endorsement, using a phrase such as "**without recourse**," can be used together with a blank endorsement or special endorsement. The use of a qualified endorsement does not affect the negotiability of an instrument.

qualified endorsement
An endorsement in which the endorser avoids liability for payment even if the maker or drawer defaults on the instrument.

without recourse
A phrase used to indicate a qualified endorsement.

EXAMPLE 23.6

▶ Mustafa, the owner of a furniture store, received a $1,000 promissory note from Huff in payment for merchandise purchased. Worried that Huff might not have sufficient funds to pay the note when it was due, Mustafa offered the note to Casler in payment of a debt at a 25 percent discount on the note on condition that Mustafa be permitted to include the words "without recourse" in her endorsement. If Casler were to accept the offer and Huff failed to pay the note at maturity, Casler could look only to Huff, not to Mustafa, for payment. Mustafa's qualified endorsement would pass title to the note and relieve her of all liability on the note.

23.3 OBLIGATIONS, WARRANTIES, AND DISCHARGE OF ENDORSERS

The endorser of a promissory note or the drawer or endorser of a draft or check is liable for the payment of the instrument if the following conditions are met:

1. It has been properly presented for payment to the maker of the note or to the drawee of the draft or check.
2. Payment has been refused by the maker or drawee.
3. Notice of the refusal has been given to the drawer or endorser.

To ensure the negotiability of commercial paper, the UCC assumes the following warranties in every endorsement (UCC 3-417):

1. The instrument is genuine. If the maker's or drawer's signature is forged, the endorser is liable to a subsequent holder for payment of the paper.

2. All prior parties were qualified to enter into a legally binding contract. If the maker or a prior endorser refuses to pay because they are a minor or otherwise incompetent, any endorser whose name follows that of the incompetent party is liable for payment of the instrument.
3. The instrument is for a valid and existing obligation. If the maker refuses to pay because the paper has been materially altered, because it was given for a gambling debt, or for any other illegal reason, the holder can recover against the endorser.
4. The endorser will pay what is due on the paper to the holder or to any subsequent endorser who had to pay on the instrument if it was not paid when presented for payment. Only an endorser who wrote "without recourse" above their name is exempt from this warranty.
5. The endorser is the true owner of the paper (has good title to it). If they found or stole the paper and transferred it to another by endorsement, the endorser is liable for any loss suffered by the endorsee.

EXAMPLE 23.7

John Lynch received a check in the mail intended for James Lynch, who lived in the same building. Even though John knew that the check was not intended for him, he endorsed it and gave it to a merchant in payment for goods he had purchased. After the merchant deposited the check in the bank, he was informed that payment had been stopped by the drawer. The merchant can hold John Lynch liable for the amount on the basis of Lynch's implied warranty that he had good title to the instrument.

An endorser of an instrument is released from liability by (1) any act that completes the negotiation of the instrument, such as payment; (2) the release of a prior party's obligation or the release of the debtor; (3) the intentional cancellation of the endorser's signature by the holder; (4) a valid tender of payment by a prior party; or (5) an agreement binding on the holder to extend the due date of the instrument.

EXAMPLE 23.8

Kappo executed a note to Wenner in payment of a debt. Wenner then negotiated the note to Wise by endorsing it. When Wise presented the note at maturity for payment, Kappo told him that she would pay the note in full if given two weeks' more time. If Wise were to agree to Kappo's request for an extension of time, Wenner would be discharged from liability.

holder in due course
A holder who has taken a negotiable instrument in good faith and for value, before maturity, and without actual or constructive notice of any defects in the instrument.

23.4 HOLDER IN DUE COURSE

A holder in due course of commercial paper, according to the UCC (UCC 3-302), is one who has taken the paper in good faith and for value, before maturity, and without actual or constructive notice (notice inferred from circumstances) of any defects in the instrument.

They are sometimes called a "*bona fide* holder for value without notice" (*bona fide* is a Latin term meaning "in good faith").

For a person to be a holder in due course of a negotiable instrument, the following must be true:

1. The paper must be complete and regular on its face. If it is apparent from the appearance of the instrument that it has been altered, the holder is not considered a holder in due course.
2. The paper must have been acquired on or before the due date. The fact that commercial paper is past due is considered notice that something might be wrong with it. According to the UCC, if the buyer of overdue negotiable paper did not have notice or knowledge that it was overdue, they could be a holder in due course. However, a person who accepted a demand instrument (a promissory note payable upon demand) later than a reasonable length of time after it was issued is considered to have been aware that it was overdue (in the case of a check, 30 days is deemed to be a reasonable time).
3. The paper must have been acquired for a valuable consideration. The consideration may have been the reasonable value of the instrument itself, or it may have been any detriment, injury, or loss suffered by the holder in taking the instrument.
4. The paper must have been taken in good faith and for value. A person who has acquired a commercial paper for a sum much smaller than the face value of the instrument appears to have acted in bad faith unless the person can show that they acted prudently by checking into the reasons for the low value before accepting it.

Any holder of an instrument, other than the payee, who might know of a fraud or learn of it before negotiating the instrument to a holder in due course cannot later become a similar holder, even if title to the instrument is transferred to them from the holder in due course.

EXAMPLE 23.9

▶ Svensson had a $500 note that had been made payable to him by Pappas. He offered the note to Manchester at a 60 percent discount. Simple prudence suggests that Manchester should have tried to find out why Svensson was willing to sell the note at such a low price—or large discount. In short, she should have looked for a defect in the instrument. Without such a search, she would not be considered a holder in due course. If Manchester transferred the instrument before maturity to Cho, who paid value for it, not knowing that Manchester had purchased the note at a 60 percent discount, then Cho would be considered a holder in due course. However, if Manchester later reacquired the note from Cho, Manchester would not be considered a holder in due course because one cannot benefit from one's own wrongdoing.

23.5 DEFENSES AGAINST PAYMENT OF COMMERCIAL PAPER

A defense against payment of commercial paper that may be used against any party except a holder in due course is called personal defense. A defense against payment of commercial paper that claims the instrument was void from the beginning is known as real defense or *absolute defense*. Real defenses may be used by the maker or drawer against any party to a paper, including a holder in due course.

personal defense
A defense against payment of commercial paper that may be used against any party except a holder in due course.

real defense
A defense against payment of commercial paper that claims the instrument was void from the beginning.

PERSONAL DEFENSES

Personal defenses against payment of commercial paper relate to the acts or circumstances leading to the issue of the paper rather than to the paper itself. These defenses include lack of consideration; fraud, duress, or undue influence; breach of warranty; nondelivery of a completed instrument; nondelivery of an incomplete instrument; payment before maturity; and counterclaim.

Lack of Consideration Although consideration is presumed to have been given for a promissory note, draft, or check, proof by the maker or drawer that consideration was in fact lacking can be used as a defense against paying the instrument.

EXAMPLE 23.10

▶ Moser gave his brother a 90-day promissory note as a gift. Before the maturity date, he changed his mind, and when the note came due, Moser refused to pay it. If sued on the note by his brother, Moser could avoid paying it by proving lack of consideration as a personal defense.

Fraud, Duress, or Undue Influence If fraud, duress (threat of harm to person or property), or undue influence was used to induce a person to sign a negotiable instrument, the injured person may use any of these as a personal defense against any person who is not a holder in due course.

The UCC provides that, unless a person who takes an instrument has the rights of a holder in due course, their claim for payment is subject to "all defenses of a party which would be available in an action on a simple contract" (UCC 3-306).

Breach of Warranty In the event of a breach of warranty, the injured party may assert the breach as a personal defense. If, for example, payment for plumbing repairs is made by check, but the repairs do not meet applicable building codes, the drawer may claim the breach of warranty as a personal defense.

Nondelivery of a Completed Instrument Sometimes, a completed negotiable instrument comes into the possession of an immediate party (the payee indicated on the instrument) before the maker or drawer has delivered it. In such a case, the payee cannot collect on the instrument. If the payee, however, negotiates the instrument to a holder in due course, the new holder in due course can enforce payment by the maker. Thus the personal defense of nondelivery is not valid against a holder in due course.

EXAMPLE 23.11

▶ Tomar, a wholesaler, agreed to accept Brinner's note in payment for goods. When Tomar went to Brinner's office to collect the note, no one was there, but on Brinner's desk Tomar found the completed note made out to him. If Tomar took the note without waiting for delivery by Brinner, he could not enforce payment if Brinner refused to pay it. But if Tomar sold the note to Nehru, who becomes a holder in due course, Nehru could collect on the instrument from Brinner, who in turn could sue Tomar.

Nondelivery of an Incomplete Instrument Under the UCC, no distinction is made between lack of delivery of a completed and an incomplete instrument. In either case, it is treated as a personal defense, not effective against a holder in due course (UCC 3-306).

Payment before Maturity Suppose the maker of an instrument paid it before maturity but failed to get the paper itself back. In this case, they would be discharged from further liability to immediate parties (the payees) but would remain liable on the note if it should come into possession of a holder in due course.

counterclaim
When the maker of a note or other drawer or acceptor of a bill of exchange may deduct from the amount demanded by an immediate party any amounts owed them by the payee.

Counterclaim The maker of a note or the drawer of a check or draft may deduct from the amount demanded by an immediate party any amounts owed them by the payee. This type of personal defense is called a counterclaim.

Commercial paper is void when the signature of the maker or drawer has been forged.
James Lauritz/Getty Images

REAL DEFENSES

Real, or absolute, defenses to payment of commercial paper, good against anyone, including holders in due course, include forgery, material alteration, lack of intent to execute commercial paper, incapacity of the parties to contract, bankruptcy, and illegality created by law.

Forgery Commercial paper on which the signature of the maker or drawer has been forged is void. Even a holder in due course cannot collect on an instrument if they obtained title after a forgery. Endorsers of a forged instrument who negotiate the paper are liable. The reason is there are implied warranties of endorsers that an instrument is genuine, that the endorser has good title to it, and that all prior parties had the capacity to contract.

EXAMPLE 23.12

▶ Misuki found a blank check that belonged to Pierce, a neighbor. Misuki filled out the check for $500, made it payable to himself, and signed Pierce's name—a forgery. He then endorsed the check and transferred it to Bader with a special endorsement in payment of a debt. Bader endorsed the check and cashed the check at Pierce's bank. When the forgery is discovered—as it will be when Pierce reviews his monthly statement—the bank must return the money to Pierce's account because it cashed a forged check. It will, however, look to the endorsers, Misuki and Bader, to recover the loss.

Material Alteration Any change made to an instrument that affects the rights of the parties is called a material alteration. The maker or drawer is responsible to pay the paper according to its original terms, not the altered terms. Changing the place or date of paper, or adding or changing an interest rate, are examples of material alterations.

material alteration
A deliberate change or alteration of an important element in a written contract that affects the rights or obligations of the parties.

The UCC provides that the loss falls upon the party whose conduct in signing a blank instrument made the fraud possible–that is, whose negligence or recklessness invited alterations by subsequent holders (UCC 3-406).

EXAMPLE 23.13

Stirks used a check to pay Moore, a merchant, $100 for a purchase. Moore raised the amount of the check to $1,000, endorsed it, and cashed it at a bank other than the one on which it was drawn. When the check was returned to Stirks's bank for collection, the bank noted the alteration and refused to pay it. The bank that cashed the check can hold Stirks liable only for $100, the amount for which the check was originally drawn.

Lack of Intent to Execute Commercial Paper A person cannot be held liable, even by a holder in due course, if they sign an instrument that is apparently not negotiable and the paper is later fraudulently converted into a negotiable instrument. Fraud in executing an instrument is a real, or absolute, defense, but fraud related to the circumstances surrounding the issuing of a paper and not to the paper itself is a personal defense.

EXAMPLE 23.14

Jackson believed she was signing a receipt for the delivery of an appliance when, in fact, she was signing a note. If she can prove that she had not been negligent and that she was tricked into signing the paper, she may use fraud in the execution of the instrument as a defense. This real, or absolute, defense is good against any holder, including a holder in due course. If, instead, Jackson had paid for merchandise with a note and later found that the goods were not of the quality contracted for, her defense against payment would be fraud in the making of the contract. This is a personal defense valid against anyone except a holder in due course.

Incapacity of Parties to Contract An incompetent person, such as a minor, who makes, signs, and delivers a negotiable instrument cannot be held liable for its payment. The real defense of incompetence is valid against anyone, even a holder in due course.

Discharge in Bankruptcy If a bankruptcy court discharges a debt secured by commercial paper during a bankruptcy proceeding, the maker of the commercial paper is released from all liability associated with it (see Chapter 21). In such a case, the maker of the commercial paper has a real defense against payment.

Illegality Created by Law Often, state statutes expressly declare that commercial paper given for gambling transactions or at usurious rates of interest is void. Paper issued under such circumstances is unenforceable, no matter who holds it.

23.6 PRESENTMENT OF COMMERCIAL PAPER

In order to establish the liability of the endorsers of commercial paper, the holder must engage in what is known as presentment: tendering a note to the maker and demanding its payment, or showing a draft or check to the drawer and requesting its acceptance or payment, on or after the maturity date at the place stated in the instrument.

presentment
When the holder of a note tenders it to the maker and demands payment, or shows drafts to the drawer and requests its acceptance or payment, on or after the maturity date at the place stated in the instrument.

The UCC states that presentment may be made by mail or at the place of acceptance of payment specified in the instrument. If no place is specified, presentment may be made at the place of business or residence of the party who is to accept or pay. Because the liability of the maker of commercial paper is absolute, presentment, and demand are not necessary to bind them.

Commercial paper must be presented for payment during business hours on the due date given on the instrument. A demand instrument such as a note or check must be presented for payment within a reasonable time after the date of issue.

EXAMPLE 23.15

▶ Chilton bought merchandise from Ramos and paid with a 60-day note. Ramos negotiated the note to Brill for value. Brill presented the note to Chilton for payment several weeks after the maturity date. When Chilton refused to pay, Brill attempted to collect from Ramos. She could not do so. Ramos, as an endorser, was released from liability when the holder, Brill, failed to present the note for payment when it became due.

23.7 DISHONOR OF COMMERCIAL PAPER

A negotiable instrument is considered dishonored if it is not accepted when presented, if it is not paid when presented for payment at maturity, or if presentment is excused or waived and the instrument is past due and unpaid.

dishonored
When a negotiable instrument is not accepted when presented for acceptance, it is not paid when presented for payment at maturity, presentment is excused or waived, or the instrument is past due and unpaid.

The holder of dishonored commercial paper must give notice of the dishonor immediately—a bank by midnight, and by any other person by midnight of the third business day after dishonor—to the drawer and to all endorsers in order to hold them liable on the instrument. Any drawer or endorser to whom such notice is not given is relieved from liability (UCC 3-503).

CHAPTER SUMMARY

23.1 The purpose of an endorsement is to transfer ownership of commercial paper from one party to another. When the transferee receives the endorsed instrument, that person becomes the new holder, or owner, of it.

23.2 There are four kinds of endorsements: (a) a blank endorsement is one in which the name of the payee is written by the payee on the back of a negotiable instrument; (b) a special endorsement is one in which the payee specifies the person to whom, or to whose order, it is to be paid; (c) a restrictive endorsement is a signature in which words have been added restricting further endorsement of the instrument; and (d) a qualified endorsement is one in which the endorser avoids liability for payment even if the maker or drawer defaults on the instrument.

23.3 The endorser of a promissory note or the drawer or endorser of a draft or check is liable for the payment of the instrument provided it has been properly presented for payment to the maker of the note or to the drawee of the draft or check, payment has been refused by the maker or drawee, and notice of the refusal has been given to the drawer or endorser. The UCC assumes the following five warranties exist in every endorsement: (a) the instrument is genuine, (b) all prior parties were qualified to enter into a legally binding contract, (c) the instrument is for a valid and existing obligation, (d) the endorser will pay what is due on the paper to the holder or to any subsequent endorser who had to pay on the instrument if it was not paid when presented for payment, and (e) the endorser is the true owner of the paper.

23.4 The four requirements for being a holder in due course are (a) the paper must be complete and regular on its face, (b) the paper must have been acquired on or before the due date, (c) the paper must have been acquired for a valuable consideration, and (d) the paper must have been taken in good faith and for value.

23.5 Personal defenses against payment of commercial paper can be used against anyone except a holder in due course; real defenses can be used against any party, including a holder in due course. Personal defenses include lack of consideration; fraud, duress, and undue influence; breach of warranty; nondelivery of a completed instrument; nondelivery of an incomplete instrument; payment before maturity; and counterclaim. Real defenses include forgery, material alteration, lack of intent to execute commercial paper, incapacity of the parties to contract, bankruptcy, and illegality created by statute.

23.6 Presentment of commercial paper occurs when a holder tenders a note to the maker and demands its payment, or shows a draft to the drawer and requests its acceptance or payment, on or after the maturity date at the place stated in the instrument.

23.7 A commercial paper is deemed dishonored if it is not accepted when presented for acceptance, it is not paid when presented for payment at maturity, or if presentment is excused or waived and the instrument is past due and unpaid.

CHAPTER TWENTY-THREE ASSESSMENT

MATCHING LEGAL TERMS

Match each of the numbered definitions with the correct term in the following list.

a. bearer instrument
b. blank endorsement
c. counterclaim
d. dishonored
e. holder in due course
f. endorsee
g. endorsement
h. endorser
i. material alteration
j. personal defense
k. qualified endorsement
l. presentment
m. real, or absolute, defense
n. restrictive endorsement
o. special, or full, endorsement

1. An endorsement by which the payee of an instrument transfers it to the order of another person. **1.** _____
2. The person who writes their name on the back of an instrument. **2.** _____

3. The person to whom an instrument is transferred. **3.** _____

4. The practice of the holder of commercial paper of writing their name on the back of an instrument. **4.** _____

5. An endorsement that transfers an instrument but limits the liability of the endorser. **5.** _____

6. An endorsement that transfers an instrument to whoever has possession of it. **6.** _____

7. An endorsement that limits the transfer of an instrument to a particular person or for a particular purpose. **7.** _____

8. A person who has accepted commercial paper in good faith, for value, before maturity, and without notice of any defects in the instrument. **8.** _____

9. A claim for not paying commercial paper that relates to the circumstances leading to the issuing of the paper rather than to the paper itself. **9.** _____

10. A claim that states that the instrument was void from the beginning. **10.** _____

11. The deduction of amounts owed claimed by the maker of a note or the drawer of a draft from the amount demanded by an immediate party. **11.** _____

12. Important changes to an instrument that affect the rights of the parties. **12.** _____

13. Exhibiting a note to its maker and demanding payment. **13.** _____

14. Refusal to pay a commercial paper. **14.** _____

15. An instrument that is payable to anyone who is in possession of it. **15.** _____

TRUE/FALSE QUIZ

Indicate whether each of the following statements is true or false.

16. The writing a holder puts on the back of a negotiable instrument is known as a negotiation. **16.** _____

17. An endorsement of an instrument must be for the entire amount. **17.** _____

18. The Uniform Commercial Code attributes an implied warranty to an endorsed instrument that the signature is genuine. **18.** _____

19. An endorser of an instrument is released from liability by any act that discharges the instrument, such as payment. **19.** _____

20. If it is apparent that an instrument has been altered, the holder is not a holder in due course. **20.** _____

21. An instrument endorsed in blank is payable to anyone in possession of it. **21.** _____

22. An instrument with a special, or full, endorsement is payable only to the person named in the endorsement. **22.** _____

23. A restrictive endorsement prevents further negotiation of an instrument. **23.** _____

24. If an instrument endorsed in blank is lost, the finder may not legally negotiate it. **24.** _____

25. The words “For deposit only” constitute a blank endorsement. **25.** _____

MULTIPLE CHOICE QUIZ

Indicate the correct answer from the choices after each question.

26. "Pay to the order of Jane Smith" written on the back of commercial paper is a (a) special endorsement (b) blank endorsement (c) restrictive endorsement (d) qualified endorsement. **26.** ____

27. "For Deposit Only" with the drawer's name written on the back of commercial paper is a (a) special endorsement (b) blank endorsement (c) restrictive endorsement (d) qualified endorsement. **27.** ____

28. A person endorses a check by signing their name on the back of the check with no other language. However, the check was forged by the original maker, who was not the endorser. In this case, (a) the endorser is not liable to the subsequent holder (b) the subsequent holder is liable to the endorser (c) the endorser is liable to the subsequent holder (d) none of the above. **28.** ____

29. A holder of a negotiable instrument is given commercial paper as a birthday present from a friend. In this case, the holder is (a) a holder in due course (b) not a holder in due course because the instrument is not complete (c) not a holder in due course because the instrument is overdue (d) not a holder in due course because it was not acquired for valuable consideration. **29.** ____

30. After presentment of commercial paper for payment, the payor refuses to pay because the original transaction was based on fraud. In this case, (a) the payor is correct regardless of the holder status (b) the payor is correct if the holder is a holder in due course (c) the payor is correct unless the holder is a holder in due course (d) none of the above. **30.** ____

31. After presentment of commercial paper for payment, the payor refuses to pay based on forgery and material alteration of the document. In this case, (a) the payor is correct regardless of holder status (b) the payor is correct if the holder is a holder in due course (c) the payor is correct unless the holder is a holder in due course (d) none of the above. **31.** ____

DISCUSSION QUESTIONS

Answer the following questions and discuss them in class.

32. Why would a person who receives a check want to limit its negotiability, and how would this be done?

____

____

33. Under what circumstances are a minor's checks valid?

____

____

34. What kind of an endorsement allows an endorser to avoid liability for payment even if the maker or drawer defaults on the instrument?

35. Describe the defenses against payment of commercial paper that are concerned with the acts or circumstances leading to the issue of the paper rather than to the paper itself.

36. What is the difference between a contract and a negotiable instrument as it concerns consideration?

37. State statutes usually declare that commercial paper that is given for gambling transactions or at usurious rates of interest is void. Can a person pay off an illegal gambling debt by check?

THINKING CRITICALLY ABOUT THE LAW

Answer the following questions, which require you to think critically about the legal principles that you learned in this chapter.

38. Delivery of Negotiable Instrument If all other requirements of a negotiable instrument have been met except delivery, should payment depend on delivery, and, if so, why?

39. Liability of Endorser The innocent endorser of a forged instrument who negotiates commercial paper is liable. Is this fair?

40. Endorsements Should an endorsement written in pencil be legally acceptable? Why or why not?

41. Material Alteration How do significant changes made in an instrument affect the rights of the parties to it?

____

____

42. A Question of Ethics Is it ethical for direct mail marketers to include a document that resembles a check made payable to the addressee, when closer examination reveals certain conditions such as "good only toward the purchase of . . ."?

____

____

CASE QUESTIONS

Study each of the following cases. Answer the questions that follow with Yes or No.

43. Raised Check Sikonen gave his check for $5 to Rivera, but in so doing he neglected to fill in the customary wavy line following the amount in the words. Rivera endorsed the check to Montana, who easily increased the amount to $500 and then presented the check to Sikonen's bank for payment.

a. Will Sikonen be required to bear the loss because of his negligence in writing the check? **a.** _____

b. Will Rivera have to bear the loss because of his negligence in endorsing a check that could be so easily altered? **b.** _____

c. Will the bank be required to bear the $495 loss for cashing an altered check? **c.** _____

44. Defenses Laredo found a checkbook belonging to Waldron, drew a check, signed Waldron's name to it, and gave it to Kelly. The payee, Kelly, endorsed the check to a holder in due course, who presented it to the bank for payment. The bank refused to pay the check.

a. Will Waldron's account be charged for the check because he lost the checkbook? **a.** _____

b. Is forgery a real defense? **b.** _____

c. May the defense be used against the claims of a holder in due course? **c.** _____

d. Is a holder in due course protected against all types of defenses? **d.** _____

45. Stale Check Church accepted a three-year-old check that Field endorsed to her. When Church presented the check for payment, the bank refused to honor it and informed Church that the account had been closed for a year.

a. Is a person who accepts a demand instrument, such as a check, subsequent to a reasonable time after issue considered to have been given notice that the instrument is overdue? **a.** _____

b. Is the drawer of a check responsible to all holders in due course for a period of seven years? **b.** _____

c. Can Church sue the drawer to collect the check? **c.** _____

CASE ANALYSIS

Study each of the following cases carefully. Briefly state the principle of law and your decision.

46. Bearer Instrument McCutchon wrote a check payable to "cash" while he was in a supermarket. Before he got to the cashier, he realized that he had lost the check. Is this a bearer instrument, payable to any holder?

Principle of Law:

____

____

Decision:

____

____

47. Personal Defense Poulakis sold a computer using fraudulent means to Welson, who paid for the machine with a promissory note for $1,200. When Welson discovered the fraud, she refused to honor the note when it was presented for payment by a subsequent holder. Welson claimed fraud as a defense. Will Welson succeed in avoiding payment to a holder in due course?

Principle of Law:

____

____

Decision:

____

____

48. Negotiability Locke gave two promissory notes to Consumer Food Inc. in payment for merchandise he purchased. The notes said, "Buyer agreed to pay to seller." Consumer Food assigned the notes to Aetna Acceptance Corporation. Were these notes negotiable instruments? [*Locke v. Aetna Acceptance Corporation,* 309 So. 2d 43 (Florida)]

Principle of Law:

____

____

Decision:

____

____

49. Postdated Check Gentilotti, father of an illegitimate son, drew a check for $20,000 in 1969 payable to the son's order. The check was dated July 1, 1985, but provided on the face of the check that, should Gentilotti die before that date, "this check shall be payable immediately." Gentilotti issued the check to the son's mother, the legal guardian. Gentilotti died on July 4, 1980. Despite the available funds, the bank, acting on orders of Gentilotti's executor, refused payment when the check was presented. The drawer's executor refused payment on the grounds that the obligation was not due. Was the postdated check valid? [*Smith v. Gentilotti,* 359 N.E.2d 953 (Massachusetts)]

Principle of Law:

Decision:

LEGAL RESEARCH

Complete the following activities. Share your findings with the class.

50. Working in Teams Working in teams of three or four, interview personnel at your local bank to describe the circumstances under which the bank might refuse to cash a check drawn on an account held at the bank.

51. Using Technology Using the Internet and search engines, find items for sale in which the form of payment accepted is a check. How should such checks be written and endorsed?

PART 5

Property

Brand X Pictures/Getty Images

chapter 24
Real and Personal Property

LEARNING OUTCOMES

After studying this chapter and completing the assessment, you will be able to

24.1 Describe the characteristics of property and provide examples of items considered property.

24.2 Distinguish between real and personal property.

24.3 Identify and discuss common ways in which title to personal property can be acquired.

24.4 Discuss the different forms of property ownership.

24.5 Discuss the characteristics of real property.

24.6 Describe ownership interests in real property in terms of freehold and leasehold estates.

24.7 Discuss the transfer of real property, including (a) the various types of deeds, (b) the delivery and recording of deeds, and (c) transfers made through eminent domain and adverse possession.

LEGAL terms

- real property
- personal property
- *inter vivos* gift
- gift *causa mortis*
- accession
- severalty
- joint tenancy
- tenancy by the entirety
- tenancy in common
- community property
- easement
- freehold estate
- leasehold estate
- fee simple
- life estate
- deed
- condemnation
- eminent domain
- title insurance
- adverse possession

REAL AND PERSONAL PROPERTY

"Real estate cannot be lost or stolen, nor can it be carried away. Purchased with common sense, paid for in full, and managed with reasonable care, it is about the safest investment in the world."

Franklin D. Roosevelt, 32nd president of the United States

M Stock/Alamy Images

24.1 CHARACTERISTICS OF PROPERTY

To many people, the term *property* suggests land. Actually, property should be viewed more broadly because it also includes tangible goods such as automobiles, furniture, clothing, and even pets. In addition, there are intangible possessions, such as patents, rights to drill for oil on someone else's land, and copyrights of creative works such as books. These intangible possessions are also property. Consequently, the broad term *property* includes, in addition to land, both tangible and intangible personal property.

Personal property includes all property other than real property, both tangible and intangible.
John Lund/Sam Diephuis/Blend Images LLC

24.2 DISTINCTION BETWEEN REAL AND PERSONAL PROPERTY

The law distinguishes between real and personal property and governs each in different ways.

REAL PROPERTY

Under common law, ownership of real property extended from the center of the earth to the highest point in the sky. A person owned not only a portion of the earth's crust but also the ground under it and the airspace above it. As a result, real property comprises land and everything attached to the land. This would include minerals such as oil, iron ore, and others. Real property includes any permanent additions to the land, such as houses, buildings, and trees.

real property
The ground and everything permanently attached to it, including land, buildings, trees, and shrubs; the airspace above and the ground below the land also are included.

PERSONAL PROPERTY

Personal property includes all property other than real property, both tangible and intangible. Examples of tangible personal property include furniture, clothing, books, and pets. Examples of intangible personal property include patents, copyrights, goodwill, trademarks, and service marks (discussed in Chapter 28).

personal property
Tangible and intangible property that is not real property.

REAL PROPERTY CAN BECOME PERSONAL PROPERTY

Because real property consists of land and things permanently attached to it, it follows logically that when things are removed from real property, they become personal property. When a tree is cut down, for example, it becomes personal property. So, too, grain growing in a field becomes personal property when it is harvested.

EXAMPLE 24.1

▶ Blanchard owned one-half acre of vacant property. He hired a contractor to build a house on the property and to plant various trees and shrubs. A year later, Blanchard became dissatisfied with the planting, uprooted the trees and shrubs, and sold them to a neighbor. In this case, the building materials and trees were personal property that became real property. When the trees and shrubs were uprooted, they became personal property once again.

PERSONAL PROPERTY CAN BECOME REAL PROPERTY

Personal property, such as trees or shrubbery purchased at a nursery, become real property when they are planted. Similarly, personal property items, such as lumber and bricks, become real property when they are used to erect a building on real property.

24.3 ACQUIRING TITLE TO PERSONAL PROPERTY

Title to personal property is the actual ownership of property, not just the evidence of ownership, such as a certificate of title (see Chapter 16). Title (ownership) can be transferred from one person to another in a number of ways, including finding lost property, gift, sale, inheritance (see Chapter 27), and other ways that will be discussed later in this chapter.

FINDING LOST PERSONAL PROPERTY

The saying "Finders keepers, losers weepers" has no basis in law. The finder of lost property holds it in trust–that is, in safekeeping, at least for a time, for the real owner. As a result, the finder is a custodian acting for the true owner. The finder of lost property has ownership rights superior to everyone except the true owner.

Responsibility of the Finder A person who finds property has a legal responsibility to make reasonable efforts to return the property to its rightful owner. Statutes in many states provide that if the finder of lost property has made reasonable efforts to locate the owner without success within a period specified by statute, title to the property then transfers to the finder.

EXAMPLE 24.2

Chan, while walking through a park, found an envelope containing a bundle of cash and documents that identified the owner. As soon as Chan found and took possession of the envelope, he assumed responsibility for safeguarding the money and returning it to the rightful owner.

Distinction between Lost and Mislaid Property Courts frequently make a distinction between lost and mislaid property. An object has been "mislaid," rather than lost, when it was intentionally left in a certain place and then forgotten by the owner. Objects forgotten in this way are considered to have been transferred willingly and placed in the custody of the person with whom the object was left and, thus, are not lost at all. On the other hand, an object that has not been intentionally left in the custody of someone else and then forgotten is considered lost, not mislaid.

EXAMPLE 24.3

McAvoy, a customer in Medina's barbershop, found a briefcase containing certain valuables that had been left there but forgotten by another customer whose identity could not be determined. A dispute arose over who should get the briefcase and its contents. The court awarded possession to Medina, stressing that the owner had intentionally left the briefcase and then forgotten it and, thus, had entrusted it to Medina's care.

In a similar but distinct case, an entirely different finding resulted.

EXAMPLE 24.4

▶ Bridges found a parcel of cash on the floor of Hassan's store. Both Bridges and Hassan claimed ownership. The court ruled that the cash was not intentionally left on the floor and that there was no custody on the part of Hassan. Possession was awarded to Bridges.

The distinction between the situations described in Examples 24.3 and 24.4 is that the former case illustrates mislaid property, while the latter case illustrates lost property.

Property Found in Public versus Private Places Courts also have made a distinction between objects found on a private portion of a person's property and objects found in areas open to the public. The thinking behind the distinction is that an owner of property that is not open to the public is presumed to possess both the place itself and whatever it contains. In an area that is open to the public, however, the finder is more likely to gain ownership of a found object than is the owner of the land.

EXAMPLE 24.5

▶ Patillo, a worker for a swimming pool maintenance company, was cleaning the pool at the Red River Motel when he found a valuable diamond ring. Both Patillo and the owner of the motel, Calkins, claimed ownership. The court decided that because Calkins had the right to say that the pool should be cleaned in any way he thought fit, and to direct what should be done with anything found in the pool, Calkins should be presumed to have the right to exercise control over any object found in or on it. The finder, Patillo, would probably have been granted possession if the ring had been found in the parking lot or on the floor in the motel lobby because these areas are open to the public.

Statutory Remedies Many states have enacted statutes that govern who owns lost and mislaid property. Typically, these statutes require the finder of lost or mislaid property to notify a specific government official who maintains records of the property found. If, by the end of a period of time set by statute, the true owner does not claim the property, title to such property is transferred to the finder. If the true owner does not come forward and the finder does not wish to claim ownership, title to the property transfers to the state after the period of time specified in the statute.

ABANDONED PROPERTY

Personal property is considered abandoned when the owner disposes of it with the apparent intention of disclaiming ownership. Title to such property is transferred to the first person who takes control over it.

GIFTS

A *gift* is the voluntary transfer of property by one person to another without consideration or payment of any kind. While gift giving is a common act, it takes on added dimensions when viewed from a legal standpoint. Three requirements must be met for property to be transferred as a gift:

1. The *donor* (the person giving the gift) must intend to make a gift.
2. The gift, or a written statement of the donor's intention, must actually be delivered to the *donee* (the person who is to receive the gift).
3. The donee must accept the gift.

Once these three requirements are met, the donor cannot rescind the gift.

***inter vivos* gift**
A gift between the living that meets all of the legal requirements for a gift.

gift causa mortis
A gift, given by a living person who expects to die from a known cause, that meets all of the legal requirements for a gift.

***Inter Vivos* Gifts** An *inter vivos* gift refers to property given while both parties are alive. *Inter vivos* is a Latin term meaning "between the living."

Gifts *Causa Mortis* A gift given by a living person who expects to die from a known cause is known as a gift *causa mortis*, a Latin term meaning "in contemplation of death." If the donor does not die from the expected cause or dies as a result of some other cause, the gift can be reclaimed by the donor or the donor's estate.

EXAMPLE 24.6

Eisermann suffered from terminal cancer. Recognizing the seriousness of his condition, he signed over several valuable stock certificates to his son, despite the objections of his wife and other children. On the way home from the hospital, he was killed in an automobile accident. The executor of his estate could justifiably claim that the gift *causa mortis* to the son may be revoked and that the stock certificates should be included in the estate.

accession
The right of an owner of property to any increase in the property.

ACCESSION

Accession is the right of an owner of property such as plants or animals to any increase in the property. The owner of a cow, for example, owns the calves born to the cow.

The owner of a horse owns the foal born to the horse.
filmfoto/Getty Images

24.4 OWNERSHIP OF REAL OR PERSONAL PROPERTY

Title (discussed in Chapter 16) is actual ownership, not just evidence of ownership. At this point, different forms of ownership will be introduced. Many of the following descriptions of single- and multiple-person ownership apply to both real and personal property.

SEVERALTY OWNERSHIP

Ownership is held in severalty when all the rights of ownership in a particular piece of property are held by one person. Although one might at first think that the word *severalty* suggests several people, in fact *several* means "separate" in this context.

severalty
Ownership of a particular piece of property that is held by one person.

MULTIPLE OWNERSHIP

For various reasons, it is sometimes desirable for multiple people to own real or personal property jointly. However, certain types of property, such as businesses, boats, cars, and planes, cannot be divided among the owners. Obviously, one of the co-owners of an airplane could not very well claim the wings of the plane and indicate that the engine belonged to the other owner.

Joint Tenancy A joint tenancy exists when two or more persons own equal shares of property. The death of one person transfers their interest to the surviving joint tenants.

In cases of joint tenancy, the owners are said to have an *undivided interest:* Each owner can claim ownership of the entire estate, subject to the same right of the other joint tenants. Generally, a person's part interest in property may be sold just as a severalty interest may be sold, unless specifically prohibited. To underscore the intention of the parties, agreements generally include the phrase "with right of survivorship." In this sense, "survivorship" means that in the case of one owner's death, ownership of the portion owned by the deceased passes to the survivors.

joint tenancy
When two or more persons own equal shares of personal property with right of survivorship.

EXAMPLE 24.7

▶ McGrath and Connell were partners who owned both a retail business and the real property on which the store was built as joint tenants. Each owner had a spouse and children. McGrath died and Connell assumed McGrath's ownership of the business and the property. McGrath's spouse and children inherited neither of these two assets.

Tenancy by the Entirety A tenancy by the entirety is a form of joint ownership of property by spouses in which both have the right to the entire property, and, upon the death of one, the other has title (the right of survivorship).

tenancy by the entirety
A form of joint ownership of property by husband and wife in which both have a right to the entire property and the right of survivorship.

Tenancy in Common A tenancy in common is a form of joint ownership of property by two or more persons. The ownership interest of any one of the owners can be sold, transferred, or inherited. In this type of joint ownership, the owners may own different, unequal interests, such as two-thirds and one-third.

The distinction of tenancy in common is that an owner's interest does not pass to the persons who share ownership at the time of their death. Rather, the interest of a tenant in common passes to that person's heirs.

tenancy in common
A form of joint ownership of property by two or more persons in which any owner's interest can be sold, transferred, or inherited.

TABLE 24.1 Community Property States

Arizona	New Mexico
California	Texas
Idaho	Washington
Louisiana	Wisconsin
Nevada	

EXAMPLE 24.8

▶ Assume that McGrath and Connell, in the previous example, own the retail business and the real property as tenants in common. McGrath dies, and his share of the jointly held property passes to his heirs.

community property
Property acquired during marriage that, in some states, belongs to both spouses.

Community Property Some states have enacted statutes that provide that property acquired by either one of the spouses during a marriage is the community property of both spouses; that is, the property acquired belongs to both parties. Statutes in these states vary in the determination of what happens to property at the time of death or in the case of divorce. Generally, the law provides that property owned by either party before the marriage, or property received as gifts or inheritances by either party during the marriage, remains the property of the individual and does not become community property. For a listing of community property states, see Table 24.1.

24.5 REAL PROPERTY

Real property is distinguished from personal property in a number of ways. Unlike most forms of personal property, the supply of land is limited. Moreover, land is unique, and one piece of land is not the same as any other. One piece, for example, may contain valuable minerals and another might have little value.

LAND

As previously stated, the law relating to real property treats land as extending down to the center of the earth and also includes things that are permanently attached to it, such as houses, buildings, and trees. Moreover, rights to land include the airspace above the land to an indefinite height, subject to the rights of aircraft in flight that do not pose a hazard to persons or property on the land. Land also includes rights to minerals such as oil, coal, or iron ore, except in states where the state retains an interest in certain minerals.

BUILDINGS AND FIXTURES

A *building* is a structure built on land. Such a structure can be almost any building permanently placed or constructed on or beneath the surface of the land. When items of personal property are added to land or to buildings in such a way that they become a part of the real property, they are known as *fixtures.* Planted shrubbery and trees are examples of fixtures to land. Kitchen cabinets would be an example of a fixture to a building. When real property is sold, the fixtures are included in the sale unless otherwise agreed by the parties.

RIGHTS IN LAND OTHER THAN OWNERSHIP

Rights in land can be separated from the land itself, except in the case of easements. Examples of such rights are discussed in the following paragraphs.

Subterranean Rights The right to extract minerals, such as oil or coal, from land is known as *subterranean rights.* The right to extract minerals can be sold without altering the ownership of the land itself.

EXAMPLE 24.9

▶ Quepos owns land under which natural gas deposits are found. Quepos can sell the rights to extract the gas to Energy Extraction Inc. If Quepos sells the land to Gallacher, Energy Extraction still has the right to extract the natural gas after the land has been sold and transferred.

Air Rights The right to build on or over the land is known as *air rights.* Air rights are of particular significance in crowded urban areas where the right to erect a building over some other use of the land might be sold. An example of such use would be the sale of the right to erect an apartment building over railroad tracks or a highway.

Easements An **easement** is a right or interest in land granted to a party to make beneficial use of the land owned by another. The distinction between easements and other real property rights is that easements "run with the land." That is, they cannot be sold or transferred once they are recorded. An example of an easement is the right granted to a public utility company to enter the land of another to maintain telephone lines or electrical equipment.

easement
A right or interest in land granted to a party to make beneficial use of the land owned by another.

Profits A *profit* is a right to enter another person's land and remove some product of the land or its natural resources. If, for example, an individual has the right to enter a neighboring property to remove timber for their logging company, they have a profit. A profit includes an implied easement to allow access to the property; but in addition to the easement, a profit is a right to take something of value from the land.

Licenses The owner of land may grant a party the right to enter the land for a specific purpose. For example, a landowner may grant someone the right to build a temporary stand to sell fruits and vegetables or souvenirs to passing motorists, or the owner of a service station may license someone to sell Mother's Day flowers on a portion of the property. Generally, the landowner receives payment or a share of profits in exchange for the license. Licensing agreements may be written or oral. The temporary interest created in the land does not run with the land.

EXAMPLE 24.10

▶ The Downtowner Motel allowed Rubin to use a small area in the corner of the lobby to display and sell his sculptures. The arrangement required Rubin to pay the motel owner a small commission on any sculptures sold. After several years, the motel manager informed Rubin that the arrangement was over. Rubin disagreed, claiming that the arrangement was a lease. Rubin is incorrect. In this instance, the arrangement is clearly a license, not a lease.

24.6 INTERESTS IN REAL PROPERTY

freehold estate
An estate in which a person owns the land for life or forever.

leasehold estate
An estate in which a person has an interest in real property that comes from a lease.

Interests in real property can relate to either ownership or possession. The term *estate* is used to identify the interest or the right a person has in real property. An estate can be either a freehold estate, by which a person owns the land either for life or forever, or a leasehold estate, by which a person has an interest in real property that comes from a lease. A leasehold estate is not ownership, but only the right to possess real property, subject to the provisions of a lease (see Chapter 26).

FREEHOLD ESTATES

There are a number of ways in which freehold estates can be held that provide absolute (total) ownership lasting either for the lifetime of the holder or forever. Consequently, a holder of a freehold estate in land can transfer the estate (ownership) by sale, by gift, or by leaving it to their heirs. A holder of a freehold estate also can create and transfer an interest in the estate that lasts only for a lifetime. Such an estate, called a *life estate,* will be discussed later in this section.

fee simple
When an owner of a freehold estate holds it absolutely.

Estate in Fee Simple The owner of a freehold estate who holds it absolutely is said to hold it in fee simple. The owner of a freehold estate who holds real property in fee simple can sell it, give it away, or leave it to their heirs. The person to whom it is transferred then owns it in fee simple. The holder of a freehold estate in fee simple is not, however, allowed to use the property in any way that violates local zoning rules, or the rights of others, or restrictive covenants in the deed. For example, a restrictive covenant in a deed may prohibit the alteration, destruction, or removal of a historic structure. Any restrictive covenant must be for a lawful purpose. A restrictive covenant prohibiting a sale because of the race or religion of the prospective buyer, for example, would not be lawful.

life estate
A freehold estate in which a person has an ownership interest only for their lifetime.

Life Estates A person who holds a freehold estate (ownership interest) only for their lifetime is said to hold a life estate in the property. A life estate is usually created by deed (the document used to transfer ownership in real property) or by inheritance.

If real property is transferred from *A* to *B* for *B*'s lifetime, and *B* dies, the property is then returned to *A*, if they are still alive, or to *A*'s heirs. The interest that *A* holds while *B* is still alive is known as a *reversion estate* because the property reverts to *A* upon *B*'s death. But suppose that *A* decides that upon *B*'s death the property should belong to *C*. *C* is said to have a *remainder estate.*

EXAMPLE 24.11

▸ Arnaz, a middle-aged man, owned several houses and was concerned about his older brother's poor financial situation. The brother had one son, but Arnaz disliked his nephew. Arnaz wished to grant one of his houses to his brother. Instead of granting the brother the house in fee simple, which would mean that the disliked nephew would likely inherit the house upon Arnaz's brother's death, Arnaz granted his brother a life estate in the house. Once the property was granted to the brother, Arnaz had a reversion estate because the property would revert to him. If, however, Arnaz had specified that upon the brother's death, the house was to become the property of Arnaz's daughter, she would then have a remainder estate during Arnaz's brother's lifetime.

LEASEHOLD ESTATES

An estate that does not involve an ownership interest in real property is known as a leasehold estate. A leasehold estate provides the holder with certain rights during the period covered by the lease (see Chapter 26).

deed
The instrument, or document, that conveys an interest in real property between parties.

24.7 TRANSFER OF REAL PROPERTY

The transfer of real property is, in many ways, more complex than the transfer of personal property. Consequently, a number of specialized terms are used. A deed is the instrument, or document, that conveys an interest in real property between parties. The parties are the *grantor,* the party who conveys real property, and the *grantee,* the party to whom the real property is conveyed. Unlike a contract, no consideration is required to effect a transfer of real property. Real property, like personal property, can be sold or given as a gift during one's life or in the form of an inheritance. A deed, however, is needed in any kind of transfer of ownership.

The transfer of real property is more complex than the transfer of personal property.
Brand X Pictures/Getty Images

TYPES OF DEEDS

Deeds can be classified by the kind of ownership interest being transferred.

A *quitclaim deed* transfers whatever interest a grantor has in real property, if any. It states that the grantor claims no interest in the property for which the deed is given. Quitclaim deeds are often used when transferring property to family members or divorcing spouses, or in other transactions between people well known to each other. Quitclaim deeds also are used to resolve questions of full title when a person has a possible, but unknown, interest in the property, and for tax sales at public auction. Quitclaim deeds do not warrant good title.

A *warranty deed* is one in which the grantor asserts that they have title and that the property is free of the claims of others. In the *general warranty deed,* the seller promises to warranty the entire chain of title to the buyer, that is, any prior problems with the title, not just problems that may have occurred during the seller's ownership of the property. In the *special warranty deed,* the seller limits their warranty to those title problems that occurred during the time the seller owned the property.

A *bargain and sale deed* simply states that the grantor is transferring the real property to the grantee. No particular warranties are given, but state statutes assume that certain implied warranties are present.

Deeds are classified by the kind of ownership interest being transferred.
Stockbyte/Getty Images

DELIVERY AND RECORDING OF DEEDS

When a deed has been completed and signed by the grantor, it must be delivered to the grantee to bring about a legally enforceable transfer of ownership. While most such deliveries are made in person in the offices of a real estate broker, a bank, a title company, or an attorney, no particular form or place of delivery is required. The deed can be handed in person to the grantee (buyer), mailed to them, or given to another person with instructions for delivery.

Recording a deed with the appropriate public official, such as a county recorder of deeds, is not legally required, but it is an important step that notifies everyone of its existence and minimizes the possibility of another person's claim to the property surfacing at a later date.

OTHER TRANSFERS OF REAL PROPERTY

In addition to those just described, there are two other ways in which real property may be transferred: under the doctrines of eminent domain and adverse possession.

Eminent Domain Real property can be taken from an owner by action of government or other public authority for the benefit of the public. Such actions are taken when a governmental body wishes to build a highway or school, for example, and the needed property is privately held. The legal process that occurs when property is taken by the government against the will of the property owner is known as condemnation.

condemnation
The legal process that occurs when property is taken by the government against the will of the property owner.

eminent domain
When ownership of real property is taken by the government and the previous owner is compensated at the fair market value of the property.

When private property is taken by eminent domain, compensation is made at the fair market value of the property. In recent years, some localities have used the doctrine of eminent domain in a highly controversial manner–to justify the taking of private property for use in economic development, such as when a city takes private homes in order to erect a hotel or shopping center. In the event of a dispute, the owner can pursue remedies available through state and federal courts [see *Kelo v. City of New London,* 545 U.S. 469 (2005)]. In response to the *Kelo* case, some states have enacted legislation restricting the use of eminent domain to take property for private economic development projects.

EXAMPLE 24.12

▶ In 2003, New York State, working with a private developer, unveiled plans to build a new arena complex to house the New Jersey Nets basketball team. Because the 22-acre project did not fit the planned site in Brooklyn, the state exercised its power of eminent domain to acquire necessary properties from their owners. New York State promised redevelopment of a blighted area. However, owners of some of the properties appealed the court's decision. They protested the condemnation of their properties, stating the fact that their properties were not blighted. In 2009, the New York State Supreme Court found that although some of the properties were recently remodeled, including several condominium complexes, there was significant evidence of blight and unsanitary conditions, enough to justify the use of eminent domain to acquire the properties necessary to build the arena.

title insurance
Coverage that protects individuals against financial loss resulting from defects in their title to real property or from issues associated with their mortgage liens.

Title Insurance Title insurance protects individuals against financial loss resulting from defects in their title to (ownership of) real property or from issues associated with their mortgage liens. Persons who purchase real property almost always procure title insurance; indeed, most banks and other financial institutions require such coverage when they finance the purchase by providing a mortgage. It is generally simply added on as a part of the purchasers' closing costs.

adverse possession
When title to land is acquired by a person's exclusive, continuous, open, known, and hostile use of the property over a period of time.

Adverse Possession Title to land also can be acquired as a result of a person's use of land over a period of time. For title to pass through an adverse possession, it must be proved that there was actual and exclusive continuous possession or use, the possession must have been for a period of years specified by state statute (typically 10 years), possession must have been open and known to the owner, and the land was used with hostility and adversely (i.e., without the owner's permission).

EXAMPLE 24.13

An alley adjacent to a retail store was commonly used by customers to park their cars, without permission but with the alley owner's knowledge. A customer was surprised one day to find that she was blocked from her favorite parking place by a chain. Upon inquiry, the clerk explained that the owner of the alley was required to briefly demonstrate his ownership in order to prevent adverse possession of the alley. The customer would be welcome to park there the following day.

CHAPTER SUMMARY

24.1 Property includes land; tangible goods such as automobiles, furniture, clothing, and pets; and intangible possessions, such as patents, rights to drill for oil on someone else's land, and copyrights of creative works such as books. Consequently, the broad term *property* includes, in addition to land, both tangible and intangible personal property.

24.2 Real property is the ground and everything permanently attached to it, including land, buildings, trees, and shrubs. The airspace above and the ground below the land also are included. Personal property is everything, tangible and intangible, that is not real property.

24.3 A finder of lost property has a responsibility to make a reasonable effort to find the true owner. However, property that is abandoned with the apparent intention of disclaiming it belongs to the first person who takes control of it. An object is considered mislaid, rather than lost, when it has been intentionally left in a certain place and then forgotten by the owner. If an object has not been intentionally left in the custody of someone else, it is considered lost. A gift *inter vivos* is one between the living; a gift *causa mortis* is given by a living person who expects to die from a known cause.

24.4 Title is actual ownership, not just evidence of ownership. Different forms of ownership include single- and multiple-person ownership, which apply to both real and personal property. Severalty ownership exists when all the rights of ownership in property are held by one person. Joint tenancy occurs when two or more people own equal shares in property with the right of survivorship. Tenancy by the entirety is a form of joint ownership by spouses in which both have a right to the entire property and the right of survivorship. Tenancy in common is a form of ownership by two or more persons that can be sold, transferred, or inherited. Community property is property acquired during marriage that, in some states, belongs to both spouses.

24.5 The law relating to real property treats land as extending down to the center of the earth and also includes things that are permanently attached to it, such as houses, buildings, and trees. Moreover, rights to land include the airspace above the land to an indefinite height, subject to the rights of aircraft in flight that do not pose a hazard to persons or property on the land. Land also includes rights to minerals such as oil, coal, or iron ore, except in states where the state retains an interest in certain minerals.

24.6 A freehold estate is one in which a person owns the land for life or forever. A leasehold estate is one in which a person has an interest in real property that comes from a lease. One type of freehold estate is an estate in fee simple, in which the owner of a freehold estate holds it absolutely. A second type of freehold estate is a life estate, in which the owner owns the estate only for their lifetime.

24.7 The transfer of real property may be effected by deed, eminent domain, or adverse possession. A deed is an instrument that conveys an interest in real property between parties. Types of deeds include a quitclaim deed, a warranty deed, and a bargain and sale deed. Real property also can be transferred by eminent domain (when it is taken by the government and the owner is compensated) or adverse possession (when land is acquired as a result of a person's actual, continuous, open, known, and hostile use of land for a certain period of time).

CHAPTER TWENTY-FOUR ASSESSMENT

MATCHING LEGAL TERMS

Match each of the numbered definitions with the correct term in the following list.

a. accession
b. adverse possession
c. *causa mortis*
d. eminent domain
e. fee simple
f. freehold estate
g. grantee
h. *inter vivos*
i. joint tenancy
j. leasehold estate
k. life estate
l. quitclaim deed
m. severalty
n. subterranean rights
o. tenancy in common

1. A gift between the living. **1.** ____

2. The right of an owner of property to the product of such property—a calf born to a cow, for example. **2.** ____

3. Ownership of property held by one person. **3.** ____

4. A gift given in anticipation of death. **4.** ____

5. A document of transfer of real property. **5.** ____

6. Absolute ownership of real property. **6.** ____

7. The right of a governmental or public body to acquire privately held real property needed for a public purpose. **7.** ____

8. The interest in real property that relates to ownership. **8.** ____

9. The person to whom real property is conveyed. **9.** ____

10. The interest a person has in real property that lasts until they die. **10.** ____

11. The interest in real property that relates to possession. **11.** ____

12. A form of co-ownership of property in which one owner's share of the property passes to the other owners upon their death. **12.** ____

13. The passing of title to land that can result from a nonowner's use of the land. **13.** ____

14. Rights that allow a person to extract minerals from land. **14.** ____

15. A form of joint ownership of property in which one owner's share of the property can be sold, transferred, or passed to heirs. **15.** ____

TRUE/FALSE QUIZ

Indicate whether each of the following statements is true or false.

16. *Property* refers to both personal and real property. 16. _____

17. Fixtures are additions to personal property. 17. _____

18. Personal property can be either tangible or intangible. 18. _____

19. There is no distinction between lost and mislaid personal property. 19. _____

20. A finder of personal property has a responsibility to try to return the property to the rightful owner. 20. _____

21. Title to abandoned property resides with the state. 21. _____

22. Some state statutes provide that property acquired before a marriage is the community property of both spouses. 22. _____

23. An easement is the right or interest in land granted for the benefit of one party to make beneficial use of the land of another. 23. _____

24. The person who holds a life estate in real property can sell absolute ownership or pass it on to their heirs. 24. _____

25. A grantor of a life estate in real property maintains a reversion estate. 25. _____

MULTIPLE CHOICE QUIZ

Indicate the correct answer from the choices after each question.

26. Planted shrubs in a residential yard are (a) tangible personal property (b) tangible real property (c) intangible real property (d) intangible personal property. 26. _____

27. Shrubs stored in pots for sale at a retail nursery are (a) tangible personal property (b) tangible real property (c) intangible real property (d) intangible personal property. 27. _____

28. The patent filed to protect the patent related to the equipment to plant the shrubs is (a) tangible personal property (b) tangible real property (c) intangible real property (d) intangible personal property. 28. _____

29. A sells B their interest in real estate. A received a life estate in the real estate from their parent. B will own the real estate (a) until B decides to transfer or sell the real estate (b) until B's death (c) until A's death (d) until both A and B's deaths. 29. _____

30. A transfers property to B with a deed that promises A has title to the property "free and clear of all claims," including any claims prior to A's ownership. This deed is a (a) general warranty deed (b) special warranty deed (c) quitclaim deed (d) bargain and sale deed. **30.** _____

31. A and B are unmarried partners who own real estate as joint tenants. A dies. After A's death, B (a) no longer owns the real estate (b) owns all of the real estate (c) owns half the real estate (d) none of the above. **31.** _____

32. A and B are unmarried partners who own real estate as tenants in common. A dies. After A's death, B (a) no longer owns the real estate (b) owns all of the real estate (c) owns half the real estate (d) none of the above. **32.** _____

33. A and B are married spouses who own real estate as tenants by the entirety. A dies. After A's death, B (a) no longer owns the real estate a (b) owns all of the real estate (c) owns half the real estate (d) none of the above. **33.** _____

DISCUSSION QUESTIONS

Answer the following questions and discuss them in class.

34. Distinguish between real and personal property.

35. Discuss both *inter vivos* gifts and gifts *causa mortis.*

36. Discuss severalty ownership, tenancy in common, joint tenancy, and community property.

37. Discuss real property as it relates to land, buildings, and fixtures. How does personal property convert to real property?

38. Identify and provide examples of rights in real property.

39. Explain the characteristics of various kinds of deeds, and explain transfers of real property through eminent domain and adverse possession.

THINKING CRITICALLY ABOUT THE LAW

Answer the following questions, which require you to think critically about the legal principles that you learned in this chapter.

40. Real and Personal Property Why do you think it is necessary to distinguish between real and personal property?

____

____

41. Sale of Property The transfer of real property is much more complex than the transfer of personal property. What could be done to simplify real property transactions?

____

____

42. Gifts Can a gift given *causa mortis* be assumed to be as freely given as a gift given *inter vivos*? Why or why not?

____

____

43. Multiple Ownership of Real Property Various forms of multiple ownership of real property–such as joint tenancy, tenancy by the entirety, tenancy in common, and so on–have evolved from our English legal roots. Are these designations relevant today?

____

____

44. A Question of Ethics An oceanfront community wanted to limit the use of its beach to residents only. A group contested this exclusion, claiming the ocean was public property. Is it fair for residents to exclude nonresidents from access to the beach?

____

____

CASE QUESTIONS

Study each of the following cases. Answer the questions that follow with Yes or No.

45. Property Ownership Roche and Hecht owned a boat, which they used for weekend fishing trips. Because both were married and had children, they set up their agreement to own the boat in such a way that if either one died, from any cause, the heirs of the deceased party would inherit his interest.

a. Is this an example of joint tenancy? **a.** _____

b. Is this an example of tenancy in common? **b.** _____

c. Does Hecht's interest in the boat indicate a severalty interest? **c.** _____

46. Found Property Weber, a customer at a restaurant owned by Hegler, found a wallet on the floor under the table. It contained money but no identification. In an attempt to return it to its rightful owner, she gave it to Hegler with the understanding that if the owner did not return, or could not be located, Weber would claim it. When the owner did not return after a period of a month, Weber claimed the wallet. Hegler refused to give it to Weber, claiming it as his own.

a. Does Weber have a lawful claim to the wallet? **a.** _____

b. Does Hegler have a lawful claim to the wallet? **b.** _____

c. Would a court regard the wallet as misplaced? **c.** _____

47. Community Property Prior to their marriage, LeRoi and her husband, Pillsbury, each held substantial assets. During their marriage, they jointly purchased a home with the income they earned, and LeRoi inherited a substantial amount of money. After four years, they agreed to divorce. The marriage ceremony and divorce action were both in a state with community property laws.

a. Is the property owned by both husband and wife before marriage considered community property? **a.** _____

b. Is LeRoi's inheritance considered community property? **b.** _____

c. Is the home considered community property? **c.** _____

48. Real and Personal Property Noguchi and his wife purchased a newly built house that had no lawn or any other landscaping. Over several years, they spent many weekends landscaping with expensive and exotic shrubbery and trees. They also had a large above-ground pool installed in the yard. Because of a transfer to another city, the Noguchis were forced to sell their home. After the sale but before moving away, the Noguchis began uprooting several shrubs and removing the pool to take these with them. The buyer objected to the removal, claiming that the shrubbery and the pool were real property and were included in the sale of the house. Noguchi claimed that the shrubbery and pool were all personal property.

a. Is the shrubbery real property? **a.** _____

b. Is the house real property? **b.** _____

c. Is the pool real property? **c.** _____

CASE ANALYSIS

Study each of the following cases carefully. Briefly state the principle of law and your decision.

49. Adverse Possession Bryer purchased a suburban home. At the time of the sale, the real estate salesperson pointed to a decorative stone fence as the boundary of the property. Because Bryer had several dogs he wanted to keep on his property, he erected a chain-link fence on what he believed to be the property line. His neighbor watched the work being done and did not object. Twenty years later, as a result of a new survey by the town, Bryer was surprised to learn that the fence was 18 inches inside the neighbor's property. Can Bryer claim ownership of all the property on his side of the fence?

Principle of Law:

____

____

Decision:

____

____

50. Easement Rae owned a farm and each summer allowed a neighbor, Fuller, to set up a stand on Rae's property to sell worms to people who drove by on their way to fish in the nearby lake. After 10 years of regularly using the small piece of property, Rae and Fuller had a dispute and Rae forbade Fuller from using his land again. Fuller claimed that he now had the right to continue using the small piece of property as he had in the past, insisting that an easement had been created. Did Fuller's continued use of the property create an easement?

Principle of Law:

____

____

Decision:

____

____

51. Gifts Harry and Marilyn Owen were divorced after a short marriage and entered into an agreement to divide assets. In addition to the division of personal property as agreed to and as recorded by the court, Marilyn claimed ownership of a Chevrolet automobile and one-half of a $24,000 certificate of deposit, insisting that they were both gifts from her former husband, Harry. Both the car, registered in Harry's name, and the certificate were purchased by Harry before the marriage. He denied having given the car and a one-half interest in the certificate of deposit. Does it appear that the requirements of an *inter vivos* gift have been met, and will Marilyn be awarded the disputed property? [*Owen v. Owen,* 351 N.W.2d 139 (South Dakota)]

Principle of Law:

____

____

Decision:

____

____

52. Lost and Mislaid Property Paset, a renter of a safety deposit box at Old Orchard Bank and Trust Company, found $6,325 in currency on the seat of a chair in an examination booth in the safety deposit vault. The chair was partially under a table. Paset notified officers of the bank and turned the money over to them. She was told by bank officials that they would try to locate the owner and that she could have the money if the owner was not located within one year. The bank wrote to everyone who had been in the safety deposit vault area on the day of, or on the day preceding, the discovery, stating that property had been found. The money remained unclaimed, and after a year Paset claimed the money under the state statute governing the disposition of lost and found property. The bank refused, claiming that the money was mislaid, not lost, and was therefore property of the bank. Was the money lost or mislaid, and will the court award the money to Paset? [*Paset v. Old Orchard Bank,* 378 N.E.2d 1264 (Illinois)]

Principle of Law:

Decision:

LEGAL RESEARCH

Complete the following activities. Share your findings with the class.

53. Working in Teams Working in teams of three or four, interview personnel at the nearest governmental authority (federal, state, or local) that handles cases of eminent domain, or the taking of private property for public use. Structure the interview so that the process is discussed and ask them about some recent cases and whether there has been state or local legislation limiting the use of eminent domain for private economic development projects.

54. Using Technology Some state and local governments are investigating the use of blockchain technology to maintain real property records. Investigate the status of these efforts and critique the advantages and disadvantages of using the technology for this purpose.

chapter 25
Bailments

LEARNING OUTCOMES

After studying this chapter and completing the assessment, you will be able to

25.1 Define and explain the purpose of a bailment.

25.2 Discuss the characteristics of bailments, including the six typical reasons for transferring goods and creating a bailment.

25.3 Distinguish among the four kinds of bailments and discuss the level of care a bailee is required to give for each one.

BAILMENTS

"Here, Cher, will you hold my meat purse?"

Lady Gaga, singer and songwriter

Tyler Olson/Shutterstock

LEGAL terms

- bailment
- bailor
- bailee
- bailment for the sole benefit of the bailee
- bailment for the sole benefit of the bailor
- mutual-benefit bailment
- warehouser
- bailee's lien
- hotelkeeper
- transient
- common carrier
- consignor
- consignee
- carrier's lien
- constructive bailment

25.1 BAILMENT DEFINED

Earlier chapters have examined numerous kinds of agreements and contracts for many different purposes. A bailment is a special kind of contract that is widely used in business and in personal affairs.

bailment
A transaction in which the owner of tangible personal property transfers it (not as a gift) to another party while still retaining ownership.

Specifically, a bailment is a transaction in which the owner of tangible personal property transfers the property to another party while still retaining ownership of such. For example, taking clothes to a dry cleaner transfers possession, but not ownership (or title), of the clothes.

25.2 CHARACTERISTICS OF BAILMENTS

A bailment allows the owner of personal property to transfer possession of it to another individual for any of the following purposes:

1. *Sale.* For example, a manufacturer ships goods to a retailer to either sell them or return them to the manufacturer (this transaction is known as *consignment*).
2. *Transportation.* For example, a business hires a transporter of goods–a truck line or rail or air carrier–to ship such goods.
3. *Repair or service.* For example, a motorist leaves an automobile at a service station for an oil change.
4. *Rental.* For example, a traveler rents an automobile from a car rental company or skis from a lodge.
5. *Storage.* For example, a company stores goods in a warehouse, a diner places a coat in a checkroom, or a driver leaves a car in a parking lot.
6. *Security for a loan.* For example, a borrower leaves valuable goods with a lender until his or her loan is paid.

bailor
The party in a bailment who retains ownership and transfers possession of the goods.

bailee
The party in a bailment who receives the goods.

In the preceding instances, the person who retains ownership and transfers possession is the bailor, and the person who receives the goods is the bailee. The agreement reached between the bailor and the bailee is a bailment.

Taking clothes to a dry cleaner transfers possession, but not ownership, of the clothes.
Andrew Resek/McGraw Hill

BAILMENT CREATED BY POSSESSION OF GOODS

Actual ownership of goods is not necessary to create a bailment. Anyone in possession of goods can create the bailment relationship and become a bailor–a borrower, a finder, or a thief.

EXAMPLE 25.1

▶ Castro rented a car for use during a business trip. While making a sales call on a downtown firm, Castro parked the car in a parking garage. The parking attendant surrendered the car to someone else by mistake. The parking garage was still responsible for the car and its contents. Although Castro was not the owner, he was a bailor.

BAILEE MUST INTEND TO POSSESS GOODS

The transfer of goods from bailor to bailee must actually take place. Unless there is some other understanding, the bailee must actually accept the goods.

EXAMPLE 25.2

▶ Goldstein had her car serviced regularly at Centre Service Station and knew the owner well. One evening, after the station had closed for the night and all the employees had gone home, Goldstein parked on the station property while she attended a social function. When she returned, the car was gone. The owner of Centre Service denied responsibility because no bailment existed. The service station owner is correct because the station did not accept the car.

BAILEE MUST RETURN IDENTICAL GOODS

Except for a bailment that requires alteration, such as a suit left for cleaning and alterations, or when fungible goods, such as grain or fuel oil, are stored, the identical goods must be returned.

EXAMPLE 25.3

▶ Roth left her smartphone with the Tech Fix store for repair. As a result of an error, her phone was repaired and given to another customer, who left town and could not be located. The owner of the repair shop offered Roth a newer, higher-quality smartphone instead. Roth refused, claiming that the replacement would not be compatible with her hands-free bluetooth car kit. Tech Fix must replace the exact item left for repair or pay damages.

TERMINATION OF BAILMENTS

If a bailment is for a specific term, the bailment ends when the term lapses. Otherwise, a bailment is terminated when its purpose is satisfied, when the parties mutually agree to end it, when either party makes a demand to end it, or if the bailee acts inconsistently with the terms of the bailment.

25.3 KINDS OF BAILMENTS AND CARE DURING CUSTODY

In all types of bailments, the bailee has at least a minimum duty of care to ensure the safety of the bailor's property. The level of care with which a bailee must treat a bailor's goods varies depending on the kind of bailment.

Bailments are often classified into four categories:

1. *Bailments for the sole benefit of the bailee.* An example of this kind of bailment is when one borrows an article, such as a calculator, from a friend.
2. *Bailments for the sole benefit of the bailor.* An example of this kind of bailment is when one agrees to store a friend's car in their garage while the friend is out of town.
3. *Bailments for the benefit of both the bailee and the bailor.* An example of this kind of bailment, also called *mutual-benefit bailment,* is when one leaves their car with an attendant in a parking garage (see Example 25.1).
4. *Constructive bailments.* An example of this kind of bailment is when goods, such as an umbrella, are thrust upon you by a person who unintentionally leaves property behind in your home.

Parties to a bailment are free to increase or decrease the bailee's duty to care for the bailor's goods by contract.

BAILMENTS FOR THE SOLE BENEFIT OF THE BAILEE

bailment for the sole benefit of the bailee
A bailment relationship in which only the bailee receives any benefit from the relationship.

A bailment for the sole benefit of the bailee usually results in a borrowing/lending transaction. The person who borrows an article (the bailee) gets the only benefit. However, the owner (the bailor) must warn the bailee of any defects or hazards that might exist. Because the bailee is getting something for nothing, the law generally expects the bailee to exercise great or extraordinary care while in possession of the article.

EXAMPLE 25.4

Fordyce lent his car to a friend, Dyani, to use while taking a short trip. Fordyce knew but failed to mention that the brakes were worn and in need of repair. Dyani was injured when the brakes failed and the car crashed into a tree. Fordyce would be held liable for failure to warn Dyani of the unsafe brakes.

However, in Example 25.4, if Dyani had been drinking alcohol and was at fault for the accident, he could be held liable for failing to use great or extraordinary care.

BAILMENTS FOR THE SOLE BENEFIT OF THE BAILOR

bailment for the sole benefit of the bailor
A bailment that exists when the bailor entrusts an article to the bailee for storage or safekeeping without charge, as a favor.

A bailment for the sole benefit of the bailor exists when the owner (the bailor) entrusts an article to another person (the bailee) for storage or safekeeping without being charged. Because the bailee is doing a favor for the bailor, the law requires that he or she exercise only slight care when in possession of the article.

EXAMPLE 25.5

▶ Berens was traveling for several months and asked a friend, Zanicky, to care for a valuable painting. Zanicky left the painting leaning against the wall in a spare room. While he was out for an evening, the painting was stolen. Zanicky would not be liable because he was required to provide only slight care.

MUTUAL-BENEFIT BAILMENTS

By far the most common bailment is the kind in which consideration is present. Recall from Chapter 10 that consideration is the exchange of promises by the parties to an agreement to each give up something of value they have a right to keep, or to do something they are not otherwise required to do.

A mutual-benefit bailment is one in which both the bailee and bailor derive some benefit, and, as a result, each has rights and duties. The bailor has the duty to warn the bailee of any defects in the property that could cause harm. The bailee has the duty to exercise reasonable or ordinary care in the use of the property. Each party has the right to expect the other party to fulfill the duty imposed on them.

mutual-benefit bailment A bailment in which both the bailee and the bailor derive some benefit, and, as a result, each has rights and duties.

In Example 25.5, if Zanicky had hung the painting in his living room, thereby gaining some benefit, he would have been required to use ordinary care because it would have been a mutual-benefit bailment.

Bailment for Storage Both individuals and businesses sometimes need to place articles in storage. The person or firm that provides storage facilities is known as a warehouser. The Uniform Commercial Code (UCC) provides that when goods are turned over to a warehouse for storage, the warehouser will provide a receipt for the goods and will accept the responsibility for loss of, or damage to, the goods caused by a lack of care that a reasonable person would exercise under similar circumstances (UCC 7-204).

warehouser A person or firm that provides storage facilities.

Parking Lot Bailment Parking a car in a parking lot or parking garage is a common transaction. It is important to remember, however, that a bailment is created only if the parking lot attendant actually takes control of the vehicle. If a customer parks their own automobile,

A bailment is created when the parking lot attendant actually takes control of the vehicle.
merrymuuu/Shutterstock

locks it, and retains the key, a bailment does not exist–only a license to use the parking space. In most cases, the parking lot has no responsibility for the car. However, even when the customer locks their own vehicle and retains the key, if the parking lot provides a substantial number of attendants and makes express or implied assurances that security will be provided, the court may interpret the facts of the case as suggesting that the parking lot had, in fact, gained control of the car and that a bailment existed.

EXAMPLE 25.6

Mandel was often disturbed when he would witness parking lot attendants recklessly driving automobiles with much squealing of tires and racing of engines. For this reason, he preferred to patronize "park-and-lock" garages. On one occasion, he left his vehicle in such a lot, and when he returned he found that the car had been broken into and the radio and cellular telephone had been stolen. The court would find that this was not a bailment because the attendant had no control over the car, and the transaction was merely a license to use the parking space.

Suppose that, in Example 25.6 the parking lot had a number of attendants who were parking and moving the cars of those customers who had left their keys; the attendant admitted that there had been break-ins; and the attendant assured Mandel, "We'll keep an eye on your car." In such a situation, it is likely that a court would find that a bailment did exist, and the parking lot would be liable for the radio and cellular telephone.

Bailment for Work and Services Whenever one person turns over property to another with the understanding that certain work is to be performed on the property, a bailment for work and services is created. For example, when the owner of an automobile (the bailor) leaves it at a garage (the bailee) to have repairs made, or the owner of fabric (the bailor) turns it over to a tailor (the bailee) to have a garment made, a bailment for work and services is created.

bailee's lien
The right of the bailee in a bailment for work and services to hold and, if necessary, sell the property if the bailor does not pay for the services or work done.

In transactions of this kind, there are actually two legal relationships. The bailor-bailee relationship is concerned with the care of the property. The contractual relationship is concerned with the kind and the quality of work done and the payment for services performed. The bailee in a bailment for work and services is entitled to hold and, if necessary, sell the property if the bailor does not pay for the services or work done. This provision of the law is known as a bailee's lien. (A *lien* is a claim against the property of another as security for a debt.)

EXAMPLE 25.7

Surry instructed the service manager of an automobile service station to perform a tune-up and "check it over carefully and get it ready for the winter." When Surry picked up the car, he got a bill for $385, which included numerous repairs and parts. He refused to pay and the service station refused to release the car, claiming a bailee's lien. The service station has the right to hold the property until Surry (the bailor) pays for the services done. Ultimately, a court would have to decide what services were reasonable to prepare the car for winter.

hotelkeeper
A person or firm in the business of offering lodgings or temporary shelter to guests and transients.

Hotel Bailments A bailment relationship exists between a guest (as bailor) and a hotelkeeper (as bailee) with regard to the guest's property that is specifically placed in the care of the hotelkeeper. A hotelkeeper, sometimes called an *innkeeper,* is in the business of offering lodgings or temporary shelter to transients. The shelter may be in a hotel, motel, hostel, or bed and breakfast. A transient is a guest whose stay is relatively uncertain—a day, a week, a month, or more. Under common law, the hotelkeeper's liability for the property of guests was near absolute, but state statutes today limit a hotel's liability to that of an ordinary bailee or limit liability to the amount listed in a posted notice in the room. Typically, a hotel will have a sign on the room door stating that the hotel's liability extends only to property deposited in the hotel safe. Such statutes also allow the hotel to place a dollar limit on the hotel's liability.

transient
A guest whose stay is relatively uncertain.

Common-Carrier Bailments A common carrier is an individual or firm in the business of transporting goods between certain points as allowed by the various state commissions that regulate the carriers. The law requires that a common carrier must accept all shipments that it is authorized to handle. When a shipper, known as the consignor, turns over goods to a common carrier, a mutual-benefit bailment is created that is terminated only when the common carrier delivers the goods to the party designated by the shipper, known as the consignee. The mutual-benefit bailment gives the carrier (the bailee) certain rights and duties:

common carrier
An individual or firm in the business of transporting goods between certain points as allowed by the various state commissions that regulate carriers.

consignor
The person or party shipping goods in a bailment relationship.

consignee
The person or party receiving goods in a bailment relationship.

1. The right to determine and enforce reasonable rules and requirements concerning the operation of its services. For example, a carrier may refuse to accept improperly packed goods or, during certain times of the year, it may refuse to accept goods that could be damaged by freezing temperatures.
2. The right to payment for services provided. The carrier has a legal right to hold a shipment until payment is made. Withholding payment for transportation charges enables the carrier to hold goods on the basis of a carrier's lien.
3. The right to payment from either the consignor or consignee (depending upon the contract of consignment) during the time when the carrier's equipment is rendered unavailable while it is being loaded or unloaded.

carrier's lien
A carrier's legal right to hold a shipment until payment is made.

A common carrier is responsible for any loss or damage to goods that occurs while the goods are in its custody. However, a common carrier can avoid liability if goods are lost or damaged as a result of goods improperly packed by the sender, an act of God, or the nature of the goods themselves. A common carrier is permitted by contract to limit the amount of compensation paid in the event of lost or damaged goods.

The law requires that a common carrier must accept all shipments that it is authorized to handle.
Andrew Resek/McGraw Hill

CONSTRUCTIVE BAILMENTS

There are instances in which goods are thrust upon a bailee who does not have any choice about whether they wish to serve as bailee. An example might be if a guest in your home accidentally leaves behind their property or if a package addressed to your neighbor is accidentally delivered to you. Many people would argue that such instances are not bailments at all. Still, the courts have been unwilling to dismiss the idea of bailment altogether. As a result, the idea of involuntary bailment, or constructive bailment, has come about.

constructive bailment
A bailment in which goods are thrust upon a bailee who does not have any choice about whether they wish to serve as bailee.

EXAMPLE 25.8

▶ Mr. and Mrs. Burnside were having dinner in the dining room of the hotel in which they were overnight guests. After dinner Mrs. Burnside left her handbag, containing expensive jewelry, at the table. It was then found by the server, who gave it to the cashier. The cashier gave the handbag to the assistant manager, who disappeared with the handbag and its contents. A court would hold that a constructive bailment had been created and that the hotel was responsible for providing reasonable care, which it did not.

CHAPTER SUMMARY

25.1 A bailment is a special kind of contract that is widely used in business and in personal affairs. Specifically, it is a transaction in which the owner of tangible personal property transfers the property to another party while still retaining ownership of the property.

25.2 A bailment allows the owner of personal property to transfer possession of it to another individual. The six typical reasons for creating a bailment are sale, transportation, repair or service, rental, storage, and security for a loan.

25.3 The four types of bailments are as follows:

1. A bailment for the sole benefit of the bailee, which occurs when only the bailee benefits from the agreement. Because the bailee is getting something for nothing, they are expected to exercise great or extraordinary care in using the property.
2. A bailment for the sole benefit of the bailor, which occurs when only the bailor benefits from the agreement. In this case, the bailee receives no benefit and must exercise only slight care.
3. A mutual-benefit bailment, in which both the bailee and bailor benefit. In this situation, the bailee is required to exercise reasonable or ordinary care.
4. A constructive bailment, which occurs when goods are thrust upon a bailee who does not have a choice about whether he or she wishes to serve as bailee. In constructive bailments, the bailee is usually expected to exercise reasonable care.

CHAPTER TWENTY-FIVE ASSESSMENT

MATCHING LEGAL TERMS

Match each of the numbered definitions with the correct term in the following list.

a. bailee
b. bailment
c. bailor
d. carrier's lien
e. common carrier
f. consignee
g. consignor
h. constructive bailment
i. lien
j. transient

1. A relationship concerned with the transfer and possession of personal property without the passage of title. 1. _____
2. A relationship in which the bailee comes into possession by having goods thrust upon them. 2. _____
3. An individual or firm in the business of transporting goods between certain points for anyone. 3. _____
4. A person or firm who ships goods. 4. _____
5. A claim against the property of another as security for a debt. 5. _____
6. A person to whom goods are shipped. 6. _____

7. The person in a bailment relationship who transfers possession of goods to another. 7. _____

8. The person whose stay in a place of lodging is indefinite. 8. _____

9. The claim of a carrier against the owner of property for unpaid transportation charges. 9. _____

10. The person who receives goods as part of a bailment relationship. 10. _____

TRUE/FALSE QUIZ

Indicate whether each of the following statements is true or false.

11. A bailment requires that title pass at the time the bailment is created. 11. _____

12. Bailments can be express or implied. 12. _____

13. A bailment for the sole benefit of the bailee usually exists in agreements for the rental of equipment. 13. _____

14. In a bailment for the sole benefit of the bailee, the bailee is required to extend only slight care. 14. _____

15. A mutual-benefit bailment does not exist if there is a lack of consideration. 15. _____

16. The Uniform Commercial Code does not cover bailments for storage. 16. _____

17. The bailee in a bailment for work and services is entitled to hold and sell the property if the bailor does not pay for work or services done. 17. _____

18. A hotelkeeper has almost total liability for the property of guests. 18. _____

19. When a parking lot operator allows a motorist to lock a car and retain the key, a bailment relationship is created. 19. _____

20. When goods are stored in a warehouse, the warehouser becomes the bailor. 20. _____

21. In a mutual-benefit bailment, the bailee is required to extend extraordinary care. 21. _____

22. When fungible goods are stored, the identical goods must be returned. 22. _____

MULTIPLE CHOICE QUIZ

Indicate the correct answer from the choices following each question.

23. Which of the following is not a bailment? (a) Transportation of goods (b) Storage of goods in a warehouse (c) Sale of goods to a retailer (d) Holding of automobile at repair shop 23. _____

24. A leaves a diamond ring for repair at a jewelry store, which accidentally sells the diamond ring. The store offers to give A a different diamond ring from their inventory, which has the same value. In this case, the store had a bailment relationship with the customer and (a) satisfied their obligation by offering a ring with the same value (b) must return the identical goods (c) does not have any duty to return goods (d) must pay the value of the ring and return the identical goods. **24.** _____

25. Parking a car in a lot where an attendant has the keys to the car creates a bailment where the parking lot is required to (a) exercise extraordinary care (b) exercise reasonable care (c) exercise slight care (d) exercise no care. **25.** _____

26. A borrows a car from B for a short trip and so has created a bailment relationship. In this case, A is required to (a) exercise extraordinary care (b) exercise reasonable care (c) exercise slight care (d) exercise no care. **26.** _____

27. A asks B to store their car for them as a favor. In this case, B is the bailee and is required to (a) exercise extraordinary care (b) exercise reasonable care (c) exercise slight care (d) exercise no care. **27.** _____

DISCUSSION QUESTIONS

Answer the following questions and discuss them in class.

28. Discuss the six typical reasons for transferring goods and creating a bailment.

29. Discuss the importance of acceptance, possession, and return of goods as they apply to bailments.

30. Distinguish among (a) bailment for the sole benefit of the bailee, (b) bailment for the sole benefit of the bailor, (c) mutual-benefit bailment, and (d) constructive bailment, and provide examples of each.

31. Discuss the special requirements of mutual-benefit bailments concerned with (a) storage, (b) parking lots, (c) work and services, (d) hotels, and (e) common carriers.

32. Discuss the level of care a bailee is required to give for each of several kinds of bailments.

33. Discuss constructive bailments and explain how they differ from other kinds of bailments.

THINKING CRITICALLY ABOUT THE LAW

Answer the following questions, which require you to think critically about the legal principles that you learned in this chapter.

34. Mutual Benefit Bailment A car left in a parking garage is damaged and the attendant disclaims responsibility. While, in theory, the owner of the car (the bailor) would seem to have the law on their side, how can they prove the claim? In practice, will the owner be able to collect for the damages?

35. Care of Bailments The law of bailments requires that the bailee extend either slight care, reasonable care, or extraordinary care–depending on the circumstances. Why does the law allow such variations?

36. Hotel Bailments A guest's laptop computer is stolen from her hotel room. Should the hotel bear some responsibility for the loss?

37. Common-Carrier Bailments Should a common carrier be required to accept *all* goods for shipment that it is authorized to transport? Could there be grounds for refusing some shipments?

38. A Question of Ethics A renter of a power tool, ignoring safety warnings, injures himself while using it. The renter later denies that he had seen or read the warnings. The company renting the tool denies any knowledge of the defects in the power tool despite being aware of these defects. Is one party behaving more unethically than the other? Why or why not?

CASE QUESTIONS

Study each of the following cases. Answer the questions that follow with Yes or No.

39. Bailment Ky operated a service station on a road near the Canadian border. As a favor to customers, he frequently stored, without charge, certain items that travelers preferred not to take into Canada. Rowan had planned to cross the border for a day's visit but did not wish to take with her a bolt of fabric she had in her car. She left the fabric with Ky, saying that she would pick it up later in the day.

a. Is the service Ky offers a bailment for the sole benefit of the bailee? **a.** _____

b. Is Ky the bailor? **b.** _____

c. Is Ky required to extend extraordinary care? **c.** _____

d. Is Rowan the bailee? **d.** _____

40. Bailment Ziess, a college student, owned some furniture, a portable TV, and a small refrigerator. At the end of the spring semester, she arranged to store her property in a storage room in her dorm building provided by her college for no charge. The college made it clear that all storage was at students' risk.

a. Is this storage arrangement a bailment for the sole benefit of the bailee? **a.** _____

b. Is this arrangement a mutual-benefit bailment? **b.** _____

c. Can Ziess take any action against the college in the event of loss of her property? **c.** _____

41. Bailment Kenworth took his very expensive watch to Gervey Jewelry for repairs and cleaning. During the week in which the watch remained with the jeweler, it was placed in the store's vault each night. One night, burglars were able to bypass the burglar alarm, break into the store, and use explosives to open the vault. Kenworth's watch was among the goods stolen. Kenworth brought suit, charging that Gervey should have provided greater care in this bailment. Specifically, he charged that Gervey should have had a 24-hour security guard.

a. Is this an example of a mutual-benefit bailment? **a.** _____

b. Did Gervey provide at least ordinary care of the bailed property? **b.** _____

c. Is it likely that a court would rule in favor of Kenworth? **c.** _____

CASE ANALYSIS

Study each of the following cases carefully. Briefly state the principle of law and your decision.

42. Parking Lot Bailment Wall parked his car in the parking lot at O'Hare Airport in Chicago. After he received a parking ticket from a ticket-dispensing machine, an automatic gate was raised and he entered the lot and parked his car in a space of his choosing. On the reverse side of the parking ticket was printed, "This is a lease of parking space only and not a bailment." When he returned the next day, he discovered that his car was missing and was presumed stolen. The car was later found, but it had been extensively damaged by the thieves. Wall brought suit for $1,846, claiming that a bailment existed and that the parking lot operator was responsible. Did a bailment exist and is the parking lot operator responsible for Wall's loss? [*Clifford L. Wall et al. v. Airport Parking Company of Chicago,* 244 N.E.2d 190 (Illinois)]

Principle of Law:

____

____

Decision:

____

____

43. Bailment Noble, a resident of Washington, D.C., ordered a stereo tuner from a store in Maine. The unit was shipped and was received by McLean, the receptionist/switchboard operator in Noble's apartment building. She placed the tuner in a small room where packages for tenants were kept. When McLean went off duty at 4 p.m., the package was still in the room. By the next day it was gone; only the empty box in which the unit had been shipped was found outside the building. Noble brought suit, claiming that a bailment existed. The landlord, Bernstein, denied responsibility and pointed out a provision in the lease that the landlord is not responsible for the property of tenants and that, even if an employee of the landlord does store, move, or handle a tenant's property, he or she does so as the tenant's agent. Did a bailment exist and is Bernstein responsible for the loss? [*Howard Bernstein, et al. v. Richard Noble,* 487 A.2d 231 (District of Columbia)]

Principle of Law:

____

____

Decision:

____

____

44. Bailment Gilder entered a parking garage enclosed within the Washington Hilton Hotel, where he was directed to a parking space by an attendant. Some of the spaces were designated for park-and-lock and others were not. He locked the car and kept the keys. When Gilder had entered the garage, he saw a number of employees: a manager, a cashier, and three attendants. After Gilder parked his car, he opened the trunk in plain view of a group of employees, placed his friend's cosmetic bag in it, and locked the trunk. Upon his return, he found the trunk lid damaged from being pried open. Gilder brought suit, charging the garage with failure to provide adequate care. On appeal, the garage denied responsibility, claiming that there was no bailment.

Did a bailment exist, and is the garage responsible? [*Parking Management, Inc. v. Mark Gilder,* 343 A.2d 51 (District of Columbia)]

Principle of Law:

Decision:

45. Bailment The Marglin family moved from Indianapolis to New York and rented an apartment smaller than the one they had left. Marglin arranged to have the excess furniture stored at Global Transportation and Storage Company. During the year that the furniture was in storage, Global stored some animal hides near the furniture. When Marglin picked up the furniture, he found that it had a very unpleasant odor. When Marglin complained, Global insisted that it had provided storage as agreed. Marglin brought suit for negligence and claimed that Global had failed to provide the ordinary care required. Will Marglin succeed?

Principle of Law:

Decision:

LEGAL RESEARCH

Complete the following activities. Share your findings with the class.

46. Working in Teams In teams of three or four, visit several hotels and motels to determine their policies regarding stolen or missing property. Ask particularly about experiences with guests' complaints.

47. Using Technology Using the Internet and search engines, look for legal cases involving bailments and sample bailment contracts. Identify the types of bailments in such cases and contracts.

chapter 26
Landlord–Tenant Relations

LEARNING OUTCOMES

After studying this chapter and completing the assessment, you will be able to

26.1 Discuss the landlord–tenant relationship.

26.2 Describe the four types of tenant interests in real property.

26.3 Discuss the rights and duties of landlords and tenants.

26.4 Explain several reasons for termination of leases.

26.5 Explain how liability is determined and whether the landlord or tenant is likely to be found liable.

LANDLORD–TENANT RELATIONS

"Service to others is the rent you pay for your room here on earth."

Muhammad Ali, former professional boxer, philanthropist, and social activist

sirtravelalot/Shutterstock

LEGAL terms

- landlord
- tenant
- lease
- lessor
- lessee
- covenant
- conditions
- Fair Housing Act
- periodic tenancy
- tenancy for years
- tenancy at will
- tenancy at sufferance
- warranty of habitability
- mitigate
- quiet enjoyment
- eviction
- assignment of lease
- sublease

26.1 THE LANDLORD–TENANT RELATIONSHIP

Part of the American dream is owning a home of one's own. For many people, however, home ownership is either an unattainable dream or an unattractive choice. Renting a house or an apartment, therefore, is often an option selected by many individuals and households. In Chapter 24, leasehold estates (possession interests in real property) were introduced. These were distinguished from freehold estates (ownership interests). This chapter examines the landlord-tenant relationship and the major points of law that affect and govern leasehold estates.

landlord
The owner of real property who gives up their right of possession.

tenant
The person who agrees to pay for the use of real property.

lease
The document in which the terms of a rental agreement are written.

lessor
The landlord in a lease agreement.

lessee
The tenant in a lease agreement.

The landlord is the owner of real property who gives up their right of possession, and the tenant is the person who agrees to pay for the use of real property. The relationship between the two involves a tenant's possession, use, and control of real property in exchange for payment of rent. The document in which the terms of the agreement are spelled out is the lease. The landlord is referred to as the lessor, and the tenant is referred to as the lessee.

THE DIFFERENCE BETWEEN A LEASE AND A LICENSE

Both leases and licenses give nonowners certain rights in real property. A lease transfers to a lessee the right of possession; a license does not. A *license* merely gives a person (the licensee) the right to use real property for a specific purpose and can be canceled at the will of the landowner (the licensor). As a result, a lease creates an estate (interest) in real property; a license merely gives permission to use the real property.

ESSENTIAL ELEMENTS OF THE LANDLORD–TENANT RELATIONSHIP

The essentials of the landlord-tenant relationship are

- The tenant can occupy a landlord's property only with the consent of the landlord.
- The tenant's rights in the property are inferior to those of the landlord.
- The property must revert (be returned) to the landlord at the termination of the lease.
- The parties must agree that the tenant has a right of immediate possession.

THE LEASE IS THE BASIS OF THE RELATIONSHIP

The landlord-tenant relationship can be created by an express or an implied contract. While oral contracts of lease are valid under common law, most state statutes require written leases in instances where the term of the lease is greater than one to three years. In addition, recall from Chapter 13 that the Statute of Frauds requires that contracts that cannot be completed in less than one year must be in writing to be enforceable.

covenant
An agreement made by either a landlord or a tenant to do certain things.

conditions
Restrictions that limit the use of the property.

Covenants A covenant is an agreement or promise in a lease to do a particular thing—such as when a tenant promises to use the property for certain purposes or a landlord promises to make certain repairs and to ensure the tenant's quiet enjoyment.

Conditions A condition, or restriction, included in a lease limits the use of the property. If the lease stipulates that the premises will be used as a retail bookstore, for example, opening a nightclub would not be permissible. The landlord may cancel the lease if a tenant fails to respect the conditions specified.

EXAMPLE 26.1

▶ Whitehorse, the lessee/tenant, leased an apartment from Mirov, the lessor/landlord, for $600 per month. Mirov included in the written lease a statement that pets were not allowed. Whitehorse's promise to pay the rent is a covenant, and the "no pet" clause in the lease is a condition. Mirov can cancel the lease if Whitehorse either fails to pay the rent or allows a dog to live on the premises.

The Law Relating to Leases The Fair Housing Act prohibits discrimination in housing on the basis of race, color, sex, familial status, national origin, religion, or handicap. Under the Fair Housing Act, it is generally illegal for a landlord to discriminate against these protected classes by refusing to rent property, or by claiming that property is already rented when in fact it is available. It is also illegal for a landlord to alter the terms, privileges, or conditions of a lease so that they are unfavorable to a protected class.

Fair Housing Act
A federal law that prohibits discrimination in housing on the basis of race, color, sex, familial status, national origin, religion, or handicap.

In addition to the Fair Housing Act, under common law, the parties to a lease were relatively free to include whatever terms were acceptable to and agreed upon by the parties. Increasingly, however, leases are subject to many more legal restrictions than they were in the past. Also, because leases are now viewed as contracts, commercial leases are subject to certain provisions of the Uniform Commercial Code (UCC) regarding unconscionability (UCC 2-302).

26.2 TYPES OF TENANT INTERESTS IN REAL PROPERTY

The type of possession interest a tenant has in real property can vary considerably depending on the agreements between the parties and the provisions of the lease. The following types of possession interests are most common.

periodic tenancy
A possession interest in which the lease continues for successive periods for the same length of time.

tenancy for years
The most common type of possession interest in which the lease is for a specific period of time.

PERIODIC TENANCY

A periodic tenancy is a possession interest in which the lease continues for successive periods for the same length of time–weekly, monthly, annually, and so forth. A periodic tenancy is somewhat open-ended because it is automatically renewed at the end of the period unless the landlord or tenant gives notice of their intent to not renew the lease.

In such a case, either the landlord or tenant must give the other party timely notice in order to comply with applicable state laws. The amount of advanced notice generally equals the term of the lease, but varies greatly from state to state. For example, Connecticut requires a three-day notice prior to the termination of a periodic tenancy, while Delaware requires a 60-day notice.

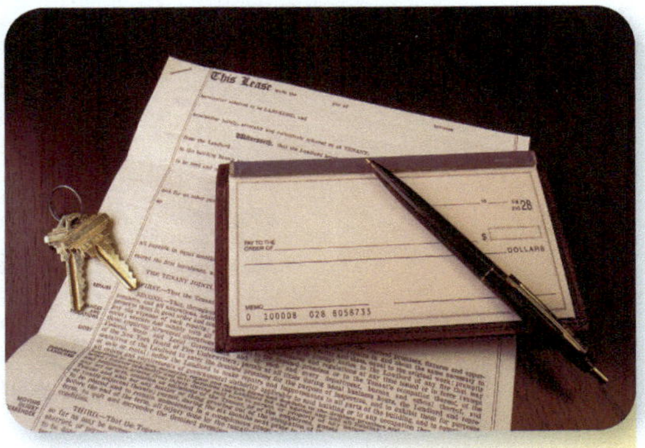

Because leases are now viewed as contracts, commercial leases are subject to certain provisions of the UCC.
Comstock Images/Getty Images

TENANCY FOR YEARS

The most common type of possession interest is a tenancy for years. This type of lease is for a specific period of time–weeks, months, years, or the like. A tenancy of this type automatically terminates on the stated expiration date.

TENANCY AT WILL

tenancy at will
A possession interest in which no specific time of lease is agreed upon.

A tenancy at will is a possession interest in which no specific time of lease is agreed upon. The lease continues indefinitely until one of the parties notifies the other of a desire to terminate the lease. Most state statutes provide that the landlord must give the tenant a specified minimum number of days' notice of their intent to terminate the lease. Sometimes such notice must be in writing.

EXAMPLE 26.2

▶ Commisky was transferred from Chicago to Los Angeles. While she searched for a suitable house, she rented a furnished apartment with the understanding that her stay would be only a few weeks to a few months. She paid rent weekly and could terminate her lease at any time by giving the landlord one week's notice. The lease is an example of a tenancy at will.

TENANCY AT SUFFERANCE

tenancy at sufferance
A tenancy that exists only when a tenant wrongfully extends their tenancy beyond the term agreed upon.

A tenancy at sufferance (also referred to as a *holdover tenancy*) exists only in one limited situation—when a tenant wrongfully extends their tenancy beyond the term agreed upon. Tenancy at sufferance is really not a true tenancy at all because the status of the tenant in this situation is uncertain. The landlord can choose either to evict the tenant and treat them as a trespasser or to hold the tenant to another term of the lease. Thus, it is important to note that if a tenant extends their tenancy by just a few days, the landlord may hold the tenant to a new tenancy—even if the tenancy is unwanted by the tenant.

EXAMPLE 26.3

▶ Segura rented a house from Daly for two years. Uncertain about a pending job relocation, Segura was in no hurry to vacate the premises. At the end of the lease, the two parties had several conversations about Segura staying on, but nothing was agreed upon and no additional rent was paid. Segura's status was that of a tenancy at sufferance. Daly could evict Segura or hold him to another term of the lease, even though Segura had not indicated any desire to renew his lease.

26.3 RIGHTS AND DUTIES OF THE PARTIES

While the rights and duties of the parties are usually stated in the lease (whether the lease is oral or in writing), these rights may be expanded or modified by relevant laws and regulations.

LANDLORD'S WARRANTY OF HABITABILITY

As discussed in Chapter 18, a warranty is a promise or guarantee made by the seller that goods offered for sale are what they claim they are—or what a reasonable person has a right to expect. In the case of the landlord-tenant relationship, the law assumes another kind of promise—an implied warranty of habitability. This means that the landlord assures the tenant that the premises are reasonably fit for occupancy and that there are no defects that would impair the health, safety, or well-being of the occupants of the premises. The landlord must also maintain the property in a habitable condition throughout the duration of the lease. Thus, the landlord usually reserves the right to enter and inspect the premises to make any necessary repairs.

warranty of habitability An implied warranty in which the landlord guarantees that the premises are reasonably fit for occupancy and that there are no defects that would impair the health, safety, or well-being of the occupants.

EXAMPLE 26.4

▶ Dexter had been living in a college dormitory for three years and decided to rent an off-campus apartment for her senior year. Somewhat naïve and eager to be independent, she hurriedly signed a one-year lease and moved in soon afterward. It was not long before she had cause to regret her hasty decision. She discovered that she had the unwelcome company of mice, and there was neither hot water nor heat. In addition, because the door lock was defective and the windows could not be locked, an intruder entered her apartment and stole her laptop computer. When the landlord refused to make necessary repairs, she moved out after one month. The landlord sued, claiming that Dexter had violated the terms of the one-year lease. Dexter claimed that the landlord had breached his warranty of habitability. A court in all likelihood would rule that the landlord had breached the contract by violating the warranty and would agree that Dexter could terminate her lease.

LANDLORD'S RIGHT TO RENT, TO REGAIN POSSESSION, TO EVICT, AND TO RETAIN A TENANT'S SECURITY DEPOSIT

A landlord has the right to collect the agreed-upon rent as provided in the lease. Also, a landlord has the right to regain possession of the property in good condition at the end of the lease. In addition, a landlord has the right, subject to limitations by state statutes and local ordinances, to evict a tenant for nonpayment of rent, illegal use of the premises, or other material violations of the terms of the lease.

Finally, in certain circumstances, a landlord has the right to retain a tenant's security deposit. A security deposit is collected by a landlord to offset their losses resulting from tenant-caused property damage or nonpayment of rent. Most states require landlords to provide tenants with a written account of any damages and their subsequent repair costs within 30 days of the termination of the lease. If a landlord does not provide a tenant with such written account, a tenant will be able to collect their security deposit, even if they damaged the rental property.

EXAMPLE 26.5

▶ Itoh leased an apartment from Fodor, stating that he would occupy the premises by himself. Within three months, he began using the apartment as a gathering place for drug users. Other tenants complained to Fodor, who shortly thereafter began an eviction action. Fodor would be successful in evicting Itoh.

During the COVID-19 pandemic, various government entities, including the Federal Centers for Disease Control and Prevention, implemented bans on landlord evictions of residential tenants during the public health emergency. While those bans have been lifted for the COVID-19 pandemic, the action set a precedent for future public health emergencies.

LANDLORD'S RIGHT TO KEEP FIXTURES AND PERMANENT IMPROVEMENTS

A tenant may wish to make improvements by attaching fixtures to the land or to the premises. Two issues raised by such actions are

1. Does the tenant have the right to make attachments?
2. Does the tenant have the right to remove the fixtures they attached at the end of the lease?

Generally, the law gives a tenant the right to make reasonable modifications to the leased property in order to make it suitable for use under the circumstances. For example, it might be quite reasonable for a tenant with a long-term lease to add a patio. On the other hand, it might not be reasonable for a tenant with a one-year lease to add new wiring.

Tenants should understand that the law allows a landlord to keep any personal property added that is deemed a fixture and thus part of the real estate (see Section 24.5).

EXAMPLE 26.6

▶ Liebman rents a building to house his restaurant and makes extensive renovations for the business, including state of the art kitchen preparation counters and storage cabinets. Because these would likely be considered fixtures, Liebman would have to leave those counters and storage cabinets when the lease terminates.

LANDLORD'S DUTY TO MITIGATE DAMAGES

mitigate
The obligation of the injured party to protect the other party from any unnecessary damages.

In most states, a landlord has a duty to make reasonable efforts to reduce, or mitigate, their losses resulting from a tenant's *abandonment* (the voluntary surrender of possession of leased premises). A landlord must make a reasonable effort, for example, to find a new tenant to occupy the abandoned premises. If the landlord fails to make such reasonable effort, the tenant would be relieved of their obligation under the lease to pay the rent for the remaining time of the lease.

EXAMPLE 26.7

▶ Polin rented an apartment for one year for $800 per month. After occupying the apartment for two months, she was transferred to another city and abandoned her rented apartment. The landlord made no attempt to rent the vacated apartment, instead using the time to make repairs and paint it. After nearly a year had passed, the landlord brought suit to collect the rent that would have been paid by Polin had she not abandoned the premises. It is unlikely that a court would award the full amount of lost rent because the landlord had an obligation to mitigate damages (to reduce the loss caused by Polin's abandonment) and to rent the apartment—even at a lower rent. Of course, the landlord could sue for the difference between the lower rent and the rent specified in Polin's lease, plus any foreseeable and reasonable expenses associated with finding a new tenant.

TENANT'S RIGHT TO QUIET ENJOYMENT

quiet enjoyment
The right to use the leased premises without unreasonable interferences from the landlord or third parties.

Most written leases provide covenants (promises) of quiet enjoyment of the premises, and in many states, this is an implied right. The right to quiet enjoyment includes the use of the leased premises without unreasonable interference from the landlord or third parties.

While the landlord is not always responsible for the actions of third parties over which they have no control, some courts have held that the landlord was responsible for the actions of a tenant who denied another tenant their right to quiet enjoyment.

EXAMPLE 26.8

▶ Foden, a marriage counselor, leased a ground-floor professional office from Ganley, the owner of an office building. The lease included Ganley's covenant to provide for Foden's quiet enjoyment. The lease also included a condition that the office space would be used only for a professional practice. If Ganley rented an adjoining office to a rock music recording studio, he would have violated his covenant. If Foden changed her line of work and used the property as a nursery school, she would have violated a condition of the lease.

TENANT'S RIGHT TO ACQUIRE AND RETAIN POSSESSION

When agreeing to lease property, the landlord promises that the tenant will have possession of the premises on the agreed-upon date. If the premises are occupied by the previous tenant or under construction, the landlord must take reasonable steps to ensure that the premises are available on the specified date.

The law gives a tenant the right to make reasonable modifications to the leased property in order to make it suitable for use.
Imagemakers_Creative_Studio/iStock/360/Getty Images

The tenant has the right to possession of the leased premises for the duration of the lease. If the landlord interferes with the tenant's right of possession by evicting them without a court order of eviction, the tenant has the right to terminate the lease. An eviction is a legal action that denies the tenant the use of the premises. An *actual eviction* occurs when the tenant is denied the physical use of the premises, whether or not such an eviction was approved by a court.

A *constructive eviction* results when the tenant's use or enjoyment of the property has been substantially lessened as a result of certain actions, conditions, or behavior on the part of the landlord or other tenants. A tenant's use or enjoyment would be substantially lessened, for example, by excessive noise, foul odors, or the use of nearby premises for illegal purposes. When the tenant claims constructive, rather than actual, eviction, they cannot terminate the lease or stop paying rent unless they abandon the premises.

eviction
An action that denies the tenant the use of the premises.

assignment of lease
When a tenant transfers their entire interest in the entire premises for the remaining length of the term of the lease.

sublease
A transfer of the tenant's interest in part of the term of the lease and/or part of the premises.

TENANT'S RIGHT TO ASSIGN OR SUBLEASE

Often a tenant will transfer their interest in the property to a third person An assignment of lease is a transfer of the tenant's interest in the entire premises for the entire length of the term of the lease. A sublease is a transfer of the tenant's interest for a part

A constructive eviction can result from excessive noise.
Image Source/Getty Images

of the premises or for a part of the term of the lease. Most leases provide that a tenant may not assign or sublease without the landlord's consent. Also, a provision may be added that a landlord may not unreasonably refuse consent for an assignment or sublease. Of course, the landlord is prohibited from refusing consent for reasons that would result in illegal discrimination.

EXAMPLE 26.9

In Example 26.7, Polin had to abandon her apartment as a result of being transferred to another city. Suppose Polin had a friend who agreed to take over the remaining portion of Polin's lease. The arrangement between Polin and her friend would be a sublease. If, however, Polin had learned of the transfer prior to the commencement of the lease, and the friend had agreed to take over the entire premises for the entire period, the arrangement would have amounted to an assignment of lease. Of course, the landlord would have the right to approve or disapprove the sublease or assignment, as long as such approval or disapproval was reasonable and not for an illegal reason.

26.4 TERMINATION OF LEASES

A lease may be terminated for several reasons.

LEASE EXPIRATION

The most common reason for termination is the expiration of the lease, whether the tenancy is periodic, for years, or at will. When the lease is terminated for this reason, the landlord is required to return to the tenant any security deposit the tenant had paid unless there are damages to the premises that are above and beyond normal wear and tear.

TENANT'S ABANDONMENT

If the tenant has abandoned the premises, they are not relieved of the obligation to pay the agreed-upon rent. If, however, the landlord has violated their express or implied duty to provide the tenant with quiet enjoyment, the tenant may abandon the premises under the doctrine of constructive eviction, and this action will terminate the lease.

TERMINATION BY FORFEITURE (BREACH)

Most leases contain a provision that gives the landlord the right to terminate the lease if the tenant fails to pay rent or violates any other material lease provision–for example, making excessive noise, disturbing other tenants, or using residential premises for business purposes. However, the tenant's breach must be *material*–that is, involve an important matter. It is unlikely that a court would allow a termination if the tenant is only a few days late with the rent payment.

26.5 TORT LIABILITY

When a person is injured on leased premises, the question of liability arises. Generally, the person in control of the area in which the injury took place is held to be responsible. The landlord remains in control of common areas, such as hallways, stairways, and laundry rooms.

EXAMPLE 26.10

▶ Bonder, a new tenant in an apartment building owned by Mei, suffered serious injuries when he fell on a broken step while descending a stairway in his apartment building. The landlord was held liable for Bonder's injuries because he was negligent in failing to keep the stairway in good condition.

The tenant is responsible for injuries occurring on their own leased premises. For this reason, apartment dwellers' insurance policies are sold to protect the tenant policyholder against liability losses resulting from injuries that occur on the tenant's premises, but not losses that result from injuries that occur in common areas or in the physical structure itself.

EXAMPLE 26.11

▶ While visiting a friend's apartment, McIlhenny tripped on a torn area rug, hit her head on the sharp corner of a table, and was seriously injured. McIlhenny, reluctant to sue her friend, sued the landlord of the building instead, charging him with the tort of negligence. A court would hold that the responsibility for maintaining safe premises was the tenant's, not the landlord's.

CHAPTER SUMMARY

26.1 A landlord is an owner of real property who gives up their right of possession, and a tenant is a person who agrees to pay for the use of real property. The relationship between the two involves a tenant's possession, use, and control of real property in exchange for payment of rent. A lease transfers to a lessee the right of possession. A license does not transfer possession but gives the licensee only the right to use real property and can be canceled at will by the landowner. Covenants are promises by either the landlord or the tenant to do certain things. Conditions are restrictions on the use of the property.

26.2 The four kinds of tenant interests in real property are the following: (a) periodic tenancy (a possession interest in which the lease continues for the same length of time), (b) tenancy for years (a lease for a specific period of time), (c) tenancy at will (a possession interest in which no specific time of the lease is agreed upon), and (d) tenancy at sufferance (when a tenant wrongfully extends their tenancy beyond the term agreed upon).

26.3 The law imposes on the landlord the warranty of habitability and the duty to mitigate damages if a lease is breached. In return, the landlord has the right to rent, regain possession, evict, and keep fixtures and permanent improvements to the property. Tenants have the right to property that is reasonably fit and safe for occupancy; to the quiet enjoyment of the premises; and to acquire, possess, assign, or sublease the premises subject to the terms of the lease.

26.4 The most common reason that a lease is terminated is by expiration. Leases also can be terminated by abandonment or by breach of the terms of the lease.

26.5 Liability is generally determined by who has control of the premises at the time and place of injury. The tenant is responsible for injuries occurring in their own leased premises. The landlord is responsible for injuries that occur in common areas.

CHAPTER TWENTY-SIX ASSESSMENT

MATCHING LEGAL TERMS

Match each of the numbered definitions with the correct term in the following list.

a. abandonment	**f.** lease	**k.** sublease
b. assignment	**g.** lessee	**l.** tenancy at will
c. condition	**h.** lessor	**m.** tenancy at sufferance
d. covenant	**i.** periodic tenancy	**n.** tenancy for years
e. eviction	**j.** quiet enjoyment	**o.** warranty of habitability

1. The legal term in a landlord–tenant relationship that refers to the landlord. **1.** _____

2. The agreement between landlord and tenant. **2.** _____

3. The legal term in a landlord–tenant relationship that refers to the tenant. **3.** _____

4. A promise made by a landlord or a tenant in a lease. **4.** _____

5. A restriction in a lease that allows cancellation if the landlord or tenant fails to honor the limitation. **5.** _____

6. A lease in which the lease period continues for successive periods for the same length of time. **6.** _____

7. A lease for a specific period of time—weeks, months, years, or the like. **7.** _____

8. A lease in which no specific period has been agreed. **8.** _____

9. The status when a tenant wrongfully extends tenancy beyond the term of the original lease. **9.** _____

10. A landlord's promise that the premises are reasonably fit for occupation and that there are no defects that would impair the health, safety, or well-being of the occupants. **10.** _____

11. A tenant's voluntary surrender of possession of leased premises. **11.** _____

12. The right of a tenant to use the premises without unreasonable interference from the landlord or third parties. **12.** _____

13. An action by the landlord that denies the tenant the use of the premises. **13.** _____

14. A transfer of the tenant's interest in the entire premises for the entire term of the lease. **14.** _____

15. A transfer of the tenant's interest for part of the premises or for part of the term of the lease. **15.** _____

TRUE/FALSE QUIZ

Indicate whether each of the following statements is true or false.

16. A tenant can legally occupy a landlord's property only with the consent of the landlord. **16.** _____

17. The landlord-tenant relationship can be created by express or implied contract. **17.** _____

18. The unconscionability clause of the Uniform Commercial Code can be applied to the landlord-tenant relationship. **18.** _____

19. A tenancy at sufferance describes the relationship that exists when a tenant wrongfully extends their stay beyond the terms of the lease. **19.** _____

20. A warranty of habitability is the tenant's promise that they will inhabit the property according to the terms of the lease. **20.** _____

21. If a tenant abandons the premises, the landlord is permitted to continue charging rent while taking no other action. **21.** _____

22. The covenant of quiet enjoyment refers to a tenant's promise to remain quiet after 10 p.m. **22.** _____

23. A landlord is liable for all injuries that occur on the leased premises. **23.** _____

MULTIPLE CHOICE QUIZ

Indicate the correct answer from the choices following each question.

24. A tenant executes a written lease for a term of 12 months. In this case, the tenant has (a) periodic tenancy (b) tenancy for years (c) tenancy at will (d) tenancy at sufferance. **24.** _____

25. After a written lease term ends, the tenant remains in the leased space, continuing to pay rent, and has (a) periodic tenancy (b) tenancy for years (c) tenancy at will (d) tenancy at sufferance. **25.** _____

26. A tenant leases space for a retail store that they discover is infested with termites. As a result, the municipal authority will not allow the store to open. In this case, the tenant may (a) not terminate the lease (b) terminate the lease due to violation of the tenant's right to quiet enjoyment (c) terminate the lease due to violation of warranty of habitability (d) terminate the lease due to the right to retain possession. **26.** _____

27. A tenant leases space from a landlord for a law practice and, after taking possession, finds that the landlord has installed surveillance cameras without tenant's approval. In this case, the tenant may (a) not terminate the lease (b) terminate the lease due to violation of the tenant's right to quiet enjoyment (c) terminate the lease due to violation of warranty of habitability (d) terminate the lease due to the right to retain possession. **27.** _____

28. A landlord owns a strip mall, and a tenant leases one of the commercial spaces in the mall. Under the lease, the tenants are responsible for maintaining their leased spaces, and the landlord is responsible for maintaining the common areas, including the walkways in front of each space. In this case, the tenant will be liable for injury resulting (a) only in their leased space (b) in their leased space as well as the walkways in front of their space (c) in their leased space as well as all common areas of the strip mall (d) in all leased spaces of the mall, but not the common areas. **28.** _____

29. A written lease states that the tenant may not operate a commercial business in their leased residence. The tenant decides to open a consulting business and work from the leased residence space. The landlord (a) must wait until the end of the lease term and terminate due to lease expiration (b) may terminate due to the tenant's abandonment (c) may terminate due to the tenant's breach (d) not terminate the lease. **29.** _____

DISCUSSION QUESTIONS

Answer the following questions and discuss them in class.

30. Discuss the difference between a lease and a license, and state the advantages and disadvantages of each.

31. If a tenant chooses to use leased premises for purposes other than the one stipulated in the lease, why would a new agreement be required?

32. If a landlord should fail to make the repairs promised in the lease, what recourse does the tenant have?

33. Should a tenant have the right to remove fixtures they have added to the premises? Why or why not?

34. Explain several reasons for termination of leases.

35. Explain how liability for injuries suffered by a tenant's guests in common areas is determined and whether the landlord or tenant is likely to be found liable.

THINKING CRITICALLY ABOUT THE LAW

Answer the following questions, which require you to think critically about the legal principles that you learned in this chapter.

36. Landlord's Rights Under what circumstances should a landlord have the right to withhold their permission to assign or sublet premises?

37. Tenant's Rights Most residential leases prohibit the premises being used for business purposes. Would activities such as writing, dressmaking, or accounting be sufficient reason for eviction?

38. Warranty of Habitability What recourse does a tenant have when the landlord fails to provide reasonable habitability?

39. Liability of Landlord Under what circumstances should a landlord be held liable for injuries suffered by a tenant who is a victim of a crime in their premises?

____

____

40. Eviction Bans Should public health considerations allow government to restrict landlord eviction of tenants?

____

____

41. A Question of Ethics Are tenants justified in withholding rent on the grounds that another tenant's behavior has interfered with their right to quiet enjoyment?

____

____

CASE QUESTIONS

Study each of the following cases. Answer the questions that follow with Yes or No.

42. Tenancy Maldanado signed a written lease for office space in a commercial building. The lease covered a period of two years, and rent was to be paid monthly. At the end of the two years, Maldanado and the landlord began discussions over the terms of a new lease. During the period of negotiations, Maldanado paid the same rent that he had during the original lease, and the landlord accepted the payments.

a. Was a tenancy at sufferance created? **a.** _____

b. Was the original lease a periodic tenancy? **b.** _____

c. Was a periodic tenancy automatically created during the period of negotiations? **c.** _____

43. Landlord Rights Patsos rented a vacant warehouse for five years with the stated purpose of opening a wholesale meat distribution company. It was necessary to install a number of large refrigerators and other kinds of equipment to process and store meat. At the end of the five years, Patsos decided to build his own warehouse and did not renew the lease. The day he began to remove his equipment, the landlord appeared and stopped the activity, claiming that the refrigerators and other equipment were fixtures because they were permanently installed and thus now belonged to the landlord.

a. Is it likely that a court would consider the refrigerators and other equipment to be fixtures and therefore the property of the landlord? **a.** _____

b. Is the determination of whether the landlord's property will suffer damage an issue in this case? **b.** _____

c. Is there any way that Patsos could have conducted his business without installing the equipment? **c.** _____

44. Conditions of Lease Perez rented a vacant building, signing a lease indicating that he would open a movie theater. When Perez began operations, the theater specialized in art and classic films. After several months, however, it became apparent that the business was doomed to failure and, in an attempt to salvage his business, Perez changed his policy and began showing adult pornographic films. The change helped the business but attracted a different clientele. The landlord began an eviction action, claiming that Perez had violated the terms of his lease.

a. Is it likely that the landlord will be successful in evicting Perez? **a.** _____

b. Is the landlord asking the court to grant an order for constructive eviction? **b.** _____

c. Could the landlord have prevented the disagreement by including more specific terms in the lease agreement? **c.** _____

CASE ANALYSIS

Study each of the following cases carefully. Briefly state the principle of law and your decision.

45. Covenants Knight purchased an apartment building that was occupied by tenants Hallsthammer, Decaprio, and Breit. The day after acquiring the building, Knight informed the tenants that their rent was being increased. A week later, Breit, on behalf of himself and other tenants, informed Knight that the tenants intended to withhold their rent because of the state of disrepair of the building. In their complaint, the tenants cited wall cracks, peeling paint, water leaks, heating and electrical fixture problems, broken or inoperable windows, rodents and cockroaches, and lack of sufficient heat. The tenants accused Knight of a breach of his warranty of habitability, and for this reason they withheld rent payments. Knight defended his actions, stating that the tenants had not given him time to remedy the problems. Does it seem likely that the court would support the actions of the tenants? [*Knight v. Hallsthammer,* 623 P.2d 268 (California)]

Principle of Law:

____

____

Decision:

____

____

46. Liability An intruder entered through a window and sexually assaulted McCutchen in her apartment. McCutchen sued the landlord, Ten Associates, for failure to provide adequate security and failure to warn her of the risk of intrusion through a window. Ten Associates claimed that they had no way of anticipating an intruder. Evidence was introduced that revealed the landlord knew or should have known of a prior sexual assault and numerous intrusions through apartment windows. Does it appear that Ten Associates was negligent in providing for the security of tenants? [*Ten Associates v. McCutchen*, 398 So. 2d 860 (Florida)]

Principle of Law:

Decision:

47. Landlord Responsibility Harmon, the owner of a suburban house, rented it for one year to the Wagners, who had just moved into the city from another state. Two months after moving into the house, the Wagners divorced, and the spouses moved to smaller facilities. The house remained vacant for 10 months. At the end of one year, Harmon brought suit to collect the rent for these 10 months. The Wagners protested, claiming that the landlord should have tried to rent to someone else. The landlord said that it was the Wagners' responsibility to sublease the house. Is it likely that Harmon would be successful in his suit?

Principle of Law:

Decision:

LEGAL RESEARCH

Complete the following activities. Share your findings with the class.

48. Working in Teams In teams of three or four, investigate whether your local community has a housing or landlord-tenant court. What are some of the disputes decided by this court?

49. Using Technology Using the Internet and search engines, investigate sample leases. What are some of the covenants and conditions typically contained in these leases?

chapter 27 Wills, Intestacy, and Trusts

LEARNING OUTCOMES

After studying this chapter and completing the assessment, you will be able to

27.1 Identify the purpose of a will.

27.2 Recognize the language used to describe the various people, and the court, involved with a will.

27.3 Discuss the types of gifts covered by a will.

27.4 Identify the requirements for a valid will.

27.5 Explain how a will is revised or revoked.

27.6 Explain the way the court distributes the estate of someone who dies intestate.

27.7 Discuss trusts, including the major types of trusts and the role of a trustee.

WILLS, INTESTACY, AND TRUSTS

"There is something about wills which brings out the worst side of human nature. People who under ordinary circumstances are perfectly upright and amiable, go as curly as corkscrews and foam at the mouth, whenever they hear the words 'I devise and bequeath.'"

Dorothy L. Sayers, English author, from her novel *Strong Poison*

Comstock Images/Getty Images

LEGAL terms

- decedent
- will
- testator
- probate court
- personal representative
- executor
- administrator
- intestate
- beneficiary
- legacy
- bequest
- ademption
- devise
- holographic will
- nuncupative will
- testamentary capacity
- codicil
- trust
- trustee
- settlor

27.1 THE PURPOSE OF A WILL

The law in the United States with regard to wills, estates, and trusts has been developed to achieve certain objectives that are quite unlike those of the common law that existed in England prior to the early 20th century. Much of early English law and tradition concerning wills and estates was intended to maintain a feudal system in which all land belonged to the king.

In the United States, the law recognizes the concept of private property and the right of an individual to dispose of property as they wish. Moreover, the law reflects an attempt by the state to protect the family of the deceased person, who is known as the decedent, by providing for the needs of a surviving spouse and children, even if the decedent failed to do so.

decedent
A deceased person.

will
A person's declaration of how they wish property to be distributed upon their death.

A will, sometimes referred to as a *testament,* is a person's declaration of how they wishes property to be distributed upon their death. The primary purpose of a will is to allow an individual to designate what will happen to their property after death. This intention of the decedent is known as *testamentary intent.*

The law, reflecting both recent tradition and current public policy, states that when a person dies, arrangements will first be made to pay their final expenses, such as the cost of an appropriate burial, medical expenses, taxes, and legitimate debts. Also, all of the decedent's property will be converted to cash and applied to payment of these expenses, with the remainder to be distributed as the decedent wished or as the law provides.

testator
The person who makes a will.

probate court
The court responsible for accepting a will that meets all statutory requirements and for supervising the operation of a will.

27.2 THE LANGUAGE OF WILLS

personal representative
The person responsible for settling the affairs of the decedent.

executor
A personal representative named in a will to handle matters involving the estate of a deceased person.

administrator
A personal representative named by the court to perform as the executor would in instances in which the deceased person has not left a will.

intestate
The state in which a person dies without a will.

beneficiary
An individual who receives gifts of personal or real property by will.

The person who makes the will is known as the testator. The court responsible for accepting a will that meets all statutory requirements and for supervising the operation of a will is known as the probate court. The person responsible for settling the affairs of the decedent is known as the personal representative.

If the personal representative has been named in the will, they are known as the executor. If the executor is deceased, declines to serve, or is lacking in capacity, or if the decedent dies without making a will, the court will appoint a personal representative, known as an administrator. The personal representative is responsible for managing the affairs of the estate with prudence. They may be held liable for any loss suffered by the estate as a result of misconduct or lack of good judgment.

For various reasons, some people do not execute a will. When a person dies without a will, they are said to have died intestate.

The term *heir* is a broad term that refers to a person who inherits property either under a will or from someone who dies intestate. A beneficiary is an individual who receives gifts of personal or real property pursuant to a will.

27.3 TYPES OF GIFTS UNDER WILLS

legacy
A gift of money by will.

bequest
A gift of personal property by will.

To be precise, a gift of money under a will is known as a legacy, while a gift of personal property is known as a bequest. Currently, however, the two terms are often used synonymously. A legacy or bequest is *specific* when it identifies the personal property given or *general* when it does not identify such property. When a bequest is specific, ademption occurs when the personal property is disposed of before the death of the testator. In such a case, the bequest is considered ineffective because a will can distribute only property that the testator owned at the time of their death. Finally, a legacy or bequest can be *residuary* when it provides for the disposition of the balance of the estate. A gift of real property is known as a devise.

ademption
When a specific bequest of personal property is made, but the personal property is disposed of before the death of the testator.

devise
A gift of real property by will.

EXAMPLE 27.1

▶ Pieper drafted a will leaving a large estate, including a power snow blower, to her brother-in-law; $25,000 to her nephew; a summer home to her sister; and the remainder of her estate to her life partner. The power snow blower is a specific bequest, the $25,000 is a general legacy, the summer home is a devise, and the remainder of the estate is a residuary legacy.

27.4 REQUIREMENTS OF A VALID WILL

A will must comply with legal requirements that are intended to ensure that the wishes of the testator are met and that there are no obstacles to the smooth transfer of the property. The law governing wills varies from one state to another, but most states are consistent in specifying certain requirements.

REQUIREMENT OF WRITING

In most cases, a will must be in writing, dated, and signed to be effective. The writing need not be formal, as long as it meets the legal requirements. A holographic will is one that is completely handwritten. Holographic wills have been challenged because they included some words that were not handwritten, such as the letterhead on stationery. As a result, some states require only the material portions and signature to be handwritten in order for a holographic will to be considered valid. Like other wills, a holographic will must be signed and dated.

holographic will
A will that is completely handwritten.

nuncupative will
An oral will.

A nuncupative will, the term used for an oral will, might be valid in only the most unusual circumstances (e.g., where the testator was under the imminent danger of death). A tape recording of a decedent's voice, offered as a nuncupative will, would be invalid.

While several states have considered allowing electronic signatures for digital copies of wills, most states still require a written signature for a valid will.

In most cases, a will must be in writing, dated, and signed to be effective. Except in very rare circumstances, wills must be in writing.
NotarYES/Shutterstock

REQUIREMENT OF WITNESSES

A formal, printed will must be signed by the testator and witnessed. In most states, there are no age requirements for witnesses, but they must be legally competent. That is, minors may witness a will as long as they have an adequate understanding of what they are signing and could testify regarding the facts related to the execution of the will if such becomes necessary. The number of witnesses required varies depending upon state law (it usually numbers two or three). It is necessary, however, that the witnesses see the testator sign the document because they may be called upon later to attest that they actually saw the testator sign. For this reason, it is generally advisable to have witnesses who are younger than the testator and who live nearby (not that all younger persons will outlive the testator, but it is more likely that they will). Witnesses generally also must be aware that the document being signed is a will.

Witnesses are expected to be satisfied that the testator is of sound mind at the time of signing. Frequently, testators video themselves and their witnesses during the signing of the will to demonstrate their own competence and the presence of witnesses. However, the video itself is not a valid will. In some states, witnesses cannot also be beneficiaries under the will. There have been instances in some states when wills that have not been witnessed have been accepted as valid.

TESTAMENTARY CAPACITY

testamentary capacity
The requirement that a testator be of sound mind and legal age.

Just as contracts require competent parties, the law relating to wills requires testamentary capacity; that is, a testator must be of sound mind and legal age. There is some variation among the states as to the minimum age. In most states, the age of majority for the purpose of executing a will is 18.

While the testator's age is something that can be determined easily, a person's mental capacity is not so readily provable. It is essential that the testator be of sound mind when the will is made, even though, as often happens, mental capacity may deteriorate with the passing years. From a legal perspective, a testator is considered of sound mind if they are adequately rational to understand the act of making a will, realize the nature and disposition of their property, and recognize their heirs. A person with mental illness can still be considered of testamentary capacity if they make a will during a lucid period.

If it can be established that the testator lacked testamentary capacity, the will is void.

UNDUE INFLUENCE

The expression *undue influence* (see Chapter 9) describes the pressure that might be applied to a testator to change their true wishes for the disposition of property. Undue influence can take many forms, from threats of harm to more subtle suggestions. Very often, it is difficult for a court to decide whether the attention given to an elderly relative, for example, is undue influence or is simply loving concern shown by one of the parties named in the will.

EXAMPLE 27.2

Marley had worked for Phan, a 62-year-old executive, for 15 years as an administrative assistant. When he was 60, Phan had executed a will leaving his entire estate to Marley. Two years later he died. Phan's grown children, who were effectively disinherited by the will, challenged the will, claiming that because of Marley's and Phan's confidential relationship, Marley had exercised undue influence over their father. The court held that the confidential relationship in itself could not be viewed as undue influence. Lacking evidence of undue influence, the will was allowed to stand, and the entire estate passed to Marley.

27.5 REVISING AND REVOKING WILLS

During the lifetime of the testator, a number of circumstances may prompt the testator to revise or revoke their will. Intended beneficiaries, for example, may die while the testator is alive or may fall out of favor.

REVISIONS

Any alterations to a will, such as erasures, words crossed out, or handwritten insertions, usually invalidate the document. To make legal changes in a will, a separate document, called a codicil, is prepared to revoke, alter, or revise the will. The execution of a codicil has formal requirements and is very much like writing a new will. It must be witnessed and dated. There is no limit on the number of codicils that can be made. In the case of a relatively simple, straightforward will, it is often just as easy to execute an entirely new will. Also, with the use of word processing, it is easy to recall the existing will and make whatever changes are desired. On the other hand, a lengthy, complex will may be more easily revised by writing a codicil.

codicil
A document, separate from the will, in which a person can make legal changes to their will.

EXAMPLE 27.3

▶ Kassim, a widower, executed a will in which he left his entire estate to his two children, Robert and Susan, equally. As the years passed, Robert married, fathered three children, and struggled to make ends meet. Susan, on the other hand, remained single and enjoyed great financial success. Kassim felt that Robert needed money more than Susan did. To change the distribution of his estate so that a greater portion went to Robert, Kassim executed a new will.

REVOCATIONS

Many wills include a statement that the testator is revoking all previous wills. Even without such a statement, the most recent will, if valid, automatically revokes all prior wills made by the testator.

Revocations by operation of law can include those that result from marriage or remarriage of the testator, divorce or annulment of a marriage, and the birth or adoption of children after the will was made, all of which can change the disposition of gifts.

27.6 INTESTACY

When a person dies without a will, or had a will that failed to meet the requirements of the law, they are said to have died intestate. In such a case, the law of the state in which the deceased person was domiciled (where they lived) governs the disposition of their property, even though the death may have occurred elsewhere. These laws vary by state. Generally, a surviving spouse and children receive the entire estate. But even this seemingly fair division can create problems, as shown in Example 27.4.

If a person dies without a will, generally the surviving spouse and children will receive the entire estate.
ColorBlind Images/
Blend Images LLC

EXAMPLE 27.4

Kaslick, a man of modest means, died intestate, leaving his wife, a full-time homemaker, and two young children. Under state law, Kaslick's estate was divided in half between his wife and their children. Because of their ages, the children's share was held in trust until they reached the age of majority. Because the children's half was not available to her, Kaslick's wife not only had to support herself, but also her children with her one-half of the estate. If Kaslick had prepared a will, he might have left the entire estate, or at least most of it, to his wife, with perhaps a smaller amount to the children.

If a person dies intestate leaving a spouse but no children, the surviving spouse usually receives the entire estate. If there are children but no surviving spouse, the children usually receive the estate. State laws on intestacy also cover other situations, such as when a person dies without either a spouse or children. In these cases, other relatives, including parents, grandchildren, and siblings (brothers and sisters), are then included in the distribution. If no surviving heirs or ancestors of the deceased can be located, the decedent's property passes to the state.

EXAMPLE 27.5

Aiken, a college student with very few assets who believed he did not need a will, was killed in an airplane crash and died intestate. Aiken's estate settled the case with the airline for several hundred thousand dollars. Aiken's father, who had abandoned him as an infant, will likely share in the settlement, despite the fact that Aiken probably would not have wished for this result.

27.7 TRUSTS

trust
A device or mechanism that permits personal or real property to be held by one party, the trustee, for the benefit of another, the beneficiary.

trustee
A person who is entrusted with the management and control of another's property or the rights associated with that property.

A **trust** is a device or mechanism that permits personal or real property to be held by one party, the **trustee**, for the benefit of another, the *beneficiary.* Some trusts have some of the characteristics of a will in that they allow a person to control the disposition of their property after death. One of the benefits of a trust is that it allows the legal title of property to be separated from the benefits of ownership. A trust allows parents, for example, to transfer benefits, such as income derived from property, to children and still withhold actual ownership until the children are older and presumably wiser. In addition, the creation of the trust under these circumstances could result in favorable tax treatment for the parents.

Another use for a trust would be if, for example, Jones put property in trust for Smith's lifetime so that she could benefit from the income the property might produce, and at Smith's death, the property would then pass on to Browne, another beneficiary of the trust.

TYPES OF TRUSTS

There are two main types of trusts. A *testamentary trust* is created by a will. It becomes effective only upon the death of the testator. The names of the parties—beneficiaries and trustee—are specified in the will.

Note that, in Example 27.6, the final disposition of the property is still undetermined. The question of what happens to the property held in trust when the last of the children dies remains unanswered. To avoid such ambiguity, a trust should provide for final distribution of the property once the objective of the trust has been met.

EXAMPLE 27.6

Neurman, a wealthy merchant, was concerned that if he died, his three grown—but irresponsible—children would quickly squander their inheritances. To avoid the problems he foresaw, he established a testamentary trust in his will that provided that upon his death his entire estate, after paying final expenses, would be placed in trust and that the trustee would pay each of his children a yearly allowance.

A *living trust* (also known as an *inter vivos* trust) is established while the person, known as the settlor, who wishes to set up the trust is still alive. The settlor transfers the legal title to the property to the trust to be held for the benefit of either a beneficiary or the settlor themselves, possibly providing tax advantages to the settlor.

settlor
A person who sets up a trust while still alive.

THE ROLE OF THE TRUSTEE

The responsibility of the trustee is that of a fiduciary and, as suggested by the name, is one of great trust. They must manage the property according to the wishes of the settlor, who may be deceased. Appointment as a trustee should not be accepted unless one has the temperament, knowledge, and skills necessary to minimize the risks inherent in the position of trustee. Typically, banks, trust companies, attorneys, and other fiduciary organizations offer professional skills in the administration of trusts. Like all other fiduciaries, a trustee has a *duty of loyalty* and a *duty of care* (see Chapter 20 for detailed descriptions of these obligations).

Trustee's Powers The trustee has certain nondelegable powers granted by law or by the trust instrument itself. Powers usually granted by law include the authority and responsibility to invest trust property; to sell, exchange, or rent property; to contract with others in matters relating to the trust; to borrow funds using trust property as security; and to distribute income to beneficiaries.

Trustee's Duties The trustee has the duty to maintain appropriate records and to provide a full accounting of the trust property; to pay taxes; and to use good judgment in managing the property, including making good investment decisions. The trustee may purchase securities that are of very low risk and that appear on a document referred to as a *legal list.*

Trustee's Accountability A trustee whose performance of duty in managing the trust property is called into question can be held liable unless a court rules that the trustee exercised sound judgment.

CHAPTER SUMMARY

27.1 The purpose of a will is to recognize the concept of private property and give a person the right to dispose of their property as they wish. A will is also important for protecting the family of the deceased person.

27.2 The person who makes the will is known as the testator. The court responsible for accepting a will that meets all statutory requirements and for supervising the operation of a will is known as the probate court. The person responsible for settling the affairs of the decedent is known as the personal representative. If the personal representative has been named in the will, they are known as the executor. If the executor is deceased, declines to serve, or is lacking in capacity, or if the decedent dies without making a will, the court will appoint an administrator. A person who dies without a will is said to have died intestate. An heir is a person who inherits property either under a will or from someone who dies intestate. A beneficiary is an individual who receives gifts of personal or real property pursuant to a will. The person who makes the will is known as the testator.

27.3 A gift of money is known as a legacy and a gift of personal property is known as a bequest, although both terms are often used synonymously. A bequest can be specific, general, or residuary.

27.4 The requirements for a valid will vary by state but often include that the will be written, dated, signed, and witnessed. The testator also must have testamentary capacity and be free from undue influence. The requirements for testamentary capacity are that the testator be of legal age and of sound mind when the will is created.

27.5 A codicil is prepared to revoke, alter, or revise a will. The most recent will, if valid, automatically revokes all prior wills made by the testator.

27.6 When a person dies intestate, the law of the state in which the deceased was domiciled governs the disposition of their property. Usually a surviving spouse and children receive the entire estate. If there is no surviving spouse or children, other relatives (including parents, grandchildren, and siblings) are then included in the distribution.

27.7 The purpose of a trust is to allow a person to control the disposition of their property after death by having it held by one party, the trustee, for the benefit of another, the beneficiary. The two kinds of trusts are a testamentary trust, which is created by a will, and a living trust, which is established while the settlor is still alive. A trustee has a fiduciary duty to manage property according to the wishes of the settlor. Powers usually include the ability to sell, exchange, or rent property; borrow funds; contract with others in matters pertaining to the trust; and distribute income to beneficiaries. Duties include maintaining records of the property, providing a full accounting of trust property, and using good judgment.

CHAPTER TWENTY-SEVEN ASSESSMENT

MATCHING LEGAL TERMS

Match each of the numbered definitions with the correct term in the following list.

a. beneficiary
b. bequest
c. codicil
d. decedent
e. devise
f. executor
g. holographic will
h. *inter vivos*
i. intestate
j. personal representative
k. residuary
l. settlor
m. testamentary capacity
n. testamentary intent
o. testator

1. The legal term for a deceased person. **1.** _____
2. The individual who is either named in a will or appointed by a court to administer an estate. **2.** _____
3. A gift of real property left in a will. **3.** _____

4. A gift of personal property left in a will. **4.** _____

5. The wishes of a person for the distribution of their property as expressed in a will. **5.** _____

6. The person named in a will to administer the estate. **6.** _____

7. A person who makes a will. **7.** _____

8. A person who receives gifts of personal property in a will. **8.** _____

9. The balance of an estate remaining after all other distributions have been made. **9.** _____

10. A completely handwritten will. **10.** _____

11. The requirement that a person be of legal age and sound mind to prepare a will. **11.** _____

12. A document that revokes, changes, or revises a will. **12.** _____

13. The state of a person who dies without a will. **13.** _____

14. A trust set up while a person is still living. **14.** _____

15. A person who sets up a living trust. **15.** _____

TRUE/FALSE QUIZ

Indicate whether each of the following statements is true or false.

16. When a person dies intestate, the court appoints an executor to settle the estate. **16.** _____

17. A tape recording is an acceptable form of will. **17.** _____

18. Making a codicil has similar requirements to making a new will. **18.** _____

19. One of the primary purposes of setting up a trust is to receive favorable tax treatment. **19.** _____

20. An *inter vivos* trust is created by a will. **20.** _____

21. A trustee who fails to use prudent judgment in managing a trust can be held liable. **21.** _____

22. A trustee never has authority to make investments. **22.** _____

MULTIPLE CHOICE QUIZ

Indicate the correct answer from the choices following each question.

23. A is very ill but mentally competent and makes a will by telling their doctor, in the company of two nurses, how they want their assets distributed after death. The doctor writes the wishes out for A, but A dies before signing. In this case, (a) A has made a valid will (b) A has not made a valid will because it is not in writing (c) A has not made a valid will because there are no witnesses (d) A has not made a valid will because they lack testamentary capacity. **23.** _____

24. A is very ill and keeps forgetting their children have come to visit every day. A has a caregiver who convinces them that their children do not care and have not been visiting. A executes a will that leaves all assets to the caregiver. In this case, (a) A has made a valid will (b) A has not made a valid will because they lack testamentary capacity (c) A has not made a valid will because of undue influence (d) both b and c. **24.** _____

25. A executes a valid will dated January 15, 2015. After the birth of their first grandchild, A executes another will dated March 20, 2019, which includes the grandchild. After an argument with one of their children, A crosses out the child's name and bequest from the March will. A dies and (a) the laws of intestacy will take effect since there is no valid will (b) the will dated March 20, 2019 is valid (c) the will dated January 15, 2015 is valid (d) both the will dated March 20, 2019 and the will dated January 15, 2015 are valid. **25.** _____

26. A's will states that their diamond ring should be given to B. At A's death, B receives (a) a general bequest (b) a specific bequest (c) a residuary bequest (d) no bequest. **26.** _____

27. A's will states that their diamond ring should be given to B, but A sells the ring before their death. At A's death, B receives (a) a general bequest (b) a specific bequest (c) a residuary bequest (d) no bequest. **27.** _____

28. A is a wealthy person with three children and no spouse. A would like to ensure that their children are gainfully employed and working before receiving money from A or from their estate. In this case, what would you recommend as the best solution for A? (a) Leave all assets to their children as general bequests in their will. (b) Set up a testamentary trust that leaves assets to their children when they reach a certain age. (c) Set up an *inter vivos* trust that only distributes income to children who have demonstrated employment. (d) Set up an *inter vivos* trust that leaves assets to their children when they reach a certain age. **28.** _____

DISCUSSION QUESTIONS

Answer the following questions and discuss them in class.

29. Discuss the reasons a person prepares a will.

____

____

30. Discuss types of legacies, bequests, and devises covered by a will.

____

____

31. Explain each of the requirements of a valid will.

32. Explain why the law requires the testator to have testamentary capacity.

33. Charges of undue influence are frequently made by those who are denied benefits in a will. What steps might a testator take, while still alive, to reduce the likelihood of these charges being made?

34. Explain the way the court distributes the estate of someone who dies intestate.

THINKING CRITICALLY ABOUT THE LAW

Answer the following questions, which require you to think critically about the legal principles that you learned in this chapter.

35. Wills and the Law Should the law dictate that a person must provide for a spouse and children either by a will or by state law of intestacy? Why or why not?

36. Testamentary Intent If a person dies intestate, is there any way their heirs could prove what their testamentary intent would have been?

37. Holographic Will Why should a holographic will be legally valid while a transcript of a voice or video recorded will is invalid?

38. Electronic Signatures Should states allow electronically prepared and signed wills? What would you suggest to authenticate the signature?

39. Trusts What are the alternatives available to a testator who is considering the creation of a testamentary trust?

____

____

40. A Question of Ethics What is the most ethical way for one to distribute their children's portion of an estate: to bequeath equal shares to each child or to make the distribution reflect the individual's needs?

____

____

CASE QUESTIONS

Study each of the following cases. Answer the questions that follow with Yes or No.

41. Testamentary Capacity Gruen suffered from Alzheimer's disease (a form of progressive mental illness that generally occurs during old age) and lived in a nursing home. His sister, whom he had not seen since they were teenagers, instituted proceedings to have him declared mentally incompetent. A physician testified that Gruen was permanently mentally disabled and that his condition would get progressively worse. Gruen's sister was appointed his guardian. Six months later Gruen executed his last will, leaving his entire estate to his sister. When he died, Gruen's other relatives challenged the will, claiming that Gruen had lacked testamentary capacity.

a. Does it appear that Gruen had testamentary capacity? **a.** _____

b. Does it appear that the will embodied testamentary intent? **b.** _____

c. Does it appear that the sister exerted undue influence? **c.** _____

42. Requirements of a Valid Will Popov despised lawyers and refused to have one prepare his will. Instead he went online, got information about estate planning, and wrote a will in his own handwriting in which he left his entire estate to his brother and $1 to each of his three children. The will was not witnessed by anyone. After his death, his children challenged its legality and validity.

a. Are witnesses always necessary for a handwritten will to be valid? **a.** _____

b. Is this an example of a holographic will? **b.** _____

c. Will the validity of the will be rejected by the court because it was not prepared by an attorney? **c.** _____

43. Trusts Harley set up a trust, naming himself as trustee, and transferred his entire estate to the trust. The trust was intended to provide him with a lifetime income. After his death, the income from the trust was to be paid to his wife. After her death, the income from the trust was to go to three of their four children, after which the trust would be terminated. The trust specifically stated that one child, Nancy, was not named in the trust because other arrangements had been made for her. When the trust began paying to the three children, but not Nancy, she challenged the validity of the trust, claiming that the trust was a testamentary trust that did not comply with the state statute on wills.

a. Was this a testamentary trust? **a.** _____

b. Was this an *inter vivos* trust? **b.** _____

c. Will Nancy succeed in overturning the trust? **c.** _____

CASE ANALYSIS

Study each of the following cases carefully. Briefly state the principle of law and your decision.

44. Executor Misconduct Corbin was named as executor in his father's will. While going through his late father's papers, he discovered a promissory note made by Fulsom in the amount of $10,000 that reflected a personal loan the decedent had made before he died. Corbin approached Fulsom and indicated that he would accept $5,000 cash in exchange for the note. Obviously Fulsom's payment would not be included in the assets of the estate. One of the heirs discovered the cash payment and brought suit, charging misconduct. Will Corbin be required to cover the loss suffered by the estate?

Principle of Law:

____

____

Decision:

____

____

45. Responsibilities of Personal Representatives Aversa, the personal representative of her late father's estate, was presented with evidence that there was still $12,000 owing on his automobile. Rather than have the car repossessed, she borrowed $6,000 and refinanced the balance. Objection was made on the grounds that she had exceeded her authority. Is it likely that the court will approve her actions?

Principle of Law:

____

____

Decision:

____

____

46. Trustee Responsibilities The trustees of a labor union pension fund delivered various stocks and bonds to a bank under an agreement that provided that the bank would act as the trustees' agent in investing the fund's assets. The agreement also provided that the bank was "authorized to invest any assets . . . of the investment fund or to dispose of any such asset or property and invest the proceeds of such disposition, as in its absolute and uncontrolled discretion it deem(ed) suitable." The results of the bank's investments were disappointing. The trustees claimed that since trustees may not delegate their power, the bank breached its contract of agency by making unauthorized investment decisions that decreased the value of the fund. Does it appear that the trustees delegated power to the bank to make the investments? [*Local Union 422, U.A. of Joliet, v. The First National Bank of Joliet,* 417 N.E.2d 1077 (Illinois)]

Principle of Law:

Decision:

47. Testamentary Intent Before Dora Diggs, a widow, died, she left a handwritten document that read, "I want Tom R. Preston and Mattie Price to be the administrators (executors) to settle my estate." Following this she listed various assets. A dispute arose about whether the decedent, Diggs, intended to give Preston and Price general power to dispose of her property. If this were the interpretation, Preston and Price would be the beneficiaries. Other relatives claimed (a) the document was not really a will at all, (b) Diggs merely wanted to name executors, (c) the document lacked testamentary intent, and (d) Diggs died intestate. If this were the case, state intestacy laws would determine the distribution of property. The other relatives would benefit significantly if this position was the decision of the court. Did the disputed document fail to qualify as a will because of the lack of testamentary intent? [*Preston v. Preston,* 617 S.W.2d 841 (Texas)]

Principle of Law:

Decision:

LEGAL RESEARCH

Complete the following activities. Then share your findings with the class.

48. Working in Teams In teams of three or four, interview members of the trust department of a local bank to learn how they handle trusts and perform as executors of estates.

49. Using Technology Using the Internet and search engines, investigate cases that embody the terms *testamentary intent, testamentary capacity, holographic will,* and *intestacy.*

PART 6

Business and Technology

ColorBlind Images/Blend Images LLC

chapter 28
Intellectual Property

LEARNING OUTCOMES

After studying this chapter and completing the assessment, you will be able to

28.1 Discuss intellectual property and explain how it is protected.

28.2 Explain why trade secrets are so important to a firm and recognize how they may be protected using restrictive covenants and agreements not to compete.

28.3 Discuss when computer software is protected by trade secret law and when it is protected by licensing.

28.4 Distinguish between the types of trademarks.

28.5 Discuss how trademark law can be applied to cyberspace.

28.6 Explain copyrights and how the doctrine of fair use applies to them.

28.7 Describe how copyright law can be applied to software and cyberspace.

28.8 Identify the requirements for obtaining a patent.

28.9 Explain the challenges associated with applying patent requirements to computer hardware and software.

terms

LEGAL

- intellectual property
- trade secret
- Economic Espionage Act of 1996
- restrictive covenant
- agreement not to compete
- trademark
- trade dress
- cybersquatting
- copyright
- infringement
- fair use
- substantial similarity test
- patent
- design patent

INTELLECTUAL PROPERTY

"Intellectual property has the shelf life of a banana."

Bill Gates, founder of Microsoft Inc.

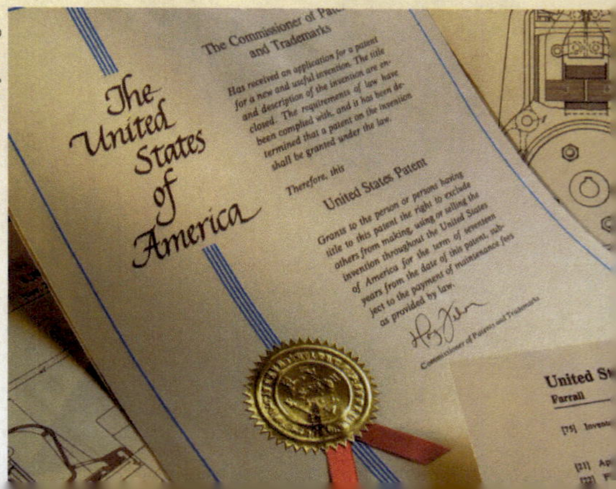

Photodisc/Getty Images

28.1 INTELLECTUAL PROPERTY DEFINED

As described in Chapter 24, individuals and businesses own both real and personal property. Most people think of property as including only tangible items, such as land and buildings (real property) and automobiles, clothing, and cash (personal property). We now examine another form of personal property, which includes knowledge, ways of doing things, and expressions of ideas. This property is commonly referred to as intellectual property or *intellectual capital.* Often the expressions of such intellectual property are stored in computers and on web pages. Intellectual property is protected through the use of trade secrets, trademarks, copyrights, and patents. This chapter addresses how the law protects intellectual property stored on computers and in other locations.

intellectual property
Personal property that includes knowledge, ways of doing things, and expressions of ideas.

28.2 TRADE SECRETS

A trade secret is specialized knowledge associated with a particular business. It includes information gained during employment about such matters as manufacturing processes, practices, devices, customer lists, and other confidential information that, in the hands of a competitor, would place a firm at a serious disadvantage. The use of a secret process or a scientific formula, for example, might be part of a worker's job, or the work itself might be so critical that disclosing it would result in injury or loss to the employer. When trade secrets are made public, the firm loses the advantage it had while the secrets were undisclosed. Accordingly, most firms take precautions to make certain that their trade secrets remain confidential.

trade secret
Specialized knowledge associated with a particular business, including information gained during employment about such matters as manufacturing processes, practices, devices, customer lists, and other confidential information.

In an effort to protect firms from the theft of trade secrets, the Economic Espionage Act of 1996 was passed. This statute makes the misappropriation or outright theft of trade secrets a federal crime. Many states have adopted the Uniform Trade Secrets Act that give owners of trade secrets a private cause of action to sue for civil damages for misappropriation of trade secrets. In 2016, Congress adopted the Defend Our Trade Secrets Act, which allows trade secret owners nationwide to bring a federal case for civil damages, thus expanding the private cause of action for trade secret theft.

Economic Espionage Act of 1996
A statute that makes the misappropriation or outright theft of trade secrets a federal crime.

EXAMPLE 28.1

▶ Starwood Hotels Inc. filed suit against Hilton Hotels Corp., claiming that Hilton unlawfully acquired Starwood trade secrets. According to the lawsuit, Hilton executives enticed two senior Starwood executives to steal confidential research and strategic plans, leave the company, and use the data to launch a luxury hotel line for Hilton. If Starwood can substantiate these claims, the company will likely be entitled to recover monetary damages.

PROTECTING TRADE SECRETS

To protect its business and its trade secrets, an employer may, within reasonable bounds, impose restrictions of secrecy on an employee or forbid the employee to work in the same line of business or for a competing firm if they leave the company. This is accomplished by requiring the employee to sign an employment contract, which governs the relationship between the employer and the employee. Often included in this contract is a clause, or paragraph, called a restrictive covenant.

restrictive covenant
An agreement in which the employee agrees not to work in similar employment within a certain geographic area or within a specified period of time.

Restrictive Covenants A restrictive covenant is an agreement in which the employee agrees not to work in similar employment. Nearly all restrictive covenants are enforceable; the most important factor is whether the covenant is reasonable. For example, it would be reasonable for a firm with a highly secret process to require its key people or scientists to agree not to work for a competitor for, say, three years. But if the same company were to require all employees—including shipping clerks, accountants, and maintenance personnel—to sign such an agreement, it would be unreasonable. Similarly, it would be unreasonable to require even key employees to avoid employment with a competitor for 20 years. It also would be unreasonable to restrict such employees from working anywhere in the world, unless perhaps the company could prove that it faced competition internationally. It must be noted that restrictive covenants could be drafted in such a way so as to prevent the employee from working for a competitor even if the employee is terminated, with or without cause.

EXAMPLE 28.2

Copley, a scientist with specialized knowledge in the field of superconductivity, was hired by the Conductol Company to work on the development of highly secret ceramics materials. Copley agreed in writing not to work for any other firm within the same state engaged in the same line of research for three years after leaving Conductol. This contract would be enforceable because Copley's leaving Conductol and joining a competitor would place Conductol at a serious competitive disadvantage because of the possibility of Copley disclosing Conductol's scientific know-how.

agreement not to compete
An agreement in which the seller of a business agrees not to begin or operate a similar business within a certain geographic area or within a specified period of time.

Agreements Not to Compete When an established business is sold, included in the sale are trade secrets that the business owns (e.g., the names and addresses of the firm's customers). Accordingly, the contract for sale usually includes an agreement not to compete, similar to the restrictive covenant placed in an employment contract. In this case, the seller agrees not to begin or operate a similar business within a certain geographic area or within a specified period of time. Again, such agreements are generally held valid provided the restrictions are reasonable.

Such agreements are highly recommended and legally enforceable because the sale of a business includes more than just a firm's physical property, such as land, buildings, inventory, cash, and so on; the sale also includes the firm's *goodwill*—that is, the name and good reputation of the firm.

EXAMPLE 28.3

Gavlick agreed to sell her dry cleaning business to Dotzel. The agreement included a provision that Gavlick would not open another dry cleaning business for five years. Two years later, Gavlick opened a dry cleaning business in a community across the state, 300 miles away. Dotzel, still angry at Gavlick for what he considered a bad bargain in terms of the profit potential of the firm, initiated legal action and pointed to the agreement not to compete that prevented Gavlick from opening a similar business within five years. It is doubtful that a court would enforce the agreement because the new firm was located so far away that it would present no real competition.

28.3 APPLICATION OF TRADE SECRET LAW TO COMPUTER SOFTWARE

Some developers of commercial software have attempted to protect against pirated copying by claiming that the program is a trade secret. Because most software is prepared for wide distribution, it is difficult to protect a computer program from being copied by making this argument. However, if a program, such as a complex accounting and budgeting program, is highly specialized and not intended for wide distribution, it would likely be considered a trade secret.

It is important, however, to recognize that a computer program distributed to a limited number of users is usually not sold; rather, the producer of the program generally retains ownership and licenses the use of it.

EXAMPLE 28.4

▶ The Grish Corporation employed 76 workers, each with their own desktop computer. Each employee needed access to software such as word processing, database management, spreadsheet, and presentation preparation. The Grish Corporation licensed all of these from Tecknisoft, a computer software firm, and all 76 employees had the software loaded onto their desktops. Included in the license agreement was a promise by Tecknisoft to update all 76 desktops with the latest versions of the software as these became available.

Producers of computer software have an incentive to treat their works as trade secrets because there is no set time limit on the protection available for trade secrets as there is for trademarks, patents, and copyrights, to be discussed later in this chapter.

Some producers of software sold to the general public that is intended for wide distribution have attempted to use licensing to protect against losses that would result from widespread copying. Frequently, such producers require that individual users who have purchased the software register their ownership. This is often accomplished by requiring the user to access the producer's home page on the web and enter some personal data. Registration then takes place automatically.

28.4 TRADEMARKS

A **trademark**, according to the *Lanham Trademark Act of 1947,* is "any word, name, symbol, or device or combination thereof adopted and used by a manufacturer or merchant to identify his (or her) goods and distinguish them from goods manufactured or sold by others." Ownership may be designated in advertising or on a label, package, or letterhead by the use of the word *Registered,* the symbol ®, or the symbol ™. Trademark registrations are issued at the federal level by the *U.S. Patent and Trademark Office* of the Department of Commerce for renewable periods of 10 years. The person in whose name a trademark is registered or to whom it has been assigned may prevent others from (1) using the trademark

trademark
Any word, name, symbol, or device or combination thereof adopted and used by a manufacturer or merchant to identify their goods and distinguish them from goods manufactured or sold by others.

in connection with competing goods, (2) using the trademark in the same or in a similar line of business, or (3) using marks or names so similar to those registered that reasonable people might confuse them. Some famous trademarks have high degrees of consumer recognition and are directly associated with a specific product or service. To prevent the dilution of these trademarks, they are afforded a higher level of protection and may even be shielded from unrelated, noncompeting uses. Some examples of famous trademarks are "Coca-Cola," "Google," and "Nike."

Symbols used to identify services, as distinguished from goods, are called *service marks.* Because the legal requirements for service marks are very similar to those for trademarks, both are often referred to simply as trademarks. The trademark law also protects other such distinguishing identifiers as *trade characters*–fictional characters such as Betty Crocker, the Green Giant, the Pillsbury Doughboy, and the Marlboro man; *trade names*–the name under which a firm does its business, such as Microsoft or General Motors; and *brand names*–the registered names for products such as Windows or Cadillac. In some cases, a firm may use the same trade name and brand name–for example, Quaker Oats Company and Quaker Oats.

EXAMPLE 28.5

The National Football League (NFL) takes a proactive role in preventing the unauthorized commercial use of its trademarked phrases "NFL," "Super Bowl," and "Super Sunday." In lieu of the trademarked phrase "Super Bowl," there have been frequent commercial uses of the phrase "the Big Game." When the NFL attempted to trademark that phrase as well, two colleges that have referred to their game as "the Big Game" for more than 100 years objected. The NFL rescinded its trademark application.

Starbucks Coffee Company is a registered trademark of Starbucks Corporation.
Jill Braaten/McGraw Hill

TRADE DRESS

trade dress
A distinctive, nonfunctional feature that distinguishes a merchant's or manufacturer's goods or services from those of another.

Trade dress is a distinctive, nonfunctional feature that distinguishes a merchant's or manufacturer's goods or services from those of another. The trade dress of a product relates to its total image and can include the color of the packaging or the configuration of goods. Examples of trade dress include the packaging for Wonder Bread, the tray configuration for Healthy Choice frozen dinners, and the color scheme of Subway sandwich shops. Seeking protection against trade dress infringements can be vital to the survival of a business.

EXAMPLE 28.6

▶ Anheuser-Busch, in a controversial marketing ploy, produced and distributed Bud Light beer in cans that prominently displayed local colleges' team colors. Some colleges objected to this marketing scheme and informed Anheuser-Busch that the company was infringing on school trade dress. Rather than risk being sued for trade dress infringement, Anheuser-Busch complied with all official requests to cease producing beer cans displaying school colors.

HOW TRADEMARKS ARE LOST

Most firms that have registered trademarks spend considerable amounts of money to research, design, register, and advertise their trademarks. These firms naturally regard them as valuable property and take appropriate measures to protect them. Yet many trademarks have been lost because they were so successful, or so often misused, that they entered the language as ordinary words. That is, to the general public, the trademark came to mean the same as the product, no matter who had manufactured it. Such words that become a common part of the language are called *generic.* Many trademarks that were once the proud possessions of particular companies have been lost in this way. Examples of these former trademarks include *escalator, kerosene, cellophane, aspirin, frisbee,* and *spearmint.*

EXAMPLE 28.7

▶ Escalator was the registered trademark for a moving staircase manufactured by the Otis Elevator Company. The Escalator brand of moving staircase was widely advertised, and the general public began to use the word *escalator* to mean "moving staircase." The manufacturer even advertised in *Architectural Forum* magazine that Otis provided "the utmost in safe, efficient, economical elevator and escalator operation." Because the term *escalator* had become generic, Otis lost its registered trademark.

In Example 28.7, by using the word *escalator* in a generic way, Otis failed to distinguish between the trademark for its own product (escalator) and the generic term for another product (elevator). Otis itself thus helped to prove that *escalator* had become a synonym for "moving staircase." The magazine advertisement was used as evidence in proceedings in the Patent and Trademark Office, which led to the cancellation of the Otis trademark.

PROTECTING A TRADEMARK

Under federal law, the owner of a trademark loses rights to it "when any course of conduct of the registrant, including acts of omission or commission, causes the mark to lose its significance as an indication of origin." It is important that all executives, all employees, and the firm's advertising agency try to protect the firm's trademark by following a few basic rules:

- *Never use the trademark without the generic name of the product.* A trademark is a proper adjective and should never be used as a common descriptive adjective, verb, or noun. For example, it is incorrect to say "a xerox machine" (common adjective), "Please xerox these papers" (verb), or "The xerox is down the hall" (noun). Correct usage would be "A Xerox photocopy machine," "Please photocopy these papers," and "The Xerox photocopier is down the hall."
- *Never use the trademark in the possessive form.* It is incorrect to say, "Ford's excellent performance." The correct form would be "the excellent performance of Ford automobiles."
- *Never use the trademark in the plural.* It is incorrect to say, "The doctor prescribed Prozacs." The correct form would be, "The doctor prescribed Prozac antidepressant medication."
- *Always identify trademarks.* A trademark must always be used in a manner that will distinguish it from the surrounding words. Trademarks should be completely capitalized, given initial capital letters and put in quotation marks, or at least given initial capitals. The generic name should not be capitalized. Correct examples are SECRET deodorant, "Secret" deodorant, and Secret deodorant. Trademarks also may be identified by the symbol ® or ™.
- *Continuously monitor the way others use your trademarks.* Most firms use a clipping service that reports periodically on the appearance of a firm's name in publications monitored by the service. Any improper use of the firm's trademarks should be brought to the attention of the editor or writer responsible. Should a challenge to the firm's ownership of a trademark arise, the record of these efforts could be used as evidence that the firm had taken positive action to protect its trademark.

28.5 APPLICATION OF TRADEMARK LAW TO CYBERSPACE

A business needs to be extremely vigilant to ensure that its valuable trademark is protected in cyberspace.

DOMAIN NAMES

A *domain name* is a unique identifier that serves as an address for a web page. It consists of several characters and numerals, followed by a suffix that can be *.com, .org, .gov, .edu,* or the like. It is extremely important to companies that they own the sequence of characters and numerals in order that web users may be properly directed to the company's site, on which the user may wish to place an order to purchase goods or services, to contact the company, or to find out more about the company's products or business. Accordingly, the law of trademarks applies to the ownership of domain names.

A business needs to ensure that its trademark is protected in cyberspace.
Jacob Lund/Shutterstock

Currently, a private firm is responsible for assigning domain names. An individual or company, however, will not be granted use of a domain name unless he or she first promises not to infringe upon anyone else's trademark.

Registering or using another person's or company's domain name in bad faith for the purpose of earning a profit is referred to as cybersquatting. The *Anti-Cybersquatting Consumer Protection Act of 1999* makes this illegal. One of the many purposes of the law is to prevent someone from buying up domain names and then reselling these back to the companies who own the trademark. To win a lawsuit using this law, a firm would need to demonstrate to the court that

cybersquatting
Registering or using another person's or company's domain name in bad faith for the purpose of earning a profit.

- There was bad faith on the part of the cybersquatter.
- The company owns the trademark.
- The trademark is distinctive.
- The domain name being used by the cybersquatter is identical to (or confusingly close to) the trademarked name owned by the complaining party.

28.6 COPYRIGHTS

A copyright is a valid, government-granted protection given to creators of literary, creative, or artistic works such as books, magazines, music, dramatic works, maps, works of art, motion pictures, computer programs, computer games, and videos. In order to receive

copyright
A valid, government-granted protection given to creators of literary, creative, or artistic works.

copyright protection, such works must be (1) original, (2) creative, and (3) expressed in a tangible form. Works produced and copyrighted in one country are protected under the laws of most other countries (see Chapter 36). A copyright cannot prevent the copying of an idea, but only the way it is expressed. Under the current copyright law, a created work is protected for the lifetime of the creator plus 70 years. If the work is produced as a result of the creator's employment, the term is 95 years from the first publication or 120 years after the creation of the work, whichever is shorter. Material that has been copyrighted is often noted by the symbol ©. If the creator of the work wishes, a formal application for a copyright may be made to the Federal Copyright Office of the Library of Congress. Copying without permission is referred to as **infringement** (the word *infringement* also applies to trademarks and patents).

infringement
Copying another's literary, creative, or artistic works without permission.

EXAMPLE 28.8

Harwood was the author of a cookbook. After her book had been published, Harwood discovered another cookbook written by Pauling that was published three years after hers. She noticed that at least one-third of Pauling's book was a direct, word-for-word copy of hers. Harwood or her publisher could bring legal action charging copyright infringement.

fair use
Limited copying allowed when the copyrighted material is copied without authorization for use in connection with criticism, news reporting, research, education, or parody.

FAIR USE

The law sometimes does allow limited copying if such copying falls under the doctrine of **fair use**. Fair use applies when the copyrighted material is copied without authorization for use in connection with criticism, news reporting, research, education, or parody.

EXAMPLE 28.9

Johansson, the mayor of a city, delivered a speech in which he made several promises. McSwain, a "shock disk jockey" on a local radio station, altered the speech so that it made Johansson appear silly and irresponsible. Because the alterations were clearly made to criticize and parody Johansson's real words, this unauthorized copying would be considered a fair use.

28.7 APPLICATION OF COPYRIGHT LAW TO SOFTWARE AND CYBERSPACE

The *Computer Software Copyright Act of 1980* defines a computer program as a "set of statements or instructions to be used directly or indirectly in a computer in order to bring about a certain act." Pursuant to this law, however, it is not an infringement if the owner of a computer program makes a single copy. Indeed, sellers of computer programs at times encourage the user to make a "working copy" and to safeguard the original CD or disk. The chief concern of software developers is widespread copying and the loss of revenue that would result.

substantial similarity test
A test that is used to determine whether an ordinary reasonable observer comparing two works would have to conclude that the work being questioned was copied from the other.

In cases where there is the need to determine whether a person or business has violated the copyright of another, courts use the **substantial similarity test**. This test is used to determine whether an ordinary reasonable observer comparing two works would have to conclude that the work being questioned was copied from the other. While this test, which applies the judgment of the ordinary reasonable person, seems to resolve most cases involving conventional copyrighted works, the courts rely heavily on the testimony of expert witnesses and professionals in cases involving allegations of computer software copyright infringement.

It should be noted that the substantial similarity test used to determine infringement in computer software cases is nearly identical to that used to judge the claim of a songwriter who alleges that their music or lyrics have been wrongfully copied.

EXAMPLE 28.10

▶ A website named BlueBeat began offering cheap downloads of hundreds of Beatles songs. The owner of BlueBeat claimed that he was the copyright owner of these songs because he altered them with a "psycho acoustic simulation" device. Because the songs sounded almost identical to the original Beatles recordings, the court found in favor of the Beatles' music rights holders and ordered BlueBeat to remove the songs from the website. [*Capitol Records, LLC, et al. v. Bluebeat, Inc., et al.*, Case No. CV 09-8030-JFW (JCx) United States District Court (CA)]

There is no legal distinction between copying from a hard copy and copying electronically. Thus, the individual who downloads a newspaper article from a website or who copies a posting from a blog and then pastes it into a word processing file is liable for infringement. In general, it is also deemed illegal to copy, or even trade, online music without first obtaining permission. The legal issues associated with distributing and sharing online music and other forms of entertainment will be discussed more fully in Chapter 31.

28.8 PATENTS

A **patent** is a valid, government-granted protection awarded to inventors that gives the patent holder the exclusive right to manufacture, use, and sell the invention for 20 years. Generally, a patent cannot be renewed. The purpose of patents is to encourage inventors to develop new products and new ideas and to reward them for having done so. Patents, like trademarks, are issued by the U.S. Patent and Trademark Office in Washington, D.C. Patents are issued for devices that are useful, novel, and nonobvious creations. Anyone who manufactures or sells, without permission, a product that has been patented by another can be charged with infringement. A person who profits from unauthorized use of a patented invention is liable to the patent holder for all profits resulting from such unauthorized use and for any other penalties provided by the patent laws.

patent
A valid, government-granted protection awarded to inventors that gives the patent holder the exclusive right to manufacture, use, and sell the invention.

Historically, patents have been granted for such inventions as machines, processes, or certain chemical compounds, but patents also have been issued for scientifically engineered bacteria as well as genetically engineered life forms. Recently, there has been a question as to whether DNA strains should be patentable. The U.S. Supreme Court ruled that human genes (and therefore also DNA) cannot be patented since they are "products of nature." However, as noted in Example 28.11, other biological uses may be patented.

EXAMPLE 28.11

▶ Chakrabarty, a biologist, developed a new strain of bacteria that could alter the nature of crude oil. Recognizing the potential of the discovery for breaking down oil spills, he applied for a patent. Initially the Patent and Trademark Office refused to issue a patent because the development did not meet the usual standards for inventions. After Chakrabarty brought suit, the Patent and Trademark Office widened its qualifications for acceptance, and the patent was issued.

28.9 APPLICATION OF PATENT LAW TO COMPUTER HARDWARE AND SOFTWARE

In order for a patent to be issued, several requirements must be met. The requirements, and their application to computer hardware and software, are described as follows:

- *The invention must be a device.* This is a term that has broad application in patent law and may include a design or process. In the case of computer-related inventions, the requirement that an invention be a device is often difficult to meet because many computer features are not devices at all, but rather they are based on mathematical formulas or on the manipulation of electronic signals and data.
- *The invention must be useful.* Because patent law requires that an invention be useful, in order to be patentable, a computer program must be more than just an amusing curiosity.
- *The invention must be novel (or new).* Because, to be patentable, a computer program must be original, merely adapting another, similar program would not satisfy the requirement that the invention be novel.
- *The invention must be nonobvious.* A computer program, for example, that merely computes the total of a series of numbers would not satisfy the requirement that the device be nonobvious. Because many computer programs are designed to do certain tasks electronically that have previously been done mechanically, it is often difficult to satisfy the novelty and nonobviousness requirements.

EXAMPLE 28.12

▶ Forlee, a secondary school teacher, invented a handheld device for use in grading examination papers. The invention enabled the user to pass the device over a specially designed student answer sheet. The device could identify correct answers, store the information gathered, and then feed the information into a separate personal computer. A specialized program included in the device could enable the computer to generate various statistical analyses of student and class achievement. Forlee applied for a patent for the handheld device, including the computer program. The Patent and Trademark Office would probably grant a patent because, taken together, the device and the computer program meet the requirements that the invention be a device, useful, novel, and nonobvious.

DESIGN PATENTS

Combining some of the characteristics of both patents and copyrights, a design patent is awarded to individuals or business firms to protect distinctive patterns, figures, and shapes and to prevent unauthorized copying. Design patents have been issued for soft drink bottles, wine decanters, silverware patterns, and other unique designs. Design patents, however, are granted for periods of less than 20 years.

design patent
A patent awarded to individuals or business firms to protect distinctive patterns, figures, and shapes and to prevent unauthorized copying.

CHAPTER SUMMARY

28.1 Intellectual property is a form of personal property. It includes knowledge, ways of doing things, and expressions of ideas. Intellectual property is protected through the use of trade secrets, trademarks, copyrights, and patents.

28.2 When its trade secrets are made public, a firm loses the advantage it had while the secrets were undisclosed. To protect its trade secrets, an employer or seller of a business may, through a restrictive covenant or an agreement not to compete, impose restrictions of secrecy on an employee or buyer of the business or forbid them from working in the same line of business or for a competing firm.

28.3 If a computer program is highly specialized and not intended for wide distribution, it would likely be considered a trade secret. A computer program distributed to a limited number of users is usually not sold; rather, the producer of the program generally retains ownership and licenses the use of it.

28.4 A trademark is any word, name, symbol, or device or combination thereof adopted and used by a manufacturer or merchant to identify their goods and distinguish them from goods manufactured or sold by others. Symbols used to identify services, as distinguished from goods, are called service marks. Trade characters are fictional characters; trade names are the names under which a firm does its business; and brand names are the registered names for products. Trade dress is a distinctive, nonfunctional feature that distinguishes a merchant's or manufacturer's goods or services from those of another.

28.5 A domain name is a unique identifier that serves as an address for a web page. To protect its domain name from a cybersquatter, a firm would need to demonstrate to the court that (a) there was bad faith on the part of the cybersquatter, (b) the firm owns the trademark, (c) the trademark is distinctive, and (d) the domain name being used by the cybersquatter is identical to (or confusingly close to) the trademarked name owned by the complaining party.

28.6 A copyright is a valid, government-granted protection given to creators of literary, creative, or artistic works such as books, magazines, music, dramatic works, maps, works of art, motion pictures, computer programs, computer games, and videos. Fair use applies when the copyrighted material is copied without authorization for use in connection with criticism, news reporting, research, education, or parody.

28.7 Courts determine whether a person or business has violated the copyright of another's computer software through the use of the substantial similarity test. This test is used to determine whether an ordinary reasonable observer comparing two programs would have to conclude that the software being questioned was copied from the other.

28.8 To obtain a patent on an invention, it must be a device that is useful, novel, and nonobvious.

28.9 It is difficult to patent computer-related inventions because many of these are not devices; are mere curiosities; adapt other, similar programs; or are designed to do certain tasks electronically that have previously been done mechanically.

CHAPTER TWENTY-EIGHT ASSESSMENT

MATCHING LEGAL TERMS

Match each of the numbered definitions with the correct term in the following list.

a. goodwill
b. trade name
c. trade secret
d. brand name
e. trademark

1. Specialized knowledge associated with a particular business. 1. _____
2. The name and good reputation of a firm. 2. _____
3. A word, name, symbol, device, or combination thereof adopted and used by a manufacturer or merchant to identify their goods and distinguish them from goods manufactured or sold by others. 3. _____
4. The name under which a firm does its business. 4. _____
5. The registered name for a product. 5. _____

TRUE/FALSE QUIZ

Indicate whether each of the following statements is true or false.

6. A contract in which an employee agrees not to work for a competitor for a reasonable period of time is unenforceable. 6. _____
7. A buyer who purchases a business from a seller receives title to the physical assets but does not gain the goodwill of the business. 7. _____
8. There is no set time limit on the legal protection available for trade secrets. 8. _____
9. Ownership of a trademark is typically noted by using the letter *O* in a circle. 9. _____
10. Trademark registrations are issued by the U.S. Patent and Trademark Office of the Department of Commerce. 10. _____
11. Words or terms that become a common part of the language are referred to as *generic.* 11. _____
12. The Anti-Cybersquatting Consumer Protection Act of 1999 makes cybersquatting illegal even if the cybersquatter acts in good faith. 12. _____
13. Because a copyright covers only an expression in words, works of art cannot be protected under copyright law. 13. _____
14. A person who profits from unauthorized use of a patented invention is liable to the patent holder for all profits resulting from such unauthorized use and for any other penalties provided by the patent laws. 14. _____

MULTIPLE CHOICE QUIZ

Indicate the correct answer from the choices following each question.

15. A has developed a new device to use in electric car steering systems. A would like to ensure that others cannot copy this device or use this device without their consent. In this case, A should (a) file a patent application (b) file a trademark application (c) file a copyright application (d) file a trade secret application. **15.** _____

16. B has a recipe for delicious chocolate chip cookies that they want to make and sell in grocery stores. B does not want anyone to see the recipe and has plans to ensure that no employees know the full recipe. In order to protect this recipe, B should take steps to protect it (a) with a patent application (b) with a trademark application (c) with a copyright application (d) as a trade secret. **16.** _____

17. C has a company that uses a computer-generated talking bird in all of its advertisements. The talking bird has become quite popular, and C would like to ensure that no other company can use this bird to advertise its business. In this case, the bird would be protected (a) with a patent (b) with a trademark (c) with a copyright (d) with a trade secret. **17.** _____

18. D has developed a television advertisement that they would like to ensure is not copied or used by any other entity. The advertisement video would be best protected by (a) a patent (b) a trademark (c) a copyright (d) a trade secret. **18.** _____

19. Trade secret protection is created by (a) filing an application with the U.S. government (b) filing an application with the state government where the creator is located (c) internal procedures to maintain secrecy (d) an exclusive court order. **19.** _____

20. E has produced a video for their business that they published on social media. E includes their copyright statement at the end of video. A local news station decides to report on this video in the evening news because many people in the community have commented on the video. In this case, E can (a) make a claim of copyright infringement, and the news station has no defense (b) not claim any copyright protection (c) claim copyright protection, but the news station can claim fair use (d) claim copyright protection, but the news station creates a new copyright with the story. **20.** _____

21. The advantage of trade secret protection over other forms of intellectual property protection is that (a) there is public notice based on a government agency filing (b) the protection has no defined time limit (c) the business seeking the protection does not have to do anything to get the protection (d) the company seeking the protection can always file an infringement claim. **21.** _____

22. The distinctive color combination that a company consistently uses to identify a business would be defined as (a) trade dress (b) trade colors (c) trade characters (d) service marks. **22.** _____

DISCUSSION QUESTIONS

Answer the following questions and discuss them in class.

23. Name five rules that a firm, or its advertising agency, should follow to protect its trademarks.

24. What must a firm prove in court to win a lawsuit filed against a cybersquatter?

25. Give several examples of literary, creative, or artistic works for which a company may be granted a copyright.

26. When does the fair use doctrine apply to copyrighted works?

27. Name the requirements that must be met for an invention to receive a patent.

28. Distinguish between design patents and other forms of patents.

THINKING CRITICALLY ABOUT THE LAW

Answer the following questions, which require you to think critically about the legal principles that you learned in this chapter.

29. Intellectual Property Why is it important to society that the law protect intellectual property?

30. Protecting Trade Secrets Should an individual who is offered an employment position sign an employment contract that contains a restrictive covenant?

____

____

31. How Trademarks Are Lost What is the justification for allowing a trademark owned by a company to become generic?

____

____

32. Domain Names Who should be responsible for assigning domain names: a private company or the federal government?

____

____

33. A Question of Ethics In your opinion, is it acceptable conduct for a firm that publishes adult websites to take over the domain name of another, well-known company after the time allotted to use that name has expired?

____

____

CASE QUESTIONS

Study each of the following cases. Answer the questions that follow with Yes or No.

34. Restrictive Covenants Morales owns a bakery that makes and sells the popular "Morales Chocolate Chip Cookie" nationally to gourmet stores. The recipe for the cookie is a closely held trade secret and has never been published. Morales hires Ng as a production manager and has Ng sign an employment agreement. The agreement specifies that Ng "will not disclose any of the recipe or ingredients for the Morales Chocolate Chip Cookie to any person or entity at any time, now or in the future." In addition, the agreement specifies that if Ng leaves Morales' employment, Ng "will not be employed by, own, or operate a bakery for a period of three years anywhere in the United States."

a. May Ng argue that the restrictive covenant not to disclose trade secrets is unenforceable? **a.** _____

b. Does Morales need to have the restriction on disclosure in order to protect the trade secret? **b.** _____

c. May Ng argue that the restrictive covenant not to compete is unenforceable? **c.** _____

35. Trademarks Hanna developed a refreshing drink using banana extract. She started a business, the Hanna Soft Drink Corporation, and began bottling and selling her soft drinks under the name "Hanna Banana." After a short time, she realized that she would need to protect her intellectual property.

a. May Hanna register the trade name "Hanna Soft Drink Company"? **a.** _____

b. May Hanna register the brand name "Hanna Banana"? **b.** _____

c. Is it possible that "Hanna Banana" could ever become generic? **c.** _____

36. Copyrights Legin, a professional writer, discovered that substantial amounts of a copyrighted article he had written 10 years earlier were included in a commercially published textbook written by Gant. When Legin confronted the publisher of the book, the publishing company denied knowledge of the use of Legin's copyrighted article and also pointed out that the text was intended for educational use.

a. Does Legin have recourse to a legal remedy? **a.** _____

b. Does the educational use of the textbook have any bearing on the case? **b.** _____

c. Does the fact that the article had been written 10 years earlier affect Legin's copyright protection? **c.** _____

CASE ANALYSIS

Study each of the following cases carefully. Briefly state the principle of law and your decision.

37. Application of Trademark Law to Cyberspace Calvin Designer Label developed a website using the terms *Playboy* and *Playmate* to direct users to the site. Calvin also used both terms in the body of its web pages to which users were directed. Playboy Enterprises Inc. owned the trademarks to both words *Playboy* and *Playmate.* Playboy Enterprises filed a lawsuit seeking to have the court issue an injunction ordering Calvin to cease using the two words. Is the court likely to grant Playboy an injunction? [*Playboy Enterprises, Inc. v. Calvin Designer Label,* 985 F. Supp. 1218 (California)]

Principle of Law:

____

____

Decision:

____

____

38. Domain Names Webster R. McGee developed a website using the domain name of "Card Service." Cardservice International Inc., a separate company, maintained that the term used by McGee was confusingly similar to the word owned by Cardservice. Cardservice filed a lawsuit requesting that the court issue an injunction directing

McGee to cease using the term "Card Service." Is Cardservice likely to be successful in obtaining the permanent injunction? [*Cardservice International, Inc., v. Webster R. McGee et alia,* 950 F. Supp. 737 (Virginia)]

Principle of Law:

____

____

Decision:

____

____

39. Copyrights Rural Telephone Service Company was a public utility providing telephone service to several communities in Kansas. Rural published a typical telephone directory consisting of white pages and yellow pages. Feist Publications was a publishing company specializing in publishing telephone directories for large geographical areas. Feist copied much of the white pages of Rural's directory without permission. Rural sued Feist for copyright infringement and won. Feist appealed to the Supreme Court of the United States. Is the Supreme Court likely to rule that Rural's copyright is valid? [*Feist Publications, Inc. v. Rural Telephone Service Company,* 499 U.S. 340 (Kansas)]

Principle of Law:

____

____

Decision:

____

____

40. Application of Copyright Law to Computers Six freelance writers sold articles for publication in print to a variety of popular newspapers and magazines, including *The New York Times, Newsday,* and *Sports Illustrated.* Nexis allowed computer users to retrieve the online version of these articles, which also were placed electronically onto CD-ROMs. The six freelance writers filed a lawsuit, arguing that, while they had granted permission to have their work appear in print form, they had never granted permission to have their work appear in electronic form. Are the plaintiffs likely to succeed in this lawsuit? [*Tasini v. New York Times Co.* 206 F.3d 161 (1999)]

Principle of Law:

____

____

Decision:

____

____

LEGAL RESEARCH

Complete the following activities. Share your findings with the class.

41. **Working in Teams** In teams of three or four, assume that you are the co-owners of a business that has created a new invention with an innovative trade name. Create a policy to protect that trade name from generic use. Find examples of trade names or tradeamarks that you feel are in danger of being lost to generic use.

42. **Using Technology** Using the Internet and search engines, locate a governmental website that addresses the issue of how to obtain a patent. What information is available on this website? If you had developed or created an invention, would you find the information helpful in protecting your intellectual property?

chapter 29 Computer Privacy and Speech

LEARNING OUTCOMES

After studying this chapter and completing the assessment, you will be able to

29.1 Discuss computer privacy and explain the possible threats to a person's right to privacy.

29.2 Describe computer crime and identify ways in which the unauthorized access to computers invites violations of rights.

29.3 Explain the major provisions of the Electronic Communications Privacy Act, the Computer Fraud and Abuse Act, the Electronic Funds Transfer Act, and other federal and state legislation that covers computer crime.

29.4 Discuss the concept of speech in a traditional context, as well as in relation to computer usage.

29.5 Explain how the Federal Trade Commission protects consumers from deception in online advertising, a form of commercial speech.

COMPUTER PRIVACY AND SPEECH

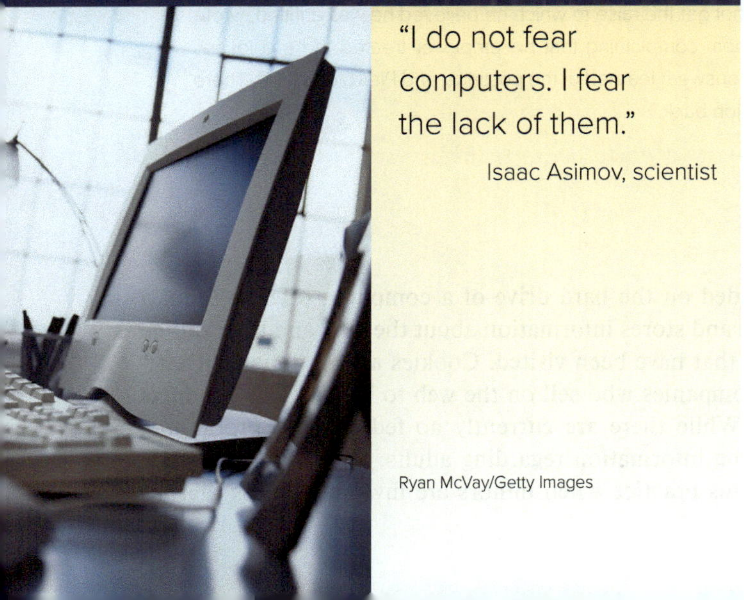

"I do not fear computers. I fear the lack of them."

Isaac Asimov, scientist

Ryan McVay/Getty Images

LEGAL terms

- cookie
- spyware
- phishing
- spoofing
- hacker
- virus
- Electronic Communications Privacy Act (ECPA)
- USA Patriot Act
- Computer Fraud and Abuse Act (CFAA)
- worm
- Electronic Funds Transfer Act (EFTA) of 1978
- public figure
- spam
- Controlling the Assault of Non-Solicited Pornography and Marketing Act (CAN-SPAM)
- Federal Trade Commission (FTC)
- deceptive advertisement

29.1 COMPUTER PRIVACY

The great majority of people in the United States either own or have access to a computer and the Internet. As a result, there is a new and increasingly significant threat to individual privacy. Most experts agree that the rapid advances in technology being experienced today make it difficult for people to maintain online anonymity or distance between themselves and powerful interests. Online marketers of products and services have quickly recognized that learning about consumers' online behavior presents a real opportunity to increase their sales. Similarly, there are those in our society who, for thrill or personal gain, seek to discover personal information about individuals. Many federal and state statutes have been passed to address these issues, but laws are developed slowly and methodically while technology expands at a rapid rate.

There are two distinct rights of privacy generally recognized in the United States. The first is a constitutional right to privacy, which is upheld by the U.S. Supreme Court (see Appendix). Generally, courts have interpreted the Constitution to give a right to privacy when a person or entity has a reasonable expectation of privacy. However, there is a second kind of privacy that, prior to the prominence of computer use, did not need much protection. This privacy protects information about individuals from widespread distribution. Where people shop, what mobile applications they download, how much life insurance they have, and what kind of pets they own are all bits of personal information that people may or may not wish to share with others. In the past, when such information was stored in the home, individuals were protected by laws against trespass. No one could enter a home without permission and gather this information. Now that this information is stored on computers and across networks, the law has had a difficult time providing as much protection.

There are also times when people may make statements on the Internet pertaining to their views on certain issues. These views may be expressed in chat rooms, on websites, on blogs, or in email messages. In most cases, a person's privacy is not protected when they make such statements by using these technologies.

EXAMPLE 29.1

▶ Pietro, who works for Howard Sportswear, received an employee evaluation that was not very laudatory. Pietro, angry that he did not get the raise to which he believed he was entitled, wrote a series of statements in a chat room complaining that his employer treated the employees poorly. The president of Howard Sportswear learned of the postings, and Pietro was fired. There is little that Pietro can do to get his job back.

COOKIES

cookie
A file that is embedded on the hard drive of a computer, often without a person's knowledge, that collects and stores information about the user and their online behavior, including websites that have been visited.

A cookie is a file that is embedded on the hard drive of a computer, often without a person's knowledge, that collects and stores information about the user and their online behavior, including the websites that have been visited. Cookies are an important marketing tool because they allow companies who sell on the web to know which products and services interest a person. While there are currently no federal laws prohibiting the use of cookies when gathering information regarding adults, the *Children's Online Privacy Protection Act* prohibits this practice when minors are involved, unless there is parental consent.

Information gathered from minors through cookies is regulated by the Children's Online Privacy Protection Act.
Thomas Barwick/Getty Images

In addition to cookies, some websites secretly install spyware, which is software that can change a computer's security settings or steal a victim's personal information, such as email addresses, bank account numbers, and credit card numbers. Closely related to spyware are phishing, which is the practice of tricking individuals into disclosing personal information via email, and spoofing, in which a legitimate website is reproduced to fool users into thinking that they are connected to a trusted site. Again, to address these problems, federal statutes have been proposed but not yet enacted.

Consumers who believe that their right to privacy is being violated by the embedding of software can complain to the Federal Trade Commission, a federal regulatory agency with responsibility to ensure that companies do not use unfair trade practices.

spyware
Software that can change a computer's security settings or steal a victim's personal information, such as email addresses, bank account numbers, and credit card numbers.

phishing
The practice of tricking individuals into disclosing personal information via email.

spoofing
A practice in which a legitimate website is reproduced to fool users into thinking that they are connected to a trusted site.

ELECTRONIC MAIL

Frequently, federal and state courts will determine a person's right to privacy by what an individual might reasonably expect under the circumstances. For example, if an individual mails a letter to a friend, they could reasonably expect that no one other than the recipient will read the letter. Similarly, persons who provide information via electronic mail (email) from their homes can reasonably expect their statements to be private; hence, the content of email messages is considered protected. The *Electronic Communications Privacy Act (ECPA)*, discussed in more detail in Section 29.3, makes it a federal crime to monitor email during real time—when it is being sent or received. It should be pointed out, however, that law enforcement officials may monitor email when they are granted such right by a court.

The law relating to email is applied differently when a person is at work. Employees have no reasonable expectation of privacy while they are on the job, and in fact, an employer may read an employee's email at any time, even without first obtaining the employee's consent. The ECPA specifically provides that employers may view email. Despite the fact that the law expressly grants this right to employers, it should be noted that most employers nonetheless have policies to the effect that email sent or received while on the employer's premises, or while using the employer's computer equipment, may be read by the employer. These also may state that an employee is forbidden to encrypt messages or install passwords unknown to the employer or without the employer's permission.

Even if an employer promises not to read the employee's email messages, courts in some states have still ruled that the promise does not create a reasonable expectation of privacy, and the employer may change their mind later without letting the employee know.

EXAMPLE 29.2

Fritz, an employee of Xu Manufacturing Co., regularly placed orders for raw materials with Nasso, an employee of Kleinman Glass Corporation. He spoke frequently on the telephone with her, and they developed a friendly relationship. Fritz then sent Nasso an email asking her to go out to dinner with him. Fritz's immediate supervisor at Xu read the email, wrote a memorandum disciplining him for violating company policy, and placed a copy of the memorandum in his personnel file. Fritz's discipline would be upheld by a court, and should he apply for another position at a different company, the contents of the email could be disclosed to the prospective employer.

The ECPA also grants an *Internet service provider (ISP)* the right to monitor email messages without the subscriber's consent. Despite possessing this legal right, most ISPs have their subscribers electronically sign a service agreement in which the subscriber acknowledges that the ISP may examine the contents of both sent and received email, and that there is no expectation of privacy.

DATA PRIVACY

Many companies will collect data electronically from customers and may use data gathered directly from customers, may sell data gathered from customers to others, and may disclose data in a nonsales transaction. Under current federal law, as long as these terms are disclosed to customers, the company may use or sell the data. However, several states have passed legislation to require the affirmative approval of customers before using, selling, or disclosing data.

29.2 COMPUTER CRIME

Many computer crimes, particularly those in which a computer is used as a means of engaging in criminal activity, are simply technologically advanced versions of standard crimes. A bank employee, for example, who programs the bank's computer to make deductions from one or several accounts and to deposit the funds to an account set up and controlled by the employee could be prosecuted for embezzlement even though they had not touched actual currency.

Another type of computer crime concerns unauthorized access to computer data. Computers are often linked to other computers by telephone, modems, cable lines, or satellite so that funds or data can be transferred from one to another. While a password is needed to gain access to a computer, often simple, obvious passwords are unwisely chosen, and as a result, unauthorized individuals can easily guess what they are and gain access. Lack of security relating to confidential passwords also results when these keys to entry fall into the wrong hands.

Unauthorized access to computers invites the following violations of rights:

- Invasion of privacy.
- Unauthorized use of the computer itself (using another person's property without permission).
- Manipulation of financial, medical, and other records.
- Unauthorized access to databases.

EXAMPLE 29.3

- City Central College had facilities for student use of computers and access to the Internet. Students had special passwords that enabled them to access an information database through the City Central College Library. Elkin learned Wilbur's password and used it to access the database to gather information for a term paper. The charges incurred by Elkin's unauthorized use of the password appeared on Wilbur's credit card. This use is not very different from Elkin using Wilbur's credit card to purchase merchandise at the local department store.

Examples of unauthorized use of computers include transferring funds from one bank account to another, changing students' grades in college computer files, and crediting accounts for purchases made.

A person who gains unauthorized access to computers, either for mischief or with criminal intent, is called a **hacker**. For personal gain or simply for the thrill, a hacker may cause the spread of a **virus**. The term *virus* in this context refers to instructions hidden in software with the potential to cause significant damage to both hardware and software; it has come into use because of the many similarities between these hidden software messages and a biological virus. Like a biological virus, a computer virus can lie dormant in a computer for long periods and spring into action at a predetermined date and time, or when a certain event occurs. Because software provides instructions to a computer, instructions contained in the virus can direct the computer to do any number of things, including erase data, generate data that take up valuable storage space, or conceal the virus itself. Some viruses are little more than a hacker's prank, consisting of instructions that tell the computer to display "Gotcha" or some other message on the screen on a certain date and time. Not all viruses are pranks, however, and some cause major disruptions in computer operations. Frequently, viruses are spread by attaching themselves to the user's email list, located in the computer's address book on the hard drive.

hacker
A person who gains unauthorized access to computers either for mischief or with criminal intent.

virus
Instructions hidden in software with the potential to cause significant damage to both hardware and software.

29.3 COMPUTER CRIME LEGISLATION

Specific computer crime statutes have been enacted by both federal and state legislatures. These statutes include the Electronic Communications Privacy Act, the USA Patriot Act, the Computer Abuse and Fraud Act, the Electronic Funds Transfer Act, and other laws that govern cyberspace activities.

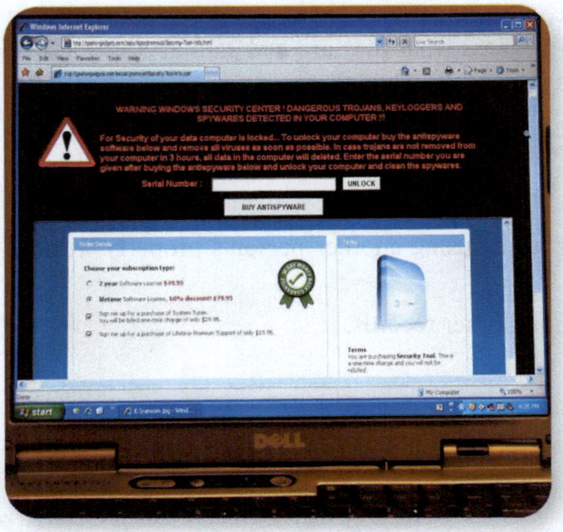

A virus has the potential to cause significant damage to both hardware and software.
Mark Dierker/McGraw-Hill Education

Electronic Communications Privacy Act (ECPA)
A federal statute that addresses hacking and other forms of illegal conduct by making it a crime to gain unauthorized access to any communication that is stored on a computer system.

THE ELECTRONIC COMMUNICATIONS PRIVACY ACT

The Electronic Communications Privacy Act (ECPA) is a statute that addresses hacking and other forms of illegal conduct by making it a federal crime to gain unauthorized access to any communication that is stored on a computer system. This law states that individuals may not gain access without permission to an electronic communication system or to exceed the authorization they have been granted. It is important to note that in the case of the ECPA, the individual must act intentionally in order to commit a crime. In other words, accidentally intruding on another person's computer files is not a crime under the ECPA.

It is also a crime under the ECPA to disclose to a third party the contents of stored computer information that has been obtained without permission. This is logical; if a person does not have permission to retrieve information, they also do not have permission to disclose it to someone else.

The USA Patriot Act
A federal statute that lowers the standards required for law enforcement officials and government agents to monitor email and personal electronic information, allows increased government cybersurveillance, and makes it easier to charge persons with serious computer-related crimes.

THE USA PATRIOT ACT

The USA Patriot Act (which stands for *Uniting and Strengthening America by Providing Appropriate Tools Required to Intercept and Obstruct Terrorism*) was passed in response to the events that transpired on September 11, 2001. Specific provisions of the USA Patriot Act include (1) lowering the standards required for law enforcement officials and government agents to monitor email and personal electronic information, (2) allowing increased government cybersurveillance, and (3) making it easier to charge persons with serious computer-related crimes.

Computer Fraud and Abuse Act (CFAA)
A federal statute that prohibits unlawful access to computers used in national defense, by financial institutions, or by governments.

THE COMPUTER FRAUD AND ABUSE ACT

The Computer Fraud and Abuse Act (CFAA), the first federal computer crime statute in the United States, covers the following areas:

- *National defense.* It is an unlawful use of a computer to gain access to secret information that could affect national security.
- *Financial institutions.* It is unlawful to use without authorization a computer to gain access to the financial records of a financial institution–including information held in any file maintained by a consumer reporting agency.
- *Government computers.* It is unlawful to access without authorization any department or agency computer used for federal government business.

In addition, the CFAA at times expands upon the ECPA, discussed earlier. While under the ECPA there must be an intent to exceed authorization for a crime to be committed, the CFAA does not require such intent if the intrusion onto another person's computer-stored information causes damage. In other words, even if a person's intent is good, if their conduct accidentally causes damage, they may be prosecuted for a federal crime under the CFAA.

EXAMPLE 29.4

▶ Witkowski released a worm (a type of virus that replicates itself and uses memory but cannot attach itself to other programs) to demonstrate vulnerabilities in the Maslow Company's computer system. Witkowski created the worm in such a way that its presence could be detected by experts but was not expected to create any problems. Unfortunately for both Witkowski and the Maslow Company, the worm attached itself to the company's mainframe and spread to all the personal computers and terminals in the company, creating millions of dollars in damage due to lost and corrupted files. Witkowski is guilty of violating the CFAA, despite his good intentions.

THE ELECTRONIC FUNDS TRANSFER ACT

The Electronic Funds Transfer Act (EFTA) of 1978 makes it a federal offense to use any device that is part of an electronic transfer mechanism to steal money, goods, or services or to alter data, interrupt wire transmissions, or use stolen codes or passwords, when the purpose of such activity is to obtain something of value unlawfully.

worm
A type of virus that replicates itself and uses memory but cannot attach itself to other programs.

Electronic Funds Transfer Act (EFTA) of 1978
A federal statute that makes it an offense to use any device that is part of an electronic transfer mechanism to steal money, goods, or services or to alter data, interrupt wire transmissions, or use stolen codes or passwords, when the purpose of such activity is to obtain something of value unlawfully.

GENERAL CRIMINAL LAW

Various federal criminal statutes, not originally concerned with computers, are still frequently used to prosecute those who commit computer crimes. The most widely used of these statutes are those that prohibit fraudulent activity using the U.S. mail, known as *mail fraud.* Also used to prosecute computer crime are the statutes that prohibit the use of the telephone and other electronic communication equipment (e.g., a fax machine) for fraudulent activity, known as *wire fraud.*

COMPUTER GAMBLING

Closely related to the issue of computer crime is that of online gambling. Federal laws make some forms of gambling illegal. However, there are numerous exceptions to these regulations in terms of the form of gambling (e.g., state lotteries and horse racing) and the location where the gambling takes place (e.g., Las Vegas and Atlantic City).

In addition, some states have legalized online gambling generally, although these laws vary from state to state and can only allow gambling within that state. Further, most states have regulations that would restrict how and when such gambling may take place. For example, many would argue that even if online gambling were to be legal, it should be restricted to those over 18 years of age. It is important to note that the rules relating to legal purpose and competent parties in contract law apply to agreements made in the form of wagers placed online.

Federal legislation disallows most, but not all, online gambling. For example, multistate lotteries, Native American casinos, and racetracks may continue their operations as before and venture into online forms of gambling as well.

The federal statute that regulates interstate online gambling is the *Unlawful Internet Gambling Enforcement Act of 2006 (UIGEA).* The UIGEA prohibits online gambling businesses from accepting payments related to Internet gambling in violation of federal or state law, and it requires all financial institutions to block payments to unlawful online gambling businesses.

Much more problematic is the issue of how to regulate offshore gambling, where consumer protection laws generally do not apply. Because obtaining jurisdiction over the companies that operate online gambling is difficult, special legislation would need to be enacted to allow federal officials to take action when necessary. It also remains to be seen whether federal regulations will address the way in which the bets are placed–for example, prohibiting the use of credit cards and electronic transfers for the purpose of gambling. The entire issue is not trivial. It is estimated that billions of dollars per year are wagered in online gambling.

EXAMPLE 29.5

▶ Antigua and Barbuda, a small, twin-island nation and haven for the Internet gambling industry, has filed a trade dispute claim against the United States with the World Trade Organization (WTO) (see Chapter 36). Antigua and Barbuda seek to gain access to the American gambling market and to recover a reported $3.4 billion in damages resulting from the United States' blocking Americans' access to offshore gambling websites. Because the United States does not ban all forms of online gambling, the WTO found the U.S. policy to be discriminatory and ruled in favor of Antigua.

29.4 COMPUTER SPEECH

Many of the laws that protect an individual's right to freedom of speech in traditional contexts, such as in public or in print, also apply to the expression of ideas using computers or network technologies, such as the Internet.

HARMFUL SPEECH

The United States has always had a deep commitment to maintaining an individual's right to *freedom of speech.* Protection afforded to freedom of speech is embodied in the First Amendment to the U.S. Constitution (see Chapter 5). A person's right to make statements that are unpopular, and at times even offensive or annoying, must be zealously guarded.

However, the freedom of speech is not absolute. Laws that prohibit speech, but that would be constitutionally acceptable, include the following:

- *Obscene statements.* What constitutes obscenity is the cause of much disagreement. In general, obscenity is that which is judged as such by local community standards.
- *Defamatory statements.* Speech that harms a person's reputation is referred to as defamation. This speech would include both slander, which is spoken, and libel, which is written or published (see Chapter 4).
- *Certain one-to-one communications.* Several statutes require that telemarketers, for example, cease telephoning when specifically requested.
- *Verbal or written threats to person or property.*
- *Intentional infliction of emotional distress.* When the objective is to cause another person to sustain severe anxiety, the injured party may sue the offending party.

EXAMPLE 29.6

▶ Alves had a long-standing feud with Caione. One evening, Alves called Caione and, disguising her voice, pretended to be an official from a local hospital. Alves then fabricated a story that Caione's daughter had been in an automobile accident and was severely injured. Caione rushed to the hospital only to learn of the deception. Alves is liable to Caione for intentional infliction of emotional distress.

It is important to note that the rules of defamation vary depending on whether one is a public figure. By becoming a public figure, such as a mayor, a baseball star, a rapper, or a rock musician, one implicitly allows others to write about them in newspapers and magazines and discuss their conduct on television and radio. These same principles hold true in cyberspace. Private figures, but not public figures, would be able to recover damages in the event statements were made about them in chat rooms or blogs. Of course, truth is an absolute defense to a charge of defamation, even in cyberspace.

public figure
A well-known person who implicitly allows others to write about them in newspapers and magazines and discuss their conduct on television and radio.

It is also important to note that the rules of libel vary depending on where the libelous statements are printed. In the case of newspapers, the defamed individual may not recover unless they can show that the newspaper acted with actual malice, reckless disregard for the truth, or knowledge by the newspaper that what it printed was false. Recently court cases have held that these same rules apply in cyberspace because numerous news and wire services distribute information online.

People in cyberspace frequently do not disclose their identities but use fictitious names instead.
JupiterImages/Getty Images

LIABILITY OF AN INTERNET SERVICE PROVIDER

When a person is defamed in cyberspace, often they are not able to determine the identity of the individual who made the defamatory statements. People in chat rooms, blogs, and in mass emails frequently do not disclose their identities but use fictitious names instead.

When individuals learn that someone has posted an untruth about them, especially when such untruth harms them professionally, they often attempt to hold their ISP liable. Courts have consistently held, however, that ISPs are not liable for defamatory statements made while using their service unless they had prior knowledge of such.

EXAMPLE 29.7

Cardone was a well-respected attorney engaging in the practice of divorce law. Cardone represented Mr. Hakim when he was sued by Mrs. Hakim for high alimony payments. Cardone accurately portrayed Mrs. Hakim as guilty of spousal abuse, and no alimony was awarded. Mrs. Hakim, while concealing her identity, posted several notices in a computer forum that stated that Cardone had never actually passed the bar examination. While Cardone strongly suspected that it was Mrs. Hakim who was the author of the untruths, he could not prove it because the ISP refused to disclose Mrs. Hakim's online identity. Cardone then sued the ISP but was unable to recover.

However, suppose we add some additional facts to Example 29.7. One month after Cardone complained to the ISP, Mrs. Hakim struck again, this time depicting Cardone as having a criminal record. Cardone would most likely recover this time against the ISP because it had prior knowledge of the defamation and, as a result, would now have an obligation to protect Cardone from additional defamatory statements.

OBSCENITY

Sometimes pictures or words that are contained on websites are alleged to be obscene. These pictures and words–both are considered speech–are legally obscene if they depict sexual conduct in a manner that is patently offensive under contemporary community standards; appeal to the prurient interest; and, taken as a whole, lack serious literary, scientific, artistic, or political value.

Many experts argue that the problem with this legal definition of obscenity is that it is too vague and ambiguous. As a result, a federal statute passed to regulate websites that contain obscene material or child pornography has now been ruled by the courts to violate due process of law–that is, to be unconstitutional. The dilemma facing many ISPs and search engines is that they are uncertain whether specific web pages, postings, and email content are obscene when matched against this definition.

SPAM

spam
Unsolicited emails sent for commercial purposes.

Not all email messages are welcomed, requested, or expected. Unsolicited emails sent for commercial purposes are popularly referred to as spam. Spam is undesirable because it can drain an ISP's resources, strain network bandwidth, and clog a user's email folders. Spam should be distinguished from email messages that are sent at the recipient's request; for example, when a person purchases an item from a brick-and-mortar company and provides their email address to the seller, it is with the expectation that they may receive email solicitations.

Spam is desirable from the originator's point of view because it is inexpensive. It has been estimated that several thousand recipients can be reached with spam for less than $100, while it would cost many thousands of dollars to reach the same number of individuals using a postal service mailing. Suppliers are therefore induced to collect email addresses, often culling these from newsgroups and web pages. It is technologically possible to stop spammers, but such is not commonplace. From a legal standpoint, it is perfectly allowable for a seller to solicit via email.

In 2003 a federal statute, the Controlling the Assault of Non-Solicited Pornography and Marketing Act (CAN-SPAM Act), went into effect. Under this statute, it remains allowable for a seller to solicit via email. However, the law provides that in most situations

- Email solicitations for products and services must be identified clearly and conspicuously.
- Commercial email senders are barred from using misleading or bogus subject lines to conceal their origins.
- Commercial solicitations must give the recipient the ability to "opt out" of additional email messages from the sender.
- In addition to its legitimate email address, the sender must provide its postal address.

Controlling the Assault of Non-Solicited Pornography and Marketing Act (CAN-SPAM)
A federal statute that limits the circumstances under which commercial email may be utilized.

29.5 ADVERTISING ON THE WEB

Another form of speech affected by the Internet is commercial speech, particularly advertising. The federal agency responsible for ensuring that advertising in the United States is truthful is the Federal Trade Commission (FTC). In addition, there are numerous state and local consumer protection agencies, as well as private not-for-profit companies, that can be of assistance in the event a consumer is misled by a deceptive advertisement.

A deceptive advertisement is defined as one that contains a material (important) misrepresentation, omission, or practice likely to mislead a consumer who acts reasonably under the circumstances.

Ads placed on web pages are required to meet the same standards as ads placed in other media, such as print, billboards, television, and radio. If the FTC determines that a web-based ad is deceptive, it has several options:

- The FTC can issue a cease -and-desist order, in effect compelling the publisher to eliminate the Internet reference.
- The FTC can order an affirmative disclosure, requiring the publisher to revise the web reference to include additional, truthful information.
- The FTC can require corrective advertising to inform future visitors to the web page that the previous information was deceptive.
- The FTC can seek fines and other civil remedies.
- In extreme cases involving fraud, the FTC can ask the U.S. Justice Department to file criminal charges, which can lead to imprisonment.

Federal Trade Commission (FTC)
The federal agency responsible for ensuring that advertising in the United States is truthful.

deceptive advertising
An advertisement that contains a material misrepresentation, omission, or practice likely to mislead a consumer who acts reasonably under the circumstances.

EXAMPLE 29.8

- Pluto Stationery sells silver-plated pen and pencil sets for $19.99. On its website, it advertised silver-plated pens for $19.99 and added that there would be a "free" silver-plated pencil provided with the purchase of a pen. Because the pencil is not really free at all, Pluto Stationery is guilty of creating a deceptive ad on its website and can be required to pay a fine.

CHAPTER SUMMARY

29.1 The rapid advances in technology being experienced today present a new and increasingly significant threat to individual privacy. Cookies can be used to invade a person's privacy because they contain information about an Internet user's behavior, including the sites they visit on the web. Spyware can change a computer's security settings or steal a victim's personal information, such as email addresses, bank account numbers, and credit card numbers. Phishing can trick individuals into disclosing personal information via email. Email also can be used to violate a person's privacy because it can sometimes be intercepted and read by unintended recipients.

29.2 Unauthorized access to computers invites the following violations of rights: invasion of privacy; unauthorized use of the computer itself; manipulation of financial, medical, and other records; and unauthorized access to databases.

29.3 The ECPA is a federal statute that makes it a crime to gain unauthorized access to any communication stored on a computer system. The USA Patriot Act lowers the standards required for law enforcement officials and government agents to monitor email and personal electronic information, allows increased government cybersurveillance, and makes it easier to charge persons with serious computer-related crimes. The CFAA protects the electronic communications systems involved in government, finance, and national defense. The EFTA makes it a federal offense to use a device that is part of an electronic transfer mechanism to steal money, goods, or services or to alter transmissions, steal passwords, and so forth for the purpose of obtaining something of value illegally. Other statutes, many not intended to cover computers, are now applied to computers and networks.

29.4 While the U.S. Constitution guarantees the First Amendment right to freedom of speech, this right is not absolute. Regulated or prohibited speech includes obscenity, defamation, certain one-to-one communications, threats to person or property, and the intentional infliction of emotional distress. Laws to protect computer users from obscenity and spam are currently developing. Obscene material can be illegal if it is deemed patently offensive by community standards, appeals to prurient interests, and lacks any serious value. Spam is legal but is subject to the provisions of the CAN-SPAM Act.

29.5 The FTC protects consumers from deceptive online advertising by ensuring that advertising is truthful and by taking a variety of measures against online advertising that is false or misleading. If the FTC finds that web-based advertising is deceptive, it has several options: It can issue a cease-and-desist order; require an affirmative disclosure; order corrective advertising; seek fines and order civil remedies; and, in severe cases alleging fraud, ask the Justice Department to file criminal charges.

CHAPTER TWENTY-NINE ASSESSMENT

MATCHING LEGAL TERMS

Match each of the numbered definitions with the correct term in the following list.

a. defamation
b. worm
c. hacker
d. cookie
e. spam

1. A file that is embedded on the hard drive of a computer, often without a person's knowledge, that collects and stores information about the user. 1. _____
2. A person who gains unauthorized access to a computer either for mischief or with criminal intent. 2. _____
3. A small, self-contained program that invades all computers in a network. 3. _____
4. An unsolicited email sent for commercial purposes. 4. _____
5. Speech that harms a person's reputation. 5. _____

TRUE/FALSE QUIZ

Indicate whether each of the following statements is true or false.

6. Individuals making statements in chat rooms have an absolute right to privacy. 6. _____
7. There are currently no laws prohibiting the use of cookies in the case of adult computer users. 7. _____
8. Employees have no reasonable expectation of privacy while they are at work; hence, employers may read their email without first receiving the employee's consent. 8. _____
9. Internet service providers have the legal right to monitor email without the subscriber's consent. 9. _____
10. Employees who transfer money from their employer's account into their own account without authorization can be prosecuted for the crime of embezzlement. 10. _____
11. There are numerous state, but no federal, regulations covering the misuse of computers and data. 11. _____
12. In order to violate the Computer Fraud and Abuse Act, an individual must act with intent. 12. _____
13. Because most forms of gambling are illegal, most forms of online gambling are also illegal. 13. _____
14. A deceptive advertisement is one that contains a material misrepresentation, omission, or practice likely to mislead a consumer who acts reasonably under the circumstances. 14. _____
15. The Federal Trade Commission is responsible for ensuring that advertising in the United States is truthful. 15. _____
16. A newspaper that prints a story about a public figure, with knowledge that the story is untrue, could be held liable for defamation. 16. _____

17. The law mandates that all Internet service providers require subscribers to use their true names when entering cyberspace. **17.** _____

18. Pictures and words are legally obscene if they depict sexual conduct in a manner that is patently offensive under contemporary community standards; appeals to the prurient interest; and, taken as a whole, lacks serious literary, scientific, artistic, or political value. **18.** _____

19. When an individual purchases an item from a brick-and-mortar company and provides their email address to the seller, the individual is implicitly consenting to the receipt of email solicitations. **19.** _____

20. Spam is illegal in the United States. **20.** _____

MULTIPLE CHOICE QUIZ

Indicate the correct answer from the choices following each question.

21. An employer seeks to monitor its employees email correspondence during working hours to ensure that its anti-harassment policies are being followed. Under current law, that employer (a) may not monitor the email under the regulations of the Electronic Communications Privacy Act (ECPA) (b) may monitor the email under the regulations of the ECPA (c) may not monitor the email due to the USA Patriot Act (d) may monitor the email under the USA Patriot Act. **21.** _____

22. A consumer often shops on an online shopping site. The consumer discovers that the site has been gathering data about all of the site users shopping habits and selling that data to marketing firms. In this case, (a) federal law will allow the data sale, and state law does not apply (b) federal law does not allow the sale (c) federal law allows the sale, but state law may limit the sale (d) neither state law nor federal law allow the sale. **22.** _____

23. Unauthorized access to a computer or computer files may give rise to a claim of (a) use of property without permission (b) invasion of privacy (c) both a and b (d) neither a nor b. **23.** _____

24. B publishes an online article that contains false information about C. C may (a) bring a claim against B under the ECPA (b) bring a claim of defamation against B (c) not bring a claim against B because of B's First Amendment rights (d) not bring a claim against B because of the CAN-SPAM Act. **24.** _____

25. D has an online advertisement that makes false and misleading claims about its product. The Federal Trade Commission can (a) not regulate this advertisement since it is online (b) seek to remove the advertisement from the Internet (c) not regulate this advertisement since that regulation is a violation of the First Amendment (d) not regulate this advertisement since the Federal Trade Commission does not regulate advertising. **25.** _____

DISCUSSION QUESTIONS

Answer the following questions and discuss them in class.

26. Explain how the law protecting the privacy of email differs depending on whether the email is sent from home or from work.

27. Identify at least three typical company policies that restrict email sent or received by employees while on the employer's premises.

28. Name four rights that may be violated when individuals gain access to computers without proper authorization.

29. Give three examples of unauthorized uses of computers that can result in criminal prosecution.

30. Distinguish the Electronic Communications Privacy Act from the Computer Fraud and Abuse Act in terms of intent to commit a crime.

31. Identify five types of laws that restrict speech but would, nonetheless, be constitutionally permissible.

THINKING CRITICALLY ABOUT THE LAW

Answer the following questions, which require you to think critically about the legal principles that you learned in this chapter.

32. USA Patriot Act Where should the line be drawn between the responsibility of the government to thwart terrorism and the rights of Americans to be free from governmental intrusions into their privacy?

33. Cookies How does the presence of cookies on the hard drive of a user's computer harm an individual's right to privacy?

____

____

34. Email What justification might there be for an employer to be legally entitled to view an employee's email without the employee's permission?

____

____

35. Spam What are some advantages and disadvantages of legally restricting spam in cyberspace?

____

____

36. A Question of Ethics Do you feel that it is ethical for companies to have customers agree to data policies by agreeing to terms of agreement rather than an affirmative agreement (or right to opt out) to those policies?

____

____

CASE QUESTIONS

Study each of the following cases. Answer the questions that follow with Yes or No.

37. Advertising on the Web Dragos was interested in obtaining memorabilia relating to her favorite 1980s heavy metal band, Deaf Panther. Through a search engine, Dragos found a company called WebPix, which offered autographed photographs of various celebrities, including Deaf Panther band members. Dragos ordered the photographs and charged the cost of these to her credit card. The signatures turned out to be forgeries.

a. Can Dragos complain to the Federal Trade Commission? **a.** _____

b. Can Dragos sue WebPix for breach of contract? **b.** _____

c. Can Dragos sue WebPix for a violation of securities law? **c.** _____

38. Computer Crime Schroeder, a student at Plymouth College, entered a computer lab on campus, overrode the password system, entered the college's computer without authorization, and changed her grade in a Business Law course from D to a B+.

a. Can Schroeder be charged with the crime of embezzlement? **a.** _____

b. Is Schroeder hacking? **b.** _____

c. Can Schroeder be charged with unauthorized access to databases? **c.** _____

39. Spam WeAreTravel Corp., a retail travel agency doing business in Pennsylvania, regularly sent computer messages to all persons who signed onto the firm's mailing list. In addition, the company sent email to all persons residing in the same town as the agency.

a. Does WeAreTravel Corp. have a legal right to send spam to the persons who signed onto the mailing list? **a.** _____

b. Does WeAreTravel Corp. have a legal right to send spam to the persons who are residents of the town in which the company is located? **b.** _____

c. Does WeAreTravel Corp. have a legal right to send 200 emails per day to these individuals? **c.** _____

CASE ANALYSIS

Study each of the following cases carefully. Briefly state the principle of law and your decision.

40. Computer Privacy Timothy R. McVeigh (no relation to the Oklahoma City bomber) was a highly decorated, 17-year veteran of the U.S. Navy. McVeigh was a gay male who, while using an alias, sent an email message to a civilian Navy volunteer through AOL. The volunteer searched through AOL's member profile directory and learned some information about the sender; eventually, this information and McVeigh's identity found their way to senior officials in the Navy. McVeigh was then found to be in violation of the military's policy of "Don't ask, don't tell," an offense that warrants discharge for homosexuality. McVeigh brought suit, attempting to prevent the military from ordering his discharge. Will McVeigh be allowed to offer as an argument that his email to the volunteer cannot be used against him due to his right to privacy? [*McVeigh v. Cohen,* 983 F. Supp. 215 (Washington, D.C.)]

Principle of Law:

____

____

Decision:

____

____

41. Email Michael A. Smith was a regional operations manager for the Pillsbury Company. In this capacity, he regularly used the company's email server. The company regularly assured its employees that all email communications would remain confidential and privileged. While at home, Smith then exchanged email messages with his supervisor. Pillsbury read these email messages, claimed that they were inappropriate and unprofessional, and terminated Smith's employment. Smith brought a lawsuit for wrongful termination, and Pillsbury requested that it be dismissed. Will the court allow Smith's lawsuit to proceed, or will the case be dismissed? [*Smith v. Pillsbury,* C.A. No. 95-5712 (Pennsylvania)]

Principle of Law:

____

____

Decision:

____

____

42. Computer Crime Legislation Robert Tappan Morris released onto the Internet a worm that spread and multiplied. The worm found its way into computers at several educational and military sites, causing these computers to crash. Morris was charged with violating section 2(d) of the Computer Fraud and Abuse Act of 1986. Morris was able to prove during a jury trial that, while in fact he had released the worm, he did not do so intentionally. Nonetheless, Morris was found guilty of violating the law. He appealed his conviction on the grounds that his access to these educational and military computers was not without authorization because Morris did not intend to access them. Will Morris be successful in his appeal of the guilty verdict? [*United States v. Morris,* 928 F.2d 504 (Washington, D.C.)]

Principle of Law:

____

____

Decision:

____

____

43. Liability of an Internet Service Provider *Rumorville,* a daily online newspaper, was part of a journalism forum on the Internet published by Fitzpatrick. Subscribers to CompuServe, an Internet service provider, had access to *Rumorville.* Skuttlebut was a service that distributed news and gossip about journalism. *Rumorville* published items about Skuttlebut that were alleged to be defamatory and untrue. Skuttlebut sued CompuServe, arguing that this Internet service provider was liable for the defamatory statements carried by the service. Will Skuttlebut be successful in a suit against CompuServe? [*Cubby v. CompuServe,* 776 F. Supp. 135 (New York)]

Principle of Law:

____

____

Decision:

____

____

LEGAL RESEARCH

Complete the following activities. Share your findings with the class.

44. Working in Teams In teams of three or four, draft a federal statute that might be enacted that would address the issue of online gambling. Be certain to include who is covered and what forms of gambling are being regulated.

____

____

45. Using Technology Using the Internet and search engines, visit a website that provides a free download to detect spyware.

____

____

chapter 30
Social Media and the Law

PERFORMANCE OBJECTIVES

After studying this chapter and completing the assessment, you will be able to:

30.1 Define *social media* and identify the categories of legal issues related to social media.

30.2 Explain how privacy expectations in social media use may be affected by business considerations, particularly with respect to employment and use as evidence in civil cases.

30.3 Identify crimes associated with social media.

30.4 Discuss the ways in which social media speech can affect business, including defamation, intellectual property infringement, and deceptive advertising.

30.5 Describe emerging issues such as social media.

LEGAL terms

- social media
- concerted action
- cyberstalking
- intellectual property infringement
- username squatting
- impersonation
- improper affiliation
- Equal Credit Opportunity Act (ECOA)

SOCIAL MEDIA AND THE LAW

"What is interesting is the power and the impact of social media. . . . So we must try to use social media in a good way".

Malala Yousafzai, Pakistani education activist and Nobel Peace Prize Laureate

Mark Dierker/McGraw Hill

30.1 SOCIAL MEDIA

Social media refers to online technology in which large groups of people interact while creating, sharing, and exchanging information, ideas, and personal messages in virtual communities and networks. The laws surrounding social media are essentially identical to those affecting other forms of public communications media, including television, radio, mass emails, and websites. As is true for all other forms of mass communication, individuals who post on social media may be held legally responsible for defamation, libel, invasion of privacy, deception in advertising, fraud, intellectual property infringement, and all forms of criminal activity. Because communication through social media is relatively new, the law is evolving. As with Chapter 29 Computer Privacy and Speech, this chapter organizes the discussion based on privacy, crime, and speech as these topics relate to social media.

social media
Online technology allowing large numbers of people to interact and share information.

30.2 PRIVACY IN SOCIAL MEDIA

EMPLOYER ACCESS AND MONITORING

Employers have valid reasons for needing access to employees' social media accounts. As discussed in Chapter 28, businesses that protect intellectual property as trade secrets must have systems in place that ensure the protection of those trade secrets. Thus, an employer may need to monitor social media posts by employees and others with access to those trade secrets as part of the documented process of maintaining the secrecy. In order to mitigate the impact of this monitoring, businesses should only examine the posts of those with access to the protected information.

Employers may be liable for the harassing behavior of their employees in the workplace if the employer knew or should have known of the behavior. Because some of that behavior may occur in social media, it is reasonable for employers to monitor social media activity of employees. While employers may view public posts, many companies are requiring that employees and potential employees provide their passwords and usernames as a requirement of employment. Numerous states have passed laws that restrict this practice, but currently there is no federal protection for employees from the requirement to provide passwords and usernames.

Another legal problem for employers restricting use of social media by employees is that they are also restricting concerted action by those employees. Concerted action is protected by Section 7 of the National Labor Relations Act in order to allow employees to share information about wages, benefits, and working conditions. Thus, any policy must ensure that employees are allowed to continue to share information on those topics without recourse.

concerted action
Employee ability to freely discuss wages, benefits, and working conditions.

USE IN EMPLOYMENT DECISIONS

Employers typically use application information and interviews as their primary data in making employment decisions. However, social media use by potential employees gives much more data for evaluation. Employers have used social media behavior to make initial employment decisions, as well as decisions related to discipline and termination.

EXAMPLE 30.1

▶ Winn Inc. is seeking a new sales manager and compares one applicant's résumé provided to the firm as part of his application to information provided by the same applicant in his LinkedIn social media site profile. When the information does not correspond, Winn Inc. decides not to hire the applicant.

EVIDENCE IN CIVIL TRIALS

Evidence used in civil trials must meet certain standards in order to be allowed by the court. Social media activity in some cases may help a party in proving their case. The Federal Rules of Civil Procedure have recognized the role of social media as evidence in trial. Whether or not social media activity is admissible in a civil trial depends on whether the social media activity seeking to be introduced can prove or disprove a fact or elements of a case. Any use of social media posts or activity as evidence must be authenticated and must originate from a specific, identifiable account with proof of authorship.

30.3 CRIME AND SOCIAL MEDIA

CYBERSTALKING

cyberstalking
Posting hurtful, threatening, or embarrassing messages online.

Cyberstalking, also referred to cyberbullying, occurs when hurtful, threatening, or embarrassing messages or images are posted online. Cyberstalking may be perpetrated by an identified or unidentified entity, and both businesses and individuals may be victims. Anonymous behavior of this sort complicates efforts at criminal prosecution. For businesses, cyberstalking by employees or others related to the business may create vicarious liability (see Chapter 4) for that business, particularly if the cyberstalking creates a hostile work environment (to be discussed in Chapter 33).

IDENTITY THEFT AND FRAUD

Many social media sites encourage users to post personal information, including hobbies, family pictures and information, vacation destinations, and other news to update followers or friends. While most viewers would not take advantage of such data, it is possible that those seeking to access accounts could use the information posted to answer security questions, for example, that are designed to protect the account holder.

30.4 SOCIAL MEDIA AND SPEECH

Social media sites have given consumers, employees, businesses, and others tremendous opportunities to disseminate information, voice opinions, and attempt to effect change.

EXAMPLE 30.2

▶ Vicenza learned that her bank had just instituted a policy of charging customers a $5 monthly fee if debit cards were used for purchases. Vicenza began a social media campaign on Facebook and Twitter to encourage others to sign an online petition on Change.org. This social media campaign attracted the attention of national news outlets and together with the pressure of the online petition, the bank eliminated the fee.

However, with that opportunity comes risks of liability related to speech. These legal issues include defamation, intellectual property infringement, and deceptive advertising.

DEFAMATORY AND OFFENSIVE SPEECH

As discussed in Chapter 4, *defamation* is the harming of reputation by communication of a false statement. Both persons and businesses can be defamed. Because social media encourages free expression of opinions and posting of information, the danger of posting false information has been heightened. An additional complication occurs when the one posting the false information is not able to be identified. Defamation requires that the statement be presented as a fact, not as an opinion. Often, social media posts fail to distinguish between the two and present posts as facts when they are actually opinions. Many social media sites encourage reviews of products and services. While these reviews are often positioned as opinions, there are instances when they purport to state facts about a business that are not true.

EXAMPLE 30.3

▶ A user posts a review of a hotel on a popular social media site. The review gives the hotel a very poor grade and states that "our hotel room had roaches, a dirty sink, and blood on the carpet." That statement is one of fact, not opinion, and subject to a defamation claim if it is not true.

INTELLECTUAL PROPERTY INFRINGEMENT

Intellectual property, described in Chapter 28, includes trade secrets, trademarks, copyrights, and patents. Businesses invest significant resources in the creation of intellectual property and thus need to safeguard against intellectual property infringement, or unauthorized use of intellectual property. While "fair use" of intellectual property allows use of intellectual property, such as trade names, in reviews or similar opinion posting, social media activity has given rise to several categories of concerns with intellectual property including username squatting, impersonation, and improper affiliation.

intellectual property infringement
Unauthorized use of trademarks, trade secrets, copyrights, or patents.

Username squatting occurs when someone registers a username with a social media site for the purpose of selling that name to a going concern with the same name. The Anti-Cyber Squatting Consumer Protection Act described in Chapter 29 also applies to usernames in social media.

username squatting
Registration of username that is similar or the same as an existing entity in order to gain profit.

EXAMPLE 30.4

▶ Tony LaRussa, a well-known baseball manager, discovered that an unknown user had registered the name Tony LaRussa on Twitter and began posting derogatory messages about the baseball team LaRussa was managing. Presumably, this user was trying to force LaRussa to pay the user for the name.

impersonation
Imposters' use of names similar to existing businesses on social media.

Impersonation of existing companies on social media has also been a problem related to unauthorized use of trademarks or trade names. In these scenarios, imposters using the names of known businesses or persons register with social media sites and either post comments related to the business or attempt to entice action by others.

EXAMPLE 30.5

▶ Nine West Shoes is a well-known women's shoe brand. A fake Nine West Shoes group page was created on Facebook by a user known as "Nine West Shoes." This site solicited women for model auditions and requested submission of photographs and contact information. The women responding to this solicitation believed they were responding to a reputable business, when, in fact, an imposter was gathering the information for his own purposes.

improper affiliation
Unauthorized, inappropriate social media activity that implies a tie with a business.

Companies have begun to recognize the value of fan clubs and other social media groups in marketing campaigns. However, companies do not always have control over these groups and run the risk of **improper affiliation**, which includes activity that is inappropriate or damaging to the company.

EXAMPLE 30.6

▶ An unknown user created a username and profile on Snapchat called "LoboSnaps" and featured the athletics logo of the University of New Mexico Lobos. The implication was that this site was a fan club of the Lobos athletic teams. However, when the site began to post explicit photos, the University of New Mexico sued to have the site taken down by the host.

DECEPTIVE ADVERTISING

Businesses have begun to formally incorporate social media into their marketing plans in a variety of ways, relying on it to test markets, publicize new products and ideas, and mobilize consumers. Social media allows consumers, employees, and others to market products, services, and businesses by posting information and reviews. However, these posts do not always clearly state the position of the person providing the information. While a consumer may give their opinion without recourse for deception, the Federal Trade Commission has held that employees of a company posting information or reviews related to their employer's products or services must disclose their status.

EXAMPLE 30.7

▶ Rose Enterprises decides to "appoint" 25 employees as brand ambassadors of their new product, giving the employees the product to wear for free. Employees are also encouraged to share information and pictures on social media about the product. Under FTC rules, each time an employee posts information touting that product, the employee must disclose that they are an employee of the company producing the product.

30.5 EMERGING ISSUES IN SOCIAL MEDIA

DETERMINING CREDITWORTHINESS

In August 2015, the social media company Facebook secured a patent for a product that would use social media networks to determine creditworthiness of users. Another company, Lenddo, has developed an algorithm, or mathematical formula, that analyzes big data from social media activity to develop credit assessments as well. Both of these companies have developed algorithms that claim to use data from social media to predict whether a borrower will repay a loan. These examples of using social media networks and activity to evaluate a person's propensity to repay, however, must ensure that lenders are not discriminating against borrowers based on age, gender, race, or religion. The Equal Credit Opportunity Act (ECOA) is a federal law that prohibits any lender from discriminating in offering credit, and the law is enforced in part by comparing lending activity in a community with the demographic characteristics of that community. Thus, if a lender's credit decisions based on data from social media has discriminatory impact, a lender will be in violation of the ECOA.

Equal Credit Opportunity Act (ECOA)
Federal legislation protecting borrowers from discrimination.

SECURITIES LAW DISCLOSURE ON SOCIAL MEDIA

Federal and state securities laws require timely, fair, and accurate disclosure of material information to all investors or potential investors of securities. Some have argued that social media is an ideal medium for companies to disseminate timely information. Others have argued that while social media may be one method to disseminate information, it should not replace the traditional filings and press releases currently being used.

REMOVAL OF SOCIAL MEDIA ACCOUNTS

Recently, social media platforms have garnered publicity for removing high profile accounts that violate their policies. While many argue that the sites not only have the right, but also the duty, to remove certain accounts, others have argued that platforms' actions are arbitrary and tend to favor certain groups over others. Currently there is no law or regulation of social media duties with regard to monitoring or removal of accounts.

CHAPTER SUMMARY

30.1 Social media involves online activity by large groups of people who interact by sharing information, ideas, and messages. As with other online activities, legal issues may arise in relation to privacy, criminal activity, and speech, as well as other emerging issues.

30.2 Expectations of privacy in social media use have been affected by cases of employers using social media activity to monitor employees and to make employment decisions. In addition, social media activity may be used as evidence in court when it has value in proving a case and can be authenticated.

30.3 Crimes have been committed using social media, including cyberstalking, identity theft, and fraud. While these same crimes could be committed using online forums other than social media, the public nature of the activity and the ability of the criminal to remain anonymous has created additional concerns for law enforcement.

30.4 Social media has had a tremendous impact on commercial speech since it gives individuals the power to spread information, voice opinions, and try to affect change. However, this speech can be defamatory or offensive and is governed by the same legal principles that apply to all speech. In addition, social media username squatting, impersonation, and improper affiliation can all lead to intellectual property infringement claims. Finally, businesses must guard against social media activity leading to claims of deceptive advertising, particularly when they encourage employees to use the medium to post information or opinions about a product or service.

30.5 Social media is evolving rapidly, and so there are emerging issues that the law will need to address. For example, lenders using social media activity to make credit decisions may face discrimination claims. Companies disclosing important information on social media must ensure that they are complying with all applicable securities laws.

CHAPTER THIRTY ASSESSMENT

MATCHING LEGAL TERMS

Match each of the numbered definitions with the correct term in the following list.

- **a.** social media
- **b.** cyberstalking
- **c.** improper affiliation
- **d.** Equal Credit Opportunity Act
- **e.** username squatting
- **f.** concerted action
- **g.** impersonation
- **h.** intellectual property infringement

1. Employee ability to freely discuss wages, benefits, and working conditions. **1.** _____
2. Posting hurtful, threatening, or embarrassing messages online. **2.** _____
3. Online technology allowing large numbers of people to interact and share information. **3.** _____
4. Federal legislation protecting borrowers from discrimination. **4.** _____
5. Unauthorized use of trademarks, trade secrets, copyrights, or patents. **5.** _____
6. Unauthorized, inappropriate social media activity that implies a tie with a business. **6.** _____
7. An imposter's use of names similar to existing businesses on social media. **7.** _____
8. Registration of a username that is similar or the same as an existing entity in order to gain profit. **8.** _____

TRUE/FALSE QUIZ

Indicate whether each of the following statements is true or false.

9. Employers in all states are prohibited from asking for social media passwords. **9.** _____

10. Defamatory social media speech is a tort. **10.** _____

11. Employers are not allowed to implement any restrictions on employee use of social media to protect trade secrets. **11.** _____

12. Unlike domain names, usernames are not subject to laws preventing cybersquatting. **12.** _____

13. Social media posts may be used in certain circumstances as evidence. **13.** _____

14. Social media fan group pages are always designated improper affiliation. **14.** _____

15. Current securities law disclosure allows a company to only use social media for disclosing information to investors. **15.** _____

16. Social media posts may be considered advertising subject to FTC restrictions on deceptive advertising. **16.** _____

17. Employees posting positive reviews of products on behalf of employers are not required to disclose their employment status. **17.** _____

18. Employers may use social media activity as a consideration in making employment decisions. **18.** _____

MULTIPLE CHOICE QUIZ

Indicate the correct answer from the choices following each question.

19. A posts derogatory comments about their supervisor on A's social media account, which they also use to post family pictures and other personal information. The supervisor can (a) not access the social media comments because the social media site is used for personal information (b) can access the comments and can fire the employee (c) can access the comments but federal law may not allow the firing (d) not access the social media comments under federal law. **19.** _____

20. B discovers that an unidentified party has been posting false and inflammatory statements about B on a social media site. In this case, B (a) will not have a cause of action since the perpetrator is unidentified (b) has a cause of action for identity theft even though the perpetrator is unidentified (c) has a cause of action for cyberstalking even though the perpetrator is unidentified (d) will not have a cause of action because defamation is allowed on social media with free speech rules. **20.** _____

21. C has a business that has enthusiastic customers. Some of the customers decide to set up a "fan club" using C's business name. Unfortunately, dissatisfied customers begin posting on this open site as well, damaging C's reputation. In this case, C may (a) bring a claim of improper affiliation against the fan club, assuming that C did not approve or control the site (b) bring a claim of improper affiliation against the fan club whether or not C approved or controlled the site (c) bring a claim of impersonation against the fan club (d) not bring any claim against the fan club. **21.** _____

22. D has a social media site and discovers that E has been opening credit cards in D's name without D's consent. E obtained D's personal information from unauthorized access to D's social media site, where D often posts personal information. In this case, D may (a) not bring any action against E since D posted the personal information used by E (b) bring an action for improper affiliation against E (c) bring an action for identity theft against E (d) bring an action for defamation against E. **22.** _____

23. Which of the following is currently not allowed under federal law?
(a) Access to information on social media to make employment decisions
(b) Access to information on social media to make credit decisions
(c) Access to information on social media to use as evidence in a trial
(d) None of the above. **23.** _____

DISCUSSION QUESTIONS

Answer the following questions and discuss them in class.

24. Explain why an employer would restrict an employee's speech on social media.

____

____

25. Identify two crimes that could be carried out using social media.

____

____

26. How does evaluating social media use for determining creditworthiness potentially violate federal law?

____

____

27. What are some of the legal problems with using social media posts as evidence?

____

____

28. What are three ways that social media could be used that would infringe on trademark rights of a company?

____

____

29. When posting reviews on social media, what might be a defense to a claim of defamation?

____

____

30. How does social media facilitate identity theft?

____

____

THINKING CRITICALLY ABOUT THE LAW

Answer the following questions, which require you to think critically about the legal principles that you learned in this chapter.

31. Should the government (state and federal) implement laws that restrict employers from requiring password and username information from employees or potential employees?

____

____

32. Why would a creditor want information about a potential borrower's social media use?

____

____

33. Are there instances when social media posts should not be used as evidence?

____

____

34. Should social media be used by companies to disclose information to investors?

____

____

35. Should companies monitor, restrict, or ban unaffiliated group pages that purport to boost a company's products?

____

____

36. How should prosecutors deal with anonymous crimes on social media? Should host sites be held responsible?

____

____

37. Are there instances when an employer should not make an employment decision based on an employee's social media use?

____

____

38. What emerging issues do you see for businesses as the use of social media expands and develops?

____

____

CASE QUESTIONS

Study each of the following cases. Answer the questions that follow with Yes or No.

39. Intellectual Property Infringement Jones, a popular radio personality, uses the name "Rocky Shores" on his show. The name "Rocky Shores" has been registered for trademark protection by the station's owner. In addition, the station has developed a contest format for Jones's show called "Twitter of the Day," in which Jones's Twitter followers would call in answers to questions posted on the Twitter account for prizes. Jones is terminated from his position with the station and starts his own radio show on an Internet platform using the name "Rocky Shores," and he also has a daily contest called "Twitter of the Day." Jones is not able to access the same Twitter account, but registers "Ricky Shores" for the new Twitter account.

a. Is Jones liable for trademark infringement for use of the name "Rocky Shores"? **a.** _____

b. Is Jones liable for infringement in using the Twitter of the Day contest? **b.** _____

c. Would Jones be liable under any other theory for using the Twitter of the Day contest? **c.** _____

40. Use of Social Media as Evidence Workers' compensation claims by employees injured at the workplace allow for compensation for lost wages and medical expenses while employees remain unable to work. Rachelle was injured at work and received workers' compensation, including wages while she was recovering. During recovery and while Rachelle is still listed as not able to work, Rachelle's sister posts pictures on social media of Rachelle waterskiing with the caption, "had fun yesterday at the lake."

a. Would this post be admissible as evidence in a civil trial? **a.** _____

b. What authentication would the court likely require? **b.** _____

41. Employment Decision Stanley is employed as a truck driver by a national company. As he is traveling on a cross-country trip, he discovers a closed road. After several attempts, he is unsuccessful in reaching his employer's on-call dispatcher to notify the customer of the delay in delivery. Once he returns and discovers that the lack of communication was due to improper phone set-up, he posts on his personal Facebook page complaining about the inability of his employer to handle such basic technology.

a. Should the employer take action against Stanley for his social media post? **a.** _____

b. Would the employer have grounds to terminate Stanley? **b.** _____

c. Would Stanley have an argument against any disciplinary action? **c.** _____

CASE ANALYSIS

Study each of the following cases carefully. Briefly state the principle of law and your decision.

42. Defamation Axeler and AvePoint are competitors producing software products, primarily for the military market. Axeler employees tweeted that "Ouch . . . Another #Federal Deployment Finds Out Where the Competition is Developed . . . #RedDragon." Red Dragon referred to a symbol that is often used to refer to China. In addition, Axeler created a false LinkedIn account under the name Jim Chung, whose profile included that he was a "software engineer at AvePoint" and that he was located in Xinjiang, China. AvePoint sued for defamation based on these activities because its software products were not made in China and, in fact, were required to be manufactured in the United States as part of the military requirements. Are these statements and actions defamatory against AvePoint? [*AvePoint, Inc. v. Power Tools, Inc.,* 981 F. Supp. 2d 496 (Virginia)]

Principle of Law:

____

____

Decision:

____

____

43. Concerted Action An employee posted on her personal Facebook page that her manager "does not feel that we help customers enough–I've had it. My fellow coworkers–How do U feel?" Other coworkers responded on Facebook, indicating that they were also frustrated by the lack of appreciation for their efforts at the workplace. The supervisor in question attempts to discipline all workers posting on Facebook about the workplace environment. Is the supervisor able to use these social media conversations as a basis for discipline? [*Hispanics United of Buffalo,* 2012 NLRB Lexis 852]

Principle of Law:

____

____

Decision:

____

____

LEGAL RESEARCH

Complete the following activities. Share your findings with the class.

44. Working in Teams In teams of three or four, discuss what forms of social media each team member uses. How does each member use that form of social media to communicate or share information?

____

____

45. Using Technology Find three online reviews for businesses that each team member knows. Based on the experience of the team members, are the reviews accurate?

____

____

chapter 31 Conducting Business in Cyberspace

LEARNING OUTCOMES

After studying this chapter and completing the assessment, you will be able to

31.1 Identify five key settings in which the law applies to conducting business on the web.

31.2 Discuss the role of the Securities and Exchange Commission in the sale and trading of securities online.

31.3 Identify the copyright issues associated with selling music and other forms of entertainment online.

31.4 Explain how contracts formed online are offered, accepted, and signed.

31.5 Discuss how legal disputes can be settled online using alternative dispute resolution.

31.6 Discuss the current rules pertaining to states' levying sales taxes for purchases made online.

CONDUCTING BUSINESS IN CYBERSPACE

"In fact, blockchain has the potential to fundamentally change how we share information, buy and sell things, interact with government, prove our identity, and even verify the authenticity of everything—from the food we eat to the medicine we take to who we say we are."

Julie Sweet, American technology executive

Chris Ryan/Age Fotostock

LEGAL terms

- Securities and Exchange Commission (SEC)
- Securities Act of 1933
- primary market
- prospectus
- Securities Exchange Act of 1934
- secondary market
- touting
- insider trading
- Dodd-Frank Wall Street Reform and Consumer Protection Act of 2010
- crowdfunding
- Digital Millennium Copyright Act (DMCA) of 1998
- Electronic Signatures in Global and National Commerce Act (ESIGN) of 2000
- alternative dispute resolution (ADR)
- mediation
- arbitration
- personal jurisdiction
- nexus
- Internet Tax Freedom Act

31.1 BUSINESS, THE INTERNET, AND BLOCKCHAIN

The 1990s ushered in a whole new way of doing business. Words like *e-business,e-tailing, e-marketing,* and *e-contracts* found their way into the English vocabulary, and companies started taking the Internet seriously as an important new means of doing business. Firms that conduct business on the web, however, are subject to the same legal restrictions as are traditional brick-and-mortar firms. This chapter examines five key settings in which the law applies to conducting business on the web. These key settings include selling securities, selling entertainment, entering into contracts, settling disputes, and paying taxes.

While this chapter focuses on business use of the Internet, blockchain technology (described in Chapter 7) is rapidly becoming part of the business landscape as well. This technology is particularly useful for self-executing transactions and for storing information.

31.2 SELLING SECURITIES ON THE WEB

There are two main federal statutes that cover the sale and distribution of securities in the United States. The federal agency responsible for administering these two statutes, as well as several others laws and regulations, is the Securities and Exchange Commission (SEC).

Securities and Exchange Commission (SEC)
The federal agency responsible for administering the statutes relating to the sale and trading of securities.

SECURITIES ACT OF 1933

The Securities Act of 1933 covers the sale of securities (stock, bonds, and other forms of investments) in the primary market, defined as the place where a corporation (an issuer) sells its securities to the public. This act requires that issuers of securities that are selling them publicly must make certain necessary disclosures when the securities are issued. The act includes the following important provisions:

Securities Act of 1933
The federal law covering the sale of securities (stocks, bonds, and other forms of investment) in the primary market.

primary market
The place where a corporation (an issuer) sells its securities to the public.

- Issuers of securities must register the securities with the Securities and Exchange Commission.
- A registration statement must be filed that includes information about the securities offered, historical and current data about the issuing company, and how the company plans to use the proceeds from the offer.
- The issuing company must provide prospective investors with a prospectus, a document that provides relevant and important information about the company, its businesses, and its prospects.

prospectus
A document that provides relevant and important information about a company, its businesses, and its prospects to prospective investors.

In 1992, the SEC created a computerized system, known as the Electronic Data Gathering, Analysis, and Retrieval (EDGAR) system, that allows companies to upload required information directly into the government's computers. This system is also useful to the public, which can now access company information electronically.

SECURITIES EXCHANGE ACT OF 1934

The Securities Exchange Act of 1934 covers the trading of these same securities in the secondary market, defined as the place where one member of the public sells securities to another member of the public. This act requires that companies periodically release important business information to the public and to investors. Among other things, it requires that insiders, or officers of the corporation, file a statement disclosing any equity securities they may hold in the company.

Securities Exchange Act of 1934
The federal law covering the trading of securities (stocks, bonds, and other forms of investment) in the secondary market.

secondary market
The place where one member of the public sells securities to another member of the public.

It is important to note that when we use the term *place* in the previous definitions, we are not necessarily referring to a physical location. The web, or cyberspace, is also considered a place, and securities are regularly bought and sold electronically.

EXAMPLE 31.1

▶ The Washington Company sold common stock to O'Brien, who held the stock for several years and then resold it at a profit to Gupta. The Washington Company, the issuer in this example, is governed by the 1933 act when it sold the stock to O'Brien and by the 1934 act because O'Brien is legally entitled to resell the stock to Gupta.

The SEC attempts to ensure that prospective investors have access to full and correct information about the companies whose securities they are interested in purchasing. Accordingly, the SEC requires that companies prepare forms and documentation containing financial and other information so prospective investors can, if they so desire, review this information prior to investing money.

Securities are regularly bought and sold electronically on the web.
Ryan McVay/Getty Images

Since 1995, the SEC has addressed the issue of selling securities electronically by publishing a series of guidelines relating to such sales. The rules relating to online sales of securities can be summarized as follows:

- Information that is distributed electronically will satisfy the transmission requirements of the federal securities laws provided that the distribution results in delivery of information substantially equivalent to what the prospective investors would have received in paper form.
- There must be timely and adequate notice to prospective investors of the availability of this information.
- The electronic delivery must afford access to the information that is comparable to that afforded by paper copies.
- There must be evidence to demonstrate that delivery of the information to prospective investors was successful.

The SEC also acts to make certain that investors do not violate the SEC's anti-touting rules. Touting occurs when an investor who owns shares of a company's stock posts notices online–in chat rooms, on web pages, on blogs, and elsewhere–that indicate that the value of the stock will increase. If enough individuals who read these postings believe that the touter is a disinterested expert, the demand for the shares will increase, and the touter has the opportunity to earn large amounts of money by selling the shares at the inflated price.

touting
An activity in which an investor who owns shares of a company's stock posts notices online–in chat rooms, on web pages, on blogs, and elsewhere–that indicate that the value of the stock will increase.

EXAMPLE 31.2

▶ Felmuth, a 15-year-old computer maven, entered chat rooms and placed postings on numerous occasions, pretending to be a financial analyst with an MBA from a respected university. Felmuth falsely implied that she had inside information that the Daya Corporation, a drug manufacturer, was on the verge of a major breakthrough in discovering a cure for a deadly disease. The Daya Corporation's stock rose fivefold in less than a week, and Felmuth made several hundred thousand dollars when she sold the stock for a huge profit. Felmuth is guilty of violating federal securities laws, will be required to repay all profits, and could spend some time in a juvenile detention center.

INSIDER TRADING

insider trading
An illegal activity in which a person who has confidential information about a particular company purchases shares of the company's stock with the intention of selling these shares for a higher price when the information is released to the general public.

Insider trading, a type of securities fraud (see Chapter 3), occurs when a person who has confidential information about a particular company purchases shares of the company's stock with the intention of selling these shares for a higher price when the information is released to the general public. The illegal activity of using insider information for personal gain is considered a "manipulative and deceptive practice," which is illegal under the 1934 act. It is important to note that trading in the stock of the firm by company officials is also called *insider trading,* but as long as it is reported, it is not illegal.

The confidential information may come from various sources. In one case, an individual had prior access to newspaper and magazine articles that, upon publication, affected the price of a company's stock. By making the appropriate investment in the stock of the firm discussed in the news item, the individual experienced a financial windfall. In another case, a top official of a company, having advance knowledge of a development that affected the price of the firm's stock, gave the information to friends and relatives, who then speculated in the company's stock, sharing profits with the wrongdoer. The official used friends and relatives in the scheme because federal law requires upper management to report their trading in the stock of the company with which they are associated.

EXAMPLE 31.3

Feng, president of China Imports, learned that his proposal to expand the firm's operations had been approved by the regulatory authorities and, as a result, China Imports would increase its business considerably. As soon as the news of this development became public, the price of the stock of China Imports would increase. Feng suggested to his brother-in-law that they could share the profit if the brother-in-law bought several thousand shares of the company's stock before the news was made public. By engaging in this illegal activity, Feng has violated federal regulations that prohibit an officer in a corporation from trading in the stock of his corporation without disclosure. Using his brother-in-law to purchase the stock was merely a clumsy attempt to evade the law.

RECENT TRENDS IN FINANCIAL REGULATIONS

In recent years, technological improvements that allow real-time market data to be transmitted over cyberspace have altered the way securities trading takes place. Automated trades are frequently transacted by computer programs that analyze market data received in cyberspace. As a result, thousands of trades can now be made within seconds. In light of the impact such advances have had on the securities markets, the SEC is currently attempting to establish new regulations to promote and improve the financial markets.

Dodd-Frank Wall Street Reform and Consumer Protection Act of 2010
A federal law that provides for significant regulatory changes over the financial system.

The federal government continues to respond to significant issues in the securities market with legislation. For example, in response to the recession of the late 2000s the Dodd-Frank Wall Street Reform and Consumer Protection Act was signed into law in 2010 in order to regulate specific types of securities that created the market issues. That law may be amended or rescinded due to other changes in the market, and regulation of the financial market continues to evolve.

EXAMPLE 31.4

▶ On May 6, 2010, a large computerized stock trade of $4.1 billion triggered a series of events that resulted in one of the quickest stock market crashes and subsequent recoveries in U.S. history. This market crash, referred to as the "Flash Crash," occurred when a large, computerized stock trade made a sufficient impact on the market to prompt numerous automated trades. These trades flowed into the market at a rate of thousands per second and resulted in an immediate decrease in stock prices.

Another law, the Jumpstart Our Business Startups (JOBS) Act of 2012 allows securities offering to the public through registered crowdfunding websites, which raise money for businesses from many small investments. The SEC has imposed a maximum annual amount that issuers can raise and requires disclosure about the investments and risks.

Crowdfunding
Raising money through a website solicitation from many small investments.

EXAMPLE 31.5

▶ Legion M, a new film company, decided to offer securities for sale using the website WeFunder, which was properly registered with the SEC for crowdfunding sales. Legion M prepared a business plan that was posted to the WeFunder site and available to all interested investors. Three thousand people invested $1 million for this successful crowdfunding offering.

31.3 SELLING ENTERTAINMENT ON THE WEB

It has become quite popular for people to download music from the web onto digital storage devices.
McGraw-Hill Education

In recent years, it has become quite popular for people to trade and download music and other forms of entertainment (movies, games, etc.) from the web onto compact disks and other digital storage devices. The legal issue associated with this is copyright infringement, discussed in detail in Chapter 28. Because the rightful owners of the music often have not granted permission and do not receive royalties from the pirated music, they have made efforts to stop companies from distributing music online. While the issue is still far from settled, several court decisions have held that copyright infringement takes place even if the company merely provides a forum for music to be "shared" among subscribers.

Another related issue is to what extent Internet service providers (ISPs), discussed in Chapter 29, are liable when a copyright infringement occurs while computer users are online.

THE DIGITAL MILLENNIUM COPYRIGHT ACT

Digital Millennium Copyright Act (DMCA) of 1998
A federal statute that provides that ISPs are not liable for copyright infringements by their subscribers so long as they adhere to certain requirements.

Among numerous provisions, the federal Digital Millennium Copyright Act (DMCA) of 1998 provides that ISPs are not liable for copyright infringements by their subscribers if they abide by the following:

- Adopt and reasonably implement a policy of terminating, in appropriate circumstances, the accounts of subscribers who are repeat infringers.
- Accommodate, and do not interfere with, the identification or protection of copyrighted works.

The DMCA further protects ISPs from liability for copyright infringement even for information residing on their users' systems or networks, provided that

- The ISP did not have knowledge of the infringing activity.
- The ISP did not receive financial benefit directly attributable to the infringing activity.
- Upon receiving proper notification of claimed infringement, the ISP expeditiously blocked access to the infringed material.

31.4 ENTERING INTO CONTRACTS ON THE WEB

The ability of parties to enter into agreements in cyberspace raises numerous questions. Offers are readily available on the web, and some questions that may arise include these:

- How are offers in cyberspace accepted?
- Are agreements entered into on the web contracts of adhesion?
- How does a computer user sign a contract made on the web, especially a contract that must be in writing pursuant to the Statute of Frauds?

ACCEPTING OFFERS ON THE WEB

Remember that it is the offeror who determines how offers may be accepted (see Chapter 8). But also remember that silence on the part of the offeree generally does not constitute acceptance of an offer. These same rules are applicable in cyberspace.

Frequently, offers on websites include a button to be clicked by the user with their mouse that indicates acceptance. Most courts acknowledge that by clicking the button, the offer has been accepted. It should be pointed out that the button need not explicitly read "I accept." It could, for example, use terms such as "I agree," "Yes," "I consent," or any other expression indicating that the offeree has read the offer and is accepting the terms. Computer users who frequent websites, therefore, should be especially careful to click their mouse only after they have read the entire agreement and accepted all of the terms.

Simply visiting a website does not constitute acceptance of an offer that is contained on that website. In other words, silence (not clicking the "I accept" button) does not constitute acceptance on the part of the user.

But what happens when the user has accepted the offer by clicking their mouse but has not read all the terms of the agreement?

CONTRACTS OF ADHESION ON THE WEB

In Chapter 9, it was explained that there are many instances when contracts are formed without there being any real negotiating or bargaining by the parties. It also was pointed out that these agreements, termed *contracts of adhesion,* are nonetheless valid unless they contain terms that are unreasonable. These same rules apply in cyberspace. If the website visitor has had an ample opportunity to read the terms, and if those terms are not unreasonable, a valid contract exists. Of course, all of the other elements of a contract must be met as well; for example, if the individual accepting the offer is a minor, the contract is voidable, and so forth.

EXAMPLE 31.6

▶ Motomba surfed to a web page for her favorite pop group, which indicated that for a $3 monthly fee, she could subscribe to a monthly electronic newsletter by clicking the "I subscribe" button. Motomba did not read the lengthy offer but simply clicked the button with her mouse. Later, Motomba learned that the terms of the subscriber agreement stated in small print that, in addition to the newsletter, she would receive the latest CD performed by the pop group and would be billed $25. Motomba will be required to pay for the monthly newsletter but will not be required to purchase the CD.

ELECTRONIC SIGNATURES

In Chapter 13, it was explained that the Statute of Frauds requires that certain types of contracts must be in writing and signed by the party to be charged to be enforceable. In addition, even if the Statute of Frauds is not applicable, many parties to contracts prefer them to be in writing so that the terms are clearly spelled out.

Contracts made on the web can easily be reduced to writing by simply printing the portion of the website containing the offer and the important terms of the contract. But how are these written contracts signed?

The Electronic Signatures in Global and National Commerce Act (ESIGN) of 2000, a federal statute, states that electronic contracts containing electronic signatures are just as enforceable as those that are printed on paper. Clicking the computer mouse on the "I agree" button, therefore, constitutes an electronic signature that satisfies the writing requirement of the Statute of Frauds.

Electronic Signatures in Global and National Commerce Act (ESIGN) of 2000
A federal statute that provides that electronic contracts containing electronic signatures are just as enforceable as those that are printed on paper.

Of course, many new technologies are now needed to ensure that the person who is supposedly accepting the contract is actually the person who is clicking the button. Some of these new, emerging technologies include

- Allowing the computer user to verify a digital signature using an encrypted code that is registered with a third party.
- Providing the computer user with hardware that can read the user's fingerprint or scan the user's retina.
- Providing the computer user with hardware that can electronically read the user's handwriting and thus electronically register the user's signature.

Finally, it must be pointed out that ESIGN does not apply to electronic signatures that appear on

- Wills, codicils, and related testamentary documents.
- Adoption or divorce papers.
- Court papers such as orders, pleadings, and motions.
- Notices of cancellation or interruption in utility services.
- Notices of defaults, repossessions, foreclosures, and evictions.
- Notices of cancellation or termination of life or health insurance benefits.
- Certain notices relating to recalls of defective products.
- Documents relating to the transportation of hazardous materials.

31.5 SETTLING DISPUTES IN CYBERSPACE

Because it is expensive to proceed against a defendant in a court case, a person who is the victim of a breach of contract will frequently seek to have the dispute resolved using alternative means. Alternative dispute resolution (ADR) is a system in which contract disputes and other disagreements are resolved by using means other than a lawsuit. Means of ADR include mediation, in which a neutral third party meets with the disputants in order to have them come to some form of settlement agreement; and arbitration, in which a neutral third party actually decides a case as if they were the judge and jury. (Many "court" shows on television actually depict arbitration proceedings.)

alternative dispute resolution (ADR)
A system in which contract disputes and other disagreements are resolved by using means other than a lawsuit.

mediation
A process for dispute resolution in which a neutral third party meets with the disputants in order to have them come to some form of settlement agreement.

arbitration
A process for dispute resolution in which a neutral third party decides a case as if they were a judge and jury.

The advantages to ADR include

- *Speed.* The matter is resolved quickly.
- *Finality.* Unless there is some type of misconduct, ADR results may not be appealed.
- *Informality.* ADR does not use the same strict rules of evidence that a court does.
- *Privacy.* ADR proceedings are not generally open to the public, as civil trials usually are.
- *Financial savings.* Because ADR is faster, with fewer legal motions, witnesses, and so on, they are much less expensive for the disputants than are court trials.

In cyberspace, numerous websites have been established for the purpose of providing forums for both mediation and arbitration of contract disputes. Parties involved in a contract dispute can simply access an Internet search engine to locate an organization that will assist with the ADR process.

If parties do not agree to ADR and must go through a court proceeding to resolve a dispute, one question that has become more prominent with Internet transactions is when a court has personal jurisdiction, or the right to hear a case, over a nonresident defendant. The law requires that the defendant have sufficient contact with the state where the court is located in order to be subject to personal jurisdiction in the state.

personal jurisdiction
The power of a court to hear a case involving a nonresident defendant.

EXAMPLE 31.7

Banto had an Internet site selling handmade jewelry that he made in North Carolina. Banto made his first sale to a customer in California. After the customer was injured by a sharp object on the jewelry, Banto was sued in California court. With only one isolated sale in California, Banto would not be subject to personal jurisdiction in California court, but Banto could be sued by the customer in North Carolina court.

31.6 PAYING TAXES ON INTERNET SALES

In 2018, the Supreme Court of the United States ruled that states could impose sales tax on Internet sales, overturning the previous commerce clause interpretation requiring that a state have some nexus, or connection, with an Internet seller in order to impose a sales tax. The buyer, not the seller, pays the sales tax, although the seller typically collects the tax from the buyer and then turns the proceed over to the state.

nexus
The link or tie that a location must have to a sale in order for the location to collect sales tax.

EXAMPLE 31.8

▶ Lebeda is a soap crafter who requires lye for her soap making. Because Lebeda resides in a rural area of Pennsylvania, she purchases the lye in quantity online from a manufacturer in California. Even though the California seller has no physical operations in Pennsylvnia, Lebeda can be required to pay Pennsylvania sales tax on the the lye she purchases.

TAXING INTERNET ACCESS SERVICES

In 1998, Congress passed the Internet Tax Freedom Act, which established a moratorium on taxing ISPs on the services they provide to computer users. The moratorium, which is a period of time during which no state may levy sales taxes on these ISPs, was permanently extended by Congress in the Permanent Internet Tax Freedom Act. Again, many states and localities are seeking changes to the law so that they may begin to tax the monthly fees that people pay for Internet access.

Many retailers who operate traditional brick-and-mortar enterprises also do business on the web.
JGI/Jamie Grill/Blend Images LLC

Internet Tax Freedom Act A federal statute that placed a moratorium on taxing Internet service providers on the services they provide to computer users.

CHAPTER SUMMARY

31.1 Five key settings in which the law applies to conducting business on the web include selling securities, selling entertainment, entering into contracts, settling disputes, and paying taxes.

31.2 For online securities sales, the SEC requires that information distributed electronically to potential investors is to be substantially equivalent to what would have been provided in paper form; access to information is to be comparable to that afforded by paper copies; there must be adequate notice to prospective investors of the availability of the information; and there must be evidence demonstrating that delivery of information to prospective investors was successful. Crowdfunding is a newly authorized method of selling securities on the web to the public.

31.3 The copyright issues associated with selling music and other forms of entertainment online involve the problem that the rightful owners often do not grant permission for its availability online and do not receive royalties when it is pirated.

31.4 Offers can be made online in much the same way that they are made by other means, and the rules of acceptance are also similar. For example, by clicking a button that reads "I accept" or something similar, a user can accept and be bound by the terms of an agreement. Silence, or not clicking such a button, cannot be used as grounds for accepting an offer.

31.5 Advantages of using alternative dispute resolution (ADR) include speed, finality, informality, privacy, and financial savings. Means of ADR include mediation and arbitration. These methods are also available on numerous websites that have been established on the Internet to provide forums for parties to resolve their problems. If parties do use the court system, the court must have personal jurisdiction over the defendant.

31.6 States are losing a great deal of potential tax revenue because they are not collecting taxes on sales made over the Internet. The reasons include the difficulty of establishing a nexus for the transaction in Internet-based transactions. The Internet Tax Freedom Act established a moratorium on taxing the services that ISPs provide to computer users. However, many states and localities are seeking to change the law so people can be taxed on the monthly fees they pay to have Internet access.

CHAPTER THIRTY-ONE ASSESSMENT

MATCHING LEGAL TERMS

Match each of the numbered definitions with the correct term in the following list.

a. mediation
b. primary market
c. nexus
d. secondary market
e. arbitration

1. The place where a corporation sells its securities to the public. **1.** _____

2. The place where one member of the public sells securities to another member of the public. **2.** _____

3. A process in which a neutral third party meets with disputants to have them come to some form of settlement agreement. **3.** _____

4. A process in which a neutral third party decides a case as if they were the judge and jury. **4.** _____

5. A location's link or tie to a sale required in order for the location to collect sales tax. **5.** _____

TRUE/FALSE QUIZ

Indicate whether each of the following statements is true or false.

6. The Securities and Exchange Commission requires that prospective investors review all of a firm's financial information prior to purchasing any stock in the company. **6.** _____

7. Touting occurs when an investor who owns shares of a company's stock posts notices online indicating that the value of the company's stock will increase. **7.** _____

8. Selling securities on crowdfunding sites was just made illegal. **8.** _____

9. Insider trading that is properly reported to the SEC is legal. **9.** _____

10. The SEC has an electronic filing system for public companies that the public may access to obtain information. **10.** _____

11. Companies that provide websites that are forums for music to be shared without permission of the owners may be liable for copyright infringement. **11.** ____

12. Most courts will acknowledge that by clicking the "I accept" button, the user has accepted the offer contained on the web page. **12.** ____

13. Simply visiting a website can sometimes indicate an acceptance by the user of the terms contained on the site. **13.** ____

14. Contracts of adhesion in cyberspace are valid unless they contain terms that are unreasonable. **14.** ____

15. An electronic signature will not satisfy the Statute of Frauds. **15.** ____

16. The Electronic Signatures in Global and National Commerce Act pertains only to cases in which the offeror and the offeree are from different countries. **16.** ____

17. Mediation is a form of alternative dispute resolution in which a neutral party decides a case as if they were the judge and jury. **17.** ____

18. A disadvantage to alternative dispute resolution is that it is far more time-consuming than litigation. **18.** ____

19. A state wishing to collect a sales tax levies the tax on the buyer of goods but usually requires the seller to collect the tax. **19.** ____

MULTIPLE CHOICE QUIZ

Indicate the correct answer from the choices following each question.

20. A company seeking to sell shares of stock in order to get financing for a new venture must (a) comply with the Securities Exchange Act of 1934 (b) comply with the Electronic Data Gathering, Analysis, and Retrieval Act (c) comply with the Insider Trading Act (d) comply with the Securities Act of 1933. **20.** ____

21. When a company's securities are traded on a national exchange, the company must (a) prepare periodic reports available to the public (b) ensure regular disclosure of any important information (c) ensure that the public have access to full and correct information (d) all of the above. **21.** ____

22. An entity sharing music online without the permission of the copyright owner (a) is not liable for infringement because the transaction is online (b) is liable for infringement but the site used to share the music is not liable (c) both the entity sharing and the sharing platform are liable for infringement (d) neither the entity sharing nor the platform are liable for infringement. **22.** ____

23. E-signatures on contracts or other legal documents are valid unless they are (a) for sales over $500 (b) for employment contracts (c) for a will (d) for purchase of a business. **23.** ____

24. Two businesses are contracting for the sale of supplies and agree that they do not want to have to go to court to settle disputes. Instead, they would like to draft a contract provision that allows timely and decisive settlement of any dispute they may have. In this case, the contract should include a provision that requires which type of alternative dispute resolution? (a) Arbitration (b) Mediation (c) Personal jurisdiction (d) None of the above **24.** _____

25. A business selling goods on the web (a) does not have to collect sales tax unless the business is located in a state that requires sales tax collection (b) must collect sales tax in states requiring the collection (c) must collect sales tax on all transactions regardless of state law (d) never collects sales tax. **25.** _____

DISCUSSION QUESTIONS

Answer the following questions and discuss them in class.

26. Compare and contrast the two main statutes that cover the sale and distribution of securities in the United States.

27. State the four rules relating to online sales of securities and explain the importance of these.

28. When is insider trading of securities illegal?

29. How can Internet service providers protect themselves against a charge of copyright infringement?

30. Identify types of legal documents for which electronic signatures are not valid and explain why the law excludes these.

31. Name five advantages for individuals who select alternative dispute resolution over litigation and give an example of each.

THINKING CRITICALLY ABOUT THE LAW

Answer the following questions, which require you to think critically about the legal principles that you learned in this chapter.

32. Selling Securities on the Web How can the law better protect individuals who are considering making investments over the web?

____

____

33. Crowdfunding Currently there is a $5 million limit on the amount a company may raise in 12 months through crowdfunding. Should investors have more opportunities to purchase securities over the Internet through crowdfunding?

____

____

34. Entering into Contracts on the Web Why and how are contracts of adhesion especially problematic for offers made on the web?

____

____

35. Electronic Signatures Describe some ways in which technology might be used to ensure that computer users signing contracts with e-signatures are in fact the persons they are representing themselves to be.

____

____

36. A Question of Ethics Several representatives of the entertainment media have suggested that a federal statute be enacted that would require all computers sold in the United States to incorporate software that would prevent making digital copies of music and video. Is it fair that consumers would lose the right to use their computers to make additional digital copies, for their own use, of songs and movies that they purchased legally?

____

____

CASE QUESTIONS

Study each of the following cases. Answer the questions that follow with Yes or No.

37. Selling Securities on the Web Mikai developed an exercise device that she sold on a website. Sales were brisk, and she soon discovered that she would need additional funds to purchase materials. She included on the website an invitation to the public to invest in her company by purchasing shares of stock.

a. Must Mikai register these securities with the Federal Trade Commission? **a.** ______

b. If Mikai does not register the securities, can she be charged with violating the Securities Act of 1933? **b.** ______

c. Must Mikai provide financial information to investors prior to selling securities online? **c.** ______

38. Crowdfunding Iago started a restaurant specializing in vegetarian dishes that quickly grew. In order to raise more funds for growth, Iago decided to sell stock in the company to investors through UsFunding, a registered crowdfunding website. Iago intends to keep the offering open for six months.

a. Does Iago have to prepare disclosure for posting on the UsFunding site? **a.** _____

b. May Iago raise $2 million in this six-month offering? **b.** _____

c. Can this offering be open to anyone in the public? **c.** _____

39. Settling Disputes in Cyberspace Kule purchased an antique doll for $700 from Elliott through an auction website known as e-Auction. The description of the doll provided by Elliott stated that it was in "good condition," but when Kule received the doll, she noted that it had a damaged leg. Both Kule and Elliott agreed to be bound by the decision of a representative of e-Auction, which inspected the doll.

a. Is the contract between Kule and Elliott valid despite the fact that it was entered into in cyberspace? **a.** _____

b. Is the representative from e-Auction an arbitrator? **b.** _____

c. If Kule wishes to resolve the dispute as quickly as possible, would she be better off by filing a lawsuit against Elliott? **c.** _____

CASE ANALYSIS

Study each of the following cases carefully. Briefly state the principle of law and your decision.

40. Selling Securities on the Web Jonathan G. Lebed was a 15-year-old Internet maven who, over about a six-month period, on 11 separate occasions "engaged in a scheme in which he purchased large blocks of thinly traded stocks and, within hours of making such purchases, sent numerous false and misleading messages over the Internet touting the stocks that he had just purchased." Lebed sold these shares, usually by the next day. From these activities he realized a total profit during the period of $272,826. Is Lebed guilty of violating the securities laws? [*In the Matter of Jonathan G. Lebed, a Minor, through his Guardian,* Administrative Proceeding, File No. 3-10291 (Washington, D.C.)]

Principle of Law:

____

____

Decision:

____

____

41. Personal Jurisdiction Kenneth Zippo Manufacturing Co. (ZMC) manufactured lighters at its facility in Bradford, Pennsylvania, and sold the lighters internationally. Zippo Dot Com Inc. (ZDC) is a California company that operated a website that allows subscribers to access sexually explicit material. ZMC sued ZDC for trademark infringement in Pennsylvania, but ZDC argued that they should not have to travel to

Pennsylvania to defend themselves. [*Zippo Manufacturing Co. v. Zippo Dot Com, Inc.*, 952 F. Supp. 1119 (Pennsylvania)]

Principle of Law:

____

____

Decision:

____

____

42. Selling Entertainment on the Web Napster Inc. provided a free service for visitors to its website that allowed users to share music digitally. Napster did not receive permission from the owners of the music. Several large recording studios that owned much of the music that was being shared filed a lawsuit against Napster, requesting that a federal court order Napster to cease its free online file-sharing service. Will the recording studios be successful in convincing the court to order Napster to cease these operations? [*A&M Records Inc. v. Napster*, 239 F.3d 1004 (California)]

Principle of Law:

____

____

Decision:

____

____

43. Entering into Contracts on the Web Netscape offered all visitors to its website free "SmartLoad" software provided the visitor clicked their mouse on a designated box labeled "Download." A reference to a license agreement appeared on the screen in which the "Download" box was located, but the license agreement itself appeared on the next screen. The license agreement contained a clause requiring that any dispute between the parties proceed to arbitration, rather than to court. Six plaintiffs later filed suit against Netscape relating to the software. Netscape demanded that the suit be dismissed and that all the plaintiffs be compelled to have their claims arbitrated instead. Will the plaintiffs be required to have their disputes resolved by an arbitrator, or will the court rule that the license agreement was not a part of the contract? [*Specht et al. v. Netscape et al.*, 150 F. Supp. 2d 585 (New York)]

Principle of Law:

____

____

Decision:

____

____

LEGAL RESEARCH

Complete the following activities. Share your findings with the class.

44. Working in Teams In teams of three or four, contact several retail stores in your city or town. Ask them if they maintain websites for consumers. Visit these websites, compare and contrast them, and present to the class your conclusions as to which of these are most effective in encouraging consumers to purchase the retailers' products and services.

45. Using Technology Using the Internet and search engines, find several websites that offer products and services for sale. In addition to clicking an "I accept" button, how are computer users requested to accept offers? List several means.

PART 7

Legal Environment of Business

Ryan McVay/Getty Images

chapter 32
The Employer–Employee Relationship

LEARNING OUTCOMES

After studying this chapter and completing the assessment, you will be able to

32.1 Describe the duties of an employer and employee to each other.

32.2 Distinguish between employees and independent contractors.

32.3 Explain the doctrine of employment at will.

32.4 List some typical clauses in an employment contract.

32.5 Identify some typical policies contained in an employee handbook.

32.6 Explain how employers expose themselves to legal liability when they provide employee references.

32.7 Discuss the impact of the Fair Labor Standards Act on the employer–employee relationship.

terms

LEGAL

- respondeat superior
- independent contractor
- employment at will
- employment contract
- employee handbook
- Fair Labor Standards Act of 1938

THE EMPLOYER–EMPLOYEE RELATIONSHIP

"The most common way people give up their power is thinking they don't have any."

Alice Walker, American novelist

DW labs Incorporated/Shutterstock

32.1 DUTIES OF EMPLOYER AND EMPLOYEE TO EACH OTHER

One of the most important legal relationships is that of employer-employee. This chapter examines some of the ways in which the law affects this relationship.

The employer owes several legal duties to their employee. An employer must pay an employee the agreed-upon wage, subject to company policy, union contracts, and government mandates, for their services. The employer must protect the employee by providing a safe and sanitary place to work, proper tools and machinery for the job to be performed, careful and competent employees with whom to work, and an environment free of discrimination and harassment (see Chapter 33). The employer must warn the employee of any danger that exists in connection with the work. Under *workers' compensation laws* (also covered in Chapter 33), any employee who is injured in the course of employment is permitted to recover compensation for the injury regardless of its cause unless the injury was due to the injured person's gross negligence or intentional act. An employee must obey their employer's lawful orders concerning the employment, exercise good faith toward the employer, and do their work carefully and conscientiously.

The acts of an employee committed while performing employment duties are considered the acts of the employer. This comes from a legal doctrine known as respondeat superior, a Latin term meaning "let the master answer." Therefore, the employer is liable to third parties for injuries caused by an employee, whether the acts are willful or negligent, so long as the acts were committed by the employee within the ordinary course of employment. The employee is also personally liable for wrongful acts that result in injuries to a third party, whether they are intentional or the result of negligence.

respondeat superior
A legal doctrine that holds that the acts of an employee committed while performing duties are considered the acts of the employer.

EXAMPLE 32.1

▶ Marek was employed in the shipping department of Margo Stores Inc. Otler, a customer, came to the department to pick up a shipment, and Marek carelessly ran into him with a hand truck and injured Otler's leg. Both Margo Stores and Marek are liable to Otler for the injury. As a practical matter, an injured third party who is interested in receiving a financial settlement will usually sue the employer because the employer generally has more financial resources as well as insurance.

32.2 EMPLOYEES VERSUS INDEPENDENT CONTRACTORS

The distinction between an employee and an agent was addressed in Chapter 19. Similarly, an employee is also distinct from an independent contractor. It is important to recognize these distinctions because in order to apply the law, a court first needs to determine whether an employer-employee relationship actually existed. In all cases, it is not the worker's title, or the tax treatment they receive, that determines whether they are an employee. Rather, what the individual does on the job defines the relationship.

INDEPENDENT CONTRACTORS

independent contractor One who contracts to do a job and who retains complete control over the methods employed to obtain completion.

An independent contractor is a person or firm that performs services for another. Examples of independent contractors include freelance writers and photographers, private-duty nurses, painters, and plumbers. Independent contractors are not under the direct control of the person who engages them. It is important to distinguish between employees and independent contractors because employees usually cannot sue their employers for on-the-job injuries, whereas independent contractors can sue the person with whom they made the contract. An employer is responsible for an employee's torts committed within the scope of employment; the person who engages an independent contractor, on the other hand, is generally not responsible for the independent contractor's torts.

EXAMPLE 32.2

Chu, a retired magazine editor, was engaged by Fifth National Bank to write and edit a monthly employee newsletter. She often spent time in the offices of the bank interviewing various staff members but was paid a flat fee for each issue of the newsletter. Chu is an independent contractor. She would not be considered a member of the bank's staff and did not have the legal status of an employee.

In Example 32.2, if Chu were to libel someone in her newsletter, she, but not the bank, would be responsible for the tort (although the bank would probably be named as a codefendant in a suit). Also, if Chu were injured while in the offices of the bank, unlike an employee, she would not be prevented from suing the bank for its negligence.

A plumber is an example of an independent contractor.
kurhan/123RF

THE INTERNAL REVENUE SERVICE TEST

The Internal Revenue Service (IRS) publishes a kind of test that is used to aid individuals in determining whether a worker fits the status of an employee or an independent contractor. This test includes items such as who provides instruction, training, and tools; who sets hours; who determines where the work is performed and the sequence of work; and how payment is made to the worker. This explicit IRS test aids businesses and individuals in distinguishing employees from independent contractors. Understanding this distinction affects how an individual pays federal income taxes, Social Security taxes, and Medicare taxes. It also determines whether the individual receives a W-2, a tax form provided to employees, or a 1099, a tax form provided to independent contractors.

EXAMPLE 32.3

▶ Pirrone worked for wages of $14 per hour during regularly scheduled hours for Bluesky Travel, answering telephones, responding to email, and greeting clients. At the end of each year, Bluesky sent Pirrone a Form 1099 rather than a W-2 form. Pirrone's duties at her job clearly make her an employee, with Bluesky her employer, irrespective of the tax form she was provided.

If the IRS discovers that a company has misclassified employees as independent contractors, it may impose substantial penalties on the company. In a case of a deliberate misclassification, IRS penalties are harsh and may amount to millions of dollars for large companies. Thus, it is crucial to correctly classify workers as either employees or independent contractors.

For additional information relating to the IRS test on employees versus independent contractors, visit www.irs.gov/pub/irs-pdf/p1779.pdf.

32.3 THE DOCTRINE OF EMPLOYMENT AT WILL

Deeply rooted in U.S. tradition is the doctrine of employment at will, which states that, just as an employee may choose to terminate their employment at any time they wish, so too an employer may terminate an employee's employment at any time for a good reason, a bad reason, or no reason at all. Of course, an employer could not exercise this doctrine when that would breach an employment contract. In addition, over a long period of time, this doctrine has been eroded by federal, state, and local statutes; by court decisions; and by public policy. Early exceptions to the doctrine disallowed an employee from being terminated for jury duty service, for being called to active duty in the military, and for *whistleblowing* (e.g., reporting the employer's criminal acts to the authorities). Later it became illegal to terminate an employee for reasons that amounted to illegal discrimination (see Chapter 33). Today, there are numerous reasons for which it would be illegal to terminate an employee.

employment at will
A doctrine that states that an employer may terminate an employee's employment at any time for a good reason, a bad reason, or no reason at all.

EXAMPLE 32.4

▶ Smoko worked as a mechanic for Lots and Lots Used Cars. Zlotuca, the manager, ordered him to roll back the odometer on an automobile that was for sale so that it would command a higher price. Smoko, knowing that such conduct was illegal, refused and Zlotuca fired him. Smoko sued for lost wages, and Lots and Lots argued that Smoko was employed at will. Smoko will probably be successful in his lawsuit.

32.4 EMPLOYMENT CONTRACTS

employment contract
An agreement that specifies that the employer agrees to pay, and the employee agrees to work, for a specified period of time at a specified salary.

There are many instances in which an employer and employee enter into a formal, written employment contract that specifies that the employer agrees to pay, and the employee agrees to work, for a specified period of time at a specified salary. These contracts frequently have clauses related to maintaining confidentiality with respect to trade secrets, restrictive covenants (see Chapter 28), and agreements to arbitrate in the event of a dispute between the parties (see Chapter 31). The U.S. Supreme Court has ruled that arbitration clauses in employment contracts are enforceable provided the employee

- Has signed the agreement.
- Has a reasonable time to file a claim.
- Has access to the same remedies that a court could provide.
- Has access to an arbitrator with expertise in employment law.
- Has the right to be represented by an attorney.
- Does not have to pay the cost of arbitration.

EXAMPLE 32.5

Zebramai and One Furry Creation, a dog grooming store, entered into an employment contract wherein Zebramai would be employed for one year as a groomer at a salary of $400 per week. When Zebramai received her first paycheck, she noticed that the amount of salary was only $300. When Zebramai complained, she was immediately fired. Zebramai filed a lawsuit, and One Furry Creation argued that it was company policy that all employee claims go to arbitration. Because Zebramai never agreed to the policy, she will be allowed to have her case resolved by a court rather than an arbitrator.

32.5 EMPLOYEE HANDBOOKS

employee handbook
A manual published by an employer that contains the many policies of the firm.

Many employers provide employees with employee handbooks, manuals that contain the many policies of the firm. In some states, the provisions contained in the handbook are considered a kind of contract between the employer and the employee, while in other states, legislatures and courts have made it clear that employee handbooks are not to be construed as contracts.

Typically, the employee handbook contains the following information:

- *History* of the company, including its mission and philosophy.
- *Hiring procedures,* including a statement that the company complies with federal and state antidiscrimination laws.
- *Hours of employment,* including how schedules are crafted and time card policies.
- *Payment of salaries,* including the conditions under which employees may receive advances.
- *Salary increments and promotions,* including procedures for employee evaluation and appeals that may be available.

- *Termination procedures,* including exit interviews and the requirement that employees must return all company property.
- *Benefits,* including those legally required, such as unemployment insurance, Social Security contributions, and workers' compensation; and those not legally required, such as medical insurance, disability insurance, vacation and personal days, sick leave, holidays, education benefits, and profit sharing.
- *Leaves of absence,* including maternity leave, jury duty, military leave, and leaves for marriage or religious purposes.
- *Safety and security,* including medical and security emergencies, vandalism, tobacco and alcohol policies, drug testing, and computer usage and passwords.
- *Miscellaneous policies,* including parking regulations, lost and found, employee dress codes, eating and drinking on company premises, telephone usage, business travel, and employees' right to access their personnel files.

EXAMPLE 32.6

- Hegde was employed for five months by a medium-size accounting firm. She was planning a European holiday for next year and was interested in knowing how much vacation time the company offered. She consulted the employee handbook, which provided the information she needed to make her plans.

32.6 EMPLOYEE REFERENCES

Often, employers are asked to provide references for employees who are currently working for them or who have worked for them in the past. Employers need to be extremely careful in how they respond to these requests. Providing either negative or incomplete references can subject a previous employer to three kinds of lawsuits brought by either former employees or prospective employers: invasion of privacy, defamation, and negligent misrepresentation.

At times, employers are asked to provide references for employees.
Keith Brofsky/Getty Images

INVASION OF PRIVACY

Disclosing personal, irrelevant information about a former employee amounts to invasion of privacy, irrespective of whether such information is true or false. An employer can safely disclose information about a current or former employee in the following areas:

- The employee's prior employment and educational history.
- The employee's character as such relates to the job (teamwork, leadership abilities, etc.).
- The employee's performance capabilities.
- The employer's willingness to rehire the employee.

EXAMPLE 32.7

▶ Verret applied for a position at a local bank, using her former manager, Abusir, as a reference. When the human resources manager at the bank telephoned Abusir to learn more about Verret's employment history, Abusir explained that Verret had engaged in an extramarital affair and was about to get divorced. When the bank did not hire Verret, she sued Abusir for invasion of privacy.

DEFAMATION

In general, a current or former employee may sue their employer for defamation if the employer provides information to a third party that is untrue, irrespective of whether it relates to the employee's job performance. Such defamation is considered slander, if spoken, or libel, if written (see Chapter 4).

EXAMPLE 32.8

▶ Caswell applied for a position at a local bank, using his former manager, Panganibin, as a reference. When the human resources manager at the bank telephoned Panganibin to learn more about Caswell's employment history, Panganibin lied and stated that Caswell had stolen money from his employer. When the bank did not hire Caswell, he sued Panganibin for slander, a form of defamation.

It is important to note that many states have enacted laws to shield employers from the risk of liability for defamation, provided the previous employer has a good-faith belief that the statements made in the reference are truthful and has documentation supporting the claims.

NEGLIGENT MISREPRESENTATION

Occasionally, employers attempt to reduce their risk of liability in providing references by withholding negative reference information or simply not responding to reference requests. However, if a prospective employer hires an employee based on an incomplete reference and then suffers damages that may have been avoided had the previous employer provided an accurate reference, the prospective employer may sue the previous employer for negligent misrepresentation.

EXAMPLE 32.9

▶ Central State University fired Baez, one of the clerks in its registrar's office, for stealing money paid by students for their tuition. Baez later applied for a position as a financial aid officer at Kingsman College and, knowing that her former employer had a policy of not providing references, used Central State as a reference. Baez was hired by Kingsman and, a short time later, stole several thousand dollars and fled the country. Kingsman would probably be successful in a lawsuit against Central State for negligent misrepresentation.

32.7 FAIR LABOR STANDARDS ACT OF 1938

The Fair Labor Standards Act of 1938 (FLSA) is a law that sets standards for the minimum age an employee can be, the minimum wages an employee can earn, and the rate at which an employee is paid if they work more than a certain number of hours in a given workweek. Currently, the federal minimum wage is $7.25, and the overtime pay rate for employees who work more than 40 hours in a workweek is one and a half times their regular wages. While some states and local governments have adopted a minimum wage higher than $7.25, states are not allowed to have a minimum wage less than $7.25.

Fair Labor Standards Act of 1938 (FLSA)
The FLSA is a law that sets standards for the minimum age an employee can be, the minimum wages an employee can earn, and the rate at which an employee is paid if they work more than a certain number of hours in a given workweek.

Many industries are covered by FLSA; however, four categories of employees are excluded from coverage: executives, professional employees, outside sales associates, and administrative employees. Of course, independent contractors are not covered by the provisions of the FLSA.

CHAPTER SUMMARY

32.1 An employer must pay an employee the agreed-upon wage for their services and provide the employee with a safe and sanitary workplace, proper tools for the job to be performed, careful and competent employees with whom to work, and an environment free of discrimination and harassment. The employer also must warn an employee of any danger that exists in connection with the work. The employee must obey their employer's lawful orders concerning employment, exercise good faith toward the employer, and do their work carefully and conscientiously.

32.2 Unlike employees, independent contractors can sue their employer for on-the-job injuries. An employer is also liable for an employee's torts, but not those of an independent contractor, that are committed within the scope of employment. The Internal Revenue Service publishes a test to aid individuals in determining whether a worker fits the status of an employee or an independent contractor.

32.3 The doctrine of employment at will states that, just as an employee may choose to terminate their employment at any time they wish, so too an employer may terminate an employee's employment at any time for a good reason, a bad reason, or no reason at all.

32.4 Employment contracts frequently have clauses related to maintaining confidentiality with respect to trade secrets, restrictive covenants, and agreements to arbitrate in the event of a dispute between the parties.

32.5 Typically, an employee handbook contains the history of the company, hiring procedures, hours of employment, payment of salaries, salary increments and promotions, termination procedures, benefits, leaves of absence, safety and security, and miscellaneous policies.

32.6 Employers who are asked to provide references for employees need to be extremely careful. Providing either negative or incomplete references can subject a previous employer to three kinds of lawsuits brought by either former employees or prospective employers: invasion of privacy, defamation, and negligent misrepresentation.

32.7 The FLSA is a law that sets standards for the minimum age an employee can be, the minimum wages an employee can earn, and the rate at which an employee is paid if they work more than a certain number of hours in a given workweek.

CHAPTER THIRTY-TWO ASSESSMENT

MATCHING LEGAL TERMS

Match each of the numbered definitions with the correct term in the following list.

a. 1099
b. employment at will
c. employment contract
d. employee handbook
e. independent contractor
f. respondeat superior
g. W-2

1. An agreement that specifies that the employer agrees to pay, and the employee agrees to work, for a specified period of time at a specified salary. **1.** _____

2. A tax form provided to employees. **2.** _____

3. A person or firm that performs services for another. **3.** _____

4. A tax form provided to independent contractors. **4.** _____

5. A doctine that states that, just as an employee may choose to terminate their employment at any time they wish, so too an employer may terminate an employee's employment at any time. **5.** _____

6. A manual published by an employer that contains the policies of the firm. **6.** _____

7. A legal doctrine that holds that the acts of an employee committed while performing employment duties are considered the acts of the employer. **7.** _____

TRUE/FALSE QUIZ

Indicate whether each of the following statements is true or false.

8. Acts of an employee while performing duties of employment are considered the acts of the employer. **8.** _____

9. Workers' compensation laws are designed to ensure that all employees are paid fairly. **9.** _____

10. Independent contractors are under the direct control of the person who engages them. **10.** _____

11. An independent contractor can sue the person with whom they made the contract. **11.** _____

12. The doctrine of employment at will has been eroded by federal, state, and local statutes; by court decisions; and by public policy. **12.** _____

13. Arbitration clauses in employment contracts are never enforceable. **13.** _____

14. In some states, the provisions contained in an employee handbook are considered a kind of contract between the employer and the employee. **14.** _____

15. In some states, legislatures and courts have made it clear that employee handbooks are not to be construed as contracts. **15.** _____

16. A current or former employee may sue their employer for defamation if the employer provides information to a third party that is untrue, irrespective of whether it relates to the employee's job performance. **16.** _____

MULTIPLE CHOICE QUIZ

Indicate the correct answer from the choices following each question.

17. An employee delivering goods to a customer has a car accident that injures a driver in another car. The injured driver may (a) sue only the employee driving the car (b) sue only the employer (c) sue both the employee and the employer (d) not sue either the employee or the employer. **17.** _____

18. A business hires a trucking company to deliver goods to a customer, and one of the trucks has a car accident that injures a driver in another car. The injured driver may (a) sue only the trucking company (b) sue only the business hiring the trucking company (c) sue both the trucking company and the business hiring the trucking company (d) not sue either the trucking company nor the business hiring the trucking company. **18.** _____

19. An employer hires an employee to manage their retail store. After a period of three months, the employer decides to terminate the employee. In this case, the employer may (a) terminate the employee only if there was a contract (b) terminate the employee only if the employee committed a crime (c) terminate the employee unless there was a contract for employment or such termination would violate the law (d) terminate the employee in any case. **19.** _____

20. An employer has a business that makes a food product using a recipe that is a trade secret. When hiring an employee who would have access to the recipe, the employer (a) cannot require confidentiality as part of the employment contract (b) should require confidentiality as part of the employment contract (c) may rely on the law to enforce confidentiality (d) none of the above. **20.** _____

21. An employer would like to include a clause in its employment contracts that requires all disputes relating to employment be resolved using arbitration. In this case, the employer (a) may include that the employee cannot obtain legal representation (b) may include that the employee does not have access to all remedies available in court (c) may include that arbitration be final (d) may require that the employee pay the full cost of arbitration. **21.** _____

22. An employer receiving a request for a reference for a former employee should not disclose which of the following in order to avoid a claim of invasion of privacy? (a) The former employee's address and telephone number (b) The former employee's educational history (c) The former employee's performance capabilities (d) The employer's willingness to rehire the former employee **22.** _____

23. Employers must balance the potential claims of defamation and negligent misrepresentation when asking for a reference about a former employee. The best practice to balance those claims is (a) to make claims regardless of documentation (b) to refuse to answer any questions (c) to make claims that have basis in documentation (d) to make partial claims and check documentation later. **23.** _____

24. Which of the following jobs would be entitled to minimum wage under federal law? (a) An attorney employed by a law firm (b) A consultant hired as a contractor (c) A retail clerk (d) A vice president of marketing **24.** _____

DISCUSSION QUESTIONS

Answer the following questions and discuss them in class.

25. Describe the duties of an employer and employee to each other.

26. Distinguish between independent contractors and employees.

27. List some exceptions to the doctrine of employment at will.

28. Describe the conditions under which arbitration clauses in employment contracts are enforceable.

29. List some items typically found in an employee handbook.

30. Identify the standards established by the Fair Labor Standards Act of 1938.

THINKING CRITICALLY ABOUT THE LAW

Answer the following questions, which require you to think critically about the legal principles that you learned in this chapter.

31. Duties of Employer Should an employer be held liable for an employee's negligent act even though the employer is not at fault?

32. Employees versus Independent Contractors Does it place an unnecessary burden on a third party to determine whether they are dealing with an employee or an independent contractor?

____

____

33. Employment at Will Should the law allow an employer to fire an employee without having a good reason?

____

____

34. Employee Handbooks Should promises made in an employee handbook legally bind an employer?

____

____

35. A Question of Ethics When providing a reference for a former employee, is it ethical to withhold truthful negative information for fear of being sued?

____

____

CASE QUESTIONS

Study each of the following cases. Answer the questions that follow with Yes or No.

36. Duty of Employer Zanucky was employed by a furniture store as a driver of a delivery truck. While making a delivery, he negligently drove through a red light, and the delivery truck struck a vehicle operated by Gittins, who was injured in the accident.

a. Can Gittins sue Zanucky for her injuries? **a.** _____

b. Can Gittins sue the furniture store for her injuries? **b.** _____

c. Can the furniture store sue Zanucky for damages to the truck? **c.** _____

37. The Doctrine of Employment at Will Packerd owned a restaurant that employed several employees as servers. When sales began to decline, Packerd decided to fire three servers. He selected Artemuk, who had numerous complaints about her service; Bednerz, who would soon be leaving for jury duty; and Tondruck, who had just been called up for active military service.

a. May Packerd legally fire Artemuk? **a.** _____

b. May Packerd legally fire Bednerz? **b.** _____

c. May Packerd legally fire Tondruck? **c.** _____

38. Employee Handbooks Killian was hired as a human resources manager for a company that employed about 75 people. She decided that it would be a good idea to publish an employee handbook explaining the many policies of the firm. She began to consider what provisions the handbook should have.

a. Should the employee handbook have a section on procedures for employee evaluation and appeals? **a.** _____

b. Should the employee handbook have a section on the Internal Revenue Service test? **b.** _____

c. Should the employee handbook have a section on the number of vacation and personal days available to employees? **c.** _____

CASE ANALYSIS

Study each of the following cases carefully. Briefly state the principle of law and your decision.

39. Employment Arbitration The GDGS Corporation adopted an arbitration policy and announced it to its employees via email. The policy stated that arbitration was the exclusive means of resolving legal disputes between employees and the company. When Campbell, one of the employees of GDGS, was fired, he filed a lawsuit against the company despite the fact that he was aware of the policy. GDGS insisted that the case goes to arbitration. Will Campbell be required to take his claim to arbitration, or can the case be heard by a court? [*Campbell v. General Dynamics Government Systems Corp.,* 321 F. Supp.2d 142 (Massachusetts)]

Principle of Law:

____

____

Decision:

____

____

40. Invasion of Privacy Dasey was employed as a state trooper by the Massachusetts Department of State Police. In his employment application, Dasey stated that he had not used illegal drugs during the previous five years. Later, during an unrelated homicide investigation, a videotape surfaced that depicted Dasey smoking marijuana. Dasey was fired for lying on his application. He filed a lawsuit alleging, among other things, that he had been denied his right to privacy. Has Dasey's privacy been invaded, and will Dasey be successful in his lawsuit? [*Dasey v. Anderson et al.,* 304 F.3d 148 (Fed. 1st Cir. 2002)]

Principle of Law:

____

____

Decision:

____

____

41. Employees versus Independent Contractors Wojewski, a cardiothoracic surgeon, became a member of the medical staff at Rapid City Regional Hospital. Wojewski's staff status entitled him to admit patients, use the hospital's facilities, and perform surgery. Wojewski could also use nurses to assist him in surgery. Wojewski leased separate office space and maintained his own staff, whom he hired and paid. Medical staff membership required Wojewski to provide appropriate patient care, abide by medical staff bylaws, prepare required medical records, abide by ethical principles, attend an orientation program, participate in continuing medical education, and schedule operating room time. Wojewski also agreed to take calls from the emergency room for heart-related emergencies. Wojewski billed his patients directly, and the patients remitted payments directly to him. The hospital did not issue a form W-2 or 1099 to Wojewski and did not pay his Social Security taxes or provide benefits, such as health and malpractice insurance. When Wojewski had a dispute with the hospital, he argued that he was afforded protection as an employee. Does Wojewski hold the legal status of an employee? [*Wojewski v. Rapid City Regional Hospital, Inc.*, 450 F.3d 338 (Fed. 8th Cir., 2006)]

Principle of Law:

Decision:

LEGAL RESEARCH

Complete the following activities. Share your findings with the class.

42. Working in Teams In teams of three or four, interview managers of local businesses. Ask them if they have ever provided a negative reference for a former employee.

43. Using Technology Using the Internet and search engines, investigate the Internal Revenue Service to determine how the agency distinguishes between employees and independent contractors.

chapter 33

Employment Law

LEARNING OUTCOMES

After studying this chapter and completing the assessment, you will be able to

33.1 Discuss federal and state laws that protect employees, including workers' compensation and the Occupational Safety and Health Act.

33.2 Identify the major federal statutes concerning discrimination in employment, and identify several forms of conduct that can constitute sexual harassment.

33.3 Discuss labor unions and the rights of employees, unions, and employers under federal law.

33.4 Discuss an employee's rights to medical leave and unemployment benefits.

terms

LEGAL

- workers' compensation
- exclusive remedy
- Occupational Safety and Health Act of 1970
- Occupational Safety and Health Administration (OSHA)
- ergonomics
- affirmative action plans
- Civil Rights Act of 1964
- Title VII
- Equal Employment Opportunity Commission (EEOC)
- Equal Pay Act of 1963 (EPA)
- Age Discrimination in Employment Act of 1967
- Pregnancy Discrimination Act of 1978
- Americans with Disabilities Act (ADA) of 1990
- Civil Rights Act of 1991
- sexual harassment
- labor unions
- National Labor Relations Board (NLRB)
- collective bargaining agreement
- wildcat strike
- slowdown
- lockout
- Family and Medical Leave Act of 1993 (FMLA)
- unemployment insurance

EMPLOYMENT LAW

"Society as a whole benefits immeasurably from a climate in which all persons, regardless of race or gender, may have the opportunity to earn respect, responsibility, advancement, and remuneration based on ability."

Sandra Day O'Connor, former associate justice of the U.S. Supreme Court

ml/Shutterstock

33.1 WORKER SAFETY AND HEALTH

Numerous federal and state laws protect employees from accidents and sicknesses that are job-related. At the state level, there are workers' compensation statutes, which pertain to how a worker may recover damages for work-related injuries and illnesses. At the federal level, several statutes require that employers maintain a safe and healthy work environment. The most important of these federal statutes is the Occupational Safety and Health Act of 1970.

workers' compensation
A type of insurance that allows employees to recover damages for work-related injuries and illnesses without having to prove negligence on the part of the employer.

WORKERS' COMPENSATION

Workers' compensation is a type of insurance that allows employees to recover damages for work-related injuries and illnesses without having to prove negligence on the part of the employer.

EXAMPLE 33.1

▶ Seely, an employee of Gorr Floors, installs carpeting in customers' homes. After an installation, and while on the way back to the Gorr warehouse, Seely stopped at a local tavern for a few beers. He then became engaged in a dispute with another patron and was struck in the face, resulting in the loss of several of Seely's teeth. Seely is not able to file for workers' compensation because his injury is not work related. He is, however, allowed to try to collect damages for his injuries from the other patron or perhaps from the owner of the tavern for failing to provide a safe environment.

exclusive remedy
A doctrine that states that an employee who sustains a work-related injury or illness can recover damages only through workers' compensation and may not file a lawsuit against their employer.

Because workers' compensation is mandatory in most industries, and because it provides employees with nearly automatic recovery, it is considered to be the exclusive remedy: An employee who sustains a work-related injury or illness can recover damages only through workers' compensation and may not file a lawsuit against their employer.

EXAMPLE 33.2

▶ Kwan was injured when he tripped on a slippery floor while working for Nambeesan Mini-Markets. Kwan sued Nambeesan, arguing that she should be allowed to recover for her injuries due to Nambeesan's negligence in not maintaining a dry floor. Kwan's case will be dismissed because workers' compensation is her exclusive remedy.

Of course, the fact that an employee is prohibited from suing their employer for a work-related injury or illness does not preclude the employee from suing a third party, even if the injury or illness occurred while the employee was on the job.

EXAMPLE 33.3

LeBlanc worked in an office where an outside contracting company was painting the walls. While LeBlanc was walking to the office conference room, a paint can fell from scaffolding and struck him in the head, causing a concussion. LeBlanc may file a workers' compensation claim against his employer and also may file a lawsuit against the contracting company. Should LeBlanc be successful in his lawsuit against the contracting company, his employer (or its insurance company) will be reimbursed for any monies paid to LeBlanc under the workers' compensation claim.

Workers' compensation provides that employees may recover damages for work-related injuries.
Tetra Images/Getty Images

It must be pointed out, however, that employees may still sue their employers if the employer's intentional or grossly negligent conduct caused the injury or illness.

In recent years, the number of workers' compensation claims that have been filed has increased dramatically, causing a large increase in costs associated with the program. Many employees have filed claims for stress-related illnesses, which are compensable if the stress was not the result of the employee's ordinary duties on the job. Many employers have *employee assistance programs* in place, a company benefit that provides opportunities for counseling and stress reduction.

Occupational Safety and Health Act of 1970
A federal statute designed to promote safety and health in the workplace.

EXAMPLE 33.4

Correa worked as a teller at a bank. An individual entered the bank building, pointed a pistol at her head, and ordered her to turn over the money in her till. Correa complied and, fortunately, was not harmed. Subsequently, Correa needed to take time off from her position to attend counseling. This stress-related condition is compensable under workers' compensation.

Occupational Safety and Health Administration (OSHA)
The federal agency that administers the many provisions of the Occupational Safety and Health Act of 1970.

OCCUPATIONAL SAFETY AND HEALTH ACT

The Occupational Safety and Health Act of 1970 was passed to promote safety and health in the workplace. The law created a federal agency, the Occupational Safety and Health Administration (OSHA), to administer its many provisions. OSHA requires that companies maintain records of employee work-related accidents and sicknesses and post data regarding these every February. OSHA inspects workplaces (at times using administrative search warrants to gain entry) to be certain that these worksites comply with safety and health standards. In the event if violations are found to exist, OSHA can impose penalties ranging from fines to closing the facility; however, in extreme cases, such as those in which deliberate and repeat violations result in a fatality, penalties may reach $500,000 plus prison time. OSHA also requires that all violations be corrected and often will revisit the facility to ensure that the unsafe conditions have been corrected.

OSHA inspects workplaces to be certain worksites comply with safety and health standards.
Burak Karademir/Getty Images

As a response to OSHA standards, companies are paying greater attention to the developing science of ergonomics, which deals with designing workplaces to promote safety and health. Examples would include desk and office chair design, computer screen protections, tilted keyboards, and so forth.

ergonomics
A developing science that deals with designing workplaces to promote safety and health.

33.2 DISCRIMINATION IN EMPLOYMENT

While the traditional employer-employee relationship in law allows termination at will, numerous federal, state, and local statutes prohibit employers from discriminating in employment. Discrimination against employees who are members of a protected class is illegal throughout the employment process, including outreach (e.g., how the employer advertises the position), hiring, job classification, salary, promotions, benefits, discipline, layoffs, termination, and so on. In specific, limited instances required by courts, companies must maintain and report detailed records to demonstrate that their employment practices are nondiscriminatory. These reports are referred to as affirmative action plans.

affirmative action plans
Detailed records that demonstrate that an employer's practices are nondiscriminatory.

THE CIVIL RIGHTS ACT OF 1964

The Civil Rights Act of 1964 is a federal statute designed to protect individuals from illegal discrimination. This law is divided into parts, referred to as *titles,* that prohibit discrimination in various situations. Discrimination in employment is covered in Title VII of the law.

The Civil Rights Act of 1964 created the Equal Employment Opportunity Commission (EEOC), a federal agency responsible for administering laws prohibiting discrimination in employment. Since 1972, the EEOC has had standing to sue companies that are alleged to be in violation of the law.

Discrimination in employment is prohibited on the basis of race, creed, color, sex, religion, and place of national origin. Over the years, these classes have been expanded to include others, to be discussed later in this chapter.

Civil Rights Act of 1964
A federal statute designed to protect individuals from illegal discrimination.

Title VII
The portion of the Civil Rights Act of 1964 that deals with discrimination in employment.

Equal Employment Opportunity Commission (EEOC)
A federal agency responsible for administering laws prohibiting discrimination in employment.

EXAMPLE 33.5

Bruno applied for a clerical position at Larkville National Bank and Trust. During her interview with the human resources manager, she was questioned about where her husband worked and whether she planned to have children. When she hesitated in responding, she was informed that she would not be offered the position. Bruno complained to the EEOC, which will likely impose penalties on the bank for discriminating on the basis of sex in the hiring process.

While many states and municipalities have passed specific laws protecting employment rights based on sexual orientation, the federal government has not passed any such legislation. However, the U.S. Supreme Court has ruled that Title VII protection based on gender includes protection based on sexual orientation or gender identity.

Title VII cases may be proven in four different ways: direct evidence, express policy, disparate treatment, and disparate impact. Direct evidence requires that a plaintiff prove facts showing that an employer took specific action to discriminate. An employer may also have a policy that, on its face, is discriminatory. If that is the case, the employer must have a good-faith reason based on the job qualifications for that policy. This reason is known as a bona fide occupational qualification (BFOQ) for the policy.

EXAMPLE 33.6

Ballantine Bathing Suits places an advertisement requesting female models for its new advertising campaign. This advertisement is expressly discriminatory based on gender, but Ballantine would argue that having females model women's bathing suits is a BFOQ.

Disparate treatment does not require oral or written evidence of discrimination but allows a court to infer discrimination from behavior of the parties. With disparate treatment, employers must have documentation to prove that they took the alleged discriminatory action for legitimate, nondiscriminatory reasons.

EXAMPLE 33.7

Liu, a manager at a consulting firm, interviews two candidates for a consultant position at the firm: Katya, a woman, and Diego, a man. Both meet the qualifications for the position. In his interview, he asks both about their qualifications but adds questions to Katya about whether she intends to have children. Liu hires Diego instead of Katya. Katya would have an initial case for discrimination based on disparate treatment since a man was hired instead of her. Liu and the firm would have to show that they made their decision to hire Diego based on legitimate, nondiscriminatory reasons.

Disparate impact actions may be brought by employees of a protected class if they are negatively affected by a policy or procedure that, on its face, is nondiscriminatory. Like disparate treatment, employers must prove that the policy or procedure is a business necessity despite its discriminatory impact.

EXAMPLE 33.8

▶ Xavier Manufacturing has equipment that requires users to be at least 5 feet 7 inches tall and 160 pounds. This policy is not discriminatory on its face because height and weight are not protected classes. However, women will tend to be less likely to meet these requirements and so have a case for disparate impact discrimination with this policy. Xavier will have to show that this requirement is a business necessity.

THE EQUAL PAY ACT OF 1963

The Equal Pay Act of 1963 (EPA), enacted prior to Title VII, was the first federal statute to address discrimination against women in the workplace. The act prohibits any employer from engaging in wage discrimination based on sex. Under this law, all employees performing substantially similar jobs must be compensated equally. However, there are some situations in which wage disparity between sexes is permissible, such as when wages are based on seniority or tenure within an organization. In lawsuits under the Equal Pay Act, the statute of limitations resets each time an employer issues a discriminatory paycheck to an employee (the *Lilly Ledbetter Fair Pay Act of 2009*).

Equal Pay Act of 1963 (EPA)
A statute that prohibits any employer from engaging in wage discrimination based on sex.

THE AGE DISCRIMINATION IN EMPLOYMENT ACT

The Age Discrimination in Employment Act of 1967 is a federal statute designed to protect individuals from illegal discrimination in employment on the basis of age. The protected class created pursuant to this statute is persons over the age of 40. It should be noted that several states have laws making it illegal to discriminate on the basis of age against persons who are younger than 40.

Age Discrimination in Employment Act of 1967
A federal statute designed to protect individuals from illegal discrimination in employment on the basis of age.

EXAMPLE 33.9

▶ Bookshire was a 67-year-old manager for a telecommunications company. Over a period of 42 years, he rose from being a mailroom clerk to a manager, attaining significant salary increments during his tenure. Senior management officials within the company repeatedly commented to Bookshire that, to retain his position, he would need to improve his technology skills. Bookshire underwent an extensive company training program, performing admirably, and took computer courses at a nearby college as well. Nonetheless, Bookshire was terminated and replaced by a 21-year-old applicant with no experience, at a significantly lower salary than Bookshire had earned. Bookshire filed a complaint with the EEOC, which will likely impose penalties on the company for discriminating in employment on the basis of age.

THE PREGNANCY DISCRIMINATION ACT

The Pregnancy Discrimination Act of 1978 is a federal statute designed to protect individuals from illegal discrimination in employment on the basis of pregnancy. Under the act, employers must treat women affected by pregnancy in the same manner as any other employee who suffers from a temporary disability.

Pregnancy Discrimination Act of 1978
A federal statute designed to protect individuals from illegal discrimination in employment on the basis of pregnancy.

EXAMPLE 33.10

Yashiv worked on an assembly line for a manufacturer of plastic containers. The position required that she stand on her feet for long hours. She performed her duties well and continually received outstanding evaluations. Yashiv then informed the company that she had become pregnant and requested a temporary transfer to a clerical position that was vacant and for which she was qualified. The company refused, and when Yashiv entered the latter stages of her pregnancy, she was no longer able to perform her assembly-line duties. The company then terminated her employment. Yashiv filed a complaint with the EEOC, arguing that the company should have honored her reasonable request for a temporary transfer. The EEOC will likely impose penalties on the company for discriminating in employment on the basis of pregnancy.

The ADA requires that employers make reasonable accommodation for an otherwise qualified employee with a disability.
Keith Brofsky/Getty Images

THE AMERICANS WITH DISABILITIES ACT

The Americans with Disabilities Act (ADA) of 1990 is a federal statute designed to protect individuals from illegal discrimination in employment on the basis of disability. The ADA defines *disability* as a physical or mental impairment that substantially limits one or more of the major activities of life. Persons considered to have a disability under the ADA would include individuals who are sight impaired, are hearing impaired, or use a wheelchair. Persons who have diseases such as cancer, diabetes, alcoholism, AIDS, epilepsy, manic depression, or schizophrenia are protected under this law. Also protected from discriminatory practices by employers are persons who were prior (not current) drug users or who have learning disabilities or psychologically based eating disorders.

Americans with Disabilities Act (ADA) of 1990
A federal statute designed to protect individuals from illegal discrimination in employment on the basis of disability.

The ADA also protects persons who do not currently have a disability but who have a record of a covered disability. In addition, the statute protects persons who have a relationship with an individual who has a covered disability (e.g., if the employee's spouse is HIV positive). Furthermore, even if an employer incorrectly believes that an employee has a covered disability, the employee is then protected from discriminatory practices.

The ADA requires that employers make reasonable accommodation for an otherwise qualified employee with a disability, unless to do so would cause undue hardship. Courts have been asked on numerous occasions to determine what constitutes a "disability," a "reasonable accommodation," and an "undue hardship."

EXAMPLE 33.11

▶ Chambers worked for Jaeger Department Stores as a salesperson. Like all store employees, he was entitled to a one-hour lunch break period. Because Chambers was diabetic and because he was not allowed to have food at his post, he requested that he be given four 15-minute break periods in lieu of the one-hour break period so that he could maintain a healthy blood sugar level. Because diabetes is a covered disability, and because this reasonable accommodation is not likely to cause undue hardship for the employer, Jaeger Department Stores will be required under the ADA to grant Chambers's request.

THE CIVIL RIGHTS ACT OF 1991

The Civil Rights Act of 1991 is a federal statute that provides two important additional remedies to an employee who can prove that they were a victim of discrimination:

1. An employee may collect *punitive damages* (in effect, to punish the employer).
2. An employee may recover for emotional distress associated with being the victim of discrimination.

Civil Rights Act of 1991
A federal statute that provides additional remedies to an employee who can prove that they were a victim of discrimination.

SEXUAL HARASSMENT

Sexual harassment is unwelcome sexual attention, whether verbal or physical, that affects an employee's job condition or creates a hostile working environment. Sexual harassment is a form of discrimination on the basis of sex and is illegal under federal and state law. Same-sex harassment is also illegal.

sexual harassment
Unwelcome sexual attention, whether verbal or physical, that affects an employee's job condition or creates a hostile working environment.

There are numerous forms of sexual harassment. Examples may include:

- *Unwelcome sexual advances,* such as repeated propositions for dates by a supervisor, coworker, or even a third party (such as a delivery person), whether these occur on or off company premises.
- *Coercion,* such as asking for a date while implying either a promise of benefit or threat of reprisal.
- *Favoritism,* such as granting a promotion as a result of a relationship (even if the relationship was consensual).
- *Indirect harassment,* such as an employee who continually witnesses other employees being sexually harassed.
- *Physical conduct,* such as unseemly gestures or touching.
- *Visual harassment,* such as graffiti or inappropriate photographs and pictures.
- *Verbal harassment,* such as improper teasing, and joking.

If a case of sexual harassment winds up in court, the employer can attempt to defend against this lawsuit by demonstrating that there was an effective sexual harassment program in force.

33.3 LABOR UNIONS

Labor unions consist of groups of employees who bargain with employers for improved wages, benefits, and working conditions. Since the 1930s, labor unions have played a vital role in both the U.S. economy and its politics. Although the number of employees in the private sector who are members of labor unions has declined in recent years, it is important

labor unions
Groups of employees who bargain with employers for improved wages, benefits, and working conditions.

to understand the rights under the law that pertain to employees, unions, and employers. All of these rights are protected by the National Labor Relations Board (NLRB), a federal agency responsible for administering laws relating to labor unions. A select sample of these rights follows.

National Labor Relations Board (NLRB)
A federal agency responsible for administering laws relating to labor unions.

RIGHTS OF EMPLOYEES

Under federal law, employees have the right to form, join, and assist a labor union (or not to do so) and the right to bargain collectively through representatives of their own choosing. They also have the right not to be discriminated against because of their union activities. In addition, employees have the right to vote for union leadership in democratically held elections. If an employee has a dispute with their union, they may retain an attorney and file a lawsuit. Employment contracts (discussed in Chapter 32) that limit these rights are unenforceable.

Under Section 7 of the National Labor Relations Act, concerted action by all employees, regardless of union membership, is protected. This law ensures that employee communication and action regarding wages, benefits, and working conditions must not be restricted by employers.

RIGHTS OF THE UNION

The union has the right to represent all employees of a company who are a part of the bargaining unit. The union then has the right to negotiate a contract with the employer, called a collective bargaining agreement, that covers all terms and conditions of employment. During the negotiation process, the union has the right to ensure that the employer *bargains in good faith,* making an honest effort to reach an agreement. In the event an agreement is not reached, the union has the right to call a strike. At times, employees engage in a wildcat strike (a strike without the union's consent) or a slowdown (where employees report to work but intentionally decrease their productivity).

collective bargaining agreement
A contract between a union and an employer that covers all terms and conditions of employment.

wildcat strike
A strike without the union's consent.

slowdown
An action wherein employees report to work but intentionally decrease their productivity.

RIGHTS OF THE EMPLOYER

The employer has the right to be free from *featherbedding* (hiring unproductive workers) and *secondary boycotts* (being targeted by a union when the union's dispute is really with another employer). During the negotiation process, the employer has the right to ensure that the union *bargains in good faith.* In the event an agreement is not reached, the employer has the right to engage in a lockout—that is, not allow employees to return to work.

lockout
An action by which an employer does not allow employees to return to work in the event a collective bargaining agreement is not reached.

33.4 ADDITIONAL EMPLOYEE RIGHTS

While numerous additional employee rights are granted to employees as a result of federal and state legislation, two notable rights are the right to medical leave and the right to unemployment benefits.

FAMILY AND MEDICAL LEAVE ACT

The Family and Medical Leave Act of 1993 (FMLA) is a federal statute that provides eligible employees with the right to take up to 12 weeks of unpaid leave for personal medical reasons or to care for a child, spouse, or parent. The FMLA applies to all employers with 50 or more employees. To be eligible, an employee must have worked for their current employer for at least 1,250 hours in the previous year.

Family and Medical Leave Act of 1993 (FMLA)
A federal statute that provides eligible employees with the right to take up to 12 weeks of unpaid leave for personal medical reasons or to care for a child, spouse, or parent.

UNEMPLOYMENT BENEFITS

Unemployment insurance provides financial stability, in the form of unemployment compensation, to eligible employees who lose their jobs. In the United States, unemployment insurance is established by state and federal statutes that create a system whereby employers are required to pay federal and state unemployment insurance taxes. Laws pertaining to unemployment compensation vary from state to state; however, generally, in order for employees to be eligible to receive unemployment compensation, they must have lost a job through no fault of their own, and they must meet the minimum state requirements for wages or time worked during an established period. To learn more about the specifics of unemployment compensation, visit https://www.dol.gov/general/topic/unemployment-insurance.

unemployment insurance Unemployment insurance provides financial stability, in the form of unemployment compensation, to eligible employees who lose their jobs.

CHAPTER SUMMARY

33.1 Workers' compensation is a type of insurance that provides that employees may recover damages for work-related injuries and illnesses without having to prove negligence on the part of the employer. It is considered to be the exclusive remedy: An employee who sustains a work-related injury or illness can recover damages only through workers' compensation and may not file a lawsuit against their employer. The Occupational Safety and Health Administration administers the many provisions of the Occupational Safety and Health Act. OSHA requires that companies maintain records of employee work-related accidents and sicknesses; inspects workplaces for safety and health standards; and, in the event violations are found to exist, can impose penalties ranging from fines to closing the facility.

33.2 The major federal statutes designed to protect individuals from discrimination in employment are the Civil Rights Act of 1964, the Age Discrimination in Employment Act of 1967, the Pregnancy Discrimination Act of 1978, the Americans with Disabilities Act of 1990, and the Civil Rights Act of 1991. Forms of conduct that can constitute sexual harassment include unwelcome sexual advances, coercion, favoritism, indirect harassment, physical conduct, visual harassment, and verbal harassment.

33.3 Under federal law, employees have the right to form, join, and assist a labor union (or not to do so); the right to bargain collectively; the right not to be discriminated against because of their union activities; the right to vote for union leadership in democratically held elections; and the right to retain an attorney and file a lawsuit. The union has the right to represent all employees who are a part of the bargaining unit, the right to negotiate a collective bargaining agreement, the right to ensure that the employer bargains in good faith, and the right to call a strike. The employer has the right to be free from featherbedding and secondary boycotts, the right to ensure that the union bargains in good faith, and the right to engage in a lockout.

33.4 Two notable employee rights are the right to medical leave and the right to unemployment insurance. The Family and Medical Leave Act of 1993 (FMLA) is a federal statute that provides eligible employees with the right to take up to 12 weeks of unpaid leave for personal illness or to care for a child, spouse, or parent. Unemployment insurance provides financial stability, in the form of unemployment compensation, to eligible employees who lose their jobs.

CHAPTER THIRTY-THREE ASSESSMENT

MATCHING LEGAL TERMS

Match each of the numbered definitions with the correct term in the following list.

a. Civil Rights Act of 1964
b. EEOC
c. Equal Pay Act of 1963
d. Family Medical Leave Act of 1993
e. OSHA

1. A federal agency that promotes safety and health in the workplace. **1.** _____
2. A federal statute that provides eligible employees with the right to take up to 12 weeks of unpaid leave. **2.** _____
3. A federal statute designed to protect individuals from illegal discrimination. **3.** _____
4. A statute that prohibits any employer from engaging in wage discrimination based on sex. **4.** _____
5. A federal agency responsible for administering laws prohibiting discrimination in employment. **5.** _____

TRUE/FALSE QUIZ

Indicate whether each of the following statements is true or false.

6. An employee may sue a third party for a work-related injury or illness, even if the injury or illness occurred while the employee was on the job. **6.** _____
7. Federal law requires that employers establish employee assistance programs. **7.** _____
8. In recent years, the number of workers' compensation claims that have been filed has increased dramatically, causing a large increase in costs associated with the program. **8.** _____
9. Stress-related illnesses are compensable under workers' compensation if the stress was not the result of the employee's ordinary duties on the job. **9.** _____
10. OSHA can impose a fine for a health or safety violation, but it does not have the authority to close a business. **10.** _____
11. Discrimination in employment is covered in Title III of the Civil Rights Act of 1964. **11.** _____
12. The protected class created pursuant to the Age Discrimination in Employment Act is persons over the age of 50. **12.** _____
13. Persons who are living with AIDS are not protected by the provisions of the Americans with Disabilities Act. **13.** _____

14. Employees who are victims of illegal discrimination may recover for lost earnings but not for emotional distress. 14. _____

15. Employees who are victims of illegal discrimination may recover punitive damages. 15. _____

16. Improper teasing, joking, and so forth can constitute sexual harassment. 16. _____

17. A company may terminate an employee because the employee has joined a labor union. 17. _____

18. Under federal law, during contract negotiations, employers are required to bargain in good faith, while unions are not. 18. _____

19. An employer has the right to be free from featherbedding. 19. _____

20. In the event a collective bargaining agreement between a union and an employer is not reached, the employer has the right to engage in a lockout. 20. _____

MULTIPLE CHOICE QUIZ

Indicate the correct answer from the choices following each question.

21. An employee is injured and seeks a claim against their employer. The employee may (a) not seek workers' compensation (b) seek workers' compensation regardless of the injury (c) seek workers' compensation if the injury is work related (d) seek workers' compensation if the injury is work related and caused by employer negligence. 21. _____

22. Which of the following classes are protected under Title VII of the Civil Rights Act? (a) Race, age, national origin, gender, religion (b) Race, gender, national origin, disability (c) Race, color, age, national origin, religion (d) Race, color, national origin, religion, gender 22. _____

23. An employer conducting interviews asks female candidates if they intend to have children but does not ask the same question of the male candidates. Which is the most applicable type of Title VII claim? (a) Direct evidence (b) Express policy (c) Disparate treatment (d) Disparate impact 23. _____

24. A 35-year-old employee is terminated, and the employer hires a new 25-year-old employee. In this case, the 35-year-old employee (a) has a claim of age discrimination against the employer (b) does not have a claim of age discrimination because the age difference is only 10 years (c) does not have a claim of age discrimination because they are too young (d) none of the above. 24. _____

25. The Pregnancy Discrimination Act (a) requires that employers hire pregnant women who apply (b) prohibits firing any woman who is pregnant (c) requires that employers have parity in benefits for pregnant women (d) none of the above. 25. _____

26. Which of the following is a disability under the Americans with Disabilities Act? (a) Alcoholism (b) Depression (c) Blindness (d) All of the above **26.** _____

27. A group of employees gathers at the workplace to compare their salaries and working conditions. This meeting (a) is protected as concerted action under the National Labor Relations Act (b) is not protected as concerted action since the meeting is at the workplace (c) is not protected as concerted action unless the employees are union members (d) is not protected as concerted action since the employees are disclosing salaries. **27.** _____

DISCUSSION QUESTIONS

Answer the following questions and discuss them in class.

28. Describe the major provisions of workers' compensation laws.

29. Explain how OSHA ensures that companies maintain safe and healthful work environments.

30. Identify parts of the employment process in which discriminatory practices are illegal.

31. How does the Americans with Disabilities Act define *disability*? Provide some examples.

32. Define *sexual harassment* and identify some forms of conduct that can constitute it.

33. List the rights of employees who are members of labor unions.

THINKING CRITICALLY ABOUT THE LAW

Answer the following questions, which require you to think critically about the legal principles that you learned in this chapter.

34. Workers' Compensation Is it fair that workers do not have the right to sue their employers for negligence?

35. OSHA Should OSHA require that all safety violations be corrected, even if the cost of correcting a violation is extremely high?

36. ADA Should persons with relatively minor disabilities, such as being required to wear corrective lenses, be considered disabled under the ADA?

37. Sexual Harassment Should it be illegal for a supervisor to ask their subordinate for a date?

38. Labor Unions How can the NLRB determine whether an employer is bargaining in good faith?

39. A Question of Ethics If a union and a company have agreed to a collective bargaining agreement, is it ethical for employees who disagree with its terms to engage in a slowdown?

40. Employment Discrimination Should employees be protected from discrimination based on sexual orientation or gender identity? If so, how is it best addressed: by state or local laws, federal law, or court decision?

CASE QUESTIONS

Study each of the following cases. Answer the questions that follow with Yes or No.

41. The Americans with Disabilities Act Melski was a truck driver with a large shipping company. Pursuant to company policy, all drivers were required to undergo random drug testing. After being tested, Melski was informed that the results were positive. Melksi admitted to being addicted to cocaine, and her employment was terminated. Melski sued, arguing that she was disabled.

a. Is Melski protected under the Americans with Disabilities Act? **a.** _____

b. Must the shipping company make reasonable accommodation for Melski? **b.** _____

c. Is the shipping company required to provide Melski with the services of an employee assistance program? **c.** _____

42. Labor Unions Widra was a cashier at a large clothing store in her town. Believing her wages were below those offered by the store's competitors, she began to speak with her co-employees about the possibility of becoming affiliated with a national union. The manager of the clothing store heard about these conversations and warned her not to have these discussions. When Widra refused, the manager fired her.

a. Does Widra have the right to discuss the possibility of becoming affiliated with a union despite her manager's objections? **a.** _____

b. Does the manager have the right to warn Widra not to have these discussions? **b.** _____

c. Does Widra have the right to hire an attorney to represent her? **c.** _____

d. Would it matter if the wages at the clothing store were higher than those of competitors? **d.** _____

43. Workers' Compensation Garafolo was employed as a salesclerk at a liquor store. An armed robber entered the store one day and demanded the cash in the register. When Garafolo hesitated, the robber struck him with a pistol, causing a deep laceration. The robber left without further incident, and Garafolo was treated in the emergency room of a nearby hospital, receiving several stitches. At the insistence of his physician, Garafolo then visited a therapist, who treated him for stress.

a. Can Garafolo collect workers' compensation for the laceration he suffered during the robbery? **a.** _____

b. Can Garafolo collect workers' compensation for the stress he experienced as a result of the robbery? **b.** _____

c. If Garafolo collects any form of workers' compensation, and the robber is later apprehended, could Garafolo sue the robber for both the laceration and the stress? **c.** _____

CASE ANALYSIS

Study each of the following cases carefully. Briefly state the principle of law and your decision.

44. Workers' Compensation Ryder, a police officer in Philadelphia, was alone in his patrol car when he received a radio call of a "man with a gun." Ryder was the first officer to arrive and was confronted by a suspect brandishing an AR-15 semiautomatic rifle pointed at him. Ryder was able to subdue him and place him into the back of his police cruiser. Backup units arrived approximately 12 minutes after the initial call. The weapon used by the suspect was later found fully loaded with the safety off. Subsequently, Ryder began to experience severe anxiety and stress from answering routine police calls, feeling that either he would be killed or have to kill somebody. A physician diagnosed Ryder as having post-traumatic stress disorder. Would Ryder be entitled to benefits under workers' compensation laws? [*Ryder v. City of Philadelphia,* 565 Pa. 265, 772 A.2d.962 (2000)]

Principle of Law:

____

____

Decision:

____

____

45. Sexual Harassment Gentry, an employee of Export Packaging Company, reported directly to Broughton. Gentry alleged among other things that, during a period of approximately four months, Broughton subjected her to "40 hugs, 15 shoulder rubs, [and] a kiss on her cheek." She also alleged that she was referred to as a "sex-retary." Gentry sued her employer for sexual harassment, and the jury awarded her both compensatory and punitive damages. The company appealed. Will the company be successful in setting aside the award for damages? [*Gentry v. Export Packaging Company,* 238 F.3d 842 (Texas)]

Principle of Law:

____

____

Decision:

____

____

46. Labor Unions Roll and Hold Warehouse, the employer, began circulating a new company policy relating to employee attendance. The union representing the company's employees objected to the policy, claiming that it had never been negotiated. The company argued, among other things, that the policy was not material (important) and, therefore, that it did not need to be negotiated. The union charged the company with violating the law by failing to negotiate all terms and conditions of employment and by failing to bargain in good faith. Is the union correct in its position that the attendance policy should have been negotiated and that the company failed to bargain in good faith? [*NLRB et al. v. Roll and Hold Warehouse and Distribution Corporation,* 162 F.3d 513 (California)]

Principle of Law:

Decision:

LEGAL RESEARCH

Complete the following activities. Share your findings with the class.

47. Working in Teams In teams of three or four, interview several local businesses. Ask them how they maintain a safe and healthful workplace.

48. Using Technology Using the Internet and search engines, navigate to the web pages of your state to determine the criteria under which a worker may receive unemployment benefits.

chapter 34
Product Liability

LEARNING OUTCOMES

After studying this chapter and completing the assessment, you will be able to

34.1 Describe product liability and the tort upon which it is based.

34.2 Discuss several bases of claims often used against manufacturers and sellers in product liability lawsuits.

34.3 Identify the kinds of businesses that can be charged with product liability.

34.4 Explain the legal reasoning behind the concept of strict liability.

34.5 Describe three ways in which the federal and state governments reduce unreasonable risk of injury and death associated with consumer products.

34.6 Summarize the testing procedure required by the Food and Drug Administration in order to gain approval to sell a drug.

34.7 Identify examples of consumer products regulated by the Consumer Product Safety Commission.

34.8 Describe how federal and state statutes regulate tobacco products and explain some provisions of the Master Settlement Agreement.

34.9 Describe how the National Highway Traffic Safety Administration is responsible for the safety of automobiles sold in the United States.

PRODUCT LIABILITY

Kim Steele/Photodisc/Getty Images

"My name is on every car. You have my personal commitment that Toyota will work vigorously and unceasingly to restore the trust of our customers."

Akio Toyoda, president of Toyota Motor Company

LEGAL terms

- product liability
- product flaw
- failure to warn
- design defect
- strict liability
- Food and Drug Administration (FDA)
- Consumer Product Safety Commission (CPSC)
- Master Settlement Agreement
- National Highway Traffic Safety Administration (NHTSA)

34.1 PRODUCT LIABILITY AND TORT LAW

In Chapter 18, the issue of breach of warranty was discussed. A breach of warranty lawsuit is based upon contract law; that is, the buyer of a product sues the seller for breaching either an express or implied promise that in part formed the basis of a contract.

Many purchasers or users of products, or even third parties, who sustain injury or property loss as a direct result of using the product, however, file a civil lawsuit based not on contract law, but on tort law. Product defects that cause injury and property loss are often the result of negligence, a tort, which was discussed in detail in Chapter 4. The liability of a manufacturer or seller for injury to purchasers, users, and third parties is known as **product liability**.

product liability
The liability of a manufacturer or seller for injury to purchasers, users, and third parties.

In general, a plaintiff must prove four elements to be successful in proving the defendant's negligence in a product liability lawsuit. These are

1. *Duty.* The plaintiff must show that the defendant owed them a duty to either perform an action or not perform an action. In a product liability lawsuit, retailers, manufacturers, and others owe all persons who are foreseeable purchasers or users of the product such a duty. They also owe a duty to all third persons who could foreseeably be injured by the product.
2. *Breach.* The plaintiff must show that the defendant either acted improperly or failed to act. In a product liability lawsuit, breach is often difficult to prove because the plaintiff usually needs the opinions of expert witnesses who can evaluate whether the defendant negligently manufactured or sold the product.
3. *Proximate cause.* The plaintiff must show that the defendant's act or failure to act directly caused the injury or loss.
4. *Damages.* The plaintiff must prove, as in all civil lawsuits, that they were injured or sustained some other loss as a result of the defendant's act or failure to act.

34.2 BASES FOR PRODUCT LIABILITY INJURY CLAIMS

Certain product characteristics often become the bases of claims against manufacturers and sellers.

product flaw
An abnormality or a condition that was not intended and that makes a product more dangerous than it would have been had it been as intended.

PRODUCT FLAW

A **product flaw** is an abnormality or a condition that was not intended and that makes a product more dangerous than it would have been had it been as intended.

EXAMPLE 34.1

Ritchie purchased a new toaster produced by a reputable household appliance manufacturer. Unfortunately, the particular toaster that Ritchie purchased had a defect in the wiring system. When Ritchie plugged the toaster into the electrical socket, a fire erupted, causing damage to his home amounting to several thousand dollars. Ritchie's product liability lawsuit against the manufacturer based on product flaw was successful. Even though the manufacturer had never met Ritchie, the firm could reasonably foresee that a purchaser would plug in the toaster. The manufacturer's negligence in producing this particular toaster proximately caused the damage to Ritchie's property.

FAILURE TO WARN

Manufacturers and sellers have a duty to advise purchasers and users of dangers inherent in a product. A failure to warn is a dereliction of this duty.

failure to warn
The dereliction of a duty to advise purchasers and users of dangers inherent in a product.

EXAMPLE 34.2

▶ Poggi purchased a container of hot coffee from a fast-food retailer. When she entered her automobile with the coffee, the contents of the cup spilled onto her lap, causing third-degree burns. Poggi's product liability lawsuit based on failure to warn was successful. The retailer had a duty to warn purchasers and users that the contents were extremely hot and that extraordinary care in handling the container was required.

DESIGN DEFECT

Manufacturers have a duty to design products in a manner that is not negligent. A design defect is a fault in a product that creates a hazardous condition that causes injury.

A design defect is a hazardous condition that exists throughout an entire product line, as opposed to a product flaw, discussed previously, which is an abnormality or condition in a single unit of the product.

design defect
A fault in a product that creates a hazardous condition that causes injury.

EXAMPLE 34.3

▶ An automobile manufacturer produced cars in the United States that had the feel of a "European model." The accelerator pedal was not elongated but had the same shape as the brake pedal. In addition, both the accelerator pedal and the brake pedal were located slightly to the left of where these would be positioned on other cars. Several drivers were involved in accidents, claiming unintended acceleration. In reality, these drivers had been inadvertently applying pressure to the accelerator rather than to the brake. The drivers' suits for product liability based on design defect were successful. Shaping the accelerator pedal in the manner that had been done and positioning the accelerator and brake pedals to the left were considered design defects.

34.3 WHO CAN BE HELD LIABLE FOR PRODUCT-RELATED INJURIES?

In a product liability case, the most obvious target of an injured party is the manufacturer of the defective product. However, others in the distribution channel also may be found liable, including retailers, wholesalers, manufacturers of component parts, assemblers of products, endorsers of products, licensors of trademarks, and licensors of patents.

Retailers are particularly vulnerable when the product manufacturer is insolvent or is a corporation that has been dissolved or is unreachable–such as a manufacturer in a foreign country. Consequently, retailers need to be particularly careful to choose product manufacturers that act responsibly and are also financially secure.

34.4 STRICT LIABILITY

As discussed earlier, under traditional tort law, the injured party must prove that the manufacturer was negligent in producing a product. It is often difficult for injured parties to prove negligence for a number of reasons, and the defenses of manufacturers are often very effective. The financial burden to society and the hardships suffered by injured parties that result are of grave concern to many legal scholars and jurists.

Courts in some states have held that it should not be necessary for an injured person to prove negligence on the part of the manufacturer. They have expressed the notion that the producer is in a better position than the user of a product to prevent injuries because the company has the opportunity and expertise to design safe products. Also, they believe that the manufacturer is in a position to pay for the damages suffered by a user of a product, regardless of whether the firm was in fact negligent, because the manufacturer can buy insurance that pays the injured party. The company can then pass on the cost of insurance to all users of the product. This legal reasoning has given rise to the doctrine of strict liability—that is, liability without the necessity of proving fault.

strict liability The doctrine under which persons may be liable for injuries to others whether or not they have been negligent or committed an intentional tort. This establishes liability without the necessity of proving fault.

Today, the concept of strict liability is generally accepted, although its application from state to state varies greatly. In some states, strict liability applies only to products that are *inherently dangerous,* such as firearms, fireworks, knives, and so forth. In other states, the doctrine applies only when the manufacturer is in violation of a statute.

In a product liability case, the most obvious target of an injured party is the manufacturer of the defective product. Studiohio/McGraw Hill

Despite the advent of strict liability, there is considerable activity in various state legislatures with a view toward *tort reform* and other efforts to curb abuses of the system. One consequence of strict liability is that companies are sometimes hesitant to introduce new or innovative products because of the fear of liability lawsuits.

34.5 PRODUCT SAFETY

The previous sections of this chapter related to lawsuits that are filed as a result of a product causing injury or loss to a purchaser, user, or third party. The remaining sections of this chapter address some of the federal statutes and administrative rules that are in effect to promote safety for consumers and users of products.

The federal and state governments enact these numerous statutes and rules to reduce unreasonable risk of injury and death associated with consumer products. This is achieved by governments' providing safety information to the public, developing voluntary and mandatory standards, and pursuing recalls of dangerous products. The following sections provide a small sample of requirements that manufacturers and retailers face as they sell various types of products in the United States.

34.6 DRUGS

The federal agency responsible for the safety of food and drugs sold in the United States is the Food and Drug Administration (FDA). The FDA requires that all drugs sold be thoroughly tested to ensure that they are both safe and effective. After experimentation in the laboratory and animal studies, pharmaceutical companies subject drugs to four phases of testing:

Food and Drug Administration (FDA)
The federal agency responsible for the safety of food and drugs sold in the United States.

- In *Phase I,* a small number of people are tested to determine safety and dosage and to identify side effects that result from taking the drug.
- In *Phase II,* the effectiveness of the drug is measured by comparing subjects who receive the drug to those who receive a *placebo* (usually a water pill that will have no impact).
- In *Phase III,* the safety and effectiveness of the drug are evaluated in trials involving a great number of people.
- In *Phase IV,* continued testing occurs subsequent to FDA approval of the drug.

The process of FDA approval has come under some criticism in recent years, as concerns over the costs and length of time for obtaining approval of prescription drugs have emerged. For a drug to be approved, it is estimated that it costs a pharmaceutical company approximately $700 million and takes about 12 years for the process to unfold. Interestingly, only one of 5,000 chemicals ultimately is approved for sale as a drug, and only one-third of approved drugs become profitable. Furthermore, one-fifth of all drugs that are approved have alleged safety problems.

Because of the costs and time involved in the manufacture of prescription drugs, they have become very expensive to consumers. Many individuals have turned to the Internet, seeking drugs from Canada and other countries. Several unscrupulous firms sell drugs online, offering weaker dosages, mislabeled drugs, and illegal drugs, often from unlicensed pharmacies or firms misrepresenting their facilities as being in Canada. It is expected that federal and state statutes will continue to address this situation.

Furthermore, a pharmaceutical company earns most of its profits from a drug only during the time that the patent for the drug is effective, either 17 or 20 years, depending on the coverage of the patent (see Chapter 28). After the patent expires, other companies may produce alternative versions of the drug, referred to as *generics.* To recoup its costs, therefore, it is necessary that the pharmaceutical company charge high prices that will allow it to continue its research and development (R&D) on this and other drugs.

Advertising of drugs is legal, so long as detailed information about the drug being advertised is disclosed. The Federal Trade Commission (FTC) is responsible for ensuring that advertising is truthful (see Chapter 29). Pharmaceutical companies may advertise a drug only for the ailment for which it was approved for use. Doctors, however, may prescribe a drug for other purposes as they deem appropriate (referred to as *off-label* uses).

Toys are regulated by the CPSC.
Cade Martin/CDC

34.7 CONSUMER PRODUCTS

Consumer Product Safety Commission (CPSC) The federal agency responsible for the safety of consumer products sold in the United States.

The federal agency responsible for the safety of consumer products sold in the United States is the Consumer Product Safety Commission (CPSC). Examples of products that are regulated by the CPSC include clothing, hazardous household cleaners and substances, electronic devices, appliances, furnishings, building materials, toys, and other juvenile products.

Some consumer products with restrictions on them include the following:

- Wool products, fur products, and textile fiber products–all of which must be properly labeled and identified.
- Flammable products–which must incorporate flame-retardant materials.
- Hazardous substances–those that are toxic, corrosive, irritant, or flammable, which must be properly labeled with appropriate warnings.
- Children's toys–which may not contain electrical, thermal, or mechanical hazards.
- Paint–which generally may not contain lead.
- Radiation-emitting products–such as televisions, computer screens, cellular telephones, and microwave ovens, which must contain appropriate safeguards.

The CPSC regularly conducts tests of these products and other consumer products sold in the United States. If the agency determines that a product is dangerous, it can order the manufacturer to recall it. For additional information, visit the agency's website at www.cpsc.gov.

34.8 TOBACCO

Numerous federal and state statutes strictly regulate cigarettes and other tobacco products. Federal law disallows advertising of these products on television and radio, and FTC regulations require disclosure of tar and nicotine levels on cigarette packages. In addition, all cigarette packages must contain a warning from the surgeon general regarding the dangers of smoking.

In 1997, the major cigarette manufacturers in the United States entered into a contract, referred to as the Master Settlement Agreement, in which the companies agreed not to engage in certain advertising strategies. The companies agreed not to advertise using cartoon characters (such as Joe Camel); not to place advertising on billboards or stadium signs; not to pay for product inclusion in films and television shows; not to provide free caps, T-shirts, and so forth; not to distribute free samples of cigarettes; and not to target youth markets by sponsoring concerts, athletic events, and so on. The companies also support the American Legacy Foundation, which provides education regarding the dangers of addiction to tobacco products.

Master Settlement Agreement
A contract in which the major cigarette manufacturers in the United States agreed not to engage in certain advertising strategies.

The *Tobacco Control Act* gives the FDA authority to regulate tobacco products in order to discourage children and young adults from smoking. The FDA has introduced new labeling restrictions/requirements for packaging and has banned the production, distribution, and sale of flavored cigarettes.

EXAMPLE 34.4

▶ Djarum, an Indonesian clove cigarette manufacturer, responded to the FDA ban on flavored cigarettes by introducing a new line of clove cigars in the United States. Like cigarettes, these small cigars are filtered and contain paper in the wrapping. Because the FDA's ban on flavored cigarettes applies to any product that matches a cigarette's profile, it is illegal to sell or distribute Djarum clove "cigars" in the United States.

34.9 AUTOMOBILES

The federal agency responsible for the safety of automobiles sold in the United States is the National Highway Traffic Safety Administration (NHTSA). The NHTSA

- Requires that automobiles contain appropriate safety features, such as air bags and seat belts.
- Routinely proposes both stricter crash test requirements for automakers and, as technology advances, new regulations to provide vehicle occupants with maximum safety benefits.
- Investigates potential safety defects in automobiles and has the authority to require automakers to issue recalls to repair dangerous defects and, in extreme cases, cease production of automobiles.

National Highway Traffic Safety Administration (NHTSA)
The federal agency responsible for the safety of automobiles sold in the United States.

EXAMPLE 34.5

The NHTSA received hundreds of reports from consumers describing the unintended, sudden acceleration of their Toyota vehicles, which were equipped with computer-controlled accelerators. An initial investigation determined that the automobiles' floor mats had a tendency to push on the gas pedals and were at least partially responsible for the acceleration problems. However, despite a recall by Toyota to replace the floor mats, consumers continued to report new incidents of sudden acceleration—some resulting in fatal crashes. Finally, Toyota executives revealed that the company had traced the problem to a faulty plastic part in the accelerator pedal. Because Toyota did not have enough replacement parts in stock to issue a comprehensive recall, the NHTSA ordered Toyota to cease production of automobiles and imposed a fine of $16.4 million, the maximum allowable.

While the NHTSA administers to the safety of automobiles, the responsibility of controlling automobile emissions rests with the Environmental Protection Agency (see Chapter 37).

The NHTSA is responsible for the safety of automobiles sold in the United States.
Monty Rakusen/Cultura/Getty Images

CHAPTER SUMMARY

34.1 Product defects that cause injury and property loss are often the result of negligence, a tort. The liability of a manufacturer or seller for injury to purchasers, users, and third parties is known as product liability. The four elements that generally prove the defendant's negligence in a product liability lawsuit are duty, breach, proximate cause, and damages.

34.2 A product flaw is an abnormality or a condition that was not intended and that makes a product more dangerous than it would have been had it been as intended. A failure to warn is a dereliction of a duty to advise purchasers and users of dangers inherent in a product. A design defect is a fault in a product that creates a hazardous condition that causes injury.

34.3 Manufacturers, retailers, wholesalers, manufacturers of component parts, assemblers of products, endorsers of products, licensors of trademarks, and licensors of patents are the kinds of businesses that can be charged with product liability.

34.4 The doctrine of strict liability arose because courts believe that the manufacturer is in a better position than the user of a product to prevent injuries and that the manufacturer is in a position to pay for the damages suffered by a user of a product, regardless of whether the firm was in fact negligent, because the manufacturer can buy insurance that pays the injured party.

34.5 The federal and state governments enact numerous statutes and rules to reduce unreasonable risk of injury and death associated with consumer products. This is achieved by governments' providing safety information to the public, developing voluntary and mandatory standards, and pursuing recalls of dangerous products.

34.6 The FDA requires that, after experimentation in the laboratory and animal studies, pharmaceutical companies subject drugs to four phases of testing: (a) Phase I, during which a small number of people are tested to determine safety and dosage and to identify side effects that result from taking the drug; (b) Phase II, during which the effectiveness of the drug is measured by comparing subjects who receive the drug to those who receive a placebo; (c) Phase III, during which the safety and effectiveness of the drug are evaluated in trials involving a great number of people; and (d) Phase IV, continued testing that occurs subsequent to FDA approval of the drug.

34.7 Examples of consumer products regulated by the CPSC include wool products, fur products, and textile fiber products; flammable products; hazardous substances; children's toys; paint; and radiation-emitting products.

34.8 Numerous federal and state statutes strictly regulate cigarettes and other tobacco products. Federal law disallows advertising of these products on television and radio, and FTC regulations require disclosure of tar and nicotine levels on cigarette packages. In addition, all cigarette packages must contain a warning from the surgeon general regarding the dangers of smoking. In the Master Settlement Agreement, the major cigarette manufacturers in the United States agreed not to advertise using cartoon characters; not to place advertising on billboards or stadium signs; not to pay for product inclusion in films and television shows; not to provide free caps, T-shirts, and so forth; not to distribute free samples of cigarettes; not to target youth markets by sponsoring concerts, athletic events, and so on; and to support a foundation that provides education regarding the dangers of addiction to tobacco products.

34.9 The NHTSA requires that automobiles contain appropriate safety features, such as air bags, seat belts, and so forth; routinely proposes stricter crash test requirements for automakers and, as technology advances, new safety regulations; and investigates potential safety defects in automobiles and has the authority to require automakers to issue recalls to repair dangerous defects and, in extreme cases, cease production of automobiles.

CHAPTER THIRTY-FOUR ASSESSMENT

MATCHING LEGAL TERMS

Match each of the numbered definitions with the correct term in the following list.

a. product flaw
b. design defect
c. strict liability
d. Master Settlement Agreement
e. product liability
f. failure to warn

1. A fault in a product that creates a hazardous condition that causes injury. **1.** _____

2. Liability without the necessity of proving fault. **2.** _____

3. The liability of a manufacturer or seller for injury to purchasers, users, and third parties. **3.** _____

4. An abnormality or a condition that was not intended and that makes a product more dangerous than it would have been had it been as intended. **4.** _____

5. The dereliction of a duty to advise purchasers and users of dangers inherent in a product. **5.** _____

6. A contract in which the major cigarette manufacturers in the United States agreed not to engage in certain advertising strategies. **6.** _____

TRUE/FALSE QUIZ

Indicate whether each of the following statements is true or false.

7. Both breach of warranty and product liability lawsuits are based on tort law rather than contract law. **7.** _____

8. The four elements of a product liability lawsuit are duty, breach, proximate cause, and damages. **8.** _____

9. A design defect is a hazardous condition that exists throughout an entire product line. **9.** _____

10. An alteration that a buyer makes in a product is known as a product flaw. **10.**

11. Manufacturers and retailers have a duty to warn users of dangerous or hazardous characteristics of products. **10.** _____

12. Only manufacturers can be held liable in product liability lawsuits. **12.** _____

13. The manufacturer is in a better position than the user of a product to prevent injuries because the company has the opportunity to design safe products. **13.** _____

14. One consequence of strict liability is that companies are sometimes hesitant to introduce new or innovative products because of the fear of liability lawsuits. **14.** _____

15. In Phase II of the drug-testing process, the effectiveness of the drug is measured by comparing subjects who receive the drug to those who receive a placebo. **15.** _____

16. It is perfectly safe to purchase prescription drugs over the Internet. **11.** _____

17. Advertising of drugs is legal so long as detailed information about the drug being advertised is disclosed. **17.** _____

18. The Consumer Product Safety Commission regularly conducts tests of consumer products sold in the United States. **18.** _____

19. Under the terms of the Master Settlement Agreement, cigarette packages must contain a warning from the surgeon general regarding the dangers of smoking. **19.** _____

20. The National Highway Traffic Safety Administration has the responsibility of controlling automobile emissions. **20.** _____

MULTIPLE CHOICE QUIZ

Indicate the correct answer from the choices following each question.

21. Which of the following parties would *not* owe a duty to a plaintiff in a product liability case? (a) Federal regulator of the product (b) Retail seller of the product (c) Assembling manufacturer of the product (d) Wholesale seller of the product **21.** _____

22. A hair dryer is sold with faulty heat controls due to an error from the component manufacturer of the controls. In this case, the hair dryer has a (a) product flaw (b) flaw in failure to warn (c) design flaw (d) no flaw. **22.** _____

23. A hair dryer has heat controls that allow the air to be sufficiently hot to burn skin if targeted in one area too long. In this case, the hair dryer has a (a) product flaw (b) flaw in failure to warn (c) design flaw (d) no flaw. **23.** _____

24. A hair dryer's heated air is directed through a mechanism that allows it to regularly overheat. In this case, the hair dryer has a (a) product flaw (b) flaw in failure to warn (c) design flaw (d) no flaw. **24.** _____

25. ABC, Inc. has developed a new antibiotic for sale. The safety of this product will be regulated by (a) the Consumer Product Safety Commission (b) the Product Liability Prevention Agency (c) the Food and Drug Administration (d) none of the above. **25.** _____

DISCUSSION QUESTIONS

Answer the following questions and discuss them in class.

26. Describe product liability and the tort upon which it is based.

27. Identify the kinds of business that can be charged with product liability.

28. Explain the legal reasoning behind the concept of strict liability and weigh its consequences for businesspeople and consumers.

29. Summarize the testing procedure required by the Food and Drug Administration in order to gain approval to sell a drug.

30. Identify examples of consumer products regulated by the Consumer Product Safety Commission.

31. Explain some provisions of the Master Settlement Agreement.

THINKING CRITICALLY ABOUT THE LAW

Answer the following questions, which require you to think critically about the legal principles that you learned in this chapter.

32. Failure to Warn Is it obvious to the reasonable consumer that disposable containers containing coffee and other beverages are hot? Should retailers be required to warn customers to exercise care in handling these containers?

33. Who Can Be Held Liable Where should the responsibility lie for product safety: manufacturers, retailers, users, or government regulators?

34. Strict Liability Why would a company that is subject to strict liability be hesitant to introduce new or innovative products?

35. Drugs Should the federal and state governments allow consumers to purchase drugs from Canada and other countries on the Internet?

36. Tobacco Because tobacco is known to cause health problems, should it be illegal to use?

37. A Question of Ethics Is it ethical for a pharmaceutical company to charge high prices for prescription drugs when these drugs are needed by persons who cannot afford them and whose lives depend upon them?

CASE QUESTIONS

Study each of the following cases. Answer the questions that follow with Yes or No.

38. Failure to Warn Kriz, an elderly man who was quite overweight, purchased a power lawnmower from a nationally known retailer. To start the lawnmower, the user needed to bend down to draw the starter cord. When Kriz bent over, he suffered a heart attack. Kriz sued the retailer, arguing that the lawnmower should have contained a warning advising older, overweight users not to bend over.

a. Is this lawsuit an example of a product liability based upon product flaw? **a.** _____

b. Is this lawsuit an example of a product liability based upon design defect? **b.** _____

c. Will Kriz be required to prove that the lawnmower was the proximate cause of his ailment? **c.** _____

39. Who Can Be Held Liable Eddington operated a toy store and carried merchandise from both domestic as well as foreign manufacturers. As the holiday season approached, he found that he could reduce his costs by importing a stuffed toy from a country with relatively little safety regulation. One of the toys was responsible for an injury to a child, and the parents brought a product liability suit against Eddington. He claimed that he was unaware of the defects of the toy because he did not manufacture it but only sold it.

a. Do the parents of the injured child have the right to sue Eddington instead of the manufacturer? **a.** _____

b. Can a retailer be held liable for defective products? **b.** _____

c. Is there anyone else who could be named in the suit? **c.** _____

40. Drugs/Failure to Warn Parker, a person with no medical training, gave a prescription drug to Zimmerman, a friend, to alleviate back pain Zimmerman had been experiencing. After taking the drug, Zimmerman drove his automobile, became disoriented, and struck a telephone pole with his vehicle. Zimmerman sued, claiming he had never been warned about the drug's side effects.

a. Can Zimmerman recover the costs associated with the accident from the manufacturer of the drug? **a.** _____

b. Can Zimmerman recover the costs associated with the accident from Parker? **b.** _____

c. Can Zimmerman recover the costs associated with the accident from the Food and Drug Administration? **c.** _____

d. Was Zimmerman a foreseeable user of the drug? **d.** _____

CASE ANALYSIS

Study each of the following cases carefully. Briefly state the principle of law and your decision.

41. Drugs/Failure to Warn Merck, a major pharmaceutical company, produced a popular painkiller called Vioxx. Despite the drug being approved by the FDA, several studies linked usage of it to cardiovascular risks relating to heart attacks and strokes. Internal emails indicated that, for approximately four years, the company was aware that academics and others had concerns over the drug's safety. Finally, Merck voluntarily discontinued distribution of Vioxx. Several lawsuits were then brought by the families of those who had suffered heart attacks after taking the drug. Will the lawsuits against Merck be successful?

Principle of Law:

____

____

Decision:

____

____

42. Tobacco From the early 1950s until his death from smoking-related lung cancer in 1997, Williams smoked cigarettes, primarily the Marlboro brand, eventually developing a habit of three packs a day. At that point, he spent half his waking hours smoking and was highly addicted to tobacco, both physiologically and psychologically. Although, at the urging of his wife and children, he made several attempts to stop smoking, each time he failed, in part because of his addiction. When his family told him that cigarettes were dangerous to his health, he replied that the cigarette companies would not sell them if they were as dangerous as his family claimed. When one of his sons tried to get him to read articles about the dangers of smoking, he responded by finding published assertions that cigarette smoking was not dangerous. However, when Williams learned that he had inoperable lung cancer, he felt betrayed, stating, "Those darn cigarette people finally did it. They were lying all the time." He died about six months after his diagnosis. Williams's widow sued, demanding both compensatory and punitive damages, claiming that the manufacturer of the cigarettes was responsible for her husband's death. Is Williams's widow likely to be successful in her lawsuit? [*Philip Morris USA, Inc. v. Williams,* 540 U.S. 801, 124 S. Ct. 56, 157 L. Ed. 2d 12 (Oregon)]

Principle of Law:

____

____

Decision:

____

____

43. Automobiles/Design Defect Grimshaw, a 13-year-old girl, was a passenger in a Ford Pinto driven by a neighbor. The Pinto stalled and, while motionless, was hit from behind by another car. Moments later, the Pinto's fuel tank exploded, with the result that the driver was killed and Grimshaw was burned over 90 percent of her body. Grimshaw's family sued Ford Motor Company, claiming that Ford was negligent in designing the Pinto so that the fuel tank was in a dangerous position, with "conscious disregard of public safety." The jury awarded the family of the driver \$666,000 and Grimshaw \$2,841,000 as compensation for her injuries. In addition, the jury awarded Grimshaw another $125,000,000 as punitive damages (i.e., to punish Ford). Ford appealed the decision. Will the decision of the jury be upheld? [*Grimshaw et al. v. Ford Motor Company,* 119 Cal. App. 3d 757, 1981 Cal. App. LEXIS 1859, 174 Cal. Rptr. 348 (California)]

Principle of Law:

Decision:

LEGAL RESEARCH

Complete the following activities. Share your findings with the class.

44. Working in Teams In teams of three or four, interview several local businesses to learn what types of complaints they have received regarding defective products. Are these complaints examples of product flaw, failure to warn, or design defect?

45. Using Technology Using the Internet and search engines, navigate to the websites of several cigarette manufacturers. What warnings regarding tobacco use do these companies provide?

chapter 35 Professionals' Liability

LEARNING OUTCOMES

After studying this chapter and completing the assessment, you will be able to

35.1 Explain the characteristics of a professional.

35.2 Distinguish between the malpractice of professionals and other forms of negligence by nonprofessionals.

35.3 Explain how the elements of a malpractice lawsuit are applied to professionals.

35.4 Provide examples of professional malpractice that might be caused by health care providers, accountants, financial planners, architects and engineers, attorneys, insurance agents and brokers, and others.

35.5 Explain how professionals protect themselves against the losses that might result from being found liable for malpractice or negligence.

LEGAL terms

- professional
- malpractice
- Good Samaritan laws
- loss of consortium
- churning
- statute of limitations
- whole life insurance
- term insurance

PROFESSIONALS' LIABILITY

"What I always say is, 'Do every job you're in like you're going to do it for the rest of your life, and demonstrate that ownership of it'."

Mary Barra, CEO
General Motors

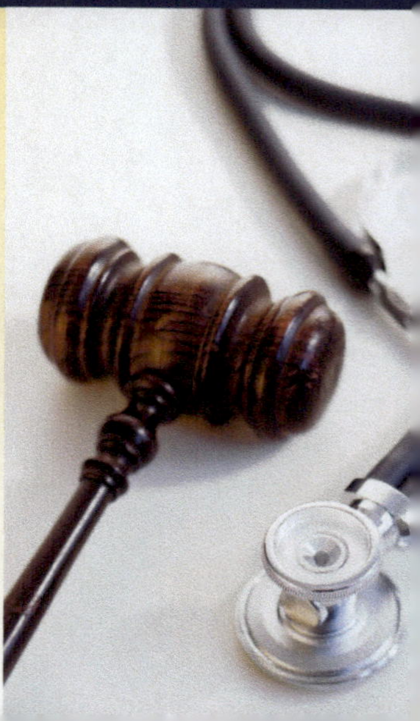

Tom Grill/Corbis

35.1 PROFESSIONALS

All competent parties are liable for their negligence or their failure to meet their contractual obligations. This chapter is devoted to the common law liability of a special category of persons–professionals–because their specialized work poses great risk of personal injury or financial loss to others, and they need to remedy these injuries and losses.

A professional is a person who performs highly specialized work that depends on special abilities, education, experience, and knowledge. Professionals generally are members of state and national professional societies, such as bar associations or medical societies, that establish entry requirements, set levels of competence for performance, accredit educational institutions, develop ethical standards, and discipline members. Many professionals must pass a state-administered examination and gain accreditation, certification, or a license before they are permitted to work in their field. Examples of professionals include health care providers (e.g., physicians, psychiatrists, nurses, and pharmacists), accountants, financial planners, architects and engineers, attorneys, insurance agents and brokers, and others.

professional
A person who does highly specialized work that depends on special abilities, education, experience, and knowledge.

While everyone is subject to a lawsuit for negligence, suits by injured or damaged parties charging negligence frequently target professionals. In some cases, third parties who were not patients or clients of the professional also can sue if they are able to show, among other things, that they suffered injury or financial loss as a direct result of a professional's negligence.

In addition to common law liability discussed in this chapter, professionals may also face contractual and statutory liability.

35.2 MALPRACTICE

Malpractice refers to a professional's improper or immoral conduct in the performance of their duties through carelessness or lack of knowledge. While the term is usually applied to physicians, dentists, attorneys, and accountants, it may be applied to all professionals. In law, malpractice is a specific type of negligence; that is, the malpractice lawsuit is really a negligence lawsuit in which a professional is the defendant. The distinction that developed between malpractice and other forms of negligence stems from the fact that the performance of certain professionals is known as a "practice" and the people served are referred to as "patients" or "clients" rather than customers. For the purpose of the law, however, there is little difference between malpractice and negligence (see Chapter 4).

malpractice
A professional's improper or immoral conduct in the performance of their duties through carelessness or lack of knowledge.

35.3 ELEMENTS OF MALPRACTICE

As was true for product liability lawsuits, discussed in Chapter 34, a claim of negligence must generally prove each of four elements; if even one of these is not present, an action for negligence will be dismissed. These elements, and their application to malpractice wherein a professional is the defendant, are as follows:

- *Duty.* The plaintiff must show that the defendant owed them a duty to either perform an action or not perform an action. In a malpractice lawsuit, the professional owes their client, as well as all third parties who are foreseeably affected by the professional's work, such as duty. The specific duty for a professional may depend on a set of standards set by a professional governing board specific to that profession.

- *Breach.* The plaintiff must show that the defendant either acted improperly or failed to act. In determining whether a defendant has breached their duty in a malpractice lawsuit, the defendant's act or failure to act is measured against the standard of care required by a reasonable professional in the same field. As a result, breach is often difficult to prove because the plaintiff will need the opinions of (often reluctant) expert witnesses in the same field who can evaluate whether the defendant acted negligently.
- *Proximate cause.* The plaintiff must show that the professional defendant's act or failure to act directly caused the injury or loss.
- *Damages.* The plaintiff must prove, as in all civil lawsuits, that they were injured or sustained some other loss as a result of the professional defendant's act or failure to act.

35.4 LIABILITY FOR PROFESSIONAL MALPRACTICE

The following discussion explains how specific professionals can commit malpractice or engage in behavior that might result in a charge of negligence.

LIABILITY OF HEALTH CARE PROVIDERS

A medical professional commits malpractice when their actions demonstrate that they have failed to observe accepted standards of performance and, as a result, the patient suffers injury or death. It is important to note, however, that certain laws exist to shield medical professionals from malpractice claims during extreme circumstances. For example, many statutes provide medical professionals who render emergency care or treatment to injured individuals outside the scope of their regular employment immunity from malpractice lawsuits. Known as Good Samaritan laws, these statutes vary significantly from state to state. However, they usually will not protect a medical professional from a malpractice lawsuit if they act in a reckless manner while providing emergency care or treatment.

Good Samaritan laws
Statutes that provide medical professionals who render emergency care or treatment to injured individuals outside the scope of their regular employment immunity from malpractice lawsuits.

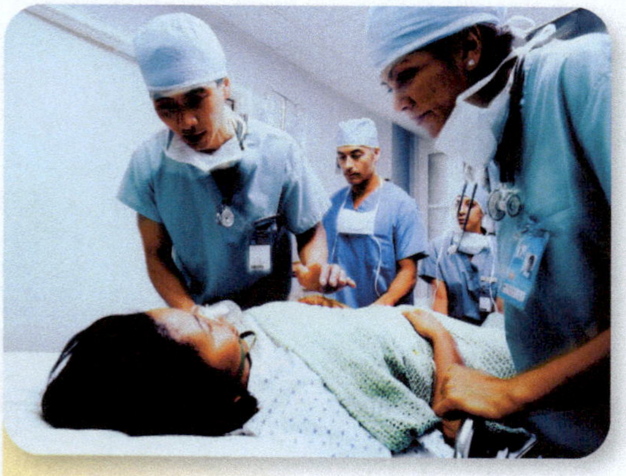

A physician can be liable for failing to inform a patient of the risks involved in a particular surgery.
Digital Vision/Getty Images

Physicians A physician's malpractice might involve their failure to render a correct diagnosis of a patient's condition, failure to order appropriate tests, failure to prescribe appropriate medications, or failure to render an accurate prognosis. Medications prescribed must be appropriate in terms of what is needed to effect a remedy and with due concern for possible side effects and allergic reactions. A physician also can be liable for failing to inform a patient of the risks involved in a particular treatment or surgery, or of available alternatives. Physicians also must have the informed consent of their patients prior to rendering treatment (exceptions may apply in emergency situations).

Typically, the malpractice of a physician does not cause injury or loss to third parties, except in cases where the physician's negligence results in a patient's death or permanent disability. In the case of a patient's death, the physician can be held liable to a surviving spouse, children, or parents for wrongful death. If the physician's negligence results in either a patient's death or disability, a spouse may request damages for loss of consortium, or the loss of companionship.

loss of consortium
In a lawsuit by a spouse, a request for damages for loss of companionship.

Psychiatrists Psychiatrists and other counselors, such as clergy, psychologists, and social workers, who learn from a patient that they intend to do harm to another have the legal responsibility to inform the possible victim and the appropriate authorities. Failure to do so is considered malpractice and is also unethical.

Nurses Even though nurses customarily work under the supervision of physicians, a nurse can be found negligent, for example, for incorrectly administering prescribed medications or failing to properly monitor a patient's condition.

EXAMPLE 35.1

▶ Simmons, a nurse-anesthetist, was charged with negligence in administering a spinal anesthetic that resulted in a patient's paralysis. Expert testimony introduced at the trial showed that it was standard practice in the area to place a pillow under the patient's head when giving a spinal anesthetic to prevent the rise of the anesthetic into the spinal canal. Because Simmons failed to use the pillow, she was held to have been negligent.

Pharmacists Pharmacists who dispense drugs other than those specifically prescribed by authorized professionals such as physicians also can be charged with malpractice if the incorrectly dispensed drugs cause injury to the legal user. Pharmacists are also liable if they dispense multiple medications that, when taken together, cause injury.

LIABILITY OF ACCOUNTANTS

Accounting professionals are liable to their clients and to third parties when they fail to observe established standards for their profession and if such failure has caused clients or third parties to suffer a loss.

For example, an accountant is liable to a client when, as a result of their negligence, the accountant fails to discover or conceals evidence that a client's employee has been embezzling funds. Likewise, an accountant is also liable if they fail to file appropriate and timely tax returns with the result that penalties are assessed against the client.

Previously, it was generally held that an accountant had a responsibility only to their client. Now, in almost all states, accountants' liability has grown to the point that they have been found liable to third parties who have relied on the accountant's work, such as creditors (e.g., banks, suppliers, bondholders) or investors (e.g., shareholders, partners).

EXAMPLE 35.2

▶ The accounting firm of Casey and Ming prepared an analysis and audit of the Referral Publishing Company that was used in securing a loan from First National Bank. The analysis and audit incorrectly depicted Referral as a solvent firm in good financial condition. First National relied on the report and approved the loan. When Referral Publishing failed, the loan could not be repaid. First National sued Casey and Ming, charging negligence. Casey and Ming claimed that the bank had no course of action against them because they had been retained by Referral Publishing and their only duty of care was to their client. Because the use of the analysis and audit in securing a loan from a bank was a reasonably foreseeable event, First National did, indeed, have a cause of action against Casey and Ming.

In Example 35.2, if Casey and Ming's inaccurate audit resulted from their own deliberate actions, and with full knowledge of the inaccuracies, it would not have been the tort of negligence but rather the tort of fraud, and it may have subjected the accounting firm and the partners to criminal prosecution as well as civil liability.

LIABILITY OF FINANCIAL PLANNERS

Financial planning is a profession in which practitioners attempt to advise their clients, who can be either individuals or businesses, on the best ways to manage their financial affairs. The work of financial planners involves an initial analysis of the client's personal and financial situation–including age, income, dependents, assets, and debts–as well as the client's desire to accept or avoid risk. The analysis leads to recommendations that typically involve insurance, investments, and pensions. When the client relies on the financial planner's recommendations and suffers a loss, the financial planner can be sued for negligence, but each of the four elements of negligence must be proved.

EXAMPLE 35.3

Hoover, who had just inherited a large sum of money, engaged the services of Orio, who was certified as a financial planner. After a careful analysis of Hoover's financial and personal situation, Orio recommended that Hoover invest in several specific mutual funds. Quite unexpectedly, the stock market declined and Hoover lost several thousand dollars. He sued Orio for malpractice. However, Orio was able to prove that her financial advice had been sound and met the standards for professionals in her field. Hoover's suit was unsuccessful.

Most lawsuits against financial planners involve one or more of the following:

churning
A financial planner's unreasonably excessive buying or selling of securities to generate commissions.

- *Churning*: the financial planner's unreasonably excessive buying or selling of securities to generate commissions.
- *Unauthorized trading:* the financial planner's exceeding their authority as agreed to by contract between the financial planner and the client.
- *Unsuitability:* the financial planner's recommendation of investments that are inconsistent with the client's particular situation, needs, and desires.
- *Fraud or misrepresentation:* the financial planner's intentional or negligent misstatement or nondisclosure of a material fact relating to an investment.
- *Transfer of account problems:* the financial planner's deliberate obstruction of the client's desire to transfer one or more accounts to another professional.
- *Failure or delay in processing:* the financial planner's neglect in complying with the client's wishes to purchase or sell securities in a timely fashion.

LIABILITY OF ARCHITECTS AND ENGINEERS

Architects design and supervise the construction of buildings and other large structures. Engineers usually design devices or installations of a complex nature, such as bridges and power-generating stations. The engineering profession includes a number of specialties, including mechanical, electrical, and civil engineering. Each specialty involves work that, if done negligently, could result in injury to others. Both architects and engineers are subject to lawsuits for negligence if their work results in injury to parties with whom they have contracted or to third parties.

Architects are subject to lawsuits for negligence if their work results in injury to parties with whom they have contracted.
Morsa Images/Getty Images

Typically, architects and engineers are licensed by states and must demonstrate their competence by passing various examinations and providing evidence of a certain level of education. These professionals do not actually build structures but design them and often supervise the construction. If an architect, for example, negligently designs a building and supervises its construction, and during or after construction it turns out that some of the windows fall out on windy days, the architect is liable both to the firm that hired the architect and to any innocent passerby who may have been killed or injured by the falling windows. The architect is also liable for wrongful death to the spouse, children, or parents of the innocent victim.

EXAMPLE 35.4

▶ Vokes hired the architectural firm of Wilkins and Co. to design and supervise the construction of a four-bedroom colonial house. Two years after the house was completed and Vokes and his family had moved in, Vokes noticed cracks in the foundation. A consulting engineer determined that the house had been built on unstable soil and consequently would continue to settle and ultimately be uninhabitable. Vokes demanded that Wilkins and Co. correct the problem, charging negligence for failing to conduct the soil tests that would be customary for this kind of project. If the problem could not be corrected, Vokes could collect monetary damages.

LIABILITY OF ATTORNEYS

An attorney is liable to a client if they fail to exercise due care in handling a client's affairs. If the attorney is in general practice, the standard of performance is that of other attorneys engaged in similar practices in the area. If the attorney is in a specialized practice, such as real estate, family law, or immigration law, it is the performance of other attorneys engaged in a similar practice by which they will be judged.

An attorney can be found to have committed malpractice if they fail to act in a timely fashion in filing claims or bringing suit before the statute of limitations (a legal time limit) expires. Malpractice also can be established if an attorney fails to properly investigate matters related to a client's case, such as seeking clear title to property in real estate matters or interviewing witnesses in criminal matters.

statute of limitations A legal time limit in which to initiate a lawsuit.

Most instances of attorney malpractice involve only the attorney and their client. In recent years, however, in some states, third parties have successfully sued attorneys who have negligently drawn wills with the result that a third party failed to inherit property as was intended. In other cases, attorneys have been held liable to third parties when an attorney planned an estate in such a way that higher taxes were required as a result of the attorney's malpractice.

EXAMPLE 35.5

Montoya, an attorney, was engaged by Jallon to handle the legal matters concerning the purchase of a residence. Jallon was in a hurry to move into the house and, knowing this, Montoya neglected to conduct a proper title search or to purchase title insurance, a form of insurance that assures the buyer of real property that there are no other claims to ownership. Two years later, when Jallon attempted to sell the house, the buyer's attorney complained that the title to the property included an *easement* (the right of access to the property) that gave the town the right to extend a road through a portion of the backyard. The buyer was willing to purchase the property despite this impediment but at a greatly reduced price. Jallon sued Montoya, charging malpractice, and sought damages for the amount of the difference between the lower selling price and the price at which the property could have been sold without the impediment to the title.

Buyers of insurance look to agents and brokers to recommend appropriate coverage.
Devonyu/iStock/Getty Images

LIABILITY OF INSURANCE AGENTS AND BROKERS

Insurance agents (representatives of specific companies) and insurance brokers (representatives of insurance buyers who deal with multiple companies) are deemed to possess superior knowledge of insurance and to have the ability to use their expertise to protect buyers against various kinds of losses. As a result, buyers of insurance look to agents and brokers to recommend appropriate coverage. When an agent or broker fails to recommend appropriate insurance and the buyer suffers a financial loss that could have been prevented or lessened, the agent or broker can be charged with negligence.

Malpractice on the part of insurance agents and brokers generally relates to either their failure to recommend the purchase of the right kind of insurance to protect against a specific type of loss or their failure to recommend appropriate amounts of coverage. Malpractice of agents and brokers can occur with all forms of insurance, including life, health, automobile, fire, theft, flood, disability, renter's, property, key person, and casualty. An agent or broker must be able to explain each of these to their client and make the appropriate recommendation. For example, the agent or broker must distinguish to their client whole life insurance, a relatively costly form of life insurance protection that includes a savings feature, from term insurance, a form of pure life insurance with no savings feature.

whole life insurance
A relatively costly form of life insurance protection that includes a savings feature.

term insurance
A form of pure life insurance with no savings feature.

EXAMPLE 35.6

▶ Gurchi was concerned about the welfare of his wife and two children and what would happen to them in the event of his untimely death. He discussed his concerns with a life insurance agent, who recommended a whole life policy with a face value of $100,000. For the same cost, Gurchi could have purchased $700,000 of term insurance. Within a year Gurchi was killed in an automobile accident. The proceeds of the policy, $100,000, barely replaced Gurchi's earnings for two years. When the widow realized how little benefit she received as compared to the benefits she would have received had her late husband purchased term insurance, she sued the agent and the insurance company whom the agent represented, charging that the agent had sold her husband an inappropriate form of insurance. During the trial, it was revealed that the agent earned a higher commission for selling the whole life policy than he would have received for selling the term policy. Both the agent and the company were found liable for negligence.

EXAMPLE 35.7

▶ Petras was involved in an accident with an uninsured driver. Petras then learned that his own insurance policy had only minimum coverage that was inadequate to cover his loss. He also learned that for an additional $25 per year, he could have had maximum coverage that would have covered the complete loss. Petras sued the agent for malpractice for failing to inform him about the other insurance options available.

OTHER PROFESSIONALS' LIABILITY

Most other types of professionals are subject to lawsuits for negligence when they fail to perform according to the standards expected of them. Educators and their schools have been sued for failure to educate students to an expected level. Travel agents have been sued for selling substandard hotels and tours.

Directors and officers of corporations have been successfully sued for breach of their duty of loyalty and duty of care (see Chapter 20), resulting from negligence, error, or omission. Shareholders of corporations have sued directors and officers, demanding reimbursement from the company for financial losses resulting from an action or inaction by the director or officer. Lawsuits also have been brought by third parties such as creditors, competitors, and the government.

35.5 REDUCING PROFESSIONALS' RISK OF LIABILITY

Nearly all professionals carry some form of liability insurance to protect against the possibility of being adjudged negligent. However, professionals need to consider additional precautions. Many professional groups conduct workshops and training sessions to help members of the profession reduce the risks that lead to negligent actions and the lawsuits that frequently result. Associations of insurance agents, for example, instruct their members on how best to conduct themselves in dealing with clients in order to minimize the risk of negligence. Many states require continuing education for certain professionals in order for the individuals in the professions to retain their licenses.

CHAPTER SUMMARY

35.1 A professional is a person who performs highly specialized work that depends on special abilities, education, experience, and knowledge. Professionals generally are members of state and national professional societies, such as bar associations or medical societies, that establish entry requirements, set levels of competence for performance, accredit educational institutions, develop ethical standards, and discipline members. Many professionals must pass a state-administered examination and gain accreditation, certification, or a license before they are permitted to work in their field.

35.2 Malpractice is a specific type of negligence; that is, the malpractice lawsuit is really a negligence lawsuit in which a professional is the defendant. The distinction that developed between malpractice and other forms of negligence stems from the fact that the performance of certain professionals is known as a "practice" and the people served are referred to as "patients" or "clients" rather than customers.

35.3 In a malpractice lawsuit, the professional owes their client, as well as all third parties who are foreseeably affected by the professional's work, a duty to either perform an action or not perform an action. In determining whether a defendant has breached their duty, the defendant's act or failure to act is measured against the standard of care required by a reasonable professional in the same field. The plaintiff must show that they were injured or sustained some other loss as a direct result of the professional defendant's act or failure to act.

35.4 Examples of professional malpractice include a physician who fails to prescribe the proper treatment, a psychiatrist who fails to alert the authorities and intended victim of a client's plan to cause harm, an accountant who fails to file a tax return in a timely manner, a financial planner who fails to explain investment risks, an architect who fails to design a structure with proper materials, an attorney who fails to inform a client of their legal options, and an insurance agent who fails to recommend the correct kind of insurance.

35.5 Professionals can protect themselves against the possibility of being adjudged negligent by purchasing liability insurance. In addition, many professional groups conduct training to help members of the profession reduce the risks that lead to negligent actions and the lawsuits that frequently result. Many states require continuing education for certain professionals to retain their licenses.

CHAPTER THIRTY-FIVE ASSESSMENT

MATCHING LEGAL TERMS

Match each of the numbered definitions with the correct term in the following list.

a. malpractice
b. professional
c. term insurance
d. Good Samaritan
e. whole life insurance

1. A form of pure life insurance with no savings feature. **1.** _____

2. A professional's improper or immoral conduct in the performance of their duties through carelessness or lack of knowledge. **2.** _____

3. A person who performs highly specialized work requiring special abilities, education, experience, and knowledge. **3.** _____

4. A person who renders emergency care or treatment. **4.** _____

5. A relatively costly form of life insurance protection that includes a savings feature. **5.** _____

TRUE/FALSE QUIZ

Indicate whether each of the following statements is true or false.

6. While the term *malpractice* is usually applied to physicians, dentists, attorneys, and accountants, it may be applied to all professionals. **6.** _____

7. Good Samaritan laws provide medical professionals who render routine care or treatment to individuals immunity from malpractice lawsuits. **7.** _____

8. The four elements of a malpractice lawsuit are duty, breach, proximate cause, and damages. **8.** _____

9. In determining whether a defendant has breached their duty in a malpractice lawsuit, the defendant's act or failure to act is measured against the standard of care required by a reasonable professional in the same field. **9.** _____

10. A psychiatrist who learns from a patient that the patient intends to do harm to another has the legal duty to inform the intended victim or the authorities. **10.** _____

11. A pharmacist can be sued if they dispense multiple medications that, when taken together, cause injury. **11.** _____

12. Nurses cannot be found to be negligent because they work under the direct supervision of a doctor. **12.** _____

13. A financial planner can be sued for deliberately obstructing their client's desire to transfer one or more accounts to another professional. **13.** _____

14. Accounting professionals have a duty only to their client. **14.** _____

15. An accountant who deliberately falsifies financial data can be charged only with negligence. **15.** _____

16. An insurance agent or broker can be charged with negligence only if they cancel a policy against the wishes of the owner. **16.** _____

17. An insurance agent or broker can be charged with negligence for failing to recommend appropriate amounts of insurance coverage. **17.** _____

18. An architect who designs a building that is later destroyed in a windstorm cannot be charged with negligence because architects have no control over the weather. **18.** _____

19. Clergy cannot be charged with negligence. **19.** _____

20. Directors and officers of corporations can be charged with breach of their duty resulting from action or inaction. **20.** _____

MULTIPLE CHOICE QUIZ

Indicate the correct answer from the choices following each question.

21. In a case of professional malpractice, the plaintiff must prove (a) only that the professional caused them damages (b) that the professional caused damages by violating a professional duty (c) that the professional caused damages by violating a professional duty and the violation of duty caused the damages (d) that the professional caused damages by violating a professional duty, the violation of duty caused the damages, and that the professional was not licensed.

22. A, an accountant, prepares financial statements for their client, B. B tells A that the statements will be used in documentation for the sale of their business to C. After B sells the business to C, C discovers that the financial statements have substantial errors and the business is not as valuable as they thought. In this case, (a) C may not sue A for malpractice because they were not the client (b) C may not sue A for malpractice because C should have used their own accountant (c) C may sue A because they relied on the statements (d) C must sue B, who must sue A.

23. A is a financial planner who also gets commissions when trading stocks for clients. A's client B notices that their account has an unusually large amount of trading activity when compared to other accounts. In this case, which is the most likely lawsuit to succeed against A? (a) Churning (b) Fraud (c) Unauthorized trading (d) Misrepresentation

DISCUSSION QUESTIONS

Answer the following questions and discuss them in class.

24. Discuss why the malpractice of professionals is considered more serious by society than negligence by nonprofessionals.

25. Of the four elements of negligence, is one of them more critical than the others?

26. Explain how the malpractice or negligence of a professional might cause injury to third parties.

27. Identify a financial loss suffered by a third party for which an accountant can be found liable.

28. Distinguish between insurance agents and brokers. Do you think that one should bear greater responsibility than the other for advising buyers about their insurance needs?

29. What are some ways that professionals can reduce their risk of negligence lawsuits?

THINKING CRITICALLY ABOUT THE LAW

Answer the following questions, which require you to think critically about the legal principles that you learned in this chapter.

30. Licensing of Professionals Does the licensing of professionals guard against negligence? Advance arguments for and against.

31. Malpractice Insurance Does having malpractice insurance lessen the care taken by professionals?

32. Malpractice Insurance Because most professionals carry liability insurance, what is the role of the insurance industry in promoting the competence of professionals?

33. Churning Where should the line be drawn between a reasonable number of securities transactions and churning?

____

____

34. A Question of Ethics The purchase of life insurance often involves the client choosing between whole life insurance, which includes a savings feature, and term insurance, which provides only protection. The sales commission also varies depending on the type of policy. Is it ethical for an insurance company to base the agent's commission on the type of policy sold, regardless of the buyer's needs?

____

____

CASE QUESTIONS

Study each of the following cases. Answer the questions that follow with Yes or No.

35. Liability of Accountants Weiss, an accountant, prepared the usual accounting records for Malucic, the owner of a clothing store. Malucic entered into negotiations with Walling for the sale of the business, using the records prepared by Weiss to justify a high purchase price. After the transaction was complete, Walling discovered that the business potential had been greatly exaggerated and there was little chance the clothing store would ever reach the potential suggested by the records. After discussing the matter with his own accountant, Walling concluded that he had been deceived by Weiss's financial reports.

a. Does Walling have a course of action against Malucic? **a.** _____

b. Does Walling have a course of action against Weiss? **b.** _____

c. Do accountants have a responsibility to persons other than their clients? **c.** _____

36. Liability of Physicians Philasen underwent minor surgery for the removal of his tonsils. Serious complications developed when he was administered penicillin, to which he was allergic. The doctor denied responsibility because he did not know about the allergy.

a. Does it seem that Philasen has a cause of action against the doctor? **a.** _____

b. Does it seem that Philasen has a cause of action against the hospital? **b.** _____

c. Was Philasen partly responsible for failing to voluntarily tell the doctor about his allergy? **c.** _____

37. Liability of Architects Li, an architect, designed a large ranch-type house for Spadacini. Within two years after construction, the house began to tilt to one side. Li argued that he was not to blame as the house was designed properly and that the problem was due solely to the negligence of the contractor. Spadacini produced the original contract, which called for Li to supervise the work of the contractor.

a. Can the architect be held responsible for the substandard work of the contractor? **a.** _____

b. Does the architect have a course of action against the contractor? **b.** _____

c. Can Spadacini share some of the blame for not supervising the work as well? **c.** _____

CASE ANALYSIS

Study each of the following cases carefully. Briefly state the principle of law and your decision.

38. Liability of Attorneys Smith was represented by Lewis, an attorney, in a divorce action against her husband, General Smith. General Smith was employed by the California National Guard and, as a state employee, belonged to the State Employees' Retirement System. Lewis advised Smith that her husband's retirement benefits were not community property and thus would not be considered in the divorce litigation or distributed by the trial court. Six months after the divorce was final, Lewis petitioned the court to amend the decree because of his mistake in not including the retirement benefits as community property in the divorce action. It was pointed out that major authoritative reference works, which attorneys routinely consult for a brief and reliable discussion of the law, provided that vested retirement benefits were generally subject to community property treatment. The court refused Lewis, and Smith brought suit against her attorney for malpractice. Will Lewis be found to be liable for malpractice? [*Smith v. Lewis,* 530 P.2d 589 (California)]

Principle of Law:

____

____

Decision:

____

____

39. Liability of Accountants The Irvin family had retained Jones as the family accountant for many years. Under the contractual arrangement, Jones paid all bills, provided bookkeeping services, invested family funds, and prepared all tax returns for the family. After the family received notice of a tax lien on their personal residence, investigation revealed that Jones had failed to properly prepare the tax returns and had failed to pay bills as directed. Further discovery showed that Jones also made poor investments that caused the family to lose significant amounts of money. Is the Irvin family likely to succeed in their suit against Jones? In addition to accounting malpractice, are there other common law principles of liability in this case? [*Irvin v. Jones,* 38 Misc. 3d. 1203 (New York)]

Principle of Law:

Decision:

40. Liability of Insurance Agents Mansfield contacted his insurance agent and asked him to obtain an automobile insurance liability policy to be effective as of February 10. On February 14, Mansfield was involved in an accident while operating his car. The agent provided a policy with an effective date of February 24, which did not cover the loss resulting from the accident. Mansfield charged the agent with a breach of the contract to procure insurance as well as negligence in the performance of his responsibilities. Will Mansfield succeed in his suit? [*Mansfield v. Federal Services Finance Corp.,* 111 A.2d 322 (New Hampshire)]

Principle of Law:

Decision:

41. Liability of Financial Planners Chard completed an educational program in financial planning and was awarded the certification offered by a national association of financial planners. He set up a business to offer his financial planning services to the general public. One of his first clients, Roblee, sought Chard's advice on investments and insurance. Chard prepared a written report that included a recommendation to purchase shares in a real estate venture. Because Chard neglected to verify the financial status of the real estate venture, Roblee lost a significant amount of the money he had invested in the venture. With almost no prospect of ever recovering the investment, he sued Chard, charging negligence. Is Roblee likely to succeed in the suit?

Principle of Law:

Decision:

LEGAL RESEARCH

Complete the following activities. Share your finding with the class.

42. Working in Teams Working in teams of three or four, interview local insurance agents and brokers to learn about various forms of insurance, such as life, health, automobile, fire, theft, flood, disability, renter's, property, key person, casualty, and professional liability.

43. Using Technology Using the Internet and search engines, investigate a case of professional liability and the basis upon which it was decided.

chapter 36
International Business Law

LEARNING OUTCOMES

After studying this chapter and completing the assessment, you will be able to

36.1 Discuss global business and cite reasons for the increased need for international law.

36.2 Define *international law* and identify its major sources.

36.3 Discuss the doctrine of comity.

36.4 Explain the purposes of several major international trade institutions.

36.5 Discuss the international legal environment and state how trade sanctions and embargoes, export and import controls, and boycotts are utilized by governments to achieve economic and political ends.

36.6 Discuss the Foreign Corrupt Practices Act, the treaty known as Contracts for the International Sale of Goods, and the Foreign Sovereign Immunities Act.

36.7 Discuss the international laws governing intellectual property.

terms

LEGAL

- international law
- comity
- transnational institutions
- General Agreement on Tariffs and Trade (GATT)
- World Trade Organization (WTO)
- International Monetary Fund (IMF)
- World Bank
- United States-Mexico-Canada Agreement (USMCA)`
- European Union (EU)
- trade sanctions
- tariff
- quota systems
- boycott
- Foreign Corrupt Practices Act (FCPA)
- Contracts for the International Sale of Goods (CISG)
- Foreign Sovereign Immunities Act (FSIA)
- World Intellectual Property Organization (WIPO)

INTERNATIONAL BUSINESS LAW

"I do believe that international trade agreements benefit both parties, always."

Phil Knight, co-founder and chairman emeritus of Nike Inc.

BananaStock/Getty Images

36.1 GLOBAL BUSINESS

The increasing volume of international trade and tourism, the globalization of the marketplace, the growing incidence of multinational business organizations, and cultural exchanges have given rise to the need for international law. Although the use of English as the language of business is increasing, cultural differences, disparate legal systems, and fluctuating exchange rates remain major obstacles to conducting business internationally.

36.2 WHAT IS INTERNATIONAL LAW

International law is the broad study of the legal systems of major countries, treaties, practices, tariffs and nontariff trade barriers, and import and export quotas. Also included in the study of international law are organizations–national and international–that regulate personal and commercial activity and facilitate international trade.

international law
The broad study of the legal systems of major countries, treaties, practices, tariffs and nontariff trade barriers, and import and export quotas.

SOURCES OF INTERNATIONAL LAW

To fully appreciate the complex legal relationships that exist among nations, it is important to recognize that international law often develops to address the many issues that emerge from international trade.

International laws resulting from the trading relationships among nations have a rich history. In ancient times, the Romans ruled the Western world; however, contrary to popular belief, their reign was based primarily on economic, rather than on military, might. Exercising control over trade through the Roman legal system (the international law of the day) allowed the Roman government to rule the world by maintaining order and peace. The philosophy of Roman international law controlling trade and commerce in a peaceful way came to be known as *Pax Romana* (Roman peace), and the phrase itself appeared on their minted coins.

While signing peace treaties is as old as war, efforts to negotiate peaceful solutions to international disputes culminated in the formation of the League of Nations following World War I. Unfortunately, the League was short-lived and failed to prevent another war. Following World War II, the world's nations again organized a forum for peaceful negotiations and established the United Nations–an organization that now is involved in such diverse social and economic functions as the International Labour Organization (ILO), the Food and Agriculture Organization (FAO), and the General Agreement on Tariffs and Trade (GATT).

In modern times, customary practices and treaties are the major sources of international law, and these are recognized in the Statute of the International Court of Justice (Article 38). More than 200 sovereign nations have the capacity to negotiate treaties and create legal obligations.

In the United States, Article II of the Constitution states that treaties are negotiated by the president and must be ratified by two-thirds of the senators present (see Appendix). However, in practice, other methods are sometimes used.

36.3 APPLYING OTHER COUNTRIES' LAWS—THE DOCTRINE OF COMITY

A major legal principle involved in international law is the doctrine of comity, which holds that the courts of one country should refrain from deciding cases involving the acts of persons from another country. The doctrine is discretionary, and courts of individual countries decide whether or not to apply it based on the facts of each case.

comity
A discretionary doctrine that holds that the courts of one country should refrain from deciding cases involving the acts of persons from another country.

transnational institutions
Organizations whose purpose is to maintain legal and economic order in trade.

General Agreement on Tariffs and Trade (GATT) An international agreement that provides a set of rules to ensure that there is no discrimination in trade by its signatories and also spells out a process for resolving international trade disputes.

World Trade Organization (WTO) An organization with responsibility for overseeing the implementation of all multinational trade agreements negotiated now or in the future.

International Monetary Fund (IMF) An organization whose purpose is to maintain a stable environment for the economies and the currencies of its members by providing protection against large fluctuations in the value of one currency versus another.

36.4 INTERNATIONAL TRADE INSTITUTIONS

Trade among nations remains a vital ingredient in the economic health of the world's population. While countries are sovereign and create and interpret their own sets of laws, the goal is that trade be governed by transnational institutions, whose purpose is to maintain legal and economic order in trade. These transnational institutions are established contractually by several countries that agree to be legally bound by the rules of the organization. A discussion of some of these transnational institutions follows.

THE WORLD TRADE ORGANIZATION

In 1947, an international agreement called the General Agreement on Tariffs and Trade (GATT) was entered into by a multitude of nations. Among its many provisions, GATT provided a set of rules to ensure that there is no discrimination in trade by its signatories and also spelled out a process for resolving international trade disputes. Pursuant to GATT, a country can be granted "normal trade relations" status by its neighbors in order to maintain an efficient and effective means of managing imports (goods from another country coming into the nation) and exports (goods being sold to other countries by companies from within the nation).

A transnational institution's purpose is to maintain legal and economic order in trade.
John W Banagan/Getty Images

By 1995, tariffs had become far less commonplace, and most nations came to recognize that GATT was no longer sufficient. Accordingly, the new World Trade Organization (WTO) was formed. The WTO is responsible for overseeing the implementation of all multinational trade agreements negotiated now or in the future.

In addition to GATT (described previously), the WTO has authority for

- GATS: The General Agreement on Trade in Services.
- TRIPS: The Agreement on Trade-Related Aspects of Intellectual Property Rights.
- TRIMs: Trade Related Investment Measures.

THE INTERNATIONAL MONETARY FUND

In 1944, several nations formed the International Monetary Fund (IMF). The purpose of this organization is to maintain a stable environment for the economies and the currencies of its members by providing protection against large fluctuations in the value of one currency versus another.

Most international experts agree that the IMF has performed its job admirably to date, but the IMF has come under great pressure due to various economic downturns in several nations. The IMF also is criticized for failing to respond adequately to the economic challenges created in the early 1990s, subsequent to the dissolution of the Soviet Union and the heavy borrowing by developing countries during the mid-1990s.

THE WORLD BANK

In 1944, to provide relief to the countries suffering from the ravages of World War II, the International Bank for Reconstruction and Development was created. Now popularly referred to simply as the World Bank, this organization works closely with the IMF to ensure that developing countries have access to funds to stimulate their economies.

The World Bank also has come under a great deal of criticism for the following reasons:

- It has often provided funds to countries with arguably corrupt regimes that have squandered the funds rather than provide real relief to their economies.
- It has provided funds to developing countries, but, despite the large inflow of money, major improvements in these economies have not been realized.

World Bank
The popular name given to the International Bank for Reconstruction and Development, an organization that works closely with the International Monetary Fund to ensure that developing countries have access to funds to stimulate their economies.

United States Mexico-Canada Agreement (USMCA)
As economic agreement aimed at promoting and facilitating trade among the United States, Canada, and Mexico.

European Union (EU)
An entity that established a legal and political relationship among its members that promotes economic growth as well as social and cultural affiliations.

REGIONAL TRADE ORGANIZATIONS AND AGREEMENTS

In addition to the previously described worldwide organizations, numerous regional agreements and entities exist for the purpose of providing legal, political, and economic processes to maintain an orderly relationship among the members.

For example, to promote trade, the United States, Canada, and Mexico have agreed to follow the rules of the United States-Mexico-Canada Agreement (USMCA). Unlike many other regional agreements, the focus of USMCA is on economic trade and its impact on each member country rather than on the political interrelationships among the three countries.

In 1993, 12 countries in Europe formed what is expected to eventually become "Euroland," an economic and political integration of the members into one entity. As a step in this direction, the European Union (EU) established a legal and political relationship among its members that promotes economic growth, as well as social and cultural affiliations. An example of the kind of interconnection among the members is the inauguration of the *euro* (€), the monetary currency of the EU. Table 36.1 shows the 28 member states of the EU. Table 36.2 lists the countries that use the euro.

The euro (€) is the monetary currency used by the majority of countries in the European Union.
Maryna Pleshkun/Shutterstock

TABLE 36.1 Countries in the European Union

- The European Union is composed of 28 independent sovereign countries that are known as member states:
  Austria, Belgium, Bulgaria, Croatia, Cyprus, the Czech Republic, Denmark, Estonia, Finland, France, Germany, Greece, Hungary, Ireland, Italy, Latvia, Lithuania, Luxembourg, Malta, the Netherlands, Poland, Portugal, Romania, Slovakia, Slovenia, Spain, and Sweden.
- There are eight official candidate countries: Albania, Bosnia and Herzegovina, Moldova, Montenegro, Republic of Macedonia, Serbia, Turkey, and Ukraine.

TABLE 36.2 Countries Using the Euro

Andorra	Luxembourg
Austria	Malta
Belgium	Monaco
Cyprus	Montenegro
Estonia	Portugal
Finland	Netherlands

TABLE 36.2 Countries Using the Euro (*Cont*)

France	San Marino
Germany	Slovakia
Greece	Slovenia
Ireland	Spain
Italy	Vatican City
Kosovo	

36.5 THE INTERNATIONAL LEGAL ENVIRONMENT

Companies that conduct business in several countries face the challenge of having to comply with a variety of legal systems that sometimes conflict with one another.

The United States, for example, requires that foreign firms that conduct business here comply with all of the regulations that govern American companies. Likewise, many American companies doing business internationally face the challenge of adapting to local customs and practices.

EXAMPLE 36.1

Kleinsdorf Inc., a German automobile manufacturing company, is opening a plant in the United States. Kleinsdorf will be required to follow all Environmental Protection Agency regulations pertaining to emissions, all National Labor Relations Board regulations pertaining to employees' right to join unions, and all Occupational Safety and Health Administration regulations pertaining to employee accident and sickness prevention.

In addition, companies that conduct business in other countries are frequently required to follow the laws of the country in which their headquarters are located.

EXAMPLE 36.2

NuCloz Corp., a U.S. firm, entered into a contract with the Xiang Company, a Chinese firm, in which Xiang agreed to manufacture men's designer shirts. NuCloz learned that Xiang did not obtain the necessary permission from the designer of the shirts who owned the trademark. Irrespective of the law in China, NuCloz could be liable for the tort of trademark infringement, and for the crime of counterfeiting in the United States, unless NuCloz desists from selling the shirts bearing the designer's logo.

trade sanctions
Legal restrictions, such as embargoes, placed on trade to achieve desired political results.

TRADE SANCTIONS AND EMBARGOES

Many governments place legal restrictions on trade to achieve desired political results. Countries that enact laws prohibiting trade with specific countries are said to be using trade sanctions, sometimes referred to as *embargoes.* These activities by nations are acceptable under international law and are indeed incorporated in the charter of the United Nations. The charter also expressly allows trade sanctions and embargoes by regional organizations, such as the Organization of American States, the Organization for African Unity, and the Arab League.

EXPORT AND IMPORT CONTROLS

In addition to trade sanctions and embargoes, at times a country will impose a tariff, a form of tax, or other restrictions, on imports or exports to attain economic results, such as protecting domestic industries or facilitating the production of certain crops.

tariff
A form of tax, or other restrictions, on imports or exports to attain economic results, such as protecting domestic industries or facilitating the production of certain crops.

Export licenses can be used as an adjunct to national security. The United States, for example, requires that exporters obtain a license prior to shipping certain goods to purchasers in other countries. If the product being sold is considered a threat to national security, for example, the export license will be denied and the exporter will not be allowed to fulfill the contract.

In addition, many countries, to maintain a positive balance of trade (i.e., ensuring that the monetary value of exports exceeds that of imports), place restrictions on the numbers and kinds of products that may enter their nation. These restrictions are referred to as quota systems.

quota systems
Restrictions on the numbers and kinds of products that may enter into a nation.

GOVERNMENTAL ACTIONS

Many governments attempt to maintain control over the actions of foreign businesses operating within their countries by controlling the ownership of the foreign companies' assets. These attempts can take three forms:

1. *Expropriation* is the act of a host country taking title to all the assets of a foreign company. In this case, the host country compensates the owners of the foreign company.
2. *Confiscation,* as is the case with expropriation, also involves the host country taking title to all the assets of the foreign company. However, in the case of confiscation, no compensation is given to the owners of the foreign company.
3. *Domestication* occurs when the host country mandates that at least partial ownership of the foreign company be sold to local citizens or companies prior to the foreign company's conducting business within the host country's borders.

BOYCOTTS

At times, citizens of a particular country refuse to purchase goods made by businesses located in other countries. This action, whether supported by the government or not, is referred to as a boycott.

boycott
Citizens' refusal to purchase goods made by a particular business—for example, a business located in another country.

EXAMPLE 36.3

▶ Morandim Corporation, a Canadian company, manufactures chemicals and regularly sells these to firms in the Middle East. Several of its customers, who are Arabic, organized a boycott and now refuse to purchase Morandim chemicals unless the company agrees to provide written documentation demonstrating that it does not conduct business with firms in Israel.

36.6 DOING BUSINESS IN FOREIGN COUNTRIES

Organizations that opt to conduct business in foreign countries must follow numerous laws and regulations. These include the Foreign Corrupt Practices Act; the treaty relating to the Contracts for the International Sale of Goods; and the Foreign Sovereign Immunities Act.

THE FOREIGN CORRUPT PRACTICES ACT

Foreign Corrupt Practices Act (FCPA)
A federal statute designed to provide executives of American companies with rules and restrictions relating to paying persons in foreign countries to expedite business in these foreign nations.

Contracts for the International Sale of Goods (CISG)
A treaty created to establish a universal set of legal procedures to be applied to contracts covering international transactions.

In some countries, it is perfectly acceptable and indeed expected that there will be payments made to individuals in order to secure their business. In the United States, however, this type of activity amounts to bribery, which is both illegal and ethically unacceptable. In 1977 the United States passed the Foreign Corrupt Practices Act (FCPA), a federal statute designed to provide executives of American companies with rules and restrictions relating to paying persons in foreign countries to expedite business in these foreign nations. Because customs and practices vary so greatly between countries, the law has helped numerous executives recognize what is and what is not acceptable conduct for U.S. firms, irrespective of acceptable ethical standards in the foreign country.

The FCPA makes it unlawful to bribe foreign government officials to obtain or retain business. Illegal activities include direct bribes paid by U.S. companies, as well as bribes paid through intermediaries. Bribes include money, gifts, or anything of value paid to a foreign governmental official or to a foreign political party.

In some countries outside the United States, it is perfectly acceptable and indeed expected that there will be payments made to individuals in order to secure their business.
BananaStock/Getty Images

The FCPA makes it clear that in order to violate the law, the payment must be made "corruptly." The statute defines *corruptly* as "connoting an evil motive or purpose, an intent to wrongly influence the recipient."

While many executives have complained that they are unfairly restrained when doing business in foreign countries, most experts maintain that by reducing bribery, the quality of goods and services produced abroad increases, while international prices are kept at optimal levels. Most would agree that U.S. companies are simply being held to ethical standards generally accepted by the American people.

In 1990, the FCPA was amended so that corporations and their executives were less likely to be prosecuted for making payments to foreign officials. This amendment was intended to offset what was viewed as an unfair advantage enjoyed by firms from other countries that had no such restraints.

CONTRACTS FOR THE INTERNATIONAL SALE OF GOODS

Sometimes, parties to an international transaction disagree over the legal provisions of the contract based on the laws of their native countries. These disagreements can delay and stifle international business. To resolve such problems, a treaty known as the United Nations Convention on Contracts for the International Sale of Goods (CISG) was drafted to establish a universal set of legal procedures to be applied to contracts covering international transactions.

Countries that have signed the treaty are bound to the terms of the CISG. Because the United States has ratified this treaty, the CISG supersedes the provisions of the Uniform Commercial Code (UCC) in certain cases. Note that the CISG differs from the UCC in only a few areas. For example, the CISG does not have a written requirement for contracts involving more than $500, whereas the UCC has a written requirement for such contracts (see Chapter 7).

FOREIGN SOVEREIGN IMMUNITIES ACT

In the United States, it had been tradition that foreign sovereign nations were granted immunity from all lawsuits brought by private individuals. However, the Foreign Sovereign Immunities Act (FSIA), a federal law passed in 1976, established certain exceptions to foreign sovereign immunity. Under this statute, a U.S. court may allow a lawsuit against a foreign sovereign nation to proceed provided the plaintiff can prove that the foreign nation engaged in one or more of the following:

Foreign Sovereign Immunities Act (FSIA) A federal law passed in 1976 that established certain exceptions to foreign sovereign immunity.

- Commercial activity that occurred in the United States in connection with foreign activity.
- Commercial activity outside the United States that caused a direct effect on U.S. commerce.
- Commercial antitrust actions (see Chapter 12).
- Expropriation, terrorism, or torture.
- Other torts committed in the United States.

INTERNATIONAL TREATMENT OF BANKRUPTCIES

In order to promote cooperation between U.S. courts and those of foreign countries in bankruptcy cases, the *Bankruptcy Abuse Prevention and Consumer Protection Act* added Chapter 15 to the federal bankruptcy law. This law allows foreign courts to interact with U.S. courts in resolving bankruptcy cases. In order to judge whether or not to cooperate with the foreign court, the U.S. court first reviews expert testimony in order to make a determination whether the foreign court conducts its proceedings in a fair and equitable manner, and whether the foreign bankruptcy law violates U.S. public policy. The U.S. court will consider how the foreign country treats creditors, how assets are distributed, and whether there would be bias against U.S. creditors (see Chapter 21).

36.7 INTERNATIONAL LAW AND INTELLECTUAL PROPERTY

Individuals, as well as companies, have rights and duties in foreign countries. These rights and duties are increasingly important in the context of the international laws governing intellectual property.

Intellectual property includes both artistic and industrial property rights. Copyrights, patents, and trademarks are the principal areas involved (see Chapter 28). Related to these rights is industrial "know-how" or technology–particularly in developing countries where technology is transferred between firms in different countries that have joint venture agreements. Nations and businesses have long had an interest in maintaining an orderly process by which intellectual property rights are protected.

The World Intellectual Property Organization (WIPO), a specialized agency of the United Nations, is an international organization that administers numerous treaties concerning protection of intellectual property rights. In 1994, the WIPO announced the formation of a center for the arbitration of disputes involving intellectual property rights.

World Intellectual Property Organization (WIPO) A specialized agency of the United Nations that administers numerous treaties concerning protection of intellectual property rights.

COPYRIGHTS

Copyrights protect the authors or creators of literary, artistic, or musical works and (in some countries) computer programs. These laws prohibit the reproduction or alteration of an author's work without their permission. Copyrighted materials are given at least minimal protection in most countries.

PATENTS

Patents are a statutory privilege granted by a nation to inventors for a fixed period of years to exclude all others from manufacturing, using, or selling a patented product without permission from the inventor. A U.S. firm can take advantage of world markets by licensing foreign firms to either manufacture a patented product or use an innovative manufacturing process in the manufacture of a product. A firm might seek *parallel patents* in each of the countries that maintain a patent system.

TRADEMARKS

Trademarks, trade names, service marks, and certification marks are valuable tools used by businesses to identify their products and services. In most cases, the treatment of these valuable properties in international commerce does not greatly differ from domestic treatment. Trademarks are viewed as property and thus can be transferred or licensed to others. Although not true in the United States, in most countries registration is a prerequisite for ownership and protection of the mark. Often, a foreign licensee must meet certain product quality requirements so that the use of the mark does not deceive the consumer or lessen the value of the mark to the owner.

CHAPTER SUMMARY

36.1 Giving rise to the need for international law are the increasing volume of international trade and tourism, the globalization of the marketplace, the growing incidence of multinational business organizations, and cultural exchanges.

36.2 *International law* may be defined as the broad study of the legal systems of major countries, treaties, practices, tariffs and nontariff trade barriers, and import and export quotas. Also included in the study of international law are organizations–national and international–that regulate personal and commercial activity and facilitate international trade. The sources of international law in modern times are customary practices and treaties, which are recognized in the Statute of the International Court of Justice. More than 200 sovereign nations have the capacity to negotiate treaties and create legal obligations.

36.3 The doctrine of comity holds that the courts of one country should refrain from deciding cases involving the acts of persons from other countries. The doctrine is discretionary, and courts of individual countries decide whether or not to apply it based on the facts of each case.

36.4 The World Trade Organization is responsible for overseeing the implementation of all multinational trade agreements negotiated now or in the future. The International Monetary Fund maintains a stable environment for the economies and the currencies of its members by providing protection against large fluctuations in the value of one currency versus another. The World Bank ensures that developing countries have access to funds to stimulate their economies. The United States-Mexico-Canada Agreement governs economic trade among the United States, Canada, and Mexico. The European Union represents a legal and political relationship among its members that promotes economic growth, as well as social and cultural affiliations.

36.5 Trade sanctions and embargoes, export and import controls, and boycotts are all measures used by governments and citizens of one country to restrict the economic activities of businesses from other countries, by not allowing these foreign firms free access to markets.

36.6 The Foreign Corrupt Practices Act is a federal statute designed to provide executives of American companies with rules and restrictions relating to paying persons in foreign countries to expedite business in these foreign nations. The treaty known as Contracts for the International Sale of Goods (CISG) was created to establish a universal set of legal procedures to be applied to contracts covering international transactions. The Foreign Sovereign Immunities Act is a federal law that established certain exceptions to foreign sovereign immunity.

36.7 Copyrights, patents, and trademarks are the principal areas involved in international laws governing intellectual property. Copyrighted materials are given at least minimal protection in most countries. Through the use of patents, a U.S. firm can take advantage of world markets by licensing foreign firms to either manufacture a patented product or use an innovative manufacturing process in the manufacture of a product. The treatment of trademarks in international commerce does not greatly differ from domestic treatment in most cases.

CHAPTER THIRTY-SIX ASSESSMENT

MATCHING LEGAL TERMS

Match each of the numbered definitions with the correct term in the following list.

a. comity
b. transnational institutions
c. General Agreement on Tariffs and Trade
d. World Trade Organization
e. International Monetary Fund
f. United States-Mexico-Canada Agreement
g. European Union
h. trade sanctions and embargoes
i. import and export controls
j. tariffs
k. quota systems
l. Foreign Corrupt Practices Act

1. Restrictions on the numbers and kinds of products that may enter a nation. **1.** _____

2. An organization that provides protection against large fluctuations in the value of one currency versus another. **2.** _____

3. A doctrine that holds that the courts of one country should refrain from deciding cases involving the acts of persons from another country. **3.** _____

4. Organizations established contractually by several countries that agree to be legally bound by the rules of the organization. **4.** _____

5. Government use of legal restrictions on trade to achieve desired political results. **5.** _____

6. Agreement that provides a set of rules to ensure that there is no discrimination in trade by its signatories. **6.** _____

7. An entity established to achieve economic and political integration of member countries. 7. _____

8. A form of tax, or other restrictions, on exports or imports to attain economic results, such as protecting domestic industries or facilitating the production of certain crops. 8. _____

9. An organization responsible for overseeing the implementation of all multinational trade agreements negotiated now or in the future. 9. _____

10. A broad category that includes various activities, including licensing the sale of some goods to foreign buyers, intended to affect the balance of trade. 10. _____

11. An agreement among the United States, Canada, and Mexico that focuses strictly on economic trade. 11. _____

12. A U.S. law that makes it unlawful to bribe foreign government officials to obtain or retain business. 12. _____

TRUE/FALSE QUIZ

Indicate whether each of the following statements is true or false.

13. International law is the broad study of the legal systems of major countries, treaties, practices, tariffs and nontariff trade barriers, and import and export quotas. 13. _____

14. There is little or no relationship between international law and international trade. 14. _____

15. The activities of the United Nations are limited to international law. 15. _____

16. The doctrine of *comity* holds that the courts of one country should refrain from deciding cases involving the acts of persons from another country. 16. _____

17. The purpose of transnational institutions is to maintain legal and economic order in trade. 17. _____

18. The purpose of the International Monetary Fund is to provide a clearinghouse for checks drawn on foreign banks. 18. _____

19. The European Union established a legal and political relationship among its members that promotes economic growth, as well as social and cultural affiliations. 19. _____

20. In some countries, it is common that there will be payments made to individuals in order to secure their business. 20. _____

21. The United Nations Convention on Contracts for the International Sale of Goods is a treaty created to establish a universal set of legal procedures to be applied to contracts covering international transactions. 21. _____

22. Most countries recognize U.S. patents but not copyrights. 22. _____

MULTIPLE CHOICE QUIZ

Indicate the correct answer from the choices following each question.

23. Four countries have negotiated a trade agreement that imposes tariffs on certain goods but allows free trade for other goods. In this case (a) only the General Agreement on Tariffs and Trade (GATT) rules apply (b) only the World Trade Organization (WTO) rules apply (c) both the GATT and WTO rules apply (d) neither the GATT nor the WTO rules apply. **23.** _____

24. Country A would like to ensure that certain electronic technology does not get exported at all to Country B in order to avoid having Country B obtain a military advantage over Country A. In this case, Country A should (a) impose a tariff on the import of that electronic technology (b) impose a tariff on the export of that electronic technology (c) impose an embargo on the export of that technology (d) impose an embargo on the import of that technology. **24.** _____

25. Company A (a U.S. company) has routinely paid import officials in other countries payments to ensure that its goods get preferential treatment in those countries, including expedited approvals and priority in access to transport services. In this case, Company A has (a) not violated any U.S. statutes (b) has violated the Foreign Corrupt Practices Act (c) has violated the Contracts for the International Sale of Goods (d) has violated the Foreign Sovereign Immunities Act. **25.** _____

26. Company A has produced a training video for the use of its products that it sells to customers as part of every transaction. Company A has learned that the video is being illegally copied in other countries and being sold by other entities to its customers for a lower price. In this case, the dispute between Company A and the other entities would be (a) decided only by a U.S. court (b) decided by the World Trade Organization (WTO) (c) decided by the World Intellectual Property Organization (WIPO) (d) decided only by a court in the country where the illegal sales are occurring. **26.** _____

DISCUSSION QUESTIONS

Answer the following questions and discuss them in class.

27. Cite reasons for the increased need for international law in recent years.

_____

_____

28. Discuss some of the ways international trade is regulated by international law.

_____

_____

29. What are some reasons for trade sanctions and embargoes? How do they differ from export and import controls?

_____

_____

30. How do tariffs protect domestic industries, and how do they hinder world trade?

31. Discuss the goals of the USMCA, an intercountry trade agreement, and the means it uses to achieve these goals.

32. Discuss five exceptions to foreign sovereign immunity pursuant to the Foreign Sovereign Immunities Act.

THINKING CRITICALLY ABOUT THE LAW

Answer the following questions, which require you to think critically about the legal principles that you learned in this chapter.

33. Laws and Culture Assuming that the law of a country reflects its customs, identify and discuss selected laws in foreign countries and how customs influenced the enactment of these laws.

34. International Financial Institutions Discuss the goals and criticisms of the IMF and the World Bank.

35. Trade Sanctions Because trade sanctions often affect the people of a country more severely than their government, are sanctions a good way of achieving political goals?

36. GATT Pursuant to GATT, countries could receive "normal trade relations" status based on economic criteria. Later this designation was awarded to countries that had achieved specific human rights objectives. Should economic inducements be used to foster moral goals?

37. A Question of Ethics Should the FCPA impose U.S. ethical standards on the activities of U.S. businesses in international trade, even though this law may put these businesses at a competitive disadvantage with their foreign counterparts?

____

____

CASE QUESTIONS

Study each of the following cases. Answer the questions that follow with Yes or No.

38. International Court Katsoulas, a U.S. car dealer, had a contract with a Korean automobile manufacturer for the delivery of several cars. When the manufacturer failed to deliver the cars as promised, Katsoulas threatened to bring the case to the International Court of Justice for a determination.

a. Does Katsoulas have a course of action against the car manufacturer? **a.** _____

b. Can Katsoulas successfully pursue his threat to take his complaint to the International Court of Justice? **b.** _____

c. If Katsoulis is unsuccessful in his threat to take his case to the International Court of Justice, does he have other avenues of redress? **c.** _____

39. Foreign Government Control Straley Corporation, a manufacturer of hand tools, had been exporting its products to several countries in Europe for 10 years and decided to establish a manufacturing operation there. The directors of the company met to select a country in which to begin operations. After much discussion, the board selected the country of Alvinia as the site. Following the selection, additional research revealed that the government of Alvinia had a record of taking over foreign businesses. Even if the government took over the firm, would any of the following types of appropriation be acceptable to the company?

a. Expropriation **a.** _____

b. Confiscation **b.** _____

c. Domestication **c.** _____

40. Foreign Corrupt Practices Act Bryerly, a U.S. sales representative for a U.S. firm, Zoom Airplane Company, was attempting to close a deal with a foreign government for the purchase of 14 jet reconnaissance planes. He knew that competitors from two other countries were also bidding for the contract. Eager for the business, he offered a bribe to the government official who would be instrumental in making the decision.

a. Can Bryerly be prosecuted under the Foreign Corrupt Practices Act? **a.** _____

b. If salespersons from other countries can bribe officials, and those from the United States cannot, are the U.S.-based personnel arguably at a competitive disadvantage? **b.** _____

c. Are there other inducements Bryerly could legally offer the official? **c.** _____

CASE ANALYSIS

Study each of the following cases carefully. Briefly state the principle of law and your decision.

41. Treaties Before boarding an El Al Israel Airlines flight from New York to Tel Aviv, Tseng, a passenger, was physically subjected to an intrusive security search. Although not injured bodily, Tseng sued El Al for damages, asserting, among other charges, assault and false imprisonment. A federal court dismissed the case on the basis of the Warsaw Convention, a treaty that precludes a passenger from maintaining an action for damages resulting from personal injury when the claim does not satisfy certain conditions for liability. The Convention expressly does not "permit recovery for psychic or psychosomatic injury." Will Tseng be successful in her suit? [*El Al Israel Airlines, Ltd. v. Tsui Yuan Tseng,* 122 F.3d 99, reversed]

Principle of Law:

Decision:

42. Trademarks Johnson, a passionate bicyclist, wanted to go into the business of manufacturing high-quality bicycles. He found that both labor and component parts were quite inexpensive in Taiwan. Even adding the shipping charges to the United States, it was economically advantageous to assemble the bicycles in Taiwan. He chose the name "Winner's Choice" and a logo that he registered with the Taiwan government. Business boomed, but his success was his downfall when his bicycles caught the attention of an American corporation that manufactured motorcycles and had previously registered the same trademark in the United States. The American firm brought suit against Johnson, contending that he violated the Lanham Act, which regulates trademarks. Johnson maintained that his was a foreign company and therefore not subject to U.S. trademark laws. Is Johnson correct in his defense?

Principle of Law:

Decision:

43. Boycotts Yikes, a U.S.-based manufacturer of shoes, had plants in several countries in Southeast Asia and enjoyed considerable success in world markets as a result of a number of factors, including its excellent products, low prices, efficient production, low labor costs, and widespread consumer product acceptance. In the midst of its success, a grassroots group took exception to the corporation's policies, particularly the firm's labor policies, which the grassroots group referred to as "sweatshop" conditions. The grassroots group set up a website on which numerous disparaging criticisms and a call for a worldwide boycott of Yikes's products were disseminated. In the opinion of Yikes's management, the criticisms were without merit; yet the unfavorable publicity that would surely result from a defamation suit against the grassroots organization did not seem to offer much encouragement either. The mass media joined the fray, and Yikes became increasingly defensive. The company mounted a public relations campaign to defend its practices. What would be a recommended course of action for Yikes?

Principle of Law:

____

____

Decision:

____

____

LEGAL RESEARCH

Complete the following activities. Share your findings with the class.

44. Working in Teams In teams of three or four, interview local small and medium-size businesses to learn about the experiences of the interviewees in dealing with various aspects of international law.

____

____

45. Using Technology Using the Internet and search engines, investigate the terms and international organizations discussed in this chapter.

____

____

chapter 37 Business and the Environment

LEARNING OUTCOMES

After studying this chapter and completing the assessment, you will be able to

37.1 Describe the history of federal statutes dealing with environmental protection.

37.2 Explain how the federal government regulates itself in the area of environmental protection.

37.3 Describe how the government regulates businesses in relation to the environment.

37.4 Discuss how major federal legislation aims to reduce pollution.

37.5 Describe the theories of law under which private citizens may sue persons and businesses that harm the environment.

37.6 Identify several types of pollution that are of great concern to society.

37.7 Identify several factors that influence the changing global climate.

37.8 Identify other environmental issues for which there is growing concern.

terms

LEGAL

- National Environmental Policy Act (NEPA) of 1970
- environmental impact statement (EIS)
- Environmental Protection Agency (EPA)
- Clean Air Act of 1970
- Clean Water Act of 1972
- Superfund
- public nuisance
- private nuisance
- particle trespass
- acid rain
- greenhouse effect

BUSINESS AND THE ENVIRONMENT

"We won't have a society if we destroy the environment."

Margaret Mead, cultural anthropologist

Image Source/Getty Images

37.1 THE DEVELOPMENT OF ENVIRONMENTAL PROTECTION

The United States has an abundance of natural resources, including waterways, wetlands, precious minerals, arable land, wildlife, coal, and forests. It was recognized early in the country's history that laws needed to be enacted to protect its physical environment.

Early federal statutes dealing with environmental issues concerned themselves primarily with conservation of forests and wildlife. Because manufacturing had not yet reached a stage that caused significant harm to the environment, few laws regulated business activities with respect to the environment.

In the 1960s, this view changed. Citizens of the United States began to insist that strict environmental laws be enacted to maintain purity of air and water. The first Earth Day was celebrated on April 22, 1970, and became a symbol of the political activism of the time. It was realized that the operations of business firms significantly affected the environment. As businesses manufacture goods for use by consumers, pollution is an unfortunate by-product. What is problematic for policymakers is balancing the importance of allowing businesses to produce at optimal levels while maintaining a watchful eye over the environment.

There are laws that protect the abundance of natural resources in the United States.
Neil Beer/Getty Images

Today, environmental regulation is a distinct area of the law, and firms strive to comply with myriad statutes, regulations, and ordinances that cover the relationship between businesses and the environment.

37.2 GOVERNMENT'S REGULATION OVER ITSELF

In an effort to ensure that the federal government itself does not contribute to the destruction of the environment, Congress passed the National Environmental Policy Act (NEPA) of 1970. This law requires that any project (such as a dam, a stadium, a canal, or a highway) with significant federal involvement (such as federal financing) must have an approved environmental impact statement (EIS) prior to the commencement of any work on the project. The Council on Environmental Quality issues guidelines for EISs. To be approved, an EIS must provide responses to several questions:

- What is the environmental impact of the proposed project?
- What negative environmental effects will result from the proposed project?
- What are the alternatives to the proposed project (including taking no action)?
- What short-term and long-term destruction of environmental resources will result from the proposed project?
- What irreversible and irretrievable commitments of resources will be consumed by the proposed project?

National Environmental Policy Act (NEPA) of 1970
A federal statute that requires that any project with significant federal involvement (such as federal financing) must have an approved environmental impact statement prior to the commencement of any work on the project.

environmental impact statement (EIS)
An assessment of the environmental consequences of a planned project that must be approved prior to commencement of any project with significant federal involvement (such as federal financing).

EXAMPLE 37.1

Several groups in New York proposed that a new highway be constructed in New York City, to be called Westway. Plans for the highway included destruction of some old wooden piers located in the Hudson River. Destroying the piers could have had an adverse impact on the striped bass, whose habitat was in the river. It was alleged that the EIS failed to adequately address the striped bass issue, and Westway was never built.

37.3 GOVERNMENT REGULATION OF BUSINESS

Environmental Protection Agency (EPA)
The federal agency that conducts environmental research, assists states and municipalities with grants and technical advice, and administers the federal pollution laws that cover businesses.

In 1970 Congress created the Environmental Protection Agency (EPA), which has the responsibility of regulating business activities as these relate to the environment. The EPA

- Conducts environmental research.
- Assists states and municipalities with grants and technical advice.
- Administers the federal pollution laws that cover businesses.

37.4 MAJOR FEDERAL LEGISLATION PROTECTING THE ENVIRONMENT

Important federal legislation aimed at protecting the environment includes the Clean Air Act, the Clean Water Act, and the Comprehensive Environmental Response, Compensation, and Liability Act, also known as Superfund.

THE CLEAN AIR ACT

Clean Air Act of 1970
A federal statute that requires all states to develop air quality standards that are at least as rigorous as the federal standards. This statute sets primary and secondary standards and regulates both stationary and mobile pollution.

The Clean Air Act of 1970 was created with recognition of the fact that pollution sometimes crosses the boundary lines of local jurisdictions and extends into two or more states. In effect, this law emphasized that when it comes to protecting the environment, state regulation is insufficient and federal law is needed. At the international level, environmental protection is attained by treaties among countries (see Chapter 36).

Pursuant to the Clean Air Act all states are required to develop air quality standards that are at least as rigorous as the federal standards. Such standards include

- *Primary standards,* which protect human life and health.
- *Secondary standards,* which protect property, vegetation, climate, and aesthetic values.

In addition, the Clean Air Act covers two forms of pollution:

- *Stationary pollution,* which is caused by factories and other production facilities. This form of pollution is sometimes corrected by the use of scrubbers on smokestacks.
- *Mobile pollution,* which is caused by automobiles, trains, airplanes, and so forth. This form of pollution is in part addressed by the EPA monitoring automobile manufacturers to ensure that they meet the standards for minimum gasoline mileage.

In 1990, the Clean Air Act was amended with a law exceeding 1,100 pages. These amendments require that emissions from automobiles contain fewer pollutants, that gasoline sold in the United States be cleaner, and that factories install new technologies to reduce the discharge of pollutants into the air.

THE CLEAN WATER ACT

The Clean Water Act of 1972 set minimum standards for water purity in a manner similar to the Clean Air Act described previously. Included in such standards is "fishable and swimmable," an intermediate standard of water quality that allows U.S. navigable waterways to be used for propagation of fish, shellfish, and wildlife and also allows such waterways to be used for recreational purposes.

Clean Water Act of 1972
A federal statute that sets minimum standards for water purity.

The ultimate goal of the Clean Water Act is to eliminate the discharge of pollutants into the nation's waters. Under the Clean Water Act, both municipalities and major industries that discharge wastewater must obtain a permit, which states the maximum amount of pollutants that may be emitted into a waterway.

EXAMPLE 37.2

- An offshore oil drilling rig, owned by BP and operating in the Gulf of Mexico, exploded in 2010. The partially drilled well then began spewing up to an estimated 60,000 barrels of oil per day. After several months, BP was successful in its efforts to permanently cap the well. However, the leak resulted in a massive oil slick that substantially damaged coastal areas and marine life. BP was found to be in violation of the Clean Water Act and was liable for substantial civil fines.

SUPERFUND

In 1980 Congress passed the *Comprehensive Environmental Response, Compensation, and Liability Act (CERCLA)*. More popularly referred to as Superfund, this law regulates the dumping of waste onto land. If business firms illegally dump waste material, they can be held responsible for three times the actual cost of the cleanup.

Superfund
A federal statute (also known as the Comprehensive Environmental Response, Compensation, and Liability Act) that regulates the dumping of waste onto land.

Superfund designates specific sites, placing them on the *National Priorities List* and mandating that these locations be cleaned up by their owners. The EPA has authority to

- Conduct cleanups when immediate action needs to be taken.
- Enforce penalties against potentially responsible parties.
- Ensure community involvement.
- Involve states.
- Ensure long-term protectiveness.

Superfund regulates the dumping of waste onto land.
Steve Allen/Brand X Pictures

The law also created a *Hazardous Substance Trust Fund* to help defray costs in addressing environmentally scarred land. Despite the national attention paid to this problem, however, applying the provisions of Superfund has not been an easy process, nor has it met with uniform success.

EXAMPLE 37.3

The Yellow Rock Coal Company went bankrupt in 1977. Yellow Rock owned 20,000 acres of environmentally damaged land and had numerous creditors who had not been paid. The land was designated as a Superfund site. A not-for-profit company called Earth Saviors received a federal grant to purchase the land but will need to engage in a massive cleanup before reclaiming the land for use as a park and wildlife preserve.

37.5 LAWSUITS BY PRIVATE CITIZENS

In the event a business firm creates pollution or damages the environment, in addition to being required to pay a fine, it may be held liable to private persons as well. There are several theories of law under which a private individual may bring a lawsuit against a business for creating pollution.

NEGLIGENCE

Negligence is a tort that allows a plaintiff to bring a lawsuit against a defendant under state law for causing personal injury or property damage when there has been a failure to use reasonable care (see Chapter 4). Businesses that create pollution frequently cause injury to people or damage to their property, and these businesses may be found liable by a court for the tort of negligence.

NUISANCE

Most states have laws prohibiting the creation of a nuisance, a condition that affects a person's health, causes property damage, or interferes with a person's well-being (see Chapter 4).

Businesses that cause pollutants to enter the air or water are in fact creating a nuisance. There are two categories of nuisances:

public nuisance
A nuisance that affects public property.

private nuisance
A nuisance that affects private property.

- A **public nuisance** is created when the nuisance affects public property, such as a navigable river or a state park. If a business causes pollution that enters a river or park, members of the public could file a lawsuit.
- A **private nuisance** is created when the nuisance affects private property, such as a residence. If a business causes pollution that enters a person's private property, the affected individual could bring a lawsuit. Generally, state laws mandate that the affected individual must notify the business in writing of the pollution's impact. If the business does not correct the problem, the affected individual may abate the nuisance (reduce the negative impact) on their own and charge the business for the work.

EXAMPLE 37.4

Festa owned a home adjacent to a small manufacturing company owned by Hedberg that placed numerous bags of unprotected trash near the property line. Festa observed the presence of vermin on her property and wrote Hedberg a letter requesting the removal of the trash—that is, the abatement of the private nuisance. When Hedberg refused to attend to the problem, Festa hired a company to remove the trash and sent Hedberg the bill.

TRESPASS

Trespass is the unauthorized entry onto another person's property. Businesses that cause pollution are, in effect, sending pollutants onto another person's land or water. Most states recognize a cause of action for particle trespass, accepting the theory that businesses are trespassing on another person's property with their pollution particles.

particle trespass The unauthorized entry of pollutants onto another person's land or water.

37.6 TYPES OF POLLUTION

The most widely discussed forms of pollution are those that affect air, water, and land, discussed in some detail earlier in this chapter. However, numerous other types of pollution and environmental issues are of great concern to society and are the subject of federal statutes.

NOISE POLLUTION

Excess noise (as measured in decibels) can affect people's health and well-being. Exposure to loud noise for extended periods can affect an individual's ability to hear, can cause mood swings, and is even alleged to injure fetuses. Noise pollution also may result in lower real estate values, as homeowners who live near airports can frequently attest.

PESTICIDE CONTROL

There are currently more than 1,000 chemicals used in the preparation of more than 20,000 pesticides. The continued use of a pesticide often causes insects to become immune to the chemical compounds, and as a result, the pesticide becomes ineffective. Stronger pesticides must then be created. In addition, many individuals are not comfortable with having their food grown in environments wherein pesticides are used.

SOLID WASTE DISPOSAL

Most products are packaged in containers and wrappers that require disposal. The sheer volume of this waste material makes it extremely difficult to manage its disposal. Accordingly, numerous municipalities require that businesses and homeowners recycle paper, plastic, glass, and metal products. Of course, the time and money necessary to manage a recycling program efficiently and effectively to some extent offsets the value of the program itself. Accordingly, it is well accepted that longer-term solutions must be found. Many companies are going "green," making products and packaging them in environmentally friendly ways. These companies have quickly discerned the positive public relations value of their concern for the environment.

The advancement of technology has contributed to the problem of solid waste disposal. Seventy percent of this waste consists of electronic scrap (*e-waste*). It is estimated that an astounding 150 million cellular telephones are taken out of circulation each year, 20 million of which end up as solid waste. Nearly 90 percent of retired computers sit in landfills or storage. Although there are no federal laws currently addressing e-waste, several states have passed statutes, and the EPA has drafted rules relating to recycling cathode ray tubes (traditionally used in televisions and computer monitors).

TOXIC SUBSTANCE DISPOSAL

Of great concern is the quantity of waste materials that can cause great harm to humans who are exposed to them. These toxic substances include medical waste and chemicals.

Pursuant to the *Toxic Substance Control Act of 1976,* manufacturers are required to test chemicals thoroughly prior to introducing them into commerce. These tests must be conducted to determine the chemicals' effect on human health and on the environment.

In addition, the *Resource Conservation and Recovery Act of 1976 (RCRA)* governs the storage and disposal of toxic substances. Under the RCRA, the EPA has the authority to regulate facilities that generate, transport, treat, store, or dispose of hazardous waste. The EPA requires such facilities to abide by a "cradle-to-grave" tracking system in which toxic substances are continuously tracked from the point of generation to the point of disposal.

EXAMPLE 37.5

During the 1950s, a surge in the construction of new gasoline stations resulted in the burial of an enormous number of gasoline storage tanks across the nation. These unprotected steel tanks had an expected life of 30–50 years; however, many of these tanks corroded rapidly and failed much sooner. In the mid-1980s, the EPA established regulations that required owners of such tanks to upgrade or replace them with corrosion-resistant tanks that have the capacity to be monitored for future leaks.

NATURAL RESOURCE CONSERVATION

The United States has extraordinary forests and wetlands that have great aesthetic and economic value. Often, policymakers struggle with designing laws and regulations that can protect these resources without disturbing the natural ecological order. An example of this is the policy that provides that forest fires that are started by an act of nature (e.g., a lightning strike) are allowed to continue to burn so long as the fire does not threaten human life and personal property. However, there is much debate about the propriety of allowing a fire to burn, sometimes out of control, so as not to disturb the ecosystem.

ACID RAIN

acid rain
A form of pollution caused by the discharge of sulfur emissions into the atmosphere.

Sulfur emissions, created primarily by manufacturing plants located in the central portion of the United States, cause pollutants to be discharged into the atmosphere and result in so-called acid rain. Because the jet stream flows from west to east, hardest hit by acid rain are the populated areas in the northeast portion of the United States and Canada. Acid rain creates problems for forests and crops, kills fish, and destroys the paint finishes on automobiles.

37.7 A CHANGING GLOBAL ENVIRONMENT

Several factors influence the changing global climate, including the release of carbon dioxide into the atmosphere, the destruction of rain forests, and the destruction of the ozone layer.

THE GREENHOUSE EFFECT

There has been great concern that global temperatures are increasing over time. Many scientists believe that the increased burning of fossil fuels (coal, gas, and oil) has loaded the atmosphere with heat-trapping carbon dioxide (CO_2), creating global warming, a condition known as the greenhouse effect. The resulting rising temperatures can melt the polar icecaps, causing rising sea levels throughout the world. The result will be damage to coastal areas, as well as a host of ecological changes to the environment.

greenhouse effect
The rising of global temperatures due to the increased burning of fossil fuels that has loaded the atmosphere with heat-trapping carbon dioxide.

DESTRUCTION OF RAIN FORESTS

In recent years, there has been a growing recognition that economic interests are causing the gradual destruction of the world's rain forests found in tropical climates. This deforestation alters the distribution and circulation of water, which in turn can lead to drought, flooding, soil erosion, and changes in wind and ocean currents and in rainfall distribution. Another serious result of deforestation is that absorption of carbon dioxide from the atmosphere is substantially reduced.

There has been a growing recognition that economic interests are causing the gradual destruction of the rain forests.
Stockbyte/Getty Images

DESTRUCTION OF THE OZONE LAYER

It is now recognized that the release of chlorofluorocarbons into the air has damaged the ozone layer in the atmosphere. A hole in the ozone layer is most manifest over the South Pole and is causing concern over its potential impact on human health. Chlorofluorocarbons are present primarily in aerosol cans and in freon, a cooling substance historically found in refrigerators and air conditioners.

Because the ozone layer protects the environment from the ultraviolet rays of the sun, damaging this protective shield could well lead to major problems for agricultural products, forests, and wildlife. Holes in the ozone layer can affect human health by causing skin cancer and other disease. As a result, amendments to the Clean Air Act have phased out the production and use of chlorofluorocarbons.

37.8 OTHER ENVIRONMENTAL ISSUES

As our knowledge of our universe increases, so does our recognition of environmental problems. There is growing concern about biodiversity and ocean and space pollution.

BIODIVERSITY

Of concern to environmentalists is the notion that thousands of species are becoming extinct at an alarming rate. It is estimated that since the year 1600, approximately 260 animal species, 370 insect species, and 380 vascular plants have become extinct. Numerous federal statutes have been passed protecting some of these endangered species, but many individuals argue that not enough is being done and that not all species are being protected adequately.

OCEAN POLLUTION

A developing environmental problem is that of ocean dumping, in which waste material is illegally deposited into the waters far off coastal areas. Currently, ocean dumping is allowed under limited circumstances. The EPA is charged with the responsibility of selecting appropriate sites and types of waste that may be discarded into the oceans by U.S. organizations.

SPACE POLLUTION

Environmentalists have recently turned their attention to the increased amount of "space junk" that is orbiting the planet. Satellites no longer in use or in disrepair continue to circle the Earth. It is now estimated that there are 20,000 pieces of space debris in orbit. *NASA's Orbital Debris Program Office* monitors risk associated with space objects.

OVERPOPULATION

Due to longer life spans and declining death rates, the world's population continues to grow at an increasing, and some would add, alarming rate. There are approximately 8 billion people alive in the world today, which is 8 times the population of only about 200 years ago. Some have estimated that by the year 2050, the world's population will reach 10 billion; and by 2100, nearly 15 billion. While speculative, these numbers have raised concerns that the planet may not be able to sustain our species.

CHAPTER SUMMARY

37.1 Early federal statutes dealing with environmental issues concerned themselves primarily with conservation of forests and wildlife. In the 1960s, citizens of the United States began to insist that strict environmental laws be enacted to maintain purity of air and water. Today, environmental regulation is a distinct area of the law, and firms strive to comply with myriad statutes, regulations, and ordinances that cover the relationship between businesses and the environment.

37.2 Government regulates itself in the area of environmental protection through the National Environmental Policy Act, which requires that any project with significant federal involvement have an approved environmental impact statement prior to the commencement of any work on the project.

37.3 The Environmental Protection Agency regulates business activities as these relate to the environment. The EPA conducts environmental research, assists states and municipalities with grants and technical advice, and administers the federal pollution laws that cover businesses.

37.4 Pursuant to the Clean Air Act, all states are required to develop air quality standards that are at least as rigorous as the federal standards. The Clean Water Act sets minimum standards for water purity in a manner similar to the Clean Air Act. Superfund states that business firms that illegally dump waste material can be held responsible for three times the actual cost of the cleanup. In addition, Superfund designates specific sites, mandating that these locations be cleaned up by their owners.

37.5 Theories of law under which a private individual may bring a lawsuit against a business for creating pollution include negligence, public nuisance, private nuisance, and trespass.

37.6 Types of pollution that are of great concern to society include air pollution, water pollution, illegal dumping of waste onto land, noise pollution, pesticide control, solid waste disposal, toxic substance disposal, natural resource conservation, and acid rain.

37.7 Several factors that influence the changing global climate include the greenhouse effect, destruction of the rain forests, and destruction of the ozone layer.

37.8 Other environmental issues for which there is growing concern include biodiversity, ocean pollution, space pollution, and overpopulation.

CHAPTER THIRTY-SEVEN ASSESSMENT

MATCHING LEGAL TERMS

Match each of the numbered definitions with the correct term in the following list.

a. National Environmental-Policy Act
b. environmental impact statement
c. Environmental Protection Agency
d. Clean Air Act
e. Clean Water Act
f. Superfund
g. public and private nuisance
h. particle trespass
i. acid rain
j. greenhouse effect

1. A law that requires, prior to the commencement of any work, a declaration of the impact any major project will have on the environment. **1.** _____

2. Increasing global temperatures that result from increasing amounts of carbon dioxide released into the atmosphere. **2.** _____

3. A law that sets minimum standards for water purity. **3.** _____

4. A federal agency with responsibility for regulating business activities as they relate to the environment. **4.** _____

5. Activities that negatively affect public or private property. **5.** _____

6. A cause of action that accepts the theory that a business can illegally enter another person's property with its pollution. **6.** _____

7. A condition resulting from the discharge of pollutants into the atmosphere that creates problems for forests and crops, kills fish, and destroys the paint finishes on automobiles. **7.** _____

8. A declaration required before beginning construction of a major project that describes the impact of the project on the environment. **8.** _____

9. A law that regulates the dumping of waste onto land and designates specific sites, mandating that these locations be cleaned up by their owners. **9.** _____

10. A law that sets minimum standards for air purity. **10.** _____

TRUE/FALSE QUIZ

Indicate whether each of the following statements is true or false.

11. The United States lacks the abundance of natural resources that many other countries have. **11.** _____

12. Environmental regulation is not yet a distinct area of the law. **12.** _____

13. The Clean Air Act of 1963 deals only with pollution within the boundaries of each state. **13.** _____

14. Included in the Clean Water Act are standards for water quality that allow navigable waterways to be used for the propagation of wildlife and for recreational purposes. **14.** _____

15. Applying the provisions of Superfund has been an easy process, and it has had uniform success. **15.** _____

16. Businesses that create pollution frequently cause injury to people or damage to their property, and these businesses may be found liable by a court for the tort of negligence. **16.** _____

17. A public nuisance is created when a nuisance affects public property, such as a navigable river or a state park. **17.** _____

18. Many states recognize a cause of action for "particle trespass," accepting the theory that businesses are trespassing on another person's property with their pollution particles. **18.** _____

19. Excess noise (as measured in decibels) cannot affect human health and well-being. **19.** _____

20. Pursuant to the Toxic Substance Control Act of 1976, manufacturers are required to test chemicals thoroughly prior to introducing them into commerce. **20.** _____

MULTIPLE CHOICE QUIZ

Indicate the correct answer from the choices following each question.

21. The Army Corps of Engineers has proposed raising levees to protect from flooding. Federal law requires that the Army Corps of Engineers (a government entity) (a) examine the environmental impact of the project (b) identify the negative impacts of the project (c) propose alternatives to the project (d) all of the above. **21.** _____

22. The Clean Air Act (a) requires that states use only the federally mandated air quality standards (b) does not require any state air quality standards (c) requires that states have air quality standards at least as strict as the federal standards (d) requires that states have standards, but the standards may be more or less strict than the federal standards. **22.** ____

23. The Clean Water Act (a) allows states to regulate discharge into water by their discretion (b) requires specific types of permitting for discharges into water (c) does not have regulations about discharges into water (d) none of the above. **23.** ____

24. A plaintiff is bringing a lawsuit against a polluter for causing damage to their residential property. In this case, the plaintiff could bring a suit based on (a) negligence only (b) negligence and public nuisance (c) public nuisance only (d) negligence and private nuisance. **24.** ____

DISCUSSION QUESTIONS

Answer the following questions and discuss them in class.

25. Explain how the federal government regulates itself in the area of environmental protection.

____

____

26. Identify several types of pollution that environmental laws regulate. Which ones do you consider most important?

____

____

27. How does Superfund defray costs of cleaning polluted sites?

____

____

28. Discuss tort remedies that individuals can use against polluters.

____

____

29. The release of carbon dioxide into the atmosphere, the destruction of the rain forests, and the destruction of the ozone layer adversely affect the atmosphere. Can additional domestic relations or international treaties halt the continuing damage more effectively?

____

____

30. Despite the warnings on containers of toxic substances, injuries and accidents still occur. Should there be additional regulations, or are there other ways to protect individuals?

THINKING CRITICALLY ABOUT THE LAW

Answer the following questions, which require you to think critically about the legal principles that you learned in this chapter.

31. EPA Discuss the EPA guidelines for preparing an environmental impact statement before a project can be approved. Are they adequate?

32. Environmental Legislation What are some of the specific rules imposed by the Clean Air Act and Clean Water Act? Should these be more stringent?

33. Hazardous Substances Some substances offer both benefits and hazards. How should responsible individuals, corporations, scientists, and regulators weigh the gains and risks of these products?

34. Recycling Separating and recycling plastic, glass, paper, and metal are costly for municipalities. Should these recycling collections be continued, or should the funds be spent on other environmental objectives?

35. A Question of Ethics Most people agree that protection of the environment is an ethical issue. Society is frequently confronted with the conflict between achieving environmental goals and the economic impact on corporations, consumers, and taxpayers. How should this dilemma be addressed?

CASE QUESTIONS

Study each of the following cases. Answer the questions that follow with Yes or No.

36. Environmental Protection Agency (EPA) An electric power company was charged by the EPA with violating the Clean Air Act by allegedly polluting a small town. To solve the allegations of environmental abuse, the company simply purchased the entire town, maintaining that it needed the land to expand its plant. By buying all of the homes, however, the company believes it now avoids the potential of lawsuits by the EPA and other individuals.

a. Does buying the homes of residents and the entire town mitigate the pollution problem? **a.** _____

b. Does the agreement of the residents to sell their homes solve the potential pollution problems for those who live downwind? **b.** _____

c. Is the company acting in an ethical manner? **c.** _____

37. Private Nuisance LeatherLux Corporation, a manufacturer of upscale handbags, had been in business for 20 years and was considered a model corporate citizen. Expanding, the company developed new tanning processes that resulted in noxious fumes and odors being released into the atmosphere. The once-welcome company was no longer viewed as a good neighbor. A number of nearby residents lodged a written complaint with LeatherLux, detailing the impact of the pollution, as required by state law. LeatherLux ignored their plea. When the fumes and odors continued unabated, the residents decided to take action.

a. Do the residents have a cause of action against LeatherLux? **a.** _____

b. It is likely that a court will rule in favor of the residents? **b.** _____

c. May the residents complain to the EPA? **c.** _____

38. Toxic Substances ChemPlus Corp. manufactured DeCorr, an industrial chemical widely used to treat various metals to retard corrosion. Gianopoulos was working in a small shop immersing metal parts in a container of DeCorr when a quantity of the chemical spilled on him. After washing off the chemical, Gianopoulos developed a painful rash and blisters. A supervisor contacted ChemPlus and was told that the company had no liability for Gianopoulos's injuries because there were adequate warnings on the containers. Calls to the Environmental Protection Agency were equally unavailing because the manufacture of DeCorr was in compliance with the Toxic Substance Control Act of 1976.

a. If Gianopoulos can prove that he did not read the warning label, will he be able to recover for his injury? **a.** _____

b. Does the Toxic Substance Control Act require that all chemicals be entirely safe? **b.** _____

c. Are Gianopoulos's injuries the result of the greenhouse effect? **c.** _____

CASE ANALYSIS

Study each of the following cases carefully. Briefly state the principle of law and your decision.

39. Environmental Protection Agency Midwest Suspension and Brake supplied rebuilt brake shoes for heavy-duty trucks. During an EPA inspection, numerous emissions of asbestos were documented, and detectable amounts of asbestos were found on the shop floor. The EPA then issued a "finding" that the company had violated the Clean Air Act by releasing hazardous air pollutants. The EPA issued an administrative order (AO) requiring that (a) wastes fall into a sturdy cardboard box, instead of falling to the floor; (b) the box be securely closed and wrapped so that it would not leak when discarded; and (c) the box bear a warning label. The AO also required that the floor be vacuumed, not swept, and that the vacuum residue be tightly sealed before disposal. Finally, the AO mandated that asbestos waste be separately disposed of, without compacting, at a landfill. Midwest agreed to comply with the Clean Air Act and the AO.

Later EPA inspections found that the conditions at the Midwest facility had not been materially corrected. Asbestos-containing materials were being dropped on the shop floor, and the floor was being broom cleaned rather than vacuumed. Because Midwest had failed to correct the problems, the EPA filed suit against it in federal court, seeking injunctive relief as well as civil penalties of up to $25,000 per day for each violation. The federal district court found that Midwest had violated the Clean Air Act and ordered it to pay a $50,000 civil penalty. Midwest appealed, contending, among other things, that it did not fall under the Clean Air Act. Should Midwest be bound by the dictates of the Clean Air Act? [*United States v. Midwest Suspension and Brake,* 49 F.3d 1197 (6th Cir. 1994)]

Principle of Law:

____

____

Decision:

____

____

40. Environment/Wildlife Bronx Reptiles Inc. imported live animals, including reptiles, into the country approximately twice per week. Edelman, the owner, knew of the International Air Transport Association guidelines for importing wildlife–how specific species should be shipped and the container requirements. Yet over the years, his company has been cited, and civil fines had been paid for numerous violations. Dead animals included iguanas and boa constrictors from Colombia and small mammals from Egypt. When frogs from the Solomon Islands were found dead, Bronx Reptiles was convicted of a misdemeanor for violating a statute that made it illegal to "knowingly caus(e) a 'wild animal' to be transported to the U.S. under inhumane or unhealthful conditions." Edelman countered that because frogs were reptiles, and not wild animals, they were not covered by the statute. The judge ruled that frogs are, in fact, amphibians and, in any event, fall within the statutory proscription. Given Edelman's belief that the statute did not apply to frogs, is it possible to prove that

Edelman "knowingly" caused the inhumane conditions? *United States of America v. Bronx Reptiles, Inc.,* 26 F.Supp.2d 481 (EDNY 1998).]

Principle of Law:

Decision:

41. National Environmental Policy Act The Forest Service planned extensive timber cutting in a part of the Green Mountain National Forest but did not prepare an environmental impact statement. A coalition of conservation organizations and environmentalists, believing that the action would have potential negative impact on black bears, whose habitat would be disturbed, and would endanger the neotropical bird population, filed a lawsuit to compel the Forest Service to prepare the EIS. The district court found that the Forest Service had failed to consider all relevant factors when determining the environmental significance of its proposed action and was directed to prepare a site-specific EIS and enjoined from further timber harvesting and road building until completion of the EIS. Is it likely that the court will rule in favor of the coalition? [*National Audubon v. Hoffman,* 917 F. Supp. 280 (D. Vt. 1995)]

Principle of Law:

Decision:

LEGAL RESEARCH

Complete the following activities. Share your findings with the class.

42. Working in Teams In teams of three or four, check labels on various products such as chemicals, cleansers, insecticides, and herbicides. Look for warnings and EPA information. Discuss your findings.

43. Using Technology Using the Internet and search engines, investigate the Environmental Protection Agency. In what types of activities is this federal agency involved?

chapter 38 Health Care Law

LEARNING OUTCOMES

After studying this chapter and completing the assessment, you will be able to

38.1 Identify some of the major legal areas that affect health care.

38.2 Explain the purpose of an advance directive and discuss the two most common types.

38.3 Describe the different types of medical insurance that are commonly available to individuals and employers.

38.4 Describe six types of health-related insurance benefits typically available to employees.

38.5 Explain how state and federal regulation affects access to health insurance.

38.6 Explain the major provisions of the privacy rule in the Health Insurance Portability and Accountability Act of 1996.

terms

LEGAL

- health care law
- advance directive
- living will
- durable power of attorney for health care
- community-based insurance
- deductible
- major medical
- health maintenance organization (HMO)
- Medicare
- Medicaid
- cafeteria plans
- Consolidated Omnibus Budget Reconciliation Act of 1985 (COBRA)
- disability insurance
- single payer system
- Health Insurance Portability and Accountability Act of 1996 (HIPAA)

HEALTH CARE LAW

"If compassion is so good for us, why don't we train our health care providers in compassion so that they can do what they're supposed to do, which is to transform suffering?"

Joan Halifax, American Zen Buddhist teacher, author, and hospice caregiver

peterspiro/iStock/360/Getty Images

38.1 HEALTH CARE LAW

Health care law is the federal, state, and local statutes, rules, regulations, and judicial decisions that govern the legal relationships of patients, physicians and other medical professionals, and health care insurers to one another. Some areas of law previously covered in this text that impact health care are:

health care law
The federal, state, and local statutes, rules, regulations, and judicial decisions that govern the legal relationships of patients, physicians and other medical professionals, and health care insurers to one other.

- *Administrative law.* There are numerous federal, state, and local administrative agencies that oversee and administer to the manner in which health care is delivered by its providers, and the ways in which health care services are covered by insurers (see Chapter 6).
- *Contract law.* When a patient consults with a physician, the two parties are entering into a legally binding contract. Similarly, when an individual or an employer procures an insurance policy covering costs associated with medical treatments, a contract is also created. All of the standard rules of contract law are then applied to these agreements (see Chapters 7-15).
- *Medical malpractice.* When a physician or other health care provider acts negligently, the patient may sue for the tort of malpractice (see Chapter 35).

This chapter will address other legal issues that a patient or other person may encounter when facing decisions regarding their health. The chapter also will provide an explanation of several federal statutes that affect a patient—either with respect to procuring health care from a provider or procuring medical and related forms of coverage from an insurance carrier.

EXAMPLE 38.1

- Experiencing flu-like symptoms, Kelsey visited her physician for a checkup. The physician prescribed a drug that had not been adequately tested according to standards prescribed by the Food and Drug Administration (FDA), a federal administrative agency. When Kelsey developed an allergic reaction to the drug, she sued her physician for both breach of contract and medical malpractice. The pharmaceutical company that produced the drug was subject to penalties from the FDA.

38.2 ADVANCE DIRECTIVES

Advancing medical technology can prolong life even when there is little chance of recovery. Many are opposed to their and their loved ones' lives being prolonged by artificial life support. To address these important matters, states have enacted statutes that allow individuals to execute a device, known as an **advance directive**, which documents their expressed wishes regarding their health care in the event that they become incapacitated or permanently unconscious without hope of recovery. While the requirements for drafting and executing valid advance directives vary greatly from state to state, in general, the individual must demonstrate that they are competent and must sign the advance directive in the presence of a specified number of witnesses. The advance directive only takes effect when the individual becomes incapable of making treatment decisions which, in some states, must be confirmed by at least two licensed physicians. An advance directive does not expire, but becomes invalid only when the individual changes it or issues a replacement advance directive.

advance directive
A document that expresses an individual's wishes regarding their health care in the event that they become incapacitated or permanently unconscious without hope of recovery.

EXAMPLE 38.2

▶ Rike, a resident of Arizona, desired to prepare an advance directive that would take effect in the event he became incapacitated due to accident or illness. He researched carefully the laws of the state of Arizona and consulted an attorney licensed to practice law in that state before duly signing the directive in the presence of witnesses.

It should be noted that, in most cases, emergency medical personnel, including first responders, paramedics, and other ambulance crew, are not permitted to honor advance directives. These specially trained individuals are required to perform all medical treatments necessary to stabilize an individual so that such person may be transferred to a hospital. Physicians at the hospital can then implement the instructions stated in the advance directive.

EXAMPLE 38.3

▶ Lieber, a 92-year-old suffering from terminal cancer, sustained a massive heart attack while in his home and ceased breathing for several minutes. When emergency responders arrived, Lieber's daughter requested that they not attempt to resuscitate him, in accordance with explicit instructions Lieber had written in his advance directive. The responders, however, took all appropriate measures to save Lieber and transported him to a nearby hospital.

Emergency medical personnel, including first responders, paramedics, and other ambulance crew, are not permitted to honor advance directives and are required to perform all medical treatments necessary to stabilize an individual.
Juice Images/Glow Images

The two most commonly used advance directives are the living will and the durable power of attorney for health care.

LIVING WILLS

A living will is a document in which a person directs their physician and/or health proxy to forgo certain extraordinary (heroic) medical procedures if, for example, the person is dying or permanently unconscious. Because statutes regarding advance directives vary from state to state, a living will must be made following the precise requirements of the applicable state statute in order to be considered valid. The purpose of a valid living will is to permit a terminally ill patient to live or die with dignity and to protect the physician or hospital from liability for sustaining or withdrawing life support. Most states now have specific requirements regarding decisions about life-sustaining medical treatments.

living will
A document in which a person directs their physician and/or health proxy to forgo certain extraordinary medical procedures if the person is dying or permanently unconscious.

DURABLE POWER OF ATTORNEY FOR HEALTH CARE

A durable power of attorney for health care (sometimes referred to as a health care proxy) is a document that appoints an individual as an agent with authority to make health care decisions on behalf of the principal in the event that the principal becomes incompetent. The principal should take extraordinary care to appoint a capable and trusted individual as their attorney in fact; an agent must protect the principal's best interests and not abuse their powers (see Chapter 19). In the event that the principal regains the ability to make decisions, the agent may no longer act on the principal's behalf.

durable power of attorney for health care
A document that appoints an individual as an agent with authority to make health care decisions on behalf of the principal in the event that the principal becomes incompetent.

MATTERS COVERED BY ADVANCE DIRECTIVES

Taken together, the living will and the durable power of attorney provide individuals with the opportunity to articulate their instructions about their medical care in the event that they develop a terminal medical condition that renders them permanently unconscious. Depending upon the law of the particular state where the individual resides, the living will and the durable power of attorney can guide their agent's decisions regarding health care treatment.

Examples of matters that may be addressed in the living will, and administered to by the agent pursuant to a durable power of attorney, are:

- *Autopsy.* An individual may request that, in the event of their death, an autopsy either be performed or not be performed. It must be noted that under the laws of all states, there are specific circumstances under which an autopsy must be performed, irrespective of an individual's wishes.
- *Burial and cremation.* An individual may specify the manner of the disposition of their remains–including burial, pursuant to a specific spiritual service, or *cremation,* the use of high-temperature burning in order to reduce the remains to chemical compounds.
- *Organ donation.* Depending upon state law, an individual may state their wishes regarding donating organs, or even refusing to donate organs.

38.3 TYPES OF MEDICAL INSURANCE

Because of the soaring costs associated with health care, many individuals have a strong desire to protect themselves against severe financial loss that may result from a serious illness or injury. These individuals purchase, or arrange to have their employers purchase, medical insurance to protect themselves. The relationship between the individual or their employer, on the one hand, and the insurance company, on the other hand, is governed by both contract law and applicable federal, state, and local laws.

Individuals who have elected not to be covered by medical insurance or who have been unable to afford such insurance have run serious risk of financial ruin. Uninsured individuals will almost certainly have their costly medical bills referred to a collection agency, and the resultant judgments that might be entered against them may result in bankruptcy (see Chapter 21).

The following sections will discuss the most common of the numerous forms of medical insurance available to individuals and employers.

COMMUNITY-BASED INSURANCE

community-based insurance
Medical insurance programs provided by Blue Cross and Blue Shield.

The Blue Cross Blue Shield Association is an independent, not-for-profit organization that serves diverse communities by providing medical insurance. The organization was developed between hospitals and teachers in Dallas, Texas, in 1929. The community-based insurance programs provided by Blue Cross and Blue Shield vary greatly in different communities because of differing state laws regulating them.

While Blue Cross and Blue Shield are two separate legal entities providing insurance benefits, in general they coordinate their functions as follows:

deductible
A set amount of money for medical expenses for which the patient is responsible.

- *Blue Cross*–covers the individual's hospital expenses. Patients generally pay a deductible, that is, a set amount of money for which the patient is responsible. The patient then pays an additional portion, such as 20 percent, of the costs in excess of the deductible.
- *Blue Shield*–covers the individual's costs for surgery and other related medical procedures. The organization also serves as a reimbursement go-between for the physician.

EXAMPLE 38.4

Katulski experienced severe abdominal discomfort and, after visiting his family physician, was admitted to his local hospital for an appendectomy (removal of his appendix). His medical insurance plan with Blue Cross covered his doctor and hospital fees, and his medical insurance plan with Blue Shield covered the fees charged by his surgeon for the operation.

MAJOR MEDICAL

major medical
A form of health insurance that covers serious illnesses and lengthy hospitalizations, which generally takes effect after other benefits are exhausted.

Major medical health insurance covers serious illnesses and lengthy hospitalizations. This type of coverage serves as a kind of umbrella policy, which generally takes effect after Blue Cross, Blue Shield, and other related insurance benefits are exhausted. At times, copays or coinsurance monies are paid by the patient.

COMMERCIAL INSURANCE

This type of medical insurance is very similar to community based, as discussed earlier. However, patients and employers purchase these insurance policies from private, often for-profit, companies.

SELF-INSURANCE

When medical insurance coverage is provided by an employer, in some cases, the employer undertakes the risk itself, paying employees' medical expenses out of its own funds. Obviously, this risk can only be justified if the employer has sufficient financial resources to cover a large number of employees who are generally in better health than the overall population.

health maintenance organization (HMO)
An organization that provides health insurance by coordinating services with specific doctors, hospitals, and other health care providers.

HEALTH MAINTENANCE ORGANIZATION

A health maintenance organization (HMO) is an organization that provides health insurance by coordinating services with specific doctors, hospitals, and other health care providers. If an employer with 25 or more employees offers traditional health care insurance, under the *Health Maintenance Organization Act of 1973,* the employer is required to offer HMO plans that are federally certified to its employees.

Under an HMO plan, doctors and other health care providers agree by contract to render medical services in accordance with strict guidelines established by the HMO. While some of these guidelines are quite restrictive, participating doctors and others agree to adhere to them in order to increase the number of patients who utilize their services.

When a patient enrolls in an HMO plan, in general, they select a participating primary care physician, who tends to the patient's routine health care. Primary care physicians are usually general practitioners, family doctors, internists, or pediatricians. If a patient needs to see a specialist, they frequently need to obtain a referral. Many times, a patient pays a copay of approximately $20 to their primary care physician and, at times, a second opinion is required. When HMO coverage is combined with Blue Cross and Blue Shield insurance coverage, it is referred to as a *point of service* (POS) plan.

EXAMPLE 38.5

▶ Kayser, a semiprofessional football player, learned that he required knee replacement surgery for injuries that he had sustained while playing. Because Kayser has a POS medical insurance plan, he has the option of either using an in-network surgeon, who is a participant in his HMO, or using a specialist who is highly recommended by his cousin but who is located in a distant city. Although the latter option will be much more costly, because Kayser is financially secure, he is choosing to follow his cousin's recommendation.

MEDICARE

Medicare
A federal program that pays for specified health care expenses for individuals who are 65 years of age or older.

Medicare is a federal program that pays for specified health care expenses for individuals who are 65 years of age or older. Established in 1965 and administered to by the Department of Health and Human Services, Medicare is also available to younger persons with disabilities and certain other individuals. Medicare is divided into four parts: Part A covers hospital bills, Part B covers both physicians' fees and bills for medically necessary medical devices, Part C provides an option to choose from a variety of health care plans, and Part D covers prescription drugs. The so-called donut hole refers to the difference among the expenses covered in Parts A, B, and C, and the lower limit in catastrophic prescription drug coverage under Part D. Patients often elect to purchase *medigap* supplemental insurance, covering the difference between the expenses reimbursed by Medicare and the total amount charged.

Under Medicare, physicians are paid a scheduled fee, depending upon the specific service rendered. Physicians can require either that the patients pay themselves and subsequently be reimbursed by the federal government or, alternatively, can submit billing materials directly to the government themselves.

While persons enrolled in Medicare at times must still pay copayments and deductibles, it is nonetheless an important social program for many individuals who would otherwise have little or no health care coverage.

Approximately 15 percent of the U.S. population is covered under Medicare.

Medicaid
A federal health care program for certain individuals and families with low incomes.

MEDICAID

Medicaid is a federal health care program for certain individuals and families with low incomes. While Medicaid is funded jointly by both the federal and states' governments, it is administered to by the states. Medicaid, like Medicare, was established in 1965.

Approximately 17 percent of the U.S. population is covered under Medicaid.

38.4 HEALTH-RELATED EMPLOYEE BENEFITS

cafeteria plans
A particular benefit or package of benefits selected by an employee from a specific amount of money allocated for this purpose.

As a way of attracting and retaining more productive employees, employers have traditionally offered their workers benefit packages. These packages often include vacation time, personal and sick days, pensions and other forms of retirement benefits, child care, leaves of absences, tuition remission, legal insurance, and even employee discounts. Because many of these benefits are quite costly, often employers allocate a specific amount of money for each of its employees, who then select the particular benefit or package of benefits that best suits their individual needs. These arrangements are referred to as cafeteria plans, so-named because of their similarity to selecting different foods items in a cafeteria.

This section will address some of the more common health-related benefits offered by employers.

Consolidated Omnibus Budget Reconciliation Act of 1985 (COBRA)
A federal statute that provides employees and their families who lose health benefits the right to elect to continue group health benefits provided by their group health plan for specified limited periods of time.

MEDICAL INSURANCE

Described in the previous section, this benefit might include a community-based plan, major medical, commercial insurance, self-insurance, or an HMO plan. The Consolidated Omnibus Budget Reconciliation Act of 1985 (COBRA) provides employees and their families who lose employment health benefits the right to elect to continue group health benefits provided by their group health plan for specified, limited periods of time. This right is granted only under specific circumstances, such as voluntary or involuntary job loss, reduction in the hours worked, transition between jobs, death, divorce, and so on. Employees may be required to pay the entire premium for coverage up to 102 percent of the cost to the plan. For additional information about COBRA, visit http://www.dol.gov/dol/topic/health-plans/cobra.htm.

EXAMPLE 38.6

After being employed for eight years as a salesperson in a regional department store, Mroz was terminated from her position due to cutbacks in the workforce. While employed, Mroz had been covered by an HMO medical insurance plan paid for by her employer. Because Mroz could not find another position for several weeks, she elected to exercise her rights under COBRA, and she will continue to be covered under her former employer's group policy. She will, however, now be required to pay the entire premium for continuing her medical insurance.

FAMILY PLANS

In addition to providing medical insurance coverage for its employees, an employer may elect to procure a family plan by providing coverage for an employee's spouse, children, and other dependents. Frequently, coverage between two working spouses who are both covered is coordinated.

An employer may elect to procure a family plan by providing coverage for an employee's spouse, children, and other dependents.

disability insurance
Insurance coverage that provides supplementary income to make up for lost wages due to an illness or accident that prevents an employee from working at their regular employment.

DISABILITY INSURANCE

Disability insurance is coverage that provides supplementary income to make up for lost wages due to an illness or accident that prevents an employee from working at their regular employment. The disability may be either long term or short term and may be either permanent or temporary. Benefits are usually provided on a monthly basis so as to allow the employee to maintain their standard of living, while continuing to pay their customary expenses. At times, this form of health insurance is required by the state.

DENTAL INSURANCE

Dental insurance usually covers procedures such as cleanings, fillings, root canals, and so on, up to a specified dollar limit of usually about $1,000. Major surgery is generally covered under other forms of medical insurance, rather than dental insurance.

VISION INSURANCE

Vision insurance usually covers eye examinations, corrective

Vision insurance covers eye examinations, corrective lenses, and contact lenses.
P. Ughetto/PhotoAlto

lenses, and contact lenses. Employees are covered for each of these up to a specified dollar amount. As is true for dental insurance, major eye surgery is covered under other forms of medical insurance, rather than vision insurance.

EXAMPLE 38.7

Hetro had vision insurance coverage included in her employee benefit package. When she needed new corrective lenses due to a change in her eyesight, she visited her local eyeglass retailer. Because the designer frames Hetro selected were far more costly than her insurance would cover, Hetro elected to pay the difference out of her own funds.

GROUP LIFE INSURANCE

Group life insurance covers employees' beneficiaries in the event of loss of life. At times, the coverage extends to other events, such as critical or terminal illnesses. Premiums for group life insurance are relatively inexpensive, and coverage is usually for one or two times the employee's salary. Approximately 95 percent of employees with cafeteria benefits select group life insurance coverage as part of their employee benefits package.

38.5 STATE AND FEDERAL REGULATION OF HEALTH CARE INSURANCE

Because of the relatively high cost of health care in the United States, individuals need health insurance to access medical care, particularly procedures, surgery, and hospital services. Legal regulation at both the state and federal level has sought to guarantee individuals the ability to purchase health insurance and thus be able to access health care. One large issue with health insurance remains the high cost of premiums and the ability of most individuals to afford health insurance. However, there is a divide in the most effective way to achieve the goal of universal access to affordable health insurance and whether the federal government should be involved in the regulation at all.

Private health insurance companies are licensed by individual states to operate, thus requiring that insurance companies seeking to operate in multiple states must be licensed separately in each state. One proposal to nationally give more individuals health insurance with affordable premiums is to eliminate the need for insurance companies to be separately licensed in each state and to allow them to operate in multiple states, or even nationally, with one license. The theory is that this opening of multistate markets would increase competition among insurers and force lower costs.

Another measure to give everyone access to health care is to have a universal health care system, which often centers on a single, government insurer available to all individuals. This single payer system has been proposed in several states but not enacted. The single payer system as a federal system has been enacted in other countries, but none of the current proposals at the federal level include a single payer system.

single payer system
A health system paid for and administered by one government source.

Federal law (the *Patient Protection and Affordable Care Act of 2010*) has centered on allowing individuals access to health insurance that is made affordable either by government subsidies or by tax credits to reduce the financial burden of paying health insurance premiums. Other regulatory methods to reduce costs include such requirements as mandates that all individuals purchase insurance to subsidize the risk for health insurers, regulation of health care providers to ensure lower costs in the providing of health care, and requirements that businesses of a certain size provide health insurance benefits to employees. The debate is ongoing, resulting in a regulation system that is evolving.

For additional information regarding the Affordable Care Act, visit http://www.healthcare.gov/law/index.xhtml.

38.6 THE HEALTH INSURANCE PORTABILITY AND ACCOUNTABILITY ACT OF 1996 PRIVACY RULE

The Health Insurance Portability and Accountability Act of 1996 (HIPAA) is a federal statute that provides an individual with rights over their health information and establishes limits on who is permitted to view and receive health information.

Health Insurance Portability and Accountability Act of 1996 (HIPAA)
A federal statute that provides an individual with rights over their health information and establishes limits on who is permitted to view and receive health information.

HIPAA contains several important provisions relating to patients' privacy. Individuals have the right to view and receive a copy of their medical records and to have such corrected if these contain errors. Unless they give permission, their medical information may be used and shared only for certain purposes, and they must receive a report as to why and to whom medical information was shared. Such information includes conversations their doctor has had about their treatment with nurses and other health care professionals, information contained in their health insurer's computer system, and billing information.

Medical information may be shared without patients' authorization for the purpose of treating these patients; coordinating care with other providers; arranging for payments of fees to providers; protecting public health; and, in select situations, reporting to the police and other authorities. It may also be shared with identified members of family, relatives, friends, and others who are involved with patients' health or bills.

Clinics, doctors, HMOs, hospitals, insurance companies, Medicaid, Medicare, nurses, nursing homes, pharmacies, and numerous other individuals and organizations are subject to the provisions of HIPAA. Individuals who believe their HIPAA rights were violated may file complaints with their health provider, their insurance company, and/or the federal government.

For additional information regarding the privacy provisions of HIPAA, visit http://www.hhs.gov/ocr/privacy/index.xhtml.

Pharmacies and numerous other individuals and organizations are subject to the provisions of the Health Insurance Portability and Accountability Act of 1996 (HIPAA).
Tom Merton/Getty Images

EXAMPLE 38.8

Dolan was a customer in a convenience store when a would-be robber entered the store. During a scuffle between the perpetrator and the store clerk, the perpetrator's pistol was fired, and the bullet struck Dolan in the leg. Upon Dolan's admission to the hospital where he was to be treated, without Dolan's knowledge, the police were notified of his condition. Employees of the hospital acted appropriately and did not violate HIPAA when they notified the authorities of Dolan's medical condition.

CHAPTER SUMMARY

38.1 Some of the major legal areas that affect health care include administrative law, breach of contract, and medical malpractice.

38.2 The purpose of an advance directive is to document individuals' expressed wishes regarding their health care in the event that they become incapacitated or permanently unconscious without hope of recovery. The two most common types of advance directives are (a) the living will, a document in which a person directs their physician and/or health proxy to forgo certain extraordinary medical procedures if, for example, the person is dying or permanently unconscious; and (b) the durable power of attorney for health care, a document that appoints an individual as an agent with authority to make health care decisions on behalf of the principal in the event that the patient becomes incompetent.

38.3 Different types of medical insurance that are commonly available to individuals and employers are community-based insurance, major medical, commercial insurance, self-insurance, HMOs, Medicare, and Medicaid.

38.4 Six types of health-related insurance benefits typically available to employees are (a) medical insurance, (b) family plans, (c) disability insurance, (d) dental insurance, (e) vision insurance, and (f) group life insurance.

38.5 Both state and federal laws and regulations attempt to ensure that individuals have access to affordable health insurance. Proposals have included allowing health insurers to sell insurance nationwide under one license to increase competition, mandating that all individuals purchase insurance to spread the risk of insuring medical care, and subsidizing premium costs.

38.6 Under the federal statute, HIPAA, individuals have the right to view and receive a copy of their medical records and to have such corrected if these contain errors. Unless they give permission, their medical information may be used and shared only for certain purposes, and they must receive a report as to why and to whom medical information was shared. Medical information may be shared without patients' authorization for the purpose of treating these patients; coordinating care with other providers; arranging for payments of fees to providers; protecting public health; and, in select situations, reporting to the police and other authorities. It may also be shared with identified members of family, relatives, friends, and others who are involved with patients' health or bills. Clinics, doctors, HMOs, hospitals, insurance companies, Medicaid, Medicare, nurses, nursing homes, pharmacies, and numerous other individuals and organizations are subject to the provisions of HIPAA.

CHAPTER THIRTY-EIGHT ASSESSMENT

MATCHING LEGAL TERMS

Match each of the numbered definitions with the correct term in the list below.

a. advance directive
b. COBRA
c. disability insurance
d. durable power of attorney for health care
e. HIPAA
f. living will
g. major medical
h. Medicaid
i. Medicare
j. single payer system

1. A federal statute that provides employees and their families who lose health benefits the right to elect to continue group health benefits provided by their group health plan for specified limited periods of time. **1.** ____

2. A federal statute that provides an individual with rights over their health information and establishes limits on who is permitted to view and receive health information. **2.** ____

3. A federal program that pays for specified health care expenses for individuals who are 65 years of age or older. **3.** ____

4. A document in which a person directs their physician and/or health proxy to forgo certain extraordinary medical procedures if the person is dying or permanently unconscious. **4.** ____

5. A document that expresses an individual's wishes regarding their health care in the event that they become incapacitated or permanently unconscious without hope of recovery. **5.** ____

6. A health system paid for and administered by one government source. **6.** ____

7. A federal health care program for certain individuals and families with low incomes. **7.** ____

8. Insurance coverage that provides supplementary income to make up for lost wages due to an illness or accident that prevents an employee from working at their regular employment. **8.** ____

9. A document that appoints an individual as an agent with authority to make health care decisions on behalf of the principal in the event that the principal becomes incompetent. **9.** ____

10. A form of health insurance that covers serious illnesses and lengthy hospitalizations, which generally takes effect after other benefits are exhausted. **10.** ____

TRUE/FALSE QUIZ

Indicate whether each of the following statements is true or false.

11. When a patient consults with a physician, the two parties are entering into a legally binding contract. **11.** _____

12. When a physician or other health care provider acts negligently, the patient may sue for the tort of slander. **12.** _____

13. The requirements for drafting and executing valid advance directives are governed by federal, and not state, laws. **13.** _____

14. An individual drafting an advance directive must demonstrate that they are competent and must sign the document in the presence of a specified number of witnesses. **14.** _____

15. In most cases, emergency medical personnel, including first responders, paramedics, and other ambulance crew, are not permitted to honor advance directives. **15.** _____

16. The two most commonly used advance directives are the last will and testament and the durable power of attorney for health care. **16.** _____

17. An advance directive only takes effect when the individual becomes incapable of making treatment decisions. **17.** _____

18. An advance directive automatically expires after a period of five years has elapsed. **18.** _____

19. Blue Cross covers an individual's costs for surgery and other related medical procedures. **19.** _____

20. Under federal law, an employer may not self-insure employees for costs associated with hospital stays. **20.** _____

21. About 40 percent of the U.S. population is covered under Medicare. **21.** _____

22. Health insurance companies must be licensed by the federal government. **22.** _____

23. The United States currently has a single payer system to provide health insurance to all individuals. **23.** _____

24. Pursuant to the provisions of HIPAA, patients must receive a report as to why and to whom medical information was shared. **24.** _____

25. Because they are governmental programs, both Medicaid and Medicare are exempt from the privacy provisions of HIPAA. **25.** _____

MULTIPLE CHOICE QUIZ

Indicate the correct answer from the choices following each question.

26. A is a 75-year-old person who would like to ensure that a trusted person makes health care decisions on their behalf if and when they become unable to do so. The best legal document for this purpose is (a) a living will (b) a last will and testament (c) a durable power of attorney (d) a nondurable power of attorney. **26.** _____

27. A is a 75-year-old person who knows exactly what care they want, particularly at the end of life, and wants to make sure their wishes are followed. The best legal document for this purpose is (a) a living will (b) a last will and testament (c) a durable power of attorney (d) a nondurable power of attorney. **27.** _____

28. B has a family history of diabetes, a chronic illness affecting the ability to produce insulin. B does not have insurance with their current employer. Other members of the family have had to leave employment as a result of the illness. B wants to only get insurance needed due to cost. What type of insurance would you recommend that B obtain? (a) Disability only (b) Disability and medical (c) Disability, medical, and dental (d) Disability, medical, dental, and vision **28.** _____

29. C is a patient with a rare heart condition being treated by Dr. D. Dr. D would like to share the patient records. Which of the following would be allowed under the Health Insurance Portability and Accountability Act of 1996 privacy rule without patient consent? (a) Share information with fellow researchers of similar heart conditions. (b) Share information with C's primary care physician. (c) Share information with a and b. (d) None of these options **29.** _____

DISCUSSION QUESTIONS

Answer the following questions and discuss them in class.

30. Distinguish between the two most commonly used advance directives—the living will and the durable power of attorney for health care.

____

____

31. Identify three examples of matters that may be addressed in the living will and administered to by the patient's agent pursuant to a durable power of attorney.

____

____

32. List the most common of the numerous forms of medical insurance available to individuals and employers.

33. List six types of health-related insurance benefits typically available to employees.

34. Identify two ways that regulators propose to make health insurance more affordable.

35. Identify the major provisions of the privacy rule in the HIPAA.

THINKING CRITICALLY ABOUT THE LAW

Answer the following questions, which require you to think critically about the legal principles that you learned in this chapter.

36. Advance Directives Given that the requirements for drafting and executing valid advance directives vary so greatly from state to state, should these be regulated by the federal government in order to promote consistency?

37. Health-Related Employee Benefits What are some ways in which employers can keep the costs of providing medical insurance for employees down without eliminating this benefit?

38. Family Plans Is it fair that some employees receive health insurance benefits covering their families, while other employees, who do not have families, do not receive this benefit?

39. Health Insurance Regulation Should the current state regulation of health insurance companies be changed to a federal licensing system to allow health insurance companies to operate across state lines?

____

____

40. A Question of Ethics Is it ethical for an attorney in fact to make health care decisions for a principal based on the attorney in fact's own personal beliefs and values, regardless of the principal's views?

____

____

CASE QUESTIONS

Study each of the cases below. Answer the questions that follow with Yes or No.

41. Advance Directives Babinski prepared and duly executed a living will in which he gave explicit instructions not to be resuscitated in the event he became incapacitated or permanently unconscious without hope of recovery. Twelve years later, Babinski had a change of heart and decided that he wished to receive all appropriate treatment in such circumstances.

a. Is Babinski's living will an example of an advance directive? **a.** _____

b. Is Babinski's living will an example of a durable power of attorney for health care? **b.** _____

c. Can Babinski change his living will? **c.** _____

d. Would Babinski's living will have expired on its own by the time the 12 years had elapsed? **d.** _____

42. Health-Related Employee Benefits Dokken was employed by a company that provided both HMO and dental insurance coverage. While riding his motorcycle, Dokken had an accident in which he sustained serious injury to his jaw, causing him to lose several teeth and requiring reconstructive surgery.

a. Will Dokken's health-related expenses be covered under his HMO policy? **a.** _____

b. Will Dokken's reconstructive surgery be covered under his dental insurance? **b.** _____

c. If the accident is Dokken's fault, will he still have the right to maintain privacy under HIPAA? **c.** _____

43. Medicare Slaff, a 73-year-old retiree, was covered under Medicare for medical expenses. When Slaff experienced difficulty breathing, she visited her family doctor for assistance. Her family doctor referred her to a pulmonologist, a specialist in respiratory illnesses, who prescribed a drug to address the medical condition.

a. Can Slaff receive benefits under Medicare Part A to cover the fee charged by her general practitioner? **a.** _____

b. Can Slaff receive benefits under Medicare Part B to cover the fee charged by her pulmonologist? **b.** _____

c. Can Slaff receive benefits under Medicare Part D to cover the cost of the drug prescribed by her pulmonologist? **c.** _____

d. Is Slaff's pharmacist required to adhere to the privacy provisions included in HIPAA? **d.** _____

CASE ANALYSIS

Study each of the following cases carefully. Briefly state the principle of law and your decision.

44. Advance Directives Quinlan, a 22-year-old female, specifically made known her wish not to have her life maintained indefinitely by the use of a breathing machine. After an apparent overdose of alcohol and drugs, Quinlan fell into a coma, suffering severe brain damage. Upon admission to the hospital, she was attached to a respirator, but unfortunately entered into a persistent vegetative state. After several months, Quinlan's family requested that she be removed from the respirator and allowed to die. Her physicians, however, determining that she was not in a terminal condition, were reluctant to discontinue her life support. Will Quinlan's family be successful in their efforts to have Quinlan removed from the respirator? [*In re Quinlan,* 70 N.J. 10, 355 A.2 d 647 (1976)].

Principle of Law:

____

____

Decision:

____

____

45. Community-Based Insurance For more than 20 years, Harlick, a 38-year-old female, suffered from anorexia nervosa, an eating disorder. She was covered by her employer's health insurance plan through Blue Shield, and was treated for the disorder through this plan. Her doctors then advised her that she required residential treatment. Harlick and her doctors ultimately determined that none of the in-network facilities suggested by Blue Shield could provide effective treatment, so she registered at a residential treatment facility that specialized in eating disorders. While Blue Shield paid for the first 11 days of treatment, it then refused to pay for the rest of her treatment. Must Blue Shield pay for Harlick's treatment? [*Harlick v. Blue Shield of California,* 686 F.3 d 699 (2012)].

Principle of Law:

____

____

Decision:

____

____

46. Medicare The Department of Health and Human Services (HHS) denied Medicare coverage for the BIO-1000, a piece of durable medical equipment used to treat osteoarthritis of the knee (a degeneration of cartilage and the underlying bone). In a series of decisions, HHS ruled that this equipment had not been shown to be reasonable and necessary for treatment of this disorder. The supplier of the device, International Rehabilitative Sciences Inc., sued, arguing that the decisions were arbitrary, capricious, and not supported by substantial evidence. Will the supplier be successful in its lawsuit? [*International Rehabilitative Sciences Inc. DBA RS v. Sebelius,* 688 F.3 d 994 (2012)].

Principle of Law:

____

____

Decision:

____

____

LEGAL RESEARCH

Complete the following activities. Share your findings with the class.

47. Working in Teams In teams of three or four, interview doctors, nurses, pharmacists, and other individuals who are employed by clinics, hospitals, and insurance companies. Ask them to provide examples of individuals and organizations that have requested medical information about clients and whether and under what circumstances such information was provided.

____

____

48. Using Technology Using the Internet and search engines, investigate the types of health-related insurance benefits that are available to employees of local and regional employers.

____

____

APPENDIX
THE CONSTITUTION OF THE UNITED STATES

We the People of the United States, in Order to form a more perfect Union, establish Justice, insure domestic Tranquility, provide for the common defence, promote the general Welfare, and secure the Blessings of Liberty to ourselves and our Posterity, do ordain and establish this Constitution for the United States of America.

ARTICLE I

SECTION 1

All legislative Powers herein granted shall be vested in a Congress of the United States, which shall consist of a Senate and House of Representatives.

SECTION 2

The House of Representatives shall be composed of Members chosen every second Year by the People of the several States, and the Electors in each State shall have the Qualifications requisite for Electors of the most numerous Branch of the State Legislature.

No Person shall be a Representative who shall not have attained to the Age of twenty five Years, and been seven Years a Citizen of the United States, and who shall not, when elected, be an Inhabitant of that State in which he shall be chosen.

Representatives and direct Taxes shall be apportioned among the several States which may be included within this Union, according to their respective Numbers, which shall be determined by adding to the whole Number of free Persons, including those bound to Service for a Term of Years, and excluding Indians not taxed, three fifths of all other Persons. The actual Enumeration shall be made within three Years after the first Meeting of the Congress of the United States, and within every subsequent Term of ten Years, in such Manner as they shall by Law direct. The Number of Representatives shall not exceed one for every thirty Thousand, but each State shall have at Least one Representative; and until such enumeration shall be made, the State of New Hampshire shall be entitled to chuse three, Massachusetts eight, Rhode-Island and Providence Plantations one, Connecticut five, New-York six, New Jersey four, Pennsylvania eight, Delaware one, Maryland six, Virginia ten, North Carolina five, South Carolina five, and Georgia three.

When vacancies happen in the Representation from any State, the Executive Authority thereof shall issue Writs of Election to fill such Vacancies.

The House of Representatives shall chuse their Speaker and other Officers; and shall have the sole Power of Impeachment.

SECTION 3

The Senate of the United States shall be composed of two Senators from each State, chosen by the Legislature thereof for six Years; and each Senator shall have one Vote.

Immediately after they shall be assembled in Consequence of the first Election, they shall be divided as equally as may be into three Classes. The Seats of the Senators of the first Class shall be vacated at the Expiration of the second Year, of the second Class at the Expiration of the fourth Year, and of the third Class at the Expiration of the sixth Year, so that one third may be chosen every second Year; and if Vacancies happen by Resignation, or otherwise, during the Recess of the Legislature of any State, the Executive thereof may make temporary Appointments until the next Meeting of the Legislature, which shall then fill such Vacancies.

No Person shall be a Senator who shall not have attained to the Age of thirty Years, and been nine Years a Citizen of the United States, and who shall not, when elected, be an Inhabitant of that State for which he shall be chosen.

The Vice President of the United States shall be President of the Senate, but shall have no Vote, unless they be equally divided.

The Senate shall chuse their other Officers, and also a President pro tempore, in the Absence of the Vice President, or when he shall exercise the Office of President of the United States.

The Senate shall have the sole Power to try all Impeachments. When sitting for that Purpose, they shall be on Oath or Affirmation. When the President of the United States is tried, the Chief Justice shall preside: And no Person shall be convicted without the Concurrence of two thirds of the Members present.

Judgment in Cases of Impeachment shall not extend further than to removal from Office, and disqualification to hold and enjoy any Office of honor, Trust or Profit under the United States: but the Party convicted shall nevertheless be liable and subject to Indictment, Trial, Judgment and Punishment, according to Law.

SECTION 4

The Times, Places and Manner of holding Elections for Senators and Representatives, shall be prescribed in each State by the Legislature thereof; but the Congress may at any time by Law make or alter such Regulations, except as to the Places of chusing Senators.

The Congress shall assemble at least once in every Year, and such Meeting shall be on the first Monday in December, unless they shall by Law appoint a different Day.

SECTION 5

Each House shall be the Judge of the Elections, Returns and Qualifications of its own Members, and a Majority of each shall constitute a Quorum to do Business; but a smaller Number may adjourn from day to day, and may be authorized to compel the Attendance of absent Members, in such Manner, and under such Penalties as each House may provide.

Each House may determine the Rules of its Proceedings, punish its Members for disorderly Behaviour, and, with the Concurrence of two thirds, expel a Member.

Each House shall keep a Journal of its Proceedings, and from time to time publish the same, excepting such Parts as may in their Judgment require Secrecy; and the Yeas and Nays of the Members of either House on any question shall, at the Desire of one fifth of those Present, be entered on the Journal.

Neither House, during the Session of Congress, shall, without the Consent of the other, adjourn for more than three days, nor to any other Place than that in which the two Houses shall be sitting.

SECTION 6

The Senators and Representatives shall receive a Compensation for their Services, to be ascertained by Law, and paid out of the Treasury of the United States. They shall in all Cases, except Treason, Felony and Breach of the Peace, be privileged from Arrest during their Attendance at the Session of their respective Houses, and in going to and returning from the same; and for any Speech or Debate in either House, they shall not be questioned in any other Place.

No Senator or Representative shall, during the Time for which he was elected, be appointed to any civil Office under the Authority of the United States, which shall have been created, or the Emoluments whereof shall have been encreased during such time; and no Person holding any Office under the United States, shall be a Member of either House during his Continuance in Office.

SECTION 7

All Bills for raising Revenue shall originate in the House of Representatives; but the Senate may propose or concur with Amendments as on other Bills.

Every Bill which shall have passed the House of Representatives and the Senate, shall, before it become a Law, be presented to the President of the United States: If he approve he shall sign it, but if not he shall return it, with his Objections to that House in which it shall have originated, who shall enter the Objections at large on their Journal, and proceed to reconsider it. If after such Reconsideration two thirds of that House shall agree to pass the Bill, it shall be sent, together with the Objections, to the other House, by which it shall likewise be reconsidered, and if approved by two thirds of that House, it shall become a Law. But in all such Cases the Votes of both Houses shall be determined by yeas and Nays, and the Names of the Persons voting for and against the Bill shall be entered on the Journal of each House respectively. If any Bill shall not be returned by the President within ten Days (Sundays excepted) after it shall have been presented to him, the Same shall be a Law, in like Manner as if he had signed it, unless the Congress by their Adjournment prevent its Return, in which Case it shall not be a Law.

Every Order, Resolution, or Vote to which the Concurrence of the Senate and House of Representatives may be necessary (except on a question of Adjournment) shall be presented to the President of the United States; and before the Same shall take Effect, shall be approved by him, or being disapproved by him, shall be repassed by two thirds of the Senate and House of Representatives, according to the Rules and Limitations prescribed in the Case of a Bill.

SECTION 8

The Congress shall have Power to lay and collect Taxes, Duties, Imposts and Excises, to pay the Debts and provide for the common Defence and general Welfare of the United States; but all Duties, Imposts and Excises shall be uniform throughout the United States;

To borrow Money on the credit of the United States;

To regulate Commerce with foreign Nations, and among the several States, and with the Indian Tribes;

To establish an uniform Rule of Naturalization, and uniform Laws on the subject of Bankruptcies throughout the United States;

To coin Money, regulate the Value thereof, and of foreign Coin, and fix the Standard of Weights and Measures;

To provide for the Punishment of counterfeiting the Securities and current Coin of the United States;

To establish Post Offices and post Roads;

To promote the Progress of Science and useful Arts, by securing for limited Times to Authors and Inventors the exclusive Right to their respective Writings and Discoveries;

To constitute Tribunals inferior to the supreme Court;

To define and punish Piracies and Felonies committed on the high Seas, and Offences against the Law of Nations;

To declare War, grant Letters of Marque and Reprisal, and make Rules concerning Captures on Land and Water;

To raise and support Armies, but no Appropriation of Money to that Use shall be for a longer Term than two Years;

To provide and maintain a Navy;

To make Rules for the Government and Regulation of the land and naval Forces;

To provide for calling forth the Militia to execute the Laws of the Union, suppress Insurrections and repel Invasions;

To provide for organizing, arming, and disciplining, the Militia, and for governing such Part of them as may be employed in the Service of the United States, reserving to the States respectively, the Appointment of the Officers, and the Authority of training the Militia according to the discipline prescribed by Congress;

To exercise exclusive Legislation in all Cases whatsoever, over such District (not exceeding ten Miles square) as may, by Cession of particular States, and the Acceptance of Congress, become the Seat of the Government of the United States, and to exercise like Authority over all Places purchased by the Consent of the Legislature of the State in which the Same shall be, for the Erection of Forts, Magazines, Arsenals, dock-Yards, and other needful Buildings;—And

To make all Laws which shall be necessary and proper for carrying into Execution the foregoing Powers, and all other Powers vested by this Constitution in the Government of the United States, or in any Department or Officer thereof.

SECTION 9

The Migration or Importation of such Persons as any of the States now existing shall think proper to admit, shall not be prohibited by the Congress prior to the Year one thousand eight hundred and eight, but a Tax or duty may be imposed on such Importation, not exceeding ten dollars for each Person.

The Privilege of the Writ of Habeas Corpus shall not be suspended, unless when in Cases of Rebellion or Invasion the public Safety may require it.

No Bill of Attainder or ex post facto Law shall be passed.

No Capitation, or other direct, Tax shall be laid, unless in Proportion to the Census or enumeration herein before directed to be taken.

No Tax or Duty shall be laid on Articles exported from any State.

No Preference shall be given by any Regulation of Commerce or Revenue to the Ports of one State over those of another; nor shall Vessels bound to, or from, one State, be obliged to enter, clear, or pay Duties in another.

No Money shall be drawn from the Treasury, but in Consequence of Appropriations made by Law; and a regular Statement and Account of the Receipts and Expenditures of all public Money shall be published from time to time.

No Title of Nobility shall be granted by the United States: And no Person holding any Office of Profit or Trust under them, shall, without the Consent of the Congress, accept of any present, Emolument, Office, or Title, of any kind whatever, from any King, Prince, or foreign State.

SECTION 10

No State shall enter into any Treaty, Alliance, or Confederation; grant Letters of Marque and Reprisal; coin Money; emit Bills of Credit; make any Thing but gold and silver Coin a Tender in Payment of Debts; pass any Bill of Attainder, ex post facto Law, or Law impairing the Obligation of Contracts, or grant any Title of Nobility.

No State shall, without the Consent of the Congress, lay any Imposts or Duties on Imports or Exports, except what may be absolutely necessary for executing it's inspection Laws: and the net Produce of all Duties and Imposts, laid by any State on Imports or Exports, shall be for the Use of the Treasury of the United States; and all such Laws shall be subject to the Revision and Control of the Congress.

No State shall, without the Consent of Congress, lay any Duty of Tonnage, keep Troops, or Ships of War in time of Peace, enter into any Agreement or Compact with another State, or with a foreign Power, or engage in War, unless actually invaded, or in such imminent Danger as will not admit of delay.

ARTICLE II

SECTION 1

The executive Power shall be vested in a President of the United States of America. He shall hold his Office during the Term of four Years, and, together with the Vice President, chosen for the same Term, be elected, as follows:

Each State shall appoint, in such Manner as the Legislature thereof may direct, a Number of Electors, equal to the whole Number of Senators and Representatives to which the State may be entitled in the Congress: but no Senator or Representative, or Person holding an Office of Trust or Profit under the United States, shall be appointed an Elector.

The Electors shall meet in their respective States, and vote by Ballot for two Persons, of whom one at least shall not be an Inhabitant of the same State with themselves. And they shall make a List of all the Persons voted for, and of the Number of Votes for each; which List they shall sign and certify, and transmit sealed to the Seat of the Government of the United States, directed to the President of the Senate. The President of the Senate shall, in the Presence of the Senate and House of Representatives, open all the Certificates, and the Votes shall then be counted. The Person having the greatest Number of Votes shall be the President, if such Number be a Majority of the whole Number of Electors appointed; and if there be more than one who have such Majority, and have an equal Number of Votes, then the House of Representatives shall immediately chuse by Ballot one of them for President; and if no Person have a Majority, then from the five highest on the List the said House shall in like Manner chuse the President. But in chusing the President, the Votes shall be taken by States, the Representation from each State having one Vote; A quorum for this purpose shall consist of a Member or Members from two thirds of the States, and a Majority of all the States shall be necessary to a Choice. In every Case, after the Choice of the President, the Person having the greatest Number of Votes of the Electors shall be the Vice President. But if there should remain two or more who have equal Votes, the Senate shall chuse from them by Ballot the Vice President.

The Congress may determine the Time of chusing the Electors, and the Day on which they shall give their Votes; which Day shall be the same throughout the United States.

No Person except a natural born Citizen, or a Citizen of the United States, at the time of the Adoption of this Constitution, shall be eligible to the Office of President; neither shall any Person be eligible to that Office who shall not have attained to the Age of thirty five Years, and been fourteen Years a Resident within the United States.

In Case of the Removal of the President from Office, or of his Death, Resignation, or Inability to discharge the Powers and Duties of the said Office, the Same shall devolve on the Vice President, and the Congress may by Law provide for the Case of Removal, Death, Resignation or Inability, both of the President and Vice President, declaring what Officer shall then act as President, and such Officer shall act accordingly, until the Disability be removed, or a President shall be elected.

The President shall, at stated Times, receive for his Services, a Compensation, which shall neither be increased nor diminished during the Period for which he shall have been elected, and he shall not receive within that Period any other Emolument from the United States, or any of them.

Before he enter on the Execution of his Office, he shall take the following Oath or Affirmation:—"I do solemnly swear (or affirm) that I will faithfully execute the Office of President of the United States, and will to the best of my Ability, preserve, protect and defend the Constitution of the United States."

SECTION 2

The President shall be Commander in Chief of the Army and Navy of the United States, and of the Militia of the several States, when called into the actual Service of the United States; he may require the Opinion, in writing, of the principal Officer in each of the executive Departments, upon any Subject relating to the Duties of their respective Offices, and he shall have Power to grant Reprieves and Pardons for Offences against the United States, except in Cases of Impeachment.

He shall have Power, by and with the Advice and Consent of the Senate, to make Treaties, provided two thirds of the Senators present concur; and he shall nominate, and by and with the Advice and Consent of the Senate, shall appoint Ambassadors, other public Ministers and Consuls, Judges of the supreme Court, and all other Officers of the United States, whose Appointments are not herein otherwise provided for, and which shall be established by Law: but the Congress may by Law vest the Appointment of such inferior Officers, as they think proper, in the President alone, in the Courts of Law, or in the Heads of Departments.

The President shall have Power to fill up all Vacancies that may happen during the Recess of the Senate, by granting Commissions which shall expire at the End of their next Session.

SECTION 3

He shall from time to time give to the Congress Information of the State of the Union, and recommend to their Consideration such Measures as he shall judge necessary and expedient; he may, on extraordinary Occasions, convene both Houses, or either of them, and in Case of Disagreement between them, with Respect to the Time of Adjournment, he may adjourn them to such Time as he shall think proper; he shall receive Ambassadors and other public Ministers; he shall take Care that the Laws be faithfully executed, and shall Commission all the Officers of the United States.

SECTION 4

The President, Vice President and all civil Officers of the United States, shall be removed from Office on Impeachment for, and Conviction of, Treason, Bribery, or other high Crimes and Misdemeanors.

ARTICLE III

SECTION 1

The judicial Power of the United States shall be vested in one supreme Court, and in such inferior Courts as the Congress may from time to time ordain and establish. The Judges, both of the supreme and inferior Courts, shall hold their Offices during good Behaviour, and shall, at stated Times, receive for their Services a Compensation, which shall not be diminished during their Continuance in Office.

SECTION 2

The judicial Power shall extend to all Cases, in Law and Equity, arising under this Constitution, the Laws of the United States, and Treaties made, or which shall be made, under their Authority;–to all Cases affecting Ambassadors, other public Ministers and Consuls;–to all Cases of admiralty and maritime Jurisdiction;–to Controversies to which the United States shall be a Party;–to Controversies between two or more States;–between a State and Citizens of another State;–between Citizens of different States;–between Citizens of the same State claiming Lands under Grants of different States, and between a State, or the Citizens thereof, and foreign States, Citizens or Subjects.

In all Cases affecting Ambassadors, other public Ministers and Consuls, and those in which a State shall be Party, the supreme Court shall have original Jurisdiction. In all the other Cases before mentioned, the supreme Court shall have appellate Jurisdiction, both as to Law and Fact, with such Exceptions, and under such Regulations as the Congress shall make.

The Trial of all Crimes, except in Cases of Impeachment, shall be by Jury; and such Trial shall be held in the State where the said Crimes shall have been committed; but when not committed within any State, the Trial shall be at such Place or Places as the Congress may by Law have directed.

SECTION 3

Treason against the United States, shall consist only in levying War against them, or in adhering to their Enemies, giving them Aid and Comfort. No Person shall be convicted of Treason unless on the Testimony of two Witnesses to the same overt Act, or on Confession in open Court.

The Congress shall have Power to declare the Punishment of Treason, but no Attainder of Treason shall work Corruption of Blood, or Forfeiture except during the Life of the Person attainted.

ARTICLE IV

SECTION 1

Full Faith and Credit shall be given in each State to the public Acts, Records, and judicial Proceedings of every other State. And the Congress may by general Laws prescribe the Manner in which such Acts, Records and Proceedings shall be proved, and the Effect thereof.

SECTION 2

The Citizens of each State shall be entitled to all Privileges and Immunities of Citizens in the several States.

A Person charged in any State with Treason, Felony, or other Crime, who shall flee from Justice, and be found in another State, shall on Demand of the executive Authority of the State from which he fled, be delivered up, to be removed to the State having Jurisdiction of the Crime.

No Person held to Service or Labour in one State, under the Laws thereof, escaping into another, shall, in Consequence of any Law or Regulation therein, be discharged from such Service or Labour, but shall be delivered up on Claim of the Party to whom such Service or Labour may be due.

SECTION 3

New States may be admitted by the Congress into this Union; but no new State shall be formed or erected within the Jurisdiction of any other State; nor any State be formed by the Junction of two or more States, or Parts of States, without the Consent of the Legislatures of the States concerned as well as of the Congress.

The Congress shall have Power to dispose of and make all needful Rules and Regulations respecting the Territory or other Property belonging to the United States; and nothing in this Constitution shall be so construed as to Prejudice any Claims of the United States, or of any particular State.

SECTION 4

The United States shall guarantee to every State in this Union a Republican Form of Government, and shall protect each of them against Invasion; and on Application of the Legislature, or of the Executive (when the Legislature cannot be convened), against domestic Violence.

ARTICLE V

The Congress, whenever two thirds of both Houses shall deem it necessary, shall propose Amendments to this Constitution, or, on the Application of the Legislatures of two thirds of the several States, shall call a Convention for proposing Amendments, which, in either Case, shall be valid to all Intents and Purposes, as Part of this Constitution, when ratified by the Legislatures of three fourths of the several States, or by Conventions in three fourths thereof, as the one or the other Mode of Ratification may be proposed by the Congress; Provided that no Amendment which may be made prior to the Year One thousand eight hundred and eight shall in any Manner affect the first and fourth Clauses in the Ninth Section of the first Article; and that no State, without its Consent, shall be deprived of its equal Suffrage in the Senate.

ARTICLE VI

All Debts contracted and Engagements entered into, before the Adoption of this Constitution, shall be as valid against the United States under this Constitution, as under the Confederation.

This Constitution, and the Laws of the United States which shall be made in Pursuance thereof; and all Treaties made, or which shall be made, under the Authority of the United States, shall be the supreme Law of the Land; and the Judges in every State shall be bound thereby, any Thing in the Constitution or Laws of any State to the Contrary notwithstanding.

The Senators and Representatives before mentioned, and the Members of the several State Legislatures, and all executive and judicial Officers, both of the United States and of the several States, shall be bound by Oath or Affirmation, to support this Constitution; but no religious Test shall ever be required as a Qualification to any Office or public Trust under the United States.

ARTICLE VII

The Ratification of the Conventions of nine States, shall be sufficient for the Establishment of this Constitution between the States so ratifying the Same.

The Word, "the," being interlined between the seventh and eighth Lines of the first Page, the Word "Thirty" being partly written on an Erazure in the fifteenth Line of the first Page, The Words "is tried" being interlined between the thirty second and thirty third Lines of the first Page and the Word "the" being interlined between the forty third and forty fourth Lines of the second Page.

Attest William Jackson
Secretary

Done in Convention by the Unanimous Consent of the States present the Seventeenth Day of September in the Year of our Lord one thousand seven hundred and Eighty seven and of the Independence of the United States of America the Twelfth In witness whereof We have hereunto subscribed our Names.

The Bill of Rights: A Transcription *Note:* The following text is a transcription of the first 10 amendments to the Constitution in their original form. These amendments were ratified December 15, 1791, and form what is known as the Bill of Rights.

Amendment I [1791] Congress shall make no law respecting an establishment of religion, or prohibiting the free exercise thereof; or abridging the freedom of speech, or of the press; or the right of the people peaceably to assemble, and to petition the Government for a redress of grievances.

Amendment II [1791] A well regulated Militia, being necessary to the security of a free State, the right of the people to keep and bear Arms, shall not be infringed.

Amendment III [1791] No Soldier shall, in time of peace be quartered in any house, without the consent of the Owner, nor in time of war, but in a manner to be prescribed by law.

Amendment IV [1791] The right of the people to be secure in their persons, houses, papers, and effects, against unreasonable searches and seizures, shall not be violated, and no Warrants shall issue, but upon probable cause, supported by Oath or affirmation, and particularly describing the place to be searched, and the persons or things to be seized.

Amendment V [1791] No person shall be held to answer for a capital, or otherwise infamous crime, unless on a presentment or indictment of a Grand Jury, except in cases arising in the land or naval forces, or in the Militia, when in actual service in time of War or public danger; nor shall any person be subject for the same offence to be twice put in jeopardy of life or limb; nor shall be compelled in any criminal case to be a witness against himself, nor be deprived of life, liberty, or property, without due process of law; nor shall private property be taken for public use, without just compensation.

Amendment VI [1791] In all criminal prosecutions, the accused shall enjoy the right to a speedy and public trial, by an impartial jury of the State and district wherein the crime shall have been committed, which district shall have been previously ascertained by law, and to be informed of the nature and cause of the accusation; to be confronted with the witnesses against him; to have compulsory process for obtaining witnesses in his favor, and to have the Assistance of Counsel for his defence.

Amendment VII [1791] In Suits at common law, where the value in controversy shall exceed twenty dollars, the right of trial by jury shall be preserved, and no fact tried by a jury, shall be otherwise re-examined in any Court of the United States, than according to the rules of the common law.

Amendment VIII [1791] Excessive bail shall not be required, nor excessive fines imposed, nor cruel and unusual punishments inflicted.

Amendment IX [1791] The enumeration in the Constitution, of certain rights, shall not be construed to deny or disparage others retained by the people.

Amendment X [1791] The powers not delegated to the United States by the Constitution, nor prohibited by it to the States, are reserved to the States respectively, or to the people.

Note: The capitalization and punctuation in this version are from the enrolled original of the Joint Resolution of Congress proposing the Bill of Rights, which is on permanent display in the Rotunda of the National Archives Building, Washington, DC.

The Constitution: Amendments 11–27 Constitutional Amendments 1-10 make up what is known as The Bill of Rights. Amendments 11-27 are listed next.

Amendment XI [1795] *Note:* Article III, section 2, of the Constitution was modified by Amendment XI.

The Judicial power of the United States shall not be construed to extend to any suit in law or equity, commenced or prosecuted against one of the United States by Citizens of another State, or by Citizens or Subjects of any Foreign State.

Amendment XII [1804] The Electors shall meet in their respective states and vote by ballot for President and Vice-President, one of whom, at least, shall not be an inhabitant of the same state with themselves; they shall name in their ballots the person voted for as President, and in distinct ballots the person voted for as Vice-President, and they shall make distinct lists of all persons voted for as President, and of all persons voted for as Vice-President, and of the number of votes for each, which lists they shall sign and certify, and transmit sealed to the seat of the government of the United States, directed to the President of the Senate;–the President of the Senate shall, in the presence of the Senate and House of Representatives, open all the certificates and the votes shall then be counted;–The person having the greatest number of votes for President, shall be the President, if such number be a majority of the whole number of Electors appointed; and if no person have such majority, then from the persons having the highest numbers not exceeding three on the list of those voted for as President, the House of Representatives shall choose immediately, by ballot, the President. But in choosing the President, the votes shall be taken by states, the representation from each state having one vote; a quorum for this purpose shall consist of a member or members from two-thirds of the states, and a majority of all the states shall be necessary to a choice. [And if the House of Representatives shall not choose a President whenever the right of choice shall devolve upon them, before the fourth day of March next following, then the Vice-President shall act as President, as in case of the death or other constitutional disability of the President.–] The person having the greatest number of votes as Vice-President, shall be the Vice-President, if such number be a majority of the whole number of Electors appointed, and if no person have a majority, then from the two highest numbers on the list, the Senate shall choose the Vice-President; a quorum for the purpose shall consist of two-thirds of the whole number of Senators, and a majority of the whole number shall be necessary to a choice. But no person constitutionally ineligible to the office of President shall be eligible to that of Vice-President of the United States.

Amendment XIII [1865]

SECTION 1

Neither slavery nor involuntary servitude, except as a punishment for crime whereof the party shall have been duly convicted, shall exist within the United States, or any place subject to their jurisdiction.

SECTION 2

Congress shall have power to enforce this article by appropriate legislation.

Amendment XIV [1868]

SECTION 1

All persons born or naturalized in the United States, and subject to the jurisdiction thereof, are citizens of the United States and of the State wherein they reside. No State shall make or enforce any law which shall abridge the privileges or immunities of citizens of the United States; nor shall any State deprive any person of life, liberty, or property, without due process of law; nor deny to any person within its jurisdiction the equal protection of the laws.

SECTION 2

Representatives shall be apportioned among the several States according to their respective numbers, counting the whole number of persons in each State, excluding Indians not taxed. But when the right to vote at any election for the choice of electors for President and Vice-President of the United States, Representatives in Congress, the Executive and Judicial officers of a State, or the members of the Legislature thereof, is denied to any of the male inhabitants of such State, being twenty-one years of age, and citizens of the United States, or in any way abridged, except for participation in rebellion, or other crime, the basis of representation therein shall be reduced in the proportion which the number of such male citizens shall bear to the whole number of male citizens twenty-one years of age in such State.

SECTION 3

No person shall be a Senator or Representative in Congress, or elector of President and Vice-President, or hold any office, civil or military, under the United States, or under any State, who, having previously taken an oath, as a member of Congress, or as an officer of the United States, or as a member of any State legislature, or as an executive or judicial officer of any State, to support the Constitution of the United States, shall have engaged in insurrection or rebellion against the same, or given aid or comfort to the enemies thereof. But Congress may by a vote of two-thirds of each House, remove such disability.

SECTION 4

The validity of the public debt of the United States, authorized by law, including debts incurred for payment of pensions and bounties for services in suppressing insurrection or rebellion, shall not be questioned. But neither the United States nor any State shall assume or pay any debt or obligation incurred in aid of insurrection or rebellion against the United States, or any claim for the loss or emancipation of any slave; but all such debts, obligations and claims shall be held illegal and void.

SECTION 5

The Congress shall have the power to enforce, by appropriate legislation, the provisions of this article.

Amendment XV [1870]

SECTION 1

The right of citizens of the United States to vote shall not be denied or abridged by the United States or by any State on account of race, color, or previous condition of servitude.

SECTION 2

The Congress shall have the power to enforce this article by appropriate legislation.

Amendment XVI [1913] The Congress shall have power to lay and collect taxes on incomes, from whatever source derived, without apportionment among the several States, and without regard to any census or enumeration.

Amendment XVII [1913] The Senate of the United States shall be composed of two Senators from each State, elected by the people thereof, for six years; and each Senator shall have one vote. The electors in each State shall have the qualifications requisite for electors of the most numerous branch of the State legislatures.

When vacancies happen in the representation of any State in the Senate, the executive authority of such State shall issue writs of election to fill such vacancies: Provided, That the legislature of any State may empower the executive thereof to make temporary appointments until the people fill the vacancies by election as the legislature may direct.

This amendment shall not be so construed as to affect the election or term of any Senator chosen before it becomes valid as part of the Constitution.

Amendment XVIII [1919] [Repealed by Amendment XXI]

SECTION 1

After one year from the ratification of this article the manufacture, sale, or transportation of intoxicating liquors within, the importation thereof into, or the exportation thereof from the United States and all territory subject to the jurisdiction thereof for beverage purposes is hereby prohibited.

SECTION 2

The Congress and the several States shall have concurrent power to enforce this article by appropriate legislation.

SECTION 3

This article shall be inoperative unless it shall have been ratified as an amendment to the Constitution by the legislatures of the several States, as provided in the Constitution, within seven years from the date of the submission hereof to the States by the Congress.

Amendment XIX [1920] The right of citizens of the United States to vote shall not be denied or abridged by the United States or by any State on account of sex.

Congress shall have power to enforce this article by appropriate legislation.

Amendment XX [1933]

SECTION 1

The terms of the President and the Vice President shall end at noon on the 20th day of January, and the terms of Senators and Representatives at noon on the 3rd day of January, of the years in which such terms would have ended if this article had not been ratified; and the terms of their successors shall then begin.

SECTION 2

The Congress shall assemble at least once in every year, and such meeting shall begin at noon on the 3rd day of January, unless they shall by law appoint a different day.

SECTION 3

If, at the time fixed for the beginning of the term of the President, the President elect shall have died, the Vice President elect shall become President. If a President shall not have been chosen before the time fixed for the beginning of his term, or if the President elect shall have failed to qualify, then the Vice President elect shall act as President until a President shall have qualified; and the Congress may by law provide for the case wherein neither a President elect nor a Vice President shall have qualified, declaring who shall then act as President, or the manner in which one who is to act shall be selected, and such person shall act accordingly until a President or Vice President shall have qualified.

SECTION 4

The Congress may by law provide for the case of the death of any of the persons from whom the House of Representatives may choose a President whenever the right of choice shall have devolved upon them, and for the case of the death of any of the persons from whom the Senate may choose a Vice President whenever the right of choice shall have devolved upon them.

SECTION 5

Sections 1 and 2 shall take effect on the 15th day of October following the ratification of this article.

SECTION 6

This article shall be inoperative unless it shall have been ratified as an amendment to the Constitution by the legislatures of three-fourths of the several States within seven years from the date of its submission.

Amendment XXI [1933]

SECTION 1

The eighteenth article of amendment to the Constitution of the United States is hereby repealed.

SECTION 2

The transportation or importation into any State, Territory, or Possession of the United States for delivery or use therein of intoxicating liquors, in violation of the laws thereof, is hereby prohibited.

SECTION 3

This article shall be inoperative unless it shall have been ratified as an amendment to the Constitution by conventions in the several States, as provided in the Constitution, within seven years from the date of the submission hereof to the States by the Congress.

Amendment XXII [1951]

SECTION 1

No person shall be elected to the office of the President more than twice, and no person who has held the office of President, or acted as President, for more than two years of a term to which some other person was elected President shall be elected to the office of President more than once. But this Article shall not apply to any person holding the office of President when this Article was proposed by Congress, and shall not prevent any person who may be holding the office of President, or acting as President, during the term within which this Article becomes operative from holding the office of President or acting as President during the remainder of such term.

SECTION 2

This article shall be inoperative unless it shall have been ratified as an amendment to the Constitution by the legislatures of three-fourths of the several States within seven years from the date of its submission to the States by the Congress.

Amendment XXIII [1961]

SECTION 1

The District constituting the seat of Government of the United States shall appoint in such manner as Congress may direct:

A number of electors of President and Vice President equal to the whole number of Senators and Representatives in Congress to which the District would be entitled if it were a State, but in no event more than the least populous State; they shall be in addition to those appointed by the States, but they shall be considered, for the purposes of the election of President and Vice President, to be electors appointed by a State; and they shall meet in the District and perform such duties as provided by the twelfth article of amendment.

SECTION 2

The Congress shall have power to enforce this article by appropriate legislation.

Amendment XXIV [1964]

SECTION 1

The right of citizens of the United States to vote in any primary or other election for President or Vice President, for electors for President or Vice President, or for Senator or Representative in Congress, shall not be denied or abridged by the United States or any State by reason of failure to pay poll tax or other tax.

SECTION 2

The Congress shall have power to enforce this article by appropriate legislation.

Amendment XXV [1967]

SECTION 1

In case of the removal of the President from office or of his death or resignation, the Vice President shall become President.

SECTION 2

Whenever there is a vacancy in the office of the Vice President, the President shall nominate a Vice President who shall take office upon confirmation by a majority vote of both Houses of Congress.

SECTION 3

Whenever the President transmits to the President pro tempore of the Senate and the Speaker of the House of Representatives his written declaration that he is unable to discharge the powers and duties of his office, and until he transmits to them a written declaration to the contrary, such powers and duties shall be discharged by the Vice President as Acting President.

SECTION 4

Whenever the Vice President and a majority of either the principal officers of the executive departments or of such other body as Congress may by law provide, transmit to the President pro tempore of the Senate and the Speaker of the House of Representatives their written declaration that the President is unable to discharge the powers and duties of his office, the Vice President shall immediately assume the powers and duties of the office as Acting President.

Thereafter, when the President transmits to the President pro tempore of the Senate and the Speaker of the House of Representatives his written declaration that no inability exists, he shall resume the powers and duties of his office unless the Vice President and a majority of either the principal officers of the executive department or of such other body as Congress may by law provide, transmit within four days to the President pro tempore of the Senate and the Speaker of the House of Representatives their written declaration that the President is unable to discharge the powers and duties of his office. Thereupon Congress shall decide the issue, assembling within forty-eight hours for that purpose if not in session. If the Congress, within twenty-one days after receipt of the latter written declaration, or, if Congress is not in session, within twenty-one days after Congress is required to assemble, determines by two-thirds vote of both Houses that the President is unable to discharge the powers and duties of his office, the Vice President shall continue to discharge the same as Acting President; otherwise, the President shall resume the powers and duties of his office.

Amendment XXVI [1971]

SECTION 1

The right of citizens of the United States, who are eighteen years of age or older, to vote shall not be denied or abridged by the United States or by any State on account of age.

SECTION 2

The Congress shall have power to enforce this article by appropriate legislation.

Amendment XXVII [1992] No law, varying the compensation for the services of the Senators and Representatives, shall take effect, until an election of representatives shall have intervened.

Glossary

A

abandonment In contract law, the condition that exists when a minor has left home and given up all rights to parental support.

acceptance An indication made by the offeree that they agree to be bound by the terms of the offer.

accession The right of an owner of property to any increase in the property.

acid rain A form of pollution caused by the discharge of sulfur emissions into the atmosphere.

ademption When a specific bequest of personal property is made, but the personal property is disposed of before the death of the testator.

administrative agency A governmental body responsible for the control and supervision of a particular activity or area of public interest.

administrative hearing A trial-like judicial proceeding, without a jury, in which an administrative agency rules on matters of the law that the agency is charged with enforcing.

administrative law The body of rules, regulations, and decisions created by administrative agencies.

administrator A personal representative named by the court to perform as the executor would in instances in which the deceased person has not left a will.

advance directive A document that expresses an individual's wishes regarding their health care in the event that they become incapacitated or permanently unconscious without hope of recovery.

adverse possession When title to land is acquired by a person's exclusive, continuous, open, known, and hostile use of the property over a period of time.

affirmative action plans Detailed records that demonstrate that an employer's practices are nondiscriminatory.

Age Discrimination in Employment Act of 1967 A federal statute designed to protect individuals from illegal discrimination in employment on the basis of age.

age of majority The age at which a person is legally recognized as an adult and is bound by the terms of their contract.

agency by necessity An agency that is created when circumstances make such an agency necessary.

agency by operation of law An agency that is created when a court finds the need for an agency to achieve a desired social policy.

agency by ratification An agency that results when a principal approves an unauthorized act performed by an agent or approves an act done in the principal's name by an unauthorized person.

agent A person authorized to act on behalf of another and subject to the other's control in dealing with third parties.

agreement not to compete An agreement in which the seller of a business agrees not to begin or operate a similar business within a certain geographic area or within a specified period of time.

alternative dispute resolution (ADR) A system in which contract disputes and other disagreements are resolved by using means other than a lawsuit.

Americans with Disabilities Act (ADA) of 1990 A federal statute designed to protect individuals from illegal discrimination in employment on the basis of disability.

antenuptial or prenuptial agreement An exchange of promises made by persons planning to marry.

anticipatory breach When a party to a contract announces his or her intention to break the contract in the future.

apparent authority The authority that a third party may reasonably assume an agent possesses, despite the fact that the agent does not actually possess such authority.

arbitration A process for dispute resolution in which a neutral third party decides a case as if they were a judge and jury.

arson The willful or malicious act of causing the burning of another's property.

articles of incorporation A document that lists the general powers of a corporation.

assignee The third party to whom rights are transferred in an assignment.

assignment The transfer of a contract right to a third party who can receive the benefits of the contract.

assignment of lease When a tenant transfers their entire interest in the entire premises for the remaining length of the term of the lease.

assignor The person who transfers their rights in an assignment.

assumption of risk A defense in a case of negligence in which the defendant demonstrates that the plaintiff voluntarily assumed the risk associated with the dangerous condition caused by the defendant.

attorney in fact The person appointed as agent when the power of attorney is exercised.

auction sale A sale in which goods are sold to the highest bidder.

auction with reserve One that gives the auctioneer the right to withdraw the goods at any time before announcing completion of the sale if reasonable bids are not made.

auction without reserve One at which the goods must be sold to the highest bidder and may not be withdrawn after bidding has begun.

B

bad check A check against a bank in which the drawer has insufficient funds on deposit to cover the check or no funds at all.

bailee The party in a bailment who receives the goods.

bailee's lien The right of the bailee in a bailment for work and services to hold and, if necessary, sell the property if the bailor does not pay for the services or work done.

bailment A transaction in which the owner of tangible personal property transfers it (not as a gift) to another party while still retaining ownership.

bailment for the sole benefit of the bailee A bailment relationship in which only the bailee receives any benefit from the relationship.

bailment for the sole benefit of the bailor A bailment that exists when the bailor entrusts an article to the bailee for storage or safekeeping without charge, as a favor.

bailor The party in a bailment who retains ownership and transfers possession of the goods.

bankruptcy The legal state that occurs when a debtor is insolvent, is in default, and is unable to fulfill their obligations to pay back their creditors.

Bankruptcy Abuse Prevention and Consumer Protection Act of 2005 A federal law that instituted strict rules and eligibility requirements for debtors filing for bankruptcy.

barren promise A promise to pay an existing debt or to obey the law, or a similar promise of something already owed.

bearer instrument An instrument that is payable to anyone who is in possession of it.

beneficiary An individual who receives gifts of personal or real property by will.

bequest A gift of personal property by will.

bill of lading A receipt for goods to be shipped, acknowledging that such goods have been received and indicating agreement that the goods will be transported to the destination specified.

bill of rights The first 10 amendments of the U.S. Constitution.

bill of sale A written statement that the seller is passing ownership to the buyer.

birthday rule The modern view that a person attains a given age on the anniversary date of their birth.

blank endorsement An endorsement in which the name of the payee is written by the payee on the back of a negotiable instrument.

blue laws State statutes and local ordinances that regulate the creation and performance of certain types of contracts on Sundays and legal holidays.

boycott Citizens' refusal to purchase goods made by a particular business–for example, a business located in another country.

breach of contract When a party to a contract refuses to perform as required by the contract or performs in an unsatisfactory manner.

bribery The act of offering, giving, receiving, or soliciting something of value to influence official action or the discharge of a public duty.

burglary The illegal entering of another person's premises for the purpose of committing a crime.

burning to defraud A special category of crime providing for the punishment of persons who burn their own property with the aim of collecting insurance money.

bylaws A document that provides rules for the meetings of a corporation.

C

cafeteria plans A particular benefit or package of benefits selected by an employee from a specific amount of money allocated for this purpose.

carrier's lien A carrier's legal right to hold a shipment until payment is made.

case law The effects of court decisions that involve the same or similar facts.

cashier's check A check issued by a cashier or other designated officer of a bank and drawn against bank funds.

certified check A check that the bank has promised to pay when it is presented for payment.

champerty An agreement to encourage a lawsuit in which one or more of the parties have no legitimate interest.

check A written order drawn on a bank by a depositor that requests the bank to pay, on demand and unconditionally, a definite sum of money to the bearer of the check or to the order of a specified person.

Check 21 The term commonly used to refer to the Check Clearing for the 21st Century Act, a federal law revolutionizing the manner in which checks are handled by banks.

churning A financial planner's unreasonably excessive buying or selling of securities to generate commissions.

Civil Rights Act of 1964 A federal statute designed to protect individuals from illegal discrimination.

Civil Rights Act of 1991 A federal statute that provides additional remedies to an employee who can prove that they were a victim of discrimination.

Clean Air Act of 1970 A federal statute that requires all states to develop air quality standards that are at least as rigorous as the federal standards. This statute sets primary and secondary standards and regulates both stationary and mobile pollution.

Clean Water Act of 1972 A federal statute that sets minimum standards for water purity.

code of ethics A set of rules that a company or other group adopts to express principles of ethical behavior that are expected of its personnel.

codicil A document, separate from the will, in which a person can make legal changes to their will.

collective bargaining agreement A contract between a union and an employer that covers all terms and conditions of employment.

coming of age rule In common law, the view that a person's legal birthday is 12:01 a.m. of the day before their actual birthday.

comity A discretionary doctrine that holds that the courts of one country should refrain from deciding cases involving the acts of persons from another country.

commerce clause A provision of the Constitution that grants Congress the power to regulate trade with foreign nations, and among the several states, and with the Indian tribes.

commercial paper A number of legally binding and commercially acceptable documents that are used to transfer money from one person to another.

common carrier An individual or firm in the business of transporting goods between certain points as allowed by the various state commissions that regulate carriers.

common law The body of recorded decisions that courts refer to and rely upon when making later legal decisions.

community property Property acquired during marriage that, in some states, belongs to both spouses.

community-based insurance Medical insurance programs provided by Blue Cross and Blue Shield.

comparative negligence A form of negligence that requires the court to assign damages according to the degree of fault of each party.

competent Being mentally capable of understanding the terms of a contract.

competent party A person of legal age and at least normal mentality who is considered by law to be capable of understanding the meaning of a contract and is permitted to enter into a valid contract.

Computer Fraud and Abuse Act (CFAA) A federal statute that prohibits unlawful access to computers used in national defense, by financial institutions, or by governments.

concerted action Employee ability to freely discuss wages, benefits, and working conditions.

condemnation The legal process that occurs when property is taken by the government against the will of the property owner.

conditional sale A sale with contract provisions that specify conditions that must be met by one of the parties.

conditional sales contract A sales contract that includes conditions that must be met either before or after the sale is completed.

conditions Restrictions that limit the use of the property.

conditions precedent Conditions in a sales contract that must be met before title passes.

conditions subsequent Conditions in a sales contract that must be met after title has passed.

consideration The promise to give up something of value that a party to a contract has a legal right to keep, or to do something that the party is not otherwise legally required to do.

consignee The person or party receiving goods in a bailment relationship.

consignor The person or party shipping goods in a bailment relationship.

Consolidated Omnibus Budget Reconciliation Act of 1985 (COBRA) A federal statute that provides employees and their families who lose health benefits the right to elect to continue group health benefits provided by their group health plan for specified limited periods of time.

constructive bailment A bailment in which goods are thrust upon a bailee who does not have any choice about whether they wish to serve as bailee.

Consumer Product Safety Commission (CPSC) The federal agency responsible for the safety of consumer products sold in the United States.

contract A legally enforceable agreement that is created when two or more competent parties agree to perform, or to avoid performing, certain acts that they have a legal right to do and that meet certain legal requirements.

contract for labor and materials A sales contract for goods of special design, construction, or manufacture.

contract for sale A legally enforceable agreement that has as its purpose the immediate transfer of title to personal property in return for consideration.

contract for sale with the right of return A contract for the sale of goods that gives the buyer both title to the goods and the opportunity to return them to the seller at a later time.

contract of adhesion A contract drawn by one party that must be accepted as is on a take-it-or-leave-it basis.

contract of agency An agreement between a principal and an agent by which the agent is vested with authority to represent the principal.

contract to sell An agreement to sell future goods.

Contracts for the International Sale of Goods (CISG) A treaty created to establish a universal set of legal procedures to be applied to contracts covering international transactions.

contractual capacity The ability to make a valid contract.

contributory negligence A legal defense that involves the failure of an injured party to be careful enough to ensure personal safety.

Controlling the Assault of Non-Solicited Pornography and Marketing Act (CAN-SPAM) A federal statute that limits the circumstances under which commercial email may be utilized.

conversion The wrongful exercise of dominion and control over another's personal property.

cookie A file that is embedded on the hard drive of a computer, often without a person's knowledge, that collects and stores information about the user and their online behavior, including websites that have been visited.

copyright A valid, government-granted protection given to creators of literary, creative, or artistic works.

corporation A business formed as a separate legal entity.

counterclaim When the maker of a note or other drawer or acceptor of a bill of exchange may deduct from the amount demanded by an immediate party any amounts owed them by the payee.

counteroffer A response to an offer in which the terms and conditions of the original offer are changed.

covenant An agreement made by either a landlord or a tenant to do certain things.

cover When the seller fails to deliver the goods, the right of a buyer to buy similar goods elsewhere to substitute for those not delivered by the seller.

creditor An individual or business to which money is owed.

crime An offense against the public at large punishable by the official governing body of a nation or state.

Crowdfunding Raising money through a website solicitation from many small investments

cryptocurrency A digitally encrypted currency not connected with any country's central banking system.

custom of the marketplace What a warranty usually means in similar transactions.

cybersquatting Registering or using another person's or company's domain name in bad faith for the purpose of earning a profit.

cyberstalking Posting hurtful, threatening, or embarrassing messages online.

D

debtor An individual or business that owes money.

decedent A deceased person.

deceptive advertising An advertisement that contains a material misrepresentation, omission, or practice likely to mislead a consumer who acts reasonably under the circumstances.

deductible A set amount of money for medical expenses for which the patient is responsible.

deed The instrument, or document, that conveys an interest in real property between parties.

defamation The harming of a person's reputation and good name by the communication of a false statement.

default The state in which a debtor fails to meet one or more financial obligations to their creditors.

defendant The party against whom a lawsuit is brought and from whom recovery is sought.

delegation The appointment of a third party by a party to an existing contract to perform contractual duties that do not involve unique skills, talents, abilities, and so on.

design defect A fault in a product that creates a hazardous condition that causes injury.

design patent A patent awarded to individuals or business firms to protect distinctive patterns, figures, and shapes and to prevent unauthorized copying.

devise A gift of real property by will.

Digital Millennium Copyright Act (DMCA) of 1998 A federal statute that provides that ISPs are not liable for copyright infringements by their subscribers so long as they adhere to certain requirements.

disability insurance Insurance coverage that provides supplementary income to make up for lost wages due to an illness or accident that prevents an employee from working at their regular employment.

disaffirmance In contract law, to indicate by a statement or act an intent not to live up to the terms of a contract.

disclaimer A denial or repudiation in an express warranty that places specific limitations in the warranty.

dishonored When a negotiable instrument is not accepted when presented for acceptance, it is not paid when presented for payment at maturity, presentment is excused or waived, or the instrument is past due and unpaid.

divisible contract An agreement that is made up of two or more parts, each part being independent of the others.

doctrine of preemption A principle that states that when certain state or local laws are inconsistent with the federal law, the federal law must be followed.

Dodd-Frank Wall Street Reform and Consumer Protection Act of 2010 A federal law that provides for significant regulatory changes over the financial system.

draft An unconditional written order to a person instructing them to pay money to another, third person.

durable power of attorney A document that appoints an individual as an agent with authority to make decisions on behalf of the principal in the event that the principal becomes incompetent.

durable power of attorney for health care A document that appoints an individual as an agent with authority to make health care decisions on behalf of the principal in the event that the principal becomes incompetent.

duress The act of applying unlawful or improper pressure or influence to a person to gain their agreement to a contract.

duty of care A legal and ethical obligation placed upon a director to act diligently and prudently in conducting the affairs of the corporation.

duty of loyalty A legal and ethical obligation placed upon a director to administer the affairs of the corporation with personal integrity, honesty, and candor.

duty-based reasoning Ethical reasoning that is based on consequences of actions.

E

easement A right or interest in land granted to a party to make beneficial use of the land owned by another.

Economic Espionage Act of 1996 A statute that makes the misappropriation or outright theft of trade secrets a federal crime.

Electronic Communications Privacy Act (ECPA) A federal statute that addresses hacking and other forms of illegal conduct by making it a crime to gain unauthorized access to any communication that is stored on a computer system.

electronic funds transfer (EFT) A variety of electronic applications for handling money.

Electronic Funds Transfer Act (EFTA) of 1978 A federal statute that makes it an offense to use any device that is part of an electronic transfer mechanism to steal money, goods, or services or to alter data, interrupt wire transmissions, or use stolen codes or passwords, when the purpose of such activity is to obtain something of value unlawfully.

Electronic Signatures in Global and National Commerce Act (ESIGN) of 2000 A federal statute that provides that electronic contracts containing electronic signatures are just as enforceable as those that are printed on paper.

emancipation In contract law, the condition that exists when minors are no longer under the control of their parents and are responsible for their contracts.

embezzlement The wrongful taking of money or other property that has been entrusted to a person as a part of his or her job.

eminent domain When ownership of real property is taken by the government and the previous owner is compensated at the fair market value of the property.

employee handbook A manual published by an employer that contains the many policies of the firm.

employment at will A doctrine that states that an employer may terminate an employee's employment at any time for a good reason, a bad reason, or no reason at all.

employment contract An agreement that specifies that the employer agrees to pay, and the employee agrees to work, for a specified period of time at a specified salary.

endorsee The person to whom a negotiable instrument is transferred.

endorsement When the holder of commercial paper signs their name, with or without words, on the back of an instrument to transfer ownership to another.

endorser The person who signs their name to a negotiable instrument.

entire contract An agreement that is made up of two or more parts, in which each part is dependent upon the others.

environmental impact statement (EIS) An assessment of the environmental consequences of a planned project that must be approved prior to commencement of any project with significant federal involvement (such as federal financing).

Environmental Protection Agency (EPA) The federal agency that conducts environmental research, assists states and municipalities with grants and technical advice, and administers the federal pollution laws that cover businesses.

Equal Credit Opportunity Act (ECOA) Federal legislation protecting borrowers from discrimination.

Equal Employment Opportunity Commission (EEOC) A federal agency responsible for administering laws prohibiting discrimination in employment.

Equal Pay Act of 1963 (EPA) A statute that prohibits any employer from engaging in wage discrimination based on sex.

ergonomics A developing science that deals with designing workplaces to promote safety and health.

estoppel A legal bar to using contradictory words or acts in asserting a claim against another.

ethics The philosophical study of what is right and wrong, good and bad.

European Union (EU) An entity that established a legal and political relationship among its members that promotes economic growth as well as social and cultural affiliations.

eviction An action that denies the tenant the use of the premises.

exclusive remedy A doctrine that states that an employee who sustains a work-related injury or illness can recover damages only through workers' compensation and may not file a lawsuit against their employer.

exculpatory clause A statement in a contract that releases one party from liability resulting from his or her own negligence throughout the performance of a contract.

executed contract A record of an agreement that has been completed in all respects by all the parties.

executive branch The branch of a government body that consists of an elected executive, including their appointed staff.

executor A personal representative named in a will to handle matters involving the estate of a deceased person.

executory contract An agreement in which some future act or obligation remains to be performed under its terms.

existing goods Goods that physically exist and are owned by the seller at the time of sale.

express authority An agent's authority that the principal voluntarily and specifically sets forth as oral or written instructions in an agency agreement.

express contract A contract that explicitly states the agreement of the parties, either orally or in writing.

express powers Those that are specifically stated in the federal Constitution.

express warranty An explicit, specifically stated promise.

extortion The act of taking or demanding money or other property from someone by using force, threats of force, or economic harm.

F

failure to warn The dereliction of a duty to advise purchasers and users of dangers inherent in a product.

Fair Housing Act A federal law that prohibits discrimination in housing on the basis of race, color, sex, familial status, national origin, religion, or handicap.

Fair Labor Standards Act of 1938 (FLSA) The FLSA is a law that sets standards for the minimum age an employee can be, the minimum wages an employee can earn, and the rate at which an employee is paid if he or she works more than a certain number of hours in a given workweek.

fair use Limited copying allowed when the copyrighted material is copied without authorization for use in connection with criticism, news reporting, research, education, or parody.

false pretenses A broad category of crimes that involves activities intended to deceive others or to obtain goods by making false claims.

Family and Medical Leave Act of 1993 (FMLA) A federal statute that provides eligible employees with the right to take up to 12 weeks of unpaid leave for personal medical reasons or to care for a child, spouse, or parent.

Federal Trade Commission (FTC) The federal agency responsible for ensuring that advertising in the United States is truthful.

fee simple When an owner of a freehold estate holds it absolutely.

felony A crime punishable by death or imprisonment in a federal or state prison for a term exceeding one year.

fiduciary responsibility A legal requirement that a person will exercise their authority while working under a duty of loyalty and a duty of care.

FOB destination Title passes from the seller to the buyer when the goods are delivered to the buyer.

FOB shipping point Title to goods passes from the seller to the buyer when the carrier receives the shipment, and it is understood that the buyer will pay the transportation charges.

Food and Drug Administration (FDA) The federal agency responsible for the safety of food and drugs sold in the United States.

forbearance The promise to refrain from doing something that a party has a legal right to do.

Foreign Corrupt Practices Act (FCPA) A federal statute designed to provide executives of American companies with rules and restrictions relating to paying persons in foreign countries to expedite business in these foreign nations.

Foreign Sovereign Immunities Act (FSIA) A federal law passed in 1976 that established certain exceptions to foreign sovereign immunity.

forged check A check that is signed by a person other than the drawer.

forgery The false making or alteration of a writing with the intent to defraud.

formal contract A specialty contract that is written and under seal.

franchisee The independent company in a franchise agreement.

franchisor The parent firm in a franchise agreement.

fraud The intentional misstatement or nondisclosure of a material (essential) fact made by one party in an attempt to influence the actions of another party.

fraudulent transfer A transaction in which the debtor sells property for an amount far below its market value.

freehold estate An estate in which a person owns the land for life or forever.

frustration of purpose A doctrine that states that where both parties know the purpose of a contract and, through no fault of either party, the reason for the contract no longer exists, the contract is terminated.

full faith and credit clause A provision of the Constitution that mandates that each state respect and enforce both the judgments awarded by courts in other states and the statutes and case law of other states.

full warranty The promise that a defective product will be repaired without charge and within a reasonable time after a complaint has been made.

fungible goods Goods that are generally sold by weight or measure.

future goods Goods that do not exist at the time of the sales transaction but are expected to come into the possession of the seller.

G

gambling agreement An agreement in which performance by one party depends on the occurrence of an uncertain event.

general agent A person authorized to assume complete charge of their principal's business or who is entrusted with general authority to act for the principal in all business-related matters.

General Agreement on Tariffs and Trade (GATT) An international agreement that provides a set of rules to ensure that there is no discrimination in trade by its signatories and also spells out a process for resolving international trade disputes.

general release A written agreement in which an aggrieved party can discharge in whole or in part a claim resulting from an alleged breach of contract.

gift causa mortis A gift, given by a living person who expects to die from a known cause, that meets all of the legal requirements for a gift.

Good Samaritan laws Statutes that provide medical professionals who render emergency care or treatment to injured individuals outside the scope of their regular employment immunity from malpractice lawsuits.

government-granted franchise A legal monopoly in which a state or federal government grants a person or firm a license to conduct a specific business, usually an essential service.

gratuitous agent One who acts on behalf of a principal without being paid.

gratuitous promise A promise that does not require some benefit in return.

greenhouse effect The rising of global temperatures due to the increased burning of fossil fuels that has loaded the atmosphere with heat-trapping carbon dioxide.

guarantor The party who guarantees the promises assigned.

guaranty A promise to pay the debts or settle the wrongdoings of another if he or she does not make settlement personally.

H

hacker A person who gains unauthorized access to computers either for mischief or with criminal intent.

health care law The federal, state, and local statutes, rules, regulations, and judicial decisions that govern the legal relationships of patients, physicians and other medical professionals, and health care insurers to one other.

Health Insurance Portability and Accountability Act of 1996 (HIPAA) A federal statute that provides an individual with rights over their health information and establishes limits on who is permitted to view and receive health information.

health maintenance organization (HMO) An organization that provides health insurance by coordinating services with specific doctors, hospitals, and other health care providers.

holder in due course A holder who has taken a negotiable instrument in good faith and for value, before maturity, and without actual or constructive notice of any defects in the instrument.

holographic will A will that is completely handwritten.

hotelkeeper A person or firm in the business of offering lodgings or temporary shelter to guests and transients.

I

illusory promise One that consists of an indefinite, open-ended statement purporting to be an agreement.

impersonation Imposters' use of names similar to existing businesses on social media.

implied authority The authority an agent reasonably assumes they has that relates to the express authority granted by the principal.

implied contract A contract that does not explicitly state the agreement of the parties but in which the terms of the agreement can be inferred from the conduct of the parties, the customs of the trade, or the conditions or circumstances.

implied powers Those that have arisen as a result of interpretation of the express powers by the courts.

implied warranty A guarantee suggested or inferred from known facts and circumstances.

implied warranty of fitness for a particular purpose The law's assumption that goods are fit for their intended use.

implied warranty of merchantability The law's assumption that goods sold by a merchant/seller are fit to be sold and are adequate for the ordinary purposes for which such goods are sold.

impossibility of performance When unforeseen circumstances make it impossible to fulfill the terms of a contract; in these cases, the contract is considered void.

improper affiliation Unauthorized, inappropriate social media activity that implies a tie with a business.

incidental beneficiary A person who will benefit as an indirect consequence of a contract, although that was not the intent of the contracting parties.

incompetent Being unable to make binding contracts due to having an unsound mind and being unable to safeguard one's own interests and affairs.

independent contractor One who contracts to do a job and who retains complete control over the methods employed to obtain completion.

infringement Copying another's literary, creative, or artistic works without permission.

injunction A permanent court order prohibiting the performance of a certain act.

insider trading An illegal activity in which a person who has confidential information about a particular company purchases shares of the company's stock with the intention of selling these shares for a higher price when the information is released to the general public.

insolvency The state that occurs when an individual's or business's liabilities exceed assets.

intellectual property Personal property that includes knowledge, ways of doing things, and expressions of ideas.

intellectual property infringement Unauthorized use of trademarks, trade secrets, copyrights, or patents.

inter vivos gift A gift between the living that meets all of the legal requirements for a gift.

interest The charge for using borrowed money, generally expressed as an annual percentage of the amount of the loan (principal).

intermediate scrutiny A test that measures whether a particular statute is substantially related to an important government objective.

international law The broad study of the legal systems of major countries, treaties, practices, tariffs and nontariff trade barriers, and import and export quotas.

International Monetary Fund (IMF) An organization whose purpose is to maintain a stable environment for the economies and the currencies of its members by providing protection against large fluctuations in the value of one currency versus another.

Internet Tax Freedom Act A federal statute that placed a moratorium on taxing Internet service providers on the services they provide to computer users.

interstate commerce Trade between two or more states.

intestate The state in which a person dies without a will.

invitation to trade An announcement published for the purpose of creating interest and attracting a response by many people. It is not considered a valid offer because it does not contain sufficient words of commitment to sell.

involuntary filing A form of bankruptcy that occurs when creditors pressure a debtor to file.

irrevocable agency An agency contract that cannot be terminated by a principal in which the agent has an interest in the subject matter of the agency in addition to the remuneration that they receive for services.

J

joint and several liability Legal exposure such that a person with a claim against a general partnership can elect to sue either all of the partners together or any individual partner whom they choose.

joint tenancy When two or more persons own equal shares of personal property with right of survivorship.

joint venture An activity in which individuals become partners for only a short period of time or for only a single project.

judicial branch The branch of a government body that determines if there have been violations of the law and interprets the law if there are questions about what the law means in particular situations.

judicial review The process of deciding if a law is contrary to the Constitution.

jurisdiction The authority of a court, as granted by a constitution or legislative act, to hear and decide cases.

L

labor unions Groups of employees who bargain with employers for improved wages, benefits, and working conditions.

landlord The owner of real property who gives up their right of possession.

larceny The act of taking and carrying away the personal property of another without the right to do so.

lease The document in which the terms of a rental agreement are written.

leasehold estate An estate in which a person has an interest in real property that comes from a lease.

legacy A gift of money by will.

legality of purpose The requirement that the intent of a contract be legal for the contract to be enforceable.

legislative branch The branch of a government body that consists of elected representatives who have the responsibility for passing laws that represent the will of the people.

lemon laws Statutes that provide remedies to consumers for products such as automobiles that repeatedly fail to meet certain standards of quality and performance.

lessee The tenant in a lease agreement.

lessor The landlord in a lease agreement.

liable Being judged legally responsible.

libel The spreading of damaging statements in written form, including pictures, cartoons, and effigies.

life estate A freehold estate in which a person has an ownership interest only for their lifetime.

limited liability Legal exposure in which an owner of a business is not personally liable for all of the debts and obligations of the business.

limited liability company (LLC) A relatively new organizational form available in most states that provides all of the owners with limited liability.

limited partnership A business in which there are one or more general partners and one or more limited partners.

limited warranty A written warranty that does not meet the minimum requirements of a full warranty.

liquidated damages clause A statement wherein damages are explicitly set in the event one of the parties breaches an agreement.

liquidation A process in which assets are sold to obtain cash.

living will A document in which a person directs their physician and/or health proxy to forgo certain extraordinary medical procedures if the person is dying or permanently unconscious.

lockout An action by which an employer does not allow employees to return to work in the event a collective bargaining agreement is not reached.

loss of consortium In a lawsuit by a spouse, a request for damages for loss of companionship.

M

Magnuson-Moss Warranty Act A federal statute that addresses many different kinds of abuses to consumers relating to warranties.

mailbox rule A rule that states that an acceptance sent via the postal system or by courier is effective when sent.

major medical A form of health insurance that covers serious illnesses and lengthy hospitalizations, which generally takes effect after other benefits are exhausted.

malpractice A professional's improper or immoral conduct in the performance of their duties through carelessness or lack of knowledge.

Master Settlement Agreement A contract in which the major cigarette manufacturers in the United States agreed not to engage in certain advertising strategies.

material alteration A deliberate change or alteration of an important element in a written contract that affects the rights or obligations of the parties.

means test A complex formula that measures an individual's income relative to the median income of the people in the state where they reside resides.

mediation A process for dispute resolution in which a neutral third party meets with the disputants in order to have them come to some form of settlement agreement.

Medicaid A federal health care program for certain individuals and families with low incomes.

Medicare A federal program that pays for specified health care expenses for individuals who are 65 years of age or older.

memorandum A written contract or agreement.

merchant An individual who deals in goods of the kind being sold in the ordinary course of business or who presents themselves as having the skills or knowledge relating to the goods.

minor A person who has not yet reached the age of majority.

misdemeanor A less serious crime that is generally punishable by a fine and/or a prison sentence of not more than one year.

misrepresentation A misstatement of a material fact that results in inducing another to enter into an agreement to their injury.

mistake A belief that is not in accord with the facts.

mitigate The obligation of the injured party to protect the other party from any unnecessary damages.

monopoly power A situation in which one or more people or firms control the market in a particular area or for a particular product.

moral consideration Something that a person is not legally bound to do but that he or she may feel bound to do because of love, friendship, honor, sympathy, conscience, or other reason.

moral law The "law" concerned with the unenforceable obligations that people have to one another.

morals Beliefs about behavior as judged by society.

mutual agreement The state of mind that exists between an offeror and an offeree when a valid offer has been accepted and the parties know what the terms are and have agreed to be bound by them. Mutual agreement is also known as "a meeting of the minds."

mutual-benefit bailment A bailment in which both the bailee and the bailor derive some benefit, and, as a result, each has rights and duties.

N

National Environmental Policy Act (NEPA) of 1970 A federal statute that requires that any project with significant federal involvement (such as federal financing) must have an approved environmental impact statement prior to the commencement of any work on the project.

National Highway Traffic Safety Administration (NHTSA) The federal agency responsible for the safety of automobiles sold in the United States.

National Labor Relations Board (NLRB) A federal agency responsible for administering laws relating to labor unions.

necessaries Goods and services that are essential to a minor's health and welfare.

negligence The failure to exercise necessary care to protect others from unreasonable risk of harm.

negligence per se Negligence per se occurs when a defendant in a case of negligence has violated a law that was enacted in order to prevent the type of injury that occurred.

negotiability The ability to be transferred freely from one person to another and be accepted as readily as cash.

negotiable instrument An unconditional written promise to pay, or pay to the order of another party, a certain sum of money on demand or at a definite time.

negotiable warehouse receipt Proof of ownership that can be used to transfer title from one person to another.

nexus The link or tie that a location must have to a sale in order for the location to collect sales tax.

nonnegotiable warehouse receipt A receipt for the goods to be stored.

novation A situation in which all parties to a contract agree to a significant change to a contract.

nuisance An unlawful interference with the enjoyment of life or property.

nuncupative will An oral will.

O

Occupational Safety and Health Act of 1970 A federal statute designed to promote safety and health in the workplace.

Occupational Safety and Health Administration (OSHA) The federal agency that administers the many provisions of the Occupational Safety and Health Act of 1970.

offer A proposal made by one party (the offeror) to another person (the offeree) that indicates a willingness to enter into a contract.

offeree The person to whom a proposal is made.

offeror The person making a proposal.

option contract A contract that has a provision to keep an offer open for a certain period of time.

oral contract An agreement that is not in writing or signed by the parties.

order bill of lading A receipt for goods to be shipped that is negotiable and is proof of title that can be used to transfer title from one person to another.

order instrument An item of commercial paper that contains the key words of negotiability, "pay to the order of," or their equivalent.

ordinance A law that is passed by a local government, such as a city council.

outcome-based reasoning Ethical reasoning based on creating the greatest good for the most people.

P

parol evidence rule The rule that any spoken or written words in conflict with what the written contract states cannot be introduced as evidence in a court of law.

particle trespass The unauthorized entry of pollutants onto another person's land or water.

partnership A business owned and operated by two or more persons.

past consideration A promise to repay someone for a benefit after it has been received.

patent A valid, government-granted protection awarded to inventors that gives the patent holder the exclusive right to manufacture, use, and sell the invention.

perfection of security interests Process to ensure priority of claims against specific collateral.

periodic tenancy A possession interest in which the lease continues for successive periods for the same length of time.

perjury The crime of intentionally giving false oral or written statements under oath in a judicial proceeding after having sworn to tell the truth.

personal defense A defense against payment of commercial paper that may be used against any party except a holder in due course.

personal jurisdiction The power of a court to hear a case involving a nonresident defendant.

personal property Tangible and intangible property that is not real property.

personal representative The person responsible for settling the affairs of the decedent.

personal-service contract A contract in which services that require a unique skill, talent, ability, and so forth are provided by a specific person.

phishing The practice of tricking individuals into disclosing personal information via email.

plaintiff The party who begins a lawsuit by filing a complaint in the appropriate court.

pledge A promise to donate money to a church, temple, mosque, hospital, college, cultural institution, or other charitable organization.

Ponzi scheme A type of securities fraud in which large gains are promised to investors, but in reality, newer investments are used to provide a return on older investments.

postdated check One that is dated later than the date on which the check is written.

power of attorney An instrument in writing by which one person, as principal, appoints another person as agent and confers the authority to perform certain specified acts on behalf of the principal.

precedent A model case that a court can follow when facing a similar situation.

preexisting duty An obligation that a party is already bound to by law or by some other agreement. The party may not use this as consideration in a new contract.

preferential payment A transfer of funds in which the debtor gives favorable treatment to one creditor over another.

Pregnancy Discrimination Act of 1978 A federal statute designed to protect individuals from illegal discrimination in employment on the basis of pregnancy.

presentment When the holder of a note tenders it to the maker and demands payment, or shows drafts to the drawer and requests its acceptance or payment, on or after the maturity date at the place stated in the instrument.

primary market The place where a corporation (an issuer) sells its securities to the public.

principal A person who authorizes an agent to act on their behalf and subject to their control.

priority debts Debts deemed sufficiently important under Chapter 13 of the bankruptcy law that they must be paid in full.

private nuisance A nuisance that affects private property.

probable cause A reasonable belief that a prudent police officer must have that a suspect has committed, is committing, or is about to commit a crime, thereby giving the officer the authority to conduct a search.

probate court The court responsible for accepting a will that meets all statutory requirements and for supervising the operation of a will.

procedural due process A constitutional mandate that all persons affected by a legal proceeding receive notice of its subject matter, time, and place and that these proceedings be conducted by a judge who is fair and impartial.

product flaw An abnormality or a condition that was not intended and that makes a product more dangerous than it would have been had it been as intended.

product liability The liability of a manufacturer or seller for injury to purchasers, users, and third parties.

professional A person who does highly specialized work that depends on special abilities, education, experience, and knowledge.

promisee In the making of a contract, the party to whom a promise is made.

promisor In the making of a contract, the party who makes a promise.

promissory note A written note or letter in which one person promises to pay a certain amount of money to another at a definite time.

proper form The requirement that the form of a contract be correct for the terms of the contract to be enforceable.

prospectus A document that provides relevant and important information about a company, its businesses, and its prospects to prospective investors.

proxy A legal document that transfers the right to vote in a corporate election to another person.

public figure A well-known person who implicitly allows others to write about them in newspapers and magazines and discuss their conduct on television and radio.

public nuisance A nuisance that affects public property.

public offer A general offer to the public at large.

puffing A general expression of opinion, typically in a sales context, that is used to persuade a prospective purchaser to buy. It does not constitute a misrepresentation of material text.

punitive damages Damages used to punish a defendant for wrongful conduct that is willful, malicious, or fraudulent in order to deter them and others from engaging in the same type of conduct again or in the future.

Q

qualified endorsement An endorsement in which the endorser avoids liability for payment even if the maker or drawer defaults on the instrument.

quiet enjoyment The right to use the leased premises without unreasonable interferences from the landlord or third parties.

quorum The minimum number of shares necessary to be present at a corporate meeting in order for action to be taken.

quota systems Restrictions on the numbers and kinds of products that may enter into a nation.

R

raised check A check on which the amount has been raised by the payee or bearer.

ratified An approval of a contract made by a minor after reaching majority.

rational basis A test that measures whether the legislature had a reasonable, and not an arbitrary, basis for enacting a particular statute.

real defense A defense against payment of commercial paper that claims the instrument was void from the beginning.

real property The ground and everything permanently attached to it, including land, buildings, trees, and shrubs; the airspace above and the ground below the land also are included.

reasonable person A completely fictitious individual who is assumed to have the judgment and skill one would expect from a person with the strengths and limitations of the person whose behavior is being judged.

rejection The express or implied refusal by an offeree to accept an offer.

remote party A person with the right to make legitimate sales as a representative of the owner of the goods, although they are not a titleholder.

reorganization bankruptcy The name given to a Chapter 13 bankruptcy, in which the debtor agrees to pay back all or a portion of their debts over a period of from three to five years.

replevin An action to recover possession of specific goods wrongfully taken or detained by another.

request for proposal (RFP) A request for an offer or an invitation to negotiate that can be accepted or rejected by the person calling for a bid.

respondeat superior A legal doctrine that holds that the acts of an employee committed while performing duties are considered the acts of the employer.

restraining order A court order prohibiting the performance of a certain act. In some states, a restraining order is temporary.

restraint of trade A limitation on the full exercise of doing business with others.

restrictive covenant An agreement in which the employee agrees not to work in similar employment within a certain geographic area or within a specified period of time.

restrictive endorsement An endorsement with a signature to which words have been added restricting further endorsement of the instrument.

revocation The calling back of an offer by the offeror before the offer has been accepted or rejected.

RICO One of the most successful laws used to combat white-collar crime, RICO prohibits an organization's employees from engaging in a pattern of racketeering activity.

robbery The taking of property in the possession of another person against that person's will and under threat of bodily harm.

Robinson-Patman Act A federal statute that makes it unlawful to discriminate, directly or indirectly, in matters involving product pricing, advertising, and promotion.

S

sale on approval A contract for the sale of goods subject to the buyer's approval.

sale or return An agreement whereby the seller will accept the return of goods at the request of the buyer to maintain goodwill, rather than because the seller is legally obliged to accept the returned goods.

Sarbanes-Oxley A federal statute that placed an onus on upper management to monitor closely the financial dealings and disclosures of their firms and that established a board to oversee accounting practices in the United States.

secondary market The place where one member of the public sells securities to another member of the public.

secured debt A loan for which a specific asset is used as collateral.

Securities Act of 1933 The federal law covering the sale of securities (stocks, bonds, and other forms of investment) in the primary market.

Securities and Exchange Commission (SEC) The federal agency responsible for administering the statutes relating to the sale and trading of securities.

Securities Exchange Act of 1934 The federal law covering the trading of securities (stocks, bonds, and other forms of investment) in the secondary market.

securities fraud A fraud that occurs when a person or company provides false information to potential investors to influence their decisions to buy or sell securities.

security interest Interest created under state law to ensure that specific personal property assets are collateral for debt.

settlor A person who sets up a trust while still alive.

severalty Ownership of a particular piece of property that is held by one person.

sexual harassment Unwelcome sexual attention, whether verbal or physical, that affects an employee's job condition or creates a hostile working environment.

Sherman Antitrust Act A federal statute that forbids certain agreements that tend to unreasonably inhibit competition, fix prices, allocate territories, or limit production.

simple contract An informal contract made without seal—even though the subject matter of the contract may be extremely complex and may involve huge amounts of money.

single payer system A health system paid for and administered by one government source.

slander The spreading of damaging words or ideas about a person, directly or indirectly, in all other forms not considered libel.

slowdown An action wherein employees report to work but intentionally decrease their productivity.

smart contract An agreement using blockchain technology in which the terms are digitally written into the lines of code across a network that can be accessed, but not modified, by the parties to the contract.

social media Online technology allowing large numbers of people to interact and share information.

sole proprietorship A business owned and operated by one person.

spam Unsolicited emails sent for commercial purposes.

special agent A person delegated to act only in a particular transaction, under definite instructions, and with specific limits on the scope of their authority.

special endorsement An endorsement in which the payee specifies the person to whom, or to whose order, it is to be paid.

specific performance A court order directing a person to perform—or not perform—as they agreed to do in a contract.

spoofing A practice in which a legitimate website is reproduced to fool users into thinking that they are connected to a trusted site.

spyware Software that can change a computer's security settings or steal a victim's personal information, such as email addresses, bank account numbers, and credit card numbers.

stakeholders People or groups who may be affected by a firm's actions or decisions.

stale check A check presented more than six months after its date.

stare decisis The practice of relying on previous decisions in which similar disputes arose.

Statute of Frauds A law requiring certain contracts to be in writing to be enforceable.

statute of limitations A legal time limit in which to initiate a lawsuit.

statutory law The field of law involving statutes, which are laws passed by Congress or by state legislatures.

stop-payment order An instruction a depositor gives to his or her bank not to pay a particular check.

stoppage in transit When the buyer is insolvent, the right of an unpaid seller to stop goods in transit and order the carrier to hold them for the seller.

straight bill of lading A nonnegotiable receipt for goods to be shipped, acknowledging that such goods have been received and indicating agreement that the goods will be transported to the destination specified.

straight or liquidation bankruptcy The name given to a Chapter 7 bankruptcy, in which a trustee collects the debtor's nonexempt property, sells it, and dispenses the proceeds.

strict liability The doctrine under which persons may be liable for injuries to others whether or not they have been negligent or committed an intentional tort. This establishes liability without the necessity of proving fault.

strict scrutiny A test that measures whether the legislature had a compelling interest for enacting a particular statute.

subchapter S corporation A corporation that is taxed as a partnership.

sublease A transfer of the tenant's interest in part of the term of the lease and/or part of the premises.

subpoena An order requiring the recipient to appear at a legal proceeding to provide testimony.

substantial performance When a party to a contract, in good faith, executes all of the promised terms and conditions of the contract with the exception of minor details that do not affect the real intent of their agreement.

substantial similarity test A test that is used to determine whether an ordinary reasonable observer comparing two works would have to conclude that the work being questioned was copied from the other.

substantive due process A constitutional mandate that government not unreasonably interfere with an individual's life, liberty, or property rights.

Sunday agreement A contract made on a Sunday; in a small number of jurisdictions, such contracts are invalid unless they are ratified on a weekday.

Superfund A federal statute (also known as the Comprehensive Environmental Response, Compensation, and Liability Act) that regulates the dumping of waste onto land.

supremacy clause A provision of the Constitution that requires state judges to follow federal law in the event of a conflict with state law.

T

tangible personal property Personal property that can be moved.

tariff A form of tax, or other restrictions, on imports or exports to attain economic results, such as protecting domestic industries or facilitating the production of certain crops.

tenancy at sufferance A tenancy that exists only when a tenant wrongfully extends his or her tenancy beyond the term agreed upon.

tenancy at will A possession interest in which no specific time of lease is agreed upon.

tenancy by the entirety A form of joint ownership of property by husband and wife in which both have a right to the entire property and the right of survivorship.

tenancy for years The most common type of possession interest in which the lease is for a specific period of time.

tenancy in common A form of joint ownership of property by two or more persons in which any owner's interest can be sold, transferred, or inherited.

tenant The person who agrees to pay for the use of real property.

tender of goods An offer to provide the goods agreed upon that is considered evidence of a party's willingness to fulfill the terms of a contract.

tender of payment A money offer of payment of an obligation.

tender of performance An offer to perform that is considered evidence of a party's willingness to fulfill the terms of a contract.

term insurance A form of pure life insurance with no savings feature.

termination by lapse of time When an opportunity to form a contract ends because the offeree fails to accept an offer within the time specified.

testamentary capacity The requirement that a testator be of sound mind and legal age.

testator The person who makes a will.

The USA Patriot Act A federal statute that lowers the standards required for law enforcement officials and government agents to monitor email and personal electronic information, allows increased government cybersurveillance, and makes it easier to charge persons with serious computer-related crimes.

third-party beneficiary A person who is not a party to a contract but is intended by the contracting parties to benefit as a consequence of a contract.

title Ownership and the right to possess something.

title insurance Coverage that protects individuals against financial loss resulting from defects in their title to real property or from issues associated with their mortgage liens.

Title VII The portion of the Civil Rights Act of 1964 that deals with discrimination in employment.

tort A private wrong that injures another person's physical well-being, property, or reputation.

touting An activity in which an investor who owns shares of a company's stock posts notices online–in chat rooms, on web pages, on blogs, and elsewhere–that indicate that the value of the stock will increase.

trade dress A distinctive, nonfunctional feature that distinguishes a merchant's or manufacturer's goods or services from those of another.

trade libel Defamation that deals with an individual's title to property or to the quality or conduct of a business.

trade sanctions Legal restrictions, such as embargoes, placed on trade to achieve desired political results.

trade secret Specialized knowledge associated with a particular business, including information gained during employment about such matters as manufacturing processes, practices, devices, customer lists, and other confidential information.

trademark Any word, name, symbol, or device or combination thereof adopted and used by a manufacturer or merchant to identify their goods and distinguish them from goods manufactured or sold by others.

transient A guest whose stay is relatively uncertain.

transnational institutions Organizations whose purpose is to maintain legal and economic order in trade.

traveler's check A certified check, useful when traveling in foreign countries, that is issued in denominations of $10 or more by certain banks, travel agencies, and financial services companies.

treason The levying of war against the United States, or the giving of aid and comfort to the nation's enemies.

trust A device or mechanism that permits personal or real property to be held by one party, the trustee, for the benefit of another, the beneficiary.

trustee A person who is entrusted with the management and control of another's property or the rights associated with that property.

U

unconscionable contract A contract that is so one-sided that it is oppressive and gives unfair advantage to one of the parties.

undue influence The improper use of excessive pressure by the dominant member of a confidential relationship to convince the weaker party to enter a contract that greatly benefits the dominant party.

unemployment insurance Unemployment insurance provides financial stability, in the form of unemployment compensation, to eligible employees who lose their jobs.

Uniform Commercial Code (UCC) A set of laws that govern various commercial transactions and that is designed to bring uniformity to the laws of the states.

United States-Mexico-Canda Agreement (USMCA) As economic agreement aimed at promoting and facilitating trade among the United States, Canada and Mexico.

unlicensed transaction An agreement with a person who does not have a required license.

unlimited liability Legal exposure in which an owner of a business is personally liable for all of the debts and obligations of the business.

username squatting Registration of user name that is similar or the same as an existing entity in order to gain profit.

usury Charging interest higher than the law permits.

V

valid contract An agreement resulting in an obligation that is legally enforceable.

values Beliefs or standards considered worthwhile, and from which a society derives its moral rules.

vicarious liability The concept of laying responsibility or blame upon one person for the actions of another.

vicarious negligence Charging a negligent act of one person to another.

virus Instructions hidden in software with the potential to cause significant damage to both hardware and software.

void contract A contract that is not enforceable from the beginning because it lacks one of the requirements of a valid contract.

voidable contract An agreement that can be rejected by one of the parties for a legally acceptable reason.

voluntary filing A form of bankruptcy that occurs when the debtor chooses to file a bankruptcy petition.

W

warehouse receipt Much like a bill of lading except the goods are not being shipped but merely stored.

warehouser A person or firm that provides storage facilities.

warranty A guarantee or promise made by the manufacturer or seller that the goods or services offered really are what they claim to be, or that goods or services are what a reasonable person has a right to expect.

warranty of habitability An implied warranty in which the landlord guarantees that the premises are reasonably fit for occupancy and that there are no defects that would impair the health, safety, or well-being of the occupants.

whistleblower An employee who discloses to the government, media, or upper management that the company is involved in wrongful or illegal activities.

white-collar crime A term used to describe various crimes that typically do not involve force or violence committed by and against businesses.

whole life insurance A relatively costly form of life insurance protection that includes a savings feature.

wildcat strike A strike without the union's consent.

will A person's declaration of how they wish property to be distributed upon their death.

winding-up period The time after dissolution of a partnership during which there is an orderly liquidation of the partnership assets.

without recourse A phrase used to indicate a qualified endorsement.

workers' compensation A type of insurance that allows employees to recover damages for work-related injuries and illnesses without having to prove negligence on the part of the employer.

World Bank The popular name given to the International Bank for Reconstruction and Development, an organization that works closely with the International Monetary Fund to ensure that developing countries have access to funds to stimulate their economies.

World Intellectual Property Organization (WIPO) A specialized agency of the United Nations that administers numerous treaties concerning protection of intellectual property rights.

World Trade Organization (WTO) An organization with responsibility for overseeing the implementation of all multinational trade agreements negotiated now or in the future.

worm A type of virus that replicates itself and uses memory but cannot attach itself to other programs.

written contract An agreement that is reduced to writing on a permanent surface.

wrongful possession When property, such as stolen goods, is transferred without permission of the owner.

Index

A

B

D

O

P

S

U

V

W

Z